THE ESSENTIAL HISTORY
MANCHESTER CITY

IAN PENNEY

FOREWORD BY TONY BOOK

First published in 2000
by HEADLINE BOOK PUBLISHING
for WHSmith, Greenbridge Road, Swindon SN3 3LD

First published in paperback in 2002

10 9 8 7 6 5 4 3 2 1

ISBN 0 7553 1168 X

Design by designsection, Frome, Somerset
All photographs supplied by Colorsport except pages 187, 189, 190 and 197.
Cover photos: front cover clockwise (from top right) Mike Summerbee, Kevin Keegan, Francis
Lee, David White, Tony Book and Joe Corrigan (cutout); spine Ali Benarbia;
back cover City squad 1978-79, Bert Trautmann
Memorabilia supplied by the author. The information for the Complete Players' Career
Records on page 308 has been provided by www.citystat.net

The author would like to thank his wife Sheila, Gary James, Neil Woodhead,
the late John Maddocks, Philip Noble, Tony Book, Jack Rollin, Phil Alcock, Julian Flanders,
Tim Taylor, Craig Stevens, Adrian Besley, Kathie Wilson and Roland Hall.
While every effort has been made to ensure that the information in this book is correct, the
author would like to apologise for any errors or omissions.

Printed and bound in Great Britain by Clays Ltd, St Ives PLC, Bungay, Suffolk

HEADLINE BOOK PUBLISHING
A division of Hodder Headline
338 Euston Road
London NW1 3BH

www.headline.co.uk
www.hodderheadline.com

Contents

Foreword
By Tony Book

I was fortunate to spend more than thirty years employed by Manchester City and I have to say I loved almost every minute of my time there. Fortunately the times I didn't enjoy were fleeting and few and far between.

As a player the highlight for me has to be the Championship decider at Newcastle in 1968. I'd always measured my own performances on consistency over a period of time and to win the Championship was something special. The fans that day were just as they are today – brilliant. I've got great memories of the trip back home down the A1.

The highlight for me as manager was undoubtedly the 1976 League Cup final when we beat Newcastle. We had a great season the following year as well, just missing out by one point to Liverpool. Remember that was a marvellous Liverpool side which was in its pomp, and to get so close was, I think, a terrific achievement and one that is sometimes overlooked.

After Malcolm Allison and I left in 1980, I spent six months with Cardiff before being asked by John Bond to come back and look after the youth set up. That was in 1981, the year of the Centenary FA Cup final, when all the previous cup-winning captains were paraded on the pitch. At the time I was not sure whether to come back but I got such a tremendous reception from the City fans that they made up my mind for me. I stayed until the end of 1996 when new manager Frank Clark arrived and brought in his own people. I was sad to go as I still thought I had something to offer, but these things happen in football.

I'd played, managed, scouted for and coached the youth, reserve and first teams at one of the biggest clubs in the country. I have no regrets about my time spent at Maine Road and I am forever grateful to have had the opportunity to get paid all these years for a job which is also my hobby. The majority of people are not that fortunate.

After leaving City, Peter Reid rang me and said he had some part-time scouting work at Sunderland. Naturally I was pleased to be involved again and then Brian Horton rang me from Huddersfield and offered me a permanent post. I got a contract and a car on a Thursday and then Brian was sacked on the Monday so I walked out with him. Peter then spoke to me again and nowadays I work full-time for Sunderland, travelling literally anywhere and everywhere.

Anyone who spent time at Maine Road will always have a soft spot for them and wish them well. I'm no different in that respect and was delighted when Joe Royle managed two marvellous back-to-back promotions and got City back in the Premiership.

Joe's replacement Kevin Keegan has been hugely successful in his first season in charge at Maine Road. To have won the First Division Championship by such a large margin and with such an entertaining style of attacking football must surely have been beyond the dreams of even the most devoted fan at the start of last season.

When I saw Stuart Pearce parading the Championship trophy to the joyous fans after the Portsmouth game, my mind went back to 1968 when I had the privilege and pleasure to captain the last City side to win the First Division. They were great days back then with great players and I'd love to see the achievements of Joe Mercer and Malcolm Allison's sides at least equalled if not bettered by the current squad of players.

Although there will be some sadness at leaving Maine Road in twelve months time, the thought of Premiership football in a brand-new, 48,000 seater stadium is certainly something to look forward to. If everything goes to plan, we might even be returning to those fabulous Wednesday night European games as well.

When you look at the depth of talent Kevin Keegan has assembled, everything at Manchester City is geared up for success over the next few years. It's been such a long time coming and is no more than the club's fantastic supporters deserve.

Tony Book.

Chapter One: 1880-1922
In the Beginning

The name Manchester City came into being at the start of the 1894-95 season, although it was by no means the beginning of a club that would later win Football League Championships, FA Cups, League Cups and a major European trophy.

These kind of achievements made City one of the finest, most successful and best supported teams in the country as well as one of the best-known in the world. However, it had all started in the late 1870s from much more humble beginnings.

In 1865, the working class suburb of Gorton, just a few miles outside the centre of industrial Manchester, saw the arrival of religion in the shape of the newly built St Mark's Church. Situated on Clowes Street in West Gorton, the church provided a focal point for the community of terraced houses and its first reverend was a gentleman by the name of Arthur Connell.

The reverend had a young daughter, known only as Miss G. Connell, who came up with an idea in 1879, one that would influence the lives of millions of people over next 100 plus years. Her idea was to provide some kind of entertainment for the male half of the parish. She suggested a working men's club, one that 'will look after their well-being'.

Somewhat surprisingly this idea wasn't well received initially by the local men, whose main social activity up to that point seemed to be fighting with men from neighbouring districts at the slightest provocation. Miss Connell had already set up a meeting place for women two years earlier, one that was by now proving very popular, and she did not let this initial lack of interest deter her.

She recruited the services of two St Mark's wardens, Messrs Beastow and Goodyeare, to help her in her task and it was William

Beastow who initially suggested the idea of forming a cricket team, an idea that the men liked immediately. Such was the popularity of the cricket team that a football team was founded the following year. It was this football team that would become Manchester City.

The team's first organised game was against the Macclesfield Baptist Church on 13 November 1880, with St Mark's (West Gorton) going down 2-1 to its visitors from leafy Cheshire. Many historians have tried, although unfortunately without conclusive evidence, to locate the exact whereabouts of the club's first pitch. Contemporary reports and maps of the time indicate the most likely place to be an area of rough land situated at the side of the Union Iron Works on nearby Thomas Street. Running parallel to Clowes Street, Thomas Street provided the only spare ground in the area and as the iron works also employed Messrs Beastow and Goodyeare, this seems to be a fair assumption.

It is believed the club played a total of seven games in that 1880-81 season, the last being against a Stalybridge side that could only field eight men, the remainder being made up from volunteers in the crowd assembled to watch the game.

St Mark's (West Gorton)

For the beginning of the 1881-82 season the club moved to a far superior playing pitch when they played their home games at Kirkmanshulme Cricket Club. This new ground was situated on Redgate Lane in Gorton, not too far from the Zoological Gardens at Belle Vue. The club was now organising itself more professionally and began to attract players from outside the parish. Because of this, the church withdrew its patronage and St Mark's (West Gorton) changed its name to West Gorton (St Mark's). A crowd of 3,000 is reported to have watched the new club's first game, an unfortunate 3-0 defeat by Newton Heath, a team that later evolved into Manchester United. West Gorton won the return fixture later that year by a margin of 2-1.

West Gorton (St Mark's) were once again on the move at the end of that 1881-82 season. Seeing the state their pitch was now in, the cricketers had no option but to ask the footballers to find new premises. Staying in Gorton, they settled for a pitch off Hyde Road near to Queen's Road, sharing what few amenities there were, with another side, Gorton Athletic. The pitch was officially known as Clemington Park, although its condition lent itself to be known locally as 'Donkey Common'.

Despite initial friction between the management of the two sides using the one pitch, by March 1884 it appears that a combined side of the best of both sets of players was merging. Reports indicate a run of four successive victories and a crowd of 1,000 is alleged to have watched one particular game.

If things were working on the field, they most definitely weren't off it. In the summer of 1884, two West Gortonians – Walter Chew and Edward Kitchen – had had enough. They left the club to set up on their own and formed another new team; this one called Gorton AFC. It is not known what happened to Gorton Athletic. Once again a pitch was sought. This time they settled for a piece of land on Pink Bank Lane, not too far from a previous home at Kirkmanshulme Cricket Club. The land was spotted by a young Gorton inside-forward called Lawrence Furniss, a man who was destined to be a major figure in the club's history. When Manchester City won the Division 1 championship in 1937, Lawrence Furniss was President.

As with previous pitches, the stay at Pink Bank Lane would be short, lasting just the 1884-85 season, although it was a significant season for the club. They applied to (and were accepted by) the Manchester & District FA and received a donation from a local MP that paid off 50 per cent of the operating costs for the year. The church warden from St Mark's, William Beastow, was also back on board after a period away, along with senior warden James Moores on the committee. The first formal playing kit is also recorded this season, Beastow himself donating the black shirts with a large white cross.

A move to a pitch owned by the landlord of the Bull's Head Hotel on Reddish Lane followed for the start of the 1885-86 season. The club was charged £6 per annum in rent and was allowed to use the pub as its changing rooms. Gorton were now growing in stature.

CITY'S EARLY PITCHES

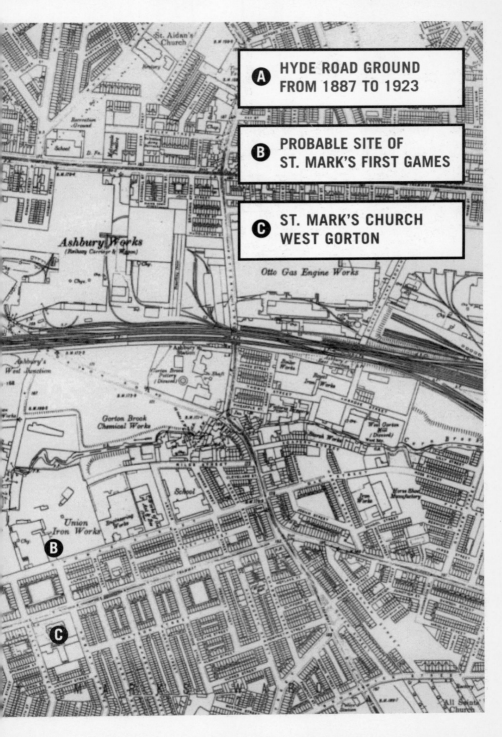

A HYDE ROAD GROUND FROM 1887 TO 1923

B PROBABLE SITE OF ST. MARK'S FIRST GAMES

C ST. MARK'S CHURCH WEST GORTON

They had a good, solid base for their home matches and managed a victory in the Manchester Cup before being soundly beaten by Newton Heath 11-1 in front of a crowd of 3,000. The end of that 1886-87 season saw a rent review by the pub landlord and Gorton either couldn't, or wouldn't pay, so, for the sixth time in seven years, the club were looking for a new home.

The question of a where to play next was answered once again by a player, this time by Gorton's captain, a Scot by the name of K. McKenzie. McKenzie was employed at Bennett's timber yard off Hyde Road, and to get to and from work every day he would take a short cut across some waste land near his home on Bennett Street. The land, owned by the Manchester, Sheffield and Lincolnshire Railway Company, was bordered on one side by their railway arches and on another by Galloway's Iron Works. To say it was unsuitable for football was an understatement.

The ground was almost entirely barren of grass and dotted with enormous puddles of water. Despite being horrified at what they first saw, the committee agreed with McKenzie when they realised the potential the land held. It gave the club an opportunity for a long-term permanent base and also had the space to provide terracing for the ever-growing football loving Manchester public. Negotiations took place between the club and the railway company and a sum of £10 was agreed for a rental period of seven months for the land. There began a huge clear-up programme and amazingly by the end of August 1887, an area was ready for football. By all accounts it wasn't the greatest playing surface ever seen but at least it was home.

A New Name

Once the new ground had been found, further discussions began concerning a new name for the club. This had come about because although the new ground was less than half a mile from its original home at St Mark's church in Gorton, technically it was in Ardwick and could therefore no longer use Gorton anywhere in its name. During the summer of 1887, Ardwick AFC came into being, formally declaring its address as Bennett Street off Hyde Road. Its headquarters were at the nearby Hyde Road Hotel, which also provided changing rooms on match days.

It was now time to attract the attention of local business and industry. The biggest benefactor at the time was Stephen Chesters-Thompson, a member of a local brewing family. At the time Chesters ale was served in the Hyde Road Hotel and later exclusively at bars situated inside the ground. Chesters-Thompson's £400 investment would prove a good deal for both parties. The nearby Galloway's Iron Works provided the necessary iron and steel for construction at the ground as well as employment for some of the players.

All was ready for the start of the 1887-88 season although Ardwick's first opponents, Salford AFC, failed to show up for their match. The following week, Hooley Hill from nearby Denton, did turn up and beat Ardwick 4-2. The club was now in a position to pay their first ever professional, the honour falling to Jack Hodgetts who was paid five shillings a week. Despite valiant efforts, the Hyde Road pitch was not up to standard and the club received many complaints and derisory reports during its first season. Ardwick also ended the season showing a £13 shortfall in the balance sheet, but in spite of these problems, with the enthusiastic Lawrence Furniss now secretary, the club was heading in the right direction.

The following season, 1888-89 saw the building of a grandstand (thanks once again to the financial assistance of Chesters-Thompson) capable of holding 1,000 spectators and a year-end profit of nearly £40. Ardwick had also narrowly lost 3-2 to Newton Heath in a floodlit charity match at Belle Vue in aid of the Hyde Colliery disaster.

By 1890 the club decided to strengthen its playing squad and Furniss travelled to Scotland to sign at least five players, including the highly-rated goalkeeper Douglas from Dundee. On the way back he raided Bolton, the prize scalp there being the England international Davie Weir. That same year also saw the club spend more than £600 on pitch improvements as well as persuading Chesters-Thompson to allow a further access to the ground by way of a pathway at the side of the pub. An estimated crowd of 5,000 watched a game against Blackburn, and although Ardwick lost 5-1, it was plain to see they were a club going places. The next step was to apply for election to the recently formed Football League and join the 'big boys'.

In October 1891 Ardwick entered the FA Cup for the first time, where their opponents were Liverpool Stanley. Davie Weir scored a hat-trick as Ardwick ran out easy winners 12-0. To date, this is still the club's record score in the FA Cup. For some unknown reason the club took no further part in the FA Cup that year. League games that season were played in the Football Alliance, a league formed out of the ashes of the now defunct Football Combination.

The Football Alliance was almost like Division 2 in standard, and opposition was provided by the likes of Sheffield Wednesday, Nottingham Forest and Small Heath, a team that would later become Birmingham City. Ardwick finished seventh out of twelve at the end of the season but did win the Manchester Cup when they beat Bolton Wanderers 4-1 in the final.

Joining the Football League

The club failed in its first bid for Football League acceptance. Despite the solid infrastructure now in place at the club, good attendances and reasonable success on the pitch, the club as a whole wasn't considered 'good enough' by the supposed more refined dignitaries of the Football League. By the time April 1892 had come around, the League was also under pressure from other clubs like Ardwick to be allowed entrance, and so, the Football League Division 2 was formed.

To all intents and purposes this was really the Alliance renamed, and Ardwick would be one of twelve teams taking part at the outset of the 1892-93 season. Other clubs included were Northwich Victoria, Lincoln City and Bootle, the team that provided Ardwick with their first League opposition. In the meantime Division 1 had been enlarged and Ardwick's rivals Newton Heath had been allowed to bypass Division 2 completely, and would start in the top division. Not surprisingly this was a decision that angered many at Hyde Road

as up until then the 'Heathens' had played their games alongside
Ardwick in the Alliance and had been only slightly more successful.

Ardwick, by now wearing their customary 'Cambridge Blue' shirts,
thrashed Bootle 7-0 in that opening game on 3 September 1892, a
game played in typical Manchester weather; heavy rain falling for
most of the day. They started the season well, but a poor run of form
after Christmas saw the side finish in fifth place. Had they finished in
the top three they would have had the opportunity to take part in the
end of season Test Matches, the forerunners of today's play-offs. All
in all though it had been a good first season in the new league, and
regular attendances in the region of 3,500 confirmed the fact that
Ardwick was by far the best supported club in Manchester.

For the start of the following season, 1893-94, Lawrence Furniss
was replaced as secretary by the smooth-talking Joshua Parlby, a man
who'd recently held a similar position with Stoke. Furniss was still a
much-respected figure at the club and was kept on because he was
also a man of considerable influence in the area. Parlby's persuasive
skills were thought to be what was required to advance the club
further in the eyes of the League hierarchy.

Unfortunately it was dreadful season both on and off the pitch and
Parlby had to earn every penny of his fifty shillings a week salary. Up
to then Furniss had not received a penny as club secretary.

A terrible run of results (including a 10-2 mauling at the hands of
Small Heath) and dropping attendances meant the club was being hit
from all directions and after being forced to sell some of its best
players, many felt they should just play out the season and then call
it a day. Parlby though would hear none of it and he began a
campaign to resurrect a club for the following season, one that 'the
whole of Manchester could be proud of'. This new club was to be
called Manchester City.

Not surprisingly there were still some die-hard Ardwick men who
wanted to fight on under the old banner, and Parlby spent many hours
trying to convince them that unfortunately those days had now
passed. It was time to move on. He also used his silver tongue to great

effect with both the railway company and the brewery as he tried to keep the ground open. On 4 April 1894, Manchester City Football Club were accepted for membership into the Lancashire FA. Twelve days later they became a registered company. The biggest stumbling block now was acceptance into the Football League. Would they see City as just Ardwick in disguise?

By all accounts, Parlby's presentation to the League was a marvel. He managed to persuade the authorities to accept a club that had no money or players but did possess a ground. Grateful Mancunians would talk about that speech for months afterwards.

On 1 September 1894, Bury beat Manchester City 4-2. It was City's first game in the Football League. Following a summer of frantic transfer activity, only one Ardwick player, Fred Dyer, played in that game. The full line-up was: Williams; Smith, Dyer; Mann, Jones, Nash; Wallace, Finnerhan, Calvey, Sharples and Little. Sam Ormerod had also been recruited to take care of team matters, leaving Parlby more time to concentrate on the administration side of the club.

After a mixed start to the season, City signed Billy Meredith from Chirk in October. Lawrence Furniss had already seen the 'Welsh Wizard' play and Finnerhan had played alongside him at Northwich confirming his opinion. It would prove to be one of the most important signings in the club's history.

Despite Meredith's obvious talent City were still an inconsistent side. For example in December 1894, they beat Woolwich Arsenal 4-0 one week, only to lose 8-0 to Burton Wanderers the next. In March the following year Notts County were beaten 7-1, and then Lincoln City 11-3, a scoreline that is still a club record victory in the league.

City ended their debut season in eighth place, 17 points behind champions Bury, but the following season showed a marked improvement. Finishing second to Liverpool only by goal average (Liverpool scored 106 goals in 30 games to City's 63), the Blues missed out on promotion when they were beaten in the Test Matches.

West Bromwich Albion and Small Heath had finished the bottom two in Division 1 and so played games against City and Liverpool to see who would play in the top division the following year. In those days promotion was not automatic.

After a 1-1 home draw with West Bromwich (when the admission price was raised from sixpence to a shilling) City lost the return game 6-1 a couple of days later. On 25 April, Small Heath were despatched 3-0 at Hyde Road in front of 9,500 spectators thanks to goals from Meredith, Davies and Rowan. However just 48 hours after this victory, City were on the wrong end of an 8-0 scoreline in the Midlands and their promotion chances had gone. Liverpool and West Bromwich Albion finally winning the four team competition.

An average Hyde Road crowd of 7,470 watched City's home games in the 1896-97 season. Meredith was leading scorer with 10 goals as they finished sixth in the league. Progress in the FA Cup was halted in the first round by Preston who cruised home easily 6-0, still City's record FA Cup defeat. Just after New Year 1897, centre-forward Billy Gillespie arrived from Lincoln City, forming an attacking partnership with Meredith that would last for the next eight years.

Seven consecutive wins greeted the start of the 1897-98 campaign. The run was halted in a 1-1 draw at Newton Heath, before Gillespie scored twice as Darwen were beaten 5-0 in the ninth game. The season ended as brightly as it had begun, with Meredith and Whitehead each scoring hat-tricks in the 9-0 victory over Burton United in the last game. It had been a good season for the Blues who finished in a creditable third place, and, but for a run of four successive draws at the end, could have finished even higher.

Ground improvements preceded the 1898-99 season, one that saw automatic promotion for the first time. Following their appearance in

Billy Meredith, the original soccer 'superstar', played for both Manchester City and Manchester United during his career.

the Test Matches of 1895-96 and narrowly missing promotion the previous season, City were determined this was going to be their year. Meredith and Gillespie began the season where they'd left the previous one, Grimsby Town suffering a 7-2 defeat at Hyde Road. December saw five straight wins, the last one being a 4-0 Boxing Day triumph over Newton Heath in front of a reported 20,000. In this game Gillespie is alleged to have bundled the ball and the Heathen's goalkeeper Barrett into the net for City's third goal.

Old adversaries Small Heath ended City's interests in the FA Cup that term, but it was in the league that the Blues' concentrated their efforts. Unbeaten in their last nine games (two draws and seven wins), City won the Division 2 championship by six points from their nearest rivals, Glossop North End. It was the club's first trophy and as reward for their efforts, both clubs played each other home and away, with the gate monies being divided equally between the players.

First Class Football for the New Century

The new century would bring Division 1 football to Ardwick for the first time. Initially there were concerns as to whether or not Hyde Road was capable of holding larger crowds, and for a while a move to the much larger Belle Vue stadium was considered. Once again with the help of Chesters-Thompson, improvements were made to the ground, including the building of a new stand and eventually all was set for the visit of Derby County on 9 September 1899, Manchester City's first home game in the top division of English football.

The season had begun the previous Saturday with the Blues putting up a good fight at Blackburn before going down 4-3 in the end. A crowd of 22,000 was at Hyde Road for the game with Derby, FA Cup finalists the previous year. They were not disappointed. Two goals from Meredith and one each from Ross and Williams secured a 4-0 victory. The team on that auspicious day was: C. Williams, Read, Jones, Moffatt, Smith B, Holmes, Meredith, Ross, Gillespie, F. Williams and Dougal. The team went on to win its next two games, scoring nine goals and conceding two. Maybe this Division 1 business wasn't that difficult after all. Unfortunately though the good form didn't last and City finished the season in seventh place. Hyde Road had an average crowd of 15,510 that year, the first time the club had averaged double figures. In the 3-1 defeat at Sunderland in April, City's consolation goal was scored by goalkeeper Charlie Williams when his long kick was assisted by the wind into the opposition net.

Centre forward Joe Cassidy joined City from Newton Heath just in time to play in the last game of the 1899-1900 season. He was leading scorer the following year, one in which City finished in 11th place, with an average crowd now more than 17,000. Meredith was reported to have had a poor season by his high standards and maybe this was one of the reasons why the Blues faired worse than the previous year. Once again they failed to negotiate the first round of the FA Cup, losing 1-0 at West Bromwich Albion, although they did manage to win the Manchester Senior Cup after beating Newton Heath 4-0 in the final.

Despite two consolidating years in Division 1, City lost exactly half of their 34 league games in the 1901-02 season and were relegated. After three games with Preston they managed to reach the second round of the FA Cup, only to be beaten 2-0 by Nottingham Forest at Hyde Road. Results like this ultimately cost manager Sam Ormerod his job. He was replaced in the close season by Tom Maley, a man who had played one game for the Blues in 1896.

Back in Division 2, Maley began looking at ways to improve the side. He brought in two forwards, Jimmy Bannister from Chorley and Sandy Turnbull from Scottish side Hurlford, playing them alongside Meredith and Gillespie, and between the four of them, they scored 77 times in the league. From the last week of January, City had a run of six consecutive victories, scoring an amazing 35 goals and conceding just three. It was goalscoring like this that gave City the Division 2 championship for the second time at the end of the season.

The following season, 1903-04, was by far the club's best to date. Having got back into Division 1, they very nearly won it, missing out to eventual (and reigning) champions Sheffield Wednesday by three points. In the meantime, Maley, still keen to improve things further, obtained the services of the 5ft 5ins (1m 65cm) Herbert the 'Mighty Atom' Burgess, a player who would go on to be the smallest full back ever to play for England.

But it was in the FA Cup that the Blues gained their greatest success. To date it had hardly proved to be a favourite competition. In the previous seven seasons, the club had only progressed to the second round twice. It had never gone any further. In 1904 though, they would go all the way. In the first round, 23,000 at Hyde Road saw the Blues victorious over Sunderland 3-2, with Meredith in fine form and the goals coming from Turnbull (2) and a Gillespie header. Woolwich Arsenal provided the opposition in round two, Sandy Turnbull again on target along with Frank Booth. The third round was also the quarter-final. City played host to Middlesbrough, a record crowd of more than 30,000 (paying £1,100) packing in to Hyde Road to witness a 0-0 draw. In the replay the following week, City won 3-1 thanks to goals from Livingstone, Gillespie and Turnbull (again), and were just one game away from the FA Cup final.

That game would be against Sheffield Wednesday, a team currently on their way to a successful defence of the Division 1 title. The venue was a rain-soaked Goodison Park and City turned in one of their best performances of the season. In the 21st minute Gillespie forced the ball home after Meredith's shot had struck the crossbar. The second half saw two more goals for the Blues, both from the prolific Turnbull, taking his tally in the FA Cup to six goals in five games. His second goal, a spectacular volley, prompted no less a player than Meredith himself to comment 'I never saw anything like it'.

And so to the Crystal Palace on 23 April 1904 for a meeting with Bolton Wanderers. For once Turnbull failed to score, the only goal of the game coming from captain Billy Meredith. At the time there was some controversy as to whether or not he was in an offside position but in the end the goal stood and City had won the FA Cup – also known as the 'Little Tin Idol', for the first time. Unfortunately they just missed out on the 'double' (a feat only achieved twice previously), but it had been a season beyond even the wildest of dreams.

Great Matches

FA CUP FINAL **Crystal Palace, London, 23 April 1904**

Bolton Wanderers 0 Manchester City 1 **Attendance 61,374**

Meredith

That day's crowd was by far the largest that City had ever played in front of, but the authorities were slightly disappointed as the Crystal Palace had seen in excess of 100,000 for previous matches. The gate receipts of only £3,000 confirmed both the difficulties and the expense incurred by rival sets of fans having to travel from 'up north'. Among the crowd that day were music hall stars George Robey and Harry Lauder, and cricketers Wilfred Rhodes and the legendary W.G. Grace.

With Bolton being a Division 2 side, it was perhaps not too surprising that City were favourites, although the Trotters did keep Hillman busy in the City goal early in the game.

Newspaper reports commented on the slick passing and style of City's play and in the 20th minute Meredith (recently voted the most popular player in the country) scored what turned out to be the decisive goal. He ran onto a long ball from Livingstone and, despite appeals for offside, crashed the ball across goalkeeper Davies and into the net. 'Loud cheers and the waving of hats and sticks' greeted the goal and one over-zealous fan ran onto the pitch to congratulate Meredith only to be 'escorted away for a time by five policemen'.

Despite failing to convert other good chances (noticeably by Gillespie and Turnbull) City remained in control of the game and Bolton's possession rarely troubled the City goal. The Cup was presented to Meredith by Colonial Secretary Alfred Lyttelton who commented on the performances of both sides before Meredith himself said a few words to the thousands who had surged onto the pitch. Meanwhile back at Hyde Road, more than 8,000 were watching a reserve game and gave a huge roar when the score from Crystal Palace was chalked up on a blackboard.

A revolutionary new way of covering the game was being tried out as reporters from *The Athletic News* hovered above the ground from a gas-filled balloon. Unfortunately for them the wind decided to blow in the opposite direction and they missed the goal. It wasn't their day but it certainly was Meredith's – and City's.

Bolton Wanderers: Davies, Brown, Struthers, Clifford, Greenhalgh, Freebairn, Stokes, Marsh, Yenson, White, Taylor.
Manchester City: Hillman, McMahon, Burgess, Frost, Hynds, Ashworth, Meredith, Livingstone, Gillespie, Turnbull, Booth.
Referee: A.J. Barker (Hanley).

The City team that won the 1904 FA Cup pose proudly with the trophy – the first major addition to the club's trophy cabinet.

The club had come a long way in a relatively short space of time, and by 1905 it had begun to make a really significant impact on English football. It was barely 10 years since the name-change from Ardwick, but since the turn of the century City had emerged as one of the top sides in the country.

However, the club's rise to the top wasn't welcomed in all quarters. The old guard running the FA were suspicious of the new professionalism creeping into the game and City were to the forefront in welcoming that professionalism. They were also proving to be a popular club with celebrity followers such as music hall star George Robey, and there was plenty of resentment at FA headquarters about how these 'upstarts from the north' had emerged so quickly to challenge the already established hierarchy clubs.

An early indication of this resentment had come late in 1904 when City as a club had been fined and had Hyde Road closed for two matches for alleged illegal payments to players. Three directors also received lengthy bans as a result of the enquiry. But City shrugged off the controversies and towards the end of the 1904-05 season were involved in a three-way tussle with Newcastle United and Everton for the Division 1 title.

City looked to have blown their chances after a disappointing 1-1 home draw against Sheffield Wednesday but the other two contenders were also faltering and a vital clash with Everton at Hyde Road could still give the Blues a lifeline. City won 2-0 but the game was a bad-tempered affair and was later investigated by the FA. Referee J.T. Howcroft was suspended for 'failing to control' a match which erupted after City winger Frank Booth had been punched in an off-the-ball incident by his Everton namesake, England international defender Tom Booth. The Blues' Scottish contingent were not slow to retaliate and the fact that no one was sent off in a foul-filled encounter was a miracle.

City's victory however, virtually ended Everton's title hopes and a 3-0 away win at Wolves the following week saw the Blues go into the last game of the season at Aston Villa with an outstanding chance of landing the title. To win it though, City needed to win at Villa Park and hope that Newcastle – who had a vastly superior goal average – would slip up in the north-east derby at Middlesbrough.

On the day City let themselves down. Villa had already won the FA Cup a couple of weeks earlier against Newcastle, denying the Geordies any chance of the double, and were keen to end the season with a flourish in front of their own supporters. City found themselves 3-0 down before half time and despite a second-half fightback which saw them pull the score back to 3-2, the match had long since turned itself into a bitter brawl similar to the Everton fixture.

THE ONLY AUTHORISED PROGRAMME.

TOPPING & SPINDLER, FLUSHING, HOLLAND.
The Oldest Established & Most Extensive Firm of Turf Commission Agents IN THE WORLD.

GREAT METROPOLITAN, CITY AND SUBURBAN, DERBY, CHESTER CUP, JUBILEE, etc.

"THE CONTINENTAL SPORTSMAN," containing latest market movements on above; also "YEAR BOOK and READY RECKONER," sent Free on receipt of Address.

All Letters to be addressed: TOPPING & SPINDLER, Flushing, Holland.
Postage 2½d. Post Cards 1d.

CRYSTAL PALACE.

OFFICIAL PROGRAMME.

English Cup Tie

SATURDAY, APRIL 23, 1904.

MANCHESTER CITY v. BOLTON WANDERERS.

TEAMS.

Frequent service of Trains after Match to all Parts

CRAMER PIANOS From 25 GUINEAS.
For HIRE, HIRE-PURCHASE SYSTEM, or for CASH.

'The only authorised programme' for City's triumphant visit to the Crystal Palace. Note that the players are numbered from 1 to 22.

Sandy Turnbull had been involved in a running battle all afternoon with his direct opponent, Villa captain and England international, Alec Leake. Leake was regarded as one of the game's gentlemen and a cool, unflustered defender, but he found his feathers ruffled by Turnbull's robust attentions and after one of several clashes between the pair, threw a handful of mud at the City player. Turnbull gestured back at him in the traditional manner prompting Leake (having first made sure that the referee was looking the other way) to swing a punch. The City player retaliated with both fists and the two players had to be separated and restrained by their team-mates.

Remarkably neither man was sent off by referee R.T. Johns – himself the later victim of an FA suspension for his poor control of the game – but that wasn't the end of the matter.

As the players were leaving the field at the final whistle, a disappointed Turnbull – one of the first City players off the pitch – was grabbed by an unidentified person and dragged into the Villa dressing room where he claimed later he was punched and kicked by a number of assailants. An angry mob of supporters then gathered outside the ground and police reinforcements had to be called in to disperse them as the City team bus was stoned.

City's protests at their treatment was backed by the north-west newspapers but not, unsurprisingly, by their Birmingham counterparts. They blamed the Manchester side exclusively for the violence, claiming that a sportsman like Alec Leake would never become involved in an incident such as the one with Turnbull without being 'severely provoked'. This stance was later supported by an FA enquiry into the game which suspended Turnbull for a month but remarkably allowed Leake to escape scot-free.

However this apparent injustice towards City paled into insignificance as a result of the next FA bombshell to hit them.

Meredith Shock

After a series of meetings behind closed doors during the summer, the football world was shocked on 5 August when it was announced that City captain Billy Meredith was to be suspended with immediate effect for attempting to bribe an opposing player. His alledged intention being to influence the outcome of the notorious Aston Villa game. The player turned out to be Alec Leake.

Meredith denied the accusations and Leake, at first, claimed he had treated the bribery attempt as the joke it was intended to be and that both men had laughed it off. As the weeks went by, however, Leake changed his tune. The FA claimed that an independent witness had overheard their conversation and after being questioned by the Commission, Leake now claimed he believed Meredith's bribery attempt had been genuine.

If City and Meredith appeared to have been harshly dealt with in the eyes of most neutrals, the FA had still not finished in its apparent vendetta against the Hyde Road club. They appointed an auditor to re-investigate the club's books for the previous few years, and as a result, another FA Commission was set up to act on his findings. This Commission met regularly throughout the 1905-06 season and by the beginning of June 1906 they were ready to announce their verdict.

It was declared that City were guilty of over-paying their players for years, that they had offered extra bonuses illegally as inducements to win matches and in transfer dealings, and had even paid amateur players on their staff. A total of 17 players were fined a combined sum of £900 and banned from ever playing for City again. Manager Tom Maley and Chairman W. Forrest were banned for life and two directors were also suspended.

City's first golden era was over, and in retrospect it appears that despite the shameful circumstances of its conclusion, they were the victims of an FA determined to teach them a lesson. Several other clubs were known to be over-paying their players at the time, but it seems City were made the scapegoats for being too successful, too soon.

Starting Over

As a club, they were now forced to start again from scratch and it took a long time to recover. Ironically, several of the players who had carried the club to success – notably Meredith and Turnbull – were later to sign for rivals Manchester United once their suspensions had ended and would help them to the first successful period in their history.

Before the 1906-07 season started, City had to find a new manager. The job was accepted Harry Newbould, former manager of Derby County. Newbould then had the unenviable task of trying to obtain players who were not only good enough, but wanted to play for this apparently controversial club. It is uncertain as to just why he took the job. Maybe he was one of many who thought City had been badly treated. On their part the club had appointed a fully trained accountant as manager. There would be no more 'creative book-keeping'.

City had just eleven players still on the books when Newbould took over. Despite having no money for transfers, he managed to prepare a side for the opening game of the 1906-07 season, at home to Woolwich Arsenal. In a game played in temperatures over 90 degrees, City lost 4-1, finishing the game with just six fit men. Two days later they were soundly beaten 9-1 at Goodison Park, to this day a record league defeat. Clearly it was going to be an extremely difficult season, but the Blues continued to battle, finishing in 17th position, fourth from the bottom. Yet again, they lost in the FA Cup first round, this time 1-0 to Blackburn Rovers in a replay. On 1 December 1906, 40,000 saw Manchester City beat Manchester United 3-0 in the first Manchester derby. Despite the problems both on and off the pitch, this season is indicative of the tremendous support the club would have over the years. Hyde Road had an average attendance of 21,670; the first time ever it had reached 20,000.

The following season was in stark contrast as a revitalised Blues' finished third in Division 1. The championship was won by Manchester United, the nucleus of their side being City's old one. One of the reasons for City's success that year was the reliability of goalkeeper Walter Smith, a £600 buy from Leicester Fosse, who played in all 38 League games. Once again the fans got behind the team with a record 23,255 being the average gate.

If 1907-08 was a good season, 1908-09 certainly wasn't. City were relegated on goal average, finishing in 19th place, just one place above the bottom club Leicester. Going into the last game at Bristol City the Blues needed a point to make certain of safety. In the 88th minute a deflected shot wrong-footed goalkeeper Smith and City were doomed. The Blues apparent dislike of the FA Cup continued, they fell at the first hurdle, this time to Tottenham by a 4-3 scoreline.

Although City were relegated, there was not a deep depression hanging over Hyde Road and the board still had faith in manager Newbould. No panic signings were made as Newbould felt he had the necessary firepower to gain promotion. The Blues had a fairly mixed start to the season, but six straight wins from Christmas-time onwards gave them a real chance. The run coincided with the arrival of inside forward George Wynn from Wrexham. With Wynn up front, ably supported by leading scorer George Dorsett, City won promotion, although it was a close-run thing with three other clubs just one point behind. It also proved a good year in the FA Cup. Unluckily drawn away in each of their four games, City won at Workington, Southampton and Aston Villa before losing 2-0 at Swindon. To celebrate promotion, extensive upgrading work at a cost in excess of £3,000 was carried out at the ground in the close season.

The topsy-turvy life of Manchester City continued next season. It was a year of extreme 'ordinariness' on the pitch with the club finishing 17th and not one player reaching double figures in terms of goals scored. Unbelievably the crowds still came in their thousands. There was a huge gate of 40,000 for the 1-1 draw with United and a season average of 24,955 was the highest to date. The only success of the season was a triumph in the Manchester Senior Cup when they beat United 3-1.

The Manchester City squad alongside other staff. This photograph dates from the start of the 1910-11 season.

A new goalkeeper arrived at Hyde Road in December 1911. His name was Jim Goodchild and he was to stay with City until 1927. He made his debut as a last minute replacement for the injured Walter Smith in a cup-tie at Preston, saving a penalty in a 1-0 win. Four wins in the last four league games helped City to a final position of 15th in the table. Like the previous season it had been a constant struggle and would ultimately cost manager Harry Newbould his job.

Just days into the new 1912-13 season, City announced their new manager. Remarkably it was to be Ernest Mangnall, a man who'd had great success at rivals United, taking them to two Division 1 titles as well as the FA Cup. Magnall's magic continued to work at Hyde Road. The club finished a highly respectable and comfortable sixth in Division 1 with George Wynn top scorer with 14. The most astonishing game that season was undoubtedly a second round FA Cup tie against Sunderland at Hyde Road on 1 February. Sunderland were one of the top sides in the country at the time; that season they won the Championship and were beaten finalists in the FA Cup. An official crowd of 41,709 was announced for the game although people actually there estimated it was nearer to 50,000 with many more thousands locked out. Not surprisingly there was considerable crowd disturbance and the ensuing pitch spillage forced the game to be abandoned and cost the club £500 in fines. The rearranged game was played four days later at Roker Park with the Blues losing 2-0.

City managed six games in the FA Cup in the 1913-14 season, although three of them were against the same opposition, Sheffield United. After two goalless draws, the Blues lost 1-0 in a second replay at Villa Park. Leading scorer in the league was inside forward Tommy 'Boy' Browell, who arrived on 31 October signing from Everton for £1,780, with 13 goals. Like many of his contemporaries, Browell lost his best playing years to war, but stayed on the club's books until 1926.

War with Germany was declared on 4 August 1914, and with many saying 'it will be over by Christmas', football continued, the new season opening four weeks later. Clubs were encouraged by the government and the FA to provide volunteers for the forces and City offered to donate 5 per cent of their wages to the Prince of Wales Fund.

Of course the fighting wasn't over by Christmas – it was to be five long years before it was over – and football's importance to the masses suffered at the turnstiles. Crowds were understandably less than in previous years although City's average of 20,205 was the highest in the division. The last two games of the season (one in which City finished 5th, just three points behind champions Everton) against Oldham and Everton, saw crowds of 40,000 and 30,000 respectively. It was obvious the fans knew that it would be end of League football for quite a while.

50 Greatest Players

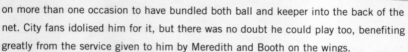

BILLY GILLESPIE Centre forward

Joined Manchester City: 1897   **From:** Lincoln City
Debut: 1897 v Darwen (league)
Appearances: 231   **Goals:** 132
Left Manchester City: 1905 (retired)
Honours won with Manchester City: Division 2 Championship
1899 & 1903, FA Cup winner 1904

Billy Gillespie earned himself a reputation as a 'bit of a boy'
during his career with City. A tough, bustling centre
forward, he took no prisoners on the pitch. He was reported
on more than one occasion to have bundled both ball and keeper into the back of the
net. City fans idolised him for it, but there was no doubt he could play too, benefiting
greatly from the service given to him by Meredith and Booth on the wings.

His reputation followed him off the pitch as well. Gillespie was notoriously poor with
regards to money matters and was also well known for liking a drink. His great friend
Meredith took him away on isolated fishing trips many times to try to calm him down.

Strathclyde-born, he signed for City on 7 January 1897, and scored on his debut
two days later. He averaged 14 goals a season during his nine years at Hyde Road.
He scored all four in a game at Blackburn in 1902 and was a key member of the
FA Cup winning side two years later, finding the net three times along the way.

A victim of the scandal that threatened to destroy the club in 1905, the colourful
Gillespie left England for the diamond mines of South Africa with his new bride.
It seemed a fitting finale for this most unorthodox of footballers.

And so it proved. For the next four years City's competitive games
were in the Lancashire Section, one of many regional leagues set up
all over the country. Sixteen sides comprised the Lancashire Section
(among them Manchester United and both Merseyside clubs) and
City finished in top spot when the first shortened season ended in
February 1916. In the last game of the season Preston were beaten
8-0, with Horace Barnes' two goals taking his total to 26 in 24 games.
In March a six-team league tournament was staged, and just to finish
the season in style, City won that as well. Again the prolific Barnes
was top scorer, this time with ten from as many games.

Despite the obvious hardships of the time – even the Hyde Road ground was used as military stables – City maintained a high standard of football throughout the Great War. After that initial success back in 1916, the club finished fourth, fourth and fifth in the Lancashire Section and picked up the subsidiary tournament for the second time in 1919. Eli Fletcher made most wartime appearances for the Blues with 133, closely followed by goalkeeper Jim Goodchild with 130. Billy Meredith (now on United's books) guested in 107 games whilst Horace Barnes led the goalscoring table by the small margin of 50, with 73 goals in 73 games.

The saddest point during the war was when news reached the club in 1917 that Sandy Turnbull, one of the players banned after the bribery investigations and currently playing for neighbours United, was killed serving in the trenches in northern France.

The war had undoubtedly stopped City from reaching the top in English football; results and players available confirm this point. Many felt that their club had once again been robbed by outside factors, just as they'd been by the FA more than a decade earlier.

Sheffield United visited Hyde Road on 30 August 1919 and shared six goals as well as the points. It was the first league game after hostilities had ceased and 30,000 people flocked to see it. Another visitor that season was King George V. He watched the Blues come from behind to beat Liverpool 2-1 in March, and by all accounts, thoroughly enjoyed the time he spent in Ardwick. City's goals that day were both scored by Horace Barnes although he was now in competition with Tommy Browell. Both had scored 22 times by the end of a season that saw City finish seventh.

A very early season ticket – City were popular from their very early days.

Great Matches

FOOTBALL LEAGUE DIVISION 1   Hyde Road, Manchester, 26 March 1921

Manchester City   3 Burnley 0   Attendance 50,000 (approx)

Barnes 2

Johnson

When the top two sides in Division 1 meet, understandably the game produces a larger than normal crowd. When the top two sides are also local rivals, this increases the gate even further. This is exactly what happened when the Blues met Lancashire neighbours Burnley in a game of vital importance to both teams.

City's average home attendance that year had been around the 31,000 mark, although there had been instances (notably against Manchester United and Sunderland) when it had been considerably higher. Although no 'official' figures are available, it was felt by fans who were there that between 50 and 55 thousand packed into Hyde Road that day. They precariously watched the game from the roof of the stand, the girders underneath as well as the pitch side itself. At one point a fire broke out in the stand but miraculously no one was seriously injured. It only confirmed the point that City had simply outgrown their present facilities and would have to find a new home.

When play did get underway, City were determined to end Burnley's impressive unbeaten run of 30 games. Two goals from Horace Barnes (one from an amazing 40-yard free-kick) and the third from Tommy Johnson underlined their superiority on the day although the Turf Moor side did gain revenge in the return game the following week. Burnley would eventually win the title by five points from City, even though the Blues did actually win one more game than them over the season.

A wonderful performance by the team only confirmed their enormous popularity. As well as the events described above, stories abounded regarding gates collapsing and people climbing into the ground on ropes. Clearly something had to be done, and the following summer the club acquired a plot of land in Moss Side which would finally eliminate these problems.

Manchester City: Goodchild, Cookson, Fletcher, Fayers, Woosnam, Hamill, Broad, Browell, Johnson, Barnes, Murphy.
Burnley: Dawson, Smelt, Jones, Bassnett, Boyle, Watson, Nesbitt, Kelly, Anderson, Cross, Mosscrop.

City's successes were by now attracting regular crowds far too big for the limited facilities at Hyde Road. The proximity of the railway arches and the iron works, as well as the housing on Bennett Street, made it impossible to extend the ground further and so the committee began to look around for new accommodation. Not for the first time, they looked at Belle Vue, a stadium very close to the club's foundations at St Mark's church in West Gorton. They also declined the offer of using the recently built 70,000 capacity stadium at Old Trafford.

Rather than rush into anything, the club decided, at least for the time being, to stay at Hyde Road. The events of Saturday, 6 November 1920 would help change their minds. A stray cigarette butt set fire to the wooden-built main stand destroying it completely. As well as providing seating for 3,000 people, it also housed the changing rooms and club offices. Determined that 'the show must go on' the club managed to patch things up (the players changed in the iron works) in time for the Huddersfield game the following week.

City ran out 3-2 winners in front of a happy, if somewhat uncomfortable, 30,000 crowd. Amazingly for the visit of Manchester United on 27 November, the club had built a brand-new, wooden grandstand, which actually increased the capacity. A reported 40,000 saw Barnes, Browell and 'Spud' Murphy score for City in the 3-0 win.

That same scoreline greeted Burnley on 26 March in a game vital for both Lancashire clubs as they focussed in on the Division 1 title. Reports suggest that anywhere between 50,000 and 55,000 crammed into the ground, some balanced precariously on the roofs while others sat on the pitch surrounds. Despite the loss, Burnley managed to beat the Blues into second place. The main talking point in the close season must surely have been a new ground.

A familiar face returned to Hyde Road prior to the start of the 1921-22 season when Billy Meredith, now aged 47, was employed as player/coach. As far as the final position goes, the Blues finished a disappointing 10th, Meredith playing in 25 of the 42 league games. Once again Browell and Barnes dominated the scoring with 41 between them. Browell also managed to score five more in the FA Cup

50 Greatest Players

BILLY MEREDITH Forward

Joined Manchester City: 1894 and 1921 **From:** Chirk and Manchester United

Debut: 1894 v Newcastle United (league)

Appearances: 390   **Goals:** 150

Left Manchester City: 1905   **For:** Manchester United
and 1924 (retired)

Honours won with Manchester City: Division 2 Championship
1903, FA Cup winner 1904, Division 2 Championship 1899,
22 Wales caps

Without doubt one of the most famous names in the history of
British football, Billy Meredith was the game's first superstar.
Born in Chirk on 30 July 1874 he joined City in October 1894.
No actual transfer fee is recorded although it is said that
Meredith received a £5 signing on fee. He made his debut in a
5-4 defeat at Newcastle on 27 October, Hyde Road fans saw him
for the first time a week later when he scored twice against
Newton Heath in the first Manchester derby. The bandy legs,
trademark toothpick and jinking runs, were loved equally by City fans and by the
cartoonists of the day, and he would draw huge crowds at any public event he attended.

Meredith's career with City was in two distinct parts. His first time was curtailed
when he was pivotal in the FA's investigations into the club and suffered an 18-month
ban, after which he moved to neighbours United. He returned to Hyde Road during the
war as both a coach and guest player. Following a dispute with United, Meredith
returned to City again and played 25 times during the 1921-22 season. By then he
was 47 years old. In August 1923 City moved to Maine Road. In 1924, the still
remarkably fit Meredith was chosen to play in the FA Cup third round clash at Brighton
in February. City won 5-1 and, not surprisingly, he scored. In front of a then record
crowd of 76,166 City were held to a goalless draw by Cardiff, before winning the
replay 1-0. Unfortunately the Blues lost to Newcastle in the semi-finals.

That game against Newcastle, on 29 March 1924, was his last competitive game. He
was 49 years and 245 days old that day, making him the oldest player ever to appear in
City's first-team as well as the oldest player to play in the FA Cup for any team.

After retiring Meredith dabbled in many business ventures, but was most successful
as landlord of the Stretford Road Hotel. He died at his home in Withington on 19 April
1958 at the age of 83.

that season, including a hat-trick against Darlington, before the Blues went down 2-1 at Tottenham in the third round. In the final game of the season, against Newcastle United, Max Woosnam broke his leg and would miss the whole of the following campaign, not returning to first team duties until 25 August 1923. That would prove to be the first game at the new stadium as well as Woosnam's only league appearance of the season. The broken leg effectively finished his career.

On 9 May 1922, the *Manchester Evening News* ran a story outlining plans for the club's new venue. A 16-acre site in Moss Side had been acquired, the plans indicating the stadium would be built in two phases, eventually holding 120,000 people. However, the club still had one more season at the old Hyde Road ground.

As far as league performances go, it showed a slight improvement on the previous season. The Blues finished eighth, but once again failed to negotiate the first round of the FA cup, going down 2-1 at Charlton. An influx of new players included defender Charlie Pringle, a half back, who, after making his debut in the opening game of the season, was an ever-present afterwards. Frank Roberts, signed from Bolton, scored 10 times, linking up well with Tommy Johnson who was back in the side after injury. Injuries kept Browell out of action for several months, leaving Barnes top scorer with 21 in the league.

The club's need to find a new home was confirmed in this edited article from the *Manchester Evening News* dated 18 August 1923:

'Manchester City players made their last appearance at the Hyde Road ground this afternoon, when a practice match was played in the presence of an attendance seriously affected by the inclement weather earlier in the day. Henceforward all games connected with the club will be played on the new ground at Moss Side.

'In spite of the heavy rain during the forenoon the playing pitch was in splendid condition, and except for a few small yards in the goalmouth it had a quite a rich growth of grass.

'A goalless first half was of no surprise to the crowd of between 7,000 and 8,000 as neither custodian had had hardly a shot worthy of the name to stop.

'The senior forwards attacked in a virile way in the second half and goals from Roberts and Johnson proved too much for the solitary reply from Browell.'

The pitch description provides ample evidence that football could still be played at Hyde Road. The facilities for the spectator, however, proved otherwise. Apart from the traditionalists who rejected change, the move to a new venue was popular with the Manchester public.

And so to Moss Side.

Great Managers 1889-93

LAWRENCE FURNISS

Lawrence Furniss was a major figure in the early development of Manchester City Football Club. During his younger days he had been a useful forward who turned out regularly for Gorton AFC, only to have his playing career curtailed by a knee injury. This injury however only seemed to make him redirect his energies into the administrative side of football at the end of the 1890s. When his playing career was over he became 'secretary/manager', a title given to someone during those embryonic professional football days, who did everything from pick the side to balance the books. Furniss was still with the club nearly fifty years later, when the Blues won the Division 1 Championship for the first time in 1937.

Gorton's move to a new ground off Pink Bank Lane in 1884 has been credited to the young Furniss who lived nearby at the time in a house on Kirkmanshulme Lane in Longsight. By the time the club had moved to Hyde Road, Furniss had become secretary, and he was involved heavily in business negotiations with local brewers Chesters in the building of a 1,000-seater stand at the ground. He also turned in a year-end profit of £33 as well as travelling to Scotland where he persuaded at least five players to try their luck in Manchester. On his way back he stopped off in Bolton and began to sign half their side as well!

When the Moss Side stadium opened its doors for the first time in August 1923, Lawrence Furniss had progressed to Chairman. His contribution to the club over the years even prompted one Mancunian to write to *The Evening Chronicle* suggesting the new ground should be named Furniss Park after him.

Arguably the greatest single thing Furniss ever did for Manchester City came when he refereed a game involving Northwich Victoria in 1894. Playing inside right that day was a player called Pat Finnerhan. Playing outside right was a certain Billy Meredith. Within six months of this game, both players were regular fixtures in the City side.

Chapter Two: 1923-36
A New Home

Under the watchful eye of Ernest Mangnall, who'd overseen Manchester United's move to Old Trafford some 14 years earlier, work began on the new stadium on 24 April 1923.

Situated off Lloyd Street on a relatively small street known as Maine Road, the new ground would be ideally located close to the city's major thoroughfares in the south as well as the corporation tramway system. It cost the club £5,500 for the land, which had recently been a refuse tip as well as providing the raw material for brick making.

Top Manchester architect Charles Swain was brought in and the construction contract was won by Sir R. McAlpine & Sons. One of the first jobs was to cover the entire proposed playing area with cinders topped by 3,000 tons of soil from nearby Wilbraham Road. The playing surface itself was two-inch thick, 100-year-old Poynton turf.

The initial plan was to build the ground in two stages. Stage one was the building of a covered grandstand (the Main Stand) to seat 15,000, with huge banks of open terracing to accommodate some 65,000, on the other three sides. Phase two, which was never completed, was to extend further and eventually cover the other three sides, taking the capacity to 120,000. The enormous terracing, 110 steps high in some places, were accessed by six capacious tunnels, one in each corner and two in the 'popular side', latterly to become known as the Kippax. The last two were still in use up until the end of the 1993-94 season when the Kippax stand was demolished. These tunnels were part of the instructions given by the club to the architect for evacuation purposes.

A veritable army of workmen took just four months to complete the entire stadium; it was ready in time for the opening game of the 1923-24 season on 25 August. The club had taken some of Hyde Road with it in the shape of the goalposts and some of the turnstiles, and it is believed that some of the old stands were sold to Halifax Town. The new pitch was both five yards wider and longer that its predecessor, prompting one reporter to comment, '...it is a picture. If footballers cannot play on that, they cannot play on anything'. The total cost of the entire project was reported as slightly more than £100,000.

The old ground was redeveloped by the tram corporation and in later life was used as a freight depot, a skidpan for training bus drivers and was home for a while to the Greater Manchester Police helicopter. Bennett Street is still there but the original houses have long gone. Indeed the only structures still standing are the railway arches; even the old Hyde Road Hotel, the Blues' first real base, has fallen foul of the bulldozers in recent times. The whole area though can still be seen clearly by daily commuters on the Manchester to Stockport line.

People gazing from the train windows across the club's first home, can see, looming on the horizon, the brand new City of Manchester

The City team that kicked off the 1923-24 season in a brand new venue – the 80,000 capacity Maine Road stadium.

Great Matches

LEAGUE DIVISION 1   **Maine Road, Manchester, 25 August 1923**

Manchester City 2   **Sheffield United 1**   **Attendance 58,159**

Barnes   Johnson

Johnson

The opening game of the 1923-24 season was a memorable one in the history of Manchester City: it was the first game to be played at their brand new stadium in Moss Side. With that in mind, it was perhaps not surprising that the local newspapers of the day concentrated their efforts more on the construction of the stadium rather than footballing matters. Indeed the new ground was a tremendous feat of engineering, being entirely constructed in just five months.

A crowd of 58,159 (described as 'a many-headed monster') watched the game that day, some loyal followers from the Hyde Road days and others just curious to have a look at this new stadium designed to hold 80,000 people. Only one stand was seated and covered (the Main Stand) with the other three sides being standing terracing, to which entrance was gained by 'capacious tunnels'.

The Lord Mayor of Manchester, Councillor Cundiffe, officially opened procedures by being introduced to the players and then carried out a ceremonial kick-off. City welcomed back two star players, Eli Fletcher and captain Max Woosnam, both of whom had been absent from the side with injuries for several months. Inside forward Horace Barnes had the honour of scoring the first goal at Maine Road when he breached the Sheffield defences in the 68th minute. Tom Johnson doubled City's lead minutes later, a goal scored at the second attempt after good work by the Sheffield goalkeeper Gough. The Blues then had a chance to increase their lead further only for Frank Roberts to have the misfortune of becoming the first player to miss a penalty at Maine Road. With just two minutes to go City looked assured of the points when a header from Sheffield United's centre forward Harry Johnson found its way past Jim Mitchell to the City net. The Blues hung on to win the game 2-1and a new era in the club's history had begun.

Manchester City: Mitchell, Cookson, Fletcher, Hamill, Woosnam, Pringle, Donaldson, Roberts, Johnson, Barnes, Murphy.
Sheffield United: Gough, Cook, Milton, Pantling, Waugh, Green, Mercer, Sampy, Johnson, Gillespie, Nunstall.
Referee: J.J. Howcroft.

Stadium, City's home from August 2003. Ironically, the new home is less than two miles from the old one.

Meredith's Swansong

A particularly wet autumn led to some problems with the new pitch but despite these difficulties the Blues entered the FA Cup in January in a comfortable mid-table position. Nottingham Forest were beaten 2-1 in the first round and then three games were needed to dispose of Halifax Town in the next round. Two goals from Roberts and one from Browell giving the Blues a 3-0 win at a neutral Old Trafford.Brighton were brushed aside 5-1 in round three with the 49 year-old Billy Meredith not only making a comeback after returning from United but also scoring one of the goals. He played his first game at Maine Road the following week when Middlesbrough were beaten 3-2 in the league.

FA Cup fourth round day fell on 8 March with Cardiff City visiting Maine Road. The expectations for this game were enormous. Five-hour queues gathered outside the ground, the gates were opened at 12.30 and a record crowd of 76,166 flooded in to see Meredith for possibly the last time. The only disappointment was that the game finished goalless and a replay was needed four days later. A crowd in the region of 50,000 saw the replay, one that City won thanks to a solitary goal from Browell. Much to the crowd's delight, the goal had been set up by man of the match Meredith who, despite being the oldest on the pitch by far, was still arguably the most skilful.

The semi-final against Newcastle United at Birmingham's St Andrew's ground proved just one step too far for both City and the 'Welsh Wizard'. The Blues lost 2-0 and Meredith saw very little of the ball. It was to be his last game in City's colours.

City had had a good Cup run, finished 11th in Division 1 and had a superb swansong for one of the greatest footballers of all time. As well as opening a brand new stadium, comparable only to the recently built Wembley, all in all, it had been a pretty good season.

Manager Ernest Mangnall's contract expired in the close season and for no apparent reason except 'new blood', the board decided not to renew it. They offered the position to Oldham Athletic's David Ashworth, a man who'd earlier won the Division 1 title with Liverpool.

Ashworth's first game in charge was the opener of the 1924-25 season, a 2-0 defeat at Bury. Little improvement was made on the previous season as City finished 10th, one place higher, but lost in the first round of the FA Cup, 4-1 at Preston. After 10 years loyal service, Horace Barnes joined the Deepdale side in November with centre half Sam Cowan arriving the following month from Doncaster Rovers.

A testimonial game was held at Maine Road on the evening of Wednesday, 29 April for Billy Meredith. Now aged 51, Meredith played in his own XI against a combined Rangers and Celtic XI in a game that finished 2-2. By all accounts it was not a great game as many of the opposition showed little interest in anything resembling a tackle on the 'old man'. But 15,000 turned out to pay tribute to Meredith and to thank him for what he had done for City.

The 1925-26 proved an eventful one if not always for the right reasons. There were some remarkable results in both the league and the FA Cup. Tommy Browell scored five goals in an 8-3 victory against Burnley whilst just two days later the scoreline was reversed as the Blues travelled to Sheffield United. A possible reason for these high scoring games could have been the introduction of the new offside law that had come in at the start of the season. Whatever the reasons, the goals kept on coming. Unfortunately for manager Ashworth though these were just the type of inconsistencies the board could not afford and in November he resigned, whether or not by mutual consent is uncertain. Not wishing to rush into a replacement, club Chairman Albert Alexander Snr took charge of team affairs until a suitable replacement could be found.

Still in the league, a 6-5 defeat at Bury in December preceded a trip to Manchester United the following month. City won 6-1 in front of 48,657 at Old Trafford to record the highest derby victory of all time. In the Cup, it took two games to beat The Corinthians before Herbert Chapman's Huddersfield Town side (currently on their way to their third consecutive Division 1 title) were beaten 4-0. Crystal Palace, at

50 Greatest Players

HORACE BARNES Forward

Joined Manchester City: 1914   **From:** Derby County

Debut: 1914 v Bradford City (league)

Appearances: 235   **Goals:** 125

Left Manchester City: 1924   **For:** Preston North End

Horace Barnes joined City in May 1914 from Derby County for £2,500, and forged a powerful attacking partnership with Tommy Browell for more than 10 years. He scored on his debut for City in the opening game of the 1914-15 season, one that saw him score 12 times in 25 league games, before the outbreak of war. He continued playing at Hyde Road during the war, scoring 73 goals in 73 games. Employed in a munitions factory throughout the hostilities, Barnes was so keen to play in a game against Stockport that he failed to turn up for work and was fined by a Manchester magistrate.

After the war Barnes continued his goalscoring feats, averaging a goal in every other game. His goals total for City has been bettered by just six players in the club's history. Barnes even had the privilege of scoring the first ever goal at the new Maine Road ground, City beating Sheffield United 2-1 on 25 August 1923.

Renowned for the ferocity of his shooting, Barnes moved to Preston in November 1924, later playing for Oldham Athletic and Ashton National. Once his footballing career was over he worked until he was 70 at an east Manchester engineering firm. Sadly he passed away at his Clayton home twelve months after his retirement.

the time a mid-table Division 3 South side, visited Maine Road on the 20 February for the fifth round tie, and although they managed to score four times themselves, City scored 11 at the other end. For City, Frank Roberts found the net five times while amazingly the Palace goalkeeper was carried off at the end of the game for his heroic performance in keeping the score down!

It was Tommy Johnson's turn in the next round, scoring a hat-trick as the Blues won 6-1 at Clapton Orient. The semi-final was to be played at the neutral venue of Bramall Lane, Sheffield, against Old Trafford, still stinging from the 6-1 defeat a few weeks earlier. Once again City ran out winners, this time only by 3-1, but it was enough to take the Blues to Wembley for the first time and a clash with Bolton Wanderers.

Unfortunately it would prove to be an unsuccessful trip with Bolton reversing the scoreline of the 1904 FA Cup Final, winning 1-0. An all-ticket crowd of 91,567 saw an even game, one that reporters said would be decided by just the one goal. Unfortunately for the Blues, it was scored by Bolton's David Jack with 12 minutes to go.

City had gone into the Cup final perilously close to the bottom of the league. Three days later they managed to win a crucial game at fellow strugglers Leeds United but still needed a point in the last game, away at Newcastle, to have any chance of survival. Unfortunately for the Blues, they lost 3-2 and were relegated along with Notts County. It had not been the greatest of weeks for City, and new manager Peter Hodge (formerly of Leicester who'd joined the club during that week) knew he had a job of work to do.

Goals Galore, But No Joy

Hodge's side started the 1926-27 season with four wins and a draw. Eli Fletcher and Tommy Browell, both long-serving players, left the club, with the only new face being Matthew Barrass from Sheffield Wednesday. Barrass seemed to fit in well from the outset and played a key role behind the strikers. He even managed a hat-trick himself when Clapton Orient were beaten 6-1 in a repeat of last year's FA Cup tie.

It was a good, consistent season for the Blues, and after Christmas they lost just twice in the league, giving them a real chance for promotion. Going into the last game, City and Portsmouth were neck and neck for second place, with Middlesbrough already promoted as champions. City had scored more goals than Portsmouth (100 against 82) but unfortunately had also conceded more, 61 against 48. Remember this was in the days of goal average not goal difference. The last game could not have gone any better for the Blues. They destroyed visitors Bradford City 8-0 with Tommy Johnson getting a hat-trick. Surely this would be enough to gain promotion? Regrettably Portsmouth beat Preston 5-1 and went up by the narrowest goal difference of all time: 1.7755 against City's 1.7705. Although these 108 goals are the most ever scored by the Blues in one season (although equalled in 2001-02), they still missed out. One more goal would have been enough.

Determined not to miss out again by such a small margin, Hodge strengthened his attack for the following term when he bought the Barnsley duo of Eric Brook and Freddie Tilson for a combined fee of

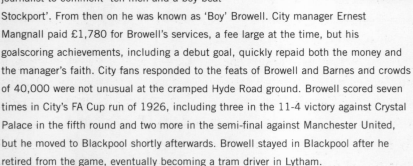

50 Greatest Players

TOMMY BROWELL Forward

Joined Manchester City: 1913	**From:** Everton
Debut:: 1913 v Sheffield Wednesday (league)	
Appearances: 247	**Goals:** 139
Left Manchester City: 1926	**For:** Blackpool

The other half of a successful goalscoring duo with Horace Barnes, Browell's reputation for goals was already well known when he arrived at Hyde Road from Merseysiders Everton in October 1913.

Hull City had first spotted his ability in 1910 prior to a move to Everton the following year. It was at Hull that the 18-year-old Browell once scored a hat-trick in a game against Stockport County, prompting one newspaper journalist to comment 'ten men and a boy beat Stockport'. From then on he was known as 'Boy' Browell. City manager Ernest Mangnall paid £1,780 for Browell's services, a fee large at the time, but his goalscoring achievements, including a debut goal, quickly repaid both the money and the manager's faith. City fans responded to the feats of Browell and Barnes and crowds of 40,000 were not unusual at the cramped Hyde Road ground. Browell scored seven times in City's FA Cup run of 1926, including three in the 11-4 victory against Crystal Palace in the fifth round and two more in the semi-final against Manchester United, but he moved to Blackpool shortly afterwards. Browell stayed in Blackpool after he retired from the game, eventually becoming a tram driver in Lytham.

Tommy Browell died on 5 October 1955.

£6,000. Once again the magical figure of 100 goals scored was achieved (with Swansea and Barnsley both being on the receiving end of seven) and the Blues lost just eight times in 42 league games. Despite losing the last game of the season 2-1 at Notts County they'd done enough to secure the Division 2 championship for the fourth time. The crowd responded to their success and attacking style of play with an average attendance of 37,468, the highest in any division.

The Blues failed to secure a win in any of the opening three games of the 1928-29 season, their only point coming from a 2-2 draw with United at Maine Road. A crowd of over 61,000 saw City take the lead through Roberts only to go in 2-1 down at half-time. Fortunately Tommy Johnson was on hand to equalise in the second half and the points were shared. Johnson's goal

Ernie Toseland was ever-present for City during the 1929-30 season.

that day was his first of a record-breaking season. He would go on to score 38 times in 39 league games, still a club record more than 70 years later.

City lost just one of their last 10 games to finish their first season back in the top division in eighth place. With a playing squad of 25 professionals, the smallest at the club for a long time, it had been a successful season, achieving what it set out to do at the start: namely establishing itself in the top flight.

Ernie Toseland had joined the club at the end of the 1928-29 season and proved to be an ever-present the following campaign. Alongside Toseland now was another newcomer, Busby, a player very nearly lost to the game for all time but for the intervention of manager Hodge.

If Hodge was seen to have made a good decision in persuading Matt Busby to come to City, he was regarded as having made a bad one by letting Johnson move to Everton for £6,000. Johnson had already scored 11 times in the league by the time he left in March and although his striking partner Tommy Tait was averaging almost a goal a game, City fans were shocked by the decision to sell their great favourite. The season ended with the Blues in third place (13 points behind champions Sheffield Wednesday), having progressed to the fifth round of the FA Cup and winning the Lancashire Senior Cup.

During that FA Cup run Swindon were humiliated 10-1 at Maine Road after a 1-1 draw four days earlier, Bobby Marshall scoring five times for the Blues.

50 Greatest Players

SAMMY COOKSON Full back

Joined Manchester City: 1918   **From:** Macclesfield Town

Debut: 1920 v Bradford City (league)

Appearances: 306   **Goals:** 1

Left Manchester City: 1928   **For:** Bradford

Before joining Macclesfield Town Sammy Cookson had previously been with Stalybridge Celtic, spending his working life down the pit and playing football purely for enjoyment at weekends. The exertions of mine work provided Cookson with a very powerful physique, one which sometimes proved deceptive to opposition forwards. Once established in the first team he formed a long-standing partnership with Eli Fletcher which earned them both the accolade 'best uncapped full backs of the era'. In nine seasons with City (which included the move from Hyde Road to Maine Road), Cookson played in 306 League and Cup games, scoring one goal, against The Corinthians in the 1926 FA Cup campaign. He went on to play against Bolton in the final that year; his runners-up medal being the only prize he would collect with the club. In 1928 he moved to Bradford and later played in a Barnsley side that won the Third Division North championship.

Cookson was by then 38 and had finally picked up a winners' medal. None of his contemporaries could begrudge him this belated reward.

After he'd retired, Cookson, who'd suffered with rheumatism during his playing days, returned to his native Manchester where he passed away in August 1955 at the comparatively young age of 59.

No Goals

The sale of Johnson could have some bearing on City's total of 75 league goals during the 1930-31 season. It was the lowest they'd scored for eight seasons. Leading scorer in the campaign was Eric Brook with 16. Tommy Tait joined Bolton in November, his place being taken by David Halliday from Arsenal. Halliday would eventually score 14 times in 24 appearances but it was simply this lack of goals that forced the club to finish the season in eighth place. Like so many other seasons before, the third round of the FA Cup was a far as they got, beaten 3-0 away at Burnley. Perhaps the only consolation for the season was a double over United and then to see the Old Trafford side relegated.

Matt Busby: an important football figure in both halves of Manchester.

The following season, 1931-32, saw a much better Cup run as the Blues reached the semi-final only to lose to Arsenal at Villa Park by the lowest possible scoreline. In the third round game at Millwall, they had to wait until the very last minute for Toseland to secure the tie at 3-2. Tilson scored a hat-trick in the next round as Brentford from Division 3 were despatched 6-1 in front of 56,190 at Maine Road. Drawn at home again in the fifth round, this time to Derby County, an even bigger crowd of 62,641 witnessed a comfortable 3-0 victory for the Blues. An all-Lancashire clash with Bury awaited City in the quarter-finals. At one point City were 4-0 in front but in the end they had to cling on desperately for a 4-3 victory.

50 Greatest Players

TOMMY JOHNSON Forward

Joined Manchester City: 1919   **From:** Dalton Casuals

Debut: 1919 v Blackburn Rovers (league)

Appearances: 354   **Goals:** 166

Left Manchester City: 1930   **For:** Everton

Honours won with Manchester City: Division 2 Championship 1928, 2 England caps

It is rumoured that City full back Eli Fletcher refused to sign a new contract at the club unless they bought Tommy Johnson from Dalton Casuals. Fortunately manager Ernest Mangnall listened to Fletcher and signed a player who would eventually become a goalscoring record breaker for City. Johnson scored twice on his League debut for the Blues and his career went on from there.

When City won the Division 2 championship in 1927-28, only Frank Roberts, with one more, bettered Johnson's tally of 19 league goals. The following season belonged solely to Johnson. He scored 38 goals in 39 league games, still a club record and one unlikely to be beaten. This included five against Everton at Goodison Park and a hat-trick against Bolton Wanderers.

By his standards he had a disappointing 1929-30, scoring 12 times in 34 outings, but it still came as a shock to many fans when he was surprisingly sold to Everton for £6,000 in March 1930.

Tommy Johnson stands second behind Eric Brook as Manchester City's top goalscorer of all time. He died in Monsall Hospital, Manchester, on 28 January 1973, aged 71.

And so to Villa Park for a game against Arsenal, the side that would finish the season as runners-up. Because of the difference in league positions, Arsenal started the game as favourites, But come the day the Blues were not in awe of the Gunners and matched them step for step. Arsenal's only chance in a goalless first half came when City right back Billy Felton cleared the ball off the line following a shot from Alex James.

In the dying moments of the game, Felton lost possession and Arsenal's centre forward Lambert crossed infield for Bastin. Bastin's shot was tipped against the bar by Langford in the City goal only for the ball to bounce down and hit the inside of the post before spinning

50 Greatest Players

FRANK ROBERTS Forward

Joined Manchester City: 1922   **From:** Bolton Wanderers

Debut: 1922 v Preston North End (league)

Appearances: 237   **Goals:** 130

Left Manchester City: 1929   **For:** Manchester Central

Honours won with Manchester City: Division 2 Championship 1928, 4 England caps

Sandbach-born Frank Roberts joined City from Bolton Wanderers in October 1922, the last season at Hyde Road. He cost somewhere in the region of £3,500, a figure thought high at the time, but Roberts immediately began to prove his worth. He played in every one of the remaining 32 League games that term, scoring 10 times and forming a deadly strike-force alongside Tommy Johnson and Horace Barnes.

The 1924-25 season proved his most prolific as he notched up 32 goals in 39 league and cup games. His efforts were rewarded that season with the first of his four England caps. In February 1926 on their way to Wembley, City thrashed Crystal Palace by an amazing 11-4 scoreline with Roberts scoring five times.

He was leading scorer for City in their successful 1927-28 Division 2 campaign with 20 goals from 26 outings.

In June 1929, after seven seasons with the club, he moved to Manchester Central. His 130 goals in 237 games in City's colours put him tenth in the overall scoring table.

over the line and into the net. It was cruel way to lose such an important game and the blame was laid firmly on Felton. Despite an otherwise sound performance, he was harshly criticised and never played for City again. By the following Saturday he was wearing Tottenham's colours.

At the end of the season Peter Hodge was lured back to his previous club Leicester, leaving the assistant manager of the past 12 years, Wilf Wild, to take over. Little did anyone know at the time, that Wild's side would be at Wembley the following May.

Wild's Side

There was little difference in the way Wild approached the side. No major signings were made and the Blues finished the 1932-33 season in 16th place, two places lower than the previous year. In the Cup though things were different, and this time the Blues went one better than last year's unfortunate defeat at the hands of Arsenal.

After a 1-1 draw at Gateshead, City won the replay 9-0, with a hat-trick from Tilson and two from captain Sam Cowan. Eric Brook scored both City's goals as Walsall were beaten in round four, once again in front of a 50,000 plus crowd at Maine Road. In the fifth round at Bolton, Brook completed a hat-trick as City won 4-2 front of nearly 70,000. Another Lancashire derby awaited the Blues in the sixth round, this time Tilson providing the only goal of the game at Burnley, and for the second year running City had reached the semi-final.

Eric Brook was in fine form during the 1932-33 FA Cup run.

Like the previous year, City's opponents in the semi-final were hot favourites. This time it was Derby County, again like last year, a team that would finish above City in the league. Unlike last year though, City, with Eric Brook in fine form, stormed into a three-goal lead with just 20 minutes left on the clock. The goals came from Toseland, Tilson and McMullan but in typical Blues' fashion, at this point they stopped playing. When Derby scored twice (the second with just three minutes left), finger nails were chewed vigorously on the packed terraces of Huddersfield's Leeds Road ground.

Nerves Account for City

Unfortunately for the Blues, leading scorer Freddie Tilson missed the final against Everton owing to a nerve problem in his leg. This meant Bobby Marshall came into the side with Alex Herd taking over Tilson's role in the centre. City wore their change kit of maroon shirts and it was also the first time numbers were worn in a Cup final.

By contemporary accounts it appears that apart from the loss of Tilson, the biggest handicap to City that day was nerves. Despite valiant efforts from both Cowan and McMullan to calm their team-mates down, City appeared the more unsettled of the two sides. Langford in the City goal was one of the most nervous and in the 40th minute he dropped a centre obligingly at the feet of outside left Jack Stein who gave Everton the lead.

Seven minutes after the interval Everton increased their lead and effectively sealed the match. As Langford attempted to hold on to a high ball from Britton, he was barged by Dixie Dean with both ball and goalkeeper ending up in the net. In the 80th minute Everton's Dunn headed home a corner to finish the day's scoring.

It was a disappointing day all round, but as captain Sam Cowan was collecting his runners'-up medal from the Duke of York, he was already thinking about the following season when he said, 'We'll be back next year and win it'.

Alex Herd – whose interest in reading nearly saw him miss the FA Cup final.

Fred Tilson scored both of City's goals in the 1934 FA Cup final.

Whether it was bravado on Cowan's part or just simply a way of cheering up his deflated troops, City were back at Wembley next May and Cowan was true to his word. The 1933-34 season also saw an improvement in the league. City finished in fifth place, their best position for four seasons. Despite this improvement, though, the league season was not without some difficulties, the lowest point being an 8-0 defeat at Wolves two days before Christmas. In the next game, a 4-1 defeat at Derby on Christmas Day, the 19-year-old Frank Swift made his debut between the posts for the Blues. Any goalkeeping worries at Maine Road could be put on hold for the next 16 years.

The third round of the FA Cup saw Blackburn Rovers visit Maine Road. With the score at 0-0 Swift made a brilliant one-handed save which seemed to inspire the whole side on to a 3-1 win. It took a replay to finally get the better of Hull City in the fourth round. After drawing 2-2 at Hull on the Saturday, goals from Tilson (2), Toseland and Marshall gave the Blues a 4-1 win at Maine Road the following Wednesday. Round five proved similar to round four. Another 2-2 draw at another Yorkshire side, Sheffield Wednesday, preceded a 2-0 win at Maine Road in the replay. A crowd of 72,841 provided Hillsborough with its record attendance, although safety features were not all they should have been and hundreds of fans were injured in the ensuing crush. At least one unfortunate supporter was reported to have been killed, the body being carried past Frank Swift in the City goal. Another vast crowd saw the replay as 68,614 (many taking unauthorised time off work) packed into Maine Road for the Wednesday afternoon game.

If the crowds to date had been large, nothing could prepare the fans for the sixth round game with Stoke City on 3 March. On that day 84,569 watched the game at Maine Road, thereby creating a record for any game outside London. It is also still the largest attendance at any club fixture. Fortunately the safety precautions in place at Maine Road were better that those at Hillsborough. The biggest complaint was thousands simply couldn't see the pitch because of the crush.

One local comic suggested that all the six footers should be placed

Goalkeeper Frank Swift (left) and full back Sam Barkas were two of City's greatest players – in one of City's greatest teams.

Great Matches

FA CUP SIXTH ROUND   Maine Road, Manchester, 3 March, 1934

Manchester City 1   Stoke City 0   Attendance 84,569
Brook

By the time City had reached the fifth round of the FA Cup during the 1933-34 season, nearly 270,000 people had watched their five matches. However, the average gate of 54,000 was well and truly bettered as a huge crowd of 84,569 (paying a total of £5,426) packed into Maine Road for the sixth-round game against Stoke City. The Potteries side were not short of support either, bringing with them thousands of their own followers. The sheer size of the crowd proved too much for some who, realising they couldn't possibly see any of the play, decided to try and leave the ground. However, such was the interest in this game that the gates were locked 20 minutes before kick-off; the first time ever in the history of Maine Road. Some people were even seen scaling 12-foot walls to get out and about a hundred or so were treated for the effects of crushing and slight abrasions. Fortunately only three people were taken to hospital.

On the pitch, a 17-year-old Stanley Matthews played for Stoke against a full-strength City side containing Swift, Cowan and Toseland, but it would be Eric Brook's name that was on everyone's lips at the end of the game. Brook scored the only goal of the game and people were talking for weeks later as to whether or not he meant it.

He was so far wide out on the left wing in front of the uncovered Kippax Stand that the Stoke defenders stood back and prepared themselves for a cross into the middle. Brook swung over a high, curling ball that goalkeeper Roy John at first appeared to have covered, only to see it apparently swerve and fly past him into the top corner of the net. Despite a late flurry from the visitors, it was enough to see City through to the semi-final and another date at Leeds Road, Huddersfield, but this time for a match against Aston Villa.

A record crowd for a game outside of London had witnessed the 'fluke from Brook' – or had they?

Manchester City: Swift, Barnett, Dale, Busby, Cowan, Bray, Toseland, Marshall, Tilson, Herd, Brook.
Stoke City: John, McGrory, Spencer, Tutin, Turner, Sellars, Matthews, Liddle, Dale, Davies, Johnson.

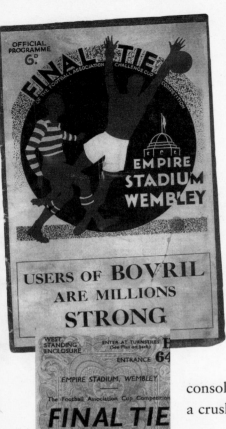

Every fan's dream –
an official programme
and a ticket for the 1934
FA Cup final.

at the back of the stand with all the five footers at the front! In the event, Brook's remarkable goal set up City's 1-0 victory and put them into the FA Cup semi-final for the second year running.

As with last year's semi-final, City once again made their way to Huddersfield, Aston Villa now being the opponents. The Blues were determined to honour Cowan's promise and stormed into a 4-0 lead before half-time. In the second half City continued in the same vein, Tilson taking his personal tally to four goals as the lead increased to six before an 86th-minute consolation Villa reply through Astley. It was a crushing victory for City.

The Big Day

The main talking point in the newspapers on the morning of the final concerned nerves. If City could overcome theirs, something they had failed to do the previous season, then it was felt they'd be victorious. In order to relax even more, the Blues spent a week at a Southport hotel prior to travelling down to Wembley. This period of rest and relaxation did the trick. Despite being a goal down at half-time, City rallied superbly after the interval and thanks to Fred Tilson, won the game 2-1 to lift the FA Cup for the first time in 30 years. On top of a good League campaign, the win at Wembley crowned a highly successful season.

A new face appeared in defence for the beginning of the 1934-35

Great Matches

FA CUP FINAL

Wembley, London, 28 April 1934

Manchester City 2 Portsmouth 1

Attendance 93,258

Tilson 2 Rutherford

City's Alex Herd nearly missed the FA Cup final of 1934, though not by injury. So engrossed was the inside forward with his Edgar Wallace thriller that the team left him behind in the dressing room! Wearing their change colours of maroon shirts, white shorts and maroon and white hooped socks, City were under pressure

early on and a constant flow of Portsmouth attacks on a damp pitch forced the nervous 20-year-old City goalkeeper Frank Swift to be alert at all times. Early in the game Brook missed a glorious opportunity to give City the lead, his shot being blocked by Pompey's Smith.

Just before the half-hour mark, Portsmouth took the lead when Rutherford struck a shot that Swift could only get his fingers to. The score remained 1-0 at half-time and in the dressing room the upset Swift commented that he thought he could have saved the shot if he'd been wearing his gloves. Fred Tilson put Swift at ease when he replied, 'Tha don't need to worry – I'll plonk in two in t'next 'arf', in his strong Yorkshire accent.

Tilson was as good as his word. In the 75th minute, after good play with Brook, he hit a left-foot shot past Gilfillan in the Portsmouth goal and City were level. There were just three minutes left when Tilson delivered his promise. After seeing Swift make a fine, diving save at the other end, he ran onto a pass from Brook to steer the ball home. The dying seconds seemed like an eternity and poor Frank Swift felt the tension even more. When referee Stanley Rous blew the final whistle, Swift turned around to pick up his gloves and fainted. 'Fancy a great big strapping fellow like me fainting in front of all these people... and the King', said a somewhat embarrassed Swift later.

Captain Sam Cowan collected the Cup from King George V, just as he'd promised he would 12 months earlier. City had won the Cup for a second time and the next day the team received a heroes' welcome as thousands thronged the streets of Manchester and packed into Albert Square to hear the speeches. Somewhat of a contrast to the side of 1904 – they were told then that Manchester 'had no time for merriment'.

Manchester City: Swift, Barnett, Dale, Busby, Cowan, Bray, Toseland, Marshall, Tilson, Herd, Brook.

Portsmouth: Gilfillan, Mackie, W Smith, Nichol, Allen, Thackeray, Worrall, J Smith, Weddle, Easson, Rutherford.

Referee: S.F. Rous.

season. Sam Barkas had arrived from Bradford City the week prior to the Cup final and had played in the last two league games. By August he'd replaced Barnett in the side and missed just one league game all season.

It was understandably a season of high expectation at Maine Road but ultimately the side failed to deliver, although the final position of fourth was higher than last year.

The FA Cup campaign that term was also a major disappointment. After three successful campaigns in a row (one semi-final and two final appearances), City lost 1-0 against Tottenham at White Hart Lane in the third round.

Frank Swift was by now earning himself great praise amongst the football writers and he played in all 42 league games of the 1935-36 season. Crowd favourites Matt

Peter Doherty, signed in 1936 from Blackpool, was possibly City's greatest ever player.

50 Greatest Players

SAM COWAN Centre half

Joined Manchester City: 1924   **From:** Doncaster Rovers

Debut: 1924 v Birmingham City (league)

Appearances: 407   **Goals:** 24

Left Manchester City: 1935   **For:** Bradford City

Honours won with Manchester City: Division 2 Championship 1928, FA Cup winner 1934, 3 England caps

Chesterfield born Sam Cowan arrived at Maine Road shortly before Christmas 1924. He was a great motivator, and captained the Blues for three years from the 1932-33 season. Cowan twice led his side out at Wembley, in 1933 against Everton, and then the following year against Portsmouth. In addition to his successes with City, he also won three England caps and represented the Football League.

An ever-present in the 1934-35 season Cowan didn't play a single game the following year and was transferred to Bradford City in October for £2,000. He eventually moved to Brighton, setting up a physiotherapist's practice in the town before being asked to return to Maine Road as manager in November 1946. Cowan guided City to promotion in his one and only season in charge, the conflicting interests of Brighton and Manchester forcing him to leave Maine Road again in July 1947. His physiotherapy work later involved him with Sussex County Cricket Club as well as the MCC. Cowan was refereeing a charity match for Sussex wicket-keeper Jim Parks in October 1964 when he collapsed and died later in the changing rooms. The only man to represent City in three FA Cup finals was 62 when the tragedy occurred.

Busby and captain Sam Cowan moved on, to Liverpool and Bradford City respectively, with the £10,000 rated Peter Doherty arriving from Blackpool. Once again it was a mixed season. There were some wonderful results in the league, with Bolton beaten 7-0, and both Liverpool and Aston Villa suffering 6-0 defeats. The FA Cup run was ended 3-2 at Grimsby in the fifth round. Peter Doherty found the net four times in his nine league appearances. The following season would confirm just what an exceptional talent he was.

Chapter Three: 1937-49
Just Champion

A season that ended with the greatest prize in English football couldn't have started in a less convincing way. By the first week in November, City had won just three of their first 14 league games. Two of these wins came in the space of four days with 10 goals being put past Leeds (four) and West Bromwich Albion (six). The Blues had even suffered defeat in the first derby in more than five years, going down 3-2 to a poor United side in front of nearly 69,000 at Old Trafford.

However things changed at Christmas. On Boxing Day, City, at the time a struggling mid-table side, beat Middlesbrough 2-1 and so embarked on an unbeaten run in the league which lasted for the rest of the season. The 'season to be jolly' lasted for more than four months. The run contained 15 wins and seven draws and pushed the Blues to the top of the table. The highlights of this run came in March when Liverpool were beaten 5-0 at Anfield in 5-1 in the return at Maine Road three days later.

When Sheffield Wednesday visited Maine Road for the penultimate game of the season on 24 April, the Blues needed two points from the last two games to clinch the title. Determined to win the championship for the first time in front of their home supporters, City set about their visitors and went in at half-time leading 3-0. A goal from each side in the second-half made the final score 4-1. City had done it: they were Division 1 champions. The last game at Birmingham finished 2-2 with Peter Doherty's admitted 'fisted' equalising goal keeping the run intact.

That goal of Doherty's was his 30th in the league for the season. He'd scored fifteen in the last twelve games and was undoubtedly the jewel in City's crown. To this day he is still thought by many to be the greatest player ever to have been on the club's books.

Great Matches

LEAGUE DIVISION 1   **Maine Road, Manchester, 24 April, 1937**

Manchester City 4   **Sheffield Wednesday 1**   **Attendance 55,000**

Brook 2   **Rimmer**

Tilson

Doherty

Nothing is certain in football. Just look at the contrasting fortunes of these two sides during the 1936-37 season. Six days before Christmas, City, languishing too near the bottom of the table for comfort, were thrashed 5-1 at Hillsborough. Just four months on, City had to win this game to clinch the Division 1 title. Wednesday had to win to have any chance of survival in the top division.

The Blues had only lost once since that defeat at Hillsborough, and that was the very next game – on Christmas Day itself – 2-1 at Grimsby. They went into this game unbeaten in 20 with six successive straight wins. Not surprisingly they were hot favourites, although they were a little tentative early on.

In the 19th minute, early nerves were settled when Doherty passed to Brook who lashed in an unstoppable shot to give City the lead. One newspaper described it as 'a piece of forked lightning', such was the power behind it. Five minutes later Tilson doubled the lead after being put through by Doherty. In the 31st minute the game was all but over. Swift's clearance found its way to Doherty and so began a slick, passing move that carved open the Wednesday defence. The move lasted some 40 yards, Tilson's final pass enabling Doherty to score his 29th goal of the season, and one of the finest ever seen at Maine Road. A standing ovation led the teams off at the interval. Wednesday did manage a consolation goal in the second half but in the dying minutes, Brook scored his second and the championship had been won. The final whistle brought a joyous pitch invasion, with the crowd bursting into choruses of 'Auld Lang Syne' and 'God Save The King'.

City, FA Cup winners two years before, were champions for the first time. Sheffield Wednesday were relegated the following weekend along with Manchester United.

Manchester City: Swift, Clark, Barkas, Percival, Marshall, Bray, Toseland, Herd, Tilson, Doherty, Brook.
Sheffield Wednesday: Smith, Ashley, Catlin, Grosvenor, Hanford, Rhodes, Luke, Robinson, Dewar, Drury, Rimmer.
Referee: R.W. Blake.

50 Greatest Players

PETER DOHERTY **Forward**

Joined Manchester City: 1936   **From:** Blackpool

Debut: 1936 v Preston North End (league)

Appearances: 131   **Goals:** 80

Left Manchester City: 1945   **For:** Derby County

Honours won with Manchester City: Division 1 Championship 1937,

16 Northern Ireland caps

Doherty signed for City on 19 February 1936, manager Wilf Wild paying a then club record fee of £10,000 for him. Right from the outset City fans could see what Wild had bought. It was difficult to find any weakness in Doherty's game. Tough in the tackle, two-footed, good in the air, and deadly in front of goal, the crowd idolised him. He was leading scorer in the championship winning 1936-37 season.

Like many others, his career was interrupted by war (he joined the RAF) although he did continue to play for City in wartime games. He also guested for 11 other clubs, and played for both the Football League and Northern Ireland.

In 1945 he moved to Derby County and helped them to FA Cup success the following year. After Derby he played for Huddersfield and Doncaster before becoming manager of the Northern Ireland side which reached the quarter-finals of the 1958 World Cup.

Peter Doherty died in Poulton-le-Fylde on 5 May 1990, aged 76.

The FA Cup run that championship year was halted in the quarter-final as City lost 2-0 at Millwall. The earlier rounds had seen a 3-1 win at Wrexham followed by a 2-0 victory against Accrington Stanley at Maine Road. The fifth round tie at Bolton proved a heated affair, with City eventually beating the ten-men Trotters 5-0.

While City were enjoying their success in May, neighbours United were relegated. Nearly 60 years later when the roles were reversed, this was the ultimate achievement as far as the successful club was concerned. Back in the 1930s nothing could be further from the truth. City fans were as disappointed as their Old Trafford counterparts and genuinely wanted United back in the First Division.

Before the new season began, the shipping company Manchester Liners launched a new ship, *The Manchester City* to commemorate the club's championship success.

Reversal of Fortune

If the 1936-37 season was one to remember, the 1937-38 one was certainly one to forget. A truly remarkable reversal of fortunes saw City relegated (despite scoring more goals than anyone else in the division) and United win promotion. Derby County were well beaten 6-1 in a game in September, perhaps the only bright spot in the season prior to Christmas. It was at Christmas-time the previous year that City's good run started, and although Derby suffered a 7-1 defeat in the return fixture in January, the winter months were not kind to City this time around. Out of a total of 10 league games in February and March, City managed just one win, against Portsmouth at home.

Their form improved slightly in April as the goals made a welcome reappearance. Charlton were beaten 5-3 (including a hat-trick from Milsom), West Bromwich Albion 7-1 (four from Brook) and Leeds United 6-2 thanks mainly to a hat-trick from Doherty. When they went to Huddersfield for the last game, both sides were amongst the seven who could be relegated. City lost 1-0, and with other results going against them, were relegated in 21st place along with West Bromwich Albion. That victory for Huddersfield ensured they finished the season eight places off the bottom.

In November City won the Charity Shield for the first time when they beat Sunderland 2-0 at Maine Road. Although their league form wasn't the best, the club enjoyed a good cup run, reaching the quarter-finals only to lose 3-2 at Aston Villa again in front of a then Villa Park record crowd of more than 75,000.

Les McDowall had arrived in March from Sunderland and Doherty was once again leading scorer, with 23 goals from 41 games. But their efforts could not prevent City from playing the next season in Division 2. Injuries to Doherty and Herd and some poor performances by Swift, meant the Blues won just two of their first ten games of the 1938-39 season. However, by November, Doherty was back in the side and the arrival of two new full backs in Eric Westwood and Bert Sproston helped shore up the defence. City began a run of five successive wins, thus preventing any further disasters.

50 Greatest Players

FREDDIE TILSON Inside forward

Joined Manchester City: 1928   From: Barnsley

Debut: 1928 v Grimsby Town (league)

Appearances: 275   Goals: 132

Left Manchester City: 1938   For: Northampton Town

Honours won with Manchester City: FA Cup winner 1934, Division 1 Championship 1937, 4 England caps

Freddie Tilson arrived at Maine Road in March 1928 and played in six games as City won promotion at the end of the season. The other half of a joint signing with former Barnsley colleague Eric Brook, he reformed the partnership on the left hand side of the attack, one that would serve the Blues well over the next 10 years.

Unfortunately for City both injuries and illness dogged his career, although he did manage to score six times in his four international appearances. Injuries also forced him to miss the 1933 FA Cup final against Everton, but he more than made up for it the following year, scoring twice – just as he'd told Frank Swift he would do – as City beat Portsmouth. Tilson was a firm favourite with the supporters. His contribution to the side in the 1930s was rewarded with a championship medal in 1937.

He moved to Northampton Town in March 1938, but that wasn't the end of his Maine Road career. In later life he was City's coach, assistant manager, and chief scout, working right up until his retirement in 1967 for his beloved Blues.

After a short illness, Freddie Tilson passed away in November 1972, aged 69.

In December centre forward Jackie Milsom showed a particular fondness for Tranmere Rovers. He scored seven times in two days as City won 9-3 away and then 5-2 at home. The Blues finished the season with a good run (beaten in just one the last of their last 11 games) but the earlier damage meant they could finish the season no higher than fifth. There proved no joy in the FA Cup either with City winning easily 5-0 at Norwich in the third round only to be beaten 2-0 at Sheffield United in round four. Disgruntled supporters wanted more. After just three games of the 1939-40 campaign, war was declared against Nazi Germany and the entire Football League programme was halted for seven seasons.

As with the advent of World War I, 25 years earlier, clubs were asked to 'do their bit' and provide men for the services. City responded with the likes of Sproston, Barkas and Westwood joining the army, whilst Albert Emptage and Joe Fagan joined the navy. Doherty and manager Wilf Wild enlisted in the RAF and Les McDowall returned to his pre-footballing skills of draughtsmanship, while Jimmy Heale became a fireman. Frank Swift made an abortive attempt at being a traffic policeman before joining the army.

On the footballing front, again like World War I, organised leagues were set up purely on a geographical basis to minimise travel and the likelyhood of huge crowds which would be difficult to evacuate in the event of an emergency.

Teams such as New Brighton and Port Vale became the regulars at Maine Road in the newly formed Western League. From the following season, 1940-41, further changes were made and City played in the North Regional League. Not surprisingly the movement around the country of enlisted footballers made the selection of regular teams virtually impossible and 'guest' players became the norm. Among the guest players for City was Harry McShane, the father of *Lovejoy* actor Ian McShane, who was then on United's books. He played 23 times during the 1940-41 season and even scored against United in a 2-0 win.

Joe Fagan (right) was at City for 1 years before making his debut.

Players' registrations were still kept by the club who also tried to impose strict rules and conditions. For instance Eric Westwood was banned from riding a bicycle at all times.

The rules of these wartime leagues restricted crowds to no more than 8,000 and called for clubs to play a minimum of 18 games prior to Christmas. When Blackpool withdrew from a couple of fixtures in 1942 things got really complicated and City were not placed in the second half of the season through no fault of their own.

50 Greatest Players

FRANK SWIFT Goalkeeper

Joined Manchester City: 1932   **From:** Fleetwood

Debut: 1933 v Derby County (league)

Appearances: 376

Left Manchester City: 1949 (retired)

Honours won with Manchester City: FA Cup winner 1934, Division 1 Championship 1937, Division 2 Championship 1947, 19 England caps

After impressing City scouts playing in goal for the amateur side Fleetwood, Frank Swift was invited down to Maine Road for a trial. He passed the trial, signed amateur forms in October 1932, and turned professional a month later.

After his not too successful debut at Derby on Christmas Day 1933, (City lost 4-1), Swift missed just one league game in the next five seasons. A larger than life character he was popular with football fans up and down the country, not just those at Maine Road. The 'hands like frying pans' could catch the ball easily and then, with no apparent effort, hurl the ball over the halfway line. He became for many, simply the best goalkeeper the game has ever produced.

He will always be remembered for fainting after the final whistle after the 1934 FA Cup final. Swift became the first keeper to captain England when he led the side out to face the Italians in Turin in 1947. England won the game 4-0. Swift retired in September 1949, his place taken by another outstanding goalkeeper, Bert Trautmann.

After retiring, Swift tried his hand in the catering business before becoming a sports journalist for the *News of the World*. It was while returning home from covering Manchester United's European Cup tie in Belgrade in February 1958 that he perished in the tragic Munich air crash.

It was not unusual for City to use up to 40 different players in any of these wartime seasons. Irish international half-back Billy Walsh played more than anyone for City during the war, clocking up 229 appearances in total, scoring eight times. The leading scorer was James Currier, a guest player from nearby Bolton Wanderers, who scored 84 times in 113 matches. Away from the actual football, former player Mickey Hamill who'd played more than 100 games for the Blues in the early 1920s was found mysteriously dead in a canal in July 1943.

Another notable event during the war was a deal struck with United (£5,000 per annum plus a share of the gate receipts) allowing the Reds to use Maine Road for their home matches. Old Trafford was badly damaged by German bombs on the night of 11 March 1941. In return City were allowed to use United's training ground in Salford for their reserve games. In October 1943 there was a reduction in the number of air raids and 60,000 fans saw England beat Scotland 8-0 at Maine Road. It is though to be the finest ever performance by an England side, which contained Frank Swift in goal and Joe Mercer at wing half.

Although wartime league games continued throughout the 1945-46 season, the FA Cup proper returned in January with games being played on a two-legged basis. In the third round against Barrow, Alex Herd scored a hat-trick in a 6-2 win at Maine Road, with the sides drawing 2-2 in the return leg. Bradford Park Avenue were beaten 3-1

50 Greatest Players

ERIC BROOK Winger

Joined Manchester City: 1928   **From:** Barnsley

Debut: 1928 v Grimsby Town (league)

Appearances: 493   **Goals:** 177

Left Manchester City: 1940 (retired through injury)

Honours won with Manchester City: FA Cup winner 1934, Division 2 Championship 1928, Division 1 championship 1937, 18 England caps

City's all-time leading goalscorer was signed in March 1928 in a £6,000 double deal with Barnsley team-mate Freddie Tilson. The successful 1936-37 season saw him score 20 of City's 107 league goals. Primarily a left-winger, he could play at both full back and centre forward and was also capable of standing in as a goalkeeper.

He was a key member of a very strong City side in the 1930s. The scorer of a 'wonder goal' in front of a record crowd of 84,569 against Stoke City in the sixth round in 1934, he was also the first player to wear the number 12 shirt in a FA Cup final. In 1933 Everton wore 1 to 11 while City (outside-left first) wore 12 to 22.

Brook was injured in a road accident travelling to Newcastle for a wartime England v Scotland game, a fractured skull finishing his playing career. After a spell coaching in his home-town of Mexborough, Brook became a pub landlord in Halifax, later returning to Manchester to work as a crane driver in Trafford Park.

He was just 57 when he passed away at his home in Wythenshawe in March 1965.

in the first leg of round four, but the Blues then contrived to lose 8-2 at Maine Road. To date it is still City's record home defeat.

Football Returns

Once the war was over City were eager to return to the top flight. Even though the club had lost the services of one of the all-time greats in Peter Doherty, players of the calibre of Swift, Sproston and Barkas and the goalscoring abilities of George Smith up front, gave City fans confidence for the restart. They began the season well with a 3-0 win at Leicester, and a 3-1 victory against Bury at Maine Road. Andy Black, signed from Hearts, scored three of City's seven against Bradford as City lost just twice in the first 12 games.

In November, Wilf Wild, after 14 years in charge, relinquished his team duties when he became club secretary. His replacement was former captain Sam Cowan, at the time a physiotherapist in Brighton. Cowan's side maintained City's good start and were unbeaten in 22 games until Newcastle won 2-0 at Maine Road on 3 May. After Fulham were beaten on New Year's Day, City remained top of the division for the rest of the season. The last game of which proved

remarkable for several reasons. Firstly, it was played on 14 June, the latest season finish ever for the Blues. Secondly, George Smith scored all five as Newport County were beaten 5-1, thereby equalling Tommy Johnson's record of 19 years standing. And last but by no means least, when Roy Clarke made his debut for Blues against Newport, he was two thirds of the way through a remarkable run that

George Smith (centre) was a great goalscorer, even netting five in one game in 1947.

would see him play three successive games in three different divisions. The disappointment of going out of the FA Cup 5-0 in the fifth round to Birmingham was suddenly forgotten as once again City had won promotion.

City started the next season without a manager. Sam Cowan was unable to combine his physiotherapy business on the south coast with the running of a Division 1 football club in Manchester and so a brief, but successful, reign was over. Former Everton player Jock Thomson became the new man in charge in November.

City averaged a home crowd of 42,725 for the season; the club's highest to date. The biggest of the season was 78,000 for the 'home' derby with United that finished 0-0. Nearly 72,000 saw the 'away' derby in April, a game that also ended in a draw, this time 1-1.

50 Greatest Players

SAM BARKAS Full back

Joined Manchester City: 1934   **From:** Bradford City

Debut: 1934 v Liverpool (league)

Appearances: 195   **Goals:** 1

Left Manchester City: 1947   **For:** Workington Town

Honours won with Manchester City: Division 1 Championship 1937, Division 2 Championship 1947, 5 England caps

A footballing defender who liked to use the ball constructively instead of just clearing the lines, Barkas was capped five times for England, one of them at inside forward, a fact confirming his ability when in possession. He missed just one league game of the 1934-35 season forming a solid partnership with his opposite full back Bill Dale that would last for three years before Dale moved to Ipswich.

Like team-mates Alex Herd and Eric Westwood, Barkas joined the army in 1939 where he kept himself fit enough to return to the City side as a 36-year-old seven years later. Barkas captained the side to the Division 2 title in that 1946-47 season, thus completing a trio of championship medals. He'd already won the Division 1 title with City in 1936-37 and the Division 3 North whilst with Bradford.

Barkas left Maine Road in the 1947 close season after scoring just once in nearly 200 appearances, to take over at Workington Town as manager. Ten years later he was back with City in a scouting capacity, a similar post he would then hold with Leeds, before working in the commercial department at his first club Bradford City.

50 Greatest Players

ALEX HERD Forward

Joined Manchester City: 1933   **From:** Hamilton Accademicals

Debut: 1933 v Blackpool (league)

Appearances: 288   **Goals:** 125

Left Manchester City: 1948   **For:** Stockport County

Honours won with Manchester City: FA Cup winner 1934, Division 1 Championship 1937, Division 2 Championship 1947

Alex Herd arrived at Maine Road from Scotland in February 1933, scoring seven times in 16 league games in his debut season. A powerful inside forward with an eye for goal, Herd became a regular in a strong Blues' side of the 1930s, playing in both FA Cup finals of the period. Alongside Tilson, Doherty and Brook, Herd provided a prolific forward line, those four players alone contributing 80 of City's 107 during the Championship winning 1936-37 campaign.

When war broke out he joined the army but continued to play football, turning out in 90 wartime games for City as well as representing the Scottish League.

In March 1948 he moved to Stockport County on a free transfer, playing 111 League games in three years for the Edgeley Park side before retiring.

Father of United's David, Alex Herd passed away in 1982, aged 70.

Although City were attracting excellent crowds, their performances on the pitch were poor and the club finished in 10th position. There was little success in the Cup either. After beating Barnsley and Chelsea, City then lost 1-0 to Preston in a fifth round tie at Maine Road.

United on the other hand, now managed by former Blue Matt Busby, were playing fine football and establishing themselves at the top of the table. It was noticed by the City board that their 'guests' were attracting more to their 'home' games than City. As they began to slowly take over the mantle of Manchester's top club, it became obvious that some football fans (as opposed to City fans) were favouring the Reds. City's generosity was now backfiring on them.

Before the 1948-49 season started, Frank Swift announced it would be his last. The man who had been praised far and wide as the best goalkeeper in the world would be very hard to replace.

The season ended with 15 wins, 15 draws and 12 defeats – no indication of which way the club was headed, although City did finish seventh, three places higher than the previous year. Again there was no joy in the FA Cup, losing 1-0 at Everton in the third round. In December matters came to a head with their 'lodgers' and United were given notice to quit. Towards the end of the season United attracted more than 80,000 for games against Bradford Park Avenue and Yeovil. Although both derbies that year ended 0-0, it was plain to see which way the power in Manchester football was swinging.

Great Managers 1932-46

WILF WILD

In March 1932 City manager Peter Hodge returned to his previous club, Leicester City, tempted by a higher salary and a five-year contract. Into his shoes stepped Wilf Wild. Wild had been with the Blues since 1920 when he was appointed assistant secretary. He graduated to secretary in 1924 and was keen to take the administrative workload off the manager, believing the manager's priorities should lie purely with matters on the pitch. When Hodge left Maine Road, ironically Wild found himself having to juggle both positions when he was given the title secretary/manager.

His first full season in charge saw City reach Wembley only to suffer defeat at the hands of the Dixie Dean inspired Everton. Twelve months later Wild's side returned to the twin towers where captain Sam Cowan lifted the cup following the 2-1 victory over Portsmouth. With the arrival of such great players as Peter Doherty, Alex Herd and goalkeeper Frank Swift, City's league performances also improved, culminating in a first Championship success in 1937. The following season, despite scoring more goals than any other team in the division, and with virtually the same side, City were relegated to Division 2. It was the lowest point in Wild's 30-year career at Maine Road.

Wild continued to manage the Blues through World War II, a period of obvious uncertainty, during which time he did an excellent job in keeping the club afloat. In November 1946 – midway through City's Division 2 Championship-winning season and after more than 14 years in charge – Wild returned to his secretarial post, handing over the reins to former captain Sam Cowan. He died while still in office in December 1950.

Chapter Four: 1950-57
Lows and Highs

Frank Swift kept his promise and retired at the end of the 1948-49 season although circumstances meant the management would have to once again ask for his services. Swift's replacement in the team should have been Alec Thurlow, a goalkeeper who'd been on the books since September 1946. Unfortunately for Thurlow, he was taken ill with tuberculosis and left for East Anglia to recuperate. Tragically Thurlow was to die of the illness in 1956, aged 34.

Swift came back for the opening game of the 1949-50 season, a 3-3 draw against Aston Villa. Ronnie Powell was in for the next two games before Swift returned for three more, finally calling it a day after the Everton game on 7 September.

By November, with Powell still in goal, City had won only three times. On 19 November, they lost 3-0 at Bolton but had yet another

Bert Trautmann guards the City goal in a league game at Villa Park in December 1949. Bert was popular with football fans from all over the country.

goalkeeper on duty. Signed from non-league St Helens, Bert Trautmann was to become one of the Blues' most popular players, as well as being arguably the best goalkeeper in the world. A former German paratrooper, Trautmann had been a prisoner of war, and not surprisingly his arrival brought about a string of protests from a Manchester public still mindful of the atrocities. Chairman Robert Smith tried his utmost to ease these worries and within a few months, Trautmann's performances on the pitch, and general demeanour off it, had won over many of his detractors.

Unfortunately for City though, things were going very badly on the pitch and despite Trautmann's heroics, the Blues lost 7-0 at Derby in one game. The main problem appeared to be the inability to score goals. The leading scorer was winger Roy Clarke with nine as City

50 Greatest Players

BERT SPROSTON Full back

Joined Manchester City: 1938　　　From: Tottenham Hotspur
Debut: 1938 v Tottenham Hotspur (league)
Appearances: 131　　　Goals: 5
Left Manchester City: 1950 (retired)
Honours won with Manchester City: Division 2 Championship 1947, 2 England caps

In the modern game, it seems inconceivable that a player would travel to an away game with his team-mates, sign for the opposition and promptly make his debut against his old club. However that is precisely what happened to full back Bert Sproston, who, in November 1938, travelled north with Tottenham Hotspur on a Friday for a game at Maine Road the following day. He joined City for £10,000 that same evening and made his debut for the Blues the next day in a 2-0 win over his former club.

These days registration deadlines would make such a deal impossible, but it was not considered particularly unusual at the time, especially as it involved an unhappy player. His move to Maine Road proved the ideal solution and he soon established a strong and reliable full back pairing with Eric Westwood. However World War II seriously impaired his career both at club and international level although he remained at Maine Road until he retired in 1950.

Sproston did some physio and scouting work for Bolton Wanderers before passing away in February 2000 at the age of 84.

managed just 36 in total from 42 League games. There were 18 games in which they failed to score at all, although they did score three times in the FA Cup against Derby, only to concede five at the other end. The season ended in relegation (along with Birmingham) and it spelt the end of Jock Thomson's reign as manager.

The New Man

The new man in charge was former player Les McDowall, recently manager at Wrexham. McDowall immediately brought in Roy Paul from Swansea, a fiercely competitive player who immediately made an impact in defence. The other two stars of the season would be Dennis Westcott and George Smith who the previous season had scored seven times between them. By the end of this season they'd scored 46.

With Trautmann and Paul at the back and Westcott and Smith up front – ably assisted by Johnny Hart – the Blues began to look like they may have a chance of returning to Division 1 after just one season. Jimmy Meadows signed in March as City lost just once in their last 11 games.

The final game was a 2-2 home draw with Grimsby Town, a point being enough to gain promotion in second place behind Preston North End. McDowall's career at Maine Road had started in best possible way.

Roy Paul made an immediate impact when he joined City in 1950.

An obvious difference in standard greeted City on their return to the top flight in August 1951. They earned a solitary point in their first three games, suffering a 5-1 defeat at Huddersfield in the second. In the return game with the Yorkshire side the following week, roles were reversed as City ran out 3-0 winners thanks to goals from Hart, Westcott and Meadows. However, wins of this kind proved hard to come by, indeed they could only manage two wins throughout the second half of the season. Newcomers Ivor Broadis and Don Revie both arrived in the space of three weeks in October but neither made any great impact as the Blues ended the season in 15th place.

Regrettably the 1952-53 season proved to be more of the same. With only one win in the first 16 games, the Blues once again faced an uphill struggle for survival. Johnny Williamson, a big, strong centre forward scored 11 times in the league, the same number as Billy Spurdle, but once again, there were problems in defence. But for the ever-present Trautmann, things might have been much worse. The FA Cup provided only slight relief, Swindon Town beaten 7-0, before City lost to Luton after a replay. Not for the first (or last) time City fans proved their loyalty to the cause in spite of a struggling side. The average crowd was slightly above 34,000, with more than 50,000

watching the games against Manchester United, Sheffield Wednesday and Arsenal.

The brightest thing about the 1953-54 season were the newly installed floodlights at Maine Road. The lights made their first appearance for a friendly against Hearts on 14 October with City winning 6-3. Ten days later, youngster Joe Hayes made his debut for City, unfortunately on the wrong end of a 3-0 scoreline at Tottenham.

Signed in 1953, the young striker Joe Hayes was an important part of the FA Cup-winning team of 1956.

50 Greatest Players

ERIC WESTWOOD Full back

Joined Manchester City: 1937   **From:** Manchester United

Debut: 1938 v Tottenham Hotspur (league)

Appearances: 260   **Goals:** 5

Left Manchester City: 1953   **For:** Altrincham

Honours won with Manchester City: Division 2 Championship 1947

Like his full back partner Bert Sproston, Eric Westwood lost the bulk of his playing career to World War II. Their careers virtually ran parallel, both making their debuts in the same game against Tottenham in November 1938, then, like a generation of players, lost their prime years to the battle against Fascism.

Manchester born, Westwood actually played as an amateur for rivals United before turning professional with City in November 1937. A sturdy and skilful left back who could also play outside left, he managed 23 wartime appearances for City, and, at a time when circumstances allowed such things, guested for Chelsea while stationed in the south and played for them in the 1944 War Cup final. At the end of the war he captained the British Army on the Rhine team which played across Europe.

Westwood's career at Maine Road spanned 16 years, during which time he won a Division 2 championship medal, Football League and England 'B' honours. He moved to Altrincham on a free transfer in 1953 and when his playing days were finally over, he went into business, first as a pub landlord and later as a newsagent.

Although these were obviously difficult times for the Blues, little money was being spent to try and improve the playing squad; indeed Ivor Broadis was actually sold to Newcastle in November after a 'heart to heart' with the manager. Some of the Broadis money went towards the signing of centre forward Billy McAdams from Irish side Distillery the following month. McAdams impressed in his 17 games that season, scoring eight times.

Tottenham knocked the Blues out of the Cup by the only goal of the game at Maine Road in the fourth round. The season ended on a high as Charlton were beaten 3-0, but yet again it had been a disappointing effort. However, plans were being tried and tested in the reserve team that would certainly improve City's standing over the next couple of years.

Ken Barnes was pivotal to the success of McDowall's 'Revie Plan'.

The Revie Plan

Manager McDowall and former player now trainer Freddie Tilson, had been experimenting with a formation which featured the centre forward playing behind the other front men instead of alongside them. This was a plan used to great effect by the Hungarian national side and had been first seen in England in 1953.

In the reserves, Johnny Williamson played this deep-lying role, with Ken Barnes being his chief ally. McDowall wanted his team to 'play football' in the new season, and so, in the first game, away at Preston, City tried out this new formation. Don Revie was to be the pivot, but the plan backfired as City lost 5-0.

Determined to persevere with the plan, Ken Barnes was brought into the side at the expense of Jock McTavish for the next game, four days later, at home to Sheffield United. With Barnes and Revie now working together, the plan worked beautifully as City won the game 5-2. A system later christened the Revie Plan had been introduced to league football and it reaped dividends for City all season. The finest example of the plan came in the Old Trafford derby in February. City won 5-0 thanks to goals from Fagan and Hayes (two each) and Hart. The plan was crucial in seeing the Blues improvement in league standing at the end of the season. They finished seventh; ten places higher than the previous year, and just two points behind runners-up Wolves.

In the FA Cup, the Blues had a terrific run, eventually losing in the final to Newcastle. Barnes, Hayes and Revie scored the goals as Derby County were beaten in the third round, and then 74,723 saw Manchester United beaten 2-0 in round four. Two goals from Roy

Clarke won the fifth round game at Luton in a blizzard, and Johnny Hart's single strike was enough to see the end of Birmingham in the quarter-final. That game at St Andrew's was described as being the hardest in the competition so far. In the semi-final at Villa Park, a game played in atrocious ground and weather conditions, Roy Clarke's flying header from a Joe Hayes cross was the only goal of the game and City were through to Wembley. Tragically Clarke was to injure a knee shortly before the end of the game which forced him to miss the final.

Striker Johnny Hart scored against Birmingham in the 1955 FA Cup quarter-final.

Another absentee from the final was Johnny Hart, City's leading scorer in the league. Hart had broken his leg in a game at Huddersfield the week before the semi-final.

Captained by Roy Paul, City came out on the famous Wembley turf dressed in tracksuits, the first side to do so in a final. There were also two more firsts that day; Bert Trautmann was the first German to play in a Wembley Cup final, and Billy Spurdle, in for the injured Clarke, was the first Channel Islander.

The Blues couldn't have got off to a worse start as Milburn headed in a corner after 45 seconds. Twenty minutes later a further tragedy struck when full back Jimmy Meadows twisted his knee and was carried off. Down to 10 men, the Blues rallied to play some good football which resulted in a header from Bobby Johnstone levelling the score by the interval.

Unfortunately for the Blues, being a man short proved too much and by the time the hour mark was reached, the game was effectively over. Two more Newcastle goals, from Mitchell and Hannah, increased their lead to 3-1 and that was it. The Revie Plan, which had served the Blues well all season, was unable to influence the biggest game of the season. At a dinner after the final, a dejected Roy Paul repeated the words of Sam Cowan in 1933, when he said: 'We'll be back next year and win it'.

The Manchester City official brochure for the 1955 FA Cup final.

The main talking point prior to the opening of the 1955-56 season was the apparent fall-out between manager Les McDowall and his major playmaker, the recently voted Footballer of the Year, Don Revie. By November, City were playing the Revie Plan without Revie, McDowall having suspended the player for 14 days. There were also rumours about another rift between Revie and the up and coming Bobby Johnstone. This rift couldn't have been helped when it was announced that Johnstone would be taking Revie's place in the side as the deep-lying centre forward.

Disagreements like these might indicate City were in for a poor season although events proved the opposite. The Blues finished the season in fourth place, a third consecutive improvement. The ever-present Joe Hayes was leading scorer with 23, with the Lancashire cricketer Jack Dyson (a player who'd been at the club for more than three years) in second place with 13.

More FA Cup Glory

As in the previous year, it was in the FA Cup that City excelled, this time winning the ultimate prize. In the third round against Blackpool, fog and heavy mud caused the game to be abandoned after 55 minutes with the score at 1-1. In the rearranged game the following week Jack Dyson and Joe Hayes scored for the Blues in a 2-1 win. There was more mud in the next round as City travelled to Southend. On a pitch covered by cockleshells to help with the drainage, Bert Trautmann played what many thought was his best ever game for City as Hayes scored the only goal of the game.

Ice was the problem for the fifth round visit of Liverpool on 18 February. The game finished goalless in front of a crowd of 70,640 with neither side being able to master the conditions sufficiently well to grab the crucial goal. In the replay four days later, a blanket of snow covered Anfield (and 57,000 spectators) in a game the Blues came from a goal down in to win 2-1, although only just. The presence of both Trautmann and Ewing couldn't prevent Liverpool's Billy Liddell from equalising in the very last minute in front of the Kop. At least they thought he had. Fortunately the referee had blown his whistle literally a second before Liddell had 'scored' and so the 'goal' would not stand. The referee (a Mr Griffiths) was a very brave man.

In the quarter-final, City played to

Roy Little clears from Newcastle's Vic Keeble in the 1955 FA Cup final.

host to the other Merseyside team, Everton, in front of another huge crowd, 76,129. As at Anfield, City came from a goal behind to win 2-1 with Hayes and Johnstone getting the all-important goals. The semi-final was against Tottenham, a team currently too near the bottom of the division for comfort, at Villa Park, the scene of last year's triumph. Like the previous year against Sunderland, one goal would be enough to decide the tie and fortunately for the Blues it came from Bobby Johnstone's header in the 40th minute.

Before the final, Bert Trautmann collected the Football Writers' Footballer of the Year Award, retaining the award won by team-mate Don Revie 12 months earlier. Little did anyone know what drama Trautmann would be a part of in the final.

The rift between McDowall and Revie had been simmering all season, and although Revie had played in the last four league games, he'd played in just one FA Cup tie and his place in the final was not certain. The papers were full of contradictory stories. On the morning of the game the decision was taken out of McDowall's hands. After a visit to the doctor, Billy Spurdle was told his outbreak of boils would keep him out of the side; Revie would play.

The 1953 final had been christened 'The Matthews Final' after the superb display

THE FOOTBALL ASSOCIATION CHALLENGE CUP COMPETITION

FINAL TIE
BIRMINGHAM CITY
v
MANCHESTER CITY
SATURDAY, MAY 5th, 1956   KICK-OFF 3 pm

EMPIRE STADIUM
WEMBLEY

Chairman and Managing Director   SIR ARTHUR J. ELVIN, MBE
OFFICIAL PROGRAMME   -   ONE SHILLING

The big day: the 1956 FA Cup final was Manchester City's second in two years.

by the Blackpool winger. The 1956 Final would soon be known as 'The Revie Final'. City beat Birmingham by a 3-1 margin, with several players, Ken Barnes included, saying it was the finest example of the Revie Plan in action.

The season had ended on a triumphant note for the Blues and it was

Great Matches

FA CUP FINAL   **Wembley, London, 5 May 1956**

Manchester City 3   **Birmingham City 1**   **Attendance 100,000**

Hayes   Kinsey

Dyson

Johnstone

For the previous couple of seasons City had been playing in a style first seen in 1953 when Hungary beat England at Wembley. This involved a deep-lying centre forward as opposed to the traditional, bustling, Nat Lofthouse-type of player. At City, Don Revie assumed this revolutionary new position and not surprisingly the tactic was christened 'The Revie Plan'. Less than three minutes after kick-off, City were a goal up thanks to the Revie Plan, Joe Hayes completing the move with a left foot shot into the corner. Eleven minutes later Birmingham equalised when a shot from Noel Kinsey beat Trautmann and went in off a post. Twenty minutes into the second half City regained the lead when Jack Dyson scored. Johnstone was on the scoresheet two minutes later to put himself in the record books as the first man to score in successive FA Cup finals.

Over the years Wembley has witnessed some dramatic moments, but perhaps none more so than when – with less than 15 minutes to go to the final whistle – City's German goalkeeper Bert Trautmann broke his neck. Diving at the feet of the incoming Peter Murphy, Trautmann was obviously seriously injured (it wasn't known just how seriously at the time) but courageously carried on to collect his Cup winner's medal. Captain Roy Paul led his victorious side up the famous Wembley steps to collect the FA Cup – just as the 'Welsh Dragon' had predicted 12 months earlier.

Manchester City: Trautmann, Leivers, Little, Barnes, Ewing, Paul, Johnstone, Hayes, Revie, Dyson, Clarke.
Birmingham City: Merrick, Hall, Green, Newman, Smith, Boyd, Astall, Kinsey, Brown, Murphy, Govan.
Referee: A. Bond.

as the English FA Cup winners that they set off on an unbeaten summer tour to Germany. Unfortunately for the Germans they were unable to see their greatest export in action because of his injuries. It was to be a further seven months before anybody saw Bert Trautmann play again.

The obvious difficulties between McDowall and Revie showed no signs of healing over the summer. The 1956-57 league campaign started badly – just two wins in the first 13 games – and in November Revie was transferred to Sunderland. The 6ft 4ins (1m 93cm) Jack Savage was Trautmann's replacement in goal, and, try as he may, his performances didn't match those of the legendary German as City continued to struggle. By December, Trautmann, still not fully fit, was back in the side.

Apart from a 7-3 defeat at Arsenal back in October, perhaps the most

50 Greatest Players

ROY CLARKE Winger

Joined Manchester City: 1947   **From:** Cardiff City

Debut: 1947 v Newport County (league)

Appearances: 370   **Goals:** 79

Left Manchester City: 1958   **For:** Stockport County

Honours won with Manchester City: Division 2 Championship 1947, FA Cup winner 1956, 22 Wales caps

Roy Clarke has served City faithfully for over 50 years, as a player, Social Club manager and latterly as a prominent member of the club's Former Players' Association.

Clarke holds a unique record in British football having played three consecutive games in three different divisions of the Football League. He played for Cardiff City in their penultimate fixture of 1946-47, who then, having already clinched the Division 3 championship, allowed him to move to City for £12,000 in time for him to make his debut for the Blues in the final game of their Division 2 championship campaign. Clarke's next game therefore was the opening game of the 1947-48 season in Division 1 when he scored in a 4-3 home victory over Wolves.

He went on to appear in successive FA Cup finals in 1955 and 1956. City's victory over Birmingham City in the latter was undoubtedly the highlight of an illustrious career that included 22 Welsh caps. He left to join Stockport County on a free transfer in 1958 but eventually returned to become a familiar and popular face on the Maine Road scene in the many years since.

50 Greatest Players

ROY PAUL Wing half

Joined Manchester City: 1950   **From:** Swansea Town

Debut: 1950 v Preston North End (league)

Appearances: 294   **Goals:** 9

Left Manchester City: 1957   **For:** Worcester City

Honours won with Manchester City: FA Cup winner 1956, 24 Wales caps

Born in the Welsh mining village of Gilli Pentre, Roy Paul began his professional career with Swansea Town who he signed for in 1938. When war broke out he joined the Royal Marines as a PT instructor. After serving in India, he returned to Swansea where he played 160 league games before, in his own words 'my South American adventure'. Along with some other British players, Paul was lured by the large sums of money on offer to play in Bogota, Colombia. He quickly realised his mistake and returned to the UK in 1950 where he was signed by City boss Les McDowall for £19,500.

The name of Roy Paul would be a regular feature on a City team sheet for the next seven seasons. He missed just one game in his debut season of 1950-51, a season that saw City return to Division 1, five points behind champions Preston North End.

Always a fierce competitor and a man who hated to lose, Paul was bitterly disappointed after the 1955 FA Cup final and commented at the after match dinner 'we'll be back next year and win it'. He was as good as his word twelve months later when Birmingham City were beaten 3-1 at Wembley. In June 1957 he joined Worcester City as player/manager.

He died from Alzheimer's Disease in a Glamorgan nursing home in May 2002 aged 82.

Bobby Johnstone scores City's third and final goal in the FA Cup final in 1956 by sliding the ball under the advancing Birmingham goalkeeper.

remarkable game of the season was in the FA Cup third round against Newcastle. After a 1-1 draw at St James' Park on the Saturday, City led 3-0 after half an hour in the replay. By the 85th minute the Geordies had levelled the score and the game went into extra time. Johnstone restored the Blues' lead before two goals from Len White won the tie 5-4 for the visitors. A crowd of nearly 47,000 had witnessed a game in which only Manchester City could have taken part.

50 Greatest Players

DON REVIE Inside forward

Joined Manchester City: 1951   **From:** Hull City

Debut: 1951 v Burnley (league)

Appearances: 178   **Goals:** 41

Left Manchester City: 1956   **For:** Sunderland

Honours won with Manchester City: FA Cup winner 1956, Footballer of the Year 1955, 6 England caps

Middlesbrough born Don Revie achieved fame as both an influential player and a highly successful manager. He began his playing career with Leicester City in 1944. He moved to Hull City in 1949 before signing for City in October 1951 for £25,000. When Revie arrived for pre-season training at Maine Road in the summer of 1954 he was surprised to find that much more emphasis had been put on ball work as opposed to traditional fitness training. This was the beginning of what would become known as the 'Revie Plan', which developed so well that it brought City the FA Cup in 1956.

Revie was voted Footballer of the Year in 1955. In 1956 he moved back to the north-east when he joined Sunderland. After two years there he moved to Leeds, where, after a spell as player/manager, he became manager full-time in May 1963. Over the next 11 years, Revie transformed an ordinary Division 2 side into one of the best teams in Europe. He left Elland Road to replace Joe Mercer as manager of England in 1974, before being offered the post as coach to the United Arab Emirates national side. In later life, Don Revie OBE, one of the game's greatest thinkers, contracted motor-neurone disease and died in Edinburgh on 26 May 1989.

Chapter Five: 1958-1964
The Darkest Hours

The 1957-58 season began with a 3-2 win against Chelsea at Stamford Bridge followed by a 5-2 triumph in the return game the next week. Sandwiched in between, however, was a 4-1 defeat at Old Trafford. The pattern for the season had been set.

Roy Warhurst had arrived in the summer from Birmingham City to replace the inspirational Roy Paul and youngsters Colin Barlow and Cliff Sear began to establish themselves in the first team.

Manager McDowall tried to evolve another plan, this time involving inside left Keith Marsden playing alongside Dave Ewing at the back in a dual centre half role. This proved to be a short-lived scheme and was abandoned after a 6-1 defeat at Preston followed by a 9-2 mauling at West Bromwich. Jack Savage had the misfortune to be standing in for the injured Bert Trautmann in both these matches.

A neutral supporter must have loved watching the Blues that season. They both scored and conceded over 100 goals and managed to finish in fifth place, thirteen places higher than the previous season. Wins such as 6-2 at home to Everton when Ken Barnes scored a hat-trick of penalties, were interspersed with defeats such as 8-4 at Leicester.

Frank Swift was killed in the Munich air disaster.

The lowest point of the season came in February with the news of the Munich air disaster. Among the many killed was Frank Swift, City's former goalkeeper, who had been covering United's European cup-tie for the *News of the World*.

85

City came back from 3-0 down to win at Burnley in the first game of the 1958-59 season. They would not win again for nine games. Once again it was a tale of inconsistency for the Blues. The previous year they had no problem in scoring (they scored 104) whereas this season proved the opposite. This year's tally was 64 and was the main reason for the club finishing just one point away from relegation. Even the arrival of inside forward George Hannah made little difference; Barlow and Hayes finishing as leading scorers. They faired badly in the FA Cup as well, going down 2-1 at home to Grimsby Town of Division 2 in a replay. The fact that Grimsby were relegated to Division 3 at the end of the season typified City's situation at the time.

50 Greatest Players

BOBBY JOHNSTONE Forward

Joined Manchester City: 1955   **From:** Hibernian

Debut: 1955 v Bolton Wanderers (league)

Appearances: 139   **Goals:** 51

Left Manchester City: 1959   **For:** Hibernian

Honours won with Manchester City: FA Cup winner 1956,

4 Scotland caps

Bobby Johnstone's name is in the record books as the first man ever to score in two successive FA Cup finals.

Already a Scottish international and member of a highly successful Hibernian side, Johnstone signed for City in March 1955 for £20,700. Just over 12 months later he had played in two Wembley finals and had become something of a cult figure amongst the City followers. He scored the equaliser against Newcastle United in 1955 and then the third against Birmingham City the following year. He also won the 1956 semi-final for the Blues with a spectacular diving header against Tottenham at Villa Park.

Johnstone played four times for Scotland while at Maine Road as well as turning out for Britain against a Rest of Europe side. His happy knack of scoring goals produced a tally of 51 from 138 appearances in a City shirt. In September 1959 he rejoined Hibs for a fee of £3,000 where he stayed for one season before joining Oldham Athletic. After spending many years in retirement in the north-west, Johnstone moved back to his native Scotland at the end of the 1990s. He died on 22 August 2001, aged 71.

Realising this kind of inconsistency couldn't continue, McDowall began to make changes in his playing staff as the new decade approached. Long-serving players such as Bobby Johnstone and Roy Little left the club to be replaced initially by the likes of Clive Colbridge and the fleeting visit of full back Andy Kerr.

Despite all McDowall's efforts there was little change on the pitch although City did finish in the relatively comfortable position of 16th. However, a close examination of the table shows their cushion of three points above second to the bottom Leeds United proves it was too close for comfort. Had it not been for Colin Barlow's late winner against Preston in the third to last match, things could have been worse.

On 15 March 1960, McDowall finally obtained the services of a striker he'd been tracking for months. His name was Denis Law and the fee was a then British transfer record of £55,000. Law scored twice in seven league appearances, leading scorer for the season being Billy McAdams with 21 goals.

With the prolific Law in the side, the 1960-61 season promised at the least, an improvement over the last couple of years. Law was joined by 17-year-old David Wagstaffe as well as summer signings Barrie Betts and Jackie Plenderleith, and City started well, remaining unbeaten in their first six games, of which three were victories.

Denis Law joined City in 1960 for a British record fee of £55,000.

A 3-1 defeat at Bolton on 5 November began a sequence of 10 games in which City lost nine and won one. This dreadful run – including a 5-1 defeat at Old Trafford – ruined all that had gone before it and jeopardised any chance the Blues had of finishing in the top 10. The rot was finally stopped with consecutive 3-3 draws against Newcastle and Cardiff and a 3-0 win against West Bromwich Albion.

The League Cup Begins

This was the first season of a new knockout competition, the Football League Cup, and after a comfortable 3-0 victory over Stockport County, City then lost 2-0 at Portsmouth who were in Division 2. The FA Cup provided a remarkable match for the Blues, and placed the name of Denis Law in the history books.

After three games with Cardiff in the third round, City were drawn away at Luton in round four. In playing conditions resembling a bog and with heavy rain still pouring down, the Blues found themselves two goals down in the first 20 minutes. Denis Law then produced a hat-trick and by half-time City were in front. He continued with his amazing feat after the break by scoring another hat-trick in less than 25 minutes and City led 6-2.

Just two minutes after Law had scored his sixth, referee Tuck decided no further play was possible and abandoned the game. In the replay four days later, (in conditions described by Denis Law as 'worse') City lost 3-1, Law's name again on the scoresheet. Unfortunately for Law, only his goal in the replay is allowed in his statistical record. Like the FA Cup clash with Newcastle four seasons earlier, this was game in which only Manchester City could have taken part.

The goalscoring achievements of Law attracted Italian giants Torino in the summer of 1961. In June he left Maine Road for a staggering £110,000, only to spend one year in Italy before returning to Manchester to spend the best years of his career with Matt Busby at Old Trafford.

McDowall spent some of this money on inside forward Peter Dobing from Blackburn and defender Bobby Kennedy from Kilmarnock.

50 Greatest Players

KEN BARNES Wing half

Joined Manchester City: 1950   **From:** Stafford Rangers

Debut: 1952 v Derby County (league)

Appearances: 283   **Goals:** 19

Left Manchester City: 1961   **For:** Wrexham

Honours won with Manchester City: FA Cup winner 1956

When City signed Ken Barnes from Stafford Rangers in May 1950 they had a surfeit of wing halves on the books. His breakthrough in the first team came in the second game of the 1954-55 season and his role soon became a pivotal one in the Blues' new style of play known as 'The Revie Plan'. Such was his importance that Revie himself commented 'Ken Barnes is the one that makes it work'.

Barnes played in the successful 1956 FA Cup winning side, and the following year he put his name in the record books when he scored a hat-trick of penalties in a thrilling 6-2 victory over Everton at Maine Road.

The club's practical joker, well known for always having a cigarette nearby, 'Beaky' became player/manager of Wrexham in 1961. The Birmingham-born midfielder's only international recognition came when he was named as reserve for The Football League against Wales in 1957. He retired from playing in 1964, returning to Maine Road six years later as first team coach. The father of two sons who have also played at Maine Road, Ken Barnes spent 18 years as chief scout for the club, discovering, among others, Steve Redmond, Paul Lake and David White.

The acquisition of Dobing proved to be a wise one as he finished the leading scorer for 1961-62 season with 22 goals, having missed just one game all season.

Like the previous season, November proved to be the start of a bad run, and by New Year City were once again at the wrong end of the table. McDowall decided to blood some of the Maine Road youngsters, and gave opportunities to Neil Young and a 15-year-old Glyn Pardoe (the youngest ever in City's first-team), both of whom would give sterling service to the club over the next 10 years. Young initially wore the number seven shirt and scored 11 times, including City's only goal in the FA Cup, from his position out on the wing. The Blues lost 2-0 at Everton in the fourth round of the FA Cup after a 1-0 win at Notts County. In the League Cup, they failed to negotiate the first round, losing 4-2 at Ipswich. The hitherto loyal fans were beginning to show their displeasure at the turnstiles. The season's average attendance of 25,626 was nearly 4,000 less than the previous year. That in turn was the first time it had been under 30,000 for thirty years.

Apart from the 1957-58 season when City had finished fifth, recent times at Maine Road could not exactly be described as successful. Despite this there was no apparent displeasure with the manager as the 1962-63 season opened with a humiliating 8-1 defeat at Wolves. Even City's goal that day was provided by their opponents. Alex Harley arrived from Third Lanark in August and would end the season's leading scorer. Thanks to a last minute goal from Harley, City won the Old Trafford derby 3-2, with Denis Law scoring twice for United.

The fierce winter of 1962-63 affected all sporting activities and between 15 December and 2 March City played just three games, although they were undefeated. It was by far their longest unbeaten run of the season! After the thaw they lost six consecutive games and by Easter they were in 21st place. With just two games remaining City were still desperate for the points as Manchester United arrived at Maine Road for the 74th league derby.

United at the time were just one point above City although they did have a game in hand. It was expected to be a tough game as the points were vital to both teams. And so it proved.

50 Greatest Players

DAVE EWING Centre half

Joined Manchester City: 1949   **From:** Luncarty Juniors

Debut: 1953 v Manchester United (league)

Appearances: 303   **Goals:** 1

Left Manchester City: 1962   **For:** Crewe Alexandra

Honours won with Manchester City: FA Cup winner 1956

Dave Ewing joined City in June 1949, but would have to wait more than three and a half years for his first-team debut which came in a 1-1 draw at Old Trafford, the first of what would be more than 300 games for City. An uncompromising 'stopper', Ewing was the archetypal centre-half, one who always gave 100 per cent, and his booming voice was synonymous with the City sides of the 1950s. The saying 'All stop at Dave's' became popular with Blues' supporters as a tribute to his attitude and determination.

He played in successive FA Cup finals in the 1950s, defending the badly injured Bert Trautmann in 1956, although at one point so keen was his enthusiasm that he actually collided with the stricken goalkeeper causing more consternation. Ewing managed just one solitary goal during his 10 years in the first team at Maine Road, against Portsmouth in 1957, a game City won 2-1.

At the end of the 1961-62 season he left Maine Road for Crewe on a free transfer. He later became manager of Hibernian. He would eventually return to Maine Road on the coaching staff. After a long illness, Dave Ewing died in July 1999.

The Blues went ahead in the ninth minute when Alex Harley's low shot beat the diving Gaskell in the United goal. Harley found the net a second time 20 minutes later only for the goal to be ruled out by a very close offside decision. After a running battle all afternoon, an ill-tempered first-half ended with United's Pat Crerand 'laying out' David Wagstaffe in the players' tunnel.

With four minutes left on the clock, Wagstaffe tried a backpass to goalkeeper Harry Dowd which fell some way short. Denis Law ran onto the ball as Dowd rushed out and took it to the side of the diving City keeper. Dowd managed to push the ball out of play as Law fell over him. Tragically for City the referee adjudged Dowd's challenge to be a foul and awarded a penalty kick. Albert Quixall converted from the spot and City were robbed of a valuable point.

Needing a win at all costs, City travelled to London only to be badly beaten 6-1 by West Ham. Nearest rivals Birmingham managed to win their last game and so City were relegated to face football in Division 2 for the first time in twelve years.

By far the club's best run in the League Cup was ended at Birmingham by a convincing 6-0 scoreline in the fifth round, Norwich won at Maine Road by the odd goal in three to end any aspirations in the FA Cup after three matches. All in all it had been a dreadful season and it would be one season too far for manager McDowall. After 13 years in charge, he was replaced by his assistant manager George Poyser in May 1963.

New Faces

The prospects of playing in Division 2 in 1963-64 didn't appeal to either Peter Dobing or Alex Harley and they both left Maine Road in the close season, to Stoke and Birmingham respectively.

Derek Kevan was a new face, a £35,000 signing from Chelsea and would finish the season top scorer with 30 goals. Centre forward Jimmy Murray came from Wolves in November and scored 21 times, combining with Kevan to form a powerful attack.

Harry Dowd had by now taken over the goalkeeping post permanently from Bert Trautmann, although his position was under threat towards the end of the season from Alan Ogley who'd signed from Barnsley the previous July. In February, City were trailing 1-0 at home to Bury thanks to a goal by future Manchester City legend

All international XI
versus a combined Manchester City
and Manchester United XI

Wednesday April 15th 1964
at Maine Road Manchester
kick off 7-30 p.m.

BERT
TRAUTMANN

testimonial
match

Official programme
one shilling

*The official programme from Bert Trautmann's testimonial. The game was a sell
out, and many people queued for hours to get in, but without success.*

50 Greatest Players

BERT TRAUTMANN Goalkeeper

Joined Manchester City: 1949   **From:** St Helens Town

Debut: 1949 v Bolton Wanderers (league)

Appearances: 545

Left Manchester City: 1964 (retired)

Honours won with Manchester City: FA Cup winner 1956, Footballer of the Year 1956

The name Bert Trautmann is not only a legend in the history of Manchester City Football Club, but also in the history of football in England. Born in Bremen in October 1923, Trautmann joined the Luftwaffe in 1941. Initially a radio operator, he became a paratrooper serving in Poland and Russia where he was captured. He managed to escape and went to France, only to be captured again. In true Hollywood style, he escaped again. He was captured for a third and final time by the Americans in Normandy who shipped him off to a prisoner-of-war camp in the Lancashire town of Ashton-in-Makerfield. At the camp he began to be recognised as quite a useful goalkeeper, and after the war he was offered the opportunity to play non-league football for nearby St Helens Town. His early promise continued and he attracted the attention of Jock Thomson, then manager at City.

On 7 October 1949, Bert Trautmann signed amateur forms for City, turning professional just a few weeks later. Reactions were mixed at the thought of having a German playing at Maine Road. However, Trautmann's performances over the next few months won over many of his initial 'enemies', and he would go on to be one of the most popular figures ever to have played at Maine Road. Nowadays he spends his time mainly between Spain and his native Germany, but when he does return to his adopted Manchester, he is still besieged for autographs wherever he goes.

Of the 545 games Trautmann played for City, he will be forever remembered for one in particular, the 1956 FA Cup final. This was the game when he broke his neck diving at the feet of the Birmingham forward Peter Murphy. City were leading 3-1 with just 14 minutes left when the incident happened. In those pre-substitute days, Trautmann bravely carried on, unaware of just how seriously injured he was. Nobody really knew the severity for several days afterwards. After retiring from playing, he took over as general manager at Stockport County in October 1965, before spending many years travelling the world as a coach.

Colin Bell. In the 54th minute of the game, Dowd broke a finger and was replaced in goal by Matt Gray, enabling Dowd to play in attack. When a shot from Derek Kevan bounced down off the crossbar, it was City's injured goalkeeper who was on hand to bundle home the equaliser.

The FA Cup campaign ended in the third round with City losing 2-1 at Swindon. In the League Cup, the Blues faired much better, eventually going down 2-1 over a two-legged semi-final to Stoke. Four wins and a draw completed the season and City finished sixth, perhaps slightly disappointing as many had tipped the Blues strongly for an immediate return.

On 15 April, 48,000 (with many more locked out) packed into Maine Road for Bert Trautmann's testimonial game. The game between a combined City and United XI and an International XI provided a fitting tribute to one of the world's greatest goalkeepers.

Bleak Prospects

The 1964-65 season was one of alarming mediocrity.

Attendances had been dropping regularly over the past few years and by the January 1965, the fans had finally had enough. City suffered an embarrassing third round FA Cup defeat against Shrewsbury Town of Division 3 and three days later only 8,015 turned up for a league game against Swindon Town. It is the lowest ever attendance for a league game at Maine Road. City even contrived to lose the match 2-1, with a certain Mike Summerbee scoring for the visitors. Another side from Division 3, Mansfield Town, knocked City out of the League Cup 5-3 in front of a meagre 8,789 at Maine Road.

Manager Poyser had brought in Irish international Johnny Crossan and given a league debut to Mike Doyle to try to improve things but it was all to no avail. Following the Swindon game angry supporters hurled bricks at the windows in the main stand as a way of showing their frustration. Across at Old Trafford, Matt Busby had successfully rebuilt his side after Munich and the ground was being upgraded for the forthcoming World Cup. City fans had every reason to be angry.

50 Greatest Players

JOE HAYES Inside forward

Joined Manchester City: 1953   **From:** Juniors

Debut: 1953 v Tottenham Hotspur (league)

Appearances: 364   **Goals:** 152

Left Manchester City: 1965   **For:** Barnsley

Honours won with Manchester City: FA Cup winner 1956

A small man – he was 5' 8" (1m 72cm) – Joe Hayes was one of the most prolific marksmen in the history of the club, in fact only two men have scored more times for City. Kearsley born, he scored four goals in a trial game at Maine Road. This convinced the club to sign him, and two months later he made his debut in the senior side, albeit it in a 3-0 defeat at Tottenham. In season 1954-55, he scored 13 times in 20 league games, a terrific ratio for someone who was still only 19 years old.

Hayes played in the side that lost to Newcastle United in the 1955 FA Cup final as well as the victorious final twelve months later. In that 1956 final, he scored the first goal as Birmingham were beaten 3-1. Capped twice at Under 23 level for England, Hayes' career was cut abruptly short when he badly injured knee ligaments during a game against Bury at Gigg Lane in December 1964. He was just 28 and never really recovered full fitness before being sold to Barnsley the following summer. His later career took him to Wigan Athletic and then player/manager with Lancaster City.

On retirement from the game Hayes worked for a finance company for a while before setting up his own greengrocery business. He died of cancer in 1999, aged 63.

At Easter, George Poyser resigned, leaving the club even more rudderless for the last few games of the season. A combination of several people, including coach Johnny Hart, selected the team until Chairman Albert Alexander felt he'd chosen the right replacement. City fans would have to wait until July for the announcement but the wait would certainly be worth it.

Chapter Six: 1965-1972
Glory Days

Joe Mercer was the man chosen as the new manager of a Manchester City side struggling in Division 2. Highly respected in the game, Mercer had been a successful player with both Arsenal and Everton and had played more than 30 times for England. He'd already managed Sheffield United and Aston Villa, taking Villa to two FA Cup semi-finals and becoming the first ever winners of the League Cup. In July 1964 he'd suffered a stroke and stepped down at Villa Park. His appointment at Maine Road was seen by some as a gamble on both parts.

Joe Mercer was a big name signing as manager of City.

Mercer's first 'signing' was a young, extrovert coach by the name of Malcolm Allison. It was the beginning of a perfect partnership, one on which Allison would later say, 'Between the two of us, we never missed a trick'.

The first thing Allison did was to dispense with the services of the current leading scorer at the club, Derek Kevan. This prompted raised eyebrows among City supporters, but Allison was adamant he didn't want anyone at the club who 'cheated' in training.

On 7 August, Dundee travelled to Maine Road for a pre-season friendly with Mercer and Allison both wondering if anyone would turn up to watch. City turned in a poor performance and lost 2-1. Clearly there was a lot of work to be done.

Mike Summerbee joined City from Swindon Town.

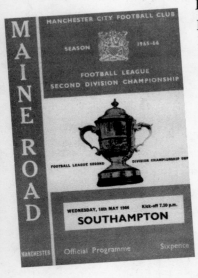

City clinched the Division 2 championship in 1966.

Mercer signed Scottish international forward Ralph Brand from Rangers, a man with a good goalscoring record north of the border. Regrettably he couldn't maintain this form with City and left the club two years later. If Brand can be perceived as a failure, the second signing most certainly can't. Mike Summerbee cost the club £35,000 from Swindon and made his debut in the opening game of the season at Middlesbrough. Summerbee played in all 42 league games in what would be his first of 10 tremendous seasons with the club.

The game at Middlesbrough finished 1-1 and began a run of seven unbeaten games. When Norwich drew 0-0 at Maine Road in October, a crowd of 34,091 witnessed the game that won a bet for Allison. Prior to the start of the season, United's Pat Crerand had bet Allison that City would never get 30,000 in the ground again. Wisecracks such as these only fuelled Allison's ambitions to rid City of the Reds' dominance even more and he was delighted to collect his winnings from the cocky Scot just two months into the season.

The new managerial partnership had already revitalised a club that was dying just a few months earlier. In the top three for most of the early part of the season, City beat leaders Huddersfield 2-0 on New Years' Day in front of more than 47,000 at Maine Road. People once

50 Greatest Players

TONY BOOK Full back

Joined Manchester City: 1966   **From:** Bath City

Debut: 1966 v Southampton (league)

Appearances: 309   **Goals:** 5

Left Manchester City: 1973 (retired)

Honours won with Manchester City: League Championship 1968, FA Cup winner 1969, Footballer of the Year (joint) 1969, European Cup Winners Cup 1970, League Cup 1970

In the early 1960s Tony Book was earning a living working as builder, and spending his spare time playing non-league football for Bath City. By the end of the decade he had captained City to both the league championship and the FA Cup and was joint winner of the Footballer of the Year trophy.

After being finally persuaded by Malcolm Allison, Joe Mercer parted with £17,000 for Book in July 1966. The 30 year-old, thought by many to be too old for top class football, missed just one league game in his first two seasons. He proved his critics wrong as he became one of the best full backs in the country and his calmness proved an invaluable asset to a City side that swept all before them at home and in Europe. He retired from playing in November 1973. The then 38-year-old became assistant manager to Ron Saunders, and within five months Book became manager.

A man who played 309 times for the Blues Book was the most successful captain the club has ever had. He should also be very proud of his achievements as manager – not many have bettered them.

again were sitting up and taking note of Manchester City.

The excellent league form carried over into the FA Cup. The Blues got through the third round after a replay against Blackpool before beating Grimsby Town of Division 3 2-0 in round four. In the fifth round, again after a replay, City beat Leicester, a side that had earlier knocked the Blues out of the League Cup.

The quarter-final saw a titanic struggle against Everton who were riding high in Division 1 that would eventually run to three games.

After two goalless draws, City finally succumbed 2-0 at Molineux. The first of these three games was watched by a crowd of 63,034, the largest attendance at Maine Road for more than six years.

Bell or Davies?

In March with City strongly pushing for promotion, Mercer and Allison were keen on two players but only had the finances for one. The choice was between Bolton's Wyn Davies and Colin Bell from Bury. Eventually they settled for the £45,000 Bell. City had bought a player many consider the best ever to wear a City shirt.

Bell scored on his debut in a 2-1 win at Derby and then headed the winner at Rotherham seven games later to guarantee promotion. When the Blues won 3-2 at Charlton in the penultimate game of the season, the Championship was theirs. The last game of the season, on Wednesday 18 May, was against Southampton, a team that would be joining the Blues in Division 1 next term. Although the game finished goalless, it provided a night of celebration for City fans as the Division 2 championship trophy was paraded. Mercer and Allison had re-established the club after just one season.

Like all promoted sides, the main priority for the 1966-67 season was consolidation. Centre half George Heslop had been signed from Everton last season, but the Mercer/Allison partnership still felt the side needed strengthening further, especially at right-back. After sizing up all the opportunities, City decided on Tony Book, a 30 year-old who'd worked with Allison at non-league Bath.

The test of just how far City had come in 12 months came in the second game of the season when reigning champions Liverpool visited Maine Road. More than 50,000 saw Colin Bell and Jimmy Murray find the net in a game the Blues won 2-1. No doubt City were on the up once again, but when United won 1-0 at Old Trafford in September, they were still unable to lay the red ghost to rest.

City's league form fluctuated for most of the season, but the FA Cup confirmed that they were definitely on an upward curve. In the third round, Leicester were once again the opposition, goals from Doyle and

Pardoe giving City a 2-1 victory. Cardiff were beaten 3-1 in a replay at Maine Road in round four and another replay was required before a 3-0 win at Ipswich. In the quarter-final City were drawn away at Leeds United. With the majority of people expecting the Blues to defend and settle for a draw, Leeds were shell-shocked by a brilliant attacking display. In the end only a hotly disputed goal from Jack Charlton settled the tie, but even Leeds admitted they were lucky to go through.

Colin Bell, a signing from Bury in 1966 – a significant Mercer/Allison purchase.

More Ways to Improve

Winger Tony Coleman arrived towards the end of a season in which City finished 15th. It was a creditable effort, but Mercer and Allison were still looking at ways to improve. Johnny Crossan left at the start of the 1967-68 season with Tony Book taking over the captaincy. Youngsters Paul Hince and Stan Bowles were given brief, but memorable, runs in the side, and City had a good September, winning five successive games. In the 12th game (a 2-0 win against Wolves) Francis Lee, a £60,000 record signing from Bolton, made his debut. Described by Mercer as 'the final piece in the jigsaw', Lee's arrival coincided with an unbeaten run of 11 games including the famous 'Ballet on Ice' defeat of Spurs in December.

The New Year arrived with the Blues in third place behind Liverpool and Manchester United. In the FA Cup, a disappointing City were held to a goalless draw by Reading but made no mistake in the replay, winning 7-0. The Blues met Leicester for the fifth time in three years in a cup-tie, but lost 4-3 in a replay in the fourth round.

In the League Cup the two sides amazingly were once again drawn against each other with Stan Bowles scoring twice in an easy 4-0 win. After a 1-1 draw at Maine Road, Blackpool were beaten in 2-0 in the replay but the Wembley trail (at least for this year) ended with City going down 3-2 at Fulham.

City's form continued in the league and in March they topped the Division. A defeat at Leeds meant the next game was crucial for the Blues to get back to winning ways. That game was at Old Trafford and couldn't have started worse. George Best scored inside the first minute and it appeared City could still not negotiate their greatest barrier. However, with Bell and Doyle in inspirational form, the Blues settled down and turned in a magnificent performance to win 3-1. Once again City fans could hold their heads high and there was a belief that the Blues could land the title.

As the season neared its close, City, United, Liverpool and Leeds all stood a chance. The Blues won three successive games, arriving at Newcastle for the last game of the season knowing another win would

*Mercer considered his team complete
after signing Francis Lee in 1967.*

be enough. By now the race had narrowed to just both Manchester clubs, with United, defending Champions and still favourites, having potentially the easier game at home to Sunderland. More than 46,000 crammed into St. James' Park to witness the proverbial 'end to end' thriller. City took the lead three times only for the home side to keep coming back at them. In the end the Blues hung on to win the game 4-3 and with it the First Division title. The trip home to Manchester down the A1 took longer than normal that night!

A delighted Allison commented

Great Matches

LEAGUE DIVISION 1   St James' Park, Newcastle, 11 May 1968

Newcastle 3   **Manchester City 4**   Attendance 46,300

Robson	Summerbee
Sinclair	Young 2
McNamee	Lee

Newcastle boss Joe Harvey said 'It's the first time we've been beaten at home before the game started' when he saw the 20,000 City fans who'd made the trip north for the last game of the 1967-68 season. A victory for the Blues would clinch the Division 1 championship for the first time in over 30 years. The only team that could stop City was neighbours United. On paper at least, reigning champions United had just to beat lowly Sunderland at Old Trafford to clinch the title, whereas City had a much more difficult game at St James' Park. Football League officials were so convinced of the outcome that they sent instructions for the trophy to be left at Old Trafford. BBC's *Match of the Day* cameras also made the wrong choice of game to cover that day.

The normally reliable George Heslop – along with several others – started the game badly, but nerves appeared to settle when Mike Summerbee opened the scoring on 12 minutes. City's joy was short-lived however, when Bryan 'Pop' Robson equalised.

Just after the half-hour mark, Colin Bell picked up a throw-in from Summerbee and passed inside to Oakes. Oakes' shot was charged down only to the unerring left foot of Neil Young and City had the lead back. Once again though nerves seemed to get the better of City and Newcastle equalised for a second time when Jackie Sinclair scored.

The teams went in level at half-time. Four minutes after, Young put the Blues back in front. It was Francis Lee's turn to get into the action next. He had a goal disallowed before giving City a two-goal cushion as he clipped the ball over the onrushing McFaul.

With four minutes to go, centre half John McNamee scored Newcastle's third to make it even more nail-biting for Blues' followers. It was a valiant effort by the Geordies but City hung on to win the title. Cries of 'Champions' could be heard well into the night, and – not that it made any difference – Sunderland won at Old Trafford.

Manchester City: Mulhearn, Book, Pardoe, Doyle, Heslop, Oakes, Lee, Bell, Summerbee, Young, Coleman.
Newcastle United: McFaul, Craig, Clark, Moncur, McNamee, Iley, Sinclair, Scott, Davies, B Robson, T Robson.
Referee: J. Thacker (Scarborough)

that City would 'be the first team to play on Mars' and they'd 'terrify Europe'. Unfortunately he was wrong with the first remark and a little premature with the second, but all City fans knew what he meant. And they believed him!

The European Dream

With new signing Bobby Owen in the side, City began the 1968-69 season where they'd left the previous. A superb attacking display destroyed West Bromwich Albion 6-1 in the Charity Shield game at Maine Road. An Achilles injury to Tony Book kept him out of the first half of the season and many thought it would be the end of his career. Despite the terrific showing against West Bromwich, it was a fairly inauspicious start to the league campaign with only one win in the first nine games. On 8 September, Turkish Champions Fenerbahce arrived at Maine Road for City's first ever European game. Regrettably City's run of poor form continued into Europe. Having squandered numerous goalscoring opportunities in the first leg at home, the Blues failed to find the net and travelled to Turkey without an advantage. When Coleman gave the Blues an early lead in the return leg things looked rosy but once again mistakes were made and two goals conceded. It was the end of the end of the European adventure, at least for this year.

Form improved slightly in the league with West Bromwich again suffering (this time 5-1) and Burnley were destroyed 7-0 in December. The season continued in much the same vein with a mixture of convincing wins and less than inspirational draws and defeats. A final position of 13th was achieved and could have meant a disappointing season had it not been for the FA Cup.

In the third round against Luton, Lee's penalty was the only thing that divided the teams. In round four, after a goalless draw at St James' Park (which marked Tony Book's return to the side), City beat the Geordies 2-0 in the replay. Young and Owen scored the goals watched by a crowd of 60,884. After several postponements, the fifth round tie eventually took place at Blackburn on 24 February. With Bell back in the side after a knee injury, City ran out 4-1

Great Matches

EUROPEAN CUP ROUND 1   Maine Road, Manchester, 18 September 1968

Manchester City 0   Fenerbahce SK 0   Attendance 38,787

The fluent, attacking style of play that took City to the Division 1 title in May 1968 had apparently deserted them when the new season began just a few months later.

By the time the club's first ever European game was due to be played, the Blues had won only one of their nine league games and were not in the best of form for the visit of the Turkish champions.

Despite having won the League and Cup double in their own country, many thought seemed to be an easy game for City. However, a look at Fenerbahce's record for the previous year showed that in 34 league games they had conceded just 12 goals. This was a statistic that would come to haunt City.

The night proved to be the kind that when no matter how long the game lasted, fans knew there was no way the Blues would ever score. They had enough chances to seal the tie in the first half at Maine Road but missed chances galore. The normally prolific Mike Summerbee and Colin Bell were the main culprits with Summerbee missing the best chance of all when – unchallenged – he failed to connect with a cross inside the six-yard box. Summerbee, who was booed by his own fans that night, later commented 'We all thought we were unbeatable and lost that edge.'

Even the Turkish reporters who travelled with the team to England described the game as a one-off and were convinced City would triumph in the return leg two weeks later. A noisy crowd of some 50,000 inside the National Stadium in Istanbul was silenced when Tony Coleman rounded the Turkish goalkeeper to give City the lead after 12 minutes and it looked like the reporters were right. Things went badly wrong in the second half however, when Fenerbahce scored twice to win the tie. The end of the game saw fireworks, riot police and more than a hundred fires on the terraces.

City had fallen at their first European hurdle. A bitterly disappointed Malcolm Allison (like his players) was determined it would never happen again.

Manchester City: Mulhearn, Kennedy, Pardoe, Doyle, Heslop, Oakes, Lee, Bell, Summerbee, Young, Coleman.
Fenerbahce: Yavuz, Sukru, Ercan, Nunweiler, Levent, Felim, Ziya, Yilhaz, Abdullah, Nedim, Can.
Referee: A. Boogaerts (Netherlands).

winners with two goals each from Coleman and Lee. The quarter-final tie with Tottenham was a very difficult game, settled only by a second-half strike from Lee that went in via a post.

For the semi-final against Everton at Villa Park, Mercer and Allison decided that their key player, future City manager Alan Ball, would prove less influential if he had the close attentions of City's utility man Dave Connor to contend with. The plan worked beautifully as Ball hardly had a kick all afternoon although it took a last minute goal from 19-year-old Tommy Booth to finally secure the game for City.

City's opponents for the final were Leicester, a a regular cup opponent over the past few years. Because of Leicester's lowly standing in the league, City were hot favourites but the game turned out to be a very close affair. In the end the destination of the FA Cup was decided by Neil Young's trusty left foot in the 23rd minute. His solitary strike a somewhat surprising statistic as both sides had several good chances. Tony Book was the victorious captain but his opposite

Neil Young scores the goal that won the 1969 FA Cup. Leicester City's Graham Cross (left) and Bobby Roberts (right) were helpless.

Great Matches

FA CUP FINAL   **Wembley, London, 26 April 1969**

Manchester City 1   Leicester City 0   **Attendance 100,000**

Young

Winger Tony Coleman was known as a firebrand long before he came to Maine Road in 1967. A typical example of his sometimes eccentric behaviour came as the teams were being introduced to Princess Anne prior to kick-off. 'Give my regards to your mum and dad' he said in front of his astonished team-mates.

Coleman, like the rest of the City team, was confident and relaxed, obeying Malcolm Allison's pre-match instructions to the letter. Perhaps the most nervous person in City's AC Milan-like red and black striped kit was eight-year-old mascot Paul Todd, the first ever mascot in a Wembley cup final. He was to take Allison's seat on the bench, the coach forced to watch the game from a seat in the stands after a touchline ban.

Leicester's record signing Allan Clarke provided the first incident forcing Harry Dowd to make a fine diving save. It was the beginning of some excellent attacking play at both ends, Coleman and Young coming close for City, before Rodrigues shot wide from inside the penalty area. In the 23rd minute, Lee took a throw-in down the line to Summerbee. He forced his way past Woollett before pulling the ball back perfectly for Neil Young who crashed an unstoppable shot high into the net.

It proved to be the only goal although there were opportunities for both sides in the second half. Harry Dowd made two splendid saves from Lochhead, ensuring the Cup came to Manchester, and Leicester would leave Wembley empty-handed yet again. To their credit they had played their part in an entertaining and sporting game, and provided the man of the match in Allan Clarke. More misfortune was to befall Leicester a few weeks later when they were relegated from Division 1. The last time a team had been runners-up in the FA Cup and relegated in the same season was 1926 – the team then was Manchester City.

Tony Book collected the FA Cup from Princess Anne – interestingly dressed in red and black – to go alongside his Footballer of the Year award won just two days earlier. It hadn't been a bad weekend's work for the 34-year-old skipper.

Manchester City: Dowd, Book, Pardoe, Doyle, Booth, Oakes, Summerbee, Bell, Lee, Young, Coleman. Sub. Connor.
Leicester City: Shilton, Rodrigues, Nish, Roberts, Woollett, Cross, Fern, Gibson, Lochhead, Clarke, Glover (Manley).
Referee: G. McCabe.

number David Nish had every reason to be proud of his side because they had more than played their part in a thoroughly enjoyable and entertaining final.

The success at Wembley meant Joe Mercer had become the first person to win the FA Cup as both a player and a manager. With Tony

Book already announced as joint Footballer of the Year (along with Dave Mackay) it meant that the season had been a great success on both a team and personal level.

Domestic Success

Joe Corrigan started as first choice keeper for the 1969-70 season having taken over from Harry Dowd and Ken Mulhearn who'd shared the duties for the past couple of seasons. The only other new face in the side was Ian Bowyer

Joe Corrigan's goalkeeping saw City through to the 1970 League Cup final.

(nowadays coach at Nottingham Forest), a useful player who would score 12 league goals in the season.

Along with the two domestic cup competitions, City also had the European Cup Winners' Cup to contend with. Taking lessons learnt from the Fenerbahce game 12 months earlier, City began their quest against Spanish side Atletico Bilbao in September. The Blues fought a really hard battle in Spain in the first leg and came away with a highly creditable 3-3 draw. At Maine Road two weeks later, goals from Oakes, Bowyer and Bell eased City through to the next round.

Their opponents would be the Belgian part-timers of SK Lierse who provided little opposition and the Blues had a comfortable 8-0 aggregate over the two legs. City would have to wait until March for their next European fixture.

The League Cup also began in September and City won 3-0 at

Southport before a much sterner test against Liverpool in round three. City had already lost twice to Liverpool in the league but managed to stop the hat-trick of defeats with a fighting 3-2 win. Everton and Queens Park Rangers were also beaten as City reached the semi-final to play their fiercest rivals United.

Tommy Booth sees off George Best in one of the Manchester derbies of the early 1970s.

The Blues took a valuable 2-1 lead into the second-leg, although the deciding goal at Maine Road from a Francis Lee penalty was hotly disputed, not surprisingly, by United at the time. George Best was so angry with the decision that he knocked the ball out of referee Jack Taylor's hands at the end of the game, an action that cost the Irishman a £100 fine and a month's ban. There was even more drama in the return leg at Old Trafford. Ian Bowyer gave City the lead on the night but United came back in force to score twice and level the tie. With eight minutes to go, Francis Lee blasted an indirect free-kick through the United wall where goalkeeper Alex Stepney instinctively tried to save it. Stepney could only manage to palm the ball down and the advancing Summerbee had great pleasure in slamming the ball into the net and sending City back to Wembley. City's dominance over their apparently more illustrious neighbours continued in the league as well, with City winning both games. The 4-0 win at Maine Road was reported in the newspapers at the time as 'the most one-side derby in history'.

European Glory

Back in Europe, City travelled to Portugal to play the student side Academica Coimbra in the quarter-final just a few days before the League Cup final against West Bromwich Albion. Conditions for the

Great Matches

LEAGUE CUP FINAL   **Wembley, London, 7 March 1970**

West Bromwich Albion 1   **Manchester City 2***   **Attendance 97,963**

Astle   Doyle

                             Pardoe

*After extra time

Wembley was like a cabbage patch for the final, having recently hosted the Horse of the Year Show. Once the horses had left, the turf had been covered with snow and several tons of straw. The match was a difficult test for City, but they passed with flying colours.

In an attempt to counter the airborne threat of England's Jeff Astle, City brought in George Heslop in place of Neil Young. It was the only change from the ECWC game in Portugal earlier in the week and prompted critics to say the Blues could never win with such a defensive line-up. After six minutes a cross from Albion's Ray Wilson evaded both Heslop and Corrigan before being met by Astle's forehead and City were a goal down.

The goal fired the Blues into action and Francis Lee began to play the game thought by many to be his best ever in City's colours. Despite constant pressure and attempts by both Lee and Summerbee, City could not find an equaliser and the score remained 1-0 at half-time. In the second half an attack by the Baggies almost gave them an unjust two-goal lead but Suggett missed a great chance. In the 65th minute Colin Bell back-headed a flick-on by Summerbee and Mike Doyle rammed home the equaliser. Summerbee sadly had to then leave the field with what turned out to be a fractured leg. The game finished 1-1 and so began a further 30 minutes on what was by then a terrible surface.

Although tired from the effects of two difficult games in four days, City's superior fitness level showed. Albion just could not compete in extra time and, following good work down the right by Lee and then Bell, Glyn Pardoe hooked home the winner. It was Pardoe's first of the season and couldn't have come at a more opportune moment. Once again Tony Book received a cup from Princess Anne. Once again City had won at Wembley in red and black. Once again they were back in Europe.

Manchester City: Corrigan, Book, Mann, Doyle, Booth, Oakes, Heslop, Bell, Summerbee (Bowyer), Lee, Pardoe.
West Bromwich Albion: Osborne, Fraser, Wilson, Brown, Talbut, Kaye, Cantello, Suggett, Astle, Hartford (Krzywicki), Hope.
Referee: V. James.

two games couldn't have been more different. In Portugal the game was played on a bone-hard pitch in temperatures in the 70s. The Blues came back to England after a hard-fought game with a 0-0 scoreline intact for the second leg.

The return leg with Coimbra proved just as difficult and it took a Tony Towers' strike deep into extra-time to finally settle the outcome. With all this cup activity, it was perhaps inevitable that the Blues would struggle to achieve some kind of consistency in the league. Their final

Alan Oakes played over 680 games in City's midfield.

position was 10th, three places better than the previous year. United had gained at least a modicum of success when they knocked City out of the FA Cup 3-0 in their fourth round match at Old Trafford.

Success in the League Cup final at Wembley was satisfying for everyone: the management, the team and for the fans. Another trophy for the cabinet and another season of European football guaranteed. However, this year's European trail had not yet ended.

City's opponents in the European Cup Winners' Cup semi-final were the very powerful German side FC Schalke 04. In the first leg in Germany, City lost 1-0. Despite this setback they remained confident of success at Maine Road two weeks later. Goalkeeper Joe Corrigan played the entire home leg with a broken nose but for most of the game stood, along with 46,361 others, as a spectator as the Blues gave a superb display of attacking football to win 5-1. Goals from Doyle, Young (2), Lee and Bell gave the scoreline an emphatic look.

Great Matches

EUROPEAN CUP WINNERS' CUP FINAL Prater Stadium, Vienna, 29 April 1970

Manchester City 2 **Gornik Zabrze 1** **Attendance 10,000 (approx)**

Young   Ozlizlo

Lee (pen)

Manchester City won their first, and to date only, European trophy – the Cup Winners' Cup – on a wet and windy night in Vienna in April 1970. Unbelievably the event went almost unnoticed in a Britain tuned in to the Leeds v Chelsea FA Cup final replay.

The Blues were in a confident mood after their demolition of crack German side Schalke in the semi-final, and not even the terrible weather conditions in the vast, open-air Prater Stadium could stop them from tearing into their opponents from the off. In the 12th minute, Francis Lee, out wide on the left, cut inside his marker and let fly with a vicious angled shot that skidded off the wet turf and could only be parried by goalkeeper Kostka. Neil Young was in like a flash on the loose ball and City were one up.

Mercer's side continued to push forward and three minutes before half-time were rewarded with a second goal. Gornik carelessly lost possession inside their own half, the ball was threaded through the middle and the elegant Young glided around Kostka only to be brought down by the despairing goalkeeper. As ever, Lee stepped up confidently to convert the resulting penalty, though he did have some luck when his low, hard-driven shot went through the legs of the luckless Kostka.

City had lost the influential Mike Doyle through injury in the first half and it was inevitable after the interval that Gornik – with nothing to lose – would try to exert some pressure. In the 68th minute their captain, Ozlizlo, pulled a goal back and it looked as if City might face a late fightback from the talented Poles. Despite one or two anxious moments, the Blues stayed solid and could have scored more as, just before the end, substitute Ian Bowyer missed a glorious chance. The one sad part of the final was that barely 10,000 were in the stadium to see Tony Book lift the trophy. However, 4,000 of them were City fans, drenched but happy, who promptly went out on the town to celebrate a night they would not forget for the rest of their lives.

Manchester City: Corrigan, Book, Pardoe; Doyle (Bowyer), Booth, Oakes, Heslop, Bell, Lee, Young, Towers.
Gornik Zabrze: Kostka, Latocha, Ozlizlo, Gorgian, Forenski (Deja), Szoltysik, Wilczek (Skowrone), Olek, Banas, Lubanski, Szarinski.
Referee: P. Schiller (Austria).

50 Greatest Players

NEIL YOUNG   Forward

Joined Manchester City: 1959   **From:** Juniors

Debut: 1961 v Aston Villa (league)

Appearances: 416   **Goals:** 108

Left Manchester City: 1972   **For:** Preston North End

Honours won with Manchester City: Division 2 1966, Division 1 1968, FA Cup winner 1969, European Cup Winners' Cup winner 1970

The Fallowfield-born Young signed amateur forms for City in 1959, making his debut two years later in a 2-1 defeat at Villa Park. In his early days, he was a left winger, but under the guidance of Mercer and Allison he became an elegant inside left, with a keen eye for goal coupled with an explosive and accurate shot.

Young's name was on the scoresheet when City won the Division 1 title at Newcastle in 1968, the FA Cup in 1969 and the following year in the Prater Stadium in Vienna as the Blues triumphed in the European Cup Winners' Cup. He played just over 10 seasons for City and was leading scorer in both the Division 2 and Division 1 championship seasons in the mid-1960s.

In January 1972, Young moved to Preston North End before finishing his career at Rochdale. Always a fans' favourite, Young fell out with City following a dispute regarding a testimonial which he was denied. His great friend Francis Lee finally persuaded him to come back and nowadays Young is a familiar figure at Former Players' functions as well as being involved in junior soccer schools.

For the final against Polish Cup winners Gornik Zabrze, City and their fans made their way to the Prater Stadium in Vienna, Austria.

City's ultimate victory made history as they became the first English side to win both a domestic and European trophy in the same season.

Domestic Disorder

It was events off the pitch rather than those on it, that provided the headlines for City as the 1970-71 season got underway. The old Open

Manchester City's youngest-ever first team player: Glyn Pardoe.

End had been demolished to make way for the North Stand, but it was in the bowels of the Main Stand where an equal amount of activity was taking place. In spite of the massive distance the club had travelled in five years, Allison thought they could go even further, but felt he was being hampered by the 'small-mindedness' of some of the board members.

On the pitch, the Blues had a good run of five successive wins, but surrendered the League Cup to Carlisle United at the first time of asking. In September they began their defence of the European Cup Winners' Cup with a tricky tie against Belfast side Linfield. Bell scored the only goal of the game in the first leg at Maine Road and fortunately scored again in the return leg. Linfield led 2-0 until Bell scored a crucial goal in the dying minutes to see the Blues through on the away goals rule.

Another difficult tie awaited City in the next round with a visit to Hungarian cup winners Honved. City dominated the game but only Lee was able to find the net in front of small crowd. Torrential rain almost caused the second leg at Maine Road to be abandoned two weeks later. In the event City adapted better to the conditions and won 2-0 thanks to goals from Bell and Lee. Like last year, the Blues could now forget about Europe until the following March.

On 24 November, stories appeared in the press concerning a new consortium set to take control of City. This new group supported Allison fully in his bid to 'improve' City but things got very messy and in fact turned some of the players against him. Because of the great success of recent years, they were of the opinion that 'if it's not broke, why fix it?' and manager Joe Mercer also stayed on the side of the present regime.

The two men who had been most influential in revitalising City's fortunes were now on opposite sides of the fence, although in a complete

Mike Doyle was a regular for City through the 1960s glory days.

50 Greatest Players

COLIN BELL Forward

Joined Manchester City: 1966   **From:** Bury

Debut: 1966 v Derby County (league)

Appearances: 501   **Goals:** 153

Left Manchester City: 1979 (retired)

Honours won with Manchester City: Division 2 Championship 1966, Division 1 Championship 1968, FA Cup winner 1969, European Cup Winners' Cup winner 1970, League Cup winner 1970, 48 England caps

Christened 'Nijinsky' by assistant manager Malcolm Allison after the legendary racehorse, Colin Bell was the most complete footballer ever to appear in a City shirt. He had tremendous pace and stamina: there was hardly a flaw in any aspect of his game.

Bell had been attracting the attention of many of the top clubs while playing for Bury in 1964. Despite Allison's now famous 'can't head it, can't pass it, he's hopeless' comments designed to dissuade any other interested parties, Bell signed for City in March 1966. He was the key member of the all-conquering City sides of the late 1960s and early 1970s and also appeared in the Mexico World Cup of 1970. He is the most capped City player of all time. It was a tragedy when, at the age of 29, he injured a knee in a collision with Manchester United's Martin Buchan during a League Cup-tie at Maine Road. Despite all his efforts he was never the same player again and he retired from playing in August 1979.

After a spell working with the Maine Road youngsters, Colin Bell left the club for a while before returning in the late 1990s in an ambassadorial role.

Great Managers 1965-71

JOE MERCER OBE

Joe Mercer was one of the all-time greats of English football. Born in Ellesmere Port in 1914, he became interested in football whilst watching his father (also called Joe) play for Tranmere Rovers. By the time he was 15 he'd been spotted by Everton, the team he supported as a youngster. In 1939 Mercer won a Championship medal with Everton and played in 27 wartime internationals before being transferred to Arsenal in 1946. He successfully continued playing at Highbury, but in April 1954 in a collision with one of his own team-mates, he broke a leg and ended his playing career. Two years later he became manager at Sheffield United, a job that proved difficult, not least when trying to balance the cheque book with success on the pitch.

In 1958 he was appointed manager at Aston Villa, but the pressures of work at Villa Park were heavy and in 1964 he suffered a stroke. In 1965 a struggling Manchester City offered Mercer the manager's job. Knowing he was no longer fit enough to train the team, he insisted that Malcolm Allison be brought in as his No. 2. For City it was a partnership made in heaven and promotion to Division I came after just one season.

Two years later they were Champions of Division I, and FA Cup, League Cup and European Cup Winners' Cup success followed over the next few glorious years. Joe Mercer presided over the most successful period in the history of the club. In 1971 he handed over team matters entirely to Allison and became General Manager, a position that unfortunately didn't work out, and the following year he moved to Coventry. In 1974 he took over as caretaker manager of the England side for seven games following the sacking of Alf Ramsey.

His later years were spent on his native Wirral and he was often seen watching Tranmere Rovers' home games. Tragically Joe became a victim of Alzheimer's disease, a complaint that eventually caused his death. On 9 August 1990, his 76th birthday, Joe Mercer passed away in his favourite armchair. The game had lost one of its finest ambassadors as well as one of its nicest men.

about turn, Mercer would eventually agree with his coach. The board felt that if they removed Allison then the threat of a take-over would go with him. After a 1-0 defeat at Leeds four days after the stories had broken, the board sacked Allison only to hear Mercer reply, 'If he goes, I go'. Obviously the board now had to retract their dismissal of Allison.

Like the Peter Swales/Francis Lee situation in the 1990s, these were uncomfortable times at Maine Road and the events off the pitch had

50 Greatest Players

MIKE SUMMERBEE Forward

Joined Manchester City: 1965   **From:** Swindon Town

Debut: 1965 v Middlesbrough (league)

Appearances: 452   **Goals:** 68

Left Manchester City: 1975   **For:** Burnley

Honours won with Manchester City: Division 2 1966, Division 1 1968, FA Cup winner 1969, League Cup Winner 1970, 8 England caps

Employed nowadays on the club's commercial side, Mike Summerbee is still a familiar and much-loved Maine Road face. He first arrived in the summer of 1965, the second signing by Joe Mercer and Malcolm Allison. A crowd-pleasing and direct player, at home both on the wing or at centre forward, Summerbee played his early football with Swindon Town. His debut for City came at the start of the 1965-66 season, a season in which he didn't miss a single game and City were crowned Division 2 Champions. An influential part of City's triumphs during his time there, his biggest disappointment was missing the 1970 European Cup Winners' Cup final with a leg injury.

A one-time part owner of a Manchester boutique with George Best, Summerbee has developed a successful shirt business alongside his work with City. His father George, and his son Nick, have also played league football, thereby guaranteeing the name Summerbee remains in the record books. A regular after dinner speaker and someone who always has time for the fans, Mike Summerbee will be forever associated with City as a member of the great trio alongside Francis Lee and Colin Bell.

an effect on the players. City's 1-0 win over Crystal Palace on 9 January, was their last that season. The side was not helped by some long-term injuries to Pardoe, Oakes, Summerbee and Bell.

The European Cup Winners' Cup came around again in the spring, and City's opponents in the quarter-finals were Gornik Zabrze, the side beaten in last year's final. Gornik won the first leg 2-0 in Poland, and the Blues levelled the tie at Maine Road thanks to goals from Doyle and young reserve Ian Mellor. A replay was required at the neutral venue of Copenhagen with City finally winning 3-1. Allison was suspended by the FA from all footballing activities prior to the all-English semi-final against Chelsea leaving Mercer in charge of team matters. Mercer selected three players who weren't completely

50 Greatest Players

FRANCIS LEE Forward

Joined Manchester City: 1967   **From:** Bolton Wanderers

Debut: 1967 v Wolverhampton Wanderers (league)

Appearances: 330   **Goals:** 148

Left Manchester City: 1974   **For:** Derby County

Honours won with Manchester City: Division 1 1968, FA Cup winner 1969, League Cup winner 1970, European Cup Winners Cup winner 1970, 27 England caps

Francis Lee will be remembered much more for his achievements on the field for Manchester City than for those off. He became Chairman of the club in 1994, following a huge wave of fans' support that finally ousted Peter Swales. In March 1998, when he left Maine Road, he had taken in five managers and two caretakers, as well as two relegations, leaving City to play in what was really Division 3 for the very first time.

If he was unsuccessful as a chairman, then the opposite is most certainly true as a player. He joined City in October 1967 for a then club record fee of £60,000; Joe Mercer describing him as 'the final piece in the puzzle'. This he was as six months later City won the Division 1 title. Over the next few years Lee was one of the stars of a team guaranteed at least one piece of silverware every season. He surprisingly left for Derby in 1974.

Francis Lee was one of the most popular players ever at Maine Road. The Mercer/Allison glory years were the most successful in the history of the club and Lee played a huge part in them. Fans should remember that as well as the fact that Lee too was enormously disappointed by the events of those four years as chairman.

fit for an unimportant league game at Newcastle two days before the first leg at Stamford Bridge. The plan backfired as Bell and Doyle were injured in the match and had to miss the Chelsea game.

End of an Era

The Blues lost 1-0 at Chelsea and again by the same scoreline in the return leg when reserve goalkeeper Ronnie Healey failed to keep out a free kick from Keith Weller. It had been a disappointing end to a season that promised so much. The boardroom problems still simmered away and were only calmed when Peter Swales, a self imposed 'peacemaker', managed to settle the waters to a degree in the summer. The players soon forgot about any boardroom wranglings and just a month into the 1971-72 season the Blues were in a very commendable fourth place. In October a further change to the structure of the club was announced when Joe Mercer was given the title General Manager with Malcolm Allison being promoted to Team Manager. It appeared that Allison had finally got what he wanted: sole charge of team affairs.

Joe Mercer was the least pleased of the two but it seemed at the time, the best way of satisfying them both and at least it would keep the two of them at the club. Under Allison, City had their best season since the Championship success four years before. Wyn Davies had proved an excellent target man and a tremendous foil for Lee who scored 35 times including a record 13 penalties.

By March City had a real chance of winning the Championship.

50 Greatest Players

WILLIE DONACHIE Full back

Joined Manchester City: 1968   **From:** Glasgow Amateurs
Debut: 1970 v Crystal Palace (league)
Appearances: 436   **Goals:** 2
Left Manchester City: 1980   **For:** Portland Timbers (NASL)
Honours won with Manchester City: League Cup winner 1976, 35 Scotland caps

It was as a midfielder that Willie Donachie first caught the eye of City scouts back in the late 1960s. Born in the Glasgow district of Gorbals, the young Donachie had been playing his football with Glasgow Amateurs, a club that provided youngsters for Celtic. He signed for City as a junior in December 1968 making his debut 14 months later coming on as a substitute for the injured Tony Book in the 1-1 home draw with Nottingham Forest. His first start was at Crystal Palace in April 1970.

Like many other players of his era, Donachie was tempted by the NASL and in March 1980 he joined Portland Timbers for £200,000. On his return to England, Donachie played for Norwich and Burnley before becoming player/manager with Joe Royle's Oldham side. When Joe Royle returned to Maine Road as manager in 1998, he reunited the partnership by appointing Donachie first team coach. City's successive promotions of recent years is testimony to the terrific job they both did during their time together at Maine Road.

50 Greatest Players

DENIS LAW Forward

Joined Manchester City: 1960 and 1973   **From:** Huddersfield Town and
Manchester United

Debut: 1960 v Leeds United (league), 1973 v Birmingham City (league)

Appearances: 82   **Goals:** 38

Left Manchester City: 1961 and 1974   **For:** Torino (and retired)

In 1960 Denis Law joined Manchester City when manager Les McDowall spent a British record fee of £55,000 on him. He made his debut in a 4-3 defeat at Leeds. The following season, 1960-61 he scored 23 times in 43 games.

   The star of a struggling City side that year, it was no surprise when Law moved to Torino in the summer for £110,000, making him Britain's first £100,000 player. He stayed in Italy for just one season before returning to Manchester in July 1962. Unfortunately for City he joined neighbours United. After 11 seasons at Old Trafford he was released on a free transfer and manager Johnny Hart had no hesitation in re-signing him for the Blues. Ironically his last game of the season would also be his last in league football. His back-heeled goal at Old Trafford effectively relegated his former club and a devastated Law left the field minutes later. He never kicked a ball in league football again. But his appearances for City had confirmed his place with the Scotland side for the 1974 World Cup, where he played two games before announcing his retirement. One of the game's most prolific and natural goalscorers, Law is liked equally by both sets of Manchester fans.

Allison then broke the club's transfer record when he signed Rodney Marsh from Queens Park Rangers for £200,000. The Blues form stuttered towards the end of the season and Marsh's style of play was said by many to be the reason the club failed to win the title. City eventually lost out to Champions Derby County by a single point.

Mercer left the club in June 1972 to join Coventry. Not feeling any animosity towards Allison, Mercer felt his contribution had gone unjustly unrecognised by the new board, and his new contract and cut in pay made him feel unwanted. Worst of all, his pride was hurt. It was the end of a great managerial partnership: a partnership that provided great success. City fans pondered for many long years what would have happened if the whole thing had been handled better.

Chapter Seven: 1973-80
Unrest Over and Loadsamoney

In the first game of the season, City, wearing their splendid new continental 'Miss World' change kit, won the Charity Shield against Aston Villa thanks to a Francis Lee penalty.

The 1972-73 league campaign started badly for the Blues with just one win in the first six games. September brought heavy defeats at both Birmingham and Stoke as well as City's first venture into the UEFA Cup. Mellor and Marsh scored for City in the first leg of the first round tie at home to Valencia (the game finishing 2-2) but with the Spaniards already having the advantage, City lost 2-1 in the second leg. The following week they were knocked out of the League Cup by Bury from Division 4.

Rodney Marsh: ever the showman at Manchester City and a crowd favourite.

City's form improved in November when three successive wins culminated in a 3-0 win against Manchester United. In a game littered with ill-feeling, Wyn Davies lined up in a red shirt, having moved to Old Trafford just a few days prior to the game.

In the FA Cup Stoke were beaten 3-2 in the third round and then brilliant psychology from Allison inspired City to a goalless draw at Anfield in the next round. A goal in each half from Colin Bell and Tommy Booth won the replay for City. A crowd of 54,478 saw the fifth round clash with Sunderland then playing in Division 2. Tony

Towers opened the scoring for City but from then on Jim Montgomery in the Sunderland goal had an outstanding game, stopping everything the Blues could throw at him. Despite constant pressure, the Blues found themselves 2-1 down later in the game and were grateful when Summerbee's corner struck Montgomery and found its way into the net for the equaliser. Unfortunately for City, Sunderland won the replay, and eventually went on to beat Leeds United in the final.

It was around this time that Allison began to feel disillusioned at the club. The board had not delivered all their promises and when he was forced to sell the promising Ian Mellor to Norwich in March it proved the final straw. He left Maine Road shortly afterwards citing 'an inability to motivate the players' as the reason for leaving. The ever popular Johnny Hart took over and City finished the season in 11th place.

The Return of Denis Law

Like the previous year, City were once again invited to contest the Charity Shield at the start of the new season. Unfortunately Burnley scored the only goal of the game this time. An old face reappeared in City's colours for the opening game against Birmingham. Denis Law had been discarded by Tommy Docherty at Old Trafford and was snapped up Johnny Hart on a free transfer. To everyone's delight he scored twice in the 3-1 victory. Glyn Pardoe made a welcome return to the first team after an absence of nearly two years following a badly broken leg sustained at Old Trafford.

In October a major announcement was made when 'peacemaker' Peter Swales became Chairman, taking over from Eric Alexander. Swales would remain in the position for 20 years. One of his first jobs was to find a successor to Johnny Hart who stood down in November.

His replacement was known disciplinarian Ron Saunders, at the time in charge at Norwich. Under Saunders there was no real improvement in the league, and with a 4-1 defeat in the FA Cup at Notts County, the League Cup provided City's only hope of a trophy. Still under Hart's control, City had begun by beating Walsall 4-0 in a second replay in round two. Carlisle United and York City were then beaten and it took two attempts to dispose of Coventry in round five.

In the semi-final Tommy Booth scored an important equaliser at Plymouth to bring the sides back to Maine Road level at 1-1 for the second leg. City won relatively easy 2-0 and were back at Wembley.

Saunders' way with people had started to irritate some of the experienced professionals at the club. Some felt he treated them like children and it wasn't a happy band of players that prepared for the final against Wolves. Summerbee, Bell, Lee, Law and Marsh made up City's forward line, but incredibly Wolves still won the game. Despite all that talent on show, the Wolves keeper Pierce had the best game of his life and pulled off a string of fine saves.

50 Greatest Players

TOMMY BOOTH Centre half
Joined Manchester City: 1965   **From:** Manchester Catholic Boys
Debut: 1968 v Huddersfield Town (League Cup)
Appearances: 491   **Goals:** 36
Left Manchester City: 1981   **For:** Preston North End
Honours won with Manchester City: FA Cup winner 1969, League Cup winner 1970, European Cup Winners' Cup winner 1970, League Cup winner 1976

Tommy Booth joined City as an amateur in 1965. Two years later he'd turned professional and his cultured performances at centre half in City's junior sides prompted Joe Mercer to give him his debut in the first team as a 19-year-old. The following month he played his first league game taking over from George Heslop.

Once established in the senior side, Booth became a permanent fixture for the next 13 years. Perhaps his most famous (and important) goal was the decider against Everton in the 1969 FA Cup semi-final. The arrival of Dave Watson and the injury to Colin Bell moved Booth into a midfield position later in his career, and he played in this position in the successful 1976 League Cup-winning side.

A central figure in the cup-winning sides of the late 60s and early 70s, Booth was a footballing centre half, likened by Joe Mercer to Stan Cullis, the great Wolves player of the 1930s and 40s. Booth won four England Under-23 caps during his time with City before a £30,000 move to Preston North End in October 1981. Nowadays Booth, a keen golfer, is employed as a television engineer with a national company.

Having gone a goal down just before the break, Colin Bell finally beat Pierce for City's equaliser on the hour. With just five minutes left, an innocuous centre struck the heel of Marsh and rolled invitingly into the path of Wolves' John Richards. Richards was one of the top strikers in the country at the time and he lashed the ball past City's £100,000 goalkeeper Keith MacRae. It was a day of dreadful luck for the Blues.

Shortly after the final, Saunders signed Dennis Tueart and Mick Horswill from Sunderland. The signing of Tueart was arguably the best thing Saunders ever did for City. With growing unrest among the players, City still struggled in the league and appeared to be going backwards instead of forwards. Fearful of the prospect of relegation, Swales sacked Saunders at Easter.

A Bitter Pill

Former captain Tony Book was put in charge for the last five games of the season. The final one was at Old Trafford and United were desperate for the points to maintain their top flight standing. The game was brought to life in the 81st minute when Denis Law back-heeled his now infamous goal past Alex Stepney. Realising what he'd done, a sick and depressed Law left the field immediately. He would never kick a ball again in the Football League. Despite attempts by United supporters to have the game abandoned the result stood. The other two teams trying to avoid the drop – Birmingham and Southampton – managed to win their games so Law's goal proved academic in the end although it did make for some good copy.

A New Era

With the much-respected Tony Book at the helm, the attitude of the players changed almost immediately and City began the 1974-75 season with a convincing 4-0 win against West Ham. Asa Hartford had arrived in the summer with Francis Lee moving to Derby, a move that angered Lee, who threatened the club had not seen the last of him. As if to prove a point, Lee had won his second Championship medal at the end of the season.

The goal he'll never forget: Denis Law scores for City at Old Trafford, condemning his old club to relegation. It was the last game he ever played in the Football League.

With just two defeats in the first ten games, City entered October in second place. They'd slipped to eighth when Lee returned to Maine Road in December with his new Derby team-mates. He thundered an unstoppable shot past Joe Corrigan to earn a 2-1 victory and the joy on his face was clear for all to see. Joe Royle signed for City on Christmas Eve despite rumours of back problems following surgery. Leading scorer for the season was Dennis Tueart who'd won many admirers with his direct style of play.

The Blues lost 2-0 to Newcastle in the third round of the FA Cup, a game played at Maine Road owing to the FA's closure of St James' Park. In the League Cup, a Colin Bell hat-trick inspired City to a convincing 6-0 victory over Scunthorpe before a disputed Gerry Daly penalty decided the game at Old Trafford in round three. A more tranquil City finished the season in eighth position.

More transfer dealings greeted the opening of the 1975-76 season. Another member of the late 60s side, Mike Summerbee, had left to join Burnley and Dave Watson had arrived from Sunderland.

This proved to be a   memorable season as Tony Book took his side to Wembley success in the League Cup – the Blues' third final in this competition in seven seasons. In the second round, a Dennis Tueart hat-trick in a second replay finally saw off Norwich. Nottingham Forest

were beaten 2-1 in the next round, setting up a fourth round tie with Manchester United at Maine Road.

Inside the first minute City took the lead through Dennis Tueart. It was the beginning of a display in which United were completely outclassed. The one major setback on the night (or possibly in the club's history) was the terrible knee

Joe Royle was a popular player at the club and went on to be a popular manager.

50 Greatest Players

JOE CORRIGAN Goalkeeper

Joined Manchester City: 1966   **From:** Sale Grammar School

Debut: 1967 v Blackpool (League Cup)

Appearances: 605

Left Manchester City: 1983   **For:** Seattle Sounders (NASL)

Honours won with Manchester City: League Cup winner 1970, European Cup Winners' Cup winner 1970, League Cup winner 1976, 9 England caps

In the entire history of Manchester City Football Club, only Alan Oakes has played more first team games than Joe Corrigan. But anyone who saw him make his debut in 1967 could be forgiven for thinking he'd be lucky to reach double figures. Given his chance because of injuries, City's third choice goalkeeper had the dreadful misfortune of letting the ball run through his legs to gift opponents Blackpool a simple goal.

By the start of the 1969-70 season, Corrigan had forced his way into the first team and would remain an almost permanent fixture for the next 14 years. It was just reward for one of the most determined players ever at Maine Road.

In 1983 he moved to NASL side Seattle Sounders for a short time before returning to England with Brighton & Hove Albion. His playing career was ended on the plastic pitch of Queens Park Rangers, where he suffered a back injury that required an operation. Nowadays Corrigan is a highly respected goalkeeping coach, currently working with the senior side at Anfield.

Great Matches

LEAGUE CUP FINAL   Wembley, London, 28 February 1976

Newcastle United 1   Manchester City 2   Attendance 100,000
Gowling   Barnes
                          Tueart

Tony Book had seen and done it all as a player with City in the late 1960s and early 1970s. By 1976 he had been manager of the side for two years, building his team into one of the best in the division. Book's team had played some fine, attacking football in the early rounds of the League Cup, scoring 23 and conceding eight in the previous games.

City's confidence was high as they went into the final, the only slight concern being Dave Watson's troublesome back. Newcastle, on the other hand, had been badly affected by a 'flu bug, but to give them credit, they never cited this as being the reason they would finish the afternoon as Wembley losers.

It was an open game right from the kick-off, with Joe Corrigan called upon to make two saves in the first 90 seconds. City's only reply was a shot by Hartford that struck team-mate Tueart. In the 12th minute City were awarded a somewhat harsh free-kick when centre half Keeley was adjudged to have fouled Joe Royle. From Hartford's ensuing cross Mike Doyle headed across goal for Peter Barnes to crash the ball home. With ten minutes to half time Newcastle equalised when Gowling turned Macdonald's cross past Corrigan. The sides went in level at the break – perhaps a fair result.

Two minutes after the interval Dennis Tueart scored a fantastic – and what turned out to be decisive – goal. Donachie's cross was knocked down by Booth for Tueart to produce a superb overhead kick and send the ball flying past the diving Mahoney into the corner of the net. It was the kind of goal dreams are made of.

Royle had a goal disallowed for offside and Booth saw a header go just wide. At the other end Corrigan was kept busy by Burns and Gowling in the Newcastle attack. In the final minute Booth had a chance to seal the game only to see his header saved. As captain Mike Doyle paraded the cup he was warmly applauded by the Newcastle fans. It just confirmed the kind of sporting atmosphere the game had been played in.

Manchester City: Corrigan, Keegan, Donachie, Doyle, Watson, Oakes, Barnes, Booth, Royle, Hartford, Tueart.
Newcastle United: Mahoney, Nattrass, Kennedy, Barrowclough, Keeley, Howard, Burns, Cassidy, Macdonald, Gowling, Craig.
Referee: J. Taylor (Wolverhampton).

Peter Barnes scored in the 1976 League Cup final.

injury to Colin Bell. The final score of 4-0 was marred by an injury that would keep Bell out of the side for two years. It was a cruel blow to the player, his club and his country.

Mansfield Town from Division 3 provided tough opposition in round five, the 4-2 scoreline in City's favour disguising a difficult game. The first leg of the semi-final took the Blues to Middlesbrough and although City played well on the night, they lost 1-0. The scores were level on aggregate just five minutes into the second leg when Ged Keegan headed in a Peter Barnes cross. A low, long distance drive from Alan Oakes made it 2-0 not long afterwards and second-half goals from Barnes and Royle sealed the tie.

By the end of the 1976 season, the unrest in the boardroom had died down, Book had assembled an excellent side, City finished eighth in the league again and had won a trophy. It had been a good year's work at Maine Road.

Former United star Brian Kidd was City's major signing in the close season. Coming back to Manchester after a spell in London with Arsenal, Kidd proved an excellent buy for the club, finishing the season top scorer with 21 league goals. Kidd scored his first goal for City in the UEFA Cup against a powerful Juventus side at Maine Road. Unfortunately it wasn't enough with the Italians scoring twice in the return leg to go through. It was also time to bid a fond farewell to the most loyal of servants in Alan Oakes who'd taken over as player/manager with Chester. To this date, no one has played more games for the Blues than the reliable midfielder.

European Qualification

City's league campaign had started well: indeed by Christmas they'd only lost twice and were posing a real threat to leaders Liverpool. The

50 Greatest Players

GLYN PARDOE Full back

Joined Manchester City: 1961   **From:** Juniors

Debut: 1962 v Birmingham City (league)

Appearances: 380   **Goals:** 22

Left Manchester City: 1976 (retired)

Honours won with Manchester City: Division 2 Championship1966, Division 1 Championship 1968, FA Cup winner 1969, League Cup winner 1970, European Cup Winners Cup winner 1970

Winsford-born Glyn Pardoe followed the same path into City's first team as his cousin Alan Oakes. Also a product of Mid-Cheshire Boys, Pardoe signed apprentice forms in July 1961. On 11 April 1962, he made his first team debut. He was just 15 years, 314 days old; the youngest player ever to appear in the Blues' senior side.

The arrival of Joe Mercer and Malcolm Allison saw him develop into a cultured left back, although he played in every position except centre half and goalkeeper during his 13 years with City. Indeed he wore the number 11 shirt when he scored the winning goal in extra time of the 1970 League Cup final. Nine months after that Wembley winner, Pardoe suffered a badly broken leg in a tackle by George Best in a 4-1 win at Old Trafford. It was nearly two years before he was back in action. He finally retired from playing in April 1976 before spending nearly 16 years on the coaching staff at Maine Road.

His 31-year relationship with City ended in 1992 when manager Peter Reid re-organised the backroom staff and Pardoe lost his job.

League Cup had proved fruitless with Ron Saunders' Aston Villa side beating City 3-0 in the second round. The league form continued into the FA Cup as well. City progressed to the fifth round (having beaten West Bromwich Albion and Newcastle on the way) before falling to a late Trevor Cherry goal at Leeds.

Following three successive wins, a 4-0 defeat at Derby at the end of April blew a big hole in the title aspirations. Although the Blues won their last game of the season at Coventry, Liverpool kept their noses in front and won the title by one point. This was a Liverpool team at the height of its powers and to come so close was quite an achievement. It also meant the club had again qualified for the UEFA Cup.

In an attempt to go one place better, Book signed the experienced England international Mike Channon from Southampton in readiness for the 1977-78 season. Channon's arrival would eventually see the departure of Joe Royle, but that was in the future as City went to the top of the league in September.

Manchester United were beaten easily 3-1 four days before City met Polish side Widzew Lodz in the UEFA Cup at Maine Road. Strolling to a two-goal lead, the Blues allowed the visitors to score twice late on in the game: goals that would make the return leg extremely difficult. And so it proved. The Blues were unable to make any impression against a Polish side who were quite happy with two away goals. The game finished 0-0 and City – not for the first time – were out of Europe through being too naive.

The League Cup began with a 1-0 win against Chesterfield and then three games against Luton, City finally progressing 3-2. Ipswich Town were then beaten 2-1 at home before City lost to Arsenal in a replay. The FA Cup lasted only two games with City gaining revenge for last year's defeat by Leeds only to lose at Nottingham Forest in round four.

The biggest cheer of the season was undoubtedly reserved for the return of Colin Bell on Boxing Day. The game against Newcastle was 0-0 when Bell came on for the second half. Not only did his appearance lift the crowd it also lifted the players, Dennis Tueart in particular. Tueart scored a hat-trick and City won 4-0 although a modest Bell said later, 'I didn't do a thing. The game just passed me by'.

Ins and Outs

After a couple of niggling injuries, Dennis Tueart found his regular place in the side in jeopardy. He asked to be put on the transfer list, and in February moved to New York to join the star-studded Cosmos. Another fine player and one of the most popular ever at Maine Road

50 Greatest Players

ALAN OAKES Midfield

Joined Manchester City: 1958   **From:** Mid-Cheshire Boys

Debut: 1959 v Chelsea (league)

Appearances: 680   **Goals:** 34

Left Manchester City: 1976   **For:** Chester

Honours won with Manchester City: Division 2 Championship 1966, Division 1 Championship 1968, FA Cup winner 1969, League Cup winner 1970, European Cup Winners' Cup winner 1970, League Cup Winner 1976

The City side that struggled in the early part of the 1960s contained several players who would become household names in the years that followed. Alan Oakes was one of them. It is difficult to see anyone overtaking Oakes' record of 680 appearances. It took him 17 seasons to achieve this after joining the club as an amateur in April 1958. He made his first-team debut the following year in a 1-1 draw with Chelsea. He made his last appearance as a sub at Old Trafford in May 1976 before moving to Chester as player/manager.

Solid and reliable in defence, Oakes also provided great service to the strikers around him. His powerful runs from midfield often resulted in long range shots at goal, and he scored memorable goals against Atletico Bilbao in the 1969-70 European Cup-Winners' Cup, and against Middlesbrough in the League Cup semi-final six years later. Alan Oakes was the 'Mr. Dependable' in the Manchester City line-up. He was a 'professional' footballer in the true sense of the word.

had left to the dismay of City supporters. Despite this, the average crowd of 41,687 for the season is still a record for the club. The season ended with the Blues in fourth place, enough to qualify for a UEFA Cup place next time out, but less than was hoped for at the outset.

Brian Kidd started the 1978-79 season in fine form with three goals in three games. The dependable Mike Doyle had moved on and was replaced by the £350,000 record signing Paul Futcher, from Luton. In November, Polish World Cup captain Kaziu Deyna signed from Legia Warsaw, for, according to Peter Swales, 'A small amount of cash, some typewriters and medical equipment. It was a strange signing!'

50 Greatest Players

MIKE DOYLE Wing half

Joined Manchester City: 1962   **From:** Stockport Boys

Debut: 1965 v Cardiff City (league)

Appearances: 572   **Goals:** 40

Left Manchester City: 1978   **For:** Stoke City

Honours won with Manchester City: Division 2
Championship 1966, Division 1 Championship 1968,
FA Cup winner 1969, League Cup winner 1970,
European Cup Winners' Cup winner 1970, League Cup
winner 1976, 5 England caps

Stockport-born Mike Doyle joined City in 1962. His early
career saw him play at both right back and centre
forward, but it was at wing-half that he turned in his best
performances. After making his debut towards the end of
the 1964-65 season, Doyle's contribution to the sky-blue
cause ensured he would be a permanent fixture in the side for the next 14 seasons.

A determined and committed player, Doyle was not afraid to give his opinion of the
'other' Manchester club, which only increased his popularity to City fans. Only Alan
Oakes and Joe Corrigan have played more games for City. Not a prolific goalscorer,
perhaps his most important strike was the equaliser in the 1970 League Cup final.
Doyle played in three League Cup finals, captaining City to success in 1976 following
a 2-1 win over Newcastle United. A £50,000 transfer took him to Stoke in June 1978.

Doyle also played for Bolton and Rochdale before retiring from football to spend
more time on the golf course.

City had most success in the UEFA Cup that term. Drawn away in
the first round first leg, Dave Watson scored a valuable away goal in
a 1-1 draw with FC Twente Enschede. City won a tight return leg 3-
2 for a 4-3 aggregate score. In round two, the Blues beat the Belgian
side Standard Liege 4-0, a scoreline that could have been much closer
had it not been for three goals in the last five minutes. Although Liege
won 2-0 two weeks later, City had done enough to progress to a third
round meeting with Italian giants AC Milan.

Thick fog postponed the first game in the San Siro; instead of a
Wednesday night, the game was played on a Thursday afternoon, and

this reduced the noise level considerably for the home support. Amazingly Brian Kidd and Paul Power gave City a 2-0 lead and were on the verge of being the first British side ever to beat Milan at home. Milan then began to play their best football and had the ball in City's net five times. Fortunately for the Blues only two of them stood, the others all being ruled out for offside. The 2-2 was terrific for City and they also had the advantage of what could be crucial away goals.

In the end away goals never entered the equation. Milan were overrun by the Blues in the return leg at Maine Road with goals from Booth, Hartford and Kidd (all in the first half) sealing a 3-0 victory.

Since the days of Mercer and Allison when City had been the dominant force in Manchester football, the nearest they'd come since was in 1976-77 when they narrowly missed out on the title to

50 Greatest Players

RODNEY MARSH Forward

Joined Manchester City: 1972	**From:** Queens Park Rangers
Debut: 1972 v Chelsea (league)	
Appearances: 152	**Goals:** 47
Left Manchester City: 1976	**For:** Tampa Bay Rowdies (NASL)
Honours won with Manchester City: 8 England caps	

By his own admission, Rodney Marsh was 'unfit and overweight' when he arrived at Maine Road in March 1972. Signed by Malcolm Allison for a then club record fee of £200,000, he was seen as the perfect rival the skills of George Best at neighbours Manchester United. Whether he was or not, no one can argue that watching Rodney Marsh on top form was one of the most enjoyable features of watching City in the 70s. Anyone who saw his goal against Derby in that 1971-72 season, or him tapping a fictitious wristwatch whilst standing on the ball at Old Trafford would have to agree.

Marsh eventually became captain at Maine Road and went on to win eight of his nine England caps whilst with City. In January 1976 he decided to try his luck in the NASL and moved to Tampa for a short period before returning to England and signing for Fulham where he joined his great friends George Best and Bobby Moore. He soon returned to Tampa where he would eventually become coach and then manager.

Now back in England permanently, Rodney Marsh is a respected (if sometimes controversial) TV pundit. He will be remembered by City fans as arguably the greatest showman the club has ever had.

50 Greatest Players

PETER BARNES Winger

Joined Manchester City: 1972	**From:** Apprentice
and 1987	**From:** Manchester United
Debut: 1974 v Burnley (league)	
Appearances: 162	**Goals:** 22
Left Manchester City: 1979	**For:** West Bromwich Albion
and 1988	**For:** Hull City

Honours won with Manchester City: League Cup winner 1976, 14 England caps

During his career Peter Barnes played for 20 different clubs, although he is best remembered for his days at City. His first appearance in the Blues' senior side came when he replaced Glyn Pardoe in a League Cup-tie at Old Trafford in October 1974. He made his first start three days later in a 2-1 defeat at Burnley. A year later his skilful wing play meant he was a permanent fixture in the side. Such were his performances during the 1975-76 season that he collected the Young Player of the Year Award. In November 1977 he picked up the first of his 22 England caps as England beat Germany 2-0 in a World Cup qualifier at Wembley. All this success and he'd only just turned 20.

In July 1979 a £750,000 transfer took him to West Bromwich Albion. He stayed in the Midlands for two seasons before setting off on his travels which would take him to Spain, Australia and the United States as well as to the somewhat less glamorous venues of Port Vale, Hull and Wrexham. He also had a second, brief spell at Maine Road during the 1986-87 season.

Liverpool. In the words of Peter Swales, 'It was now time for the final push'. His plan was revealed in January when Malcolm Allison returned to the club as 'Coaching Overlord', primarily to work alongside manager Tony Book. Unfortunately it was a plan destined for failure and would eventually cost both men their jobs and the club a lot more into the bargain.

Having been knocked out of the League Cup (albeit in the fifth round) by Southampton, the first indication of things to come was in an embarrassing fourth round FA Cup defeat at Shrewsbury – then of Division 3. Inconsistent league form followed and City finished 15th, their lowest position for 11 seasons, or put another way, their first season back after promotion from Division 2 in 1966-67.

50 Greatest Players

ASA HARTFORD Midfielder

Joined Manchester City: 1974　　　　**From:** West Bromwich Albion

　　　　　　　　　and 1981　　　　**From:** Everton

Debut: 1974 v West Ham United (league)

Appearances: 323　　　　　　**Goals:** 37

Left Manchester City: 1979　　　**For:** Nottingham Forest

　　　　　　　　　and 1984　　　　**For:** Fort Lauderdale Sun (NASL)

Honours won with Manchester City: League Cup winner 1976, 36 Scotland caps

Asa Hartford will be remembered by City fans as a tough-tackling and creative midfielder. However his name first came to prominence in 1972 for events off the pitch. At that time Hartford was playing for West Brom. His proposed move to Leeds United fell through on medical grounds when he was diagnosed as having a hole in the heart.

  Manager Tony Book paid £210,000 for him in 1974, beginning a spell at Maine Road that lasted 289 games over the next five seasons. He left Maine Road in the summer of 1979 for a very short spell at Nottingham Forest before a move to Everton. In October 1981 he was back at City. At the end of the 1983-84 season he was released by Billy McNeill to try his hand for a while in Florida with Fort Lauderdale Sun. He is the most capped Scottish player ever on the club's books.

  In the summer of 1995 he came back to Maine Road again, this time as assistant manager to Alan Ball, and has remained ever since in a variety of coaching roles. He was in charge of the reserve side in 1999-2000 that won the Pontins League Premier title.

  The UEFA Cup was the only way of securing a trophy, and in the quarter-final, played in March, City had the misfortune to be drawn against the strongest side in the tournament, Borussia Monchengladbach. A goal from Mike Channon in the first leg at Maine Road was later ruled out by a German equaliser which gave Monchengladbach the upper hand for the return leg. Eighteen year-old Nicky Reid made his debut in the first leg, the first of many shock changes Allison would make during his second spell at Maine Road. Reid played well enough to retain his place for the return leg, but unfortunately the Germans ran out 3-1 winners. City's late consolation goal was scored by Deyna and it is the club's last goal in Europe to date.

Great Managers 1965-73, 1979-80

MALCOLM ALLISON

Sometimes controversial but never short of an opinion, Malcolm Allison was one of the most flamboyant people in the game and is still recognised and popular with City fans today. Without doubt he was one of the finest tacticians and coaches of all time.

After a playing career as a centre half for Charlton and West Ham he had a bout of TB and was forced to retire from playing. His first managerial position was with Southern League side Bath City. It was at Bath that Allison first came across a player destined, like himself, to go on to great things at Maine Road. The player was Tony Book. He then moved to Plymouth Argyle (taking Book with him) for 12 months before accepting Joe Mercer's offer of employment at City in July 1965.

His training methods transformed his players into the nucleus of a side that would win both the Division 2 and Division 1 titles in just three years. Today Allison claims that his training was revolutionary only because 'they'd never had any training before I came. All they did was just run round the pitch'. Tremendously fit and strong, as well as being tactically extremely well organised, the City team led by Joe Mercer and Malcolm Allison became the top side in the country during the late 1960s and early 1970s.

Perhaps not surprisingly after six years together, Allison felt it was time for personal promotion and he was given his wish in 1972 when Mercer moved to Coventry. In March 1973, feeling he was unable to motivate the players any longer, Allison accepted the manager's position at Crystal Palace. Four more moves and six years later he returned to Maine Road, primarily as coach to then manager, Tony Book. Unfortunately his return did not prove successful and after a clearout of players, an embarrassing FA Cup defeat and some big spending, Allison was dismissed in October 1980 and returned to Crystal Palace.

Football needs people with the abilities and charisma of 'Big Mal' – a man who will always be remembered with great affection by City fans for his work with Joe Mercer.

The Big Clearout

With Allison by now team manager and making the major decisions, the summer of 1979 saw his much-chronicled clearout when he sold established stars Gary Owen, Peter Barnes, Asa Hartford and Dave Watson. Brian Kidd had gone the previous March and Mike Channon followed just four games into the new season. City supporters were confused by this alarming disposal of talent, although because it was Malcolm Allison who'd orchestrated it, they assumed there must be

Steve Daley was the biggest of Allison's restructuring signings in the late 1970s. Daley was never popular at the club and was part of a very disappointing team.

valid reasons for it. Speaking some 20 years later, Allison said that the experienced players didn't like change and simply 'didn't want to play'. There's always two sides to an argument.

What made things worse for the fans that the replacements cost vast sums of money and appeared to be poorer players than those who had left. Steve MacKenzie cost £250,000 from Crystal Palace and had yet to play a league game: Michael Robinson was a £750,000 buy from Preston whilst Yugoslavian international Dragoslav Stepanovic and Wrexham's Bobby Shinton cost nearly £450,000 between them. The *pièce de résistance* amongst all these dealings though was the signing of Steve Daley from Wolves for an amazing £1,437,500. Neither Swales or Allison could ever decide which of them had agreed the deal. Fans could see what Allison was trying to do and a lot of them supported his ideas in trying to bring new blood into the side. But it was too much too soon. Surely the way to do it had to be the way Liverpool had done it so successfully in recent times – gradually.

50 Greatest Players

DENNIS TUEART Winger

Joined Manchester City: 1974	**From:** Sunderland
and 1980	**From:** New York Cosmos
Debut: 1974 v Manchester United (league)	
Appearances: 275	**Goals:** 109
Left Manchester City: 1978	**For:** New York Cosmos
and 1983	**For:** Stoke City

Honours won with Manchester City: League Cup winner 1976, 6 England caps

A fast, attacking winger capable of scoring with both feet, Dennis Tueart signed for City in March 1974. Two years later he played in a City side that beat Newcastle in the League Cup final. Tueart scored one of the best goals ever seen at the old stadium when his spectacular overhead kick proved to be the winner.

Tueart's career at Maine Road has been in three distinct parts, two playing spells, and currently as a director. His first spell ended in 1978 when he moved to New York where he joined the glamorous Cosmos. Two years later he was back in City's colours. Tueart's ratio of goals per game is quite remarkable for a winger although he was helped in this respect by his precision from the penalty spot. Only two players – Francis Lee and Eric Brook – have scored more penalties for City than Tueart. Lee has 46 to his name, Brook 35 and Tueart 24.

Outside of football, Tueart had built up a successful corporate hospitality business before returning to Maine Road as a director just prior to Christmas 1997.

In October, City were knocked out of the League Cup by Sunderland and were in the bottom half of the table. A 2-0 derby win at Maine Road was welcome but after a victory against Everton on 22 December, the season fell apart dramatically. City failed to win in 18 league games. January also saw another humiliating FA Cup defeat, this time at Halifax from Division 4.

Peter Swales still continued to provide money to back Allison's judgement when Dennis Tueart returned from New York and he also authorised £1,200,000 for the purchase of Kevin Reeves a couple of weeks before the transfer deadline. A traumatic season ended with City in a hugely disappointing 17th place. Something would need to be done quickly to prevent the club from slipping any further.

Chapter Eight: 1981-89
Wembley to 5-1

If the 1979-80 season had ended on a comparative high – three wins and a draw in the last four games – the start of the 1980-81 season was in stark contrast. The Blues did not win a game until 22 October when Tottenham were beaten at Maine Road. It was a run of 12 games and it finally saw the end of both Tony Book and Malcolm Allison. Book left for a short spell with Cardiff City and Allison returned to former hunting ground Crystal Palace.

The new man in charge was John Bond, a former playing colleague of Allison's at West Ham in the 1950s. Bond quickly made three signings: Bobby McDonald and Tommy Hutchison from Coventry and Gerry Gow from Bristol City. All were experienced campaigners and City lost just four more league games before the end of February.

In the League Cup, City had beaten Stoke City and Luton Town before destroying Notts County 5-1, thanks to four goals from Dennis Tueart. West Bromwich Albion were then beaten 2-1 to set up a two-legged semi-final against Liverpool, and City were unlucky to lose the tie 2-1 on aggregate. In the first leg at Maine Road Kevin Reeves had a perfectly good goal ruled out for a foul on Clemence and the Merseysiders went on to win 1-0. In the second leg Dave Bennett hit the bar and the game finished 1-1.

Tommy Hutchison was one of John Bond's early signings.

The irony of football brought Malcolm Allison back to Maine Road with his Crystal Palace side for the third round of the FA Cup in

January. Bond's revitalised City easily won 4-0 and a further irony brought Bond's former side Norwich in the fourth round. City won even more convincingly this time, scoring six without reply from the visitors.

A potential banana skin at Fourth Division Peterborough was successfully negotiated thanks to a solitary goal from Tommy Booth and it then took a replay to eventually beat Everton. Paul Power was the hero of this tie, scoring in both games. He would prove to be so in the semi-final as well. It was still goalless in extra-time when he curled a beautiful free-kick around the Ipswich wall to send City to Wembley.

City tasted victory in the 1981 FA Cup semi-final.

The 100th FA Cup Final

City's opponents for the 100th FA Cup Final were Tottenham, a team including two of Argentina's 1978 World Cup-winning side – Osvaldo Ardiles and Ricky Villa. When Tommy Hutchison gave City the lead with a flying header it looked as though it would be City's day and the

Tommy Hutchison scores with a stunning diving header in the 1981 FA Cup. Unfortunately he also scored an own goal at the other end to leave the scores level.

Kevin Reeves scored from the spot in the 1981 FA Cup final replay. His goal put
City 2-1 up, but they couldn't hold on to the lead.

events of recent years would soon be forgotten. However, with just 10 minutes left the hero turned villain he deflected a Glenn Hoddle free-kick past Corrigan who was diving in the opposite direction.

The following Thursday the two teams met again for the replay at Wembley. Villa gave Spurs the lead early on in the game only for his effort to be surpassed just moments later by a superb volley from City's Steve MacKenzie. Five minutes into the second half Bennett was fouled in the Spurs penalty area and Kevin Reeves scored from the spot.

For the second time the Blues had one hand on the cup. Regrettably though, again it wasn't enough. Garth Crookes brought the scores level before Villa scored perhaps the most replayed goal ever at Wembley. Joe Corrigan was spot on with his assessment: 'We should never have let him get that far.' For the second time in four days, Lady Luck had deserted Manchester City.

The final position of 12th showed a marked improvement on the past couple of seasons – City even managed to take three points off neighbours United who finished eighth.

Book Comes Back

At the request of John Bond, Tony Book made a welcome return to the club in the summer to work as an assistant to Ken Barnes on the scouting side. On the pitch, Martin O'Neill had arrived from Norwich, and after just two games of the season, Trevor Francis signed from Nottingham Forest for £1.2 million. Francis was obviously a very talented player, scoring twice on his debut against Stoke, and was popular with the fans. He scored 12 league goals that season. His only problem was he seemed somewhat injury prone in City's colours and moved to Italy at the end of the season. The signing was not a huge success for club or player.

In the first season of three points for a win, City finished 10th, an increase of two places on the last time out. Leeds, Swansea and Brighton were all beaten 4-0 whilst the lowest point was the 5-0 loss at Anfield. It was generally felt that if Dennis Tueart had recovered from the ankle injury that kept him out from December, the Blues would have finished much higher.

Trevor Francis scored twice on his debut against Stoke City in 1981.

Neither cup competition held City's interest for long that season. In the FA Cup, the Blues beat Cardiff 3-1 before losing to Coventry by the same score in round four, a game in which Asa Hartford was sent off. There was an unusual game with Stoke in the second round of the League Cup. Both legs were won by the home side 2-0, with City finally winning through 9-8 on penalties. Dennis

50 Greatest Players

TOMMY HUTCHISON Winger

Joined Manchester City: 1980   **From:** Coventry City

Debut: 1980 v Brighton & Hove Albion (league)

Appearances: 60   **Goals:** 5

Left Manchester City: 1982   **For:** Bulova (Hong Kong)

Tommy Hutchison's arrival coincided with the transformation of a relegation-haunted side into a powerful Cup-fighting force that reached the FA Cup final and the League Cup semi-final. Hutchison spearheaded the brief John Bond revolution at Maine Road. A tall, leggy winger, Hutchison started his football life with Alloa Athletic before moving south to Blackpool and then Coventry, where he earned Scottish international honours and played in the 1974 World Cup. A fans' favourite with all his clubs, Hutchison became something of a cult hero during his short time with City, where the crowd loved his elusive dribbling, accurate crossing and the odd vital goal thrown in for good measure. Hutchison's Indian summer at Maine Road nearly produced a golden highlight when City met Tottenham in the 1981 FA Cup final. Unfortunately it was not to be: Hutch being forever remembered for scoring at both ends in the first game that ended 1-1. In July 1982 he left Maine Road to join Hong Kong side Bulova, later returning to the UK and playing for both Burnley and Swansea.

Tueart scored twice in a 3-1 win against Northampton but a 1-0 defeat at Barnsley ended any further Wembley aspirations.

The 1982-83 season started on a high note with three consecutive wins and only one goal conceded. The 1-0 victory against Watford is memorable for the goalkeeping efforts of full back Bobby McDonald. Joe Corrigan injured a shoulder after just three minutes with the admirable McDonald keeping a clean sheet for the remaining 87.

By the time the FA Cup came around in January, City were mid-table and had already been knocked out of the League (Milk) Cup, suffering a 4-0 defeat at Southampton.

Pleat's Jig Greets City Misery

When City went to Brighton for a fourth round tie they were humbled by the same score and it immediately brought about the resignation of John Bond. There were lots or rumours as to the reason for his apparent swift decision, not least the relationship with certain directors, as well as supposed difficulties in his private life, and his number two John Benson took over.

Under Benson, City moved down the table at a remarkable pace and when the last game of the season arrived, City needed a draw to stay up. Their opponents, Luton Town, needed a win. With four minutes to go a deflected shot from Luton substitute Raddy Antic beat Alex Williams and City went down. Luton's side included future City manager Brian Horton as well as Paul Walsh, but the thing most City fans will, unfortunately, remember must surely be the delirious jig performed by Luton boss David Pleat which is now part of BBC's *Match of the Day* archives.

A club that by now was not the most buoyant financially would be playing Second Division football next season. Not surprisingly, John Benson lost his job in the summer and Swales turned his attentions to Scotland, signing up Billy McNeill. McNeill had recently left his position with Celtic and immediately recruited Jimmy Frizzell from Oldham as his number two. Despite McNeill's hands being tied because of the lack of money available, he was confident enough in the squad to predict promotion at the first attempt.

A future manager of the Irish national team: Mick McCarthy

In collaboration with Frizzell, a man who'd been used to limited finances at his previous club, McNeill began to pick up some quality players at prices the Blues could afford. He bought Jim Tolmie from Belgian side FC Lokeren, Neil McNab from Brighton and picked up Derek Parlane from Leeds on a free transfer.

By mid-October City were in second place, having won five consecutive games, the highlight of which was the 6-0 defeat of Blackburn when Parlane scored a hat-trick. Tommy Caton was sold to Arsenal in December, his replacement being Mick McCarthy from Barnsley. The £200,000 difference went some way towards pacifying City's frustrated bank manager.

The League Cup witnessed another 6-0 victory, this time against Torquay United, with Parlane again finding the net three times. The Scottish centre forward was proving to be a sound investment and would finish the season as leading scorer. Unfortunately for the Blues Aston Villa were awaiting them in the next round of the League Cup and City lost 3-1.

In the FA Cup, Fourth Division Blackpool were victorious in the third round by a 2-1 margin. Even City's goal was scored by the Seasiders.

City could now concentrate on the league and they remained in the top four for most of the season, their main rivals being the Kevin Keegan inspired Newcastle United. Three successive defeats at the end of April ruined any chances of promotion and the Blues eventually finished in fourth place, 10 points behind the Geordies who went up alongside Sheffield Wednesday and champions Chelsea.

For the opening of the 1984-85 season, City travelled to Plough Lane for a historic first league meeting with Wimbledon. The 2-2 draw gave debuts to new boys David Phillips and Tony Cunningham. The good league form of the previous season continued, so much so the side topped the division after a 1-0 win at Blackburn in the first week of March. By that time City had been knocked out of the FA Cup at Coventry in the third round and had beaten both Blackpool and West Ham in the League Cup before falling 4-1 to Chelsea in round four.

Failure to win any of six games in a month caused some concern and City went into the last game of the season knowing a win was vital to be assured of promotion. Starting the game neck and neck in the league with Alan Ball's Portsmouth, City – playing against Charlton – attacked from the outset. The final score of 5-1 underlined City's supremacy on the day. A huge crowd of 47,285 – although fans there said that figure was underestimated – saw glorious sunshine and City return to the First Division.

Back in the High Life

As with most clubs entering a higher division, the first season can be the most difficult one, and the 1985-86 campaign proved no different for City. The arrivals of big City fan Mark Lillis and former Red Sammy McIlroy gave the Blues a good start but by October they were struggling in 20th position. In that same month, the newspapers were full of stories concerning City's financial plight – one even quoting the club was £4 million in debt.

The Blues had a good January, winning all five league games, but then failed to win again for the rest of the season – a run of 13 matches. The season ended with City 15th, four points above a relegation spot. Neither was there any real success in either the FA or League Cup, as City lost in the second and third rounds respectively, to Watford and Arsenal.

However, in a new cup competition, created primarily as a result of the ban on English clubs in Europe, City faired much better. In the Full Members' Cup, the Blues went all the way to the final at Wembley, losing out 5-4 to Chelsea in a thrilling match. The game against Chelsea was played just 24 hours after the Old Trafford derby, which ended 2-2.

Steve Redmond was a successful product of City's youth team.

The high spot of the 1985-86 season was the success of City's youth team. Under the coaching of Tony Book and Glyn Pardoe, and chief scout Ken Barnes, Steve Redmond captained the young Blues to a two-leg success 3-1 against Manchester United in the final of the FA Youth Cup. Seven of the side would eventually play in City's first team. Apart from Redmond these included Hinchcliffe, White, Lake and Brightwell, all saving the Blues hundeds of thousands of pounds in the transfer market.

50 Greatest Players

PAUL POWER Midfielder

Joined Manchester City: 1973   **From:** Manchester Boys
Debut: 1975 v Aston Villa (league)
Appearances: 445   **Goals:** 36
Left Manchester City: 1986   **For:** Everton

Paul Power joined City as an amateur in August 1973.
Under Tony Book he established himself in the first team
in the 1976-77 season. His commitment to the City
cause earned him the Player of the Year trophy twice, in
1980-81 and 1984-85 and he captained the Blues for
the best part of seven seasons. The left-sided midfielder
with boundless energy scored 36 times for City, perhaps
none more important than the 1981 FA Cup semi-final
decider against Ipswich at Villa Park.

Power had the privilege to lead City out at Wembley three times, but unfortunately
never appeared on a winning side. Undoubtedly one of the club's most loyal servants
and popular players – only eight men have played more games for Manchester City.

Not surprisingly, City fans were shocked when manager Billy McNeill sold him to
Everton in June 1986. At the end of his first season at Goodison Park he'd won a
Championship medal and City fans were delighted for their former idol. A knee
injury the following year forced him to retire from football and he joined the Everton
coaching staff.

Power later worked for the PFA before returning to Maine Road in 1997 at the
request of Frank Clark. Nowadays, Power is a key figure in the success of City's
youngsters at the highly-acclaimed Platt Lane Academy. If it produces just one player
of a similar standard to Paul Power then it will be well worth the effort.

Seven games into the 1986-87 season manager Billy McNeill left
Maine Road and moved to Aston Villa. He cited reasons such as
the obvious lack of money, which prevented him from strengthening
the side, and he was unable to work with a newly-appointed
director, Freddie Pye.

City had also lost the services of the captain Paul Power who'd
joined Everton in the summer. Power won a championship medal

with Everton at the end of his first season and City fans were delighted when one of their own had been justly rewarded.

Jimmy Frizzell took over from McNeill but City still had to wait until November for their first league win when McNeill's new club were beaten 3-1 at Maine Road. By the time the two teams met again at Villa Park in April, City were struggling and were 10 games into a 14-game run without a win. The following game was a 4-2 defeat by Southampton at home and saw 'The Case Against Peter Swales' leaflet distributed amongst the supporters. The disgruntled fans were unhappy about Swales' 13-year rule and wanted his immediate resignation. That would be another seven years in coming.

The disappointment of that Southampton defeat had faded by the time West Ham visited on 9 May, the last game of the season. City lost 2-0 and were relegated once again, the second time in four years.

The '10-1'

Paul Stewart had been a £200,000 signing from Blackpool in March but could only manage two goals in 11 league outings. In the cups, City had gone out in the early rounds of all three trophies. United had won 1-0 at Old Trafford in the third round of the FA Cup although a perfectly legitimate goal by City's Imre Varadi was ruled out for 'who-knows' what reason. After beating Southend in the second round of the League Cup, the Blues went down 3-1 to Arsenal at Highbury. Once again the club's best performance was in the Full Members' Cup, where, after beating Wimbledon and Watford, City lost 3-2 to Ipswich in round four.

Mel Machin became City's 11th manager since 1970 when he took over in the summer, Jimmy Frizzell having been elevated to the position of general manager. Machin had previously been with Norwich and at Maine Road he inherited a side of experienced professionals and several members of the successful FA Youth Cup team. With Stewart, in particular, in fine goalscoring form, City had already scored four goals on four occasions by the time Huddersfield Town came to Maine Road on 7 November. Nobody could have anticipated the outcome as Malcolm Macdonald's side were destroyed 10-1.

Great Matches

Football League Division 2   Maine Road, Manchester, 7 November 1987

Manchester City 10   Huddersfield 1   Attendance 19,583

Manchester City	Huddersfield
McNab	May (pen)
Stewart 3	
Adcock 3	
White 3	

Manager Mel Machin spent just over two years in charge at Maine Road but had the privilege to preside over two games that will linger long in the fans' memories. This one was City's biggest win of the century; the other was, of, course, the famous '5-1' victory over Manchester United in September 1989. Wearing a hideous black and yellow square kit (possibly the worst ever seen at Maine Road) Huddersfield, bottom of the table, arrived for the game with new manager Malcolm Macdonald just three weeks into the job.

Despite their lowly league position, Huddersfield could have taken the lead twice in the opening ten minutes. City's Neil McNab, at his most influential that day, broke the deadlock in the 12th minute and well and truly opened the floodgates. Paul Stewart doubled the score after 29 minutes and five minutes later Tony Adcock headed the third. When David White got his first – City's fourth – just before half time, City fans jokingly thought the Blues might get eight!

The interval only prolonged the agony. In the 52nd minute Adcock hooked in his second and Stewart's header made it six a quarter of an hour later. Huddersfield had just restarted proceedings when Adcock broke through to make it 7-0 and complete his hat-trick. It took 17 minutes for the next goal, Stewart converting Andy Hinchcliffe's cross for his third and City's eighth. The last five minutes of the game produced three more goals. White's second was followed by the highlight of Huddersfield's miserable day as former Blue Andy May converted a consolation penalty. In the last minute of the game White dribbled round Cox for City's tenth. It was the first time in 25 years that three players from the same team had scored hat-tricks in a league game.

In typical City style, the Blues lost 1-0 in the return game five months later.

Manchester City: Nixon, Gidman, Hinchcliffe, Clements, Lake, Redmond, White, Stewart, Adcock, McNab, Simpson.
Huddersfield: Cox, Brown, Bray, Banks, Webster, Walford, Barham, May, Shearer, Winter, Cork.
Referee: K. Breen.

The FA Cup then brought City and Huddersfield together again, only this time it was a much closer contest. After two draws, City eventually went through 3-0 to face Blackpool in round four. After a fortunate 1-1 draw at Bloomfield Road, the Blues won the replay 2-1 thanks to goals from the two Pauls, Stewart and Simpson. In the fifth round Plymouth were beaten 3-1, setting up a quarter-final clash with Liverpool at Maine Road. At the time, the Merseysiders were marching away with the championship and were red-hot favourites to win the game. Thanks partly to two suspect refereeing decisions (both of which cost the Blues a goal) this they duly did, although the 4-0 scoreline is somewhat unfair on a City side that put up a brave fight.

City had earlier gone out of the League Cup to a Merseyside team – this time it had been Everton who'd beaten them 2-0 in round five.

In a fairly mixed season, City's talented youngsters had been watched many times by spies from the so-called bigger clubs. When Tottenham offered City £1.7 million for Paul Stewart in July, Peter Swales could not turn it down. In a season when City finished eleventh in Division 2, there was no little concern amongst fans who had just seen the club sell its leading scorer.

Andy Dibble, Brian Gayle, Wayne Biggins and Nigel Gleghorn were four new faces in City's side for the opening fixture of the 1988-89 season, a 1-0 defeat at Hull. Without a win in the first four games, City won the next five, including beating leaders Blackburn 1-0 thanks to a goal from new boy Biggins. When Bradford City were beaten 4-0 on 10 December, City went to top spot, albeit on goal difference.

There was disappointment in the FA Cup when City lost 3-1 at Third Division Brentford in the fourth round after a 1-0 win against Leicester. The Blues had lost interest in the Full Members' Cup after just one game, going down 3-2 at Blackburn whilst the League Cup was only slightly better. Plymouth were beaten 7-3 on aggregate in the second round, followed by a 4-2 victory against Sheffield United when Paul Moulden scored a hat-trick. Unfortunately, the goals ran out at Luton in round five, only David White replying to three from the home side. Meanwhile, they did continue in the league as City maintained pressure on the leaders. Hull, Ipswich, Leicester and Sunderland (away) were all on the receiving end of four as the race to catch champions Chelsea continued right up until the last few days of the season. Nerves would be settled if the Blues could beat Bournemouth in the penultimate game at Maine Road.

By half-time the Blues led 3-0 and any other club apart from the totally unpredictable Manchester City would have closed the game up in the second half. Amazingly, Bournemouth (with Ian Bishop in the side) scored twice and when Andy Hinchcliffe gave away a penalty for the equaliser in the 96th minute, City had effectively 'snatched defeat from the jaws of victory'.

'Going Bananas'

The whole season hinged on the last game at Bradford. No matter what happened elsewhere, one point would guarantee the Blues an automatic promotion place. It appeared City were determined to make their fans suffer for as long as possible and even contrived to go in at half time a goal down. News was coming through of their closest rivals Crystal Palace winning by four, even five goals. With four minutes to go it looked as though City would have to settle for a play-off spot. It was then that David White's cross reached the sliding Trevor Morley on the six-yard line and the City fans really did 'go bananas'. The Blues were back in the big time.

Having impressed in the Bournemouth game, Ian Bishop was a summer signing although the fans were disappointed when the home-grown Paul Moulden moved in the opposite direction. Another arrival was the £1 million Clive Allen from French side Bordeaux. Both these two players were highly talented and would quickly become firm favourites with the supporters, and were just the kind of players required at Maine Road. No one could foresee at the time how both players would fall out of favour with future managers, indeed Bishop wouldn't play for City once 1990 had arrived.

Not surprisingly, the start of the season proved difficult as the opening 3-1 defeat at Liverpool confirmed. The seventh game of the season was the Maine Road derby, and with City joint bottom of the table, a win was almost guaranteed for Alex Ferguson's multi-million pound – if under-achieving – side.

Biggest Ever Derby Victory

The programme from a Manchester derby that will be remembered for a long time.

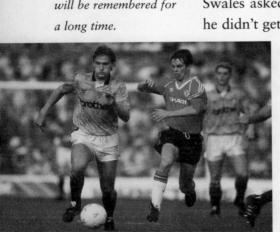

Andy Hinchcliffe outruns United's Russell Beardsmore during City's famous 5-1 destruction of United in September 1989.

The 23 September 1989 will live forever in the memories of any City fan lucky enough to be there. In weather more suited for cricket than football, City very nearly ran up a cricket score as United were humiliated 5-1. It was City's biggest ever derby victory at Maine Road and it was one of the greatest days in the club's history.

City's form continued to fluctuate over the next few weeks but a 6-0 defeat at Derby was their biggest loss in more than 25 years. It also began the rumours that Machin was on his way out. The Blues lost 3-0 at home to Nottingham Forest and then travelled to Charlton and drew 1-1. It was now that Swales asked for Machin's resignation. When he didn't get it, Swales sacked him.

The chairman said that Machin had been ousted following pressure from the fans. This proved to be a fabrication and was heavily criticised in the City fanzines over the next few issues. Machin had won promotion, bought some good players and been in charge for the by now famous '10-1' and '5-1' games but some said that he wasn't 'showbizzy' enough for the chairman.

Great Matches

LEAGUE DIVISION 1   Maine Road, Manchester, 23 September 1989

Manchester City 5   **Manchester United 1**   Attendance 43,246

Oldfield 2   Hughes

Morley

Bishop

Hinchcliffe

Mel Machin's only derby in charge of City is one of the most memorable matches in the history of the club. Promoted from Division 2 at the end of the previous season, the Blues had struggled in their six opening games and were languishing near the bottom of the league as derby day approached. Things were different at Old Trafford where the previous week United had beaten league leaders Millwall 5-1, and their side contained several million-pound players. City's side was their promotion side, and although Ian Bishop had arrived in the summer, City fans knew things wouldn't be easy against the 'old enemy'.

On a gloriously sunny afternoon United started brightly before referee Neil Midgley took both teams off the pitch because of crowd trouble. Within minutes of the restart David Oldfield had crashed the ball past Jim Leighton after a David White cross. City were one up and eager for more. They didn't have to wait long. United's defence couldn't clear the ball after good work by Paul Lake, and Trevor Morley poked home the second. Things kept getting better as Bishop scored the third after 35 minutes – hurling himself into a spectacular diving header. Harsh words from Alex Ferguson at half time seemed to pay dividends as Mark Hughes pulled a goal back on 50 minutes. City fans remembered the Bournemouth game at the end of the previous season when they'd seen their side give away a three-goal lead. This time there was no need for worry as Paul Lake set up David Oldfield's second goal just after the hour to restore the three-goal lead.

Arguably City saved the best 'til last. Bishop played the ball out wide on the right to White and his first-time cross was met by the onrushing Andy Hinchcliffe who powered a header past the hapless Jim Leighton in the United goal. The Blues had never scored five in a Maine Road derby before and the humiliation was complete.

Manchester City: Cooper, Fleming, Hinchcliffe, Bishop, Gayle, Redmond, White, Morley, Oldfield, Brightwell, Lake (Beckford).

Manchester United: Leighton, Anderson, Donaghy, Duxbury, Phelan, Pallister, Beardsmore, Ince, McClair, Hughes, Wallace.

Referee: N. Midgley.

Kendall Arrives

Swales offered the managerial post to Oldham's Joe Royle who turned it down, deciding to continue his good work at Boundary Park. On 9 December Howard Kendall watched City draw 1-1 at Southampton before officially taking over for his first game, ironically at Everton, a few days later. Kendall began to mould the team to his way of thinking and brought in two ex-Evertonians in Peter Reid and Alan Harper. Ian Bishop and Trevor Morley didn't fit into his plans and were both soon on their way to West Ham in exchange for another ex-Evertonian, Mark Ward.

Another favourite, Clive Allen, was surprisingly used sparingly in City's side that began to let very few goals in but, conversely, failed to score many at the other end.

Millwall knocked the Blues out of the FA Cup after two drawn games, whilst a 3-2 defeat at Nottingham Forest ended any aspirations in the Full Members' Cup. City did manage to progress to the fourth round of the League Cup (following wins against Brentford and Norwich) only to lose to Coventry at Maine Road.

February saw the arrival of Adrian Heath – yet another player with Everton connections – as well as the 100th First Division Manchester derby. United were still sore from the events of the previous September and were seeking revenge. It had not been too great a season at Old Trafford either and City went into the game two points higher than their supposedly more illustrious neighbours. Against the run of play Clayton Blackmore gave United the lead only for Ian Brightwell to 'welly' an unstoppable equaliser.

The draw at Old Trafford was the first of five in seven games. The last of the run was against Chelsea on 21 March, a game which saw Niall Quinn's debut and his first goal for his new club.

With four wins in four games at the end of the season and City finishing in 14th place, it looked as though Kendall was finally creating a strong side and City fans looked forward to the prospect of some success next year. However, if they were to achieve any, it wouldn't be under Kendall's guidance.

Chapter Nine: 1990-97
All Change in the Hot Seat

On the transfer front, the summer of 1990 proved no different from many others with players coming and going. A surprise deal saw Andy Hinchcliffe moving to Everton in a £600,000 deal involving Neil Pointon, causing City fans to joke about the shade of blue the team should now be wearing. Goalkeeper Tony Coton was a £1 million buy from Watford and, along with Niall Quinn, would easily become Kendall's best buy during his time at Maine Road.

The season began with a 3-1 defeat at Tottenham followed by home victories against Everton and Aston Villa. In the Villa game Paul Lake

50 Greatest Players

ANDY HINCHCLIFFE Full back

Joined Manchester City: 1985   **From:** Juniors

Debut: 1987 v Plymouth Argyle (league)

Appearances: 139   **Goals:** 11

Left Manchester City: 1990   **For:** Everton

One of the stars of City's FA Youth Cup-winning side of 1986, Andy Hinchcliffe's break into the first team was delayed by a serious back injury during the 1986-87 season.

Tony Book had described his reserve team debut as the best he'd ever seen and was already accurately predicting international honours for the classy left back. Following an assured performance in his first team debut on the opening day of the 1987-88 season, Hinchcliffe never looked back as he established himself as a crowd favourite with his quality crossing and tenacious tackling. However, he soon became known for his trademark diagonal crossfield ball to David White and the whipped-in near post corner.

Hinchcliffe was also a member of the famous '5-1' team, scoring the last goal with a spectacular header in front of a half-empty Platt Lane Stand. A falling-out with new manager Howard Kendall saw Hinchcliffe moving to Everton in a player/cash deal for Neil Pointon valued at £600,000 on 11 July 1990.

injured his knee, little knowing then what bearing it was to have on the rest of his career. For the neutral supporter there was a terrific 3-3 Maine Road derby in October, although City were bitterly disappointed to draw after being 3-1 up with 10 minutes to go.

After beating Torquay in the second round of the League Cup, City lost at home to Arsenal. On the same October night Everton were losing to Sheffield United and Colin Harvey's job was in the balance. Joe Royle's name was mentioned as his replacement but City fans were mortified when Howard Kendall took advantage of a get-out clause in his contract and returned to his 'first love' at Goodison Park.

Reid Replaces Kendall

By now the fans were genuinely sick and tired of the constant upheaval in the manager's chair and wanted a period of continuity. With this in mind they overwhelmingly supported current player Peter Reid, thinking that he could at least carry on the work started by Kendall, and so it proved. Under Reid, City prospered and played some good, attacking football, with Niall Quinn and David White forming a prolific partnership up front. The Blues lost just one of their last nine league games to finish the season in fifth place, one above United, and their highest since 1977-78 under Tony Book. In the game with Derby County, Niall Quinn deputised for Tony Coton who had been sent off after bringing Dean Saunders down in the penalty area. Quinn promptly saved the resulting spot-kick and City went on to win the game 2-1. For good measure, Quinn had already scored at the other end. White then scored four in the next game as City produced a sparkling display to win 5-1 at Villa Park.

Nearly 40,000 witnessed the last game of the season when Sunderland needed a win to avoid relegation. Once again Quinn was involved, scoring twice as City won 3-2, condemning his future club to the Second Division. It was the last game in front of the old Platt Lane Stand which was to be demolished in the summer. Although they prospered in the league, there was little joy in the FA Cup when, after away victories at Burnley and Port Vale, the Blues lost 1-0 at Notts County.

Because of the success of the previous season, 1991-92 began with a certain amount of optimism and after three straight wins the Blues topped the table. A new signing (and captain) was on board in the shape of Keith Curle, a then club record signing of £2.5 million from Wimbledon. After a disappointing September, City's form improved and by the time Steve McMahon arrived from Liverpool at Christmas, the Blues had lost once in the previous 10 games.

Middlesbrough won the third round FA Cup-tie 2-1 in January, a repeat of the fourth round League Cup game the previous month. Once again, it was White and Quinn leading the way in the goalscoring stakes, assisted now by youngster Mike Sheron.

Three defeats in four league games in March threatened to put something of a dampener on the latter part of the season but a wonderful performance against Leeds ended the barren run. Leeds and Manchester United were going neck and neck for the championship and many felt City would just lay down and die in a game watched by more than 30,000. It was a day when

David White (top) and Niall Quinn formed a prolific scoring partnership for City.

everything went right for the Blues who won handsomely 4-0. At first it was thought the win would give the title to United, but Leeds

Keith Curle captained City through some troubled times in the 1990s.

regrouped after the heavy defeat to win the title by four points.

City finished with four consecutive wins, David White again showing his fondness for the end of the season, this time by scoring a hat-trick in the 5-2 win at Oldham. For the second successive year the Blues ended fifth position. All seemed rosy in the Maine Road garden.

The Premiership Arrives

The 1992-93 season was the first of the new FA Premier League and City's first game was rescheduled to become Sky TV's first *Monday Night Football* show. Fireworks, parachutists and cheerleaders all made appearances before a three-sided crowd prior to a 1-1 draw with Queens Park Rangers.

There had been changes both on and off the pitch during the close season. Left-winger Rick Holden came from Oldham with Neil Pointon and Steve Redmond going in the opposite direction, while Wimbledon again received £2.5 million from the Blues, this time for Salford-born Terry Phelan. Off the pitch, physio Roy Bailey had been dismissed along with former player, and now youth coach, Glyn Pardoe, and chief scout Ken Barnes had retired. The loss of these three long-serving City backroom staff angered many supporters.

The Queens Park Rangers game had seen the return to the side of Paul Lake who had been out for nearly two years. In the next game, away at Middlesbrough, Lake once again injured his knee and was carried off after just eight minutes. This was his last appearance in a City shirt and he retired because of his injuries in 1996.

For no apparent reason City's start to the season had been, at best,

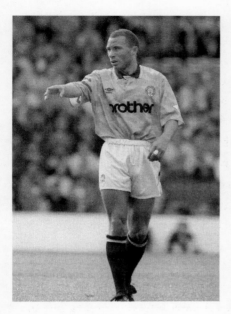

Terry Phelan became known for his skilful play at Manchester City.

inconsistent. White was yet again producing the goals but after a convincing 3-0 win at Sheffield Wednesday, City then lost the next three games by the same scoreline of 1-0. When the Blues lost in the League Cup to Tottenham in October, at the same time as the chairman said there would be no more cash for players, the rumblings once again of 'Swales Out' could be heard in Moss Side.

The FA Cup provided some highspots as City progressed to the quarter-final, only to lose again to Tottenham, a side that would beat City four times in the season. The FA Cup-tie saw the opening of the new Umbro Stand as the replacement for the old Platt Lane stand, with a crowd of more than 34,000 and a national TV audience of millions. When Mike Sheron gave City an early lead it really did look like the Blues could be on their way to Wembley.

It was then that City, in their inimitable style, shot themselves in the foot and allowed a Nayim-inspired Spurs side to score four in reply. Terry Phelan set off on one of his customary mazy dribbles and scored a second for City but his goal only seemed to tip some disgruntled fans over the edge. A strange, almost confusing, pitch invasion followed, one that was eventually dispelled by mounted police. Sheer frustration had finally proved too much for the City supporters who'd simply had enough. An opportunity to show off the new stand and prove to the country just what City could do on the pitch had backfired in the worst possible way.

In the last game of the season Everton won 5-2 at Maine Road to leave City in ninth place. With Manchester United being crowned the first-ever Premier League Champions, fans were understandably disappointed at once again being empty-handed and even more angry with the chairman who was the target for some carefully aimed eggs after the Everton game.

The Maddox Regime

One new face did materialise just as the 1993-94 season was getting under way. However, it proved to be a face which had no previous experience of professional football matters and only angered fans even more. In August, just two games into the season, the former *News of the World* journalist John Maddock was brought in by Peter Swales as general manager. Immediately Maddock told the press he was now in charge at Maine Road and, despite what many thought,

50 Greatest Players

DAVID WHITE Striker

Joined Manchester City: 1985   **From:** Salford Boys
Debut: 1986 v Luton Town (league)
Appearances: 342   **Goals:** 95
Left Manchester City: 1993   **For:** Leeds United
Honours won with Manchester City: 1 England cap

David White was one of several members of City's FA Youth Cup winning side of 1986 to make a significant impact in the first team. A tall and powerful winger with explosive pace and a shot to match, White was always a prolific marksman as a youngster and managed to transfer that ability to senior level once he was given his first team chance with a debut as a substitute at Luton in September 1986.

Over the next few years he became a permanent fixture on City's right-wing, rarely missing a game and maintaining a high goals ratio which was to earn him England B and Under 21 honours. He then won one full international cap, against Spain in Santander in 1992, when he was perhaps unfairly blamed by the press for the 1-0 defeat after he missed a glorious opportunity early in the game.

He left Maine Road in December 1993 in a player exchange deal involving David Rocastle of Leeds United. A series of injuries were to lead eventually to a premature retirement from the game in 1997. He can still be seen at Maine Road occasionally summarising the Blues' games for local radio.

he said he was not a mouthpiece for the chairman. There were also rumours of a rift between Swales and Reid. Whatever was going on behind the scenes it was clear to see that Reid's – and his assistant Sam Ellis' – days were numbered. The players backed Reid 100 per cent saying, in the words of captain Keith Curle, 'The only rift here appears to be between the hierarchy and the management.'

Perhaps Reid's popularity with the players undermined the chairman's authority and it soon became clear that Maddock had been brought in as a hatchet man. The hatchet fell on Peter Reid and Sam Ellis after four games without a win. Surely the chairman realised what the feeling among the supporters would be after this decision.

Increased protests outside the ground became the norm but the national press then began to show considerable interest in the history of Manchester City under the chairmanship of Peter Swales. Regrettably, but honestly, it did not show the club in any great light and once again City were in the news for all the wrong reasons.

Horton In, Swales Out

When Maddock announced Reid's replacement it did little to placate the, by now, irate supporters. Oxford United's Brian Horton became City's sixth manager in 10 years, but most fans hadn't even heard of him. They were expecting someone like Joe Royle or Terry Venables, both of whom had been linked with the job in the press. Admittedly, Horton wasn't a big name, but over a period of time he would become very popular with the fans – indeed, even today he still appears at some Supporters' Club functions and is regarded as a genuinely nice guy.

The arrival of Horton by no means saw the end of the off-the-pitch events that season. Francis Lee's name came into the frame as he headed a consortium aimed at ousting Swales and taking over at Maine Road. When Lee made an appearance in the director's box for the league match against Queens Park Rangers in September, City responded with their best performance of the season to win 3-0. The crowd loved not only the victory but also the arrival of the 'Messiah'. The 'Forward with Franny' campaign was now in full swing.

50 Greatest Players

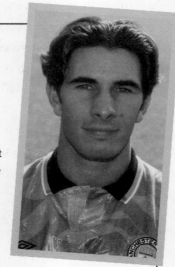

PAUL LAKE Midfielder

Joined Manchester City: 1985   **From:** Juniors

Debut: 1987 v Wimbledon (league)

Appearances: 134   **Goals:** 11

Left Manchester City: 1996 (retired)

Howard Kendall once described Paul Lake as 'the most talented footballer I ever worked with' and his versatility saw him excel in positions all over the field. Bobby Robson drafted Lake into his provisional squad for the 1990 World Cup and tipped him as a future England captain but sadly his career was brought to a premature end. On 11 March 1989 after a collision of heads in a game against Leicester at Maine Road, Lake swallowed his tongue and 22,000 watched his body convulse on the floor. Thankfully the quick thinking of physio Roy Bailey saved the day and Lake was back in action the following week. However, on 5 September 1990, Lake was not to be so lucky. Controlling an innocuous through ball against Aston Villa, the newly-installed team captain, fell to the ground in agony. He had ruptured a cruciate ligament and so began a six-year battle to regain full fitness that he was tragically to lose. He eventually started a new career as a physio.

After an extremely lively AGM, and a 3-2 defeat by United after being 2-0 up, Peter Swales eventually succumbed to the pressure and resigned on 29 November 1993. The take-over transaction was so complicated that Lee wouldn't actually gain control of the club until February.

Meanwhile, back on the pitch, it is perhaps not surprising that 1993-94 wasn't the greatest of seasons for City who finished 16th in the Premier League and struggled for goals all season with Mike Sheron top scorer in the league with a miserly six. In the League Cup City had progressed to the fourth round after victories against Reading and Chelsea only to be beaten by Nottingham Forest in a replay. Round three of the FA Cup witnessed a 4-1 victory against Leicester, thanks to a hat-trick from new signing, Norwegian international Kare Ingebrigtsen. A disappointing performance at

Cardiff in the next round saw the Blues lose 1-0 with skipper Keith Curle missing a penalty.

As the end of the season approached, City signed four players in an attempt to stave off the prospect of relegation, one that they had been dicing with for most of the season. In a player/cash deal involving David White, midfielder David Rocastle came from Leeds and the diminutive Paul Walsh cost £700,000 from Portsmouth. Peter Beagrie was a £1.1 million signing from Everton on transfer deadline day and an unknown German striker called Uwe Rosler arrived, initially on loan, from FC Nurnburg.

Rosler and Walsh both scored in the last home game of the season, a 2-2 draw with Chelsea in front of 33,594. As well as it being the last opportunity to see their beloved Blues for the next three months, many came to say farewell to the Kippax Street stand which was due for demolition in the summer.

Ups and Downs

With Lee and his chief ally Colin Barlow desperately trying to make some sense of the club's accounts during the close season, manager Brian Horton sold Mike Sheron to Norwich and David Rocastle to Chelsea. Nicky Summerbee had impressed for Swindon back in February and was bought for £1.5 million.

The season started with a 3-0 defeat at Arsenal but then came two resounding victories against West Ham and Everton at a Maine Road now reduced to a capacity of less than 20,000. The Blues continued their winning ways with a 5-2 victory against Spurs but suffered a major setback three weeks later when they were overrun 5-0 at Old Trafford.

The League Cup also witnessed the Blues in free-scoring form. After losing the first leg 1-0 at

Paul Walsh – a speedy signing from Portsmouth.

Georgiou Kinkladze's signing was a major coup for Francis Lee.

Barnet, City progressed to the third round with a 4-1 win at Maine Road in the return game. Then came a nail-biting 4-3 away win against Queens Park Rangers, despite goalkeeper Andy Dibble and Richard Edghill both being sent off. It took two games to see off Newcastle United before another poor performance at Crystal Palace in round five saw City crash out 4-0. In February, Newcastle would gain revenge for that League Cup defeat with a 3-1 triumph in the FA Cup. Not unlike the previous season, City continued to frustrate fans with a combination of excellent and dire performances. After successive defeats to Wimbledon, Crystal Palace and Tottenham, the Blues then beat Liverpool at home and the champions-elect Blackburn Rovers away.

A 0-0 draw with Newcastle heralded the opening of the new Kippax Street stand at the end of April as City finished the season without a win in their last four games. A final position of 17th and a woeful display in the 3-2 home defeat by Queens Park Rangers in the very last game proved to be the end for manager Brian Horton. Strangely, though, had City won that game they would have finished 12th and possibly Horton would have still had a job. Fortunately for Horton, he was offered a position with Huddersfield less than six weeks later.

The New Man

According to press statements from the club, 'City's new manager will be a high-profile figure with a proven track record.' When Alan Ball was appointed at the end of June the fans were once again astounded

50 Greatest Players

NIALL QUINN Striker

Joined Manchester City: 1990   **From:** Arsenal

Debut: 1990 v Chelsea (league)

Appearances: 244   **Goals:** 78

Left Manchester City: 1996   **For:** Sunderland

Honours won with Manchester City: 47 Republic of Ireland caps

Unable to command a regular spot in the Arsenal first team, manager Howard Kendall brought Niall Quinn to City in March 1990 for £800,000. His arrival helped ensure City's top-flight status and booked his ticket to Italia '90. After a highly successful tournament he returned to a prolific season of 22 goals in City's colours. He became a regular in Jack Charlton's Republic of Ireland squad and soon established himself as a firm favourite with the City supporters. A knee injury forced him to miss more than half of the 1993-94 season as well as the whole of the USA World Cup tournament. The subsequent decline in the fortunes at Maine Road manifested itself in Quinn's goals-to-games ratio and, finally, relegation from the Premiership led to his departure from the club in the summer of 1996 when he rejoined Peter Reid at Sunderland.

by the decision. Certainly Ball was high-profile, but as a player, and not as a manager. Indeed, his only claim to fame as a manager was that most of the clubs he'd been associated with had been relegated. Ball's appointment also threw doubts on Lee's ability as chairman with many people saying it was another case of 'jobs for the boys'.

Before the season started, City had once again dipped into the coffers in order to improve things. German goalkeeper Eike Immel came in as cover for the injured duo of Coton and Dibble and Kit Symons arrived from one of Ball's previous sides, Portsmouth. The best of all though was the wonderful Georgian, Georgiou Kinkladze. Kinkladze had impressed many European sides, including AC Milan and Barcelona, and for Lee to persuade him to come to Manchester was a major coup.

All three new signings made their debuts in the opening game of the season, a 1-1 draw with Tottenham at Maine Road on 19 August. It was to be City's one and only point until 21 October. Not surprisingly, City found themselves bottom of the table. It was hardly an auspicious start for the new manager. Not even a 4-0 win against Wycombe in the League Cup provided much hope. In the next round Liverpool won 4-0 then followed it up with a 6-0 league win three days later.

Amazingly, City then went unbeaten for the whole of October, a run that would earn the Manager of the Month award for Ball. Despite three wins and a draw, City scored just four times – three 1-0 victories and a 1-1 draw at Sheffield Wednesday. These very welcome points pushed City up to mid-table. But by January they'd fallen back into the losing habit and could only manage one win in nine games. In the FA Cup, City had beaten Leicester 5-0 and then, in round four, Coventry after a replay. This set up a fifth round tie at Old Trafford and City dumfounded everyone with their performance. Rosler gave City the lead and the Blues were much the better side until a ludicrous refereeing decision from Alan Wilkie changed the whole course of the game. When he penalised City's Michael Frontzeck for a 'push' on Cantona inside the penalty area he was the only person in the ground who saw it. There was not one single appeal from either United players or supporters. Not surprisingly the Frenchman converted the kick and United found a winner in the second-half. City were demoralised and out of the Cup. The 'penalty' was discussed for days afterwards with no one either in the press or on television agreeing with Wilkie's decision. When league leaders Newcastle came to Maine Road the following week, they too were surprised by City's performance. In a wonderful attacking game, City led 3-2 only to see the points shared when Newcastle levelled in the 81st minute.

Under Manager's Orders

With three games to go, City were still in the relegation zone. Despite 1-0 victories against both Sheffield Wednesday and Aston Villa, they still could not escape their nearest rivals Southampton and Coventry. The final game of the season was at home to Liverpool. The equation was simple: all three teams had 37 points – City needed to win and hope the other two slipped up.

Against a reluctant Liverpool, City managed to find themselves 2-0

50 Greatest Players

UWE ROSLER Striker

Joined Manchester City: 1994   **From:** FC Nurnburg

Debut: 1994 v Queens Park Rangers (league)

Appearances: 177   **Goals:** 64

Left Manchester City: 1998   **For:** Kaiserslautern

Uwe Rosler arrived at Maine Road on a three-month trial in March 1994 and immediately made his mark on his debut when his backheel set up David Rocastle for the equaliser at Loftus Road. Manager Brian Horton had no hesitation in making the move permanent when he handed over £500,000 to Rosler's Bundesliga club FC Nurnburg. The holder of five East German international caps, Rosler's enthusiasm, and 64 goals, made him hugely popular with City followers – in his first three full seasons he top scored with 22, 13 and 17 goals respectively. His performances even outshone his more illustrious countryman Jurgen Klinsmann and won him City's Player of the Year trophy in 1995. In April 1998 he returned home when he joined Bundesliga leaders Kaiserslautern.

Uwe Rosler was popular with fans largely due to his high level of commitment.

down. Liverpool were almost apologetic after they'd scored. A Rosler penalty and a Symons' volley levelled the score and then news reached Ball that Coventry were losing and a point would be enough for survival. Under the manager's orders the Blues began to waste time, only to find out, when it was far too late, that the information was wrong. Both Coventry and Southampton drew their games and City were relegated on goal difference. It was a huge blow for the supporters who had already lost what little faith they had in the manager and, by now, the chairman.

Despite all the problems at the club, 29,129 fans turned up for the first game of the 1996-97 season. The opponents for the televised game on Friday 16 August were Ipswich Town, a side, like City, tipped among the favourites for promotion. The Blues won 1-0 thanks to goal from Steve Lomas, but whereas Ipswich would reach the play-offs, City finally stuttered to 14th place.

Five Managers in One Season

Alan Ball resigned on 26 August. Asa Hartford stayed on a caretaker basis until former United player Steve Coppell took over on 7 October. Even though Coppell said, 'I want to be here a long time', he lasted just six games, claiming 'medical grounds' as the reason for his swift departure. Interestingly enough the 'medical grounds' did not prevent him from returning to Crystal Palace a few months later. It seemed no one wanted to take up the poisoned chalice. George Graham and Dave Bassett were both reported to have accepted the post and then turned it down. Next in line was another caretaker, this time Coppell's assistant, Phil Neal. The former Liverpool and England full back lasted from 8 November until 29 December. It was then that Frank Clark was finally announced as the new man in charge. Although he didn't actually take charge of a game until 11 January, it appeared, at last, that City had managed to acquire a much-respected figure in the game with a proven and successful record.

Clark's arrival was followed by a 4-1 victory at Oxford, a game won almost single-handedly by Kinkladze. That win began an unbeaten run of five wins and a draw as City looked a completely fresh side who were once again enjoying their football. Their confidence took them to the fifth round of the FA Cup only to lose 1-0 to Middlesbrough in a game of appalling refereeing decisions at Maine Road. Two successive 3-1 victories against West Bromwich Albion and Grimsby in April pushed City up to 14th place, their highest position for five months. Despite only one win in the last four games they were still in the same position at the end of what had been another remarkable season for all the wrong reasons.

Chapter Ten: 1998-2000
Back to Back!

Two club records and a major announcement greeted the start of the 1997-98 season. Frank Clark had spent £3 million on the Portsmouth striker and former soldier Lee Bradbury, and 16,000 season tickets had already been sold.

For the first time the club was linked with a move to the as-yet unbuilt Eastlands Stadium, the future home of the 2002 Commonwealth Games. In the months to come the proposed new stadium story gathered momentum but the purchase of Bradbury proved a major disappointment for all concerned. It raised similar questions to the one posed to Steve Daley at the end of the seventies: 'He's not a bad player but is he worth all that money?'

Bradbury's debut came in the opening game of the season, ironically a 2-2 draw against Portsmouth at Maine Road,

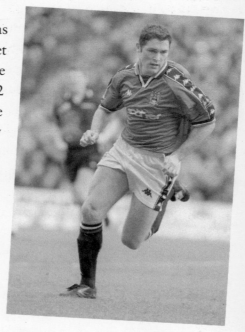

Former City manager Frank Clark splashed out £3 million for Lee Bradbury.

watched by a crowd of 30,474 including members of the Oasis rock band. The following week City visited Sunderland's brand-new Stadium of Light only to lose 3-1 with Alan Kernaghan being sent off and former Blue Niall Quinn scoring one of the goals. City then crashed out of the League Cup to Blackpool losing 4-2 in a penalty shoot-out. When Norwich won 2-1 at Maine Road on 20 September, the Blues found themselves in 20th place. Already it seemed as if the chairman's pre-season rallying call for promotion was a hopeless dream. However, the great contradiction that is Manchester City then destroyed Swindon 6-0 just seven days later.

City had dropped to 21st by the time of the AGM in October, a meeting in which Francis Lee claimed there was no money available for new players. This did not comfort the supporters who'd seen many players with average ability arrive over the past few months. A week later Georgian defender Murtaz Shelia was signed for £400,000. It appeared to be another Maine Road contradiction.

On the pitch the signs were not good. Record signing Lee Bradbury was out injured having broken a bone in his back, there was an obvious rift between the manager and Uwe Rosler, and captain Kit Symons was suffering under intense pressure from the fans. City led 1-0 at Birmingham thanks to a Shelia goal in the 87th minute only to concede two in a seven-minute injury-time period.

The FA Cup brought some cheer with a 2-0 win against Bradford City in round three, and although City lost 2-1 to West Ham United in the next round the performance showed a marked improvement and Kinkladze's goal was something special.

The Knives Are Out

Just two days before his first anniversary at Maine Road, City gave Frank Clark's previous side Nottingham Forest a three-goal lead before Shelia and Dickov gave the score, if not the performance, an air of respectability. City were still 20th and the knives were slowly coming out for Clark, with Joe Royle once again being named as a possible replacement in the Maine Road hot-seat.

The Blues' precarious state fuelled rumours concerning Kinkladze's future with the club. Newspapers linked him with almost every team in the Premiership, although Clark vehemently denied that he was for sale. There were plenty of others to choose from, though, as 15 players were on the transfer list in February.

Three days after losing 1-0 to Bury at Maine Road, City found themselves in 23rd position, just one off the bottom. On his way into work Frank Clark heard of his dismissal on the car radio. Three of his backroom staff, Alan Hill, Richard Money and Peter Edwards had also been dismissed.

Royle Appointment

After several abortive attempts to link Joe Royle with the manager's job at Manchester City in the past, this time the stories were true. Royle had 15 games to keep the club in the First Division. He immediately brought in Jim Cassell as chief scout and former City player Willie Donachie as first-team coach, both of whom he'd worked with at Oldham. His first game in charge was a 2-1 home defeat by Ipswich, but then three wins in four games moved City up

to 17th place – out of the relegation zone. Despite having more than 50 full-time professionals at the club, Royle brought in Richard Jobson, Jaime Pollock, Shaun Goater, and old favourite Ian Bishop, who gave up a testimonial at West Ham to return to Maine Road.

On 16 March Francis Lee announced he intended to stand down as chairman and handed over to fellow director David Bernstein. Lee had been in charge for four turbulent years and though, undoubtedly, the club was by now in a much better position off the pitch, he admitted himself that chairmen are judged by results on it. He also went on to say he felt he had done his very best for the club and that possibly he should have interfered more in team affairs.

As the season neared its climax,

Ian Bishop returned to Maine Road, helping out in a relegation crisis.

City suffered defeats at the hands of Oxford United, Port Vale and Bradford City, teams one would normally expect Manchester City to beat. Two more losses at home to Birmingham and then at Middlesbrough left City in 21st place. A 2-2 draw against Queens Park Rangers in the penultimate game saw them drop two more places.

The final game against fellow strugglers Stoke City saw City run out 5-2 victors but regrettably other results went against them and City were relegated to the Second Division (technically the Third) for the first time in their history. It was a bizarre day with Stoke fans taunting City supporters with 'Going down, going down', only to hear a reply of 'So are you, so are you'. Blues' fans can never have been so disappointed after seeing their side win 5-2.

Tragically, Joe Royle could not prevent a second relegation in three years. But these events had been coming for a long time and to expect a miracle was too much even for City. Just three days after the Stoke game Joe Royle and Willie Donachie signed new contracts, finally giving the impression that some long-term stability was being introduced to the club.

The Long Road Back

Crowd favourites Gio Kinkladze and Uwe Rosler both left the club in the summer, to Holland and Germany respectively, as Joe Royle began to look at ways to get out of the division as soon as possible. One new face who was in the starting line-up for the visit of Blackpool on 8 August was 19-year-old goalkeeper Nicky Weaver. Little did anyone know what an impact he would make on the season.

Not for the first time, City were favourites to go up but the club realised how difficult it would be having to play on tight pitches, in front of small crowds, against clubs who would undoubtedly raise their game against a side of City's stature. The season started well with two convincing wins but then things went badly wrong on a Friday night in Fulham. Not only did the Blues lose 3-0 in front of the Sky TV cameras, but they also lost the services of Georgian centre-half

50 Greatest Players

GEORGIOU KINKLADZE Midfielder

Joined Manchester City: 1995   From: Dynamo Tblisi
Debut: 1995 v Tottenham (league)
Appearances: 121   Goals: 22
Left Manchester City: 1998   For: Ajax Amsterdam
Honours won with Manchester City: 17 Georgia caps

The most popular player of the last ten seasons (if not more) at Maine Road, the mercurial talents of Georgiou Kinkladze were spotted by then Chairman Francis Lee on television. He'd impressed particularly in a game for Georgia against Wales in Cardiff when he scored a spectacular winner.

Fortunately for the Blues, Lee acted quickly and spent £2 million to acquire his services on 14 July, 1995 – the same day Alan Ball became manager.

Kinkladze made his debut against Tottenham on the opening day of the 1995-96 season. In that one game City fans recognised his obvious talent and skill. For a relatively small man he is extremely difficult to knock off the ball and possesses a marvellous left foot. He quickly became City's regular penalty taker and dead ball specialist, but was also capable of scoring during normal play. Any City fan who saw his goal against Southampton in March 1996 and his effort against West Ham in the FA Cup will remember them for a long time. Unfortunately for Kinkladze – the jewel in City's crown – no-one else could get anywhere near his level of play. Kinkladze was unable to find a regular place in Royle's side and was transferred to Ajax in Amsterdam.

Tskhadadze with a serious knee injury. Tskhadadze had scored in both previous games and would miss the rest of the season.

That defeat at Fulham was City's only setback in nine games before the League Cup (aka Worthington) paired them with Premiership side Derby County. The Blues had already knocked-out Notts County with an 8-2 aggregate score and they turned in a sterling performance at Pride Park, holding the home side to a 1-1- draw, with Australian Danny Tiatto scoring his first goal for City. In the return leg the following week City again played well only to lose the game 1-0. The performance prompted Royle to say, 'There weren't two divisions between the sides,' a point agreed with by City fans and things appeared to be looking good for the future.

City were in the top 10 for most of the first part of the season but only occasionally looked likely to threaten a play-off place. Humbled out of the Auto Windscreen Shield by Mansfield Town in front of 3,007, the Blues also had to negotiate the first round of the FA Cup and a tricky tie against Halifax Town. Thanks to two goals from Craig Russell and one from Shaun Goater, City won the game 3-0 and were watched by 11,108, City's lowest FA Cup gate of the century.

Defeat at York City on 19 December saw City fall to 12th place, but the Blues then went on an unbeaten run of 12 league games, culminating in a 6-0 victory at Burnley where Goater scored a hat-trick. During that time they'd lost to another Premiership side, Wimbledon, in the FA Cup, again by a solitary goal.

The good run was ended by Oldham Athletic who won 2-1 at Maine Road but, immediately, City's form picked up again and they won seven and drew one of the next eight games. Three players were instrumental in these good runs: Ian Bishop was enjoying himself in midfield, the powerful Andy Morrison gave the defence some organisation and solidity and Terry Cooke, initially on loan from Manchester United, gave the attack some width and contributed the occasional important goal.

As with the Oldham game, City then lost a game they shouldn't have when Wycombe surprised everyone with a 2-1 win at Maine Road. The highest league attendance of the season saw City's last game, a 4-0 win against York. The Blues finished in third place to face two difficult play-off games against neighbours Wigan Athletic. It had been a season of great financial rewards for Second Division clubs as the City faithful followed their side to some of the more remote outposts of the game. Of the 24 clubs in the division, 19 of them had their highest crowd of the season for City's visit.

Play-off Lottery

The play-off first leg at Wigan began disastrously as Gerard Wiekens and Nicky Weaver contrived to gift the home side a goal inside the first minute. Both players had had an outstanding season and such a lapse in concentration caused concern amongst the 9,000 fans who were watching the game on a big TV screen back at Maine Road. There were 2,500 more at Maine Road than at Wigan's Springfield Park. Being a goal down only caused the recently-found and much-talked about City team spirit to come to the fore. As they forced their way back into the game, Michael Brown hit the bar before crossing for Paul Dickov to turn in the equaliser. It was no more than City deserved and it set up the second leg at Maine Road four days later. More than 31,000 celebrated and made a tremendous amount of

Great Matches

SECOND DIVISION PLAY-OFF FINAL   **Wembley, London, 30 May, 1999**

Manchester City 2   **Gillingham 2***   **Attendance 76,935**

*After extra time (City won 3-1 on penalties)

Horlock   Asaba

Dickov   Taylor

Semi-final goals by Paul Dickov and Shaun Goater against Wigan Athletic took City through to Wembley for arguably the most remarkable game in the club's history. For City it was an opportunity to win at the Twin Towers for the first time in 23 years. For Gillingham it was an opportunity to play football in the top two divisions for the first time.

The Kent side started well, with Weaver in early action tipping over a fierce shot from Galloway. City replied with a shot from Crooks which was inches wide before Bartram saved a header from Horlock. Carl Asaba then had a goal disallowed, standing in an offside position following a knock-back from future City signing Robert Taylor.

Bishop (making his first appearance at Wembley) and Vaughan replaced Brown and Morrison in the second half just prior to Goater coming close when his shot from a narrow angle struck a post. Cooke then had a shot from outside the area spectacularly turned over by the flying Bartram. With just nine minutes left, disaster struck for City when Asaba poked the ball past Weaver. In reply, Dickov's 12-yarder at the other end was saved by Bartram's feet and there looked no way back when, in the 86th minute, Robert Taylor scored to make it 2-0. Many in the crowd thought that it was all over.

In the last minute of normal time Goater was tackled on the edge of the Gills' area and Kevin Horlock stroked the loose ball home to give City some hope. When the fourth official raised the board indicating five minutes of stoppage time, the Blues found new heart.

Dickov earned himself a place in City folklore when he crashed in a dramatic late, late equaliser (see picture below), lifting City even further and proving a psychological blow to Gillingham. Extra time produced no goals. The ensuing penalties were taken at the City end and provided yet another hero, goalkeeper Nick Weaver. He saved two penalties whilst team-mates Horlock, Cooke and Edghill all converted successfully.

Manchester City: Weaver, Crooks (Taylor), Edghill, Wiekens, Morrison (Vaughan), Horlock, Brown (Bishop), Whitley, Dickov, Goater, Cooke.
Gillingham: Bartram, Southall, Ashby, Smith, Butters, Pennock, Patterson (Hodge), Hessenthaler, Asaba (Carr), Galloway (Saunders), Taylor.
Referee: M. Halsey.

noise as City returned to Wembley thanks to the only goal of the game from Bermudan international Shaun Goater. It was Goater's 21st goal of the season and, although perhaps it wasn't the prettiest goal, it was certainly the most important. And so to Wembley.

Most City fans would have been happy with a consolidating mid-table position at the start of the 1999-2000 season but with Republic of Ireland winger Mark Kennedy a summer addition to the squad it became clear that Royle's plans were going to based on an attacking side.

Wolves won at Maine Road on the opening day but confidence was restored with convincing five and six nil wins in two of the next three

50 Greatest Players

SHAUN GOATER Striker

Joined Manchester City: 1998   **From:** Bristol City

Debut: 1998 v Bradford City (league)

Appearances: 183   **Goals:** 97

When Joe Royle signed Shaun Goater towards the end of the ill-fated 1997/98 season, it was hoped that this most prolific of strikers could find the goals necessary to secure the Blues' place in Division One. Regrettably, too much damage had been done prior to his arrival and City were doomed to the third tier of English football for the first time in their history. Since then though Goater has averaged a goal every other game and is right up there amongst the game's top marksmen. Indeed some of his goals have been the most crucial of recent times. In the back-to-back promotion campaigns, he scored 50 times, making the £400,000 fee Royle paid for him look ridiculously small.

Although missing half of the Premiership season of 2000/01 because of injury, Goater still finished top scorer, a position he has achieved in every one of his four seasons to date at Maine Road. Last season, 2001/02, saw him become the first City payer since Francis Lee back in 1971/72 to break the magical 30-goal barrier. A regular international for Bermuda, Goater is such a popular figure on his home island that he even has a day named after him. He is almost as popular back home as he is with the fans in Moss Side.

matches. After a goalless draw against Southampton in the League Cup, City won 1-0 at Walsall thanks to Shaun Goater's fourth goal of the season and were top of the division. The Blues then went down 4-3 in a thrilling second leg League Cup-tie at Southampton and suffered further losses at Ipswich and Norwich. The defeat at Norwich dropped City to fourth spot – it would be their lowest position for nearly six months.

Having already put six past Sheffield United, in November the Blues recorded four against Portsmouth (who scored first thanks to City's former record signing Lee Bradbury) to register their fifth straight win and confirm their position at the top. Three successive defeats, against Huddersfield, Wolves (again) and Stockport, knocked City off the top spot but only down to second place and still very much in the running for an automatic promotion place.

Three more successive wins meant City fans could celebrate the Millennium with their team back on top and eagerly awaiting the visit of Leeds United in the fourth round of the FA Cup. This would be City's sternest test of the season and would give a good indication as to just how far Joe Royle's team had come in such a short space of time. Despite showing their obvious fighting qualities and taking the lead twice, City ran up against a very talented Leeds side currently chasing the Premiership title and lost 5-2.

50 Greatest Players

NICKY WEAVER Goalkeeper

Joined Manchester City: 1997   **From:** Mansfield Town
Debut: 1998 v Blackpool (league)
Appearances: 179

Appearing as a raw 19-year-old on the opening day of the 1998-99 season, Nicky Weaver's confidence soon permeated through the back four and the rest of the team to help turn a losing culture into a positive environment. Some dazzling performances throughout that season's promotion campaign (not to mention a record number of clean sheets) quickly established him as a firm favourite on the terraces. His year was highlighted by his heroics at Wembley in the play-off final against Gillingham and his memorable manic sprint following his last penalty save.

His form continued throughout the successful First Division promotion season as well, but after two excellent years, he suffered slightly when coming up against the Premiership's elite. In Weaver's defence, this was a problem that was not exclusively his. A couple of individual errors led to goals conceded and he appeared to lack the confidence he'd shown up unto that point.

After losing his place to new signing Carlo Nash, Weaver battled to regain his place in the side only to lose it again midway through last year's Championship campaign because of injury.

The arrival of Peter Schmeichel and a knee operation in the summer of 2002 seem certain to limit Weaver's immediate chances of a return to the first team. However, the former England Under 21 goalkeeper has already gone down on record as saying that he is more than willing to battle for his place, and is convinced that City fans have not seen the last of him between the posts.

The Nail Biting Starts

The Blues immediately bounced back with a 4-0 win against Fulham only to slip up against Sheffield United when Michael Brown (a City player up until a week previously) scored the only goal of the game. After two wins in the next two games, there then followed a run of seven games without a victory but things were so tight that the Blues' lowest point would still be fourth. With Charlton Athletic having established a lead at the top, it seemed City's best effort would now be a place in the play-offs. This would have delighted the fans at the start of the campaign but City's performances had been so good that a play-off place could have been perceived as a comparative failure with an automatic spot still being the number-one priority.

With nine games to go and Shaun Goater still amongst the goals, City began another terrific run at just the right time. They won seven and drew two, keeping five clean sheets, more than useful in itself, as goal difference might just be the deciding factor in a very tense finish. In the penultimate game at home to Birmingham, Robert Taylor (a scorer for Gillingham in last year's play-off final) scored the only goal of the game and gave the Blues a five-point lead over second place Ipswich. Not surprisingly, the crowd went delirious at the end and staged a massive, but very high-spirited, pitch invasion. City had one game left but Ipswich had two so mathematically it was still possible for the Blues to slip up, a fact noted (and gloated) by some in the media who described the celebrations as premature. For City fans it was perhaps the last opportunity of the season to pay their respects to the players and management for their efforts over what had been a wonderful season – even if it was to end in the play-offs.

Down to the Wire

Ipswich won their game in hand the next day against a Charlton side who'd played very poorly since being crowned champions. And so the season went 'down to the wire' as many had thought it would. The Blues still had a two-point lead but faced a difficult trip to Blackburn, a team tipped by many as promotion candidates, but who had generally disappointed and were some 10 points outside a play-off spot. Under new manager Graeme Souness, Blackburn promised no favours as their players played for pride and for new contracts. Ipswich, meantime, had a home game against a Walsall side desperately needing a win to stave off relegation.

Regardless of what happened at Ipswich, City only had to avoid defeat to gain promotion back to the Premiership. At half-time the omens didn't look too good. The Blues were a goal down and had Weaver and the woodwork to thank for keeping them in the game. When news came through of Ipswich taking the lead minutes into the second-half things looked decidedly worse. It was then that Royle introduced Bishop and Dickov, substitutions that would change the course of the game and, consequently, the season. When Goater grabbed the equaliser with his 29th goal of the season, Blackburn heads went down, and although they hit the post twice more, City now appeared to have the upper hand. The first hour's performance was quickly forgotten as an own goal, and then Kennedy and Dickov sealed the game, and promotion, on a gloriously sunny day. For the record, Ipswich won 2-0 to relegate Walsall and finish in third place.

Once again the crowd invaded the pitch and amongst the joyous celebrations, the City players appeared in the stands to receive a heroes' welcome. This time there was no mention of premature celebrations. The Blues had won promotion in a way that all their supporters had by now got used to. Why do things the easy way when you can do things the Manchester City way?

'City are back' could be heard loudly and proudly all across the north-west on the night of Sunday 7 May 2000.

Chapter Eleven: 2000-02
Down, Up and the Future

After all the hyperbole and expectation preceding the 2001-02 season, City's return to the Premiership proved a disastrous one and would ultimately cost Joe Royle his job.

The Best Laid Plans, as They Say

The anticipation surrounding a clutch of new arrivals, with George Weah, record signing Paulo Wanchope, Steve Howey and Paul Ritchie all arriving in August, quickly evaporated as home form in particular began to suffer. Initially the fans' optimism looked well founded despite a shock opening day mauling at the hands of fellow Premiership newcomers Charlton Athletic who devoured the Blues 4-0 at The Valley. A couple of good wins in the next three games over Sunderland (Wanchope hitting a hat-trick on his home debut), and at Leeds, was followed by a decent performance in defeat (2-3) at Liverpool and suggested that the Charlton debacle may just have been a case of bedding in a team with several newcomers. A goalless draw at Tottenham encouraged that belief further but it soon became clear that the performance at Charlton was a truer indication of the team's Premiership potential.

To make matters worse, Weah – who, it has to be said, looked to be nearing the end of his career – fell out with the manager over the number of games he was being asked to sit out as a substitute. What must have been the final straw for the former World Footballer of the Year was to hear the reception afforded to fans' favourite Shaun Goater as he limbered up along the touchline during a home game with Bradford.

Goater, injured in pre-season, had not yet started a game but the hero's welcome he received merely for warming up must have been galling for Weah as he sat on the bench, hood up, hands deep inside his tracksuit pockets. Within days the Liberian had walked out of Maine Road, less than three months into his contract, and was quickly in print accusing Royle of showing him no respect and even swearing at him in front of his team-mates. To be fair to the manager, players and staff alike at Maine Road quickly refuted Weah's claims.

More new faces arrived in the shape of Laurent Charvet and Richard Dunne without any significant improvement in results, though a win at Southampton briefly lifted the Blues into mid-table.

However a 5-0 setback at Arsenal followed shortly afterwards, a game in which Danny Tiatto was controversially sent off and one that plunged City into a desperate November. Already they were slipping into the relegation zone. One of these November defeats was a 'derby' reversal against United at Maine Road and it was around this time that Royle fell out with another of his pre-season imports Paulo Wanchope, manager and player reportedly being kept apart by team-mates after a heavy defeat at West Ham.

A 5-0 rout of the hapless Everton at Maine Road provided a brief glimmer of hope but the bad results kept coming, culminating in another abject display against Charlton who triumphed 4-1 at the Blues' headquarters two days before New Year. It was a performance so poor that the ground was nearly half-empty by the final whistle. City's consolation against the Londoners came from Darren Huckerby, Joe Royle's latest acquisition who had joined the Blues 48 hours beforehand from Leeds United. Kevin Horlock also broke his ankle in this game, a crucial setback in the coming weeks with the midfield department now significantly weakened. Royle attempted to remedy the situation with a move for former City favourite Steve Lomas but the Irish international – who has always claimed he never wanted to leave Maine Road in the first place – turned the approach down flat, preferring instead to remain in London at West Ham.

Around this time, the form of Nicky Weaver had begun to suffer due to the pressure of being a young goalkeeper performing in a struggling side at top level. His every mistake was punished by strikers of Premiership quality and Royle moved quickly to provide

Great Managers 1998-2001

JOE ROYLE

Highly respected as a manager these days, Joe Royle had been a successful centre forward, initially with Everton, a side he joined as an apprentice in 1964. Four years later he was playing in an FA Cup final (although Everton lost 1-0 to West Bromwich Albion) and he was capped by England for the first time in 1971 against Malta. In total he played six times for England, winning five times and drawing the other one, scoring twice.

Despite rumours of a back problem, then manager Tony Book signed him for City on Christmas Eve 1974 and he became a valuable member of the Blues side which won the League Cup in 1976, and finished runners-up to Liverpool the following season. He left Maine Road to join Bristol City in November 1977 before finishing his playing career at Norwich in April 1982 after suffering a knee injury.

His first managerial appointment came just three months later when he took over from future City boss Jimmy Frizzell at Oldham, so beginning the most successful period in that club's history. Royle spent more than 12 years at Oldham before returning to Goodison Park in October 1994, guiding them to FA Cup success against Manchester United the following May.

After parting company with Everton he was out of the game for 12 months prior to his acceptance of the 'poisoned chalice' at Maine Road, a job he had been linked with several times before. His first priority was to stop the Blues' slide into Division Two but with just 15 games left at the end of the 1997/98 season it proved to be too much. Promotion next time of asking was an absolute must and although it was achieved in the most amazing way possible (a penalty shoot-out at Wembley) it was the end of a season Royle described as 'horrible'.

The following campaign, 1999/2000, was beyond everybody's wildest dreams as City won their second successive promotion with an amazing 4-1 win at Blackburn on the final day. Remarkably, Royle had returned City to the top flight in the shortest possible time. With hindsight though it was possibly a case of 'too much too soon'.

The Blues suffered throughout the Premiership season of 2000/01, a combination of many things (not least a lack of goals scored and poor home form) culminating in relegation back to the Nationwide League. After all the successes of the previous two years it was a bitterly disappointing time for the club and ultimately it would cost Royle his job in the summer.

City fans should remember Royle not only for his bustling goalscoring days on the pitch but also for those remarkable back-to-back seasons.

cover for his youthful custodian by signing Carlo Nash from neighbouring Stockport County for a bargain £100,000. Nash was soon to be followed by the loan arrival of Ukrainian winger Andre Kanchelskis from Glasgow Rangers, a move Royle agreed was 'a calculated gamble'.

Kanchelskis, a former star at rivals United, who had once scored a hat-trick against City in an Old Trafford 'derby', was well known to Royle from his days at Everton. Unfortunately the arrival once again of a 'name player' coming towards the end of his career proved to be unsuccessful and Kanchelskis had returned to Scotland before the end of the season. Laurent Charvet had by this time become unsettled because of a lack of first-team opportunities – another sure sign that all was not well with the spirit within the club.

A run in the FA Cup with home wins against Birmingham and Coventry ended in the fifth round against Liverpool at Anfield, but it was the Coventry game that saw another falling out between Wanchope and his manager. This time the Costa Rican was transfer-listed for his reaction to being substituted by Shaun Goater, ironically enough the man who headed in the last-minute winner. With Paul Dickov currently sidelined with a long-term injury, the Blues' attacking options were looking a little threadbare.

As is so often the case with teams struggling at the wrong end of the table, City also began to suffer some cruel misfortune. Danny Tiatto's spectacular solo effort would have provided the winner at Middlesbrough had it not been astonishingly ruled out by referee Alan Wiley after a linesman had flagged Darren Huckerby offside when clearly in no position to influence play. A week later Huckerby himself had a goal ruled out in a home defeat by Tottenham for allegedly impeding the visiting goalkeeper Neil Sullivan. Television replays later clearly showed it was in fact England centre-half Sol Campbell who had made contact with his own goalkeeper.

A surprise, but nevertheless welcome, single-goal victory in a blizzard at Newcastle (Goater again) gave City's long-suffering supporters a brief respite from the club's tribulations only for them to flare up again in the very next game. Against Southampton at Maine Road, Royle was given more ammunition to fire at officials when Saints defender Dan Petrescu clearly handled in the area to deny City a scoring opportunity – the player himself admitted his guilt after the game. No penalty was given and then, as if to rub even more salt in the Blues' wounds, the very same offending player proceeded to score the winner and condemn City to another home defeat.

Nicky Weaver's blunders in subsequent losses at home to Aston Villa and at Everton saw the young England goalkeeper pay the ultimate price by losing his place to Carlo Nash, whose own debut could hardly have been more nightmarish. Within half an hour of starting his first game for the Blues, Nash had picked the ball out of his net four times as Arsenal ran riot at Maine Road. Fortunately for Nash and City, the Gunners opted to declare at half-time, a situation that paved the way for some typical black humour from the faithful supporters. Cries of 'Boring, boring Arsenal' and 'Can we play you every week?' were just examples of the way City's beleaguered supporters tried to cheer themselves up.

Their self-deprecating wit and constant backing for their besieged team drew praise from an impressed Arsenal manager Arsene Wenger, with Joe Royle also joining in with his own tribute saying, 'Our fans are unique. Even a battle-hardened veteran like me found their support incredible.'

Other results by this time were also going against City. A win at Leicester (the by now reprieved Wanchope amongst the scorers) was rendered meaningless by a shock win at Arsenal by fellow strugglers Middlesbrough. On Easter weekend City found themselves without a game and had to sit back helplessly while other rivals in distress, Derby and Coventry, won at Leicester and Sunderland respectively, successes that only made the Blues' position even more precarious.

A battling draw at Old Trafford salvaged some local pride with Steve Howey grabbing a late equaliser on a day when United were awarded two penalties – Paul Scholes missing the first before Teddy Sheringham converted the second. However the game will be long remembered for the horrific 'tackle' late in the game by Reds' skipper Roy Keane on his Blues counterpart Alfie Haaland, a tackle stemming from 'bad blood' between the pair from Haaland's days at Leeds. Keane was rightly sent off though Haaland made light of the incident, joking, 'I must upgrade my insurance the next time I play against United!'

A week following the point earned at Old Trafford, a marvellous goalkeeping display by Carlo Nash somehow kept out West Ham as City edged the Londoners 1-0 thanks to a deflected effort from Goater. Regrettably, despite the events of recent weeks, City's survival chances were now remote and when Derby came away with three points from Old Trafford the result virtually left the Blues on the brink of relegation.

Royle pledged a 'fight to the finish' as City faced a crucial evening trip to Ipswich in front of Sky's television cameras. Ironically enough the Suffolk club had only followed City up via the play-offs the previous season, yet, despite spending barely any money by comparison, were heading for a top-six finish and a place in Europe. Goater again gave Royle's side brief hope with a first-half goal and although the Blues played well on the night, two late goals from the home side earned them victory and condemned City to the drop. Chairman David Bernstein immediately apologised to the fans saying he had never been so disappointed, then adding, 'We will do everything possible to make sure we return quickly.' These words proved to be highly significant in view of the events that would take place at the club over the next two weeks.

Joe Royle had refused to comment after the Ipswich game but there was no hint his future was in doubt as he announced his plans for the club immediately after the relegation. He transfer listed the disappointing Charvet as well as central defender Spencer Prior and also confirmed the club would not be taking up an option to buy Dino Topmoeller, a young German midfielder who had been on trial at Maine Road. The manager went on to praise some of the younger players, predicting golden futures for the likes of Shaun Wright-

Phillips, Chris Shuker, Rhys Day and Terry Dunfield. Unfortunately for Royle he wouldn't be there to witness whether his predictions would come true.

The last game of the season was an irrelevance (Chelsea merely adding to City's tale of woe with a 2-1 win at Maine Road) but, despite the fans' resignation to their fate, it still came as a massive shock to them 48 hours later when it was announced Royle would be leaving the club. Chairman Bernstein cited 'fundamental differences' for the split, describing his decision to part company with the manager as 'the toughest of my life, both in the sporting and business world'. Several of Royle's backroom staff, including chief scout John Hurst and goalkeeping coach Alex Stepney, were also dismissed, though his number two Willie Donachie was asked to stay on.

Preston's forward-thinking young boss David Moyes and Republic of Ireland's Mick McCarthy – himself a former City player – were among the favourites the press immediately linked with the vacancy. However one name in particular was a huge surprise – Kevin Keegan.

A surprise replacement for Joe Royle, new manager Kevin Keegan inspired City to their first trophy since 1976.

KK Arrives at Maine Road

The former Liverpool and England star, and twice European Footballer of the Year during his days in Germany with Hamburg, had been in a self-imposed six-month exile from the game since quitting as national manager following England's 1-0 defeat by Germany in the last ever international match at Wembley. During that time Keegan had become a virtual recluse, ignoring any contact with the press who had so cruelly vilified him over his decision to quit and giving no hint that he ever wished to return to the game. Because of his recent situation, it could be said that when a packed press conference on 24 May unveiled him as City's new man in charge, it was, at the very least, something of a surprise to those in attendance.

From his opening comments, though, it was clear that Keegan had rekindled all the enthusiasm that had so marked his previous successful sorties into club management at Newcastle and Fulham. Not surprisingly he said all the things any new manager was expected to say, such as 'a unique opportunity' etc but when Keegan said it, somehow it seemed to be with meaning. Within hours of that press conference, the charismatic new boss attended a hastily arranged fans' forum at Platt Lane where he quickly had his new disciples eating out of his hand.

Keegan's first three appointments in his new post were to prove hugely significant ones over the course of the forthcoming season. Within days of his arrival, his long-term mentor at managerial level, the former Newcastle and Derby boss Arthur Cox, had been installed as his unofficial number two and chief scout. Cox, credited and respected as one of the most knowledgeable people in the game, was quickly followed by Colombian fitness coach Juan Carlos Osario whose innovative training methods over the next nine months were to earn unstinted praise. The third new face (at least as far as Maine Road was concerned) was that of Stuart Pearce, a player who Keegan talked out of retirement plans and signed on a free transfer from West Ham. The legendary former England full-back, one of the fiercest and most committed defenders in the history of the game, was in his

39th year but was immediately made club captain and became Keegan's new 'dressing room leader'.

Before the players reported back for pre-season in July, Keegan had shipped out Mark Kennedy and Spencer Prior for substantial fees, brought in another ex-England coach, Peter Bonetti, to work with the goalkeepers, made Australian defender Simon Colosimo his second signing for a nominal fee and, most significantly, rejected a bid by Wolves for Shaun Goater.

Keegan's first major signing continued the summer of surprises. Israeli midfield ace Eyal Berkovic joined the Blues for a reported £1.5 million after an unhappy spell in Scotland with Celtic. Paulo Wanchope ended speculation about his future by revealing he was staying at Maine Road to become part of the 'New Revolution' and City prepared for the new season with Keegan declaring, 'We have plenty of reason to be optimistic.' The events of 2001–02 were to render that declaration a massive understatement. However the first few weeks of the new campaign were to provide some confirmation for the doubters who still sought to undermine Keegan after what they saw as his England defection.

The evergreen Stuart Pearce was talked out of retirement and captained the Blues to the First Division Championship.

A 3-0 opening day rout of one of City's predicted promotion rivals, Watford – a game strangely played on a Saturday evening to suit television requirements – was followed seven days later by a terrible afternoon at Carrow Road when the Blues not only lost to Norwich, but had Wanchope sent off and three others (Berkovic, Nash and

Whitley) carried off with serious injuries. Big wins at home to Crewe and away at Burnley followed, but a terrible defensive performance at West Bromwich Albion saw City crushed 4-0 and left Keegan fuming. He apologised to the club's travelling supporters and blasted his players, claiming they were good enough for a top six finish but 'not for automatic promotion'. Six days after the defeat at The Hawthorns, Keegan moved to remedy the situation by making arguably the most significant signing in City's recent history.

Algerian Ali Benarbia was a former French Footballer of the Year who had spent his entire career in France with a variety of clubs and had been a recognised talent in that time, if not in parochial England. Now aged 32, he was available on a free transfer from Paris St Germain and keen to try his luck in England. The Blues had also lined up a deal with another French club, Nantes, for young striker Alioune Toure who came for talks at Platt Lane and was accompanied by Benarbia with whom he shared the same agent. Benarbia was on his way up to Sunderland for discussions with former City player and manager Peter Reid but Keegan was later to claim 'he must have enjoyed the lunch we gave him while he was here!'

The mercurial Algerian Ali Benarbia, City's Player of the Year for 2001-02.

Within days Benarbia's agent had contacted the Blues' boss to say that talks with Sunderland had broken down and would he (Keegan) be keen on bringing the wonderfully gifted playmaker to City. Keegan jumped at the chance and the rest, as they say, is history. Benarbia enjoyed a stunning debut in a 3-0 home win over fancied Birmingham, an individual performance that had Keegan comparing his new midfield star with arguably City's greatest player of all time, the legendary Colin Bell. Those in the media who scoffed at his comparison were soon eating their words.

The topsy-turvy start to the season saw Coventry win a 4-3 thriller at Highfield Road after City had levelled the score three times, but in the very next game less than a week later, Benarbia inspired a 6-2 victory against Sheffield Wednesday at Hillsborough to leave Blues fans purring at the all-round quality of his performance. Walsall were then beaten and just as supporters were beginning to believe that some consistency was finally being achieved, a rude awakening was to follow at the hands of Wimbledon. Nightmare defensive lapses saw the Dons rip City apart to the tune of 4-0 at Maine Road to leave Keegan again furious and his latest signing Lucien Mettomo, a Cameroon international defender from French side St Etienne, possibly wondering what he had let himself in for as he watched from his seat in the stand.

Darren Huckerby, recalled to the starting line-up after Paulo Wanchope had flown out to America for exploratory tests on his troublesome right knee, then hit four as Birmingham were beaten 6-0 in a decidedly one-sided League Cup tie at Maine Road. Despite this particular terrific performance, League form continued to suffer with successive home draws with Stockport County and Sheffield United followed by a 2-1 setback at Preston, a game that saw Eyal Berkovic sent off for dissent by referee Mike Dean. North End's winner on that drizzly Deepdale Sunday was a sensational (if speculative) effort from 50 yards by Jonathan Macken, a player later to become City's record signing.

Keegan by this time must have been concerned as his side slowly but surely slipped towards mid-table and Croatian full-back and captain Robert Jarni became a target as the City boss looked at ways to arrest the slide. The deal was ultimately to collapse when Keegan pulled the plug over Jarni's dithering about contractual differences with his club Las Palmas, but consecutive wins over Grimsby, Barnsley and Gillingham and a draw at Nottingham Forest (thanks to the Forest keeper's glaring error and Goater's alertness) put the manager in better heart.

A move to bring in experienced centre-half David Wetherall from Leeds collapsed when the player failed a medical but two others did arrive in the shape of French midfielder Christian Negouai and young goalkeeper Kevin Stuhr Ellegaard from Danish club Farum. One person to leave in November was coach Willie Donachie, a hugely popular figure at Maine Road but a man who'd never appeared truly happy since the departure of his good friend Joe Royle in the summer. His replacement was Derek Fazackerley, a man who Keegan knew well from his days with Newcastle and England.

Fazackerley's first game saw Benarbia spare City's blushes with a late winner at home to Rotherham and though the Blues exited the League Cup at Blackburn (Negouai was sent off early in the 2-0 defeat) League form began to pick up with good away victories at Grimsby and the Lions' Den of Millwall. With hindsight the 3-2 win at Millwall may have been the turning point of City's season. Previous trouble between the rival sets of supporters had seen a ban imposed on away fans at the New Den, so City faced a hostile and intimidating night in London with (officially) no backing. To triumph in the way they did was a truly outstanding achievement. The game was also significant for Shaun Wright-Phillips who scored the late winner – his first senior goal for the club – and from that point onwards his fledgling career took off in spectacular style.

A blip at Crystal Palace was followed by another important win against promotion rivals Wolves. On a cold and foggy night at Maine Road, Kevin Horlock's first-half free-kick was enough to separate the teams and the win moved the Blues into the top two in the division. By now Keegan's philosophy was beginning to register with his players.

A goalless draw with West Bromwich Albion at Maine Road on Boxing Day proved to be a watershed – they would be the last points dropped at home for the rest of the season. Three days later League leaders Burnley arrived for a top-of-the-table showdown only to return to East Lancashire with their tails between their legs after a 5-1 thrashing thanks largely to Wanchope's hat-trick.

City went top on New Year's Day after a 3-1 victory over Sheffield United at Bramall Lane; a position they were rarely to relinquish for the rest of the campaign. Apart from a spell when Keegan's team embarked on an FA Cup run and were overtaken by a Wolves side who'd been knocked out in the third round, no one else seemed capable of catching the Blues who by now were playing some marvellously entertaining football. Two of those FA Cup ties proved beyond doubt that City would not be out of place in the higher division should promotion be finally achieved.

A 4-1 rout of Ipswich – the team that had doomed the Blues to relegation the previous May on the very same Portman Road ground – was followed by a fifth round trip to Newcastle where Keegan received a rapturous reception from his former worshippers. City went out of the Cup that night, entirely due to a hotly disputed Nolberto Solano goal and only after an exhilarating performance when for long periods Newcastle were totally outplayed on their own ground. All this despite the fact that the Blues played most of the game with ten men after Richard Dunne had been sent off.

The fact that City were able to play so well with a man short came as no real surprise to the travelling Blues as well as to the thousands who watched the game live on BBC's *Match of the Day*. Keegan's side had already proved they could do it by producing thrilling home victories over promotion hopefuls Norwich and Millwall. On both occasions victories were achieved after early dismissals, with Tiatto and Benarbia being the players asked to take an early bath.

Another new face was Danish international wing-back Niclas Jensen, a player signed from FC Copenhagen and one who would bring poise and balance to the left-hand side. His performance dovetailed beautifully with the more direct and aggressive Tiatto and was to prove another key factor in the Blues' confirmation as a real force.

Another promotion rival, Preston, was seen off at Maine Road, and the quality of play over the closing weeks of the season had the fans in raptures. They'd not seen consistent performances of such quality in a long time and how they revelled in it.

A goalless draw at Walsall, however, left City eight points adrift of leaders Wolves, a situation that forced Keegan into print with a statement suggesting the Midlanders were now clear favourites for the title. In retrospect, though, his comments could have been a psychological ploy because he must surely have known (the City supporters certainly did) that he had in his charge the best team in the division by the proverbial country mile. Four-goal hammerings of Sheffield Wednesday and Coventry confirmed what the fans already knew and these successive victories continued the Blues' relentless pursuit of Wolves at the top of the table. It was then Keegan sprang another surprise in what was already a remarkable season.

Having added to his squad further with the acquisition of Chinese international defender Sun Jihai, the Blues boss promptly shattered the club's transfer record with a swoop for Preston's Jon Macken, a Manchester-born striker who'd scored for North End in both of their games with City during the season. It was typical Keegan. On the same night as Macken signed for a reported £5 million fee, City topped 100 goals for the season with a 2-1 win at St Andrews to end Birmingham's slim hopes of an automatic promotion place, and yet City were bringing in another attacking player! Macken made his debut as a substitute at Bradford three nights later and came on to score the decisive goal in a 2-0 win. The three points earned finally overhauled Wolves and restored City to the top spot. It was a position they'd keep for the rest of the season.

Blues Close in on Promotion

Following the success at Bradford, Crewe and Crystal Palace were beaten in the space of four days before the apparently obligatory struggle against Stockport County. Macken gave City the lead at Edgeley Park only for the Blues to lose Goater (after a deliberate handball) and two goals in the last five minutes. A tricky game on a difficult pitch followed at Rotherham, where the Blues were grateful

Great Managers 2001-present

KEVIN KEEGAN

The phrase 'been there, done that' could have been originally aimed at Kevin Keegan.

From humble beginnings at Scunthorpe, Keegan became European Footballer of the Year twice whilst playing in Germany with Hamburg in the late 1970s. In between times he had signed for Bill Shankly's Liverpool for £35,000. At Anfield he won the first of his 63 England caps and established himself not only as one of the finest players in England, but also in Europe. He played 230 League games (68 goals) for Liverpool before being transferred to Hamburg in the summer of 1977. Three years later he was back in England, plying his trade with Southampton and eventually finishing his career at Newcastle at the end of the 1983–84 season.

A hugely popular player on Tyneside, Keegan took over as manager at St James' Park in 1992 after spending much of his intervening retirement years living in Spain. At Newcastle he rejuvenated a side struggling to hang on to its place in the First Division watched only by a relative handful of people. A similar description fits his time at Fulham, another club at present playing its football in the top division thanks largely to the earlier efforts of Keegan. He left Fulham to take over as England boss, a decision much heralded by press and public alike.

Alas, managing international teams on a part-time basis proved a great deal different from everyday, hands-on club matters and a bitterly disappointed Keegan resigned from his post after a defeat by Germany at Wembley in the qualifiers for the 2002 World Cup finals. Following City's relegation from the Premiership in the summer of 2001, Keegan was approached by the club to take over from Joe Royle.

At the time he was quoted as saying that City were the only club he was interested in joining and promised to give the job 'everything and more'. After just one season in charge, Keegan had guided his highly entertaining side to the First Division title, a trophy they'd not won for more than 30 years. There is no doubt that club management is Keegan's forte and he most definitely has that certain something that brings out the best in each and every one of his players. Let us all hope that Keegan's style, philosophy and success continue at Maine Road – and the new stadium – for many years to come.

for Benarbia's second-half equaliser against a team just outside the relegation zone. Fortunately the games at Stockport and Rotherham were the last two blips on a remarkable season.

When Nottingham Forest travelled to Maine Road on 30 March, they were greeted by Huckerby's second hat-trick of the season. The win set the Blues in good heart for what many said was the championship decider – a trip to Molineux. On the day, City proved there was only ever going to be one side capable of lifting the trophy. Despite lots of effort from the home side, the more skilful Blues dominated proceedings and a goal in each half from Shaun Wright-Phillips settled the outcome. It also continued Wolves' poor run of form towards the end of the season; a run so bad that they would eventually miss out on automatic promotion before losing out altogether in the lottery of the play-offs.

Relegation-bound Barnsley provided the sacrifice on 6 April. Once again Huckerby was in outstanding form; his second hat-trick in a week was supplemented with two from Macken as the visitors from Yorkshire were beaten 5-1. The victory meant no one could now catch the Blues at the top of the table. Manchester City were champions of the First Division, a feat they'd not achieved since the halcyon days of Joe

Mercer and Malcolm Allison back in 1968. A huge, fan-free, celebration took place on the pitch after the game, but Stuart Pearce would have to wait another two weeks before getting his hands on the famous old trophy.

Before that a trip to Gillingham resulted in a 3-1 win and provided City with their 12th away win of the season. And so to Portsmouth, the last game of a wonderful season. For a change in recent years, there was little pressure on the Blues in their farewell appearance. In front of another full house at Maine Road, the sun shone brightly as City won 3-1, producing some quite magnificent football along the way and confirming just how far above the other teams in the division Kevin Keegan's side was. Howey, Goater and Macken scored the goals that equalled City's scoring record of 108 in the League, a record that had stood since 1926–27.

Skipper Stuart Pearce, playing in his last game before retirement, had the opportunity to break that record – and take his own personal career tally to exactly 100 – with a penalty in the very last minute of the game. Despite everyone in the ground (including the Portsmouth players) wanting him to score, Pearce put his kick high and wide, this after Dave Beasant in the Pompey goal had even told him which side to put it. But the disappointment lasted a matter of seconds. The referee blew his whistle and City fans knew that was the signal for the celebrations to begin. Pearce lifted the trophy to arguably the biggest cheer ever heard at Maine Road before leading a wonderful lap of honour. He even stopped off to miss (twice more) and then score, an imaginary penalty.

It was the climax to a quite breathtaking season, one in which not even the most die-hard Blue could have wished for at the outset. As is normally the case when a new manager comes on board, the majority, quite rightly, wondered exactly what was in store when Kevin Keegan took over from Joe Royle the previous summer. What they got was a constant supply of entertaining and attacking football, littered with goals and a trophy at the end of it. The trophy of course meant City once again would be back in the Premiership. It is absolutely vital they stay in that division with the move to a new stadium now less than 12 months off.

A Summer Spent Spending
With a view to achieving that aim – and a top six spot to boot – Keegan strengthened his squad literally as soon as the season was

New record signing Nicolas Anelka, the man poised to lead City's assault on the Premiership.

over. Goalkeeper Peter Schmeichel, a vastly experienced Danish international and a firm favourite 'over the road' for many years, arrived shortly before Sylvain Distin and Argentinian Under-21 striker Vincente Jose Matias Vuoso. The former Independiente star took Keegan's choice of strikers to six, and an array of talent equal to the majority of those already in the Premiership. The most expensive of these six – indeed the most expensive signing in the club's history – is the French superstar Nicolas Anelka. Signed for a reported £13.5 million (one of the top six British transfers ever) Anelka came from Paris St Germain (via a loan spell at Anfield) to once again join forces with his old team-mates Benarbia and the recent acquisition Distin. It is clear that no matter which division Keegan has a side in, his philosophy of attacking football will never change, one of the reasons he is still highly thought of at his previous clubs Newcastle United and Fulham.

There is a long overdue buzz around all things connected with Manchester City Football Club. Even cautious bookmakers appear to believe in Keegan's top six comments and odds on offer are nowhere near as long as those for other newly promoted teams. Who knows, as Tony Book suggests in his foreword, maybe the days of Wednesday night European football are not that far off again. In front of 48,000 people at the new stadium, these games should be quite a sight both on and off the pitch.

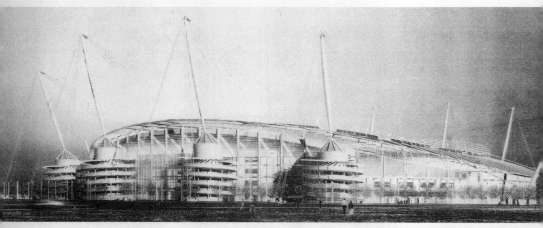

An artist's impression of the Commonwealth Stadium – City's proposed home from 2003.

THE ESSENTIAL HISTORY OF MANCHESTER CITY

CLUB STATISTICS

The Manchester City Directory

In 1884-85, Gorton AFC took its place in the Manchester and District Football League. Originally an amalgamation of two local sides – West Gorton and Gorton Athletic – Gorton AFC remained in existence for just three years before a ground move also forced a name change.

Ardwick FC came into being in 1887 and began playing its home games at the Bennett Street ground just off Hyde Road. Seven years later the club had changed its name again, this time to Manchester City. By the start of the 1923-24 season Manchester City had outgrown the resources at Hyde Road (a fire in 1920 had not helped matters) and the club moved to its present stadium at Maine Road.

- Formed: 1887 (as Ardwick FC)
- Turned Professional: 1887
- Became a Limited Company: 1894
- Nickname: City or Blues

Ground Information
- 1880-1881 Clowes Street
- 1881-1882 Kirkmanshulme Cricket Ground
- 1882-1884 Queens Road/Clemington Park – 'Donkey Common'
- 1884-1885 Pink Bank Lane
- 1885-1887 The Bull's Head Hotel
- 1887-1923 Hyde Road (1894 to 1923 as City)
- 1923-present Maine Road

Colours
Laser blue shirts, white shorts and laser and dark blue hooped socks.

Change colours 1: White shirts with black and red sash; black shorts; black, red and white hooped socks.
Change colours 2: Red and black striped shirts; black shorts; red socks

Honours
- League Division One Champions:
  1936-37, 1967-68, 2001-02
- Runners-up:
  1903-04, 1920-21, 1976-77, 1999-2000.
- Second Division Champions:
  1898-99, 1902-03, 1909-10, 1927-28, 1946-47, 1965-66
- Runners-up:
  1895-96, 1950-51, 1988-89.
- FA Cup Winners:
  1904, 1934, 1956, 1969
- Runners-up:
  1926, 1933, 1955, 1981
- Football League Cup Winners:
  1970, 1976
- Football League Cup Runners-up:
  1974
- FA Charity Shield Winners:
  1937, 1968, 1972
- European Cup-Winners' Cup Winners:
  1970
- FA Youth Cup Winners:
  1986
- Full Members Cup Runners-up:
  1986
- Central League Champions:
  1977-78, 1986-87
- Pontins League Premier Division Champions:
  1999-2000
- Division Two Play-off final: 1998-99

Records

- Record League Victory: 11-3 v Lincoln City (h), Division 2, 23 March 1895
- Record League Defeat: 1-9 v Everton (a), Division 1, 3 September 1906
- Record Cup Victory:
  12-0 v Liverpool Stanley (h), FA Cup Qualifying Round One, 4 October 1890
- Record Cup Defeat: 0-6 v Preston North End (a), FA Cup 1st round, 30 January 1897
- Most matches undefeated:
  22 in 1946-47
  22 in 1936-37
- Most League goals in a season:
  108 in 1926-27 and 2001-02
- Most League goals by one player in a season:
  38 by Tommy Johnson in 1928-29
- Most League appearances for club:
  564 by Alan Oakes (1959-76)
- Most League goals in one match:
  5 by Tommy Johnson v Everton (a) Division 1, 15 September 1928 and by George Smith v Newport County (h) Division 2, 14 June 1947
- Most goals in career:
  178 by Eric Brook between 1928 and 1940
- Most Cup goals by one player in a game: 6 by Denis Law v Luton Town (a) FA Cup 4th round, 28 January 1961 (match abandoned)
- Oldest Player:
  Billy Meredith 49 years and 245 days v Newcastle United, FA Cup semi final, 29 March 1924
- Youngest Player:
  Glyn Pardoe 15 years 314 days v Birmingham City (h) Division 1, 11 April 1962
- Most capped player:
  Colin Bell – 48 caps for England
- Record transfer fee paid: £13.5 million to Paris St. Germaine for Nicolas Anelka June 2002
- Record transfer fee received:
  £4,925,000 from Ajax Amsterdam for Georgiou Kinkladze – May 1998
- First Football League game:
  3 September 1892, Division 2, v Bootle (h), won 7-0. Douglas; McVickers, Robson; Middleton, Russell, Hopkins; Davies (3), Morris (2), Angus J. (1), Weir (1), Milarvie.
- Most League points (2 points for a win):
  62, Division 2, 1946-47, finished as Champions.
- Most League points (3 points for a win):
  99, Division 1, 2001-02, finished as Champions.

Club Information

**Maine Road, Moss Side,
Manchester. M14 7WN**

Tel: 0161 232 3000
Fax: 0161 232 8999
Ticket Office: 0161 226 2224
Dial-a-seat: 0161 828 1200
Clubcall: 0891 121191
Ticketcall: 09068 121591
Website: www.mcfc.co.uk
Chairman: David Bernstein
Ground capacity: 34,657
Pitch measurements: 116 x 79 yards
Record attendance: 84,569 v Stoke City FA Cup 6th round, 3 March 1934
Record receipts: £512,235 Oldham Athletic v Manchester United, FA Cup semi-final replay 13 April 1994

50 Greatest Players

This list was not conceived to be definitive. A list of Manchester City's 50 greatest players of all time would be impossible to compile: no two fans would agree on the same list. This one is based on my choices, and includes players that have entertained me over the years as well as some of the great old players that were around before my time. I'm sure that this list will cause discussion and maybe a little argument, but perhaps that's not a bad thing.

No. 1 Colin Bell (Midfielder) – 501 appearances, 153 goals. Nijinsky was renowned for his pace and stamina but there wasn't a single flaw in his game. The greatest City player ever (see page 115).

No. 2 Bert Trautmann (Goalkeeper) – 545 appearances. The German POW brave enough to stay on in his captive country to play football, broke his neck in the 1956 Cup final – and played on. A popular and marvellous keeper (see page 94).

No. 3 Billy Meredith (Forward) – 390 appearances, 150 goals. Football's first superstar, Meredith was as popular with the Hyde Road crowd as with the cartoonists of the day. Signed for £5 in 1894, he played his last game for City, aged 49, in 1924 (see page 34).

No. 4 Frank Swift (Goalkeeper) – 376 appearances. Popular with football fans all over England, Swift was the first goalkeeper to captain his country when he led England out against Italy in 1947. Swift was tragically killed in the Munich air disaster in 1958 (see page 65).

No. 5 Roy Clarke (Winger) – 370 appearances, 79 goals. The Welsh winger was injured for the 1955 FA Cup Final he'd helped City to reach, but was in the winning Wembley side the following season (see page 82).

No. 6 Peter Doherty (Forward) – 131 appearances, 80 goals. An idol of the City fans, Doherty was the complete footballer: tough tackling, two-footed, good in the air and deadly in front of goal (see page 61).

No. 7 Eric Brook (Winger) – 493 appearances, 177 goals. City's leading goalscorer of all time, Brook scored ten goals for England, but his prolific career was cut short after sustaining an injury in a wartime road accident. (see page 66).

No. 8 Francis Lee (Forward) – 330 appearances, 148 goals. An exciting burst of pace and an incredible shot saw Lee light up Maine Road in the glory years. He helped City win the title and stay at the top (see page 118).

No. 9 Alan Oakes (Midfielder) – 680 appearances, 34 goals. 'Mr Dependable' made more appearances than any other player. Solid and reliable, his forward runs often created and earned him crucial goals (see page 131).

No. 10 Dennis Tueart (Winger) – 275 appearances, 109 goals. Fast, direct, attacking winger who scored one of the best goals Wembley has ever seen. (see page 138).

No. 11 Tommy Browell (Forward) – 247 appearances, 139 goals. Horace Barnes' striking partner whose goals made him popular with the Hyde Road crowd (see page 44).

No. 12 Ken Barnes (Wing half) – 283 appearances, 19 goals. Crucial to City's style of play during the late 1950s, Barnes' practical jokes made him a terrace favourite (see page 89).

No. 13 Horace Barnes (Forward) – 235 appearances, 125 goals. Renowned for his fierce shot Barnes averaged a goal every other game for City in a powerful striking partnership with Tommy Browell (see page 42).

No. 14 Tommy Johnson (Forward) – 354 appearances, 166 goals. City's second highest ever goalscorer in history and the scorer of a record 38 league goals in the 1928–29 season (see page 48).

No. 15 Billy Gillespie (Centre forward) – 231 appearances, 132 goals. An unorthodox but effective goalscorer, Gillespie had a reputation as a 'bit of a boy'. He was hugely popular with the City fans (see page 30).

No. 16 Frank Roberts (Forward) – 237 appearances, 130 goals. A prolific goalscorer in the 1920s, he also won 4 England caps during his stint at City (see page 49).

No. 17 Paul Power (Midfielder) – 445 appearances, 36 goals. Strength, energy and more than a little finesse characterised City's 80s captain, who returned in 1997 to coach the Blues' youngsters (see page 147).

No. 18 Freddie Tilson (Inside forward) – 275 appearances, 132 goals. Despite a career blighted by injuries and illness, he still managed almost a goal every other game and scored 6 goals in 4 England games (see page 63).

No. 19 Alex Herd (Forward) – 288 appearances, 125 goals. A powerful inside forward, Herd was a regular fixture in the strong City sides of the 1930s (see page 69).

No. 20 Joe Hayes (Inside forward) – 364 appearances, 152 goals. An inside-right with a prolific goalscoring record, Hayes scored the first goal in the 1955 Cup final victory aged only 20 (see page 96).

No. 21 Tony Book (Full back) – 309 appearances 5 goals. A tough tackler and inspirational captain, Book led the Blues to the Championship and the FA Cup and won the Footballer of the Year award in 1969 (see page 99).

No. 22 Roy Paul (Forward) – 294 appearances, 9 goals. A 1950s regular and Welsh international, Paul was a fierce competitor who always gave his best. (see page 83).

No. 23 Sam Cowan (Centre half) – 407 appearances, 24 goals. A great motivator, Cowan captained City for three years during the early 1930s and managed the club between November 1946 and July 1947 (see page 58).

No. 24 Don Revie (Inside forward) – 178 appearances, 41 goals. A skilful and intelligent player, Revie was instrumental in Les McDowall's tactical game. He was voted Player of the Year in 1955. (see page 84).

No. 25 Neil Young (Inside forward) – 416 appearances, 108 goals. An elegant player with a fierce shot, Young rose to the big occasions, scoring in the 1969 Cup final and the 1970 Cup Winners' Cup final (see page 113).

No. 26 Bobby Johnstone (Forward) – 139 appearances, 51 goals. A cult figure amongst many supporters, he scored crucial goals in his four seasons at the club, including goals in both the 1955 and 1956 finals (see page 86).

No. 27 Dave Ewing (Centre half) – 303 appearances, 1 goal. An uncompromising stopper, Ewing always gave 100 per cent for the club. see page 91).

No. 28 Glyn Pardoe (Full back) – 380 appearances, 22 goals. The youngest ever City debutant, Pardoe developed into a cultured left back. Versatile and loyal, he got the winner in the 1970 League Cup final (see page 129).

No. 29 Mike Doyle (Wing half) – 572 appearances, 40 goals. Thoroughly committed to the Sky Blue cause, Doyle was a constant the middle of the park as City won championships and cups (see page 132).

No. 30 Tommy Booth (Defender/Midfielder) – 491 appearances, 36 goals. A footballing centre half who spent 13 years in the team and adapted well to a midfield role later in his City career (see page 123).

No. 31 Asa Hartford (Midfielder) – 323 appearances, 37 goals. The hard-tackling and creative Hartford came to City as the 'hole-in-the-heart' player – and was still there ten years later (see page 135).

No. 32 Sam Barkas (Full back) – 195 appearances, 1 goal. 1930s defender Barkas was ahead of his time in trying to play the ball out of defence (see page 68).

No. 33 Eric Westwood (Full back) – 260 appearances, 5 goals. Westwood was a sturdy and skilful defender who would have played more football for City but for the intervention of World War II (see page 75).

No. 34 Mike Summerbee (Forward) – 452 appearances, 68 goals. Summerbee's thrusting runs along the wing or through the middle delighted the Maine Road faithful in his ten glorious years at the club (see page 117).

No. 35 Shaun Goater (Striker) – 183 appearances, 97 goals. Bermudan international, 'The Goat' averages more than a goal every other game and is one of the club's most popular players of all time (see page 177).

No. 36 Peter Barnes (Winger) – 162 appearances, 22 goals. Skilful left wing-play earned Barnes honours and plaudits in his best years as a young City player (see page 134).

No. 37 Willie Donachie (Full back) – 436 appearances, 2 goals. The Scottish international included consistency and a touch of class in his defensive repertoire (see page 119).

No. 38 Bert Sproston (Full back) – 131 appearances, 5 goals. A strong, reliable England international full back, his career was curtailed by World War II (see page 72).

No. 39 Denis Law (Forward) – 82 appearances, 38 goals. In two short spells with City, Law showed why he is one of football's natural goalscorers (see page 120).

No. 40 Rodney Marsh (Forward) – 152 appearances, 47 goals. City's greatest showman ever, Marsh brought his cheek, tricks and goals to an appreciative Maine Road (see page 133).

No. 41 Niall Quinn (Forward) – 244 appearances, 78 goals. The towering Republic of Ireland star's displays proved he was not only an airbound threat but also a quick-footed and intelligent footballer (see page 165).

No. 42 Uwe Rosler (Forward) – 177 appearances, 64 goals. The East German international's bustling enthusiasm combined with a striker's instincts made him a firm favourite with the Maine Road faithful (see page 167).

No. 43 Georgiou Kinkladze (Midfielder) – 121 appearances, 22 goals. One of Blues' fans favourite ever players, the Georgian international hypnotised, tantalised and destroyed defences with his jinking runs and accurate shooting (see page 173).

No. 44 Joe Corrigan (Goalkeeper) – 605 appearances. Tall and dynamic he completely commanded his area. Corrigan was unlucky in only winning nine England caps (see page 126).

No. 45 Nicky Weaver (Goalkeeper) – 179 appearances. Capped at Under 21 level for England, Weaver is the latest in a long line of top class goalkeepers at Maine Road (see page 178).

No. 46 Tommy Hutchison (Winger) – 60 appearances, 5 goals. A tall, leggy winger whose trademark elusive dribbling and accurate crossing were vital to John Bond's City team (see page 143).

No. 47 Paul Lake (Midfielder/Forward) – 134 appearances, 11 goals. Naturally gifted with tremendous pace, Lake's career was cruelly cut short by injury (see page 162).

No. 48 Andy Hinchcliffe (Full back/Midfielder) – 139 appearances, 11 goals. A product of Maine Road's youth teams and a quality left-sided player who could cross a ball with power and accuracy (see page 155).

No. 49 David White (Winger) – 342 appearances, 95 goals. With explosive pace and a shot to match, White made his mark in the City history books (see page 160).

No. 50 Sammy Cookson (Full back) – 306 appearances, 1 goal. A former miner, Cookson's huge physique was often deceptive to opposing forwards, making him an effective defender (see page 46).

Results and Tables 1892-2002

The following pages include details of every official match played by Manchester City Football Club since their participation in Football League Division Two in 1894-5 as well as those of their forerunners Ardwick Football Club (who joined the Football League in 1892).

Each season has its own page and is dated at the top. League matches appear first, followed by individual cup competitions. The opponents played at home are written in capital letters, and appear in upper and lower case for away games. The date of the match, the score, the Manchester City (or Ardwick) goalscorers and the match attendance are also included. Full League and Cup and European competition appearances and the goalscorers are featured separately. The final league table is included at the bottom of each page as well as a Fact File which notes particularly interesting facts and figures for the season as well as any notable transfers etc.

In both the League & Cup Appearances and Goalscorers tables the category 'other' includes matches in the FA Charity Shield, Auto Windscreen Shield and the Divisional Play-offs.

Frank Swift was in his prime during World War II, playing 133 times for Manchester City. In 1947 he became the first goalkeeper to captain England.

The War Years

During the World Wars the official Football League programme was suspended. The results of matches played during the years, 1915-18 and 1939-45, are not therefore not included here. There was a huge amount of football played during the wartime years but teams were greatly disrupted with many players called up to fight and others guesting for various different teams all over the country. For these reasons, wartime football statistics, though interesting, are not regarded as 'official'.

World War I

Manchester City played in the sixteen-team Lancashire Section and a smaller subsidiary competition at the end of the season. The following are the ten players who made the most appearances in these games:

PLAYER	League		Subsidiary Tournament		TOTAL	
	Apps.	Goals	Apps.	Goals	Apps.	Goals
Fletcher, Eli	106	0	27	3	133	3
Goodchild, Jim	106	0	24	0	130	0
Meredith, Billy	85	5	22	2	107	7
Fairclough, P.	85	12	17	1	102	13
Brennan, J.	75	3	19	1	94	4
Tyler, H.	80	7	14	0	94	7
Barnes, Horace	57	56	16	17	73	73
Hughes, E.	55	2	10	0	65	2
Cartwright, J.	45	7	15	2	60	9
Broad, T.	36	2	10	0	46	2

World War II

Once again Leagues were set up on regional basis. In 1939-40 Manchester City competed in the Western League and from 1940-41 they took part in the North Regional League. The following are the ten players who made the most appearances in these games:

PLAYER	League		Wartime Cup		TOTAL	
	Apps.	Goals	Apps.	Goals	Apps.	Goals
Walsh, Billy	162	7	67	1	229	8
Clark, G.	120	0	60	0	180	0
Bray, Jackie	121	9	56	2	177	11
Eastwood, E.	104	0	59	0	163	0
Swift, Frank	102	0	31	0	133	0
McDowall, Les	82	8	32	0	114	8
Currier, James	75	69	38	15	113	84
Herd, Alec	68	46	22	14	90	60
Smith, George	68	38	22	7	90	45
Doherty, Peter	66	45	23	15	89	60

The Essential History of Manchester City

Season 1892-93

Football League Division 2

DATE	OPPONENTS	SCORE	GOALSCORERS	ATTENDANCE
Sep 3	BOOTLE	W 7-0	Morris 2, Davies 3, Weir, Angus	4,000
Sep 10	Northwich Vale	W 3-0	Russell 2, Morris	3,000
Sep 12	BURSLEM PORT VALE	W 2-0	Angus, Weir	2,000
Sep 17	Walsall Town Swifts	W 4-2	Davies 2, Angus, Lambie	1,000
Sep 24	NORTHWICH VALE	D 1-1	Middleton	2,000
Oct 1	WALSALL TOWN SWIFTS	W 2-0	Davies, Weir	4,000
Oct 8	Darwen	L 1-3	Davies	5,000
Oct 10	Burslem Port Vale	W 2-1	Weir	1,000
Oct 22	SMALL HEATH	D 2-2	Weir, Morris	6,000
Nov 5	Grimsby Town	L 0-2		2,000
Nov 26	BURTON SWIFTS	D 1-1	Russell	3,000
Dec 17	DARWEN	W 4-2	Weir, Mooney, Milvarie	6,000
Dec 24	Lincoln City	L 1-2	Forrester	1,000
Jan 14	Burton Swifts	L 0-2		1,000
Jan 21	Bootle	L 3-5	Mooney 2, Middleton	800
Jan 30	GRIMSBY TOWN	L 0-3		1,000
Feb 4	Crewe Alexandra	L 1-4	Yates	1,000
Feb 18	CREWE ALEXANDRA	W 3-1	Yates, Bowman, Milvarie	3,000
Mar 4	SHEFFIELD UNITED	L 2-3	Whittle, Bowman	2,000
Mar 25	Sheffield United	L 1-2	Yates	700
Apr 1	Small Heath	L 2-3	Yates, Carson	800
Apr 17	LINCOLN CITY	W 3-1	Yates, Mooney, Morris	2,000

FA Cup

Sep 22	Fleetwood Rangers	(QF) D 1-1		600
Oct 5	FLEETWOOD RANGERS	(R) L 0-2		2,000

League & Cup Appearances

PLAYER	LEAGUE	CUP COMPETITION FA CUP	TOTAL
Angus H	2		2
Angus J	7	1	8
Armitt	1		1
Bowman	2	2	4
Carson	3		3
Davies	12	2	14
Douglas	20	2	22
Forrester	4		4
Hopkins	20	1	21
Lambie	3		3
McVickers	17	2	19
Middleton	21	2	23
Milarvie	17	2	19
Milne	8	1	9
Mooney	9		9
Morris	19	2	21
Robson	22	2	24
Russell	17	2	19
Steele	4		4
Stones	2		2
Turner	1		1
Weir	14	1	15
Whittle	9		9
Yates	8		8

Goalscorers

PLAYER	LEAGUE	CUP COMPETITION FA CUP	TOTAL
Weir	8		8
Davies	7		7
Morris	5		5
Yates	5		5
Mooney	4		4
Russell	3		3
Angus J	3		3
Milarvie	2	1	3
Middleton	2		2
Bowman	2		2
Whittle	1		1
Forrester	1		1
Carson	1		1
Lambie	1		1

Fact File

1892 Ardwick, playing in 'Cambridge Blue' shirts, take part in the inaugural season of the Football League's Second Division.

MANAGER: Lawrence Furniss
CAPTAIN: Dave Russell
TOP SCORER: Davie Weir
BIGGEST WIN: September 3, 1892 7-0 v Bootle, Division 2
HIGHEST ATTENDANCE: October 22, 1892 (approx.) 6,000 v Small Heath, Drew 2-2, Division 2
MAJOR TRANSFERS IN: Dave Russell from Nottingham Forest

Final Division 2 Table

		P	W	D	L	F	A	Pts
1	SMALL HEATH	22	17	2	3	90	35	36
2	SHEFFIELD U	22	16	3	3	62	19	35
3	DARWEN	22	14	2	6	60	36	30
4	GRIMSBY T	22	11	1	10	42	41	23
5	ARDWICK	22	9	3	10	45	40	21
6	BURTON SWIFTS	22	9	2	11	47	47	20
7	NORTHWICH V	22	9	2	11	42	58	20
8	BOOTLE	22	8	3	11	49	63	19
9	LINCOLN C	22	7	3	12	45	51	17
10	CREWE ALEX	22	6	3	13	42	69	15
11	BURSLEM PORT VALE	22	6	3	13	30	57	15
12	WALSALL T SWIFTS	22	5	3	14	37	75	13

Season 1893-94

Football League Division 2

DATE	OPPONENTS	SCORE	GOALSCORERS	ATTENDANCE
Sep 2	Burslem Port Vale	L 2-4	Carson, Robinson	3,000
Sep 9	MIDDLESBROUGH	W 6-1	Morris 2, Bowman, Carson, Robinson, Jones	4,000
Sep 11	BURTON SWIFTS	L 1-4	Morris	1,000
Sep 16	LIVERPOOL	L 0-1		6,000
Sep 20	Burton Swifts	L 0-5		3,000
Sep 23	Middlesbrough	L 0-2		1,500
Sep 30	SMALL HEATH	L 0-1		5,000
Oct 7	BURSLEM PORT VALE	W 8-1	Morris 3, Milvarie, Steele, Middleton, Yates, o.g.	4,000
Oct 21	NEWCASTLE UNITED	L 2-3	Yates, Morris	3,000
Oct 28	NOTTS COUNTY	D 0-0		4,000
Nov 11	Woolwich Arsenal	L 0-1		4,500
Nov 18	WALSALL TOWN SWIFTS	W 3-0	Yates 2, Robertson	3,000
Dec 2	Liverpool	L 0-3		4,000
Dec 9	GRIMSBY TOWN	W 4-1	Davies, Bennett, Whittle, Middleton	4,000
Dec 26	ROTHERHAM TOWN	W 3-2	Pickford 2, Bennett	4,000
Dec 30	WOOLWICH ARSENAL	L 0-1		4,000
Jan 6	Newcastle United	L 1-2	Pickford	800
Jan 13	Grimsby Town	L 0-5		1,000
Jan 27	NORTHWICH VALE	W 4-2	Bennett 2, Whittle, Dyer	3,000
Feb 10	Northwich Vale	W 4-1	Milvarie 2, Robertson, Milne	2,000
Feb 24	Crewe Alexandra	D 1-1	Bennett	1,000
Mar 15	Notts County	L 0-5		2,500
Mar 17	Small Heath	L 2-10	Bennett, Robertson	2,000
Mar 24	Lincoln City	L 0-6		1,000
Mar 26	Rotherham Town	W 3-1	Baker, Milne, Milvarie	2,000
Mar 31	LINCOLN CITY	L 0-1		3,000
Apr 7	CREWE ALEXANDRA	L 1-2	Spittle	2,500
Apr 14	Walsall Town Swifts	L 2-5	Milne, Forrester	2,000

FA Cup

Oct 14	West Manchester	(QR) L 0-3		6,000

League & Cup Appearances

PLAYER	LEAGUE	CUP COMPETITION FA CUP	TOTAL
Baker	3		3
Bennett	12		12
Bowman	21		21
Caine	1		1
Carson	6		6
Davies	4		4
Douglas	16	1	17
Dyer	21	1	22
Edge	1		1
Egan	7		7
Forrester	6		6
Hargreaves	8		8
Hopkins	3		3
Hughes	2		2
Jones	2		2
McDowell	4		4
McVickers	9	1	10
Middleton	15	1	16
Milvarie	22	1	23
Milne	10		10
Morris	9	1	10
O'Brien	2		2
Pickford	8		8
Regan	21	1	22
Robertson	7		7
Robinson	4		4
Robson	17	1	18
Saddington	6		6
Spittle	1		1
Steele	13	1	14
Stenson	2		2
Stones	10		10
Whittle	21	1	22
Willey	1		1
Yates	12	1	13

Goalscorers

PLAYER	LEAGUE	CUP COMPETITION FA CUP	TOTAL
Morris	7		7
Bennett	6		6
Milarvie	4		4
Yates	4		4
Milne	3		3
Pickford	3		3
Robertson	3		3
Carson	2		2
Middleton	2		2
Robinson	2		2
Whittle	2		2
Baker	1		1
Bowman	1		1
Davies	1		1
Dyer	1		1
Forrester	1		1
Jones	1		1
Spittle	1		1
Steele	1		1
Opps' o.gs.	1		1

Fact File

Herbert Morris scored both goals for Wales in their 2-5 defeat by Scotland in the Home Internationals in Spring 1994.

MANAGER: Joshua Parlby
CAPTAIN: Bob Milarvie
TOP SCORER: Herbert Morris
BIGGEST WIN: October 7, 1893 8-1 v Burslem Port Vale, Division 2
HIGHEST ATTENDANCE: September 16, 1893 (approx.) 6,000 v Liverpool, lost 0-1, Division 2

Final Division 2 Table

		P	W	D	L	F	A	Pts
1	LIVERPOOL	28	22	6	0	77	18	50
2	SMALL HEATH	28	21	0	7	103	44	42
3	NOTTS CO	28	18	3	7	70	31	39
4	NEWCASTLE U	28	15	6	7	66	39	36
5	GRIMSBY T	28	15	2	11	71	58	32
6	BURTON SWIFTS	28	14	3	11	79	61	31
7	BURSLEM PORT VALE	28	13	4	11	66	64	30
8	LINCOLN C	28	11	6	11	59	58	28
9	WOOLWICH ARSENAL	28	12	4	12	52	55	28
10	WALSALL T SWIFTS	28	10	3	15	51	61	23
11	MIDDLESBROUGH	28	8	4	16	37	72	20
12	CREWE ALEX	28	6	7	15	42	73	19
13	ARDWICK	28	8	2	18	47	71	18
14	ROTHERHAM T	28	6	3	19	44	91	15
15	NORTHWICH V	28	3	3	22	30	98	9

Season 1894-95

Football League Division 2

DATE	OPPONENTS	SCORE	GOALSCORERS	ATTENDANCE
Sep 1	Bury	L 2-4	Calvey, Little	7,000
Sep 3	BURTON WANDERERS	D 1-1	Little	2,500
Sep 8	BURSLEM PORT VALE	W 4-1	Calvey 2, Mann, Finnerhan	4,000
Sep 15	Walsall Town Swifts	W 2-1	Finnerhan, Rowan	4,000
Sep 22	GRIMSBY TOWN	L 2-5	Wallace, Little	5,000
Sep 29	Woolwich Arsenal	L 2-4	Dyer, Rowan	5,000
Oct 1	Rotherham Town	L 2-3	Calvey 2	1,500
Oct 6	WALSALL TOWN SWIFTS	W 6-1	Sharples 3, Finnerhan, Rowan, Nash	3,000
Oct 13	Notts County	W 3-1	Sharples, Finnerhan, Rowan	3,000
Oct 20	DARWEN	L 2-4	Sharples, Tompkinson	6,000
Oct 27	Newcastle United	L 4-5	Sharples 2, Finnerhan, McReddie	2,000
Nov 3	NEWTON HEATH	L 2-5	Meredith 2	14,000
Nov 10	Burton Swifts	L 1-2	Finnerhan	2,000
Dec 8	BURY	D 3-3	McReddie, Rowan, Milvarie	10,000
Dec 15	WOOLWICH ARSENAL	W 4-1	Meredith 2, McBride, o.g.	5,000
Dec 26	Burton Wanderers	L 0-8		4,000
Dec 31	Crewe Alexandra	W 3-2	Meredith 2, Finnerhan	450
Jan 1	ROTHERHAM TOWN	W 1-0	Rowan	4,000
Jan 5	Newton Heath	L 1-4	Meredith	12,000
Feb 2	Burslem Port Vale	W 2-1	Finnerhan, McReddie	1,500
Feb 9	NEWCASTLE UNITED	W 4-0	Finnerhan 2, Meredith, Rowan	8,000
Mar 2	Lincoln City	W 2-0	Rowan 2	5,000
Mar 9	NOTTS COUNTY	W 7-1	Finnerhan 2, Rowan, McReddie, Sharples, Meredith, Walker	7,000
Mar 16	Leicester Fosse	L 1-3	Sharples	4,000
Mar 23	Lincoln City	W 11-3	McReddie 4, Finnerhan 2, Meredith 2, Rowan 2, Milvarie	2,000
Mar 30	LEICESTER FOSSE	D 1-1	McReddie	4,000
Apr 6	Darwen	L 0-4		2,000
Apr 12	CREWE ALEXANDRA	W 4-1	Meredith, Finnerhan, Sharples, Dyer	4,000
Apr 13	BURTON SWIFTS	W 4-1	Meredith, Sharples, Mann, o.g.	4,000
Apr 20	Grimsby Town	L 1-2	Milvarie	6,000

FA Cup

Did not enter.

League & Cup Appearances

PLAYER	LEAGUE	TOTAL
Bowman	10	10
Calvey	7	7
Dyer	12	12
Ferguson	2	2
Finnerhan	30	30
Hutchinson	7	7
Jones	18	18
Little	7	7
Mann	18	18
McBride	17	17
McReddie	20	20
Meredith	18	18
Milarvie	10	10
Nash	17	17
Robson	17	17
Rowan	24	24
Sharples	24	24
Smith	18	18
Tompkinson	6	6
Walker	19	19
Wallace	6	6
Williams	23	23

Goalscorers

PLAYER	LEAGUE	TOTAL
Finnerhan	15	15
Meredith	12	12
Rowan	12	12
Sharples	12	12
McReddie	9	9
Calvey	5	5
Little	3	3
Milarvie	3	3
Dyer	2	2
Mann	2	2
McBride	1	1
Nash	1	1
Walker	1	1
Wallace	1	1
Opps' o.gs.	2	2

Fact File

The 11-3 defeat of Lincoln City is still a club record league victory.

MANAGER: Joshua Parlby

CAPTAIN: Tom Chapman

TOP SCORER: Finnerhan

BIGGEST WIN: March 23, 1895 11-3 v Lincoln City, Division 2

HIGHEST ATTENDANCE: November 3, 1894 (approx.) 14,000 v Newton Heath, lost 2-5, Division 2

MAJOR TRANSFERS IN: Billy Meredith from Chirk

Final Division 2 Table

		P	W	D	L	F	A	Pts
1	BURY	30	23	2	5	78	33	48
2	NOTTS CO	30	17	5	8	75	45	39
3	NEWTON HEATH	30	15	8	7	78	44	38
4	LEICESTER FOSSE	30	15	8	7	72	53	38
5	GRIMSBY T	30	18	1	11	79	52	37
6	DARWEN	30	16	4	10	74	43	36
7	BURTON W	30	14	7	9	67	39	35
8	WOOLWICH ARSENAL	30	14	6	10	75	58	34
9	MANCHESTER CITY	30	14	3	13	82	72	31
10	NEWCASTLE U	30	12	3	15	72	84	27
11	BURTON SWIFTS	30	11	3	16	52	74	25
12	ROTHERHAM T	30	11	2	17	55	62	24
13	LINCOLN C	30	10	0	20	52	92	20
14	WALSALL T SWIFTS	30	10	0	20	47	92	20
15	BURSLEM PORT VALE	30	7	4	19	39	77	18
16	CREWE ALEX	30	3	4	23	26	103	10

Season 1895-96

Football League Division 2

DATE	OPPONENTS	SCORE	GOALSCORERS	ATTENDANCE
Sep 7	Woolwich Arsenal	W 1-0	Meredith	8,000
Sep 9	ROTHERHAM TOWN	W 2-0	Clifford, Little	3,000
Sep 14	LEICESTER FOSSE	W 2-0	Finnerhan, Rowan	9,000
Sep 21	Grimsby Town	L 0-5		3,000
Sep 28	WOOLWICH ARSENAL	W 1-0	Sharples	9,000
Oct 5	Newton Heath	D 1-1	Rowan	10,000
Oct 12	DARWEN	W 4-1	Rowan 2, Sharples, Chapman	10,000
Oct 19	Crewe Alexandra	W 2-0	Meredith, Finnerhan	3,000
Oct 26	GRIMSBY TOWN	W 2-1	Rowan, Little	14,000
Nov 2	Darwen	W 3-2	Meredith, Finnerhan, McReddie	4,000
Nov 4	Rotherham Town	W 3-2	McReddie 2, Rowan	5,000
Nov 16	Burton Wanderers	L 1-4	Meredith	3,000
Nov 23	BURTON WANDERERS	D 1-1	Meredith	12,000
Nov 30	Burton Swifts	W 4-1	Rowan 2, Morris 2	3,000
Dec 7	NEWTON HEATH	W 2-1	Meredith, Hill	20,000
Jan 1	Liverpool	L 1-3	Rowan	15,000
Jan 4	NEWCASTLE UNITED	W 5-2	Morris 2, Hill 2, Finnerhan	10,000
Jan 11	Lincoln City	W 2-1	Chapman, Meredith	2,000
Feb 1	Loughborough Town	W 4-2	Finnerhan 2, Davies, Hill	2,000
Feb 10	Burslem Port Vale	W 1-0	Davies	3,000
Feb 15	CREWE ALEXANDRA	W 4-0	Rowan 2, Meredith, Finnerhan	4,000
Feb 17	BURSLEM PORT VALE	W 1-0	Finnerhan	3,000
Feb 24	LOUGHBOROUGH TOWN	W 5-1	Morris 2, Davies, Meredith, Chapman	2,000
Feb 29	Notts County	L 0-3		4,000
Mar 7	BURTON SWIFTS	D 1-1	Robertson	9,000
Mar 14	LINCOLN CITY	W 4-0	Robertson, Meredith, Morris, Finnerhan	9,000
Mar 21	Newcastle United	L 1-4	Davies	12,000
Apr 3	LIVERPOOL	D 1-1	Morris	30,000
Apr 4	Leicester Fosse	W 2-1	Meredith, Robson	4,000
Apr 8	NOTTS COUNTY	W 2-0	Meredith, Morris	6,000

FA Cup

Oct 12	OSWALDTWISTLE ROVERS	(QR)*	

*Qualifying Round scratched.

League & Cup Appearances

PLAYER	LEAGUE	TOTAL
Bowman	7	7
Chapman	26	26
Clifford	4	4
Davis	11	11
Ditchfield	2	2
Dyer	1	1
Espie	1	1
Finnerhan	30	30
Gillies	3	3
Harper	21	21
Hill	9	9
Little	9	9
Maley	1	1
Mann	23	23
McBride	25	25
McCabe	1	1
McReddie	11	11
Meredith	29	29
Milarvie	1	1
Miller	2	2
Moffatt	2	2
Morris	16	16
Porteous	5	5
Read	1	1
Robertson	3	3
Robson	30	30
Rowan	21	21
Sharpels	5	5
Williams	30	30

Goalscorers

PLAYER	LEAGUE	TOTAL
Meredith	12	12
Rowan	11	11
Finnerhan	9	9
Morris	9	9
Davis	4	4
Hill	4	4
Chapman	3	3
McReddie	3	3
Little	2	2
Robertson	2	2
Sharpels	2	2
Clifford	1	1
Robson	1	1

Fact File

As runners-up in the League, City qualified for the 'Test Matches' (similar to modern day play-offs) along with Division 2 winners Liverpool and the two bottom teams in Division 1 (West Bromwich Albion and Small Heath). Liverpool and Albion were the successful teams.

MANAGER: Sam Ormerod
CAPTAIN: Billy Meredith
TOP SCORER: Billy Meredith
BIGGEST WIN: February 24, 1895 5-1 v Loughborough Town, Division 2
HIGHEST ATTENDANCE: April 3, 1895 (approx.) 30,000 v Liverpool, drew 1-1, Division 2
MAJOR TRANSFERS IN: Robert Hill from Sheffield United

Final Division 2 Table

		P	W	D	L	F	A	Pts
1	LIVERPOOL	30	22	2	6	106	32	46
2	MANCHESTER CITY	30	21	4	5	63	38	46
3	GRIMSBY T	30	20	2	8	82	38	42
4	BURTON W	30	19	4	7	69	40	42
5	NEWCASTLE U	30	16	2	12	73	50	34
6	NEWTON HEATH	30	15	3	12	66	57	33
7	WOOLWICH ARSENAL	30	14	4	12	58	42	32
8	LEICESTER FOSSE	30	14	4	12	57	44	32
9	DARWEN	30	12	6	12	72	67	30
10	NOTTS CO	30	12	2	16	57	54	26
11	BURTON SWIFTS	30	10	4	16	39	69	24
12	LOUGHBOROUGH	30	9	5	16	40	66	23
13	LINCOLN C	30	9	4	17	53	75	22
14	BURSLEM PORT VALE	30	7	4	19	43	78	18
15	ROTHERHAM T	30	7	3	20	34	97	17
16	CREWE ALEX	30	5	3	22	30	95	13

Season 1896-97

Football League Division 2

DATE	OPPONENTS	SCORE	GOALSCORERS	ATTENDANCE
Sep 5	WOOLWICH ARSENAL	D 1-1	Finnerhan	8,000
Sep 12	Gainsborough Town	D 1-1	Sharples	4,000
Sep 19	DARWEN	W 4-1	Mann 2, Ditchfield, Lewis	10,000
Sep 21	LINCOLN CITY	W 3-0	Finnerhan, Lewis, Sharples	3,000
Sep 26	Blackpool	D 2-2	Mann, Hill	5,000
Oct 3	NEWTON HEATH	D 0-0		20,000
Oct 10	Notts County	D 3-3	Meredith, Hill, Robinson	7,000
Ot 17	NEWCASTLE UNITED	L 1-2	Robinson	10,000
Oct 24	Grimsby Town	L 1-3	Sharples	3,000
Oct 31	NOTTS COUNTY	L 1-4	Meredith	12,000
Nov 7	BLACKPOOL	W 4-2	Bannister, Meredith, Sharples, Lewis	4,000
Nov 14	BURTON SWIFTS	W 3-1	Tait 2, Gunn	4,000
Nov 23	Walsall	L 2-3	Finnerhan, Mann	3,000
Nov 28	BURTON WANDERERS	W 2-1	Williams, Gunn	2,000
Dec 19	GRIMSBY TOWN	W 3-1	Meredith, Gunn, Williams	12,000
Dec 25	Newton Heath	L 1-2	Hill	18,000
Dec 26	Burton Swifts	L 0-5		6,000
Jan 1	SMALL HEATH	W 3-0	Bannister, Gunn, Sharples	16,000
Jan 6	WALSALL	W 5-0	Ray, Mann, Meredith, Lewis, Sharples	5,000
Jan 9	Darwen	L 1-3	Gillespie	1,000
Feb 6	Newcastle United	L 0-3		4,000
Feb 13	Lincoln City	W 1-0	Gillespie	1,000
Feb 27	GAINSBOROUGH TOWN	W 4-1	Gillespie, Williams 2, Meredith	9,000
Mar 6	Burton Wanderers	D 1-1	Read	3,000
Mar 13	LEICESTER FOSSE	W 4-0	Holmes, Meredith, Gillespie, Williams	6,000
Mar 17	Loughborough Town	L 0-2		2,000
Apr 12	Leicester Fosse	D 3-3	Meredith 2, o.g.	1,000
Apr 16	LOUGHBOROUGH TOWN	D 1-1	Foster	2,000
Apr 19	Small Heath	L 1-3	Meredith	5,000
Apr 28	Woolwich Arsenal	W 2-1	Hill 2	2,000

FA Cup

Jan 30	Preston North End	(Rd 1) L 0-6		6,000

League & Cup Appearances

PLAYER	LEAGUE	CUP COMPETITION FA CUP	TOTAL
Bannister	18		18
Bowman	2		2
Ditchfield	10		10
Finnerhan	25		25
Foster	6	1	7
Gillespie	11		11
Gunn	21	1	22
Harper	10	1	11
Hesham	2		2
Hill	12		12
Holmes	12	1	13
Lewis	12	1	13
Mann	18	1	19
McBride	28	1	29
McConnell	2		2
Meredith	27	1	28
Moffatt	11		11
Patterson	1		1
Platt	1		1
Ray	30	1	31
Read	8		8
Robinson	3		3
Sharples	10	1	11
Tait	4		4
Tonge	2		2
Townley	3		3
Williams C	30	1	31
Williams F	11		11

Goalscorers

PLAYER	LEAGUE	CUP COMPETITION FA CUP	TOTAL
Meredith	10		10
Sharples	6		6
Hill	5		5
Mann	5		5
Williams F	5		5
Gillespie	4		4
Gunn	4		4
Lewis	4		4
Finnerhan	3		3
Bannister	2		2
Robinson	2		2
Tait	2		2
Ditchfield	1		1
Foster	1		1
Holmes	1		1
Ray	1		1
Read	1		1
Opps' o.gs.	1		1

Fact File

Billy Gillespie scored on his debut against Darwen in January. He would partner Billy Meredith in attack for the next eight years.

MANAGER: Sam Ormerod

CAPTAIN: Billy Meredith

TOP SCORER: Billy Meredith

BIGGEST WIN: January 6, 1896 5-0 v Walsall, Division 2

HIGHEST ATTENDANCE: October 3, 1896 (approx.) 20,000 v Newton Heath, drew 0-0, Division 2

MAJOR TRANSFERS IN: Billy Gillespie from Lincoln City

Final Division 2 Table

		P	W	D	L	F	A	Pts
1	NOTTS CO	30	19	4	7	92	43	42
2	NEWTON HEATH	30	17	5	8	56	34	39
3	GRIMSBY T	30	17	4	9	66	45	38
4	SMALL HEATH	30	16	5	9	69	47	37
5	NEWCASTLE U	30	17	1	12	56	52	35
6	MANCHESTER CITY	30	12	8	10	58	50	32
7	GAINSBOROUGH T	30	12	7	11	50	47	31
8	BLACKPOOL	30	13	5	12	59	56	31
9	LEICESTER FOSSE	30	13	4	13	59	57	30
10	WOOLWICH ARSENAL	30	13	4	13	68	70	30
11	DARWEN	30	14	0	16	67	61	28
12	WALSALL	30	11	4	15	54	69	26
13	LOUGHBOROUGH	30	12	1	17	50	64	25
14	BURTON SWIFTS	30	9	6	15	46	61	24
15	BURTON W	30	9	2	19	31	67	20
16	LINCOLN C	30	5	2	23	27	85	12

Season 1897-98

Football League Division 2

DATE	OPPONENTS	SCORE	GOALSCORERS	ATTENDANCE
Sep 1	GAINSBOROUGH TOWN	W 3-0	Meredith, Gillespie, F Williams	2,000
Sep 4	Darwen	W 4-2	S Smith 2, Gillespie, Leonard	1,000
Sep 11	LOUGHBOROUGH TOWN	W 3-0	S Smith 2, Gillespie	7,000
Sep 18	Blackpool	W 2-0	S Smith, F Williams	4,000
Sep 25	WOOLWICH ARSENAL	W 4-1	S Smith 3, F Williams	7,000
Oct 2	Loughborough Town	W 3-0	Gillespie, F Williams 2	5,000
Oct 9	GRIMSBY TOWN	W 3-0	B Smith, Meredith, Gillespie	7,000
Oct 16	Newton Heath	D 1-1	Ray	20,000
Oct 23	DARWEN	W 5-0	Gillespie 2, F Williams 2, Whitehead	7,000
Oct 30	Burnley	L 1-3	o.g.	10,000
Nov 20	BURNLEY	D 1-1	Gillespie	20,000
Dec 11	LEICESTER FOSSE	W 2-1	Gillespie, Meredith	9,000
Dec 18	Grimsby Town	W 4-3	Leonard 2, Meredith, Gillespie	5,000
Dec 25	NEWTON HEATH	L 0-1		16,000
Dec 27	Small Heath	W 1-0	Leonard	10,000
Jan 1	Luton Town	L 0-3		4,000
Jan 3	WALSALL	W 3-2	Gillespie 2, Meredith	7,000
Jan 8	NEWCASTLE UNITED	D 1-1	Whitehead	16,000
Jan 15	Walsall	D 2-2	Gillespie, S.Smith	10,000
Jan 24	LINCOLN CITY	W 3-1	Meredith, Gillespie, o.g.	2,000
Feb 5	Woolwich Arsenal	D 2-2	Holmes, Gillespie	8,030
Feb 26	Gainsborough Town	L 0-1		2,000
Mar 16	Newcastle United	L 0-2		20,000
Mar 19	Lincoln City	L 1-2	Dougal	3,000
Mar 26	LUTON TOWN	W 2-1	Meredith 2	5,000
Mar 30	BLACKPOOL	D 3-3	S Smith, Gillespie, Dougal	4,000
Apr 2	Leicester Fosse	D 0-0		6,000
Apr 9	Burton Swifts	D 0-0		3,000
Apr 11	SMALL HEATH	D 3-3	B Smith, Meredith, Gillespie	2,000
Apr 16	BURTON SWIFTS	W 9-0	Meredith 3, Whitehead 3, S Smith 2, Gillespie	4,000

FA Cup

Jan 29	WIGAN ATHLETIC	(Rd 1) W 1-0	Gillespie	6,000
Feb 12	Bolton Wanderers	(Rd 2) L 0-1		14,000

League & Cup Appearances

PLAYER	LEAGUE	CUP COMPETITION FA CUP	TOTAL
Bowman	2		2
Chappell	7		7
Clare	1		1
Dougal	8		8
Dyer	2		2
Foster	1		1
Gillespie	30	2	32
Harper	2		2
Holmes	29	2	31
Leonard	15	1	16
Meredith	30	2	32
Moffatt	30	2	32
Munn	8		8
Ray	20	2	22
Read	27	2	29
Smith B	28	2	30
Smith S	24	2	26
Whitehead	20	2	22
Williams C	23	2	25
Williams F	22	1	23
Wilson	1		1

Goalscorers

PLAYER	LEAGUE	CUP COMPETITION FA CUP	TOTAL
Gillespie	18	1	19
Meredith	12		12
Smith S	12		12
Williams F	7		7
Whitehead	5		5
Leonard	4		4
Dougal	2		2
Smith B	2		2
Holmes	1		1
Ray	1		1
Opps' o.gs.	2		2

Fact File

Only a poor run of two wins in the last 11 games deprived City of a chance of promotion.

MANAGER: Sam Ormerod
CAPTAIN: Billy Meredith
TOP SCORER: Billy Gillespie
BIGGEST WIN: April 16, 1898 9-0 v Burton Swifts, Division 1;
HIGHEST ATTENDANCE: November 20, 1897 (approx.) 20,000 v Burnley, drew 1-1, Division 2
MAJOR TRANSFERS IN: William 'Stockport' Smith from Stockport County

Final Division 2 Table

		P	W	D	L	F	A	Pts
1	BURNLEY	30	20	8	2	80	24	48
2	NEWCASTLE U	30	21	3	6	64	32	45
3	MANCHESTER CITY	30	15	9	6	66	36	39
4	NEWTON HEATH	30	16	6	8	64	35	38
5	WOOLWICH ARSENAL	30	16	5	9	69	49	37
6	SMALL HEATH	30	16	4	10	58	50	36
7	LEICESTER FOSSE	30	13	7	10	46	35	33
8	LUTON T	30	13	4	13	68	50	30
9	GAINSBOROUGH T	30	12	6	12	50	54	30
10	WALSALL	30	12	5	13	58	58	29
11	BLACKPOOL	30	10	5	15	49	61	25
12	GRIMSBY T	30	10	4	16	52	62	24
13	BURTON SWIFTS	30	8	5	17	38	69	21
14	LINCOLN C	30	6	5	19	43	83	17
15	DARWEN	30	6	2	22	31	76	14
16	LOUGHBOROUGH	30	6	2	22	24	87	14

Season 1898-99

Football League Division 2

DATE	OPPONENTS	SCORE	GOALSCORERS	ATTENDANCE
Sep 3	GRIMSBY TOWN	W 7-2	Meredith 3, Gillespie 3, Whitehead	10,000
Sep 10	Newton Heath	L 0-3		15,000
Sep 17	NEW BRIGHTON	D 1-1	Cowie	6,000
Sep 24	Lincoln City	L 1-3	Whitehead	3,000
Oct 1	WOOLWICH ARSENAL	W 3-1	Read, S Smith, Dougal	6,000
Oct 8	Luton Town	W 3-0	Meredith, B Smith, Cowie	10,000
Oct 15	LEICESTER FOSSE	W 3-1	Meredith, S Smith, Gillespie	8,000
Oct 22	Darwen	W 2-0	Meredith, S Smith	7,000
Nov 5	Barnsley	D 1-1	Cowie	4,000
Nov 12	Glossop North End	W 2-1	Meredith, Gillespie	6,000
Nov 19	WALSALL	W 2-0	Jones, Gillespie	10,000
Nov 26	Burton Swifts	D 3-3	Meredith, Moffatt, Gillespie	5,000
Dec 3	BURSLEM PORT VALE	W 3-1	Meredith 2, Dougal	10,000
Dec 10	Loughborough Town	W 3-1	B Smith, Meredith, F Williams	10,000
Dec 17	LOUGHBOROUGH TOWN	W 5-0	Meredith 3, Ray, S Smith	4,000
Dec 24	Blackpool	W 4-2	Moffatt 2, Meredith, Gillespie	8,000
Dec 26	NEWTON HEATH	W 4-0	Meredith, Gillespie, Dougal, F Williams	20,000
Dec 27	Small Heath	L 1-4	Dougal	10,000
Jan 2	GLOSSOP NORTH END	L 0-2		7,000
Jan 14	New Brighton	W 1-0	Gillespie	10,000
Feb 4	LUTON TOWN	W 2-0	S Smith, Gillespie	8,000
Feb 11	Leicester Fosse	D 1-1	F Williams	10,000
Feb 18	DARWEN	W 10-0	F Williams 5, Meredith 3, Dougal, S Smith	8,000
Feb 22	LINCOLN CITY	W 3-1	S Smith, Gillespie, F Williams	5,000
Feb 25	Gainsborough Town	L 1-3	Meredith	5,000
Mar 4	BARNSLEY	W 5-0	Meredith 3, Ross 2	12,000
Mar 18	Walsall	D 1-1	Ross	6,000
Mar 25	BURTON SWIFTS	W 6-0	Meredith 2, Ross 2, Moffatt, Dougal	6,000
Mar 31	GAINSBOROUGH TOWN	W 4-0	Gillespie 2, Dougal, Ross	15,000
Apr 1	Burslem Port Vale	D 1-1	Meredith	12,000
Apr 3	Woolwich Arsenal	W 1-0	Gillespie	5,000
Apr 8	SMALL HEATH	W 2-0	F Williams 2	20,000
Apr 11	Grimsby Town	W 2-1	Meredith, Gillespie	5,000
Apr 22	BLACKPOOL	W 4-1	Meredith 2, Gillespie, Ross	10,000

FA Cup

Jan 28	Small Heath	(Rd 1) L 2-3	Meredith, Gillespie	15,399

League & Cup Appearances

PLAYER	LEAGUE	CUP COMPETITION FA CUP	TOTAL
Bowman	3		3
Chappell	1		1
Cowie	11		11
Dougal	31	1	32
Gillespie	30	1	31
Holmes	24	1	25
Jones	27	1	28
Meredith	33	1	34
Moffatt	34	1	35
Munn	6		6
Ray	24	1	25
Read	20		20
Ross	9		9
Smith B	34	1	35
Smith S	25	1	26
Whitehead	4		4
Williams C	33	1	34
Williams F	25	1	26

Goalscorers

PLAYER	LEAGUE	CUP COMPETITION FA CUP	TOTAL
Meredith	29	1	30
Gillespie	17	1	18
Williams F	11		11
Smith S	8		8
Dougal	7		7
Ross	7		7
Moffatt	4		4
Cowie	3		3
Whitehead	2		2
Jones	1		1
Ray	1		1
Read	1		1
Smith B	1		1

Fact File

With only two defeats in 1898 City swept to the top of the league winning the championship by six points.

MANAGER: Sam Ormerod
CAPTAIN: Billy Meredith
TOP SCORER: Billy Meredith
BIGGEST WIN: February 18, 1899 10-0 v Darwen, Division 2;
HIGHEST ATTENDANCE: December 26, 1898 (approx.) 20,000 v Newton Heath, won 4-0, Division 2; April 8, 1899 (approx.) 20,000 v Small Heath, won 2-0, Division 2
MAJOR TRANSFERS IN: Jimmy Ross from Burnley

Final Division 2 Table

		P	W	D	L	F	A	PTS
1	MANCHESTER CITY	34	23	6	5	92	35	52
2	GLOSSOP	34	20	6	8	76	38	46
3	LEICESTER FOSSE	34	18	9	7	64	42	45
4	NEWTON HEATH	34	19	5	10	67	43	43
5	NEW BRIGHTON TOWER	34	18	7	9	71	52	43
6	WALSALL	34	15	12	7	79	36	42
7	WOOLWICH ARSENAL	34	18	5	11	72	41	41
8	SMALL HEATH	34	17	7	10	85	50	41
9	BURSLEM PORT VALE	34	17	5	12	56	34	39
10	GRIMSBY T	34	15	5	14	71	60	35
11	BARNSLEY	34	12	7	15	52	56	31
12	LINCOLN C	34	12	7	15	51	56	31
13	BURTON SWIFTS	34	10	8	16	51	70	28
14	GAINSBOROUGH T	34	10	5	19	56	72	25
15	LUTON T	34	10	3	21	51	95	23
16	BLACKPOOL	34	8	4	22	49	90	20
17	LOUGHBOROUGH	34	6	6	22	38	92	18
18	DARWEN	34	2	5	27	22	141	9

Season 1899-1900

Football League Division 1

DATE	OPPONENTS	SCORE	GOALSCORERS	ATTENDANCE
Sep 2	Blackburn Rovers	L 3-4	Meredith, Ross, F Williams	10,000
Sep 9	DERBY COUNTY	W 4-0	Meredith 2, Ross, Gillespie	22,000
Sep 16	Bury	W 4-1	Meredith, Ross, F Williams, Leonard	13,000
Sep 23	NOTTS COUNTY	W 5-1	Ross 2, Moffatt, B Smith, Gillespie	22,000
Sep 30	Wolves	D 1-1	Ross	14,000
Oct 7	Sheffield United	L 0-3		18,000
Oct 14	NEWCASTLE UNITED	W 1-0	Ross	25,000
Oct 21	Aston Villa	L 1-2	F Williams	20,000
Oct 28	LIVERPOOL	L 0-1		25,000
Nov 4	Burnley	L 0-1		5,000
Nov 11	PRESTON NORTH END	W 3-1	Meredith, Gillespie, F Williams	8,000
Nov 25	GLOSSOP NORTH END	W 4-1	Meredith, Ross, F Williams, Dougal	16,000
Dec 2	Stoke	L 0-1		10,000
Dec 9	SUNDERLAND	W 2-1	Moffatt, Meredith	20,000
Dec 16	West Bromwich Albion	D 0-0		7,000
Dec 23	EVERTON	L 1-2	Meredith	20,000
Dec 25	SHEFFIELD UNITED	L 1-2	F Williams	3,000
Dec 27	Nottingham Forest	L 0-2		5,000
Dec 30	BLACKBURN ROVERS	D 1-1	Gillespie	10,000
Jan 6	Derby County	D 0-0		5,000
Jan 13	BURY	D 2-2	S Smith 2	15,000
Jan 20	Notts County	D 1-1	Gillespie	8,000
Feb 3	Wolves	D 1-1	Meredith	2,000
Mar 3	Liverpool	L 2-5	Meredith, Gillespie	20,000
Mar 10	BURNLEY	W 1-0	Meredith	13,000
Mar 19	ASTON VILLA	L 0-2		15,000
Mar 31	Glossop North End	W 2-0	Harvey, Davidson	7,000
Apr 7	STOKE	W 1-0	F Williams	16,000
Apr 9	NOTTINGHAM FOREST	W 2-0	Meredith 2	5,000
Apr 13	Newcastle United	D 0-0		20,000
Apr 14	Sunderland	L 1-3	C Williams	6,000
Apr 16	Preston North End	W 2-0	Gillespie, Dougal	5,000
Apr 21	WEST BROMWICH ALBION	W 4-0	Ross 2, Meredith, Gillespie	15,000
Apr 28	Everton	L 0-4		20,000

FA Cup

Jan 27	ASTON VILLA	(Rd 1)	D 1-1	Ross	22,000
Jan 31	Aston Villa	(R)	L 0-3		18,000

League & Cup Appearances

PLAYER	LEAGUE	CUP COMPETITION FA CUP	TOTAL
Cassidy	1		1
Dartnell	1		1
Davidson	5		5
Dougal	23		23
Gillespie	28	2	30
Harvey	5		5
Holmes	34	2	36
Jones	34	2	36
Leonard	1		1
Meredith	33	2	35
Moffatt	25	1	26
Munn	6		6
Ray	9	2	11
Read	28	1	29
Ross	26	1	27
Smith B	34	2	36
Smith S	5		5
Threlfall	9	2	11
Tonge	2	1	3
Williams C	34	2	36
Williams F	31	2	33

Goalscorers

PLAYER	LEAGUE	CUP COMPETITION FA CUP	TOTAL
Meredith	14		14
Ross	10	1	11
Gillespie	8		8
Williams F	7		7
Dougal	2		2
Moffatt	2		2
Smith S	2		2
Davidson	1		1
Harvey	1		1
Leonard	1		1
Smith B	1		1
Williams C	1		1

Fact File

Goalkeeper Charlie Williams scored City's goal against Sunderland in April with a wind-assisted kick.

MANAGER: Sam Ormerod

CAPTAIN: Billy Meredith

TOP SCORER: Billy Meredith

BIGGEST WIN: September 23, 1899 5-1 v Notts County, Division 1

HIGHEST ATTENDANCE: October 14, 1899 (approx.) 25,000 v Newcastle Utd, won 1-0, Division 1; October 28, 1899 (approx.) 25,000 v Liverpool, lost 1-0, Division 1

MAJOR TRANSFERS IN: Joe Cassidy from Newton Heath

Final Division 1 Table

		P	W	D	L	F	A	Pts
1	ASTON VILLA	34	22	6	6	77	35	50
2	SHEFFIELD U	34	18	12	4	63	33	48
3	SUNDERLAND	34	19	3	12	50	35	41
4	WOLVERHAMPTON W	34	15	9	10	48	37	39
5	NEWCASTLE U	34	13	10	11	53	43	36
6	DERBY CO	34	14	8	12	45	43	36
7	MANCHESTER CITY	34	13	8	13	50	44	34
8	NOTTINGHAM F	34	13	8	13	56	55	34
9	STOKE C	34	13	8	13	37	45	34
10	LIVERPOOL	34	14	5	15	49	45	33
11	EVERTON	34	13	7	14	47	49	33
12	BURY	34	13	6	15	40	44	32
13	WBA	34	11	8	15	43	51	30
14	BLACKBURN R	34	13	4	17	49	61	30
15	NOTTS CO	34	9	11	14	46	60	29
16	PRESTON NE	34	12	4	18	38	48	28
17	BURNLEY	34	11	5	18	34	54	27
18	GLOSSOP	34	4	10	20	31	74	18

Season 1900-01

Football League Division 1

DATE	OPPONENTS	SCORE	GOALSCORERS	ATTENDANCE
Sep 1	SHEFFIELD WEDNESDAY	D 2-2	Ross, Dougal	18,000
Sep 8	Bury	L 0-4		17,000
Sep 15	NOTTINGHAM FOREST	W 1-0	Cassidy	20,000
Sep 22	Blackburn Rovers	L 0-1		10,000
Sep 28	STOKE	W 2-0	Meredith, Davies	20,000
Oct 6	West Bromwich Albion	L 2-3	Holmes, Moffatt	5,000
Oct 13	EVERTON	W 1-0	Cassidy	15,000
Oct 20	Sunderland	L 0-3		10,000
Oct 27	DERBY COUNTY	W 2-0	F Williams 2	15,000
Nov 3	Bolton Wanderers	D 0-0		20,000
Nov 10	NOTTS COUNTY	W 2-0	Gillespie, Cassidy	16,000
Nov 17	Preston North End	W 4-0	Cassidy 2, Gillespie, F Williams	5,000
Nov 24	WOLVES	W 3-2	Meredith, Ross, Cassidy	16,000
Dec 1	Aston Villa	L 1-7	Cassidy	12,000
Dec 8	LIVERPOOL	L 3-4	Cassidy 2, Smith	18,000
Dec 15	Newcastle United	L 1-2	F Williams	16,000
Dec 22	SHEFFIELD UNITED	W 2-1	Meredith, Gillespie	15,000
Dec 25	SUNDERLAND	D 1-1	Gillespie	20,000
Dec 26	Sheffield United	D 1-1	Gillespie	20,000
Dec 29	Sheffield Wednesday	L 1-4	Cassidy	15,000
Jan 5	BURY	W 1-0	Cassidy	23,000
Jan 12	Nottingham Forest	L 2-4	Gillespie, Cassidy	8,000
Jan 19	BLACKBURN ROVERS	L 1-3	Meredith	8,000
Jan 26	Stoke	L 1-2	Cassidy	3,000
Feb 16	Everton	L 2-5	Meredith, Cassidy	20,000
Feb 23	PRESTON NORTH END	W 3-1	Meredith, F Williams, Dougal	10,000
Mar 2	Derby County	L 0-2		5,000
Mar 9	BOLTON WANDERERS	D 1-1	Holmes	15,000
Mar 16	Notts County	D 0-0		6,000
Mar 30	Wolves	L 0-1		3,000
Apr 5	WEST BROMWICH ALBION	W 1-0	Gillespie	23,000
Apr 13	Liverpool	L 1-3	Meredith	15,000
Apr 20	NEWCASTLE UNITED	W 2-1	Gillespie 2	20,000
Apr 27	ASTON VILLA	W 4-0	Scotson 2, Threlfall, Ross	15,000

FA Cup

Feb 9	West Bromwich Albion	(Rd 1)	L 0-1		16,000

League & Cup Appearances

PLAYER	LEAGUE	CUP COMPETITION FA CUP	TOTAL
Cassidy	30	1	31
Cox	1		1
Dartnell	3		3
Davidson	2		2
Davies	8		8
Dougal	13	1	14
Gillespie	23		23
Hallows	1		1
Harvey	2		2
Hesham	1		1
Holmes	28	1	29
Hosie	3		3
Hunter	2		2
Jones	33	1	34
Meecham	6		6
Meredith	34	1	35
Moffatt	32	1	33
Read	27	1	28
Ross	25	1	26
Scotson	5		5
Slater	3		3
Smith	32	1	33
Threlfall	4		4
Williams C	33	1	34
Williams F	23	1	24

Goalscorers

PLAYER	LEAGUE	CUP COMPETITION FA CUP	TOTAL
Cassidy	14		14
Gillespie	9		9
Meredith	7		7
Williams F	5		5
Ross	3		3
Dougal	2		2
Holmes	2		2
Scotson	2		2
Davies	1		1
Moffatt	1		1
Smith	1		1
Threlfall	1		1

Fact File

Meredith and Jones both play for Wales in the 1-1 draw with England in March. Meredith scores, his third for his country and his first at Cardiff Arms Park.

MANAGER: Sam Ormerod

CAPTAIN: Billy Meredith

TOP SCORER: Joe Cassidy

BIGGEST WIN: November 17, 1901 4-0 v Preston North End, Division 1; April 27, 1901 4-0 v Aston Villa, Division 1

HIGHEST ATTENDANCE: January 5, 1900 (approx.) 23,000 v Bury, won 1-0, Division 1; April 5, 1900 (approx.) 23,000 v West Bromwich Albion, won 1-0

Final Division 1 Table

		P	W	D	L	F	A	Pts
1	LIVERPOOL	34	19	7	8	59	35	45
2	SUNDERLAND	34	15	13	6	57	26	43
3	NOTTS CO	34	18	4	12	54	46	40
4	NOTTINGHAM F	34	16	7	11	53	36	39
5	BURY	34	16	7	11	53	37	39
6	NEWCASTLE U	34	14	10	10	42	37	38
7	EVERTON	34	16	5	13	55	42	37
8	SHEFFIELD W	34	13	10	11	52	42	36
9	BLACKBURN R	34	12	9	13	39	47	33
10	BOLTON W	34	13	7	14	39	55	33
11	MANCHESTER CITY	34	13	6	15	48	58	32
12	DERBY CO	34	12	7	15	55	42	31
13	WOLVERHAMPTON W	34	9	13	12	39	55	31
14	SHEFFIELD U	34	12	7	15	35	52	31
15	ASTON VILLA	34	10	10	14	45	51	30
16	STOKE	34	11	5	18	46	57	27
17	PRESTON NE	34	9	7	18	49	75	25
18	WBA	34	7	8	19	35	62	22

Season 1901-02

Football League Division 1

DATE	OPPONENTS	SCORE	GOALSCORERS	ATTENDANCE
Sep 2	Everton	L 1-3	Meredith	20,000
Sep 7	Sunderland	L 0-1		14,000
Sep 14	SMALL HEATH	L 1-4	Scotson	18,000
Sep 21	Derby County	L 0-2		10,000
Oct 5	Notts County	L 0-2		12,000
Oct 12	BOLTON WANDERERS	W 1-0	F Williams	20,000
Oct 19	GRIMSBY TOWN	W 3-0	Meredith, Gillespie, F Williams	18,000
Oct 26	Wolves	D 0-0		8,000
Nov 2	LIVERPOOL	L 2-3	Gillespie, F Williams	22,000
Nov 9	Newcastle United	L 0-3		8,000
Nov 23	Sheffield United	L 0-5		10,000
Nov 30	NOTTINGHAM FOREST	W 3-1	Mederith, Morgan, R Jones	15,000
Dec 7	Bury	L 0-3		9,000
Dec 14	BLACKBURN ROVERS	D 1-1	Meredith	10,000
Dec 26	Sheffield Wednesday	L 1-2	R Jones	10,000
Jan 1	Bolton Wanderers	D 3-3	Meredith, Ross, Henderson	19,853
Jan 4	SUNDERLAND	L 0-3		15,000
Jan 11	Small Heath	L 0-1		12,000
Jan 13	Stoke	L 0-3		5,000
Jan 18	DERBY COUNTY	D 0-0		18,000
Feb 1	NOTTS COUNTY	W 1-0	Threlfall	20,000
Feb 15	Grimsby Town	L 2-3	Gillespie 2	4,000
Feb 17	ASTON VILLA	W 1-0	Hosie	17,000
Feb 22	WOLVES	W 3-0	Gillespie 2, McOustra	16,269
Mar 1	Liverpool	L 0-4		20,000
Mar 8	NEWCASTLE UNITED	W 2-0	Hynds 2	20,000
Mar 17	EVERTON	W 2-0	Meredith, McOustra	22,000
Mar 22	SHEFFIELD UNITED	W 4-0	Gillespie 2, Meredith, Hosie	20,000
Mar 28	SHEFFIELD WEDNESDAY	L 0-3		25,000
Mar 29	Nottingham Forest	L 1-3	Hosie	10,000
Mar 31	Aston Villa	D 2-2	Gillespie, Drummond	18,000
Apr 5	BURY	W 2-0	Gillespie, Meredith	7,000
Apr 12	Blackburn Rovers	W 4-1	Gillespie 4	3,000
Apr 19	STOKE	D 2-2	Gillespie, Drummond	12,000

FA Cup

Jan 25	Preston North End*	(Rd 1) D 1-1	Henderson	10,000
Jan 29	PRESTON NORTH END	(R) D 0-0		7,000
Feb 3	Preston North End	(2nd R) W 4-2	Smith 3, Morgan	5,000
Feb 8	NOTTINGHAM FOREST	(Rd 2) L 0-2		16,000

*Abandoned in extra-time.

League & Cup Appearances

PLAYER	LEAGUE	CUP COMPETITION FA CUP	TOTAL
Barrett	5	4	9
Bevan	2		2
Drummond	13		13
Frost	2		2
Gillespie	24		24
Henderson	5	1	6
Hillman	14		14
Holmes	6		6
Hosie	33	4	37
Hunter	5		5
Hurst	15		15
Hynds	29	4	33
Jones D	20	4	24
Jones R	9		9
McOustra	13		13
Meredith	33	4	37
Moffatt	21	2	23
Morgan	12	3	15
Orr	23	4	27
Read	4		4
Ross	7	1	8
Scotson	3	1	4
Slater	13	4	17
Smith	16	4	20
Threlfall	18	4	22
Watson	1		1
Williams C	15		15
Williams F	13		13

Goalscorers

PLAYER	LEAGUE	CUP COMPETITION FA CUP	TOTAL
Gillespie	15		15
Meredith	8		8
Hosie	3		3
Williams F	3		3
Smith		3	3
Drummond	2		2
Hynds	2		2
Jones R	2		2
McOustra	2		2
Henderson	1	1	2
Morgan	1	1	2
Ross	1		1
Scotson	1		1
Threlfall	1		1

Fact File

7 goals in the last 4 games was not enough to save City from relegation.

MANAGER: Sam Ormerod

CAPTAIN: Billy Meredith

TOP SCORER: Billy Gillespie

BIGGEST WIN: March 22, 1902 4-0 v Sheffield United, Division 1

HIGHEST ATTENDANCE: March 28, 1902 (approx.) 25,000 v Sheffield Wednesday, lost 0-3, Division 1

MAJOR TRANSFERS IN: Jack Hillman from Burnley

Final Division 1 Table

		P	W	D	L	F	A	Pts
1	SUNDERLAND	34	19	6	9	50	35	44
2	EVERTON	34	17	7	10	53	35	41
3	NEWCASTLE U	34	14	9	11	48	34	37
4	BLACKBURN R	34	15	6	13	52	48	36
5	NOTTINGHAM F	34	13	9	12	43	43	35
6	DERBY CO	34	13	9	12	39	41	35
7	BURY	34	13	8	13	44	38	34
8	ASTON VILLA	34	13	8	13	42	40	34
9	SHEFFIELD W	34	13	8	13	48	52	34
10	SHEFFIELD U	34	13	7	14	53	48	33
11	LIVERPOOL	34	10	12	12	42	38	32
12	BOLTON W	34	12	8	14	51	56	32
13	NOTTS CO	34	14	4	16	51	57	32
14	WOLVERHAMPTON W	34	13	6	15	46	57	32
15	GRIMSBY T	34	13	6	15	44	60	32
16	STOKE	34	11	9	14	45	55	31
17	SMALL HEATH	34	11	8	15	47	45	30
18	MANCHESTER CITY	34	11	6	17	42	58	28

Season 1902-03

Football League Division 2

DATE	OPPONENTS	SCORE	GOALSCORERS	ATTENDANCE
Sep 6	LINCOLN CITY	W 3-1	McOustra 2, Bevan	16,000
Sep 13	Small Heath	L 0-4		12,000
Sep 20	LEICESTER FOSSE	W 3-1	Meredith, Gillespie, o.g.	12,000
Sep 27	Chesterfield	W 1-0	Meredith	15,000
Oct 4	Burnley	D 1-1	Miller	4,000
Oct 11	PRESTON NORTH END	W 1-0	Gillespie	16,000
Oct 18	Burslem Port Vale	W 4-1	Gillespie 2, Meredith, Drummond	5,000
Oct 22	Gainsborough Trinity	W 3-0	Gillespie 2, Miller	4,000
Nov 1	Woolwich Arsenal	L 0-1		11,000
Nov 8	BURTON UNITED	W 2-0	Gillespie, McOustra	13,000
Nov 15	Bristol City	L 2-3	Turnball, Drummond	13,000
Nov 22	GLOSSOP NORTH END	W 5-2	Gillespie 3, Turnball, o.g.	8,000
Nov 24	BARNSLEY	W 3-2	Gillespie 2, Meredith	8,000
Dec 6	STOCKPORT COUNTY	W 5-0	Meredith 2, Turnball 2, Gillespie	12,000
Dec 13	Blackpool	W 3-0	Meredith, Turnball, Gillespie	5,000
Dec 20	WOOLWICH ARSENAL	W 4-1	Gillespie 3, Turnball	25,000
Dec 25	Manchester United	D 1-1	Bannister	40,000
Dec 26	Preston North End	W 2-0	Gillespie, Drummond	10,000
Dec 27	Doncaster Rovers	W 2-1	Hynds, Gillespie	30,000
Jan 1	DONCASTER ROVERS	W 4-1	Bannister 2, Meredith, Turnball	25,000
Jan 3	Lincoln City	L 0-1		6,000
Jan 17	Leicester Fosse	D 1-1	Threlfall	7,000
Jan 24	CHESTERFIELD	W 4-2	Meredith 3, Turnball	15,000
Jan 31	BURNLEY	W 6-0	Meredith 2, Gillespie 2, Threlfall, Bannister	16,000
Feb 14	BURSLEM PORT VALE	W 7-1	Bannister 2, Gillespie 2, Turnball, Meredith, McOustra	12,000
Feb 23	SMALL HEATH	W 4-0	Meredith 2, Gillespie, Threlfall	20,000
Feb 28	GAINSBOROUGH TRINITY	W 9-0	Bannister 3, Gillespie 2, Turnball 2, Meredith, Threlfall	15,000
Mar 7	Burton United	W 5-0	Bannister 2, Gillespie 2, Meredith	5,000
Mar 14	BRISTOL CITY	D 2-2	Meredith, Threlfall	20,000
Mar 21	Glossop North End	W 1-0	Bannister	7,000
Apr 4	Stockport County	W 2-0	Gillespie, Turnball	10,000
Apr 10	MANCHESTER UNITED	L 0-2		30,000
Apr 11	BLACKPOOL	W 2-0	Meredith 2	8,000
Apr 14	Barnsley	W 3-0	Meredith, Bannister, Gillespie	5,000

FA Cup

Feb 7	Preston North End	(Rd 1) L 1-3	Turnball	8,000

League & Cup Appearances

PLAYER	LEAGUE	CUP COMPETITION FA CUP	TOTAL
Bannister	21	1	22
Bevan	6	1	7
Booth	9		9
Davidson	26		26
Dearden	3		3
Drummond	14		14
Edmondson	3		3
Frost	30	1	31
Gillespie	32	1	33
Hillman	31	1	32
Holmes	11	1	12
Hosie	3		3
Hynds	31	1	32
McMahon	17		17
McOustra	32		32
Meredith	34	1	35
Miller	8		8
Moffatt	1		1
Orr	13	1	14
Slater	2		2
Threlfall	25	1	26
Turnball	22	1	23

Goalscorers

PLAYER	LEAGUE	CUP COMPETITION FA CUP	TOTAL
Gillespie	30		30
Meredith	22		22
Bannister	13		13
Turnball	12	1	13
Threlfall	5		5
McOustra	4		4
Drummond	3		3
Miller	2		2
Bevan	1		1
Hynds	1		1
Opps' o.gs.	2		2

Fact File

An amazing run from January saw the Blues win six consecutive matches scoring 35 goals and conceding only three.

MANAGER: Tom Maley

CAPTAIN: Billy Meredith

TOP SCORER: Billy Gillespie

BIGGEST WIN: February 28, 1903 9-0 v Gainsborough Trinity, Division 2

HIGHEST ATTENDANCE: April 10, 1903 (approx.) 30,000 v Manchester United, lost 0-2, Division 2

MAJOR TRANSFERS IN: Billy Lot Jones from Rushton Druids, Jimmy Bannister from Chorley, Sandy Turnball from Hurlford

Final Division 2 Table

		P	W	D	L	F	A	PTS
1	MANCHESTER CITY	34	25	4	5	95	29	54
2	SMALL HEATH	34	24	3	7	74	36	51
3	WOOLWICH ARSENAL	34	20	8	6	66	30	48
4	BRISTOL C	34	17	8	9	59	38	42
5	MANCHESTER U	34	15	8	11	53	38	38
6	CHESTERFIELD	34	14	9	11	67	40	37
7	PRESTON NE	34	13	10	11	56	40	36
8	BARNSLEY	34	13	8	13	55	51	34
9	BURSLEM PORT VALE	34	13	8	13	57	62	34
10	LINCOLN C	34	12	6	16	46	53	30
11	GLOSSOP	34	11	7	16	43	57	29
12	GAINSBOROUGH T	34	11	7	16	41	59	29
13	BURTON U	34	11	7	16	39	59	29
14	BLACKPOOL	34	9	10	15	44	59	28
15	LEICESTER FOSSE	34	10	8	16	41	65	28
16	DONCASTER R	34	9	7	18	35	72	25
17	STOCKPORT CO	34	7	6	21	38	74	20
18	BURNLEY	34	6	8	20	30	77	20

Season 1903-04

Football League Division 1

DATE	OPPONENTS	SCORE	GOALSCORERS	ATTENDANCE
Sep 5	Stoke	W 2-1	Livingstone, o.g.	16,000
Sep 12	DERBY COUNTY	W 2-1	Turnbull 2	28,000
Sep 19	WOLVES	W 4-1	Meredith, Turnbull 2, Booth	25,000
Sep 26	Notts County	W 3-0	Hynds, Meredith, Pearson	15,000
Oct 3	SHEFFIELD UNITED	L 0-1		28,000
Oct 10	Newcastle United	L 0-1		19,730
Oct 17	ASTON VILLA	W 1-0	Gillespie	30,000
Oct 24	Middlesbrough	L 0-6		14,000
Oct 31	LIVERPOOL	W 3-2	Booth, Turnbull, Gillespie	25,000
Nov 7	Bury	W 3-1	Gillespie 2, Meredith	19,371
Nov 14	BLACKBURN ROVERS	W 1-0	Meredith	20,000
Nov 21	Nottingham Forest	W 3-0	Frost, Hynds, Gillespie	12,000
Nov 28	SHEFFIELD WEDNESDAY	D 1-1	Gillespie	8,000
Dec 5	Sunderland	D 1-1	Hynds	18,000
Dec 12	WEST BROMWICH ALBION	W 6-3	Meredith 2, Gillespie 2, Turnbull, Livingstone	14,000
Dec 19	Small Heath	W 3-0	Turnbull 2, Gillespie	12,000
Dec 26	EVERTON	L 1-3	Gillespie	28,000
Dec 28	Sheffield United	L 3-5	Gillespie 2, Threlfall	35,000
Jan 1	MIDDLESBROUGH	D 1-1	Meredith	30,000
Jan 2	STOKE	D 2-2	Frost, Turnbull	16,000
Jan 9	Derby County	W 3-2	Gillespie 2, Meredith	12,000
Jan 23	NOTTS COUNTY	W 3-0	Gillespie, Booth, Frost	15,000
Feb 13	Aston Villa	W 1-0	Gillespie	16,000
Feb 27	Liverpool	D 2-2	Gillespie, Hynds	20,000
Mar 12	Blackburn Rovers	W 5-2	Meredith 2, Dennison 2, Turnbull	12,000
Mar 21	Wolves	W 6-1	Livingstone 2, Gillespie 2, Meredith, Turnbull	6,000
Mar 26	Sheffield Wednesday	L 0-1		25,000
Apr 1	NEWCASTLE UNITED	L 1-3	Turnbull	28,000
Apr 2	SUNDERLAND	W 2-1	Turnbull 2	15,000
Apr 9	West Bromwich Albion	L 1-2	Jones	14,000
Apr 11	BURY	W 3-0	Turnbull 2, Bannister	10,000
Apr 13	NOTTINGHAM FOREST	D 0-0		10,000
Apr 16	SMALL HEATH	W 4-0	Bannister 2, J Moffatt 2	15,000
Apr 25	Everton	L 0-1		12,000

FA Cup

DATE	OPPONENTS		SCORE	GOALSCORERS	ATTENDANCE
Feb 6	SUNDERLAND	(Rd 1)	W 3-2	Turnbull 2, Gillespie	23,000
Feb 20	Woolwich Arsenal	(Rd 2)	W 2-0	Turnbull, Booth	30,000
Mar 5	MIDDLESBROUGH	(Rd 3)	D 0-0		35,000
Mar 9	Middlesbrough	(R)	W 3-1	Livingstone, Gillespie, Turnbull	33,000
Mar 19	Sheffield Wednesday	(SF)	W 3-0	Turnbull 2, Gillespie	53,000
Apr 23	Bolton Wanderers	(F)	W 1-0	Meredith	61,374

League & Cup Appearances

PLAYER	LEAGUE	CUP COMPETITION	TOTAL
		FA CUP	
Ashworth	18	4	22
Bannister	7		7
Booth	24	6	30
Burgess	27	6	33
Davidson	6		6
Dearden	6		6
Dennison	1		1
Drummond	1		1
Edmondson	6	1	7
Frost	30	6	36
Gillespie	24	6	30
Hillman	28	5	33
Holmes	8	2	10
Hynds	32	6	38
Jones	1		1
Livingstone	29	6	35
Lyon	6		6
McMahon	27	6	33
McOustra	2		2
Meredith	34	6	40
Moffatt J	4		4
Norgrove	1		1
Pearson	3		3
Robinson	1		1
Slater	2		2
Threlfall	10		10
Turnbull	32	6	38
Thornley	4		4

Goalscorers

PLAYER	LEAGUE	CUP COMPETITION	TOTAL
		FA CUP	
Turnbull	16	6	22
Gillespie	18	3	21
Meredith	11	1	12
Livingstone	5	1	6
Booth	3	1	4
Hynds	4		4
Bannister	3		3
Frost	3		3
Dennison	2		2
Moffatt J	2		2
Jones	1		1
Pearson	1		1
Threlfall	1		1
Opps' o.gs.	1		1

Fact File

The third round of the Cup saw a record 30,000 crowd squeeze into Hyde Road for the match against Middlesbrough.

MANAGER: Tom Maley

CAPTAIN: Billy Meredith

TOP SCORER: Sandy Turnbull

BIGGEST WIN: March 21, 1904 6-1 v Wolverhampton Wanderers, Division 1

HIGHEST ATTENDANCE: March 19, 1904 (approx.) 53,000 v Sheffield Wednesday won 3-0, FA Cup semi-final

MAJOR TRANSFERS IN: Irvine Thornley from Glossop North End, Herbert Burgess from Glossop North End

Final Division 1 Table

		P	W	D	L	F	A	Pts
1	SHEFFIELD W	34	20	7	7	48	28	47
2	MANCHESTER CITY	34	19	6	9	71	45	44
3	EVERTON	34	19	5	10	59	32	43
4	NEWCASTLE U	34	18	6	10	58	45	42
5	ASTON VILLA	34	17	7	10	70	48	41
6	SUNDERLAND	34	17	5	12	63	49	39
7	SHEFFIELD U	34	15	8	11	62	57	38
8	WOLVERHAMPTON W	34	14	8	12	44	66	36
9	NOTTINGHAM F	34	11	9	14	57	57	31
10	MIDDLESBROUGH	34	9	12	13	46	47	30
11	SMALL HEATH	34	11	8	15	39	52	30
12	BURY	34	7	15	12	40	53	29
13	NOTTS CO	34	12	5	17	37	61	29
14	DERBY CO	34	9	10	15	58	60	28
15	BLACKBURN R	34	11	6	17	48	60	28
16	STOKE	34	10	7	17	54	57	27
17	LIVERPOOL	34	9	8	17	49	62	26
18	WBA	34	7	10	17	36	60	24

Season 1904-05

Football League Division 1

DATE	OPPONENTS	SCORE	GOALSCORERS	ATTENDANCE
Sep 3	SMALL HEATH	W 2-1	Livingstone, Booth	30,000
Sep 10	Stoke	L 0-1		12,000
Sep 17	Notts County	D 1-1	Thornley	10,000
Sep 24	SHEFFIELD UNITED	D 1-1	Thornley	23,000
Oct 1	Newcastle United	L 0-2		22,000
Oct 8	PRESTON NORTH END	W 6-1	Turnbull 2, Livingstone 2, Booth, Gillespie	23,000
Oct 15	Middlesbrough	W 1-0	Gillespie	12,000
Oct 29	Bury	W 4-2	Gillespie, Meredith, Turnbull, Booth	12,000
Nov 9	ASTON VILLA	W 2-1	Turnbull, Booth	8,000
Nov 12	Blackburn Rovers	L 1-3	Turnbull	10,000
Nov 14	WOLVES	W 5-1	Meredith, Booth 2, Livingstone, Gillespie	11,000
Nov 19	NOTTINGHAM FOREST	D 1-1	Booth	16,000
Nov 26	Sheffield Wednesday	L 1-2	Turnbull	15,000
Dec 3	SUNDERLAND	W 5-2	Turnbull 3, Gillespie, Booth	27,000
Dec 10	Woolwich Arsenal	L 0-1		16,000
Dec 17	DERBY COUNTY	W 6-0	Turnbull 4, Gillespie 2	22,000
Dec 24	Everton	D 0-0		16,000
Dec 26	Preston North End	W 1-0	Turnbull	17,000
Dec 31	Small Heath	L 1-3	Turnbull	11,000
Jan 7	STOKE	W 1-0	Meredith	12,000
Jan 14	NOTTS COUNTY	W 2-1	Turnbull, Dorsett	10,000
Jan 21	Sheffield United	W 3-0	Dorsett 2, Turnbull	15,000
Jan 28	NEWCASTLE UNITED	W 3-2	Hynds, Dorsett, o.g.	40,000
Feb 11	MIDDLESBROUGH	W 3-2	Jones, J Moffatt, Dorsett, o.g.	18,000
Feb 25	BURY	W 3-2	Bannister 2, Meredith	16,000
Mar 4	Derby County	W 1-0	Bannister	7,000
Mar 11	BLACKBURN ROVERS	W 2-1	Meredith, Turnbull	12,000
Mar 18	Nottingham Forest	L 1-2	Meredith	10,000
Apr 1	Sunderland	D 0-0		9,000
Apr 8	WOOLWICH ARSENAL	W 1-0	Meredith	18,000
Apr 15	SHEFFIELD WEDNESDAY	D 1-1	Meredith	20,000
Apr 21	EVERTON	W 2-0	Hynds, Livingstone	40,000
Apr 24	Wolves	W 3-0	Livingstone, Jones, Pearson	15,000
Apr 29	Aston Villa	L 2-3	Turnbull, Livingstone	20,000

FA Cup

Feb 4	Lincoln City	(Rd 1) W 2-1	Meredith, Turnbull	10,000
Feb 18	BOLTON WANDERERS	(Rd 2) L 1-2	Gillespie	39,000

League & Cup Appearances

PLAYER	LEAGUE	CUP COMPETITION FA CUP	TOTAL
Bannister	6		6
Booth	33	2	35
Buchan	7		7
Burgess	26	2	28
Christie	1		1
Dearden	8		8
Dorsett	9	2	11
Edmondson	2		2
Frost	32	1	33
Gillespie	16	1	17
Hillman	32	2	34
Holmes	4		4
Hynds	33	2	35
Jones	12		12
Livingstone	26		26
McMahon	31	2	33
McOustra	2		2
Meredith	33	2	35
Moffatt J	13	2	15
Norgrove	10	1	11
Pearson	3	1	4
Threlfall	1		1
Thornley	4		4
Turnbull	30	2	32

Goalscorers

PLAYER	LEAGUE	CUP COMPETITION FA CUP	TOTAL
Turnbull	19	1	20
Meredith	8	1	9
Booth	8		8
Gillespie	7	1	8
Livingstone	7		7
Dorsett	5		5
Bannister	3		3
Hynds	2		2
Jones	2		2
Thornley	2		2
Moffatt J	1		1
Pearson	1		1
Opps' o.gs.	1		1

Fact File

Meredith and Turnbull would both be suspended as a result of bribery and violent conduct charges respectively in the last game of the season against Aston Villa. A win in the game would have given City a chance of becoming champions.

MANAGER: Tom Maley
CAPTAIN: Billy Meredith
TOP SCORER: Sandy Turnbull
BIGGEST WIN: December 17, 1904 6-0 v Derby County, Division 1
HIGHEST ATTENDANCE: January 28, 1905 (approx.) 40,000 v Newcastle Utd, won 3-2, Division 1; April 21, 1905 (approx.) 40,000 v Everton, won 2-0, Division 1
MAJOR TRANSFERS IN: George Dorsett from West Bromwich Albion

Final Division 1 Table

		P	W	D	L	F	A	Pts
1	NEWCASTLE U	34	23	2	9	72	33	48
2	EVERTON	34	21	5	8	63	36	47
3	MANCHESTER CITY	34	20	6	8	66	37	46
4	ASTON VILLA	34	19	4	11	63	43	42
5	SUNDERLAND	34	16	8	10	60	44	40
6	SHEFFIELD U	34	19	2	13	64	56	40
7	SMALL HEATH	34	17	5	12	54	38	39
8	PRESTON NE	34	13	10	11	42	37	36
9	SHEFFIELD W	34	14	5	15	61	57	33
10	WOOLWICH ARSENAL	34	12	9	13	36	40	33
11	DERBY CO	34	12	8	14	37	48	32
12	STOKE	34	13	4	17	40	58	30
13	BLACKBURN R	34	11	5	18	40	51	27
14	WOLVERHAMPTON W	34	11	4	19	47	73	26
15	MIDDLESBROUGH	34	9	8	17	36	56	26
16	NOTTINGHAM F	34	9	7	18	40	61	25
17	BURY	34	10	4	20	47	67	24
18	NOTTS CO	34	5	8	21	36	69	18

Season 1905-06

Football League Division 1

DATE	OPPONENTS	SCORE	GOALSCORERS	ATTENDANCE
Sep 2	Sheffield Wednesday	L 0-1		25,000
Sep 6	Newcastle United	D 2-2	Thornley, Dorsett	22,000
Sep 9	NOTTINGHAM FOREST	W 5-0	Dorsett 2, Livingstone, Jones, Booth	16,000
Sep 16	WOLVES	W 4-0	Jones 2, Livingstone, Booth	20,000
Sep 23	Bury	W 4-2	Thornley 2, Livingstone, Dorsett	24,000
Sep 30	MIDDLESBROUGH	W 4-0	Dorsett 2, Jones, McMahon	20,000
Oct 7	Preston North End	L 0-2		10,000
Oct 21	Aston Villa	L 1-2	Livingstone	30,000
Oct 28	LIVERPOOL	L 0-1		30,000
Nov 4	Sheffield United	W 3-1	Dorsett, Thornley, Jones	8,000
Nov 11	NOTTS COUNTY	W 5-1	Thornley 2, Turnbull, Dorsett, Buchan	14,000
Nov 18	Stoke	D 0-0		8,000
Nov 25	BOLTON WANDERERS	W 3-1	Thornley, Jones, Booth	38,000
Dec 2	Woolwich Arsenal	L 0-2		15,000
Dec 9	BLACKBURN ROVERS	D 1-1	Dorsett	16,000
Dec 16	Sunderland	L 0-2		15,000
Dec 23	BIRMINGHAM	W 4-1	Turnbull 2, Livingstone, o.g.	15,000
Dec 25	Derby County	W 2-1	Dorsett, Frost	12,000
Dec 26	NEWCASTLE UNITED	L 1-4	Burgess	35,000
Dec 30	SHEFFIELD WEDNESDAY	W 2-1	Banks, Booth	16,000
Jan 1	EVERTON	W 1-0	Thornley	25,000
Jan 6	Nottingham Forest	W 1-0	Thornley	4,000
Jan 20	Wolves	W 3-2	Thornley, Livingstone, Booth	5,000
Jan 27	BURY	W 5-2	Thornley 2, Dorsett, Booth, Turnbull	16,000
Feb 10	PRESTON NORTH END	D 0-0		12,000
Mar 3	Liverpool	W 1-0	Booth	30,000
Mar 10	SHEFFIELD UNITED	L 1-2	Bannister	18,000
Mar 14	ASTON VILLA	L 1-4	Dorsett	10,000
Mar 17	Notts County	L 0-3		12,000
Mar 24	STOKE	W 2-0	Dorsett, Thornley	8,000
Mar 31	Bolton Wanderers	W 3-1	Thornley 2, Livingstone	40,000
Apr 7	WOOLWICH ARSENAL	L 1-2	Dorsett	12,000
Apr 13	DERBY COUNTY	L 1-2	Dorsett	15,000
Apr 14	Blackburn Rovers	D 1-1	Turnbull	12,000
Apr 16	Everton	W 3-0	Thornley 2, Turnbull	10,000
Apr 17	Middlesbrough	L 1-6	J Moffatt	8,000
Apr 21	SUNDERLAND	W 5-1	Thornley 3, Whittaker, Bannister	3,000
Apr 28	Birmingham	L 2-3	Burgess, Thornley	6,000

FA Cup

Jan 13	Sheffield United	(Rd 1) L 1-4	Bannister	21,352

League & Cup Appearances

PLAYER	LEAGUE	CUP COMPETITION FA CUP	TOTAL
Banks	21	1	22
Bannister	11	1	12
Booth	28	1	29
Buchan	29		29
Burgess	32	1	33
Christie	5		5
Dearden	4		4
Dorsett	34	1	35
Edmondson	27	1	28
Frost	9	1	10
Gregory	3		3
Hillman	11		11
Hynds	33	1	34
Jones	25		25
Livingstone	26	1	27
McMahon	25	1	26
McOustra	7		7
Moffatt J	3		3
Norgrove	11		11
Pearson	1		1
Steele	4		4
Thornley	36	1	37
Turnbull	26		26
Whittaker	6		6
Young	1		1

Goalscorers

PLAYER	LEAGUE	CUP COMPETITION FA CUP	TOTAL
Thornley	21		21
Dorsett	15		15
Booth	7		7
Livingstone	7		7
Jones	6		6
Turnbull	6		6
Bannister	2	1	3
Burgess	2		2
Banks	1		1
Buchan	1		1
Frost	1		1
McMahon	1		1
Moffatt J	1		1
Whittaker	1		1
Opps' o.gs.	1		1

Fact File

Frank Booth won his one and only England cap in the 1-1 draw with Ireland at Middlesbrough in February.

MANAGER: Tom Maley
CAPTAIN: Billy Meredith
TOP SCORER: Irvine Thornley
BIGGEST WIN: September 9, 1905 5-0 v Nottingham Forest, Division 1
HIGHEST ATTENDANCE: March 31, 1905 (approx.) 40,000 v Bolton Wanderers, won 3-1, Division 1
MAJOR TRANSFERS OUT: Billy Meredith to Manchester United, Billy Gillespie (retired)

Final Division 1 Table

		P	W	D	L	F	A	Pts
1	LIVERPOOL	38	23	5	10	79	46	51
2	PRESTON NE	38	17	13	8	54	39	47
3	SHEFFIELD W	38	18	8	12	63	52	44
4	NEWCASTLE U	38	18	7	13	74	48	43
5	MANCHESTER CITY	38	19	5	14	73	54	43
6	BOLTON W	38	17	7	14	81	67	41
7	BIRMINGHAM	38	17	7	14	65	59	41
8	ASTON VILLA	38	17	6	15	72	56	40
9	BLACKBURN R	38	16	8	14	54	52	40
10	STOKE	38	16	7	15	54	55	39
11	EVERTON	38	15	7	16	70	66	37
12	WOOLWICH ARSENAL	38	15	7	16	62	64	37
13	SHEFFIELD U	38	15	6	17	57	62	36
14	SUNDERLAND	38	15	5	18	61	70	35
15	DERBY CO	38	14	7	17	39	58	35
16	NOTTS CO	38	11	12	15	55	71	34
17	BURY	38	11	10	17	57	74	32
18	MIDDLESBROUGH	38	10	11	17	56	71	31
19	NOTTINGHAM F	38	13	5	20	58	79	31
20	WOLVERHAMPTON W	38	8	7	23	58	99	23

219

Season 1906-07

Football League Division 1

DATE	OPPONENTS	SCORE	GOALSCORERS	ATTENDANCE
Sep 1	WOOLWICH ARSENAL	L 1-4	Dorsett	18,000
Sep 3	Everton	L 1-9	Fisher	16,000
Sep 8	Sheffield Wednesday	L 1-3	Conlin	12,000
Sep 15	BURY	D 2-2	Jones, Thornley	20,000
Sep 22	Derby County	D 2-2	Dorsett 2	8,000
Sep 29	Middlesbrough	W 3-2	Stewart, Thornley, Fisher	22,000
Oct 6	PRESTON NORTH END	D 1-1	Thornley	25,000
Oct 13	Newcastle United	L 0-2		22,000
Oct 20	ASTON VILLA	W 4-2	Thornley 2, Stewart, Conlin	30,000
Oct 27	Liverpool	L 4-5	Thornley 2, Stewart, Jones	20,000
Nov 3	BRISTOL CITY	L 0-1		20,000
Nov 10	Notts County	D 0-0		10,000
Nov 17	SHEFFIELD UNITED	L 0-2		20,000
Nov 24	Bolton Wanderers	D 1-1	Thornley	30,000
Dec 1	MANCHESTER UNITED	W 3-0	Stewart 2, Jones	40,000
Dec 8	Stoke	L 0-3		5,000
Dec 15	BLACKBURN ROVERS	D 0-0		12,000
Dec 22	Sunderland	D 1-1	Thornley	12,000
Dec 25	BIRMINGHAM	W 1-0	Dorsett	24,000
Dec 26	EVERTON	W 3-1	Steele, Thornley, Jones	25,000
Dec 29	Woolwich Arsenal	L 1-4	Thornley	15,000
Jan 2	MIDDLESBROUGH	W 3-1	Jones 2, Thornley	8,000
Jan 5	SHEFFIELD WEDNESDAY	L 0-1		25,000
Jan 19	Bury	L 1-3	Grieve	16,000
Jan 26	DERBY COUNTY	D 2-2	Thornley, Jones	20,000
Feb 9	Preston North End	W 3-1	Dorsett, Grieve, Jones	10,000
Feb 16	NEWCASTLE UNITED	D 1-1	Jones	35,000
Feb 23	Aston Villa	L 1-4	Stewart	15,000
Mar 2	LIVERPOOL	W 1-0	Grieve	20,000
Mar 9	Bristol City	L 0-2		12,000
Mar 16	NOTTS COUNTY	W 2-1	Grieve, Ross	18,000
Mar 23	Sheffield United	W 4-1	Grieve 2, Dorsett	15,000
Mar 29	Birmingham	L 0-4		10,000
Mar 30	BOLTON WANDERERS	D 1-1	Jones	30,000
Apr 6	Manchester United	D 1-1	Dorsett	35,000
Apr 13	STOKE	D 2-2	Stewart, Jones	12,000
Apr 20	Blackburn Rovers	L 0-4		5,000
Apr 27	SUNDERLAND	L 2-3	Stewart, Eyres	15,000

FA Cup

Jan 12	Blackburn Rovers	(Rd 1)	D 2-2	Dorsett, Thornley	20,000
Jan 16	BLACKBURN ROVERS	(R)	L 0-1		30,000

League & Cup Appearances

PLAYER	LEAGUE	CUP COMPETITION FA CUP	TOTAL
Baldwin	1		1
Banks	4		4
Blair	9		9
Blew	1		1
Buchan	28	2	30
Christie	4		4
Conlin	35	2	37
Davies	5		5
Dorsett	32	2	34
Eadie	31	2	33
Eyres	1		1
Farell	3		3
Fisher	5		5
Grieve	19		19
Hall	11		11
Hamblett	1		1
Hill	21	2	23
Jones	27	2	29
Kelso	24		24
McOustra	9		9
Norgrove	27	2	29
Rankin	2		2
Ross	6		6
Smith	22	2	24
Steele	23	2	25
Stewart	36	2	38
Thornley	29	2	31
Wilkinson	2		2

Goalscorers

PLAYER	LEAGUE	CUP COMPETITION FA CUP	TOTAL
Thornley	13	1	14
Jones	11		11
Dorsett	8	1	9
Stewart	8		8
Grieve	6		6
Conlin	2		2
Fisher	2		2
Eyres	1		1
Ross	1		1
Steele	1		1

Fact File

The first City-United derby took place in December. City emerged as 4-0 victors.

MANAGER: Harry Newbould
CAPTAIN: Irvine Thornley
TOP SCORER: Irvine Thornley
BIGGEST WIN: May 23, 1907 4-1 v Sheffield United, Division 1
HIGHEST ATTENDANCE: December 1, 1906 (approx.) 40,000 v Manchester Utd, won 3-0, Division 1
MAJOR TRANSFERS IN: David Ross from Norwich City

Final Division 1 Table

		P	W	D	L	F	A	Pts
1	NEWCASTLE U	38	22	7	9	74	46	51
2	BRISTOL C	38	20	8	10	66	47	48
3	EVERTON	38	20	5	13	70	46	45
4	SHEFFIELD U	38	17	11	10	57	55	45
5	ASTON VILLA	38	19	6	13	78	52	44
6	BOLTON W	38	18	8	12	59	47	44
7	WOOLWICH ARSENAL	38	20	4	14	66	59	44
8	MANCHESTER U	38	17	8	13	53	56	42
9	BIRMINGHAM	38	15	8	15	52	52	38
10	SUNDERLAND	38	14	9	15	65	66	37
11	MIDDLESBROUGH	38	15	6	17	56	63	36
12	BLACKBURN R	38	14	7	17	56	59	35
13	SHEFFIELD W	38	12	11	15	49	60	35
14	PRESTON NE	38	14	7	17	44	57	35
15	LIVERPOOL	38	13	7	18	64	65	33
16	BURY	38	13	6	19	58	68	32
17	MANCHESTER CITY	38	10	12	16	53	77	32
18	NOTTS CO	38	8	15	15	46	50	31
19	DERBY CO	38	9	9	20	41	59	27
20	STOKE	38	8	10	20	41	64	26

Season 1907-08

Football League Division 1

DATE	OPPONENTS	SCORE	GOALSCORERS	ATTENDANCE
Sep 2	Sunderland	W 5-2	Grieve 3, Stewart, Conlin	20,000
Sep 7	Everton	D 3-3	Thornley 3	30,000
Sep 14	SUNDERLAND	D 0-0		30,000
Sep 21	Woolwich Arsenal	L 1-2	Thornley	12,000
Sep 28	SHEFFIELD WEDNESDAY	W 3-2	Ross 2, Thornley	30,000
Oct 5	Bristol City	L 1-2	Thornley	12,000
Oct 12	NOTTS COUNTY	W 2-1	Grieve 2	10,000
Oct 19	NEWCASTLE UNITED	W 1-0	Thornley	28,000
Oct 26	Preston North End	W 4-2	Dorsett, Grieve, Thornley, Conlin	14,000
Nov 2	BURY	D 2-2	Jones, Wood	30,000
Nov 9	Aston Villa	D 2-2	Thornley 2	20,000
Nov 16	LIVERPOOL	D 1-1	Dorsett	25,000
Nov 23	Middlesbrough	L 0-2		10,000
Dec 7	Chelsea	D 2-2	Buchan, Jones	40,000
Dec 14	NOTTINGHAM FOREST	W 4-2	Wood 2, Eadie, Thornley	18,000
Dec 21	Manchester United	L 1-3	Eadie	35,000
Dec 25	Birmingham	L 1-2	Dorsett	20,000
Dec 26	BOLTON WANDERERS	W 1-0	Grieve	35,000
Dec 28	BLACKBURN ROVERS	W 2-0	Dorsett, Thornley	22,000
Jan 1	Bolton Wanderers	L 0-2		26,000
Jan 4	EVERTON	W 4-2	Grieve 2, Ross, Conlin	9,000
Jan 18	WOOLWICH ARSENAL	W 4-0	Eadie, Wood, Grieve, Jones	25,000
Jan 25	Sheffield Wednesday	L 1-5	Dorsett	11,000
Feb 8	Notts County	L 0-1		8,000
Feb 15	Newcastle United	D 1-1	Conlin	25,000
Feb 29	Bury	D 0-0		10,000
Mar 7	ASTON VILLA	W 3-2	Dorsett 3	25,000
Mar 11	SHEFFIELD UNITED	L 0-2		18,000
Mar 14	Liverpool	W 1-0	Dorsett	18,000
Mar 21	MIDDLESBROUGH	W 2-1	Webb, Thornley	35,000
Mar 28	Sheffield United	W 2-1	Thornley, Conlin	12,000
Apr 4	CHELSEA	L 0-3		25,000
Apr 6	PRESTON NORTH END	W 5-0	Buchan 2, Webb 2, Wilkinson	10,000
Apr 11	Nottingham Forest	L 1-3	Dorsett	10,000
Apr 17	BIRMINGHAM	W 2-1	Jones, Conlin	27,000
Apr 18	MANCHESTER UNITED	D 0-0		40,000
Apr 21	BRISTOL CITY	D 0-0		2,500
Apr 25	Blackburn Rovers	D 0-0		10,000

FA Cup

DATE	OPPONENTS		SCORE	GOALSCORERS	ATTENDANCE
Jan 11	Glossop North End	(Rd 1) D	0-0		6,500
Jan 15	GLOSSOP NORTH END	(R) W	6-0	Buchan, Wood, Dorsett, Grieve, Jones, Conlin	20,000
Feb 1	NEW BROMPTON	(Rd 2) D	1-1	Jones	7,000
Feb 5	New Brompton	(R) W	2-1	Buchan, Wood	12,000
Feb 22	FULHAM	(Rd 3) D	1-1	Blair	25,000
Feb 26	Fulham	(R) L	1-3	Wood	37,000

League & Cup Appearances

PLAYER	LEAGUE	CUP COMPETITION FA CUP	TOTAL
Baldwin	1		1
Bannister	1		1
Blair	34	5	39
Buchan	27	6	33
Buckley	7		7
Callaghan	2		2
Conlin	37	6	43
Dorsett	34	6	40
Eadie	29	6	35
Grieve	17	2	19
Hill	17		17
Holford	2		2
Jackson	21	6	27
Jones	24	5	29
Kelso	25	6	31
Norgrove	14		14
Ross	10	1	11
Smith	38	6	44
Steele	3		3
Stewart	10		10
Thornley	31	6	37
Webb	11		11
Wilkinson	1		1
Wood	22	5	27

Goalscorers

PLAYER	LEAGUE	CUP COMPETITION FA CUP	TOTAL
Thornley	14		14
Dorsett	10	1	11
Grieve	10	1	11
Conlin	6	1	7
Wood	4	3	7
Jones	4	2	6
Buchan	3	2	5
Eadie	3		3
Ross	3		3
Webb	3		3
Blair		1	1
Stewart	1		1
Wilkinson	1		1

Fact File

Hyde Road had a record average attendance for the season of 23,255.

MANAGER: Harry Newbould

CAPTAIN: Irvine Thornley

TOP SCORER: Irvine Thornley

BIGGEST WIN: January 15, 1908 6-0 v Glossop, FA Cup Round 1 Replay

HIGHEST ATTENDANCE: December 7, 1907 (approx.) 40,000 v Chelsea, drew 2-2, Division 1; April 18, 1908 (approx.) 40,000 v Manchester Utd, drew 0-0, Division 1

MAJOR TRANSFERS IN: Tom Holford from Stoke City, Walter Smith from Leicester Fosse

Final Division 1 Table

		P	W	D	L	F	A	Pts
1	MANCHESTER U	38	23	6	9	81	48	52
2	ASTON VILLA	38	17	9	12	77	59	43
3	MANCHESTER CITY	38	16	11	11	62	54	43
4	NEWCASTLE U	38	15	12	11	65	54	42
5	SHEFFIELD W	38	19	4	15	73	64	42
6	MIDDLESBROUGH	38	17	7	14	54	45	41
7	BURY	38	14	11	13	58	61	39
8	LIVERPOOL	38	16	6	16	68	61	38
9	NOTTINGHAM F	38	13	11	14	59	62	37
10	BRISTOL C	38	12	12	14	58	61	36
11	EVERTON	38	15	6	17	58	64	36
12	PRESTON NE	38	12	12	14	47	53	36
13	CHELSEA	38	14	8	16	53	62	36
14	BLACKBURN R	38	12	12	14	51	63	36
15	WOOLWICH ARSENAL	38	12	12	14	51	63	36
16	SUNDERLAND	38	16	3	19	78	75	35
17	SHEFFIELD U	38	12	11	15	52	58	35
18	NOTTS CO	38	13	8	17	39	51	34
19	BOLTON W	38	14	5	19	52	58	33
20	BIRMINGHAM	38	9	12	17	40	60	30

Season 1908-09

Football League Division 1

DATE	OPPONENTS	SCORE	GOALSCORERS	ATTENDANCE
Sep 1	SUNDERLAND	W 1-0	Eadie	25,000
Sep 5	BLACKBURN ROVERS	D 3-3	Thornley 2, Jones	30,000
Sep 12	Bradford City	D 0-0		30,000
Sep 19	MANCHESTER UNITED	L 1-2	Thornley	40,000
Sep 26	Everton	L 3-6	Thornley 3	20,000
Oct 3	LEICESTER FOSSE	W 5-2	Grieve 2, Ross 2, Dorsett	15,000
Oct 10	Woolwich Arsenal	L 0-3		10,000
Oct 17	NOTTS COUNTY	W 1-0	Thornley	20,000
Oct 24	Newcastle United	L 0-2		25,000
Oct 31	BRISTOL CITY	W 5-1	Thornley 2, Buchan, Dorsett, Wood	20,000
Nov 7	Preston North End	L 0-3		10,000
Nov 14	MIDDLESBROUGH	D 0-0		18,000
Nov 21	Sheffield Wednesday	L 1-3	Thornley	11,000
Nov 28	Liverpool	W 3-1	Dorsett, Conlin, Jones	15,000
Dec 5	BURY	W 6-1	Thornley 3, Dorsett 2, Stewart	30,000
Dec 12	Sheffield United	L 0-4		12,000
Dec 19	ASTON VILLA	W 2-0	Dorsett, Holford	18,000
Dec 25	CHELSEA	L 1-2	Dorsett	25,000
Dec 26	Chelsea	W 2-1	Jones, Ross	40,000
Dec 28	Nottingham Forest	W 2-0	Holford, Ross	10,000
Jan 2	Blackburn Rovers	L 2-3	Wood, Conlin	12,000
Jan 9	BRADFORD CITY	W 4-3	Holford 3, Conlin	10,000
Jan 23	Manchester United	L 1-3	Conlin	40,000
Jan 30	EVERTON	W 4-0	Holford 3, Wilkinson	30,000
Feb 13	WOOLWICH ARSENAL	D 2-2	Buchan, Holford	20,000
Feb 20	Notts County	L 1-5	Dorsett	4,000
Feb 27	NEWCASTLE UNITED	L 0-2		30,000
Mar 11	Leicester Fosse	L 1-3	Thornley	8,000
Mar 13	PRESTON NORTH END	W 4-1	Thornley 2, Yuill, Jones	12,000
Mar 20	Middlesbrough	L 0-3		10,000
Mar 27	SHEFFIELD WEDNESDAY	W 4-0	Holford 3, Jones	12,000
Apr 3	LIVERPOOL	W 4-0	Buchan, Jones, Ross, Dorsett	15,000
Apr 9	Sunderland	L 0-2		15,000
Apr 10	Bury	L 0-1		16,000
Apr 13	NOTTINGHAM FOREST	W 2-1	Thornley, Conlin	3,000
Apr 17	SHEFFIELD UNITED	L 1-3	Thornley	10,000
Apr 24	Aston Villa	L 1-2	Buchan	15,000
Apr 28	Bristol City	L 0-1		8,000

FA Cup

Jan 16	TOTTENHAM HOTSPUR	(Rd 1) L 3-4	Holford 3	20,000	

League & Cup Appearances

PLAYER	LEAGUE	CUP COMPETITION FA CUP	TOTAL
Blair	31		31
Bottomley	1		1
Broomfield	4		4
Brown	4		4
Buchan	38	1	39
Buckley	4		4
Burgess	26		26
Conlin	27	1	28
Dorsett	22	1	23
Eadie	10	1	11
Grieve	8		8
Hendren	2		2
Hitchcock	1		1
Holford	26	1	27
Jackson	22		22
Jones	29	1	30
Kelso	21	1	22
Mansfield	1		1
Norgrove	7	1	8
Ramsay	1		1
Ross	22	1	23
Smith	34	1	35
Stewart	8	1	9
Thornley	32		32
Webb	11		11
Wilkinson	17		17
Wood	6		6
Yuill	3		3

Goalscorers

PLAYER	LEAGUE	CUP COMPETITION FA CUP	TOTAL
Thornley	18		18
Holford	12	3	15
Dorsett	9		9
Jones	6		6
Conlin	5		5
Ross	5		5
Buchan	4		4
Grieve	2		2
Wood	2		2
Eadie	1		1
Stewart	1		1
Wilkinson	1		1
Yuill	1		1

Fact File

City needed a point from the last game of the season against Bristol City to avoid relegation. They were sunk by a deflected shot two minutes from time.

MANAGER: Harry Newbould

CAPTAIN: Billy Lot Jones

TOP SCORER: Irvine Thornley

BIGGEST WIN: December 5, 1908 6-1 v Bury, Division 1

HIGHEST ATTENDANCE: September 19, 1908 (approx.) 40,000 v Manchester Utd, lost 1-2, Division 1; January 23, 1909 (approx.) 40,000, v Manchester United lost 1-3 Division 1

MAJOR TRANSFERS IN: George Wynn from Wrexham

Final Division 1 Table

		P	W	D	L	F	A	Pts
1	NEWCASTLE U	38	24	5	9	65	41	53
2	EVERTON	38	18	10	10	82	57	46
3	SUNDERLAND	38	21	2	15	78	63	44
4	BLACKBURN R	38	14	13	11	61	50	41
5	SHEFFIELD W	38	17	6	15	67	61	40
6	WOOLWICH ARSENAL	38	14	10	14	52	49	38
7	ASTON VILLA	38	14	10	14	58	56	38
8	BRISTOL C	38	13	12	13	45	58	38
9	MIDDLESBROUGH	38	14	9	15	59	53	37
10	PRESTON NE	38	13	11	14	48	44	37
11	CHELSEA	38	14	9	15	56	61	37
12	SHEFFIELD U	38	14	9	15	51	59	37
13	MANCHESTER U	38	15	7	16	58	68	37
14	NOTTINGHAM F	38	14	8	16	66	57	36
15	NOTTS CO	38	14	8	16	51	48	36
16	LIVERPOOL	38	15	6	17	57	65	36
17	BURY	38	14	8	16	63	77	36
18	BRADFORD C	38	12	10	16	47	47	34
19	MANCHESTER CITY	38	15	4	19	67	69	34
20	LEICESTER FOSSE	38	8	9	21	54	102	25

Season 1909-10

Football League Division 2

DATE	OPPONENTS	SCORE	GOALSCORERS	ATTENDANCE
Sep 2	BLACKPOOL	L 1-2	Thornley	10,000
Sep 4	Leicester Fosse	W 3-1	Stewart, Ross, Conlin	9,000
Sep 11	LINCOLN CITY	W 6-2	Jones 2, Thornley 2, Dorsett, Conlin	8,000
Sep 18	Clapton Orient	L 2-3	Dorsett, Ross	15,000
Sep 25	Blackpool	D 0-0		8,000
Oct 2	Hull City	W 2-1	Jones, Dorsett	12,000
Oct 9	DERBY COUNTY	W 2-1	Holford, Conlin	20,000
Oct 16	Stockport County	W 2-1	Eadie, Conlin	12,000
Oct 23	GLOSSOP NORTH END	D 3-3	Ross 2, Holford	14,000
Oct 27	Gainsborough Town	W 3-1	Jones 3	6,000
Oct 30	Birmingham	D 1-1	Thornley	18,000
Nov 6	WEST BROMWICH ALBION	W 3-2	Holford 2, Thornley	24,000
Nov 13	Oldham Athletic	L 0-1		22,000
Nov 27	Fulham	D 1-1	Thornley	12,000
Dec 4	BURNLEY	W 4-0	Jones 2, Thornley, Dorsett	12,000
Dec 11	Leeds City	W 3-1	Thornley 2, Ross	3,000
Dec 18	WOLVES	W 6-0	Thornley 3, Dorsett 2, Ross	20,000
Dec 25	Bradford City	L 0-2		18,000
Dec 27	GRIMSBY TOWN	W 2-0	Wynn, Holford	20,000
Jan 1	BRADFORD CITY	W 3-1	Wynn, Dorsett 2	25,000
Jan 8	LEICESTER CITY	W 2-0	Jones, Holford	25,000
Jan 22	Lincoln City	W 2-0	Wynn, Conlin	9,000
Feb 12	HULL CITY	W 3-0	Conlin, Wynn, Holford	30,000
Feb 26	STOCKPORT COUNTY	W 2-1	Wynn 2	16,000
Mar 9	BARNSLEY	D 0-0		15,000
Mar 12	BIRMINGHAM	W 3-0	Eadie, Jones, Conlin	15,000
Mar 16	Derby County	L 1-3	Dorsett	12,000
Mar 19	West Bromwich Albion	D 0-0		10,000
Mar 25	Grimsby Town	W 1-0	Jones	8,000
Mar 26	OLDHAM ATHLETIC	L 0-2		40,000
Mar 28	GAINSBOROUGH TOWN	W 3-1	Dorsett, Holford, Jones	15,000
Apr 2	Barnsley	D 1-1	Dorsett	10,000
Apr 6	Glossop North End	W 3-0	Conlin 2, Gould	5,000
Apr 9	FULHAM	W 3-1	Holford 2, Wynn	16,000
Apr 13	CLAPTON ORIENT	W 2-1	Dorsett, Wynn	8,000
Apr 16	Burnley	D 3-3	Gould, Holford, Wynn	7,000
Apr 23	LEEDS CITY	W 3-0	Dorsett, Wynn, Conlin	16,000
Apr 30	Wolves	L 2-3	Holford, Conlin	10,000

FA Cup

Jan 15	Workington	(Rd 1) W 2-1	Wynn 2	5,233
Feb 5	Southampton	(Rd 2) W 5-0	Dorsett, Stewart, Jones, Conlin, Holford	15,965
Feb 19	Aston Villa	(Rd 3) W 2-1	Stewart, Jones	45,000
Mar 5	Swindon Town	(Rd 4) L 0-2		14,429

League & Cup Appearances

PLAYER	LEAGUE	CUP COMPETITION FA CUP	TOTAL
Blair	2		2
Bottomley	14	4	18
Brown	2		2
Buchan	20		20
Burgess	4		4
Chapelow	7		7
Conlin	35	4	39
Coupe	1		1
Davies	1		1
Dorsett	38	4	42
Eadie	23	4	27
Furr	3		3
Gould	6		6
Holford	30	4	34
Jackson	35	4	39
James	2		2
Jones	37	4	41
Kelso	28	4	32
Lyall	33	4	37
Norgrove	8		8
Ross	11		11
Smith	3		3
Stewart	22	4	26
Swann	1		1
Thronley	23		23
Wilkinson	9		9
Wynn	20	4	24

Goalscorers

PLAYER	LEAGUE	CUP COMPETITION FA CUP	TOTAL
Dorsett	13	1	14
Jones	12	2	14
Holford	12	1	13
Conlin	11	1	12
Thronley	12		12
Wynn	10	2	12
Ross	6		6
Eadie	2		2
Gould	2		2
Stewart	1	2	3

Fact File

City won all except one of their games in December and January this season.

MANAGER: Harry Newbould
CAPTAIN: Billy Lot Jones
TOP SCORERS: George Dorsett and Billy Lot Jones
BIGGEST WIN: December 18, 1909 6-0 v Wolverhampton Wanderers, Division 1
HIGHEST ATTENDANCE: March 26, 1910 (approx.) 40,000 v Oldham Athletic, lost 0-2, Division 1
MAJOR TRANSFERS IN: Jack Lyall from Sheffield Wednesday

Final Division 2 Table

		P	W	D	L	F	A	Pts
1	MANCHESTER CITY	38	23	8	7	81	40	54
2	OLDHAM ATH	38	23	7	8	79	39	53
3	HULL C	38	23	7	8	80	46	53
4	DERBY CO	38	22	9	7	72	47	53
5	LEICESTER FOSSE	38	20	4	14	79	58	44
6	GLOSSOP	38	18	7	13	64	57	43
7	FULHAM	38	14	13	11	51	43	41
8	WOLVERHAMPTON W	38	17	6	15	64	63	40
9	BARNSLEY	38	16	7	15	62	59	39
10	BRADFORD PA	38	17	4	17	64	59	38
11	WBA	38	16	5	17	58	56	37
12	BLACKPOOL	38	14	8	16	50	52	36
13	STOCKPORT CO	38	13	8	17	50	47	34
14	BURNLEY	38	14	6	18	62	61	34
15	LINCOLN C	38	10	11	17	42	69	31
16	CLAPTON ORIENT	38	12	6	20	37	60	30
17	LEEDS C	38	10	7	21	46	80	27
18	GAINSBOROUGH T	38	10	6	22	33	75	26
19	GRIMSBY T	38	9	6	23	50	77	24
20	BIRMINGHAM	38	8	7	23	42	78	23

Season 1910-11

Football League Division 1

DATE	OPPONENTS	SCORE	GOALSCORERS	ATTENDANCE
Sep 1	BURY	W 5-1	Wynn 3, Holford, Conlin	18,000
Sep 3	Preston North End	D 1-1	Holford	10,000
Sep 10	NOTTS COUNTY	L 0-1		30,000
Sep 17	Manchester United	L 1-2	Jones	60,000
Sep 24	LIVERPOOL	L 1-2	J Dorsett	40,000
Oct 1	Bury	L 2-5	G Dorsett, Wynn	15,000
Oct 8	SHEFFIELD UNITED	L 0-4		20,000
Oct 15	Aston Villa	L 1-2	Wall	20,000
Oct 22	SUNDERLAND	D 3-3	Norgrove, G Dorsett, Thornley	25,000
Oct 29	Woolwich Arsenal	W 1-0	J Dorsett	10,000
Nov 5	BRADFORD CITY	L 1-3	J Dorsett	12,000
Nov 12	Blackburn Rovers	L 0-2		10,000
Nov 19	NOTTINGHAM FOREST	W 1-0	Conlin	20,000
Nov 26	OLDHAM ATHLETIC	W 2-0	Thornley, Conlin	25,000
Dec 3	Everton	L 0-1		8,000
Dec 10	SHEFFIELD WEDNESDAY	L 1-2	Thornley	20,000
Dec 17	Bristol City	L 1-2	J Smith	6,000
Dec 24	NEWCASTLE UNITED	W 2-0	Wynn, Conlin	25,000
Dec 26	Middlebrough	D 0-0		30,000
Dec 27	Tottenham Hotspur	D 1-1	J Smith	25,000
Dec 31	PRESTON NORTH END	L 0-2		30,000
Jan 3	TOTTENHAM HOTSPUR	W 2-1	Ross, Jones	20,000
Jan 7	Notts County	W 1-0	Ross	10,000
Jan 21	MANCHESTER UNITED	D 1-1	Jones	40,000
Jan 28	Liverpool	D 1-1	J Smith	16,000
Feb 11	Sheffield United	D 2-2	J Smith, Ross	12,000
Feb 18	ASTON VILLA	D 1-1	Jones	25,000
Feb 25	Sunderland	L 0-4		10,000
Mar 4	WOOLWICH ARSENAL	D 1-1	Thornley	20,000
Mar 14	Bradford City	L 0-1		7,000
Mar 18	BLACKBURN ROVERS	D 0-0		35,000
Mar 25	Nottingham Forest	D 0-0		7,000
Apr 1	Oldham Athletic	D 1-1	J Smith	25,000
Apr 8	EVERTON	W 2-1	Wynn, Thornley	25,000
Apr 14	MIDDLESBROUGH	W 2-1	Thornley, Jones	35,000
Apr 15	Sheffield Wednesday	L 1-4	Jones	9,000
Apr 22	BRISTOL CITY	L 1-2	Wynn	30,000
Apr 29	Newcastle United	D 3-3	Wynn 2, Ross	11,000

FA Cup

DATE	OPPONENTS		SCORE	GOALSCORERS	ATTENDANCE
Jan 14	Stoke	(Rd 1)	W 2-1	J Smith, Jones	29,000
Feb 4	Wolves	(Rd 2)	L 0-1		25,000

League & Cup Appearances

PLAYER	LEAGUE	CUP COMPETITION FA CUP	TOTAL
Bottomley	19		19
Brooks	1		1
Brown	2		2
Buchan	6		6
Burgess	2		2
Chaplin	15	2	17
Codling	5		5
Conlin	27	1	28
Dorsett G	23	2	25
Dorsett J	26	1	27
Eadie	29	2	31
Gould	2		2
Holford	29	2	31
Humphreys R	3		3
Jackson	13		13
Jones	34	2	36
Kelso	31	2	33
Lyall	7		7
Nelson	8		8
Norgrove	13		13
Ross	10	2	12
Salt	1		1
Smith J	14	2	16
Smith W	31	2	33
Stewart	17	2	19
Thornley	18		18
Wall	10		10
Wilkinson	2		2
Wynn	20		20

Goalscorers

PLAYER	LEAGUE	CUP COMPETITION FA CUP	TOTAL
Wynn	9		9
Jones	6	1	7
Thornley	6		6
Smith J	5	1	6
Conlin	4		4
Ross	4		4
Dorsett J	3		3
Dorsett G	2		2
Holford	2		2
Norgrove	1		1
Wall	1		1

Fact File

Billy Lot Jones and George Wynn were regular members of the Welsh side in 1910-11.

MANAGER: Harry Newbould

CAPTAIN: Billy Lot Jones

TOP SCORER: George Wynn

BIGGEST WIN: September 1, 1910 5-1 v Bury, Division 1

HIGHEST ATTENDANCE: September 17, 1910 (approx.) 60,000 v Manchester United, lost 1-2, Division 1

MAJOR TRANSFERS IN: Joe Dorsett from West Bromwich Albion

Final Division 1 Table

		P	W	D	L	F	A	Pts
1	MANCHESTER U	38	22	8	8	72	40	52
2	ASTON VILLA	38	22	7	9	69	41	51
3	SUNDERLAND	38	15	15	8	67	48	45
4	EVERTON	38	19	7	12	50	36	45
5	BRADFORD C	38	20	5	13	51	42	45
6	SHEFFIELD W	38	17	8	13	47	48	42
7	OLDHAM ATH	38	16	9	13	44	41	41
8	NEWCASTLE U	38	15	10	13	61	43	40
9	SHEFFIELD U	38	15	8	15	49	43	38
10	WOOLWICH ARSENAL	38	13	12	13	41	49	38
11	NOTTS CO	38	14	10	14	37	45	38
12	BLACKBURN R	38	13	11	14	62	54	37
13	LIVERPOOL	38	15	7	16	53	53	37
14	PRESTON NE	38	12	11	15	40	49	35
15	TOTTENHAM H	38	13	6	19	52	63	32
16	MIDDLESBROUGH	38	11	10	17	49	63	32
17	MANCHESTER CITY	38	9	13	16	43	58	31
18	BURY	38	9	11	18	43	71	29
19	BRISTOL C	38	11	5	22	43	66	27
20	NOTTINGHAM F	38	9	7	22	55	75	25

Season 1911-12

Football League Division 1

DATE	OPPONENTS	SCORE	GOALSCORERS	ATTENDANCE
Sep 2	MANCHESTER UNITED	D 0-0		25,000
Sep 9	Liverpool	D 2-2	Kelso 2	15,000
Sep 16	ASTON VILLA	L 2-6	Holford, Jones	30,000
Sep 23	Newcastle United	L 0-1		10,000
Sep 30	SHEFFIELD UNITED	D 0-0		25,000
Oct 7	Oldham Athletic	L 1-4	Thornley	15,000
Oct 14	BOLTON WANDERERS	W 3-1	Wall, Wynn, Keary	25,000
Oct 21	Bradford City	L 1-4	Thornley	12,000
Oct 28	WOOLWICH ARSENAL	D 3-3	Wynn 2, Thornley	25,000
Nov 4	Preston North End	L 1-2	Kelso	10,000
Nov 11	Everton	L 0-1		15,000
Nov 18	WEST BROMWICH ALBION	L 0-2		12,000
Nov 25	Sunderland	D 1-1	J Dorsett	4,000
Dec 2	BLACKBURN ROVERS	W 3-0	Wynn 2, J Dorsett	40,000
Dec 9	Sheffield Wednesday	L 0-3		12,000
Dec 16	BURY	W 2-0	Wynn, Thornley	14,000
Dec 23	Middlesbrough	L 1-3	J Dorsett	10,000
Dec 25	Notts County	W 1-0	Young	15,000
Dec 26	NOTTS COUNTY	W 4-0	Fletcher, Wynn, Young, Jones	35,000
Dec 30	Manchester United	D 0-0		41,743
Jan 6	LIVERPOOL	L 2-3	Wynn 2	10,000
Jan 20	Aston Villa	L 1-3	J Dorsett	10,000
Jan 27	NEWCASTLE UNITED	D 1-1	Wynn	30,000
Feb 10	OLDHAM ATHLETIC	L 1-3	J Smith	25,000
Feb 17	Bolton Wanderers	L 1-2	Brooks	20,000
Feb 26	Sheffield United	L 2-6	Thornley 2	5,000
Mar 2	Woolwich Arsenal	L 0-2		12,000
Mar 9	PRESTON NORTH END	D 0-0		13,000
Mar 16	EVERTON	W 4-0	Holford 4	25,000
Mar 23	West Bromwich Albion	D 1-1	Bottomley	8,000
Mar 28	BRADFORD CITY	W 4-0	Holford 2, Wynn, Jones	10,000
Mar 30	SUNDERLAND	W 2-0	Wynn, Holford	20,000
Apr 5	TOTTENHAM HOTSPUR	W 2-1	Jones, J Dorsett	10,000
Apr 6	Blackburn Rovers	L 0-2		14,000
Apr 8	Tottenham Hotspur	W 2-0	Jones, J Dorsett	15,000
Apr 13	SHEFFIELD WEDNESDAY	W 4-0	Wynn 3, Jones	30,000
Apr 20	Bury	W 2-1	Wynn 2	18,000
Apr 27	MIDDLESBROUGH	W 2-0	Jones, J Dorsett	20,000

FA Cup

Jan 13	Preston North End	(Rd 1)	W 1-0	Wynn	15,000
Feb 3	OLDHAM ATHLETIC	(Rd 2)	L 0-1		45,000

League & Cup Appearances

PLAYER	LEAGUE	CUP COMPETITION FA CUP	TOTAL
Beeby	11		11
Bentley	1		1
Booth	4		4
Bottomley	19		19
Brooks	2		2
Davies	6		6
Dorsett G	1		1
Dorsett J	33	2	35
Eadie	26	2	28
Eden	1		1
Fletcher	35	2	37
Goodchild	15	2	17
Henry	25	2	27
Hoad	37	2	39
Holford	32	2	34
Jones	24	2	26
Keary	8		8
Kelly	7		7
Kelso	9		9
Lawrence	19	2	21
Norgrove	3		3
Ross	2		2
Smith J	4		4
Smith W	12		12
Thornley	18		18
Wall	20		20
Wynn	31	2	33
Young	13	2	15

Goalscorers

PLAYER	LEAGUE	CUP COMPETITION FA CUP	TOTAL
Wynn	17	1	18
Holford	8		8
Dorsett J	7		7
Jones	7		7
Thornley	6		6
Kelso	3		3
Young	2		2
Bottomley	1		1
Brooks	1		1
Fletcher	1		1
Keary	1		1
Smith J	1		1
Wall	1		1

Fact File

Goalkeeper Jim Goodchild saved a penalty on his debut against Preston in the FA Cup.

MANAGER: Harry Newbould

CAPTAIN: Billy Lot Jones

TOP SCORER: George Wynn

BIGGEST WIN: December 26, 1911 4-0 v Notts County, Division 1; March 16, 1912 4-0 v Everton, Division 1; March 28, 1912 4-0 v Bradford City, Division 1; April 13, 1912 4-0 v Sheffield Wednedsay, Division 1

HIGHEST ATTENDANCE: December 2, 1911 (approx.) 40,000 v Blackburn Rovers, won 3-0, Division 1

MAJOR TRANSFERS IN: Eli Fletcher from Crewe Alexandra

Final Division 1 Table

		P	W	D	L	F	A	Pts
1	BLACKBURN R	38	20	9	9	60	43	49
2	EVERTON	38	20	6	12	46	42	46
3	NEWCASTLE U	38	18	8	12	64	50	44
4	BOLTON W	38	20	3	15	54	43	43
5	SHEFFIELD W	38	16	9	13	69	49	41
6	ASTON VILLA	38	17	7	14	76	63	41
7	MIDDLESBROUGH	38	16	8	14	56	45	40
8	SUNDERLAND	38	14	11	13	58	51	39
9	WBA	38	15	9	14	43	47	39
10	WOOLWICH ARSENAL	38	15	8	15	55	59	38
11	BRADFORD C	38	15	8	15	46	50	38
12	TOTTENHAM H	38	14	9	15	53	53	37
13	MANCHESTER U	38	13	11	14	45	60	37
14	SHEFFIELD U	38	13	10	15	63	56	36
15	MANCHESTER CITY	38	13	9	16	56	58	35
16	NOTTS CO	38	14	7	17	46	63	35
17	LIVERPOOL	38	12	10	16	49	55	34
18	OLDHAM ATH	38	12	10	16	46	54	34
19	PRESTON NE	38	13	7	18	40	57	33
20	BURY	38	6	9	23	32	59	21

The Essential History of Manchester City

Season 1912-13

Football League Division 1

DATE	OPPONENTS	SCORE	GOALSCORERS	ATTENDANCE
Sep 2	Notts County	W 1-0	Heary	12,000
Sep 7	Manchester United	W 1-0	Wynn	38,911
Sep 14	ASTON VILLA	W 1-0	Wynn	32,000
Sep 21	Liverpool	W 2-1	Wynn, Dorsett	35,237
Sep 28	BOLTON WANDERERS	W 2-0	Hoad, Jones	30,000
Oct 5	Sheffield United	D 1-1	Wallace	25,000
Oct 12	NEWCASTLE UNITED	L 0-1		40,000
Oct 19	Oldham Athletic	L 1-2	Wynn	10,000
Oct 26	CHELSEA	W 2-0	Taylor, Jones	15,000
Nov 2	Woolwich Arsenal	W 4-0	Wynn, Taylor 2, Jones	8,000
Nov 9	BRADFORD CITY	L 1-3	Wynn	30,000
Nov 16	SUNDERLAND	W 1-0	Wynn	16,000
Nov 23	West Bromwich Albion	W 2-0	Jones, Walker	20,000
Nov 30	EVERTON	W 1-0	Wallace	20,000
Dec 7	Sheffield Wednesday	L 0-1		20,000
Dec 14	BLACKBURN ROVERS	W 3-1	Dorsett, Wynn, Jones	20,000
Dec 21	Derby County	L 0-2		15,000
Dec 25	TOTTENHAM HOTSPUR	D 2-2	Bottomley, Wynn	30,000
Dec 26	Tottenham Hotspur	L 0-4		12,000
Dec 28	MANCHESTER UNITED	L 0-2		36,223
Jan 2	NOTTS COUNTY	W 4-0	Wynn 2, Jones, Wallace	22,000
Jan 4	Aston Villa	L 0-2		10,000
Jan 18	LIVERPOOL	W 4-1	Howard 4	20,000
Jan 25	Bolton Wanderers	D 2-2	Wynn, Howard	25,000
Feb 8	SHEFFIELD UNITED	W 3-0	Howard, Jones, Walker	18,000
Feb 15	Newcastle United	W 1-0	Wynn	30,000
Mar 1	Chelsea	L 1-2	Dorsett	40,000
Mar 8	WOOLWICH ARSENAL	L 0-1		15,000
Mar 12	OLDHAM ATHLETIC	W 2-0	Dorsett, Jones	16,000
Mar 15	Bradford City	L 1-2	Wallace	6,000
Mar 21	Middlesbrough	D 0-0		15,000
Mar 22	Sunderland	L 0-1		20,000
Mar 24	MIDDLESBROUGH	W 3-0	Howard 2, Taylor	26,000
Mar 29	WEST BROMWICH ALBION	W 2-1	Wallace 2	20,000
Apr 5	Everton	D 0-0		12,000
Apr 12	SHEFFIELD WEDNESDAY	D 2-2	Howard, Jones	30,000
Apr 19	Blackburn Rovers	D 2-2	Howard 2	8,000
Apr 26	DERBY COUNTY	D 1-1	Wynn	15,000

FA Cup

Jan 11	BIRMINGHAM	(Rd 1) W 4-0	Wynn 2, Hoad, Taylor	17,442
Feb 1	SUNDERLAND	(Rd 2) D 0-0*		41,709
Feb 5	Sunderland	(R) L 0-2		27,974

*Abandoned in extra-time.

League & Cup Appearances

PLAYER	LEAGUE	CUP COMPETITION FA CUP	TOTAL
Bottomley	33	1	34
Dorsett	30		30
Eadie	31	3	34
Fletcher	33	3	36
Garner	2		2
Goodchild	28		28
Henry	37	3	40
Hoad	16	3	19
Holford	38	3	41
Howard	16	2	18
Hughes	5	2	7
Jobling	2		2
Jones	37	3	40
Kelly	3		3
Lawrence	1		1
McGuire	6		6
Smith	10	3	13
Taylor	22	1	23
Wallace	28	3	31
Wallace	7		7
Webb	2		2
Wynn	31	3	34

Goalscorers

PLAYER	LEAGUE	CUP COMPETITION FA CUP	TOTAL
Wynn	14	2	16
Howard	11		11
Jones	9		9
Wallace	8		8
Taylor	4	1	5
Dorsett	4		4
Hoad	1	1	2
Bottomley	1		1
Henry	1		1

Fact File

The FA Cup tie against Sunderland was abandoned when an over-full Hyde Road crowd spilled out onto the pitch.

MANAGER: Ernest Mangnall

CAPTAIN: Billy Lot Jones

TOP SCORER: George Wynn

BIGGEST WIN: November 2, 1912 4-0 v Woolwich Arsenal, Division 1; January 2, 1913 4-0 v Notts County, Division 1

HIGHEST ATTENDANCE: February 1, 1913 41,709 v Sunderland, drew 0-0, FA Cup Round 2

Final Division 1 Table

		P	W	D	L	F	A	Pts
1	SUNDERLAND	38	25	4	9	86	43	54
2	ASTON VILLA	38	19	12	7	86	52	50
3	SHEFFIELD W	38	21	7	10	75	55	49
4	MANCHESTER U	38	19	8	11	69	43	46
5	BLACKBURN R	38	16	13	9	79	43	45
6	MANCHESTER CITY	38	18	8	12	53	37	44
7	DERBY CO	38	17	8	13	69	66	42
8	BOLTON W	38	16	10	12	62	63	42
9	OLDHAM ATH	38	14	14	10	50	55	42
10	WBA	38	13	12	13	57	50	38
11	EVERTON	38	15	7	16	48	54	37
12	LIVERPOOL	38	16	5	17	61	71	37
13	BRADFORD C	38	12	11	15	50	60	35
14	NEWCASTLE U	38	13	8	17	47	47	34
15	SHEFFIELD U	38	14	6	18	56	70	34
16	MIDDLESBROUGH	38	11	10	17	55	69	32
17	TOTTENHAM H	38	12	6	20	45	72	30
18	CHELSEA	38	11	6	21	51	73	28
19	NOTTS CO	38	7	9	22	28	56	23
20	WOOLWICH ARSENAL	38	3	12	23	26	74	18

Season 1913-14

Football League Division 1

DATE	OPPONENTS	SCORE	GOALSCORERS	ATTENDANCE
Sep 1	Aston Villa	D 1-1	Taylor	10,000
Sep 6	MIDDLESBROUGH	D 1-1	Taylor	30,000
Sep 13	Sheffield United	W 3-1	Abbott, Jones, Taylor	15,000
Sep 20	DERBY COUNTY	L 1-2	Abbott	25,000
Sep 27	Tottenham Hotspur	L 1-3	Jones	30,513
Oct 4	Bradford City	L 2-3	Wynn 2	20,000
Oct 11	BLACKBURN ROVERS	L 1-2	Hughes	40,000
Oct 18	Sunderland	D 0-0		28,000
Oct 25	EVERTON	D 1-1	Taylor	30,000
Nov 1	West Bromwich Albion	D 0-0		12,000
Nov 8	SHEFFIELD WEDNESDAY	L 1-2	Browell	25,000
Nov 15	Bolton Wanderers	L 0-3		25,000
Nov 22	CHELSEA	W 2-1	Browell, Wallace	30,000
Nov 29	Oldham Athletic	W 3-1	Cumming, Howard, Browell	18,000
Dec 6	MANCHESTER UNITED	L 0-2		40,000
Dec 13	Burnley	L 0-2		20,000
Dec 20	PRESTON NORTH END	D 1-1	Browell	20,000
Dec 25	Liverpool	L 2-4	Howard 2	22,000
Dec 26	LIVERPOOL	W 1-0	Howard	25,000
Dec 27	Middlesbrough	L 0-2		12,000
Jan 1	Newcastle United	W 1-0	Browell	15,000
Jan 3	SHEFFIELD UNITED	W 2-1	Taylor, Browell	25,000
Jan 17	Derby County	W 4-2	Howard 3, Taylor	8,000
Jan 24	TOTTENHAM HOTSPUR	W 2-1	Cumming, Taylor	30,000
Feb 7	BRADFORD CITY	W 1-0	Browell	25,000
Feb 14	Blackburn Rovers	L 1-2	Browell	10,000
Feb 28	Everton	L 0-1		20,000
Mar 14	Sheffield Wednesday	D 2-2	Hughes, Taylor	17,000
Mar 18	SUNDERLAND	W 3-1	Howard 2, Hindmarsh	20,000
Mar 21	BOLTON WANDERERS	L 0-1		30,000
Mar 25	WEST BROMWICH ALBION	L 2-3	A Fairclough, Browell	15,000
Mar 28	Chelsea	L 0-1		30,000
Apr 4	OLDHAM ATHLETIC	W 2-1	Jones 2	25,000
Apr 10	ASTON VILLA	W 3-1	Browell 2, Dorsett	30,000
Apr 11	Manchester United	W 1-0	Cumming	36,440
Apr 13	NEWCASTLE UNITED	L 0-1		35,000
Apr 18	BURNLEY	W 4-1	Browell 2, Howard, Wynn	18,000
Apr 25	Preston North End	D 2-2	Hanney, Howard	8,000

FA Cup

Jan 10	FULHAM	(Rd 1)	W 2-0	Hindmarsh, Howard	25,345
Jan 31	TOTTENHAM HOTSPUR	(Rd 2)	W 2-1	Howard, Browell	36,256
Feb 21	Blackburn Rovers	(Rd 3)	W 2-1	Howard, Cartwright	41,250
Mar 7	SHEFFIELD UNITED	(Rd 4)	D 0-0		35,738
Mar 12	Sheffield United	(R)	D 0-0		46,139
Mar 16	SHEFFIELD UNITED	(2nd R)	L 0-1		23,000

League & Cup Appearances

PLAYER	LEAGUE	CUP COMPETITION FA CUP	TOTAL
Abbott	3		3
Bottomley	11		11
Browell	27	6	33
Cartwright	9	5	14
Cumming	23	5	28
Dorset	17		17
Eadie	6		6
Fairclough A	2		2
Fletcher	36	6	42
Garner	2		2
Goodchild	2		2
Hanney	24	6	30
Henry	33	6	39
Hindmarsh	24	6	30
Hoad	5		5
Holford	15		15
Howard	29	6	35
Hughes	30	6	36
Jones	14	1	15
McGuire	6		6
Smith	36	6	42
Spottiswood	6		6
Taylor	27	6	33
Wall	4		4
Wallace	15	1	16
Wynn	12		12

Goalscorers

PLAYER	LEAGUE	CUP COMPETITION FA CUP	TOTAL
Browell	13	1	14
Howard	11	3	14
Taylor	8		8
Jones	4		4
Cumming	3		3
Wynn	3		3
Abbott	2		2
Hughes	2		2
Hindmarsh	1	1	2
Dorset	1		1
Fairclough A	1		1
Hanney	1		1
Wallace	1		1

Fact File

Tommy Browell scored on his Manchester City debut against Sheffield Wednesday in November.

MANAGER: Ernest Mangnall

CAPTAIN: Billy Lot Jones

TOP SCORERS: Tommy Browell and F. Howard

BIGGEST WIN: April 18, 1914 4-1 v Burnley, Division 1

HIGHEST ATTENDANCE: March 12, 1913 41,250 v Sheffield United, drew 0-0, FA Cup Round 4 Replay

MAJOR TRANSFERS IN: Tommy Browell from Everton

Final Division 1 Table

		P	W	D	L	F	A	Pts
1	BLACKBURN R	38	20	11	7	78	42	51
2	ASTON VILLA	38	19	6	13	65	50	44
3	MIDDLESBROUGH	38	19	5	14	77	60	43
4	OLDHAM ATH	38	17	9	12	55	45	43
5	WBA	38	15	13	10	46	42	43
6	BOLTON W	38	16	10	12	65	52	42
7	SUNDERLAND	38	17	6	15	63	52	40
8	CHELSEA	38	16	7	15	46	55	39
9	BRADFORD C	38	12	14	12	40	40	38
10	SHEFFIELD U	38	16	5	17	63	60	37
11	NEWCASTLE U	38	13	11	14	39	48	37
12	BURNLEY	38	12	12	14	61	53	36
13	MANCHESTER CITY	38	14	8	16	51	53	36
14	MANCHESTER U	38	15	6	17	52	62	36
15	EVERTON	38	12	11	15	46	55	35
16	LIVERPOOL	38	14	7	17	46	62	35
17	TOTTENHAM H	38	12	10	16	50	62	34
18	SHEFFIELD W	38	13	8	17	53	70	34
19	PRESTON NE	38	12	6	20	52	69	30
20	DERBY CO	38	8	11	19	55	71	27

227

Season 1914-15

Football League Division 1

DATE	OPPONENTS	SCORE	GOALSCORERS	ATTENDANCE
Sep 1	BRADFORD CITY	W 4-1	Taylor, Howard, Barnes, Dorsett	9,000
Sep 5	Manchester United	D 0-0		20,000
Sep 12	BURNLEY	W 1-0	Howard	10,000
Sep 19	Bolton Wanderers	W 3-2	Howard, Barnes, o.g.	20,000
Sep 26	TOTTENHAM HOTSPUR	W 2-1	Taylor, Howard	20,000
Oct 3	Blackburn Rovers	W 1-0	Cartwright	22,000
Oct 10	NEWCASTLE UNITED	D 1-1	Barnes	24,000
Oct 17	Notts County	W 2-0	Howard 2	14,000
Oct 24	MIDDLESBROUGH	D 1-1	Howard	25,000
Oct 31	Sunderland	W 2-0	Howard 2	10,000
Nov 7	SHEFFIELD UNITED	D 0-0		25,000
Nov 14	Sheffield Wednesday	L 1-2	Taylor	24,000
Nov 25	ASTON VILLA	W 1-0	Howard	16,000
Nov 28	West Bromwich Albion	W 1-0	Browell	10,000
Dec 5	LIVERPOOL	D 1-4	Howard	12,000
Dec 12	Everton	L 1-4	Howard	20,000
Dec 19	BRADFORD PARK AVENUE	L 2-3	Taylor, Howard	7,000
Dec 25	Chelsea	D 0-0		15,000
Dec 26	CHELSEA	W 2-1	Taylor, Howard	25,000
Jan 1	Oldham Athletic	D 0-0		22,000
Jan 2	MANCHESTER UNITED	D 1-1	Howard	30,000
Jan 18	Burnley	W 2-1	Dorsett, Barnes	8,000
Jan 23	BOLTON WANDERERS	W 2-1	Taylor, Barnes	20,000
Feb 6	BLACKBURN ROVERS	L 1-3	Taylor	25,000
Feb 13	Newcastle United	L 1-2	Taylor	18,000
Feb 22	NOTTS COUNTY	D 0-0		20,000
Feb 27	Middlesbrough	L 0-1		8,000
Mar 6	SUNDERLAND	W 2-0	Cartwright, o.g.	20,000
Mar 13	Liverpool	L 2-3	Barnes, Howard	20,000
Mar 15	Tottenham Hotspur	D 2-2	Taylor, Barnes	7,000
Mar 20	SHEFFIELD WEDNESDAY	W 4-0	Howard 2, Barnes 2	20,000
Mar 29	Sheffield United	D 0-0		18,000
Apr 3	WEST BROMWICH ALBION	W 4-0	Taylor 2, Barnes 2	15,000
Apr 5	OLDHAM ATHLETIC	D 0-0		40,000
Apr 6	Bradford City	D 0-0		15,000
Apr 17	EVERTON	L 0-1		30,000
Apr 21	Aston Villa	L 1-4	Barnes	8,000
Apr 24	Bradford Park Avenue	L 1-3	Jones	12,000

FA Cup

Jan 9	Preston North End	(Rd 1) D 0-0		14,000
Jan 16	PRESTON NORTH END	(R) W 3-0	Barnes 2, Hughes	19,985
Jan 30	ASTON VILLA	(Rd 2) W 1-0	Cartwright	29,661
Feb 20	CHELSEA	(Rd 3) L 0-1		32,000

League & Cup Appearances

PLAYER	LEAGUE	CUP COMPETITION FA CUP	TOTAL
Barnes	25	4	29
Bottomley	1		1
Brennan	33	2	35
Browell	10	2	12
Cartwright	21	4	25
Cumming	12	1	13
Dorsett	18	3	21
Fairclough A	1		1
Fairclough P	1		1
Fletcher	37	4	41
Garner	1		1
Gartland	1		1
Gaughan	10		10
Goodchild	1		1
Hall	1		1
Hanney	37	4	41
Henderson	1		1
Henry	35	4	39
Hindmarsh	4	1	5
Hoad	6		6
Howard	33	3	36
Hughes	36	4	40
Jones	17	1	18
McGuire	3		3
Smith	37	4	41
Taylor	35	3	38
Wynn	1		1

Goalscorers

PLAYER	LEAGUE	CUP COMPETITION FA CUP	TOTAL
Howard	18		18
Barnes	12	2	14
Taylor	11		11
Cartwright	2	1	3
Dorsett	2		2
Browell	1		1
Jones	1		1
Hughes		1	1
Opps' o.gs.	2		2

Fact File

A disappointing run-in to the season saw the Blues fail to win in their last five matches and blow any chance of becoming champions.

MANAGER: Ernest Mangnall

CAPTAIN: Billy Lot Jones

TOP SCORER: F. Howard

BIGGEST WIN: March 20, 1915 4-0 v Sheffield Wednesday, Division 1; April 3, 1915 4-0 v West Bromwich Albion, Division 1

HIGHEST ATTENDANCE: April 5, 1915 (approx.) 40,000 v Oldham Athletic, drew 0-0, Division 1

MAJOR TRANSFERS IN: Horace Barnes from Derby County

Final Division 1 Table

		P	W	D	L	F	A	Pts
1	EVERTON	38	19	8	11	76	47	46
2	OLDHAM ATH	38	17	11	10	70	56	45
3	BLACKBURN R	38	18	7	13	83	61	43
4	BURNLEY	38	18	7	13	61	47	43
5	MANCHESTER CITY	38	15	13	10	49	39	43
6	SHEFFIELD U	38	15	13	10	49	41	43
7	SHEFFIELD W	38	15	13	10	61	54	43
8	SUNDERLAND	38	18	5	15	81	72	41
9	BRADFORD PA	38	17	7	14	69	65	41
10	WBA	38	15	10	13	49	43	40
11	BRADFORD C	38	13	14	11	55	49	40
12	MIDDLESBROUGH	38	13	12	13	62	74	38
13	LIVERPOOL	38	14	9	15	65	75	37
14	ASTON VILLA	38	13	11	14	62	72	37
15	NEWCASTLE U	38	11	10	17	46	48	32
16	NOTTS CO	38	9	13	16	41	57	31
17	BOLTON W	38	11	8	19	68	84	30
18	MANCHESTER U	38	9	12	17	46	62	30
19	CHELSEA	38	8	13	17	51	65	29
20	TOTTENHAM H	38	8	12	18	57	90	28

Season 1919-20

Football League Division 1

DATE	OPPONENTS	SCORE	GOALSCORERS	ATTENDANCE
Aug 30	SHEFFIELD UNITED	D 3-3	Barnes 2, Browell	30,000
Sep 1	Oldham Athletic	W 3-1	Browell 2, Cartwright	3,000
Sep 6	Sheffield United	L 1-3	Wynn	30,000
Sep 8	OLDHAM ATHLETIC	W 3-1	Browell 2, Barnes	22,000
Sep 13	BOLTON WANDERERS	L 1-4	Crawshaw	20,000
Sep 20	Bolton Wanderers	L 2-6	Taylor, Browell	30,000
Sep 27	NOTTS COUNTY	W 4-1	Barnes 3, Taylor	20,000
Oct 4	Notts County	L 1-4	Barnes	16,000
Oct 11	MANCHESTER UNITED	D 3-3	Barnes 2, Taylor	32,000
Oct 18	Manchester United	L 0-1		45,000
Oct 25	SHEFFIELD WEDNESDAY	W 4-2	Browell 2, Taylor, Goodwin	20,000
Nov 1	Sheffield Wednesday	D 0-0		20,000
Nov 8	BLACKBURN ROVERS	W 8-2	Browell 3, Barnes 2, Murphy 2, Crawshaw	25,000
Nov 15	Blackburn Rovers	W 4-1	Browell 2, Barnes 2	6,000
Nov 22	DERBY COUNTY	W 3-1	Crawshaw 2, Barnes	15,000
Nov 29	Derby County	D 0-0		7,000
Dec 6	WEST BROMWICH ALBION	L 2-3	Browell 2	30,000
Dec 13	West Bromwich Albion	L 0-2		20,000
Dec 20	Sunderland	L 1-2	Reid	20,000
Dec 25	EVERTON	D 1-1	Barnes	25,000
Dec 26	Everton	L 0-2		26,000
Dec 27	SUNDERLAND	W 1-0	Murphy	30,000
Jan 1	BRADFORD CITY	W 1-0	Murphy	30,000
Jan 3	Arsenal	D 2-2	Murphy, Barnes	32,000
Jan 17	ARSENAL	W 4-1	Browell 3, Goodwin	25,000
Jan 24	MIDDLESBROUGH	W 1-0	Browell	28,000
Feb 7	BURNLEY	W 3-1	Barnes 2, Crawshaw	30,000
Feb 14	Burnley	L 0-2		20,000
Feb 18	Middlesbrough	W 2-0	Johnson 2	15,000
Feb 28	Preston North End	D 1-1	Fletcher	17,000
Mar 13	BRADFORD PARK AVENUE	W 4-1	Barnes 2, Johnson, Crawshaw	10,000
Mar 17	PRESTON NORTH END	W 1-0	Godfrey	18,000
Mar 20	Liverpool	L 0-1		30,000
Mar 22	Bradford Park Avenue	L 1-2	Johnston	8,000
Mar 27	LIVERPOOL	W 2-1	Barnes 2	35,000
Apr 3	Chelsea	L 0-1		45,000
Apr 5	Bradford City	L 0-1		20,000
Apr 10	CHELSEA	W 1-0	Barnes	25,000
Apr 17	Newcastle United	L 0-3		36,000
Apr 24	NEWCASTLE UNITED	D 0-0		25,000
Apr 26	Aston Villa	W 1-0	Browell	45,000
May 1	ASTON VILLA	D 2-2	Johnson, Barnes	23,000

FA Cup

Jan 10	CLAPTON ORIENT	(Rd 1) W 4-1	Goodwin 2, Barnes, Murphy	25,878
Jan 31	Leicester City	(Rd 2) L 0-3		23,041

League & Cup Appearances

PLAYER	LEAGUE	CUP COMPETITION FA CUP	TOTAL
Allen	2		2
Barnes	39	2	41
Brennan	20	2	22
Broad	19	1	20
Browell	30	2	32
Cartwright	6		6
Cookson	20	2	22
Crawshaw	21	1	22
Dorsett	8		8
Fairclough A	2		2
Fairclough P	4		4
Fletcher	34	2	36
Godfrey	9		9
Goodchild	33	2	35
Goodwin	15	1	16
Gray	2		2
Hanney	7		7
Henderson	4		4
Henry	13		13
Howard	1	1	2
Hughes	6		6
Jarvis	1		1
Johnson	10		10
Knowles	2		2
Lamph	11		11
Leivesley	1		1
Murphy	36	2	38
Newton	2		2
Reid	3		3
Scott	13	1	14
Sharp	6		6
Smith	9		9
Sugden	6		6
Taylor	6		6
Tyler	41	2	43
Woosnam	16	1	17
Wynn	4		4

Goalscorers

PLAYER	LEAGUE	CUP COMPETITION FA CUP	TOTAL
Barnes	22	1	23
Browell	22		22
Crawshaw	6		6
Johnson	5		5
Murphy	5	1	6
Taylor	4		4
Goodwin	2	2	4
Cartwright	1		1
Fletcher	1		1
Godfrey	1		1
Reid	1		1
Wynn	1		1

Fact File

King George V was present at Hyde Road to see the 2-1 victory over Liverpool in March of this season.

MANAGER: Ernest Mangnall

CAPTAIN: Eli Fletcher

TOP SCORER: Horace Barnes

BIGGEST WIN: November 8, 1919 8-2 v Blackburn Rovers, Division 1

HIGHEST ATTENDANCE: April 3, 1920 (approx.) 45,000 v Chelsea, lost 0-1, Division 1; April 26, 1920 (approx.) 45,000 v Aston Villa, drew 2-2 Division 1

MAJOR TRANSFERS IN: Max Woosnam from Corinthians

Final Division 1 Table

		P	W	D	L	F	A	Pts
1	WBA	42	28	4	10	104	47	60
2	BURNLEY	42	21	9	12	65	59	51
3	CHELSEA	42	22	5	15	56	51	49
4	LIVERPOOL	42	19	10	13	59	44	48
5	SUNDERLAND	42	22	4	16	72	59	48
6	BOLTON W	42	19	9	14	72	65	47
7	MANCHESTER CITY	42	18	9	15	71	62	45
8	NEWCASTLE U	42	17	9	16	44	39	43
9	ASTON VILLA	42	18	6	18	75	73	42
10	THE ARSENAL	42	15	12	15	56	58	42
11	BRADFORD PA	42	15	12	15	60	63	42
12	MANCHESTER U	42	13	14	15	54	50	40
13	MIDDLESBROUGH	42	15	10	17	61	65	40
14	SHEFFIELD U	42	16	8	18	59	69	40
15	BRADFORD C	42	14	11	17	54	63	39
16	EVERTON	42	12	14	16	69	68	38
17	OLDHAM ATH	42	15	8	19	49	52	38
18	DERBY CO	42	13	12	17	47	57	38
19	PRESTON NE	42	14	10	18	57	73	38
20	BLACKBURN R	42	13	11	18	64	77	37
21	NOTTS CO	42	12	12	18	56	74	36
22	SHEFFIELD W	42	7	9	26	28	64	23

Season 1920-21

Football League Division 1

DATE	OPPONENTS	SCORE	GOALSCORERS	ATTENDANCE
Aug 28	Liverpool	L 2-4	Goodwin, Browell	30,000
Aug 30	ASTON VILLA	W 3-1	Browell 2, Murphy	40,000
Sep 4	LIVERPOOL	W 3-2	Browell 3	30,000
Sep 6	Aston Villa	L 1-3	Murphy	14,000
Sep 11	Arsenal	L 1-2	Browell	42,000
Sep 18	ARSENAL	W 3-1	Browell, Barnes, Murphy	30,000
Sep 25	Bolton Wanderers	L 0-3		50,000
Oct 2	BOLTON WANDERERS	W 3-1	Woodcock, Fayers, Browell	40,000
Oct 9	Derby County	L 0-3		20,000
Oct 16	DERBY COUNTY	D 0-0		35,000
Oct 23	Blackburn Rovers	W 2-0	Woodcock, Johnson	30,000
Oct 30	BLACKBURN ROVERS	D 0-0		35,000
Nov 6	Huddersfield Town	W 1-0	Barnes	22,000
Nov 13	HUDDERSFIELD TOWN	W 3-2	Browell 2, Fayers	30,000
Nov 20	Manchester United	D 1-1	Barnes	66,000
Nov 27	MANCHESTER UNITED	W 3-0	Browell, Barnes, Murphy	40,000
Dec 4	Bradford City	W 2-1	Murphy, Browell	20,000
Dec 11	BRADFORD CITY	W 1-0	Browell	30,000
Dec 18	Sunderland	L 0-1		18,000
Dec 25	WEST BROMWICH ALBION	W 4-0	Browell 2, Barnes 2	30,000
Dec 27	West Bromwich Albion	D 2-2	Browell 2	40,000
Jan 1	SUNDERLAND	W 3-1	Murphy 2, Browell	40,000
Jan 15	Chelsea	L 1-2	Murphy	35,000
Jan 22	CHELSEA	W 1-0	Browell	30,000
Feb 5	Everton	L 0-3		35,000
Feb 12	Tottenham Hotspur	L 0-2		35,000
Feb 23	EVERTON	W 2-0	Browell 2	33,000
Feb 26	Oldham Athletic	L 0-2		30,000
Mar 5	OLDHAM ATHLETIC	W 3-1	Browell, Johnson, Barnes	33,000
Mar 9	TOTTENHAM HOTSPUR	W 2-0	Browell, Barnes	30,000
Mar 12	Preston North End	W 1-0	Fayers	18,000
Mar 25	MIDDLESBROUGH	W 2-1	Johnson, Barnes	25,000
Mar 26	BURNLEY	W 3-0	Barnes 2, Johnson	50,155
Mar 28	Middlesbrough	L 1-3	Browell	29,000
Apr 2	Burnley	L 1-2	Fayers	40,000
Apr 9	SHEFFIELD UNITED	W 2-1	Browell, Johnson	20,000
Apr 16	Sheffield United	D 1-1	Barnes	23,000
Apr 20	PRESTON NORTH END	W 5-1	Browell 3, Barnes 2	20,000
Apr 23	BRADFORD PARK AVENUE	W 1-0	Browell	25,000
Apr 30	Bradford Park Avenue	W 2-1	Fayers, Barnes	10,000
May 2	NEWCASTLE UNITED	W 3-1	Barnes 2, Warner	18,000
May 7	Newcastle United	D 1-1	Browell	40,000

FA Cup

Jan 8	Crystal Palace	(Rd 1) L 0-2		18,000

League & Cup Appearances

PLAYER	LEAGUE	CUP COMPETITION FA CUP	TOTAL
Allen	7		7
Barnes	41	1	42
Brennan	2		2
Broad	23	1	24
Browell	42	1	43
Carroll	12	1	13
Cartwright	2		2
Cookson	42	1	43
Crawshaw	2		2
Edelston	6		6
Fayers	40	1	41
Fletcher	35	1	36
Goodchild	42	1	43
Goodwin	5		5
Gray	1		1
Hamill	28		28
Jarvis	1		1
Johnson	12		12
Kelly	13		13
Leyland	1		1
Murphy	40	1	41
Scott	2		2
Sharp	5		5
Taylor	1		1
Thompson J	2		2
Tyler	3	1	4
Warner	5		5
Woodcock	13		13
Woosnam	34	1	35

Goalscorers

PLAYER	LEAGUE	CUP COMPETITION FA CUP	TOTAL
Browell	31		31
Barnes	17		17
Murphy	8		8
Fayers	5		5
Johnson	5		5
Woodcock	2		2
Goodwin	1		1
Warner	1		1

Final Division 1 Table

		P	W	D	L	F	A	PTS
1	BURNLEY	42	23	13	6	79	36	59
2	MANCHESTER CITY	42	24	6	12	70	50	54
3	BOLTON W	42	19	14	9	77	53	52
4	LIVERPOOL	42	18	15	9	63	35	51
5	NEWCASTLE U	42	20	10	12	66	45	50
6	TOTTENHAM H	42	19	9	14	70	48	47
7	EVERTON	42	17	13	12	66	55	47
8	MIDDLESBROUGH	42	17	12	13	53	53	46
9	THE ARSENAL	42	15	14	13	59	63	44
10	ASTON VILLA	42	18	7	17	63	70	43
11	BLACKBURN R	42	13	15	14	57	59	41
12	SUNDERLAND	42	14	13	15	57	60	41
13	MANCHESTER U	42	15	10	17	64	68	40
14	WBA	42	13	14	15	54	58	40
15	BRADFORD C	42	12	15	15	61	63	39
16	PRESTON NE	42	15	9	18	61	65	39
17	HUDDERSFIELD T	42	15	9	18	42	49	39
18	CHELSEA	42	13	13	16	48	58	39
19	OLDHAM ATH	42	9	15	18	49	86	33
20	SHEFFIELD U	42	6	18	18	42	68	30
21	DERBY CO	42	5	16	21	32	58	26
22	BRADFORD PA	42	8	8	26	43	76	24

Fact File

Over 50,000 filled the rafters of Hyde Road to see City beat their championship rivals Burnley in March. Unfortunately a defeat in the return a week later put paid to City's title ambitions.

MANAGER: Ernest Mangnall

CAPTAIN: Horace Barnes

TOP SCORER: Tommy Browell

BIGGEST WIN: April 20, 1921 5-1 v Preston North End, Division 1

HIGHEST ATTENDANCE: November 20, (approx.) 66,000 v Manchester United, drew 1-1 Division 1

MAJOR TRANSFERS IN: Mickey Hammill from Belfast Celtic

Season 1921-22

Football League Division 1

DATE	OPPONENTS	SCORE	GOALSCORERS	ATTENDANCE
Aug 27	ASTON VILLA	W 2-1	Barnes 2	35,000
Aug 31	Liverpool	L 2-3	Barnes, Murphy	25,000
Sep 3	Aston Villa	L 0-4		30,000
Sep 7	LIVERPOOL	D 1-1	Murphy	25,000
Sep 10	ARSENAL	W 2-0	Warner, Barnes	25,000
Sep 17	Arsenal	W 1-0	Barnes	25,000
Sep 24	BLACKBURN ROVERS	D 1-1	Browell	35,000
Oct 1	Blackburn Rovers	L 1-3	Browell	25,000
Oct 8	OLDHAM ATHLETIC	W 2-1	Browell, Murphy	35,000
Oct 15	Oldham Athletic	W 1-0	Browell	25,000
Oct 22	MANCHESTER UNITED	W 4-1	Barnes 3, Warner	20,000
Oct 29	Manchester United	L 1-3	Murphy	56,000
Nov 5	Cardiff City	W 2-0	Browell, Barnes	35,000
Nov 12	CARDIFF CITY	D 1-1	Murphy	25,000
Nov 19	WEST BROMWICH ALBION	W 6-1	Barnes 3, Browell 2, Woosnam	25,000
Nov 26	West Bromwich Albion	L 0-2		30,000
Dec 3	BOLTON WANDERERS	L 2-3	Browell, Barnes	35,000
Dec 10	Bolton Wanderers	L 0-5		40,000
Dec 17	EVERTON	W 2-1	Browell, Murphy	20,000
Dec 24	Everton	D 2-2	Johnson 2	30,000
Dec 26	Huddersfield Town	L 0-2		26,000
Dec 31	SUNDERLAND	W 3-0	Browell, Johnson, Murphy	10,000
Jan 2	HUDDERSFIELD TOWN	W 2-1	Johnson, Kelly	30,000
Jan 14	Sunderland	W 3-2	Browell, Barnes, Murphy	5,000
Jan 21	MIDDLESBROUGH	D 2-2	Barnes, Browell	20,000
Feb 1	Middlesbrough	L 1-4	Browell	20,000
Feb 4	TOTTENHAM HOTSPUR	D 3-3	Browell, Johnson, Barnes	20,000
Feb 11	Tottenham Hotspur	L 1-3	Barnes	45,000
Feb 22	BRADFORD CITY	W 3-2	Browell, Barnes, Woosnam	20,000
Feb 25	Bradford City	W 2-1	Murphy, Browell	25,000
Mar 11	Preston North End	L 0-1		20,000
Mar 18	Chelsea	D 0-0		40,000
Mar 25	CHELSEA	D 0-0		26,000
Apr 1	Sheffield United	L 0-1		20,000
Apr 5	PRESTON NORTH END	W 2-0	Browell, Barnes	20,000
Apr 8	SHEFFIELD UNITED	D 2-2	Browell 2	12,000
Apr 14	BIRMINGHAM	W 1-0	Warner	35,000
Apr 15	Burnley	L 2-5	Woosnam, o.g.	15,000
Apr 18	Birmingham	L 1-3	o.g.	39,000
Apr 22	BURNLEY	W 2-0	Browell, Barnes	25,000
Apr 29	Newcastle United	L 1-5	Ingham	25,000
May 6	NEWCASTLE UNITED	W 1-0	Browell	18,000

FA Cup

Jan 7	DARLINGTON	(Rd 1) W 3-1	Browell 3	23,686
Jan 28	Bolton Wanderers	(Rd 2) W 3-1	Browell 2, Kelly	66,442
Feb 18	Tottenham Hotspur	(Rd 3) L 1-2	Kelly	53,000

League & Cup Appearances

PLAYER	LEAGUE	CUP COMPETITION FA CUP	TOTAL
Albinson	3		3
Allen	2		2
Barnes	37	3	40
Blair	38	3	41
Brennan	1		1
Browell	38	3	41
Carroll	4	1	5
Cookson	39	2	41
Crawshaw	2		2
Etherington	2		2
Fayers	32	3	35
Fletcher	38	3	41
Ford	4		4
Goodchild	4		4
Hamill	24	2	26
Ingham	2		2
Johnson	20	3	23
Kelly	11	3	14
Leyland	2		2
Lievesley	1		1
Meredith	25		25
Mulligan	2		2
Murphy	42	3	45
Pearson	1		1
Royle	1		1
Sharp	25		25
Simpson	1		1
Thompson	3	1	4
Warner	22		22
Wilson	1		1
Woodcock	2		2
Woosnam	33	3	36

Goalscorers

PLAYER	LEAGUE	CUP COMPETITION FA CUP	TOTAL
Browell	21	5	26
Barnes	20		20
Murphy	9		9
Johnson	5		5
Warner	3		3
Woosnam	3		3
Ingham	1		1
Kelly	1	2	3
Opps' o.gs.	2		2

Fact File

Billy Meredith, aged 47 returned as player-coach and played in 25 games.

MANAGER: Ernest Mangnall
CAPTAIN: Mickey Hamill
TOP SCORER: Tommy Browell
BIGGEST WIN: November 19, 1921 6-1 v West Bromwich Albion, Division 1
HIGHEST ATTENDANCE: February 18, 1922 66,442 v Bolton Wanderers, won 3-1, FA Cup Round 2

Final Division 1 Table

		P	W	D	L	F	A	Pts
1	LIVERPOOL	42	22	13	7	63	36	57
2	TOTTENHAM H	42	21	9	12	65	39	51
3	BURNLEY	42	22	5	15	72	54	49
4	CARDIFF C	42	19	10	13	61	53	48
5	ASTON VILLA	42	22	3	17	74	55	47
6	BOLTON W	42	20	7	15	68	59	47
7	NEWCASTLE U	42	18	10	14	59	45	46
8	MIDDLESBROUGH	42	16	14	12	79	69	46
9	CHELSEA	42	17	12	13	40	43	46
10	MANCHESTER CITY	42	18	9	15	65	70	45
11	SHEFFIELD U	42	15	10	17	59	54	40
12	SUNDERLAND	42	16	8	18	60	62	40
13	WBA	42	15	10	17	51	63	40
14	HUDDERSFIELD T	42	15	9	18	53	54	39
15	BLACKBURN R	42	13	12	17	54	57	38
16	PRESTON NE	42	13	12	17	42	65	38
17	THE ARSENAL	42	15	7	20	47	56	37
18	BIRMINGHAM	42	15	7	20	48	60	37
19	OLDHAM ATH	42	13	11	18	38	50	37
20	EVERTON	42	12	12	18	57	55	36
21	BRADFORD C	42	11	10	21	48	72	32
22	MANCHESTER U	42	8	12	22	41	73	28

Season 1922-23

Football League Division 1

DATE	OPPONENTS	SCORE	GOALSCORERS	ATTENDANCE
Aug 26	Sheffield United	L 0-2		25,000
Aug 28	MIDDLESBROUGH	W 2-1	Browell, Barnes	25,000
Sep 2	SHEFFIELD UNITED	D 3-3	Browell, Doran, Murphy	25,000
Sep 4	Middlesbrough	L 0-5		15,000
Sep 9	BIRMINGHAM	L 0-1		22,000
Sep 16	Birmingham	W 1-0	Johnson	30,000
Sep 23	HUDDERSFIELD TOWN	W 3-1	Johnson 2, Barnes	28,000
Sep 30	Huddersfield Town	D 0-0		16,200
Oct 7	Stoke	D 1-1	Johnson	21,000
Oct 14	STOKE	W 2-1	Johnson, Barnes	28,000
Oct 21	Preston North End	W 2-0	Barnes 2	12,000
Oct 28	PRESTON NORTH END	W 2-1	Johnson, Barnes	20,000
Nov 4	West Bromwich Albion	L 0-2		18,000
Nov 11	WEST BROMWICH ALBION	D 1-1	Johnson	25,000
Nov 18	BOLTON WANDERERS	W 2-0	Roberts, Johnson	30,000
Nov 25	Bolton Wanderers	L 1-2	Barnes	30,000
Dec 2	Blackburn Rovers	D 0-0		20,000
Dec 9	BLACKBURN ROVERS	W 2-1	Barnes 2	26,000
Dec 16	Cardiff City	L 1-3	Barnes	15,000
Dec 23	CARDIFF CITY	W 5-1	Barnes 3, Roberts, Johnson	18,000
Dec 25	Everton	D 0-0		35,000
Dec 26	EVERTON	W 2-1	Roberts, Barnes	30,000
Dec 30	OLDHAM ATHLETIC	W 3-2	Johnson 2, Roberts	20,000
Jan 6	Oldham Athletic	W 3-0	Barnes 2, Roberts	18,000
Jan 20	Arsenal	L 0-1		25,000
Jan 27	ARSENAL	D 0-0		30,000
Feb 3	Aston Villa	L 0-2		20,000
Feb 10	ASTON VILLA	D 1-1	Roberts	15,000
Feb 17	Burnley	L 0-2		14,000
Feb 24	BURNLEY	W 1-0	Barnes	20,000
Mar 3	Tottenham Hotspur	L 1-3	Browell	35,000
Mar 10	TOTTENHAM HOTSPUR	W 3-0	Roberts 2, Johnson	25,000
Mar 17	LIVERPOOL	W 1-0	Barnes	35,000
Mar 24	Liverpool	L 0-2		25,000
Mar 30	Sunderland	L 0-2		35,000
Mar 31	CHELSEA	W 3-0	Johnson 2, Barnes	15,000
Apr 2	SUNDERLAND	W 1-0	Barnes	32,000
Apr 7	Chelsea	D 1-1	Barnes	22,000
Apr 14	NOTTINGHAM FOREST	D 1-1	Roberts	14,000
Apr 21	Nottingham Forest	L 0-2		12,000
Apr 28	NEWCASTLE UNITED	D 0-0		20,000
May 5	Newcastle United	L 1-3	Roberts	15,000

FA Cup

Jan 13	Charlton Athletic	(Rd 1)	L 1-2	Johnson	28,445

League & Cup Appearances

PLAYER	LEAGUE	CUP COMPETITION FA CUP	TOTAL
Allen	27		27
Barnes	38	1	39
Browell	15		15
Calderwood	4		4
Cookson	25	1	26
Daniels	10		10
Doran	3		3
Etherington	10		10
Fayers	1		1
Fletcher	5		5
Goodchild	20		20
Hammill	41	1	42
Johnson	35	1	36
Kelly	1	1	2
Meredith	1		1
Mitchell	22	1	23
Morris	26		26
Mulligan	1		1
Murphy	32	1	33
Pringle	42	1	43
Roberts	32	1	33
Sharp	41	1	42
Thompson	10		10
Utley	1		1
Warner	7		7
Wilson	12	1	13

Goalscorers

PLAYER	LEAGUE	CUP COMPETITION FA CUP	TOTAL
Barnes	21		21
Johnson	14	1	15
Roberts	10		10
Browell	3		3
Doran	1		1
Murphy	1		1

Final Division 1 Table

		P	W	D	L	F	A	Pts
1	LIVERPOOL	42	26	8	8	70	31	60
2	SUNDERLAND	42	22	10	10	72	54	54
3	HUDDERSFIELD T	42	21	11	10	60	32	53
4	NEWCASTLE U	42	18	12	12	45	37	48
5	EVERTON	42	20	7	15	63	59	47
6	ASTON VILLA	42	18	10	14	64	51	46
7	WBA	42	17	11	14	58	49	45
8	MANCHESTER CITY	42	17	11	14	50	49	45
9	CARDIFF C	42	18	7	17	73	59	43
10	SHEFFIELD U	42	16	10	16	68	64	42
11	THE ARSENAL	42	16	10	16	61	62	42
12	TOTTENHAM H	42	17	7	18	50	50	41
13	BOLTON W	42	14	12	16	50	58	40
14	BLACKBURN R	42	14	12	16	47	62	40
15	BURNLEY	42	16	6	20	58	59	38
16	PRESTON NE	42	13	11	18	60	64	37
17	BIRMINGHAM	42	13	11	18	41	57	37
18	MIDDLESBROUGH	42	13	10	19	57	63	36
19	CHELSEA	42	9	18	15	45	53	36
20	NOTTINGHAM F	42	13	8	21	41	70	34
21	STOKE	42	10	10	22	47	67	30
22	OLDHAM ATH	42	10	10	22	35	65	30

Fact File

City lost only one home game in their last season at Hyde Road.

MANAGER: Ernest Mangnall

CAPTAIN: Mickey Hamill

TOP SCORER: Horace Barnes

BIGGEST WIN: December 23, 1922 5-1 v Cardiff City, Division 1

HIGHEST ATTENDANCE: March 17, 1923 (approx.) 35,000 v Liverpool, won 1-0, Division 1

MAJOR TRANSFERS IN: Frank Roberts from Bolton Wanderers

Season 1923-24

Football League Division 1

DATE	OPPONENTS	SCORE	GOALSCORERS	ATTENDANCE
Aug 25	SHEFFIELD UNITED	W 2-1	Johnson, Barnes	56,993
Aug 29	Aston Villa	L 0-2		15,000
Sep 1	Sheffield United	L 0-3		30,000
Sep 5	ASTON VILLA	L 1-2	Barnes	32,038
Sep 8	BOLTON WANDERERS	D 1-1	Roberts	43,601
Sep 15	Bolton Wanderers	D 0-0		35,000
Sep 22	SUNDERLAND	W 4-1	Barnes 2, Johnson, Hamill	33,954
Sep 29	Sunderland	L 2-5	Barnes 2	15,000
Oct 6	ARSENAL	W 1-0	Roberts	23,477
Oct 13	Arsenal	W 2-1	Barnes 2	32,000
Oct 20	Blackburn Rovers	W 1-0	Barnes	30,000
Oct 27	BLACKBURN ROVERS	W 3-1	Roberts 2, Barnes	32,498
Nov 3	NEWCASTLE UNITED	D 1-1	Barnes	27,652
Nov 10	Newcastle United	L 1-4	Murphy	30,000
Nov 17	CARDIFF CITY	D 1-1	Murphy	20,200
Nov 24	Cardiff City	D 1-1	Roberts	30,000
Dec 1	NOTTS COUNTY	W 1-0	Roberts	22,990
Dec 8	Notts County	L 0-2		12,000
Dec 15	EVERTON	W 2-1	Barnes, Roberts	35,000
Dec 22	Everton	L 1-6	Barnes	20,000
Dec 26	Birmingham	L 0-3		30,000
Dec 29	WEST BROMWICH ALBION	D 3-3	Barnes 2, Roberts	20,000
Jan 1	TOTTENHAM HOTSPUR	W 1-0	Johnson	40,000
Jan 5	West Bromwich Albion	L 1-2	Barnes	15,000
Jan 19	LIVERPOOL	L 0-1		22,000
Jan 26	Liverpool	D 0-0		25,000
Feb 9	Nottingham Forest	W 2-1	Johnson, Browell	10,000
Feb 13	NOTTINGHAM FOREST	L 1-3	Roberts	3,000
Feb 16	BURNLEY	D 2-2	Roberts, Hicks	24,000
Mar 1	MIDDLESBROUGH	W 3-2	Barnes 2, Roberts	20,000
Mar 15	Preston North End	L 1-4	Barnes	18,000
Mar 17	Burnley	L 2-3	Warner, Browell	12,000
Mar 22	PRESTON NORTH END	D 2-2	Barnes, Johnson	22,000
Apr 2	Middlesbrough	D 1-1	Johnson	10,000
Apr 5	CHELSEA	W 1-0	Johnson	17,000
Apr 12	Huddersfield Town	D 1-1	Roberts	11,000
Apr 18	BIRMINGHAM	W 1-0	Roberts	30,000
Apr 19	HUDDERSFIELD TOWN	D 1-1	Warner	35,000
Apr 21	Tottenham Hotspur	L 1-4	Johnson	18,000
Apr 26	West Ham United	W 2-1	Roberts, Browell	16,000
Apr 30	Chelsea	L 1-3	Browell	3,600
May 3	WEST HAM UNITED	W 2-1	Warner, Johnson	12,000

FA Cup

Jan 12	NOTTINGHAM FOREST	(Rd 1) W 2-1	Roberts, Barnes	33,849
Feb 2	HALIFAX TOWN	(Rd 2) D 2-2	Hamill, Roberts	30,970
Feb 6	Halifax Town	(R) D 0-0		21,590
Feb 11	HALIFAX TOWN	(2nd R) W 3-0	Roberts 2, Browell	28,128
Feb 23	BRIGHTON & HOVE ALBION	(Rd 3) W 5-1	Browell 2, Meredith Barnes, Sharp	24,734
Mar 8	CARDIFF CITY	(Rd 4) D 0-0		76,166
Mar 12	Cardiff City	(R) W 1-0	Browell	50,000
Mar 29	NEWCASTLE UNITED	(SF) L 0-2		50,039

League & Cup Appearances

PLAYER	LEAGUE	CUP COMPETITION FA CUP	TOTAL
Allen	14	4	18
Barnes	23	7	30
Browell	14	5	19
Calderwood	15		15
Carroll	2		2
Cookson	34	8	42
Daniels	11	1	12
Donaldson	7		7
Elwood	8		8
Fletcher	20	4	24
Goodchild	7		7
Hamil	25	7	32
Harper	4		4
Hicks	2		2
Johnson	30	5	35
Leslie	1		1
Meredith	2	4	6
Mitchell	31	8	39
Morris	31	4	35
Murphy	26	4	30
Pringle	28	8	36
Roberts	41	8	49
Sharp	34	4	38
Smith	6		6
Thompson	1		1
Warner	23	2	25
Wilson	21	4	25
Woosnam	1	1	2

Goalscorers

PLAYER	LEAGUE	CUP COMPETITION FA CUP	TOTAL
Barnes	20	2	22
Roberts	14	4	18
Johnson	9		9
Browell	4	4	8
Warner	3		3
Murphy	2		2
Hamil	1	1	2
Hicks	1		1
Meredith		1	1
Sharp		1	1

Fact File

Horace Barnes scores the first ever goal at Maine Road in the season's opener.

Billy Meredith played his last game against Newcastle in the FA Cup semi-final. Aged 49 he still is the oldest ever player in an FA Cup tie.

MANAGER: Ernest Mangnall

CAPTAIN: Max Woosnam

TOP SCORER: Horace Barnes

BIGGEST WIN: February 23, 1924 5-1 v Brighton and Hove Albion, FA Cup Round 3

HIGHEST ATTENDANCE: March 8, 1924 76,166 v Cardiff City, drew 0-0, FA Cup Round 4

MAJOR TRANSFERS OUT: Billy Meredith (retired)

Final Division 1 Table

		P	W	D	L	F	A	Pts
1	HUDDERSFIELD T	42	23	11	8	60	33	57
2	CARDIFF C	42	22	13	7	61	34	57
3	SUNDERLAND	42	22	9	11	71	54	53
4	BOLTON W	42	18	14	10	68	34	50
5	SHEFFIELD U	42	19	12	11	69	49	50
6	ASTON VILLA	42	18	13	11	52	37	49
7	EVERTON	42	18	13	11	62	53	49
8	BLACKBURN R	42	17	11	14	54	50	45
9	NEWCASTLE U	42	17	10	15	60	54	44
10	NOTTS CO	42	14	14	14	44	49	42
11	MANCHESTER CITY	42	15	12	15	54	71	42
12	LIVERPOOL	42	15	11	16	49	48	41
13	WEST HAM U	42	13	15	14	40	43	41
14	BIRMINGHAM	42	13	13	16	41	49	39
15	TOTTENHAM H	42	12	14	16	50	56	38
16	WBA	42	12	14	16	51	62	38
17	BURNLEY	42	12	12	18	55	60	36
18	PRESTON NE	42	12	10	20	52	67	34
19	THE ARSENAL	42	12	9	21	40	63	33
20	NOTTINGHAM F	42	10	12	20	42	64	32
21	CHELSEA	42	9	14	19	31	53	32
22	MIDDLESBROUGH	42	7	8	27	37	60	22

Season 1924-25

Football League Division 1

DATE	OPPONENTS	SCORE	GOALSCORERS	ATTENDANCE
Aug 30	Bury	W 2-0	Roberts 2	40,000
Sep 1	Arsenal	L 0-1		25,000
Sep 6	NOTTINGHAM FOREST	W 4-2	Barnes 2, Murphy, Roberts	31,000
Sep 13	Liverpool	L 3-5	Roberts 2, Barnes	30,000
Sep 17	ARSENAL	W 2-0	Johnson, Barnes	34,000
Sep 20	NEWCASTLE UNITED	W 3-1	Roberts 2, Johnson	35,000
Sep 27	Sheffield United	W 5-0	Roberts 3, Johnson, Barnes	20,000
Oct 4	WEST HAM UNITED	W 3-1	Roberts 2, Barnes	46,000
Oct 11	Blackburn Rovers	L 1-3	Barnes	30,000
Oct 18	HUDDERSFIELD TOWN	D 1-1	Barnes	50,000
Oct 25	BOLTON WANDERERS	D 2-2	Roberts, Johnson	50,000
Oct 29	Everton	L 1-3	Johnson	20,000
Nov 1	Notts County	L 0-2		12,000
Nov 8	EVERTON	D 2-2	Austin, Roberts	30,000
Nov 10	Tottenham Hotspur	D 1-1	Roberts	11,000
Nov 15	Sunderland	L 2-3	Johnson, Murphy	20,000
Nov 22	CARDIFF CITY	D 2-2	Roberts 2	18,000
Nov 29	Preston North End	W 3-2	Austin, Roberts, Warner	22,000
Dec 6	BURNLEY	D 3-3	Austin, Roberts, Browell	20,000
Dec 13	Leeds United	W 3-0	Roberts, Browell, Murphy	15,000
Dec 20	BIRMINGHAM	D 2-2	Austin, Browell	40,000
Dec 25	WEST BROMWICH ALBION	L 1-2	Browell	35,000
Dec 26	West Bromwich Albion	L 1-3	Johnson	50,000
Jan 3	Nottingham Forest	W 3-0	Johnson 2, Cowan	8,000
Jan 17	LIVERPOOL	W 5-0	Roberts 4, Woosnam	25,000
Jan 24	Newcastle United	L 0-2		25,000
Jan 31	BURY	D 0-0		15,000
Feb 7	West Ham United	L 0-4		25,000
Feb 14	BLACKBURN ROVERS	L 1-3	Roberts	31,000
Feb 21	Huddersfield Town	D 1-1	Roberts	18,000
Feb 23	SHEFFIELD UNITED	W 2-1	Roberts 2	12,000
Feb 28	Bolton Wanderers	L 2-4	Daniels, Hicks	25,000
Mar 7	NOTTS COUNTY	W 2-1	Roberts 2	25,000
Mar 21	SUNDERLAND	L 1-3	Roberts	30,000
Apr 1	Cardiff City	W 2-0	Austin, Johnson	8,000
Apr 4	PRESTON NORTH END	W 2-1	Warner, Browell	20,000
Apr 10	Aston Villa	L 1-2	Hicks	20,000
Apr 11	Burnley	L 0-1		14,000
Apr 13	ASTON VILLA	W 1-0	Warner	25,000
Apr 18	LEEDS UNITED	W 4-2	Austin, Browell, Johnson, Hicks	14,000
Apr 25	Birmingham	L 1-2	Johnson	13,000
May 2	TOTTENHAM HOTSPUR	W 1-0	Warner	15,000

FA Cup

Jan 10	Preston North End	(Rd 1)	L 1-4	Roberts	24,536

League & Cup Appearances

PLAYER	LEAGUE	CUP COMPETITION FA CUP	TOTAL
Austin	38	1	39
Barnes	14		14
Benzie	1		1
Browell	14	1	15
Calderwood	14		14
Cookson	37		37
Cowan	21		21
Daniels	9		9
Elwood	15		15
Fletcher	27	1	28
Goodchild	13		13
Hicks	15	1	16
Johnson	41	1	42
McCourt	4		4
Mitchell	29	1	30
Murphy	24		24
Pringle	35	1	36
Roberts	38	1	39
Sharp	40	1	41
Thompson	7	1	8
Warner	12		12
Wilson	12		12
Woosnam	2	1	3

Goalscorers

PLAYER	LEAGUE	CUP COMPETITION FA CUP	TOTAL
Roberts	31	1	32
Johnson	12		12
Barnes	8		8
Austin	6		6
Browell	6		6
Warner	4		4
Hicks	3		3
Murphy	3		3
Cowan	1		1
Daniels	1		1
Woosnam	1		1

Fact File

Frank Roberts, who won a total of four England caps, scored his only two international goals against Wales at the Vetch Field in February 1925.

MANAGER: David Ashworth

CAPTAIN: Charlie Pringle

TOP SCORER: Frank Roberts

BIGGEST WIN: September 27, 1924 5-0 v Sheffield United, Division 1;

HIGHEST ATTENDANCE: October 18, 1924 (approx.) 50,000 v Huddersfield Town, drew 1-1, Division 1; October 25, 1924 approx. 50,000 v Bolton Wanderers, drew 2-2, Division 1; December 26, 1924 approx. 50,000 v West Bromwich Albion, lost 1-3, Division 1

MAJOR TRANSFERS IN: Sam Cowan from Doncaster Rovers

MAJOR TRANSFERS OUT: Horace Barnes to Preston North End

Final Division 1 Table

		P	W	D	L	F	A	Pts
1	HUDDERSFIELD T	42	21	16	5	69	28	58
2	WBA	42	23	10	9	58	34	56
3	BOLTON W	42	22	11	9	76	34	55
4	LIVERPOOL	42	20	10	12	63	55	50
5	BURY	42	17	15	10	54	51	49
6	NEWCASTLE U	42	16	16	10	61	42	48
7	SUNDERLAND	42	19	10	13	64	51	48
8	BIRMINGHAM	42	17	12	13	49	53	46
9	NOTTS CO	42	16	13	13	42	31	45
10	MANCHESTER CITY	42	17	9	16	76	68	43
11	CARDIFF C	42	16	11	15	56	51	43
12	TOTTENHAM H	42	15	12	15	52	43	42
13	WEST HAM U	42	15	12	15	62	60	42
14	SHEFFIELD U	42	13	13	16	55	63	39
15	ASTON VILLA	42	13	13	16	58	71	39
16	BLACKBURN R	42	11	13	18	53	66	35
17	EVERTON	42	12	11	19	40	60	35
18	LEEDS U	42	11	12	19	46	59	34
19	BURNLEY	42	11	12	19	46	75	34
20	THE ARSENAL	42	14	5	23	46	58	33
21	PRESTON NE	42	10	6	26	37	74	26
22	NOTTINGHAM F	42	6	12	24	29	65	24

Season 1925-26

Football League Division 1

DATE	OPPONENTS	SCORE	GOALSCORERS	ATTENDANCE
Aug 29	CARDIFF CITY	W 3-2	Austin, Warner, Johnson	42,000
Aug 31	Birmingham	L 0-1		20,000
Sep 5	Tottenham Hotspur	L 0-1		35,954
Sep 12	MANCHESTER UNITED	D 1-1	Cowan	62,994
Sep 19	EVERTON	D 4-4	Browell 4	11,393
Sep 23	West Bromwich Albion	L 1-4	Roberts	8,287
Sep 26	Huddersfield Town	D 2-2	Warner, Johnson	19,541
Oct 3	SUNDERLAND	W 4-1	Austin 2, Warner Browell	40,000
Oct 10	Blackburn Rovers	D 3-3	Browell 2, Roberts	25,935
Oct 17	Liverpool	L 1-2	Johnson	35,000
Oct 24	BURNLEY	W 8-3	Browell 5, Roberts, Johnson, Hicks	19,740
Oct 26	Sheffield United	L 3-8	Cowan, Roberts, Johnson	8,000
Oct 31	West Ham United	L 1-3	Browell	23,000
Nov 4	SHEFFIELD UNITED	L 2-4	Austin, Roberts	7,000
Nov 7	ARSENAL	L 2-5	Warner, Browell	11,384
Nov 14	Bolton Wanderers	L 1-5	Roberts	22,326
Nov 21	NOTTS COUNTY	D 1-1	Coupland	20,000
Nov 28	Aston Villa	L 1-3	Dennison	25,000
Dec 5	LEICESTER CITY	W 5-1	Roberts 2, Johnson 2, Dennison	20,000
Dec 12	Leeds United	W 4-3	Bradford, Dennison, Johnson, Roberts	18,762
Dec 19	NEWCASTLE UNITED	D 2-2	Johnson, Murphy	35,000
Dec 25	Bury	L 5-6	Browell 2, Coupland, Johnson, Roberts	25,000
Dec 26	BURY	L 0-2		50,000
Jan 1	WEST BROMWICH ALBION	W 3-1	Austin, Dennison, Johnson	23,030
Jan 2	Cardiff City	D 2-2	Roberts 2	12,000
Jan 16	TOTTENHAM HOTSPUR	D 0-0		25,344
Jan 23	Manchester United	W 6-1	Austin 2, Roberts 2, Johnson, Hicks	48,657
Feb 6	HUDDERSFIELD TOWN	L 1-5	Roberts	36,645
Feb 10	Everton	D 1-1	Roberts	15,067
Feb 13	Sunderland	L 3-5	Austin, Browell, Nicks	25,000
Feb 27	LIVERPOOL	D 1-1	Browell	35,000
Mar 13	WEST HAM UNITED	W 2-0	Roberts, Murphy	40,000
Mar 17	BLACKBURN ROVERS	L 0-1		18,793
Mar 20	Arsenal	L 0-1		34,974
Mar 29	BOLTON WANDERERS	D 1-1	Austin	21,720
Apr 2	BIRMINGHAM	L 2-4	Austin, Hicks	60,000
Apr 3	Notts County	L 0-1		12,000
Apr 6	Burnley	W 2-1	Johnson, Hicks	19,966
Apr 10	ASTON VILLA	W 4-2	Austin, Browell, Roberts, Johnson	42,000
Apr 17	Leicester City	W 3-2	Roberts 2, Browell	20,000
Apr 27	LEEDS UNITED	W 2-1	Austin, Johnson	43,475
May 1	Newcastle United	L 2-3	Browell, Roberts	20,000

FA Cup

DATE	OPPONENTS		SCORE	GOALSCORERS	ATTENDANCE
Jan 9	Corinthians	(Rd 3)	D 3-3	Cookson, Johnson, Hicks	29,700
Jan 13	CORINTHIANS	(R)	W 4-0	Austin 2, Johnson, Hicks	42,303
Jan 30	HUDDERSFIELD TOWN	(Rd 4)	W 4-0	Hicks 2, Browell, Roberts	74,789
Feb 20	CRYSTAL PALACE	(Rd 5)	W 11-4	Roberts 5, Browell 3, Austin, Johnson, Hicks	51,630
Mar 6	Clapton Orient	(Rd 6)	W 6-1	Johnson 3, Hicks, Roberts Browell	24,600
Mar 27	MANCHESTER UNITED	(SF)	W 3-0	Browell 2, Roberts	46,450
Apr 24	BOLTON WANDERERS	(F)	L 0-1		91,547

Fact File

Despite a record 6-1 victory at Old Trafford, City's failure to gain a point from their final game of the season against Newcastle sent them to Division 2.

MANAGER: David Ashworth
CAPTAIN: Charlie Pringle
TOP SCORER: Frank Roberts
BIGGEST WIN: February 20, 1926 11-4 v Crystal Palace, FA Cup Round 5
HIGHEST ATTENDANCE: April 24, 1926 91,547 v Bolton Wanderers, lost 0-1, FA Cup Final
MAJOR TRANSFERS IN: Jimmy McMullen from Partick Thistle

League & Cup Appearances

PLAYER	LEAGUE	CUP COMPETITION FA CUP	TOTAL
Appleton	1	1	2
Austin	36	7	43
Benzie	7		7
Bradford	5		5
Browell	32	5	37
Calderwood	2	2	4
Cookson	35	6	41
Coupland	23	3	26
Cowan	38	7	45
Daniels	1		1
Dennison	8	2	10
Elwood	4	1	5
Fletcher	1		1
Goodchild	24	7	31
Hicks	35	7	42
Johnson	38	7	45
McCloy	37	4	41
McMullan	10	3	13
Mitchell	17		17
Murphy	9		9
Phillips	1		1
Pringle	36	7	43
Roberts	38	7	45
Sharp	8		8
Thompson	9	1	10
Warner	7		7

Goalscorers

PLAYER	LEAGUE	CUP COMPETITION FA CUP	TOTAL
Roberts	21	9	30
Browell	21	7	28
Johnson	15	5	20
Austin	12	3	15
Hicks	5	6	11
Dennison	4		4
Warner	4		4
Coupland	2		2
Cowan	2		2
Murphy	2		2
Bradford	1		1
Cookson		1	1

Final Division 1 Table

		P	W	D	L	F	A	Pts
1	HUDDERSFIELD T	42	23	11	8	92	60	57
2	THE ARSENAL	42	22	8	12	87	63	52
3	SUNDERLAND	42	21	6	15	96	80	48
4	BURY	42	20	7	15	85	77	47
5	SHEFFIELD U	42	19	8	15	102	82	46
6	ASTON VILLA	42	16	12	14	86	76	44
7	LIVERPOOL	42	14	16	12	70	63	44
8	BOLTON W	42	17	10	15	75	76	44
9	MANCHESTER U	42	19	6	17	66	73	44
10	NEWCASTLE U	42	16	10	16	84	75	42
11	EVERTON	42	12	18	12	72	70	42
12	BLACKBURN R	42	15	11	16	91	80	41
13	WBA	42	16	8	18	79	78	40
14	BIRMINGHAM	42	16	8	18	66	81	40
15	TOTTENHAM H	42	15	9	18	66	79	39
16	CARDIFF C	42	16	7	19	61	76	39
17	LEICESTER C	42	14	10	18	70	80	38
18	WEST HAM U	42	15	7	20	63	76	37
19	LEEDS U	42	14	8	20	64	76	36
20	BURNLEY	42	13	10	19	85	108	36
21	MANCHESTER CITY	42	12	11	19	89	100	35
22	NOTTS CO	42	13	7	22	54	74	33

Season 1926-27

Football League Division 2

DATE	OPPONENTS	SCORE	GOALSCORERS	ATTENDANCE
Aug 28	FULHAM	W 4-2	Austin, Barrass, Roberts, Hicks	34,000
Sep 1	PORTSMOUTH	W 4-0	Roberts 2, Johnson, Hicks	25,000
Sep 4	Grimsby Town	D 2-2	Roberts, Johnson	16,599
Sep 6	Oldham Athletic	W 2-1	Pringle, Austin	26,009
Sep 11	BLACKPOOL	W 2-1	Austin, Johnson	34,885
Sep 18	Reading	L 0-1		24,000
Sep 22	OLDHAM ATHLETIC	W 3-0	Roberts, Johnson, Hicks	25,676
Sep 25	SWANSEA TOWN	W 3-1	Roberts, Johnson, Hicks	35,000
Oct 1	Nottingham Forest	D 3-3	Johnson 2, W Cowan	15,121
Oct 9	BARNSLEY	D 1-1	Hicks	18,000
Oct 16	SOUTHAMPTON	L 3-4	McMullan, Austin, Johnson	30,000
Oct 23	Port Vale	W 2-0	McMullan, Johnson	14,000
Oct 30	CLAPTON ORIENT	W 6-1	Barrass 3, Roberts 2, Johnson	28,979
Nov 6	Notts County	L 0-1		6,000
Nov 13	WOLVES	W 2-1	McMullan, Austin	15,000
Nov 20	Hull City	L 2-3	Barrass, Johnson	11,582
Nov 27	SOUTH SHIELDS	L 1-2	Barrass	12,000
Dec 4	Preston North End	W 4-2	Austin 3, Barrass	25,000
Dec 11	CHELSEA	W 1-0	Bell	26,868
Dec 18	Bradford City	L 3-4	Hicks 2, Roberts	17,580
Dec 25	MIDDLESBROUGH	L 3-5	S Cowan, W Cowan, Johnson	44,077
Dec 27	Middlesbrough	L 1-2	Roberts	43,753
Jan 1	Portsmouth	L 1-2	Johnson	20,000
Jan 15	Fulham	W 5-2	Gibson 2, Austin, W Cowan, S Cowan	24,000
Jan 22	GRIMSBY TOWN	W 2-0	Johnson, Hicks	21,212
Jan 29	Blackpool	W 4-2	Hicks 2, W Cowan, Johnson	9,223
Feb 5	READING	W 3-0	Roberts, Hicks, o.g.	30,000
Feb 12	Swansea Town	W 3-1	Johnson 2, Hicks	20,000
Feb 19	Nottingham Forest	D 1-1	W Cowan	48,689
Feb 26	Barnsley	D 1-1	W Cowan	14,000
Mar 12	PORT VALE	W 4-1	Johnson 2, W Cowan, Hicks	30,000
Mar 19	Clapton Orient	W 4-2	Hicks 3, Austin	15,141
Mar 26	NOTTS COUNTY	W 4-1	W Cowan 2, Hicks 2	15,000
Apr 2	Wolves	L 1-4	W Cowan	11,361
Apr 9	HULL CITY	D 2-2	W Cowan, Bell	21,508
Apr 15	Darlington	D 2-2	Broadhurst, Johnson	10,000
Apr 16	South Shields	D 2-2	Roberts, Hicks	6,000
Apr 18	DARLINGTON	W 7-0	Broadhurst 4, Johnson 2, Bell	40,000
Apr 23	PRESTON NORTH END	W 1-0	Hicks	40,000
Apr 25	Southampton	D 1-1	Roberts	8,000
Apr 30	Chelsea	D 0-0		39,995
May 7	BRADFORD CITY	W 8-0	Johnson 3, Broadhurst 2, Hicks, Bell, Roberts	40,384

FA Cup

Jan 8	Birmingham	(Rd 3) L 1-4	Hicks	39,503

League & Cup Appearances

PLAYER	LEAGUE	CUP COMPETITION FA CUP	TOTAL
Allen	2		2
Austin	26	1	27
Barrass	27	1	28
Bell	26		26
Bennett	12	1	13
Benzie	5		5
Broadhurst	7		7
Cookson	42	1	43
Coupland	1		1
Cowan S	27		27
Cowan W	22	1	23
Elwood	4		4
Finnegan	8		8
Gibson	2		2
Goodchild	15	1	16
Gray	19		19
Hicks	42	1	43
Johnson	38	1	39
McCloy	30		30
McMullan	35	1	36
Pringle	34	1	35
Roberts	27		27
Sharp	6		6
Thompson	3	1	4
Wilson	2		2

Goalscorers

PLAYER	LEAGUE	CUP COMPETITION FA CUP	TOTAL
Johnson	25		25
Hicks	21	1	22
Roberts	14		14
Cowan W	11		11
Austin	10		10
Barrass	7		7
Broadhurst	7		7
Bell	4		4
McMullan	3		3
Cowan S	2		2
Gibson	2		2
Pringle	1		1
Opps' o.gs.	1		1

Fact File

City missed out on promotion on goal difference by the narrowest margin ever – 1.7705 against Portsmouth's 1.7755.

MANAGER: Peter Hodge
CAPTAIN: Jimmy McMullan
TOP SCORER: Tommy Johnson
BIGGEST WIN: May 7, 1927 8-0 v Bradford City, Division 2;
HIGHEST ATTENDANCE: Feburary 19, 1927 48,689 v Nottingham Forest, drew 1-1, Division 2
MAJOR TRANSFERS IN: Matthew Barrass from Sheffield Wednesday, Bert Gray from Oldham

Final Division 2 Table

		P	W	D	L	F	A	Pts
1	MIDDLESBROUGH	42	27	8	7	122	60	62
2	PORTSMOUTH	42	23	8	11	87	49	54
3	MANCHESTER CITY	42	22	10	10	108	61	54
4	CHELSEA	42	20	12	10	62	52	52
5	NOTTINGHAM F	42	18	14	10	80	55	50
6	PRESTON NE	42	20	9	13	74	72	49
7	HULL C	42	20	7	15	63	52	47
8	PORT VALE	42	16	13	13	88	78	45
9	BLACKPOOL	42	18	8	16	95	80	44
10	OLDHAM ATH	42	19	6	17	74	84	44
11	BARNSLEY	42	17	9	16	88	87	43
12	SWANSEA T	42	16	11	15	68	72	43
13	SOUTHAMPTON	42	15	12	15	60	62	42
14	READING	42	16	8	18	64	72	40
15	WOLVERHAMPTON W	42	14	7	21	73	75	35
16	NOTTS CO	42	15	5	22	70	96	35
17	GRIMSBY T	42	11	12	19	74	91	34
18	FULHAM	42	13	8	21	58	92	34
19	SOUTH SHIELDS	42	11	11	20	71	96	33
20	CLAPTON ORIENT	42	12	7	23	60	96	31
21	DARLINGTON	42	12	6	24	79	98	30
22	BRADFORD C	42	7	9	26	50	88	23

Season 1927-28

Football League Division 2

DATE	OPPONENTS	SCORE	GOALSCORERS	ATTENDANCE
Aug 27	Wolves	D 2-2	McMullan, Hicks	30,000
Aug 29	SWANSEA TOWN	W 7-4	Johnson 3, Broadhurst, Hicks, Roberts, Bell	40,000
Sep 3	PORT VALE	W 1-0	Johnson	34,000
Sep 5	Swansea Town	L 3-5	Bell, Johnson, Hicks	13,000
Sep 10	South Shields	W 1-0	McMullan	9,000
Sep 17	LEEDS UNITED	W 2-1	Johnson 2	40,931
Sep 24	Nottingham Forest	W 5-4	Johnson 2, Hicks 2, Broadhurst	12,893
Oct 1	OLDHAM ATHLETIC	W 3-1	Broadhurst 2, Johnson	25,216
Oct 8	HULL CITY	W 2-1	Barrass 2	42,038
Oct 15	Preston North End	L 0-1		28,000
Oct 22	Blackpool	D 2-2	Roberts, Hicks	17,013
Oct 29	READING	W 4-1	Austin 2, Roberts, Johnson	35,000
Nov 5	Grimsby Town	L 1-4	Smelt	12,522
Nov 12	CHELSEA	L 0-1		52,830
Nov 19	Clapton Orient	W 2-0	Austin, Roberts	14,129
Nov 26	STOKE CITY	W 4-0	Austin, Allen, Roberts, Johnson	40,000
Dec 3	Bristol City	L 0-2		30,000
Dec 10	WEST BROMWICH ALBION	W 3-1	Austin, Broadhurst, Johnson	25,000
Dec 17	Southampton	D 1-1	Broadhurst	12,000
Dec 24	NOTTS COUNTY	W 3-1	Broadhurst 2, Hicks	20,000
Dec 26	Barnsley	W 3-0	Broadhurst 2, Roberts	17,000
Dec 31	WOLVES	W 3-0	Johnson 2, Broadhurst	20,000
Jan 2	BARNSLEY	W 7-3	Austin 2, Gorringe 2, McMullan, Roberts, Johnson	30,000
Jan 7	Port Vale	W 2-1	Roberts, Hicks	15,000
Jan 21	SOUTH SHIELDS	W 3-0	Austin, Broadhurst, Johnson	30,000
Feb 4	NOTTINGHAM FOREST	D 3-3	Broadhurst, Austin, Hicks	30,037
Feb 11	Oldham Athletic	L 2-3	Bell, Broadhurst	25,426
Feb 25	PRESTON NORTH END	D 2-2	Roberts 2	60,000
Mar 3	BLACKPOOL	W 4-1	Roberts 4	40,906
Mar 10	Reading	D 1-1	Marshall	12,000
Mar 17	GRIMSBY TOWN	W 2-0	Roberts, McMullan	49,185
Mar 24	Chelsea	W 1-0	Roberts	51,813
Mar 31	CLAPTON ORIENT	W 5-3	Roberts 3, Horne, Brook	38,272
Apr 6	FULHAM	W 2-1	Marshall, Roberts	30,000
Apr 7	Stoke City	L 0-2		30,000
Apr 9	Fulham	D 1-1	Tait	27,000
Apr 14	BRISTOL CITY	W 4-2	Tait, Johnson, Marshall, Hicks	30,000
Apr 16	Hull City	D 0-0		6,088
Apr 21	West Bromwich Albion	D 1-1	Brook	14,238
Apr 25	Leeds United	W 1-0	Tait	48,470
Apr 28	SOUTHAMPTON	W 6-1	Marshall 3, Johnson, Tait, Horne	40,000
May 5	Notts County	L 1-2	Marshall	6,000

FA Cup

Jan 16	LEEDS UNITED	(Rd 3) W 1-0	Johnson	50,473
Jan 28	Sunderland	(Rd 4) W 2-1	Broadhurst, Hicks	36,658
Feb 18	STOKE CITY	(Rd 5) L 0-1		73,668

Fact File

The Second Division champions' average attendance of 37,468 was the highest in the land.

MANAGER: Peter Hodge
CAPTAIN: Jimmy McMullan
TOP SCORER: Frank Roberts
BIGGEST WIN: August 29, 1927 7-4 v Swansea Town, Division 2
HIGHEST ATTENDANCE: April 4, 1928 73,668 v Stoke City, lost 0-1, FA Cup Round 5
MAJOR TRANSFERS IN: Eric Brook and Freddie Tilson from Barnsley

League & Cup Appearances

PLAYER	LEAGUE	CUP COMPETITION FA CUP	TOTAL
Allan	6	1	7
Appleton	1		1
Austin	18	2	20
Barber	10	1	11
Barrass	28	2	30
Bell	16		16
Bennett	5		5
Broadhurst	21	3	24
Brook	12		12
Cookson	11		11
Cowan	28	2	30
Foster	3		3
Gibbons	4	1	5
Gorringe	1		1
Gray	32	2	34
Hicks	28	3	31
Horne	7		7
Johnson	35	3	38
Marshall	14		14
McCloy	38	3	41
McMullan	38	3	41
Pringle	22	1	23
Ridley	30	3	33
Roberts	26	3	29
Robertson	2		2
Sharp	11		11
Smelt	2		2
Tait	7		7
Tilson	6		6

Goalscorers

PLAYER	LEAGUE	CUP COMPETITION FA CUP	TOTAL
Roberts	20		20
Johnson	19	1	20
Broadhurst	14	1	15
Hicks	10	1	11
Austin	9		9
Marshall	7		7
McMullan	4		4
Tait	4		4
Bell	3		3
Barrass	2		2
Brook	2		2
Gorringe	2		2
Horne	2		2
Allan	1		1
Smelt	1		1

Final Division 2 Table

		P	W	D	L	F	A	Pts
1	MANCHESTER CITY	42	25	9	8	100	59	59
2	LEEDS U	42	25	7	10	98	49	57
3	CHELSEA	42	23	8	11	75	45	54
4	PRESTON NE	42	22	9	11	100	66	53
5	STOKE C	42	22	8	12	78	59	52
6	SWANSEA T	42	18	12	12	75	63	48
7	OLDHAM ATH	42	19	8	15	75	51	46
8	WBA	42	17	12	13	90	70	46
9	PORT VALE	42	18	8	16	68	57	44
10	NOTTINGHAM F	42	15	10	17	83	84	40
11	GRIMSBY T	42	14	12	16	69	83	40
12	BRISTOL C	42	15	9	18	76	79	39
13	BARNSLEY	42	14	11	17	65	85	39
14	HULL C	42	12	15	15	41	54	39
15	NOTTS CO	42	13	12	17	68	74	38
16	WOLVERHAMPTON W	42	13	10	19	63	91	36
17	SOUTHAMPTON	42	14	7	21	68	77	35
18	READING	42	11	13	18	53	75	35
19	BLACKPOOL	42	13	8	21	83	101	34
20	CLAPTON ORIENT	42	11	12	19	55	85	34
21	FULHAM	42	13	7	22	68	89	33
22	SOUTH SHIELDS	42	7	9	26	56	111	23

The Essential History of Manchester City

Football League Division 1

DATE	OPPONENTS	SCORE	GOALSCORERS	ATTENDANCE
Aug 25	Birmingham	L 1-4	Tait	45,000
Sep 1	MANCHESTER UNITED	D 2-2	Roberts, Johnson	61,007
Sep 5	Portsmouth	L 0-1		26,000
Sep 8	HUDDERSFIELD TOWN	W 3-2	Johnson 2, Marshall	34,421
Sep 15	Everton	W 6-2	Johnson 5, Brook	47,871
Sep 22	ARSENAL	W 4-1	Broadhurst 2, Tilson 2	36,223
Sep 29	Blackburn Rovers	D 2-2	Tilson, Brook	25,430
Oct 1	PORTSMOUTH	W 2-1	Austin, Johnson	20,000
Oct 6	SUNDERLAND	W 5-3	Broadhurst, Barrass, Johnson, Marshall, Brook	40,000
Oct 13	Derby County	D 1-1	Brook	25,050
Oct 20	Leeds United	L 1-4	Barrass	32,866
Oct 27	LEICESTER CITY	L 2-3	Roberts 2	30,000
Nov 3	West Ham United	L 0-3		26,000
Nov 10	NEWCASTLE UNITED	L 2-4	Johnson 2	15,000
Nov 17	Burnley	W 3-2	Cowan, Roberts, Brook	14,021
Nov 24	CARDIFF CITY	D 1-1	Broadhurst	15,000
Dec 1	Sheffield United	W 3-1	Johnson 2, Roberts	22,000
Dec 19	Aston Villa	L 1-5	Johnson	13,002
Dec 22	LIVERPOOL	L 2-3	Bacon, Johnson	20,000
Dec 25	Sheffield Wednesday	L 0-4		45,000
Dec 26	SHEFFIELD WEDNESDAY	D 2-2	Johnson 2	55,000
Dec 29	BIRMINGHAM	L 2-3	Marshall, Johnson	35,000
Jan 5	Manchester United	W 2-1	Johnson, Austin	42,555
Jan 19	Huddersfield Town	D 2-2	Tait, Brook	17,602
Jan 26	EVERTON	W 5-1	Tilson 2, Austin, Brook, o.g.	36,241
Jan 30	BURY	W 6-4	Johnson 2, Tait, Brook, Tilson, Austin	20,000
Feb 2	Arsenal	D 0-0		13,764
Feb 9	BLACKBURN ROVERS	L 1-2	Johnson	33,801
Feb 16	Sunderland	L 1-3	Johnson	10,000
Feb 23	DERBY COUNTY	L 2-3	Johnson 2	27,941
Mar 2	LEEDS UNITED	W 3-0	Johnson, Tilson, Brook	33,921
Mar 9	Leicester City	L 2-3	Johnson, Tilson	15,000
Mar 16	WEST HAM UNITED	W 4-2	Brook 2, Johnson, Austin	30,000
Mar 23	Newcastle United	L 0-4		25,000
Mar 29	BOLTON WANDERERS	W 5-1	Johnson 3, Marshall, Tilson	45,838
Mar 30	BURNLEY	W 4-1	Johnson 2, Marshall, Brook	33,166
Apr 1	Bolton Wanderers	D 1-1	Marshall	21,955
Apr 6	Cardiff City	W 3-1	Johnson 2, Tilson	10,000
Apr 13	SHEFFIELD UNITED	W 3-1	Marshall, Tilson, Brook	20,000
Apr 20	Bury	W 2-1	Johnson, Tilson	15,000
Apr 27	ASTON VILLA	W 3-0	Toseland, Johnson, Brook	25,000
May 4	Liverpool	D 1-1	Johnson	25,000

FA Cup

Jan 12	Birmingham	(Rd 3) L 1-3	Austin	25,005

League & Cup Appearances

PLAYER	LEAGUE	CUP COMPETITION FA CUP	TOTAL
Austin	38	1	39
Bacon	5		5
Barber	25	1	26
Barrass	40	1	41
Bennett	2		2
Broadhurst	5		5
Brook	42	1	43
Cowan	38	1	39
Felton	10		10
Gibbons	3		3
Gray	17		17
Heinemann	4		4
Hicks	1		1
Horne	4		4
Johnson	39	1	40
Marshall	33	1	34
McCloy	31	1	32
McMullan	38	1	39
Ridley	40	1	41
Roberts	14	1	15
Tait	8		8
Tilson	22		22
Toseland	3		3

Goalscorers

PLAYER	LEAGUE	CUP COMPETITION FA CUP	TOTAL
Johnson	38		38
Brook	14		14
Tilson	12		12
Marshall	7		7
Austin	5	1	6
Roberts	6		6
Broadhurst	4		4
Tait	3		3
Barrass	2		2
Bacon	1		1
Cowan	1		1
Toseland	1		1
Opps' o.gs.	1		1

Fact File

Tommy Johnson's 38 goals this season still stands as a City goalscoring record.

MANAGER: Peter Hodge

CAPTAIN: Jimmy McMullan

TOP SCORER: Tommy Johnson

BIGGEST WIN: September 15, 1928 6-2 v Everton, Division 1

HIGHEST ATTENDANCE: September 1, 1928 61,007 v Manchester United, drew 2-2, Division 1

MAJOR TRANSFERS IN: Ernie Toseland from Coventry City

MAJOR TRANSFERS OUT: Sammy Cookson to Bradford

Final Division 1 Table

		P	W	D	L	F	A	Pts
1	SHEFFIELD W	42	21	10	11	86	62	52
2	LEICESTER C	42	21	9	12	96	67	51
3	ASTON VILLA	42	23	4	15	98	81	50
4	SUNDERLAND	42	20	7	15	93	75	47
5	LIVERPOOL	42	17	12	13	90	64	46
6	DERBY CO	42	18	10	14	86	71	46
7	BLACKBURN R	42	17	11	14	72	63	45
8	MANCHESTER CITY	42	18	9	15	95	86	45
9	ARSENAL	42	16	13	13	77	72	45
10	NEWCASTLE U	42	19	6	17	70	72	44
11	SHEFFIELD U	42	15	11	16	86	85	41
12	MANCHESTER U	42	14	13	15	66	76	41
13	LEEDS U	42	16	9	17	71	84	41
14	BOLTON W	42	14	12	16	73	80	40
15	BIRMINGHAM	42	15	10	17	68	77	40
16	HUDDERSFIELD T	42	14	11	17	70	61	39
17	WEST HAM U	42	15	9	18	86	96	39
18	EVERTON	42	17	4	21	63	75	38
19	BURNLEY	42	15	8	19	81	103	38
20	PORTSMOUTH	42	15	6	21	56	80	36
21	BURY	42	12	7	23	62	99	31
22	CARDIFF C	42	8	13	21	43	59	29

Season 1929-30

Football League Division 1

DATE	OPPONENTS	SCORE	GOALSCORERS	ATTENDANCE
Aug 31	BURNLEY	D 2-2	Marshall, Johnson	21,196
Sep 4	ARSENAL	W 3-1	Tilson 2, Marshall	38,458
Sep 7	Sunderland	L 2-5	Johnson, Tilson	35,000
Sep 11	Arsenal	L 2-3	McMullan, Brook	23,057
Sep 14	BOLTON WANDERERS	W 2-0	Brook 2	36,972
Sep 21	Everton	W 3-2	Marshall 2, Tilson	32,711
Sep 28	DERBY COUNTY	W 3-0	Tilson 3	42,047
Oct 5	Manchester United	W 3-1	Marshall, Johnson, Brook	57,201
Oct 12	Portsmouth	D 2-2	Tait, Johnson	20,000
Oct 19	WEST HAM UNITED	W 4-3	Tait 3, Marshall	25,000
Oct 26	Liverpool	W 6-1	Tait 2, Johnson 2, Brook 2	20,000
Nov 2	MIDDLESBROUGH	W 3-1	Toseland, Tait, Harrison	33,302
Nov 9	Grimsby Town	D 2-2	Tait, Brook	14,311
Nov 16	NEWCASTLE UNITED	W 3-0	Marshall, Tait, Brook	30,000
Nov 23	Sheffield United	W 2-1	Marshall, Brook	12,000
Nov 30	HUDDERSFIELD TOWN	D 1-1	Tait	28,746
Dec 7	Birmingham	L 0-3		18,000
Dec 14	LEICESTER CITY	W 3-2	Johnson 2, Brook	10,000
Dec 21	Blackburn Rovers	W 3-1	Marshall 3	20,483
Dec 25	Aston Villa	W 2-0	Tait 2	39,803
Dec 26	ASTON VILLA	L 1-2	Tait	70,000
Dec 28	Burnley	L 2-4	Johnson, Cowan	20,239
Jan 1	SHEFFIELD WEDNESDAY	D 3-3	McMullan, Marshall, Brook	54,516
Jan 4	SUNDERLAND	D 2-2	Marshall 2	30,000
Jan 18	Bolton Wanderers	W 2-1	Johnson, Brook	42,543
Feb 1	Derby County	L 2-4	Tait, Brook	18,463
Feb 5	EVERTON	L 1-2	Marshall	24,063
Feb 8	MANCHESTER UNITED	L 0-1		64,472
Feb 22	West Ham United	L 0-3		28,000
Feb 26	PORTSMOUTH	W 5-2	Tait 3, Toseland, Brook	20,000
Mar 1	LIVERPOOL	W 4-3	Tait 2, Johnson, Brook	22,000
Mar 8	Middlesbrough	L 0-1		15,739
Mar 15	GRIMSBY TOWN	W 3-1	Tait 2, Barrass	26,462
Mar 22	Newcastle United	D 2-2	Tait, Busby	30,000
Mar 29	SHEFFIELD UNITED	W 2-1	Brook, Hedley	25,000
Apr 5	Huddersfield Town	D 1-1	Busby	14,180
Apr 12	BIRMINGHAM	L 1-4	Hedley	25,000
Apr 19	Leicester City	L 1-3	Tait	10,000
Apr 21	LEEDS UNITED	W 4-1	Tait 3, Ridding	23,578
Apr 22	Leeds United	L 2-3	Ridding, Busby	16,636
Apr 26	BLACKBURN ROVERS	D 1-1	Tait	19,868
May 3	Sheffield Wednesday	L 1-5	Tait	33,000

FA Cup

Jan 11	Tottenham Hotspur	(Rd 3) D 2-2	Toseland, Cowan	37,000
Jan 15	TOTTENHAM HOTSPUR	W 4-1	Busby 2, Toseland, Marshall	37,716
Jan 25	Swindon Town	(Rd 4) D 1-1	Cowan	23,697
Jan 29	SWINDON TOWN	(R) W 10-1	Marshall 5, Tait 3, Johnson, Brook	46,082
Feb 15	HULL CITY	(Rd 5) L 1-2	Toseland	61,574

League & Cup Appearances

PLAYER	LEAGUE	CUP COMPETITION FA CUP	TOTAL
Barber	42	5	47
Barrass	41	5	46
Bray	2		2
Brook	40	5	45
Busby	11	1	12
Cann	1		1
Cowan	40	5	45
Felton	28	5	33
Gibbons	3		3
Harrison	2		2
Hedley	2		2
Heinemann	15	3	18
Johnson	30	4	34
Marshall	31	5	36
McCloy	11	2	13
McMullan	25	3	28
Ridding	5		5
Ridley	37	2	39
Robertson	8	1	9
Tait	31	3	34
Tilson	11	1	12
Toseland	42	5	47
Wrightson	4		4

Goalscorers

PLAYER	LEAGUE	CUP COMPETITION FA CUP	TOTAL
Tait	28	3	31
Brook	16	1	17
Marshall	15	6	21
Johnson	11	1	12
Tilson	7		7
Toseland	2	3	5
Busby	3	2	5
Hedley	2		2
McMullan	2		2
Ridding	2		2
Cowan	1	2	3
Harrison	1		1
Barrass	1		1

Fact File

City start 1930 by scoring 24 goals in their first seven games.

MANAGER: Peter Hodge
CAPTAIN: Jimmy McMullan
TOP SCORER: Tommy Tait
BIGGEST WIN: January 29, 1930 10-1 v Swindon Town, FA Cup Round 4 replay
HIGHEST ATTENDANCE: December 26, 1929 (approx.) 70,000 v Aston Villa, lost 1-2, Division 1
MAJOR TRANSFERS IN: Jackie Bray from Manchester Central
MAJOR TRANSFERS OUT: Tommy Johnson to Everton

Final Division 1 Table

		P	W	D	L	F	A	Pts
1	SHEFFIELD W	42	26	8	8	105	57	60
2	DERBY CO	42	21	8	13	90	82	50
3	MANCHESTER CITY	42	19	9	14	91	81	47
4	ASTON VILLA	42	21	5	16	92	83	47
5	LEEDS U	42	20	6	16	79	63	46
6	BLACKBURN R	42	19	7	16	99	93	45
7	WEST HAM U	42	19	5	18	86	79	43
8	LEICESTER C	42	17	9	16	86	90	43
9	SUNDERLAND	42	18	7	17	76	80	43
10	HUDDERSFIELD T	42	17	9	16	63	69	43
11	BIRMINGHAM	42	16	9	17	67	62	41
12	LIVERPOOL	42	16	9	17	63	79	41
13	PORTSMOUTH	42	15	10	17	66	62	40
14	ARSENAL	42	14	11	17	78	66	39
15	BOLTON W	42	15	9	18	74	74	39
16	MIDDLESBROUGH	42	16	6	20	82	84	38
17	MANCHESTER U	42	15	8	19	67	88	38
18	GRIMSBY T	42	15	7	20	73	89	37
19	NEWCASTLE U	42	15	7	20	71	92	37
20	SHEFFIELD U	42	15	6	21	91	96	36
21	BURNLEY	42	14	8	20	79	97	36
22	EVERTON	42	12	11	19	80	92	35

Season 1930-31

Football League Division 1

DATE	OPPONENTS	SCORE	GOALSCORERS	ATTENDANCE
Aug 30	Sunderland	D 3-3	Barrass, Tait, Brook	30,000
Sep 3	BLACKPOOL	L 2-4	Toseland, Brook	34,908
Sep 6	LEICESTER CITY	L 0-2		25,000
Sep 8	Leeds United	L 2-4	Brook 2	12,295
Sep 13	Birmingham	L 2-3	Tait, Brook	17,705
Sep 17	LEEDS UNITED	W 1-0	Brook	17,051
Sep 20	SHEFFIELD UNITED	L 0-4		20,000
Sep 27	Derby County	D 1-1	Tait	14,264
Oct 4	MANCHESTER UNITED	W 4-1	Marshall 2, Tait 2	41,757
Oct 11	PORTSMOUTH	L 1-3	Marshall	30,000
Oct 18	Sheffield Wednesday	D 1-1	Tait	20,000
Oct 25	GRIMSBY TOWN	W 1-0	Marshall	24,770
Nov 1	Liverpool	W 2-0	Austin, Tilson	25,000
Nov 8	MIDDLESBROUGH	W 4-2	Tait 2, Race, Marshall	27,035
Nov 15	Chelsea	L 0-2		25,671
Nov 22	BOLTON WANDERERS	W 3-0	Halliday 2, Marshall	23,481
Nov 29	Huddersfield Town	D 1-1	Brook	14,118
Dec 6	NEWCASTLE UNITED	W 2-0	Halliday, Tilson	20,000
Dec 13	West Ham United	L 0-2		22,000
Dec 20	ASTON VILLA	W 3-1	Toseland, Halliday, Brook	30,000
Dec 25	ARSENAL	L 1-4	Tilson	56,750
Dec 26	Arsenal	L 1-3	Marshall	17,624
Dec 27	SUNDERLAND	W 2-0	Marshall, Ridding	20,000
Jan 1	Blackburn Rovers	W 1-0	Toseland	27,965
Jan 3	Leicester City	L 2-3	Halliday 2	15,000
Jan 17	BIRMINGHAM	W 4-2	Brook 2, Tilson, Wrightson	11,479
Jan 28	Sheffield United	D 2-2	Toseland, Halliday	8,000
Jan 31	DERBY COUNTY	W 4-3	Halliday 2, Toseland, Roberts	14,739
Feb 7	Manchester United	W 3-1	Brook, Toseland, Halliday	39,876
Feb 18	Portsmouth	D 1-1	Halliday	5,000
Feb 21	SHEFFIELD WEDNESDAY	W 2-0	Halliday	25,000
Feb 28	Grimsby Town	W 5-3	Toseland, Marshall, Halliday, Roberts, Brook	12,611
Mar 7	LIVERPOOL	D 1-1	Barrass	18,000
Mar 14	Middlesbrough	L 1-4	Cowan	12,661
Mar 21	CHELSEA	W 2-0	Marshall, Wrightson	27,866
Mar 28	Bolton Wanderers	D 1-1	Brook	17,398
Apr 3	BLACKBURN ROVERS	W 3-0	Brook 2, Toseland	24,392
Apr 4	HUDDERSFIELD TOWN	L 0-1		27,094
Apr 11	Newcastle United	W 1-0	Brook	20,000
Apr 18	WEST HAM UNITED	D 1-1	Cowan	15,000
Apr 25	Aston Villa	L 2-4	Toseland, Wrightson	17,000
May 2	Blackpool	D 2-2	Toseland, Ridding	18,688

FA Cup

Jan 10	Burnley	(Rd 3) L 0-3		25,893

League & Cup Appearances

PLAYER	LEAGUE	CUP COMPETITION FA CUP	TOTAL
Austin	4		4
Barber	15		15
Barnett	28	1	29
Barrass	21		21
Bray	21	1	22
Brook	42	1	43
Busby	20	1	21
Cowan	40	1	41
Felton	12		12
Halliday	24	1	25
Heinemann	2		2
Langford	27	1	28
Marshall	37	1	38
McMullan	27		27
Race	5		5
Ridding	3		3
Ridley	42	1	43
Roberts	8		8
Robertson	3		3
Tait	15		15
Tilson	17	1	18
Toseland	38	1	39
Wrightson	11		11

Goalscorers

PLAYER	LEAGUE	CUP COMPETITION FA CUP	TOTAL
Brook	16		16
Halliday	14		14
Marshall	10		10
Toseland	10		10
Tait	8		8
Tilson	4		4
Wrightson	3		3
Barrass	2		2
Cowan	2		2
Ridding	2		2
Roberts	2		2
Austin	1		1
Race	1		1

Fact File

Two impressive victories over Manchester United contributed to the relegation of City's rivals.

MANAGER: Peter Hodge

CAPTAIN: Jimmy McMullan

TOP SCORER: Eric Brook

BIGGEST WIN: October 4, 1930 4-1 v Manchester United, Division 1

HIGHEST ATTENDANCE: December 25, 1930 56,750 v Arsenal, lost 1-4, Division 1

MAJOR TRANSFERS IN: David Halliday from Arsenal

MAJOR TRANSFERS OUT: Tommy Tait to Bolton Wanderers

Final Division 1 Table

		P	W	D	L	F	A	Pts
1	ARSENAL	42	28	10	4	127	59	66
2	ASTON VILLA	42	25	9	8	128	78	59
3	SHEFFIELD W	42	22	8	12	102	75	52
4	PORTSMOUTH	42	18	13	11	84	67	49
5	HUDDERSFIELD T	42	18	12	12	81	65	48
6	DERBY CO	42	18	10	14	94	79	46
7	MIDDLESBROUGH	42	19	8	15	98	90	46
8	MANCHESTER CITY	42	18	10	14	75	70	46
9	LIVERPOOL	42	15	12	15	86	85	42
10	BLACKBURN R	42	17	8	17	83	84	42
11	SUNDERLAND	42	16	9	17	89	85	41
12	CHELSEA	42	15	10	17	64	67	40
13	GRIMSBY T	42	17	5	20	82	87	39
14	BOLTON W	42	15	9	18	68	81	39
15	SHEFFIELD U	42	14	10	18	78	84	38
16	LEICESTER C	42	16	6	20	80	95	38
17	NEWCASTLE U	42	15	6	21	78	87	36
18	WEST HAM U	42	14	8	20	79	94	36
19	BIRMINGHAM	42	13	10	19	55	70	36
20	BLACKPOOL	42	11	10	21	71	125	32
21	LEEDS U	42	12	7	23	68	81	31
22	MANCHESTER U	42	7	8	27	53	115	22

Season 1931-32

Football League Division 1

DATE	OPPONENTS	SCORE	GOALSCORERS	ATTENDANCE
Aug 29	SUNDERLAND	D 1-1	Marshall	40,000
Sep 2	Derby County	L 1-2	Halliday	10,865
Sep 5	Leicester City	L 0-4		12,000
Sep 9	DERBY COUNTY	W 3-0	Halliday 3	15,153
Sep 12	Everton	W 1-0	Halliday	32,570
Sep 14	West Bromwich Albion	D 1-1	Cowan	19,042
Sep 19	ARSENAL	L 1-3	Bray	46,756
Sep 23	WEST BROMWICH ALBION	L 2-5	Cowan, Halliday	18,000
Sep 26	Blackpool	D 2-2	Wrightson, o.g.	25,031
Oct 3	SHEFFIELD UNITED	D 1-1	Marshall	25,000
Oct 10	Blackburn Rovers	D 2-2	Halliday, Tilson	12,313
Oct 17	WEST HAM UNITED	L 0-1		18,000
Oct 24	Newcastle United	L 1-2	Marshall	20,000
Oct 31	HUDDERSFIELD TOWN	W 3-0	Halliday 2, Marshall	21,332
Nov 7	Middlesbrough	D 3-3	Toseland, Halliday, Tilson	9,142
Nov 14	GRIMSBY TOWN	W 4-1	Halliday 2, Marshall, Brook	20,352
Nov 21	Liverpool	L 3-4	Marshall, Halliday, Tilson	30,000
Nov 28	ASTON VILLA	D 3-3	Halliday 2, Tilson	30,000
Dec 5	Chelsea	L 2-3	Tilson, Toseland	27,509
Dec 12	BOLTON WANDERERS	W 2-1	Halliday, Tilson	20,283
Dec 19	Sheffield Wednesday	D 1-1	Brook	10,000
Dec 26	Portsmouth	L 2-3	Halliday, Tilson	35,000
Jan 1	PORTSMOUTH	D 3-3	McMullan, Marshall, o.g.	30,000
Jan 2	Sunderland	W 5-2	Halliday 3, Rowley 2	18,000
Jan 16	LEICESTER CITY	W 5-1	Marshall 3, Halliday, Tilson, Brook	20,000
Jan 27	EVERTON	W 1-0	Halliday	26,363
Jan 30	Arsenal	L 0-4		39,834
Feb 6	BLACKPOOL	W 7-1	Halliday 2, Brook 2, Toseland, Tilson, Cowan	24,739
Feb 15	Sheffield United	L 1-2	Rowley	10,000
Feb 20	BLACKBURN ROVERS	W 3-1	Marshall 2, Brook	24,438
Mar 2	West Ham United	D 1-1	Busby	18,000
Mar 5	NEWCASTLE UNITED	W 5-1	Tilson 2, Toseland, Marshall, Brook	28,000
Mar 19	MIDDLESBROUGH	L 1-2	Tilson	24,114
Mar 26	Grimsby Town	L 1-2	Brook	11,481
Mar 28	BIRMINGHAM	W 2-1	Marshall, Brook	20,000
Mar 29	Birmingham	W 5-1	Halliday 3, Payne, Tilson	12,000
Apr 2	LIVERPOOL	L 0-1		20,000
Apr 6	Huddersfield Town	L 0-1		22,963
Apr 9	Aston Villa	L 1-2	Brook	30,000
Apr 16	CHELSEA	D 1-1	Rowley	20,124
Apr 23	Bolton Wanderers	D 1-1	Halliday	18,680
Apr 30	SHEFFIELD WEDNESDAY	L 1-2	Toseland	15,000

FA Cup

DATE	OPPONENTS		SCORE	GOALSCORERS	ATTENDANCE
Jan 9	Millwall	(Rd 3)	W 3-2	Halliday 2, Toseland	32,091
Jan 23	BRENTFORD	(Rd 4)	W 6-1	Tilson 3, Brook 2, Halliday	56,190
Feb 13	DERBY COUNTY	(Rd 5)	W 3-0	Marshall 2, Brook	62,641
Feb 27	Bury	(Rd 6)	W 4-3	Toseland 2, Halliday, Cowan	28,035
Mar 12	ARSENAL	(SF)	L 0-1		50,337

Fact File

City's exit from the FA Cup semi-final was courtesy of a last-gasp Arsenal effort that hit the bar and the post before crossing the line.

MANAGER: Peter Hodge
CAPTAIN: Jimmy McMullan
TOP SCORER: David Halliday
BIGGEST WIN: February 6, 1932 7-1 v Blackpool, Division 1
HIGHEST ATTENDANCE: February 13, 1931 62,641 v Derby County, won 6-1, FA Cup Round 5
MAJOR TRANSFERS IN: Billy Dale from Manchester United
MAJOR TRANSFERS OUT: Billy Fenton to Tottenham Hotspur

League & Cup Appearances

PLAYER	LEAGUE	CUP COMPETITION FA CUP	TOTAL
Barnett	11		11
Barrass	2		2
Bray	20		20
Brook	42	5	47
Busby	41	5	46
Cann	8		8
Cowan	31	5	36
Dale	21	5	26
Felton	23	5	28
Gregory	3		3
Halliday	40	5	45
Langford	40	5	45
Marshall	34	5	39
McMullan	21	5	26
Payne	2		2
Race	1		1
Ridding	1		1
Ridley	21		21
Rowley	13		13
Syme	1		1
Tilson	37	5	42
Toseland	40	5	45
Walmsley	2		2
Wrightson	7		7

Goalscorers

PLAYER	LEAGUE	CUP COMPETITION FA CUP	TOTAL
Halliday	28	4	32
Tilson	13	3	16
Marshall	13	2	15
Brook	10	3	13
Toseland	5	3	8
Rowley	4		4
Cowan	3	1	4
Bray	1		1
Busby	1		1
McMullan	1		1
Payne	1		1
Wrightson	1		1
Opps' o.gs.	2		2

Final Division 1 Table

		P	W	D	L	F	A	Pts
1	EVERTON	42	26	4	12	116	64	56
2	ARSENAL	42	22	10	10	90	48	54
3	SHEFFIELD W	42	22	6	14	96	82	50
4	HUDDERSFIELD T	42	19	10	13	80	63	48
5	ASTON VILLA	42	19	8	15	104	72	46
6	WBA	42	20	6	16	77	55	46
7	SHEFFIELD U	42	20	6	16	80	75	46
8	PORTSMOUTH	42	19	7	16	62	62	45
9	BIRMINGHAM	42	18	8	16	78	67	44
10	LIVERPOOL	42	19	6	17	81	93	44
11	NEWCASTLE U	42	18	6	18	80	87	42
12	CHELSEA	42	16	8	18	69	73	40
13	SUNDERLAND	42	15	10	17	67	73	40
14	MANCHESTER CITY	42	13	12	17	83	73	38
15	DERBY CO	42	14	10	18	71	75	38
16	BLACKBURN R	42	16	6	20	89	95	38
17	BOLTON W	42	17	4	21	72	80	38
18	MIDDLESBROUGH	42	15	8	19	64	89	38
19	LEICESTER C	42	15	7	20	74	94	37
20	BLACKPOOL	42	12	9	21	65	102	33
21	GRIMSBY T	42	13	6	23	67	98	32
22	WEST HAM U	42	12	7	23	62	107	31

Season 1932-33

Football League Division 1

DATE	OPPONENTS	SCORE	GOALSCORERS	ATTENDANCE
Aug 27	Sunderland	L 2-3	Brook 2	33,000
Aug 31	BIRMINGHAM	W 1-0	Marshall	26,000
Sep 3	MIDDLESBROUGH	L 2-3	Marshall	20,211
Sep 7	Birmingham	L 0-3		20,000
Sep 10	ARSENAL	L 2-3	Tilson, Busby	36,542
Sep 17	Everton	L 1-2	Toseland	32,852
Sep 24	BLACKPOOL	W 5-1	Toseland 2, Halliday 2, Brook	25,175
Oct 1	Derby County	L 0-4		13,233
Oct 8	BLACKBURN ROVERS	L 2-3	Halliday, Tilson	8,428
Oct 15	Leeds United	L 1-2	Tilson	16,898
Oct 22	Bolton Wanderers	L 1-2	Tilson	14,468
Oct 29	LIVERPOOL	D 1-1	Marshall	10,000
Nov 5	Sheffield United	W 5-2	Race 2, Toseland, Marshall, Brook	15,000
Nov 12	WOLVES	W 4-1	Marshall 2, Comrie, Brook	26,067
Nov 19	Newcastle United	L 0-2		24,000
Nov 26	ASTON VILLA	W 5-2	Tilson 4, Brook	20,000
Dec 3	Leicester City	W 2-1	Tilson, Brook	15,000
Dec 10	PORTSMOUTH	W 3-1	Tilson 2, Cowan	10,000
Dec 17	Chelsea	L 1-3	Tilson	26,240
Dec 24	HUDDERSFIELD TOWN	W 3-0	Toseland, Tilson, Brook	21,252
Dec 26	SHEFFIELD WEDNESDAY	D 2-2	Cowan, Brook	35,000
Dec 27	Sheffield Wednesday	L 1-2	Cowan	35,000
Dec 31	SUNDERLAND	L 2-4	Toseland, Tilson	18,000
Jan 7	Middlesbrough	L 0-2		7,912
Jan 21	Arsenal	L 1-2	Tilson	32,456
Feb 1	EVERTON	W 3-0	Toseland, Tilson, Brook	10,986
Feb 4	Blackpool	L 0-1		13,399
Feb 11	DERBY COUNTY	W 2-1	Toseland, Herd	33,611
Feb 23	Blackburn Rovers	L 0-1		8,931
Mar 8	BOLTON WANDERERS	W 2-1	Cowan, Herd	19,144
Mar 11	Liverpool	D 1-1	Herd	35,000
Mar 22	SHEFFIELD UNITED	W 1-0	Tilson	20,000
Mar 25	Wolves	W 2-1	Herd, Brook	26,746
Apr 1	NEWCASTLE UNITED	L 1-2	Brook	30,000
Apr 5	LEEDS UNITED	D 0-0		16,789
Apr 8	Aston Villa	D 1-1	Marshall	20,000
Apr 14	WEST BROMWICH ALBION	W 1-0	Brook	28,200
Apr 15	LEICESTER CITY	W 4-1	Herd 2, Toseland, Marshall	22,000
Apr 17	West Bromwich Albion	L 0-4		18,988
Apr 22	Portsmouth	W 2-1	Herd, Brook	12,000
May 3	CHELSEA	L 1-4	Brook	14,827
May 6	Huddersfield Town	L 0-1		5,482

FA Cup

Jan 14	Gateshead	(Rd 3) D 1-1	Toseland	9,123
Jan 18	GATESHEAD	(R) W 9-0	Tilson 3, Cowan 2, Busby, Barass, McMullan, Brook	22,590
Jan 28	WALSALL	(Rd 4) W 2-0	Brook 2	52,085
Feb 18	Bolton Wanderers	(Rd 5) W 4-2	Brook 3, Tilson	69,920
Mar 4	Burnley	(Rd 6) W 1-0	Tilson	48,717
Mar 18	DERBY COUNTY	(SF) W 3-2	Toseland, Tilson, McMullan	51,961
Apr 29	EVERTON*	(F) L 0-3		92,900

*Played at Wembley.

League & Cup Appearances

PLAYER	LEAGUE	CUP COMPETITION FA CUP	TOTAL
Barnett	4		4
Barrass	3	1	4
Bray	30	7	37
Brook	42	7	49
Busby	39	7	46
Cann	28	4	32
Comrie	14		14
Corbett F	9		9
Cowan	32	7	39
Dale	39	7	46
Fletcher	1		1
Gregory	7		7
Halliday	8		8
Herd	16	4	20
Higgs	1		1
Langford	27	7	34
Marshall	33	3	36
McMullan	26	6	32
Naylor	1		1
Nicholls	14		14
Race	4	1	5
Ridley	4	3	7
Robertson	1		1
Rowley	5		5
Syme	1		1
Tilson	29	6	35
Toseland	42	7	49

Goalscorers

PLAYER	LEAGUE	CUP COMPETITION FA CUP	TOTAL
Tilson	17	6	23
Brook	15	6	21
Toseland	9	2	11
Marshall	9		9
Herd	7		7
Cowan	4	2	6
Halliday	3		3
Race	2		2
Busby	1	1	2
Comrie	1		1
Barrass		1	1
McMullan		2	2

Fact File

City wore their maroon 'change' shirts for the FA Cup final. It was also the first time players sported numbers in an FA Cup final.

MANAGER: Wilf Wild

CAPTAIN: Sam Cowan

TOP SCORER: Freddie Tilson

BIGGEST WIN: January 18, 1933 9-0 v Gateshead, FA Cup Round 3 Replay

HIGHEST ATTENDANCE: April 29, 1933 92,900 v Everton, lost 0-3, FA Cup final

MAJOR TRANSFERS IN: Frank Swift from Fleetwood

Final Division 1 Table

		P	W	D	L	F	A	Pts
1	ARSENAL	42	25	8	9	118	61	58
2	ASTON VILLA	42	23	8	11	92	67	54
3	SHEFFIELD W	42	21	9	12	80	68	51
4	WBA	42	20	9	13	83	70	49
5	NEWCASTLE U	42	22	5	15	71	63	49
6	HUDDERSFIELD T	42	18	11	13	66	53	47
7	DERBY CO	42	15	14	13	76	69	44
8	LEEDS U	42	15	14	13	59	62	44
9	PORTSMOUTH	42	18	7	17	74	76	43
10	SHEFFIELD U	42	17	9	16	74	80	43
11	EVERTON	42	16	9	17	81	74	41
12	SUNDERLAND	42	15	10	17	63	80	40
13	BIRMINGHAM	42	14	11	17	57	57	39
14	LIVERPOOL	42	14	11	17	79	84	39
15	BLACKBURN R	42	14	10	18	76	102	38
16	MANCHESTER CITY	42	16	5	21	68	71	37
17	MIDDLESBROUGH	42	14	9	19	63	73	37
18	CHELSEA	42	14	7	21	63	73	35
19	LEICESTER C	42	11	13	18	75	89	35
20	WOLVERHAMPTON W	42	13	9	20	80	96	35
21	BOLTON W	42	12	9	21	78	92	33
22	BLACKPOOL	42	14	5	23	69	85	33

Season 1933-34

Football League Division 1

DATE	OPPONENTS	SCORE	GOALSCORERS	ATTENDANCE
Aug 26	SHEFFIELD WEDNESDAY	L 2-3	Herd, Tilson	35,000
Aug 30	Birmingham	W 1-0	Tilson	30,000
Sep 2	Leicester City	D 0-0		25,000
Sep 6	BIRMINGHAM	W 1-0	Syme	20,000
Sep 9	Arsenal	D 1-1	Herd	43,412
Sep 16	EVERTON	D 2-2	Herd, Brook	48,826
Sep 23	Middlesbrough	L 1-2	Marshall	9,095
Sep 30	BLACKBURN ROVERS	W 3-1	Cowan, Halliday, Brook	33,343
Oct 7	Newcastle United	D 2-2	Halliday, Herd	20,000
Oct 14	LEEDS UNITED	L 0-1		22,413
Oct 21	ASTON VILLA	W 1-0	Marshall	35,000
Oct 28	Sheffield United	D 1-1	Tilson	14,000
Nov 4	SUNDERLAND	W 4-1	Brook 2, Toseland, Marshall	25,000
Nov 11	Stoke City	W 1-0	Toseland	20,000
Nov 18	HUDDERSFIELD TOWN	D 2-2	Toseland, Tilson	31,900
Nov 25	Portsmouth	L 0-2		15,000
Dec 2	TOTTENHAM HOTSPUR	W 2-0	Brook, Herd	38,021
Dec 9	Chelsea	W 2-1	Herd, Gregory	18,048
Dec 16	LIVERPOOL	W 2-1	Tilson, Herd	15,000
Dec 23	Wolves	L 0-8		20,640
Dec 25	Derby County	L 1-4	Toseland	32,320
Dec 26	DERBY COUNTY	W 2-0	Gregory, Brook	57,218
Dec 30	Sheffield Wednesday	D 1-1	Busby	24,000
Jan 1	WEST BROMWICH ALBION	L 2-7	Herd, Bray	20,996
Jan 6	LEICESTER CITY	D 1-1	Herd	20,000
Jan 20	ARSENAL	W 2-1	Marshall, Herd	60,401
Feb 3	MIDDLESBROUGH	W 5-2	Tilson 2, Brook 2, Busby	22,082
Feb 7	Everton	L 0-2		17,134
Feb 10	Blackburn Rovers	L 0-3		14,076
Feb 24	Leeds United	L 1-3	Syme	15,761
Mar 7	Aston Villa	L 0-0		20,000
Mar 10	SHEFFIELD UNITED	W 4-1	Tilson 2, Herd, Bray	18,000
Mar 21	NEWCASTLE UNITED	D 1-1	Wright	14,000
Mar 24	STOKE CITY	W 4-2	Herd 2, Cowan, Bray	20,000
Mar 31	Huddersfield Town	L 0-1		20,817
Apr 2	West Bromwich Albion	L 0-4		22,198
Apr 7	PORTSMOUTH	W 2-1	Busby, Herd	35,000
Apr 11	Sunderland	D 0-0		10,000
Apr 14	Tottenham Hotspur	L 1-5	Toseland	24,576
Apr 21	CHELSEA	W 4-2	Tilson 3, Toseland	25,861
May 2	Liverpool	L 2-3	Herd, Heale	16,000
May 5	WOLVES	W 4-0	Herd 2, Cowan, Heale	21,764

FA Cup

Jan 13	BLACKBURN ROVERS	(Rd 3) W 3-1	Toseland 2, Brook	54,336
Jan 27	Hull City	(Rd 4) D 2-2	Herd, Brook	28,000
Jan 31	HULL CITY	(R) W 4-1	Tilson 2, Toseland, Marshall	49,042
Feb 17	Sheffield Wednesday	(Rd 5) D 2-2	Herd 2	72,841
Feb 21	SHEFFIELD WEDNESDAY	(R) W 2-0	Marshall, Tilson	68,614
Mar 3	STOKE CITY	(Rd 6) W 1-0	Brook	84,569
Mar 17	ASTON VILLA	(SF) W 6-1	Tilson 4, Herd, Toseland	45,473
Apr 28	PORTSMOUTH*	(F) W 2-1	Tilson 2	93,528

*Played at Wembley.

League & Cup Appearances

PLAYER	LEAGUE	CUP COMPETITION FA CUP	TOTAL
Barkas	2		2
Barnett	38	7	45
Bray	16	3	19
Brook	38	8	46
Busby	39	8	47
Cann	5		5
Comrie	3		3
Corbett F	1		1
Corbett V	5	1	6
Cowan	32	8	40
Dale	31	8	39
Dunne	2		2
Gregory	11		11
Halliday	4		4
Heale	14		14
Herd	37	8	45
Langford	18		18
Lloyd	3		3
Marshall	34	8	42
McLuckie	27	5	32
Nicholls	2		2
Payne	2		2
Percival J	5		5
Percival R	2		2
Swift	22	8	30
Syme	7		7
Tilson	21	8	29
Toseland	40	8	48
Wright	1		1

Goalscorers

PLAYER	LEAGUE	CUP COMPETITION FA CUP	TOTAL
Herd	17	4	21
Tilson	12	9	21
Brook	8	3	11
Toseland	6	4	10
Marshall	4	2	6
Busby	4		4
Cowan	3		3
Bray	2		2
Heale	2		2
Gregory	2		2
Syme	2		2
Halliday	2		2
Wright	1		1

Fact File

19-year-old Frank Swift made his debut in the 4-1 defeat against Derby County on Christmas Day.

MANAGER: Wilf Wild
CAPTAIN: Sam Cowan
TOP SCORER: Alex Herd
BIGGEST WIN: March 17, 1934 6-1 v Aston Villa, FA Cup semi-final
HIGHEST ATTENDANCE: April 4, 1947 93,528 v Portsmouth, won 2-1, FA Cup final
MAJOR TRANSFERS IN: Sam Barkas from Bradford City

Final Division 1 Table

		P	W	D	L	F	A	PTS
1	ARSENAL	42	25	9	8	75	47	59
2	HUDDERSFIELD T	42	23	10	9	90	61	56
3	TOTTENHAM H	42	21	7	14	79	56	49
4	DERBY CO	42	17	11	14	68	54	45
5	MANCHESTER CITY	42	17	11	14	65	72	45
6	SUNDERLAND	42	16	12	14	81	56	44
7	WBA	42	17	10	15	78	70	44
8	BLACKBURN R	42	18	7	17	74	81	43
9	LEEDS U	42	17	8	17	75	66	42
10	PORTSMOUTH	42	15	12	15	52	55	42
11	SHEFFIELD W	42	16	9	17	62	67	41
12	STOKE C	42	15	11	16	58	71	41
13	ASTON VILLA	42	14	12	16	78	75	40
14	EVERTON	42	12	16	14	62	63	40
15	WOLVERHAMPTON W	42	14	12	16	74	86	40
16	MIDDLESBROUGH	42	16	7	19	68	80	39
17	LEICESTER C	42	14	11	17	59	74	39
18	LIVERPOOL	42	14	10	18	79	87	38
19	CHELSEA	42	14	8	20	67	69	36
20	BIRMINGHAM	42	12	12	18	54	56	36
21	NEWCASTLE U	42	10	14	18	68	77	34
22	SHEFFIELD U	42	12	7	23	58	101	31

The Essential History of Manchester City

Football League Division 1

DATE	OPPONENTS	SCORE	GOALSCORERS	ATTENDANCE
Aug 25	West Bromwich Albion	D 1-1	Barkas	24,480
Aug 29	LIVERPOOL	W 3-1	Marshall, Brook, o.g.	18,000
Sep 1	SHEFFIELD WEDNESDAY	W 4-1	Herd 2, Marshall, Brook	50,000
Sep 5	Liverpool	L 1-2	Tilson	32,000
Sep 8	Birmingham	W 3-1	Tilson, Herd, Brook	20,000
Sep 15	STOKE CITY	W 3-1	Tilson 3	50,000
Sep 22	Leicester City	W 3-1	Herd 2, Busby	25,000
Sep 29	Middlesbrough	W 2-1	Herd, Fletcher	9,180
Oct 6	BLACKBURN ROVERS	D 3-3	Brook 2, Heale	35,482
Oct 13	Arsenal	L 0-3		68,145
Oct 20	DERBY COUNTY	L 0-1		44,393
Oct 27	Aston Villa	L 2-4	Herd, Tilson	27,000
Nov 3	TOTTENHAM HOTSPUR	W 3-1	McLuckie, Herd, Heale	28,802
Nov 10	Sunderland	L 2-3	Brook 2	9,000
Nov 17	HUDDERSFIELD TOWN	D 0-0		36,176
Nov 24	Everton	W 2-1	Tilson, Heale	36,926
Dec 1	GRIMSBY TOWN	W 1-0	Toseland	31,642
Dec 8	Preston North End	W 4-2	Tilson 3, Brook	20,000
Dec 15	CHELSEA	W 2-0	Tilson, Heale	28,797
Dec 22	Wolves	L 0-5		27,204
Dec 25	Leeds United	W 2-1	Toseland, Heale	24,810
Dec 26	LEEDS UNITED	W 3-0	Heale 2, Brook	51,387
Dec 29	WEST BROMWICH ALBION	W 3-2	Brook 2, Herd	23,545
Jan 5	Sheffield Wednesday	L 0-1		35,000
Jan 19	BIRMINGHAM	D 0-0		25,000
Jan 26	Stoke City	L 0-2		25,000
Feb 2	LEICESTER CITY	W 6-3	Brook 2, Bray, Toseland, Herd, Tilson	20,000
Feb 9	MIDDLESBROUGH	W 6-2	Toseland, Tilson, Herd 2, Brook, o.g.	29,431
Feb 23	ARSENAL	D 1-1	Brook	79,491
Mar 2	Derby County	W 2-1	Dellow, Herd	27,020
Mar 4	Blackburn Rovers	L 0-1		11,328
Mar 9	ASTON VILLA	W 4-1	Dellow 2, Heale, Brook	25,000
Mar 16	Tottenham Hotspur	D 0-0		43,572
Mar 30	Huddersfield Town	L 0-3		18,997
Apr 6	EVERTON	D 2-2	Heale, Tilson	26,138
Apr 10	SUNDERLAND	W 1-0	Heale	18,000
Apr 13	Grimsby Town	D 1-1	Herd	13,394
Apr 19	PORTSMOUTH	L 2-4	Tilson 2	35,000
Apr 20	PRESTON NORTH END	L 1-2	Herd	18,000
Apr 22	Portsmouth	L 2-4	Dellow, Tilson	17,000
Apr 27	Chelsea	L 2-4	Heale, Tilson	22,993
May 4	WOLVES	W 5-0	Heale 2, Marshall, Toseland, Brook	15,000

FA Cup

Jan 12	Tottenham Hotspur	(Rd 3) L 0-1		48,983

FA Charity Shield

Nov 28	Arsenal	L 0-4		10,888

League & Cup Appearances

PLAYER	LEAGUE	CUP COMPETITION		TOTAL
		FA CUP	OTHER	
Barkas	41	1		42
Barnett	3		1	4
Bray	39	1	1	41
Brook	40	1	1	42
Busby	33	1	1	35
Corbett F	1			1
Cowan	42	1	1	44
Dale	39	1	1	41
Dellow	10			10
Dunne	1			1
Fletcher	4			4
Heale	27	1	1	29
Herd	37	1		38
Marshall	19			19
McLuckie	5		1	6
Percival J	9			9
Shadewell	2			2
Swift	42	1	1	44
Tilson	34	1	1	36
Toseland	32	1	1	34
Wright	2			2

Goalscorers

PLAYER	LEAGUE	CUP COMPETITION		TOTAL
		FA CUP	OTHER	
Tilson	18			18
Brook	17			17
Herd	14			14
Heale	13			13
Toseland	5			5
Dellow	4			4
Marshall	3			3
Barkas	1			1
Bray	1			1
Busby	1			1
Fletcher	1			1
McLuckie	1			1
Opps' o.gs.	2			2

Fact File

Eric Brook scored twice in England's 3-2 victory over Italy in November. The game is remembered as 'The Battle of Highbury'.

MANAGER: Wilf Wild

CAPTAIN: Sam Cowan

TOP SCORER: Freddie Tilson

BIGGEST WIN: May 4, 1935 5-0 v Wolves, Division 1

HIGHEST ATTENDANCE: February 23, 1935 79,491 v Arsenal, drew 1-1, Division 1

MAJOR TRANSFERS OUT: Matt Busby to Liverpool, Sam Cowan to Bradford City

Final Division 1 Table

		P	W	D	L	F	A	Pts
1	ARSENAL	42	23	12	7	115	46	58
2	SUNDERLAND	42	19	16	7	90	51	54
3	SHEFFIELD W	42	18	13	11	70	64	49
4	MANCHESTER CITY	42	20	8	14	82	67	48
5	GRIMSBY T	42	17	11	14	78	60	45
6	DERBY CO	42	18	9	15	81	66	45
7	LIVERPOOL	42	19	7	16	85	88	45
8	EVERTON	42	16	12	14	89	88	44
9	WBA	42	17	10	15	83	83	44
10	STOKE C	42	18	6	18	71	70	42
11	PRESTON NE	42	15	12	15	62	67	42
12	CHELSEA	42	16	9	17	73	82	41
13	ASTON VILLA	42	14	13	15	74	88	41
14	PORTSMOUTH	42	15	10	17	71	72	40
15	BLACKBURN R	42	14	11	17	66	78	39
16	HUDDERSFIELD T	42	14	10	18	76	71	38
17	WOLVERHAMPTON W	42	15	8	19	88	94	38
18	LEEDS U	42	13	12	17	75	92	38
19	BIRMINGHAM	42	13	10	19	63	81	36
20	MIDDLESBROUGH	42	10	14	18	70	90	34
21	LEICESTER C	42	12	9	21	61	86	33
22	TOTTENHAM H	42	10	10	22	54	93	30

Season 1935-36

Football League Division 1

DATE	OPPONENTS	SCORE	GOALSCORERS	ATTENDANCE
Aug 31	WEST BROMWICH ALBION	W 1-0	Herd	39,826
Sep 4	Liverpool	W 2-0	Tilson, Brook	30,000
Sep 7	Sunderland	L 0-2		45,000
Sep 11	LIVERPOOL	W 6-0	Toseland 2, Heale 2, Busby, Herd	25,000
Sep 14	BIRMINGHAM	W 3-1	Bray, Toseland, Tilson	30,000
Sep 21	Arsenal	W 3-2	Toseland, Herd, Tilson	61,250
Sep 28	PORTSMOUTH	D 0-0		40,000
Oct 5	STOKE CITY	L 1-2	Heale	35,000
Oct 12	Blackburn Rovers	L 1-4	Toseland	21,416
Oct 19	Preston North End	L 0-4		18,000
Oct 26	BRENTFORD	W 2-1	Marshall, Owen	25,000
Nov 2	Derby County	L 0-3		28,776
Nov 9	EVERTON	W 1-0	Herd	39,883
Nov 16	Bolton Wanderers	D 3-3	Brook 2, Tilson	42,110
Nov 23	SHEFFIELD WEDNESDAY	W 3-0	Owen 2, McCullough	30,000
Nov 30	Middlesbrough	L 0-2		19,438
Dec 7	ASTON VILLA	W 5-0	Toseland 2, Tilson 2, Brook	35,000
Dec 14	Wolves	L 3-4	Tilson 2, Brook	20,960
Dec 25	CHELSEA	D 0-0		36,074
Dec 26	Chelsea	L 1-2	Herd	41,732
Dec 28	West Bromwich Albion	L 1-5	McLeod	31,012
Jan 1	GRIMSBY TOWN	L 0-3		32,470
Jan 4	SUNDERLAND	L 0-1		45,000
Jan 15	HUDDERSFIELD TOWN	L 1-2	Brook	16,884
Jan 18	Birmingham	W 1-0	McLeod 1	20,000
Feb 1	Portsmouth	W 2-1	McLeod 2	20,000
Feb 8	Stoke City	L 0-1		30,000
Feb 19	BLACKBURN ROVERS	W 2-0	McLeod 2	12,498
Feb 22	PRESTON NORTH END	L 1-3	Brook	39,364
Feb 29	Everton	D 2-2	Tilson, Toseland	14,418
Mar 7	MIDDLESBROUGH	W 6-0	Herd 2, Toseland, Doherty, Brook, Tilson	20,094
Mar 11	ARSENAL	W 1-0	Percival	32,750
Mar 14	Brentford	D 0-0		35,000
Mar 21	BOLTON WANDERERS	W 7-0	Brook 3, Doherty 2, Herd, Toseland	40,779
Mar 28	Sheffield Wednesday	L 0-1		22,000
Apr 4	DERBY COUNTY	W 1-0	McLeod	25,806
Apr 10	LEEDS UNITED	L 1-3	Herd	17,175
Apr 11	Aston Villa	D 2-2	Marshall, Percival	42,000
Apr 13	Leeds United	D 1-1	Brook	38,773
Apr 18	WOLVES	W 2-1	Herd, Tilson	21,852
Apr 25	Huddersfield Town	D 1-1	Doherty	8,258
May 2	Grimsby Town	L 1-3	Brook	8,974

FA Cup

Jan 11	PORTSMOUTH	(Rd 3) W 3-1	Brook 3	53,340
Jan 25	LUTON TOWN	(Rd 4) W 2-1	Herd, McLeod	65,978
Feb 15	Grimsby Town	(Rd 5) L 2-3	McLeod, Tilson	28,000

League & Cup Appearances

PLAYER	LEAGUE	CUP COMPETITION FA CUP	TOTAL
Barkas	39	3	42
Bray	38	3	41
Brook	40	3	43
Busby	19	1	20
Cassidy	2		2
Corbett	4		4
Dale	41	3	44
Doherty	9		9
Donnelly	30		30
Heale	8		8
Herd	33	3	36
Marshall	21	2	23
McCullough	12	1	13
McLeod	9	2	11
Neilson	4		4
Owen	9	1	10
Percival	23	2	25
Rodger	4	1	5
Rogers	2		2
Swift	42	3	45
Tilson	32	2	34
Toseland	41	3	44

Goalscorers

PLAYER	LEAGUE	CUP COMPETITION FA CUP	TOTAL
Brook	13	3	16
Tilson	11	1	12
Herd	10	1	11
Toseland	10		10
McLeod	7	2	9
Doherty	4		4
Heale	3		3
Owen	3		3
Marshall	2		2
Percival	2		2
Bray	1		1
Busby	1		1
McCullough	1		1

Fact File

Peter Doherty joined in February from Blackpool and scored four times in only nine league appearances.

MANAGER: Wilf Wild

CAPTAIN: Sam Barkas

TOP SCORER: Eric Brook

BIGGEST WIN: May 21, 1936 4-1 v Bolton Wanderers, Division 1

HIGHEST ATTENDANCE: January 25, 1936 65,978 v Luton Town, won 2-1, FA Cup Round 5

MAJOR TRANSFERS IN: Peter Doherty from Blackpool

Final Division 1 Table

		P	W	D	L	F	A	Pts
1	SUNDERLAND	42	25	6	11	109	74	56
2	DERBY CO	42	18	12	12	61	52	48
3	HUDDERSFIELD T	42	18	12	12	59	56	48
4	STOKE C	42	20	7	15	57	57	47
5	BRENTFORD	42	17	12	13	81	60	46
6	ARSENAL	42	15	15	12	78	48	45
7	PRESTON NE	42	18	8	16	67	64	44
8	CHELSEA	42	15	13	14	65	72	43
9	MANCHESTER CITY	42	17	8	17	68	60	42
10	PORTSMOUTH	42	17	8	17	54	67	42
11	LEEDS U	42	15	11	16	66	64	41
12	BIRMINGHAM	42	15	11	16	61	63	41
13	BOLTON W	42	14	13	15	67	76	41
14	MIDDLESBROUGH	42	15	10	17	84	70	40
15	WOLVERHAMPTON W	42	15	10	17	77	76	40
16	EVERTON	42	13	13	16	89	89	39
17	GRIMSBY T	42	17	5	20	65	73	39
18	WBA	42	16	6	20	89	88	38
19	LIVERPOOL	42	13	12	17	60	64	38
20	SHEFFIELD W	42	13	12	17	63	77	38
21	ASTON VILLA	42	13	9	20	81	110	35
22	BLACKBURN R	42	12	9	21	55	96	33

Season 1936-37

Football League Division 1

DATE	OPPONENTS	SCORE	GOALSCORERS	ATTENDANCE
Aug 29	Middlesbrough	L 0-2		23,081
Sep 2	LEEDS UNITED	W 4-0	Herd, Tilson, Doherty, Brook	24,726
Sep 5	WEST BROMWICH ALBION	W 6-2	Herd 2, Doherty 2, Heale, Brook	25,070
Sep 9	Leeds United	D 1-1	Heale	13,933
Sep 12	Manchester United	L 2-3	Bray, Heale	68,796
Sep 16	BIRMINGHAM	D 1-1	Doherty	20,000
Sep 19	Portsmouth	L 1-2	McLeod	25,000
Sep 26	CHELSEA	D 0-0		30,044
Oct 3	Stoke City	D 2-2	Heale, Doherty	36,000
Oct 10	CHARLTON ATHLETIC	D 1-1	Heale	28,000
Oct 17	DERBY COUNTY	W 3-2	Toseland, Heale, Doherty	21,245
Oct 24	Wolves	L 1-2	Doherty	20,888
Oct 31	SUNDERLAND	L 2-4	McLeod, Doherty	35,000
Nov 7	Huddersfield Town	D 1-1	Brook	18,438
Nov 14	EVERTON	W 4-1	Rodger 2, Toseland, Brook	27,818
Nov 21	Bolton Wanderers	W 2-0	Herd, Brook	32,003
Dec 5	Arsenal	W 3-1	Rodger 2, Doherty	41,783
Dec 12	PRESTON NORTH END	W 4-1	Toseland 2, Doherty, Brook	15,000
Dec 19	Sheffield Wednesday	L 1-5	Doherty	30,000
Dec 25	Grimsby Town	L 3-5	Rodger, Doherty, Brook	17,921
Dec 26	MIDDLESBROUGH	W 2-1	Rodger, Brook	56,227
Dec 28	GRIMSBY TOWN	D 1-1	Tilson	16,146
Jan 2	West Bromwich Albion	D 2-2	Herd, Tilson	18,004
Jan 9	MANCHESTER UNITED	W 1-0	Herd	64,862
Jan 23	PORTSMOUTH	W 3-1	Toseland, Herd, Brook	25,000
Feb 3	Chelsea	D 4-4	Doherty 2, Bray, Tilson	11,620
Feb 6	STOKE CITY	W 2-1	Tilson, Doherty	30,000
Feb 13	Charlton Athletic	D 1-1	Herd	45,000
Feb 24	Derby County	W 5-0	Tilson 3, Rodger, Brook	12,572
Feb 27	WOLVES	W 4-1	Tilson 3, Herd	39,720
Mar 13	HUDDERSFIELD TOWN	W 3-0	Doherty 2, Brook	28,240
Mar 20	Everton	D 1-1	Percival	31,921
Mar 26	Liverpool	W 5-0	Brook 3, Herd, Doherty	32,000
Mar 27	BOLTON WANDERERS	D 2-2	Herd, Doherty	51,714
Mar 29	LIVERPOOL	W 5-1	Herd 2, Neilson, Tilson, Brook	25,000
Apr 3	Brentford	W 6-2	Doherty 2, Toseland, Herd, Brook, Tilson	37,000
Apr 7	BRENTFORD	W 2-1	Doherty, Brook	25,000
Apr 10	ARSENAL	W 2-0	Toseland, Doherty	74,918
Apr 14	Sunderland	W 3-1	Doherty 2, Brook	15,000
Apr 17	Preston North End	W 5-2	Doherty 3, Herd, Donnelly	16,000
Apr 24	SHEFFIELD WEDNESDAY	W 4-1	Brook 2, Tilson, Doherty	55,000
May 1	Birmingham	D 2-2	Tilson, Doherty	25,000

FA Cup

DATE	OPPONENTS		SCORE	GOALSCORERS	ATTENDANCE
Jan 16	Wrexham	(Rd 3)	W 3-1	Herd, Tilson, Brook	20,600
Jan 30	ACCRINGTON STANLEY	(Rd 4)	W 2-0	Tilson, Doherty	39,135
Feb 20	Bolton Wanderers	(Rd 5)	W 5-0	Herd 2, Doherty, Brook, Tilson	60,979
Mar 6	Millwall	(Rd 6)	L 0-2		42,474

League & Cup Appearances

PLAYER	LEAGUE	CUP COMPETITION FA CUP	TOTAL
Barkas	30	4	34
Bray	40	4	44
Brook	42	4	46
Cassidy	1		1
Clark	13	1	14
Dale	36	3	39
Doherty	41	4	45
Donnelly	7		7
Freeman	1		1
Heale	10		10
Herd	32	4	36
Marshall	38	4	42
McCullough	2		2
McLeod	3		3
Neilson	2		2
Percival	42	3	45
Regan	4		4
Rodger	9		9
Rogers	2	1	3
Swift	42	4	46
Tilson	23	4	27
Toseland	42	4	46

Goalscorers

PLAYER	LEAGUE	CUP COMPETITION FA CUP	TOTAL
Doherty	30	2	32
Brook	20	2	22
Herd	15	3	18
Tilson	15	3	18
Rodger	7		7
Toseland	7		7
Heale	6		6
Bray	2		2
McLeod	2		2
Donnelly	1		1
Neilson	1		1
Percival	1		1

Fact File

After an unbeaten run of 14 wins and 6 draws since Christmas, the Blues won the championship at Maine Road with a win over Sheffield Wednesday in April.

MANAGER: Wilf Wild

CAPTAIN: Sam Barkas

TOP SCORER: Peter Doherty

BIGGEST WIN: February 20, 1937 5-0 v Bolton Wanderers, FA Cup Round 5; February 24, 1937 5-0 v Derby County, Division 1; March 26, 1937 5-0 v Liverpool, Division 1

HIGHEST ATTENDANCE: April 10, 1937 74,918 v Arsenal, drew 1-1, Division 1

MAJOR TRANSFERS IN: Billy Walsh from Manchester United

Final Division 1 Table

		P	W	D	L	F	A	Pts
1	MANCHESTER CITY	42	22	13	7	107	61	57
2	CHARLTON ATH	42	21	12	9	58	49	54
3	ARSENAL	42	18	16	8	80	49	52
4	DERBY CO	42	21	7	14	96	90	49
5	WOLVERHAMPTON W	42	21	5	16	84	67	47
6	BRENTFORD	42	18	10	14	82	78	46
7	MIDDLESBROUGH	42	19	8	15	74	71	46
8	SUNDERLAND	42	19	6	17	89	87	44
9	PORTSMOUTH	42	17	10	15	62	66	44
10	STOKE C	42	15	12	15	72	57	42
11	BIRMINGHAM	42	13	15	14	64	60	41
12	GRIMSBY T	42	17	7	18	86	81	41
13	CHELSEA	42	14	13	15	52	55	41
14	PRESTON NE	42	14	13	15	56	67	41
15	HUDDERSFIELD T	42	12	15	15	62	64	39
16	WBA	42	16	6	20	77	98	38
17	EVERTON	42	14	9	19	81	78	37
18	LIVERPOOL	42	12	11	19	62	84	35
19	LEEDS U	42	15	4	23	60	80	34
20	BOLTON W	42	10	14	18	43	66	34
21	MANCHESTER U	42	10	12	20	55	78	32
22	SHEFFIELD W	42	9	12	21	53	69	30

Season 1937-38

Football League Division 1

DATE	OPPONENTS	SCORE	GOALSCORERS	ATTENDANCE
Aug 28	Wolves	L 1-3	Herd	39,484
Sep 1	EVERTON	W 2-0	Herd, Doherty	27,603
Sep 4	LEICESTER CITY	W 3-0	Bray, Herd, Brook	40,000
Sep 8	Everton	L 1-4	Brook	27,290
Sep 11	Sunderland	L 1-3	Doherty	30,000
Sep 15	HUDDERSFIELD TOWN	W 3-2	Herd 2, Percival	19,968
Sep 18	DERBY COUNTY	W 6-1	Doherty 2, Brook 2, Clayton, Percival	32,991
Sep 25	Portsmouth	D 2-2	Doherty, Barr	20,000
Oct 2	Arsenal	L 1-2	Clayton	68,353
Oct 9	BLACKPOOL	W 2-1	Herd, Brook	38,846
Oct 16	STOKE CITY	D 0-0		40,000
Oct 23	Middlesbrough	L 0-4		18,442
Oct 30	BIRMINGHAM	W 2-0	Doherty 2	20,000
Nov 6	Preston North End	D 2-2	Doherty, Brook	32,000
Nov 13	LIVERPOOL	L 1-3	Toseland	25,000
Nov 20	Chelsea	D 2-2	Herd, Brook	40,197
Nov 27	GRIMSBY TOWN	W 3-1	Percival 2, Herd	27,526
Dec 18	Leeds United	L 1-2	Doherty	22,144
Dec 25	BRENTFORD	L 0-2		35,000
Dec 27	Brentford	L 1-2	Herd	40,000
Jan 1	WOLVES	L 2-4	Herd, Doherty	39,776
Jan 15	Leicester City	W 4-1	Doherty 3, Heale	16,000
Jan 29	Derby County	W 7-1	Heale 3, Doherty 2, Brook, Toseland	13,625
Feb 2	SUNDERLAND	D 0-0		19,000
Feb 5	PORTSMOUTH	W 2-1	Rogers, Brook	30,000
Feb 16	ARSENAL	L 1-2	Heale	34,299
Feb 19	Blackpool	L 1-2	Tilson	19,764
Feb 26	Stoke City	L 2-3	Toseland, Doherty	30,000
Mar 9	MIDDLESBROUGH	L 1-6	Milsom	16,396
Mar 12	Birmingham	D 2-2	Doherty, Brook	25,000
Mar 16	West Bromwich Albion	D 1-1	Dunkley	10,792
Mar 19	PRESTON NORTH END	L 1-2	Doherty	45,000
Mar 26	Liverpool	L 0-2		30,000
Apr 2	CHELSEA	W 1-0	Pritchard	31,033
Apr 6	CHARLTON ATHLETIC	W 5-3	Milsom 3, Bray, Pritchard	18,000
Apr 9	Grimsby Town	L 1-3	Doherty	11,413
Apr 15	BOLTON WANDERERS	L 1-2	Milsom	53,328
Apr 16	WEST BROMWICH ALBION	W 7-1	Brook 4, Herd 2, Doherty	16,700
Apr 18	Bolton Wanderers	L 1-2	Brook	29,872
Apr 23	Charlton Athletic	D 0-0		31,000
Apr 30	LEEDS UNITED	W 6-2	Doherty 3, Percival, Heale, Brook	26,732
May 7	Huddersfield Town	L 0-1		35,100

FA Cup

Jan 8	Millwall	(Rd 3)	D 2-2	Herd 2	38,110
Jan 12	MILLWALL	(R)	W 3-1	Herd, Heale, Brook	39,559
Jan 22	BURY	(Rd 4)	W 3-1	Toseland 2, o.g.	71,937
Feb 12	Luton Town	(Rd 5)	W 3-1	Doherty, Heale, o.g.	21,099
Mar 5	Aston Villa	(Rd 6)	L 2-3	Doherty, o.g.	75,500

FA Charity Shield

Nov 4	SUNDERLAND	W 2-0	Herd, Doherty	20,000

League & Cup Appearances

PLAYER	LEAGUE	CUP COMPETITION		TOTAL
		FA CUP	OTHER	
Allmark	1			1
Barkas	30	4	1	35
Barr	1			1
Bray	28	1	1	30
Brook	36	4	1	41
Clark	22	3		25
Clayton	3	1		4
Dale	30	5	1	36
Doherty	41	5	1	47
Dunkley	3			3
Emptage	4			4
Gregg	2			2
Heale	8	4		12
Herd	35	5	1	41
Marshall	31	1	1	33
McCullough	3			3
McDowall	12			12
Milsom	13			13
Neilson	6	4		10
Percival	40	5	1	46
Pritchard	9			9
Rodger	6			6
Rogers	7	2		9
Swift	42	5	1	48
Tilson	13		1	14
Toseland	30	5	1	36
Wardle	6	1		7

Goalscorers

PLAYER	LEAGUE	CUP COMPETITION		TOTAL
		FA CUP	OTHER	
Doherty	23	2	1	26
Brook	16	1		17
Herd	12	3	1	16
Heale	6	2		8
Milsom	5			5
Percival	5			5
Toseland	3	2		5
Bray	2			2
Clayton	2			2
Pritchard	2			2
Dunkley	1			1
Rogers	1			1
Tilson	1			1
Barr	1			1
Opps' o.gs.		3		3

Fact File

City are relegated despite scoring more goals than any other team in the division.

MANAGER: Wilf Wild

CAPTAIN: Sam Barkas

TOP SCORER: Peter Doherty

BIGGEST WIN: January 29, 1937 7-1 v Derby, Division 1; April 16, 1937 7-1 v West Bromwich Albion, Division 1

HIGHEST ATTENDANCE: March 5, 1947 75,500 v Aston Vila, lost 2-3, FA Cup Round 6

MAJOR TRANSFERS IN: Les McDowall from Sunderland, Eric Westwood from Manchester United

Final Division 1 Table

		P	W	D	L	F	A	PTS
1	ARSENAL	42	21	10	11	77	44	52
2	WOLVERHAMPTON W	42	20	11	11	72	49	51
3	PRESTON NE	42	16	17	9	64	44	49
4	CHARLTON ATH	42	16	14	12	65	51	46
5	MIDDLESBROUGH	42	19	8	15	72	65	46
6	BRENTFORD	42	18	9	15	69	59	45
7	BOLTON W	42	15	15	12	64	60	45
8	SUNDERLAND	42	14	16	12	55	57	44
9	LEEDS U	42	14	15	13	64	69	43
10	CHELSEA	42	14	13	15	65	65	41
11	LIVERPOOL	42	15	11	16	65	71	41
12	BLACKPOOL	42	16	8	18	61	66	40
13	DERBY CO	42	15	10	17	66	87	40
14	EVERTON	42	16	7	19	79	75	39
15	HUDDERSFIELD T	42	17	5	20	55	68	39
16	LEICESTER C	42	14	11	17	54	75	39
17	STOKE C	42	13	12	17	58	59	38
18	BIRMINGHAM	42	10	18	14	58	62	38
19	PORTSMOUTH	42	13	12	17	62	68	38
20	GRIMSBY T	42	13	12	17	51	68	38
21	MANCHESTER CITY	42	14	8	20	80	77	36
22	WBA	42	14	8	20	74	91	36

Season 1938-39

Football League Division 2

DATE	OPPONENTS	SCORE	GOALSCORERS	ATTENDANCE
Aug 27	SWANSEA TOWN	W 5-0	Herd 2, Doherty 2, Howe	30,889
Aug 29	Chesterfield	W 3-0	Howe 2, Brook	15,000
Sep 3	Bradford	L 2-4	Herd, Brook	16,000
Sep 7	WEST HAM UNITED	L 2-4	Howe, Herd	18,671
Sep 10	LUTON TOWN	L 1-2	Howe	29,627
Sep 17	Millwall	L 1-6	Bray	27,437
Sep 24	Blackburn Rovers	D 3-3	Herd, Heale, McDowall	26,457
Oct 1	FULHAM	L 3-5	McDowall 2, Barr	25,000
Oct 8	Sheffield Wednesday	L 1-3	Brook	25,000
Oct 15	Plymouth Argyle	D 0-0		24,710
Oct 22	SHEFFIELD UNITED	W 3-2	Toseland, Milsom, Brook	29,848
Oct 29	West Bromwich Albion	L 1-3	Milsom	22,274
Nov 5	TOTTENHAM HOTSPUR	W 2-0	Milsom, Doherty	47,998
Nov 12	Southampton	W 2-1	Milsom, Brook	23,104
Nov 19	COVENTRY CITY	W 3-0	Doherty 2, Herd	38,712
Nov 26	Nottingham Forest	W 4-3	Brook 3, Herd	15,727
Dec 3	NEWCASTLE UNITED	W 4-1	Herd 2, Milsom 2	45,000
Dec 10	Burnley	D 1-1	Milsom	24,096
Dec 17	NORWICH CITY	W 4-1	Doherty 2, Herd 2	17,907
Dec 24	Swansea Town	L 0-2		15,000
Dec 26	Tranmere Rovers	W 9-3	Milsom 4, Toseland 2, Doherty 2, Herd	14,000
Dec 27	TRANMERE ROVERS	W 5-2	Milsom 3, Doherty, Pritchard	43,994
Dec 31	BRADFORD CITY	W 5-1	Herd 3, Milsom, Pritchard	32,033
Jan 14	Luton Town	L 0-3		16,000
Jan 28	BLACKBURN ROVERS	W 3-2	Heale 2, Doherty	47,089
Feb 4	Fulham	L 1-2	o.g.	24,366
Feb 18	PLYMOUTH ARGYLE	L 1-3	Brook	28,784
Feb 25	Sheffield United	L 0-1		40,000
Mar 4	WEST BROMWICH ALBION	D 3-3	Herd, Doherty, Brook	18,479
Mar 11	Tottenham Hotspur	W 3-2	Sproston 2, Freeman	27,426
Mar 13	Millwall	L 1-3	Doherty	14,000
Mar 18	SOUTHAMPTON	W 2-1	McLeod, McDowall	18,000
Mar 25	Coventry City	W 1-0	Heale	20,088
Apr 1	NOTTINGHAM FOREST	W 3-0	Herd 2, o.g.	24,758
Apr 7	Bury	W 5-1	Heale 2, Herd, Doherty, Brook	24,520
Apr 8	Newcastle United	W 2-0	Heale, Doherty	23,000
Apr 10	BURY	D 0-0		36,816
Apr 15	BURNLEY	W 2-0	Doherty 2	19,230
Apr 22	Norwich City	D 0-0		12,000
Apr 26	SHEFFIELD WEDNESDAY	D 1-1	Pritchard	24,244
Apr 29	CHESTERFIELD	W 3-1	Herd, Heale, McLeod	12,258
May 6	West Ham United	L 1-2	Heale	30,000

FA Cup

Jan 12	Norwich City	(Rd 3) W 5-0	Herd 2, Milsom 2, Doherty	20,901
Jan 21	Sheffield United	(Rd 4) L 0-2		49,795

Football League Jubilee Fund Match

Aug 20	MANCHESTER UNITED	W 2-1	Bray, Howe	27,788

League & Cup Appearances

PLAYER	LEAGUE	CUP COMPETITION		TOTAL
		FA CUP	JUBILEE	
Barr	3			3
Blackshaw	3			3
Bray	23		1	24
Brook	34	2	1	37
Cardwell	37	2		39
Clark	20	1	1	22
Doherty	28	2	1	31
Dunkley	16		1	17
Eastwood	7		1	8
Emptage	9			9
Freeman	3			3
Gregg	7			7
Heale	17			17
Herd	35	2	1	38
Howe	6		1	7
McDowall	38	2	1	41
McLeod	4			4
Milsom	19	2		21
Neilson	4		1	5
Percival	26	2		28
Pritchard	13			13
Robinson	1			1
Sproston	20	1		21
Swift	41	2	1	44
Toseland	18	2		20
Westwood	30	2		32

Goalscorers

PLAYER	LEAGUE	CUP COMPETITION		TOTAL
		FA CUP	JUBILEE	
Herd	20	2		22
Doherty	17	1		18
Milsom	15	2		17
Brook	11			11
Heale	9			9
Howe	5		1	6
McDowall	4			4
Pritchard	3			3
Toseland	3			3
McLeod	2			2
Sproston	2			2
Barr	1			1
Bray	1		1	2
Freeman	1			1
Opps' o.gs.	2			2

Fact File

Jackie Milsom scored seven times in two days in the thrashings handed out to Tranmere Rovers in December.

MANAGER: Wilf Wild

CAPTAIN: Les McDowall

TOP SCORER: Alex Herd

BIGGEST WIN: December 26, 1946 9-3 v Tranmere Rovers, Division 2

HIGHEST ATTENDANCE: April 4, 1947 49,795 v Sheffield United, lost 0-2, Division 2

MAJOR TRANSFERS IN: Bert Sproston from Tottenham Hotspur

Final Division 2 Table

		P	W	D	L	F	A	Pts
1	BLACKBURN R	42	25	5	12	94	60	55
2	SHEFFIELD U	42	20	14	8	69	41	54
3	SHEFFIELD W	42	21	11	10	88	59	53
4	COVENTRY C	42	21	8	13	62	45	50
5	MANCHESTER CITY	42	21	7	14	96	72	49
6	CHESTERFIELD	42	20	9	13	69	52	49
7	LUTON T	42	22	5	15	82	66	49
8	TOTTENHAM H	42	19	9	14	67	62	47
9	NEWCASTLE U	42	18	10	14	61	48	46
10	WBA	42	18	9	15	89	72	45
11	WEST HAM U	42	17	10	15	70	52	44
12	FULHAM	42	17	10	15	61	55	44
13	MILLWALL	42	14	14	14	64	53	42
14	BURNLEY	42	15	9	18	50	56	39
15	PLYMOUTH ARG	42	15	8	19	49	55	38
16	BURY	42	12	13	17	65	74	37
17	BRADFORD PA	42	12	11	19	61	82	35
18	SOUTHAMPTON	42	13	9	20	56	82	35
19	SWANSEA T	42	11	12	19	50	83	34
20	NOTTINGHAM F	42	10	11	21	49	82	31
21	NORWICH C	42	13	5	24	50	91	31
22	TRANMERE R	42	6	5	31	39	99	17

Season 1939-40

Football League Division 2

DATE	OPPONENTS	SCORE	GOALSCORERS	ATTENDANCE
Aug 26	Leicester City	L 3-4	Dunkley, Doherty, Brook	12,000
Aug 30	BURY	D 1-1	Doherty	20,000
Sep 2	CHESTERFIELD	W 2-0	Milsom 2	15,000

Football League programme abandoned upon outbreak of World War II.
Above games played in Division 2 before League closed down.

Western Regional League

Oct 21	Manchester United	W 4-0	Herd, Heale, Doherty, Brook	7,000
Oct 28	WREXHAM	W 6-1	Doherty 2, Pritchard 2, Heale, Brook	4,000
Nov 11	Everton	L 1-3	Heale	5,000
Nov 18	STOKE CITY	D 1-1	Percival	5,000
Nov 25	New Brighton	W 3-1	Herd, Doherty 2	3,500
Dec 2	STOCKPORT COUNTY	D 6-6	Heale 5, Wright	5,774
Dec 9	CHESTER	W 4-1	Blackshaw 2, Heale, Doherty	3,000
Dec 23	Crewe Alexandra	W 2-1	Herd 2	5,000
Jan 6	LIVERPOOL	L 3-7	Doherty 2, Rudd	5,000
Feb 10	MANCHESTER UNITED	W 1-0	Herd	5,000
Feb 24	Wrexham	L 2-3	Heale, Rudd	4,000
Mar 9	EVERTON	D 2-2	Heale, Rudd	5,000
Mar 16	Stoke City	L 1-2	Herd	5,000
Mar 23	NEW BRIGHTON	L 2-3	Doherty, Westwood	6,000
Mar 30	Stockport County	D 1-1	Herd	7,000
Apr 6	Chester	W 3-0	Herd 2, Emptage	2,500
Apr 13	TRANMERE ROVERS	W 5-1	Currier 2, Bray, Herd, Emptage	3,000
May 4	Tranmere Rovers	W 6-1	Currier 4, Herd, Doherty	2,500
May 11	Port Vale	W 5-2	Currier 4, Bray	2,000
May 13	CREWE ALEXANDRA	W 6-2	Herd 4, Burdett, Doherty	1,300
May 18	PORT VALE	W 7-0	Herd 4, Currier, Doherty, Pritchard	2,000
May 25	Liverpool	L 2-3	Pritchard, Doherty	2,000

League War Cup*

Apr 20	Manchester United	(Rd 1)	W 1-0	Worsley	21,874
Apr 27	MANCHESTER UNITED	(Rd 1)	L 0-2		21,596

*Played on two-legged home and away basis.

Football League Jubilee Fund Match

Aug 19	Manchester United	D 1-1	Milsom	20,000

City's record in the Western Regional League

P	W	D	L	F	A	Pts	Position
22	12	4	6	73	41	28	4th

League & Cup Appearances

PLAYER	LEAGUE	W.REGIONAL LEAGUE	WAR CUP	JUBILEE	TOTAL
Barkas		8			8
Blackshaw		8			8
Bray	3	19	2	1	25
Bray					0
Brook	3	4		1	8
Burdett		1			1
Cardwell	3	21	2	1	27
Clark		15	2		17
Currier		4	1		5
Davenport		1			1
Doherty	3	18	1	1	23
Dunkley	3			1	4
Emptage		9			9
Heale	2	13			15
Herd	3	21	2	1	27
McDowall	3			1	4
McIntosh		1			1
Milsom	1		1	1	3
Neilson		2			2
Percival		19			19
Pritchard		11	1		12
Robinson		3			3
Rudd		6			6
Smith G		2	1		3
Smith L		1			1
Sproston	3	10	2	1	16
Swift	3	19	2	1	25
Tilson		1			1
Toseland		1			1
Walsh		9	2		11
Westwood	3	12	1	1	17
Worsley			2		2
Wright	3				3

Goalscorers

PLAYER	LEAGUE	W.REGIONAL LEAGUE	WAR CUP	JUBILEE	TOTAL
Herd		19			19
Doherty	2	13			15
Currier		11			11
Heale		11			11
Pritchard		4			4
Brook	1	2			3
Rudd		3			3
Milsom	2			1	3
Blackshaw		2			2
Bray		2			2
Emptage		2			2
Burdett		1			1
Dunkley	1				1
Percival		1			1
Westwood		1			1
Worsley			1		1
Wright		1			1

Final Division 2 Table

		P	W	D	L	F	A	Pts
1	LUTON T	3	2	1	0	7	1	5
2	BIRMINGHAM	3	2	1	0	5	1	5
3	WEST HAM U	3	2	0	1	5	4	4
4	COVENTRY C	3	1	2	0	8	6	4
5	LEICESTER C	3	2	0	1	6	5	4
6	NOTTINGHAM F	3	2	0	1	5	5	4
7	PLYMOUTH ARG	3	2	0	1	4	3	4
8	TOTTENHAM H	3	1	2	0	6	5	4
9	WBA	3	1	1	1	8	8	3
10	BURY	3	1	1	1	4	5	3
11	NEWPORT CO	3	1	1	1	5	4	3
12	MILLWALL	3	1	1	1	5	4	3
13	MANCHESTER CITY	3	1	1	1	6	5	3
14	SOUTHAMPTON	3	1	0	2	5	6	2
15	SWANSEA T	3	1	0	2	5	11	2
16	BARNSLEY	3	1	0	2	7	8	2
17	CHESTERFIELD	2	1	0	1	2	2	2
18	NEWCASTLE U	3	1	0	2	8	6	2
19	SHEFFIELD W	3	1	0	2	3	5	2
20	BRADFORD PA	3	0	1	2	2	7	1
21	FULHAM	3	0	1	2	3	6	1
22	BURNLEY	2	0	1	1	1	3	1

Fact File

James Currier, a guest player from Bolton Wanderers, scored 11 goals
in his 5 games this season.

MANAGER: Wilf Wild
CAPTAIN: Les McDowall
TOP SCORER: Alex Herd
BIGGEST WIN: May 11, 1940 7-0 v Port Vale, Western Regional League
HIGHEST ATTENDANCE: April 20, 1940 21,874 v Manchester United,
lost 0-2, League War Cup

Season 1945-46

Football League North

DATE	OPPONENTS	SCORE	GOALSCORERS	ATTENDANCE
Aug 25	MIDDLESBROUGH	W 2-1	Dunkley, Pearson	25,000
Sep 1	Middlesbrough	D 2-2	Smith 2	14,000
Sep 8	Stoke City	L 0-2		15,000
Sep 12	SHEFFIELD WEDNESDAY	L 1-5	Sproston	8,000
Sep 15	STOKE CITY	L 0-2		15,000
Sep 22	GRIMSBY TOWN	L 0-2		20,000
Sep 29	Grimsby Town	W 2-0	Hart, Constantine	13,000
Oct 6	Blackpool	L 4-5	Constantine 3, Dunkley	20,000
Oct 13	BLACKPOOL	L 1-4	King	32,730
Oct 20	LIVERPOOL	W 1-0	Constantine	23,034
Oct 27	Liverpool	W 5-0	Herd 2, Pearson 2, Smith	34,941
Nov 3	Bury	W 3-1	Walsh, Smith, Pearson	12,216
Nov 10	BURY	W 4-1	Smith 2, Woodruffe, Pearson	24,600
Nov 17	BLACKBURN ROVERS	W 4-2	Constantine 2, Dunkley, Smith	22,177
Nov 24	Blackburn Rovers	D 0-0		9,000
Dec 1	Bradford City	W 3-2	Constantine 2, Smith	14,012
Dec 8	BRADFORD CITY	W 6-0	Herd 2, Constantine 2, Wild, Dunkley	18,525
Dec 15	Burnley	L 0-1		10,000
Dec 22	BURNLEY	L 1-2	Constantine	21,000
Dec 25	NEWCASTLE UNITED	W 4-3	Dunkley, Constantine, Pearson, Smith	29,000
Dec 26	Newcastle United	D 1-1	Smith	54,495
Dec 29	Sheffield Wednesday	D 1-1	Wild	20,000
Jan 1	HUDDERSFIELD TOWN	W 3-2	Herd 2, Constantine	25,490
Jan 12	Chesterfield	W 1-0	Herd	10,000
Jan 19	CHESTERFIELD	W 1-0	Constantine	24,245
Feb 2	Barnsley	L 0-2		20,128
Feb 9	Everton	L 1-4	Constantine	40,000
Feb 16	EVERTON	L 1-3	Constantine	35,000
Feb 23	BOLTON WANDERERS	W 1-0	Constantine	25,000
Mar 9	Preston North End	L 1-3	Herd	12,000
Mar 13	BARNSLEY	L 2-3	Constantine 2	6,662
Mar 16	PRESTON NORTH END	W 3-0	Smith 2, Constantine	20,000
Mar 23	LEEDS UNITED	W 5-1	Constantine 2, Herd, Smith, Emptage	20,000
Mar 27	Bolton Wanderers	L 1-3	Gemmell	12,000
Mar 30	Leeds United	W 3-1	Herd 2, Constantine	10,000
Apr 6	Manchester United	W 4-1	Smith 4	62,144
Apr 13	MANCHESTER UNITED	L 1-3	Smith	50,440
Apr 19	SUNDERLAND	L 0-2		31,209
Apr 20	Sheffield United	W 3-2	Woodroffe, Constantine, Smith	40,000
Apr 22	Sunderland	L 0-4		27,650
Apr 27	SHEFFIELD UNITED	W 2-1	Dunkley, Smith	19,241
May 4	Huddersfield Town	L 0-3		8,781

FA Cup

DATE	OPPONENTS		SCORE	GOALSCORERS	ATTENDANCE
Jan 5	BARROW	(Rd 3)	W 6-2	Herd 3, Constantine 3	19,589
Jan 19	Barrow		D 2-2	Dunkley, Hart	7,377
Jan 26	Bradford City	(Rd 4)	W 3-1	Smith 2, Herd	25,014
Jan 30	BRADFORD CITY		L 2-8	Constantine, Smith	15,026

League & Cup Appearances

PLAYER	LEAGUE	CUP COMPETITION FA CUP	TOTAL
Barkas	33	4	37
Bootle	1	1	2
Bray	4		4
Brown	2		2
Campbell	1		1
Cardwell	17	4	21
Clark	26	4	30
Constantine	34	4	38
Cunliffe	1	1	2
Daniels	3		3
Dunkley	29	3	32
Eastwood	8		8
Emptage	12		12
Fagan	4		4
Gemmell	2		2
Hart	4	1	5
Herd	29	3	32
Hilton	1		1
Hodgson	2		2
King	2		2
Laing	1		1
Linaker	4		4
McDowall	40	3	43
Moore	3		3
Murray	4		4
Pearson	14		14
Pimbley	2		2
Pritchard		3	3
Robinson P	2	1	3
Smith	41	4	45
Sprotson	22		22
Swift	35	4	39
Taylor	3		3
Toseland	1		1
Walker	3		3
Walsh	40	4	44
Westwood	5		5
Wild	5		5
Williams	8		8
Woodroffe	6		6

Goalscorers

PLAYER	LEAGUE	CUP COMPETITION FA CUP	TOTAL
Constantine	25	4	29
Smith	20	3	23
Herd	11	4	15
Dunkley	6	1	7
Pearson	6		6
Wild	2		2
Woodroffe	2		2
Emptage	1		1
Gemmell	1		1
Hart	1	1	2
King	1		1
Sprotson	1		1
Walsh	1		1

Fact File

City's 8-2 FA Cup defeat in the Round 3 second leg against Bradford Park Avenue remains their record home defeat.

MANAGER: Wilf Wild

CAPTAIN: Sam Barkas

TOP SCORER: James Constantine

BIGGEST WIN: December 8, 1945 6-0 v Bradford City, Football League North

HIGHEST ATTENDANCE: April 4, 1947 62,144 v Manchester United, won 4-1, Football League North

Final North Table

		P	W	D	L	F	A	Pts
1	SHEFFIELD U	42	27	6	9	112	62	60
2	EVERTON	42	23	9	10	88	54	55
3	BOLTON W	42	20	11	11	67	45	51
4	MANCHESTER U	42	19	11	12	98	62	49
5	SHEFFIELD W	42	20	8	14	67	60	48
6	NEWCASTLE U	42	21	5	16	106	70	47
7	CHESTERFIELD	42	17	12	13	68	49	46
8	BARNSLEY	42	17	11	14	76	68	45
9	BLACKPOOL	42	18	9	15	94	92	45
10	MANCHESTER CITY	42	20	4	18	78	75	44
11	LIVERPOOL	42	17	9	16	80	70	43
12	MIDDLESBROUGH	42	17	9	16	75	87	43
13	STOKE C	42	18	6	18	88	79	42
14	BRADFORD PA	42	17	6	19	71	84	40
15	HUDDERSFIELD T	42	17	4	21	90	89	38
16	BURNLEY	42	13	10	19	63	84	36
17	GRIMSBY T	42	13	9	20	61	89	35
18	SUNDERLAND	42	15	5	22	55	83	35
19	PRESTON NE	42	14	6	22	70	77	34
20	BURY	42	12	10	20	60	85	34
21	BLACKBURN R	42	11	7	24	60	111	29
22	LEEDS U	42	9	7	26	66	118	25

Season 1946-47

Football League Division 2

DATE	OPPONENTS	SCORE	GOALSCORERS	ATTENDANCE
Aug 31	Leicester City	W 3-0	McDowall, Walsh, Jackson	20,000
Sep 4	BURY	W 3-1	Dunkley, Black, Smith	28,000
Sep 7	CHESTERFIELD	D 0-0		47,319
Sep 14	Millwall	W 3-1	Constantine 3	30,000
Sep 18	Bury	D 2-2	Herd 2	11,000
Sep 21	BRADFORD CITY	W 7-2	Black 3, Smith 2, Constantine, Sproston	38,330
Sep 28	Tottenham Hotspur	D 0-0		53,253
Oct 5	West Ham United	L 0-1		32,000
Oct 12	SHEFFIELD WEDNESDAY	W 2-1	Herd, Constantine	36,413
Oct 19	SWANSEA TOWN	D 1-1	Sproston	34,436
Oct 26	Newcastle United	L 2-3	Black, Westwood	65,798
Nov 2	WEST BROMWICH ALBION	W 5-0	Black 3, Dunkley, Herd	38,821
Nov 9	Birmingham City	L 1-3	Smith	30,000
Nov 16	COVENTRY CITY	W 1-0	Dunkley	25,569
Nov 23	Nottingham Forest	W 1-0	Smith	22,000
Nov 30	SOUTHAMPTON	D 1-1	Constantine	24,867
Dec 7	Newport County	W 3-0	Dunkley, Black, Constantine	15,000
Dec 14	BARNSLEY	W 5-1	Constantine 2, o.g., Smith 2	22,210
Dec 21	Burnley	D 0-0		35,000
Dec 25	PLYMOUTH ARGYLE	W 4-3	Smith 2, Herd, Constantine	24,532
Dec 26	Plymouth Argyle	W 3-2	Constantine, Smith, o.g.	27,000
Dec 28	LEICESTER CITY	W 1-0	Constantine	43,910
Jan 1	FULHAM	W 4-0	Herd 2, Black 2	47,658
Jan 4	Chesterfield	W 1-0	Jackson	20,000
Jan 18	MILLWALL	W 1-0	Capel	36,635
Feb 1	TOTTENHAM HOTSPUR	W 1-0	Westwood	39,000
Feb 22	Swansea Town	W 2-1	Smith, Herd	26,584
Mar 1	Fulham	D 2-2	Smith, Herd	32,000
Mar 15	BIRMINGHAM CITY	W 1-0	Smith	59,535
Mar 22	Coventry City	D 1-1	Herd	26,679
Mar 29	NOTTINGHAM FOREST	W 2-1	Smith, Wharton	26,354
Apr 4	LUTON TOWN	W 2-0	Woodroffe, Smith	57,592
Apr 5	Southampton	W 1-0	Smith	25,000
Apr 7	Luton Town	D 0-0		24,000
Apr 19	Barnsley	W 2-0	McDowall, Black	26,274
May 3	NEWCASTLE UNITED	L 0-2		46,972
May 10	BURNLEY	W 1-0	Herd	67,672
May 14	Bradford City	D 1-1	Smith	15,162
May 24	WEST HAM UNITED	W 2-0	McDowall, Smith	31,980
May 26	Sheffield Wednesday	L 0-1		30,000
May 31	West Bromwich Albion	L 1-3	Black	25,000
Jun 14	NEWPORT COUNTY	W 5-1	Smith 5	24,300

FA Cup

Jan 11	GATESHEAD	(Rd 3) W 3-0	Jackson, Capel, Westwood	38,575
Jan 25	Bolton Wanderers	(Rd 4) D 3-3	Black 2, Capel	41,286
Jan 29	BOLTON WANDERERS	(R) W 1-0	Westwood	39,355
Feb 8	Birmingham City	(Rd 5) L 0-5		50,000

League & Cup Appearances

PLAYER	LEAGUE	CUP COMPETITION FA CUP	TOTAL
Barkas	33	4	37
Black	34	3	37
Capel	5	4	9
Cardwell	2		2
Clarke	1		1
Constantine	18		18
Dunkley	32	4	36
Eastwood	9		9
Emptage	29	4	33
Fagan	20	4	24
Herd	28		28
Hodgson	1		1
Jackson	7	1	8
Hope	7		7
McCormack	1		1
McDowall	35	4	39
Murray	1		1
Oakes	1		1
Percival	16		16
Rigby	1		1
Robinson J	1		1
Robinson P	1		1
Rudd	2		2
Smith	38	4	42
Sprotson	38	2	40
Swift	35	4	39
Thurlow	6		6
Walsh	13		13
Westwood	28	4	32
Wharton	3		3
Williams	7	2	9
Woodroffe	9		9

Goalscorers

PLAYER	LEAGUE	CUP COMPETITION FA CUP	TOTAL
Smith	23		23
Black	13	2	15
Constantine	12		12
Herd	11		11
Dunkley	4		4
Westwood	2	2	4
McDowall	3		3
Jackson	2	1	3
Capel	1	2	3
Sprotson	2		2
Walsh	1		1
Wharton	1		1
Woodroffe	1		1
Opps' o.gs.	2		2

Fact File

As City celebrated promotion in the final league game against Newport, George Smith equalled Tommy Johnson's 19-year old record by scoring all five of City's goals.

MANAGER: Wilf Wild/Sam Cowan
CAPTAIN: Sam Barkas
TOP SCORER: George Smith
BIGGEST WIN: September 21, 1947 7-2 v Bradford City, Division 2
HIGHEST ATTENDANCE: May 10, 1948 67,672 v Burnley, won 1-0, Division 2
MAJOR TRANSFERS IN: Andy Black from Hearts, Roy Clarke from Cardiff City

Final Division 2 Table

		P	W	D	L	F	A	Pts
1	MANCHESTER CITY	42	26	10	6	78	35	62
2	BURNLEY	42	22	14	6	65	29	58
3	BIRMINGHAM C	42	25	5	12	74	33	55
4	CHESTERFIELD	42	18	14	10	58	44	50
5	NEWCASTLE U	42	19	10	13	95	62	48
6	TOTTENHAM H	42	17	14	11	65	53	48
7	WBA	42	20	8	14	88	75	48
8	COVENTRY C	42	16	13	13	66	59	45
9	LEICESTER C	42	18	7	17	69	64	43
10	BARNSLEY	42	17	8	17	84	86	42
11	NOTTINGHAM F	42	15	10	17	69	74	40
12	WEST HAM U	42	16	8	18	70	76	40
13	LUTON T	42	16	7	19	71	73	39
14	SOUTHAMPTON	42	15	9	18	69	76	39
15	FULHAM	42	15	9	18	63	74	39
16	BRADFORD PA	42	14	11	17	65	77	39
17	BURY	42	12	12	18	80	78	36
18	MILLWALL	42	14	8	20	56	79	36
19	PLYMOUTH ARG	42	14	5	23	79	96	33
20	SHEFFIELD W	42	12	8	22	67	88	32
21	SWANSEA T	42	11	7	24	55	83	29
22	NEWPORT CO	42	10	3	29	61	133	23

251

Football League Division 1

DATE	OPPONENTS	SCORE	GOALSCORERS	ATTENDANCE
Aug 23	WOLVES	W 4-3	Black, McMorran, Smith, Clarke	67,800
Aug 27	Everton	L 0-1		53,822
Aug 30	Aston Villa	D 1-1	Clarke	50,000
Sep 3	EVERTON	L 0-1		44,000
Sep 6	SUNDERLAND	W 3-0	Black, McMorran, Clarke	53,263
Sep 10	Derby County	D 0-0		31,000
Sep 13	Grimsby Town	L 0-1		20,000
Sep 17	DERBY COUNTY	W 3-2	Smith, McMorran, Capel	35,000
Sep 20	MANCHESTER UNITED	D 0-0		78,000
Sep 27	BLACKBURN ROVERS	L 1-3	Smith	44,900
Oct 4	Blackpool	D 1-1	Wharton	30,000
Oct 11	Preston North End	L 1-2	Black	32,000
Oct 18	STOKE CITY	W 3-0	Smith 2, Herd	42,408
Oct 25	Burnley	D 1-1	Fagan	41,626
Nov 1	PORTSMOUTH	W 1-0	Smith	43,000
Nov 8	Middlesbrough	L 1-2	Black	40,000
Nov 15	CHARLTON ATHLETIC	W 4-0	Black 3, McMorran	40,000
Nov 22	Bolton Wanderers	L 1-2	Linacre	30,000
Nov 29	LIVERPOOL	W 2-0	McMorran, Smith	37,464
Dec 6	Arsenal	D 1-1	Black	43,000
Dec 13	SHEFFIELD UNITED	W 4-3	Smith 2, McMorran, Black	27,058
Dec 20	Wolves	L 0-1		33,000
Dec 26	HUDDERSFIELD TOWN	D 1-1	Linacre	56,460
Dec 27	Huddersfield Town	D 1-1	Black	32,634
Jan 3	ASTON VILLA	L 0-2		50,000
Jan 17	Sunderland	W 1-0	Black	35,659
Jan 31	GRIMSBY TOWN	W 3-1	McMorran 2, Smith	34,362
Feb 14	Blackburn Rovers	L 0-1		31,000
Feb 21	BLACKPOOL	W 1-0	Smith	28,838
Mar 6	Stoke City	L 0-3		28,000
Mar 13	BURNLEY	W 4-1	Smith 2, Clarke 2	29,605
Mar 20	Portsmouth	L 0-1		29,000
Mar 26	Chelsea	D 2-2	Linacre, Black	64,396
Mar 27	MIDDLESBROUGH	W 2-0	McMorran, Black	39,668
Mar 29	CHELSEA	W 1-0	Black	29,034
Apr 3	Charlton Athletic	W 1-0	McMorran	37,000
Apr 7	Manchester United	D 1-1	Linacre	71,960
Apr 10	BOLTON WANDERERS	L 0-2		33,800
Apr 17	Liverpool	D 1-1	Black	39,348
Apr 21	PRESTON NORTH END	L 0-3		18,393
Apr 24	ARSENAL	D 0-0		20,782
May 1	Sheffield United	L 1-2	Black	24,000

FA Cup

DATE	OPPONENTS		SCORE	GOALSCORERS	ATTENDANCE
Jan 10	BARNSLEY	(Rd 3)	W 2-1	Smith, Black	54,747
Jan 24	CHELSEA	(Rd 4)	W 2-0	Linacre, Smith	45,059
Feb 7	PRESTON NORTH END	(Rd 5)	L 0-1		67,494

League & Cup Appearances

PLAYER	LEAGUE	CUP COMPETITION FA CUP	TOTAL
Black	37	3	40
Capel	4		4
Clarke	36		36
Emptage	39	3	42
Fagan	42	3	45
Hart	1		1
Herd	4		4
Jackson	1		1
Linacre	27	3	30
McDowall	16		16
McMorran	29	3	32
Munro	5		5
Murray	6		6
Oxford	1		1
Smith	39	3	42
Sprotson	37	3	40
Swift	33	3	36
Thurlow	8		8
Walsh	30	3	33
Westwood	42	3	45
Wharton	20	3	23
Williams	5		5

Goalscorers

PLAYER	LEAGUE	CUP COMPETITION FA CUP	TOTAL
Black	16	1	17
Smith	13	2	15
McMorran	10		10
Clarke	5		5
Linacre	4	1	5
Capel	1		1
Fagan	1		1
Herd	1		1
Wharton	1		1

Fact File

This season saw both Manchester clubs playing at Maine Road and both derby matches were drawn.

MANAGER: Jock Thomson
CAPTAIN: Eric Westwood
TOP SCORER: Andy Black
BIGGEST WIN: November 15, 1947 4-0 v Charlton Athletic, Division 1
HIGHEST ATTENDANCE: September 20, 1947 78,000 v Manchester United, drew 0-0, Division 1
MAJOR TRANSFERS IN: Eric McMorran from Belfast Celtic

Final Division 1 Table

		P	W	D	L	F	A	Pts
1	ARSENAL	42	23	13	6	81	32	59
2	MANCHESTER U	42	19	14	9	81	48	52
3	BURNLEY	42	20	12	10	56	43	52
4	DERBY CO	42	19	12	11	77	57	50
5	WOLVERHAMPTON W	42	19	9	14	83	70	47
6	ASTON VILLA	42	19	9	14	65	57	47
7	PRESTON NE	42	20	7	15	67	68	47
8	PORTSMOUTH	42	19	7	16	68	50	45
9	BLACKPOOL	42	17	10	15	57	41	44
10	MANCHESTER CITY	42	15	12	15	52	47	42
11	LIVERPOOL	42	16	10	16	65	61	42
12	SHEFFIELD U	42	16	10	16	65	70	42
13	CHARLTON ATH	42	17	6	19	57	66	40
14	EVERTON	42	17	6	19	52	66	40
15	STOKE C	42	14	10	18	41	55	38
16	MIDDLESBROUGH	42	14	9	19	71	73	37
17	BOLTON W	42	16	5	21	46	58	37
18	CHELSEA	42	14	9	19	53	71	37
19	HUDDERSFIELD T	42	12	12	18	51	60	36
20	SUNDERLAND	42	13	10	19	56	67	36
21	BLACKBURN R	42	11	10	21	54	72	32
22	GRIMSBY T	42	8	6	28	45	111	22

Season 1948-49

Football League Division 1

DATE	OPPONENTS	SCORE	GOALSCORERS	ATTENDANCE
Aug 21	Burnley	L 0-1		28,000
Aug 25	PRESTON NORTH END	W 3-2	Sproston, McDowall, McMorran	45,000
Aug 28	STOKE CITY	D 0-0		42,450
Sep 1	Preston North End	W 3-1	Black, Godwin, Linacre	35,000
Sep 4	Charlton Athletic	L 2-3	Godwin 2	45,000
Sep 8	BIRMINGHAM CITY	W 1-0	Black	26,841
Sep 11	MANCHESTER UNITED	D 0-0		64,502
Sep 15	Birmingham City	L 1-4	Smith	40,000
Sep 18	PORTSMOUTH	D 1-1	McMorran	48,372
Sep 25	Newcastle United	D 0-0		58,000
Oct 2	MIDDLESBROUGH	W 1-0	Oakes	42,000
Oct 9	Sheffield United	W 2-0	Oakes, Black	26,000
Oct 16	ASTON VILLA	W 4-1	Smith 3, Oakes	38,024
Oct 23	Sunderland	L 0-3		46,979
Oct 30	WOLVES	D 3-3	Oakes, Black, Linacre	44,130
Nov 6	Bolton Wanderers	L 1-5	Smith	37,931
Nov 13	LIVERPOOL	L 2-4	Black, Clarke	21,659
Nov 20	Blackpool	D 1-1	Smith	28,000
Nov 27	DERBY COUNTY	W 2-1	Black, Clarke	42,225
Dec 4	Arsenal	D 1-1	Oakes	45,000
Dec 11	HUDDERSFIELD TOWN	W 3-1	Clarke 2, Emptage	37,717
Dec 18	BURNLEY	D 2-2	Smith, o.g.	30,000
Dec 25	Everton	D 0-0		45,000
Dec 27	EVERTON	D 0-0		30,000
Jan 1	Stoke City	W 3-2	Smith 2, Clarke	25,000
Jan 15	CHARLTON ATHLETIC	L 0-1		20,000
Jan 22	Manchester United	D 0-0		64,485
Feb 5	Portsmouth	L 1-3	Smith	34,167
Feb 19	NEWCASTLE UNITED	W 1-0	Black	48,624
Feb 26	Middlesbrough	W 1-0	Black	35,000
Mar 5	SHEFFIELD UNITED	W 1-0	Black	16,502
Mar 12	Aston Villa	L 0-1		35,000
Mar 19	BLACKPOOL	D 1-1	Hart	35,857
Mar 26	Derby County	L 0-2		29,125
Apr 2	BOLTON WANDERERS	W 1-0	Black	28,000
Apr 9	Liverpool	W 1-0	Smith	31,389
Apr 15	CHELSEA	W 1-0	Smith	30,000
Apr 16	SUNDERLAND	D 1-1	Clarke	31,345
Apr 18	Chelsea	D 1-1	Munro	25,864
Apr 25	Wolves	D 1-1	Black	45,000
Apr 27	ARSENAL	L 0-3		27,955
May 7	Huddersfield Town	L 0-1		27,507

FA Cup

Jan 8	Everton	(Rd 3) L 0-1		63,459

League & Cup Appearances

PLAYER	LEAGUE	CUP COMPETITION FA CUP	TOTAL
Black	35		35
Bootle	2		2
Clarke	34	1	35
Emptage	27	1	28
Fagan	42	1	43
Gill	1		1
Godwin	8		8
Greenwood	1		1
Hart	12	1	13
Hogan	3		3
Jones	2		2
Linacre	40	1	41
McDowall	16		16
McMorran	4		4
Munro	3		3
Oakes	34	1	35
Phillips	3		3
Smith	32	1	33
Sprotson	25		25
Swift	35	1	36
Thurlow	7		7
Walsh	39	1	40
Westwood	42	1	43
Williams	15	1	16

Goalscorers

PLAYER	LEAGUE	CUP COMPETITION FA CUP	TOTAL
Smith	12		12
Black	11		11
Clarke	6		6
Oakes	5		5
Godwin	3		3
Linacre	2		2
McMorran	2		2
Emptage	1		1
Hart	1		1
McDowall	1		1
Munro	1		1
Sprotson	1		1
Opps' o.gs.	1		1

Fact File

Frank Swift won his nineteenth and last England cap in a 4-1 defeat of Norway in Oslo in May. He conceded less than a goal a game in an era of high-scoring matches.

MANAGER: Jock Thomson

CAPTAIN: Eric Westwood

TOP SCORER: George Smith

BIGGEST WIN: October 16, 1948 4-1 v Aston Villa, Division 1

HIGHEST ATTENDANCE: September 11, 1948 64,502 v Manchester United, drew 0-0, Division 1

MAJOR TRANSFERS IN: Jackie Oakes from Blackburn Rovers

Final Division 1 Table

		P	W	D	L	F	A	Pts
1	PORTSMOUTH	42	25	8	9	84	42	58
2	MANCHESTER U	42	21	11	10	77	44	53
3	DERBY CO	42	22	9	11	74	55	53
4	NEWCASTLE U	42	20	12	10	70	56	52
5	ARSENAL	42	18	13	11	74	44	49
6	WOLVERHAMPTON W	42	17	12	13	79	66	46
7	MANCHESTER CITY	42	15	15	12	47	51	45
8	SUNDERLAND	42	13	17	12	49	58	43
9	CHARLTON ATH	42	15	12	15	63	67	42
10	ASTON VILLA	42	16	10	16	60	76	42
11	STOKE C	42	16	9	17	66	68	41
12	LIVERPOOL	42	13	14	15	53	43	40
13	CHELSEA	42	12	14	16	69	68	38
14	BOLTON W	42	14	10	18	59	68	38
15	BURNLEY	42	12	14	16	43	50	38
16	BLACKPOOL	42	11	16	15	54	67	38
17	BIRMINGHAM C	42	11	15	16	36	38	37
18	EVERTON	42	13	11	18	41	63	37
19	MIDDLESBROUGH	42	11	12	19	46	57	34
20	HUDDERSFIELD T	42	12	10	20	40	69	34
21	PRESTON NE	42	11	11	20	62	75	33
22	SHEFFIELD U	42	11	11	20	57	78	33

Season 1949-50

Football League Division 1

DATE	OPPONENTS	SCORE	GOALSCORERS	ATTENDANCE
Aug 20	ASTON VILLA	D 3-3	Smith 2, Black	39,594
Aug 24	Portsmouth	D 1-1	Munro	44,294
Aug 27	Charlton Athletic	L 1-3	Fagan	31,000
Aug 31	PORTSMOUTH	W 1-0	Smith	32,611
Sep 3	Manchester United	L 1-2	Munro	47,706
Sep 7	EVERTON	D 0-0		27,265
Sep 10	FULHAM	W 2-0	Turnbull, Clarke	42,192
Sep 17	Newcastle United	L 2-4	Turnbull, Clarke	58,141
Sep 24	BLACKPOOL	L 0-3		57,815
Oct 1	Middlesbrough	D 0-0		45,000
Oct 8	Chelsea	L 0-3		45,153
Oct 15	STOKE CITY	D 1-1	Munro	31,151
Oct 22	Burnley	D 0-0		25,063
Oct 29	SUNDERLAND	W 2-1	Murray, Turnbull	43,026
Nov 5	Liverpool	L 0-4		50,536
Nov 12	ARSENAL	L 0-2		28,288
Nov 19	Bolton Wanderers	L 0-3		35,000
Nov 26	BIRMINGHAM CITY	W 4-0	Black 2, Clarke 2	30,501
Dec 7	Derby County	L 0-7		23,681
Dec 10	WEST BROMWICH ALBION	D 1-1	Black	29,544
Dec 17	Aston Villa	L 0-1		30,000
Dec 24	CHARLTON ATHLETIC	W 2-0	Black, Clarke	32,092
Dec 26	Huddersfield Town	L 0-1		29,989
Dec 27	HUDDERSFIELD TOWN	L 1-2	Clarke	45,000
Dec 31	MANCHESTER UNITED	L 1-2	Black	63,704
Jan 14	Fulham	L 0-1		30,000
Jan 21	NEWCASTLE UNITED	D 1-1	Clarke	42,986
Feb 4	Blackpool	D 0-0		25,000
Feb 18	MIDDLESBROUGH	L 0-1		59,252
Feb 25	CHELSEA	D 1-1	Hart	32,824
Mar 4	Stoke City	L 0-2		30,000
Mar 11	BOLTON WANDERERS	D 1-1	Black	46,648
Mar 18	Birmingham City	L 0-1		30,000
Mar 29	LIVERPOOL	L 1-2	o.g.	20,000
Apr 1	Arsenal	L 1-4	Hart	42,000
Apr 8	BURNLEY	W 1-0	Westcott	31,182
Apr 10	WOLVES	W 2-1	Smith, Burnbull	36,723
Apr 11	Wolves	L 0-3		50,000
Apr 15	Sunderland	W 2-1	Oakes, Clarke	40,404
Apr 22	DERBY COUNTY	D 2-2	Smith 2	52,928
Apr 29	West Bromwich Albion	D 0-0		16,760
May 6	Everton	L 1-3	Clarke	26,627

FA Cup

Jan 7	DERBY COUNTY	(Rd 3) L 3-5	Black 2, Clarke	53,213

League & Cup Appearances

PLAYER	LEAGUE	CUP COMPETITION FA CUP	TOTAL
Alison	10	1	11
Black	33	1	34
Bootle	3		3
Clarke	37	1	38
Cunliffe	2		2
Emptage	27		27
Fagan	39	1	40
Gill	7	1	8
Hart	9		9
Jones	1		1
Linacre	8		8
Munro	17		17
Murray	13		13
Oakes	22	1	23
Phillips	30	1	31
Powell	12	1	13
Rigby	6		6
Smith	15		15
Sprotson	5		5
Spurdle	13		13
Swift	4		4
Trautmann	26		26
Turnbull	29	1	30
Walsh	27	1	28
Westcott	13		13
Westwood	40	1	41
Williams	11		11
Williamson	3		3

Goalscorers

PLAYER	LEAGUE	CUP COMPETITION FA CUP	TOTAL
Clarke	9	1	10
Black	7	2	9
Smith	6		6
Turnbull	4		4
Munro	3		3
Hart	2		2
Fagan	1		1
Murray	1		1
Oakes	1		1
Westcott	1		1
Opps' o.gs.	1		1

Fact File

In a relegation season, City had to wait until April to record their first victory of 1950.

MANAGER: Jock Thomson
CAPTAIN: Eric Westwood
TOP SCORER: Roy Clarke
BIGGEST WIN: November 29, 1949 4-0 v Birmingham City, Division 1
HIGHEST ATTENDANCE: December 31, 1949 63,704 v Manchester United, lost 2-1, Division 1
MAJOR TRANSFERS IN: Bert Trautmann from St. Helens Town (amateur), Dave Ewing from Luncarty Juniors (amateur)
MAJOR TRANSFERS OUT: Frank Swift (retired)

Final Division 1 Table

		P	W	D	L	F	A	Pts
1	PORTSMOUTH	42	22	9	11	74	38	53
2	WOLVERHAMPTON W	42	20	13	9	76	49	53
3	SUNDERLAND	42	21	10	11	83	62	52
4	MANCHESTER U	42	18	14	10	69	44	50
5	NEWCASTLE U	42	19	12	11	77	55	50
6	ARSENAL	42	19	11	12	79	55	49
7	BLACKPOOL	42	17	15	10	46	35	49
8	LIVERPOOL	42	17	14	11	64	54	48
9	MIDDLESBROUGH	42	20	7	15	59	48	47
10	BURNLEY	42	16	13	13	40	40	45
11	DERBY CO	42	17	10	15	69	61	44
12	ASTON VILLA	42	15	12	15	61	61	42
13	CHELSEA	42	12	16	14	58	65	40
14	WBA	42	14	12	16	47	53	40
15	HUDDERSFIELD T	42	14	9	19	52	73	37
16	BOLTON W	42	10	14	18	45	59	34
17	FULHAM	42	10	14	18	41	54	34
18	EVERTON	42	10	14	18	42	66	34
19	STOKE C	42	11	12	19	45	75	34
20	CHARLTON ATH	42	13	6	23	53	65	32
21	MANCHESTER CITY	42	8	13	21	36	68	29
22	BIRMINGHAM C	42	7	14	21	31	67	28

Season 1950-51

Football League Division 2

DATE	OPPONENTS	SCORE	GOALSCORERS	ATTENDANCE
Aug 19	Preston North End	W 4-2	Smith 2, Westcott, Clarke	36,294
Aug 23	CARDIFF CITY	W 2-1	Westcott, Smith	14,858
Aug 26	BURY	W 5-1	Westcott 3, Hart, Oakes	40,778
Aug 28	Cardiff City	D 1-1	Oakes	32,817
Sep 2	Queens Park Rangers	W 2-1	Smith, Clarke	21,593
Sep 6	Grimsby Town	D 4-4	Westcott 2, Spurdle, Clarke	18,529
Sep 9	CHESTERFIELD	W 5-1	Smith 2, Hart 2, Westcott	43,485
Sep 16	Leicester City	W 2-1	Burnbull, Smith	32,856
Sep 23	LUTON TOWN	D 1-1	Paul	42,333
Sep 30	COVENTRY CITY	W 1-0	Spurdle	40,839
Oct 7	Doncaster Rovers	L 3-4	Smith 3	32,832
Oct 14	BRENTFORD	W 4-0	Westcott 2, Hart, Clarke	39,497
Oct 21	Swansea Town	W 3-2	Westwood, Westcott, Cunliffe	26,000
Oct 28	HULL CITY	D 0-0		45,693
Nov 4	Leeds United	D 1-1	Haddington	30,500
Nov 11	WEST HAM UNITED	W 2-0	Haddington, Westcott	41,734
Nov 18	Blackburn Rovers	L 1-4	Haddington	37,400
Nov 25	SOUTHAMPTON	L 2-3	Haddington, Westcott	38,972
Dec 2	Barnsley	D 1-1	Westcott	29,615
Dec 9	SHEFFIELD UNITED	W 5-3	Smith 2, Westcott, Spurdle, Hart	33,172
Dec 16	PRESTON NORTH END	L 0-3		30,413
Dec 25	BIRMINGHAM CITY	W 3-1	Paul 2, Westcott	40,064
Dec 26	Birmingham City	L 0-1		32,000
Jan 13	Chesterfield	W 2-1	Smith, Clarke	12,309
Jan 2-	LEICESTER CITY	D 1-1	Hart	30,198
Jan 27	Bury	L 0-2		25,439
Feb 3	Luton Town	D 2-2	Smith 2	12,087
Feb 17	Coventry City	W 2-0	Spurdle, Clarke	29,205
Feb 24	DONCASTER ROVERS	D 3-3	Westcott 2, Oakes	38,572
Mar 3	Brentford	L 0-2		24,290
Mar 14	SWANSEA TOWN	L 1-2	Cunliffe	10,000
Mar 17	Hull City	D 3-3	Westcott 2, Hart	25,000
Mar 24	LEEDS UNITED	W 4-1	Meadows, Westcott, Smith, Hart	35,000
Mar 26	NOTTS COUNTY	D 0-0		31,948
Mar 31	West Ham United	W 4-2	Smith 2, Westcott, Hart	22,000
Apr 4	QUEENS PARK RANGERS	W 5-2	Westcott, Hart 2, Clarke	21,474
Apr 7	BLACKBURN ROVERS	W 1-0	Hart	37,754
Apr 14	Southampton	L 1-2	Hart	24,579
Apr 21	BARNSLEY	W 6-0	Smith 2, Clarke 2, Meadows, Hart	42,741
Apr 28	Sheffield United	D 0-0		24,500
Apr 30	Notts County	D 0-0		13,873
May 5	GRIMSBY TOWN	D 2-2	Westcott, Smith	30,284

FA Cup

Jan 6	Birmingham City	(Rd 3) L 0-2		30,057

League & Cup Appearances

PLAYER	LEAGUE	CUP COMPETITION	TOTAL
		FA CUP	
Alison	9		9
Branagan	10	1	11
Clark	39		39
Cunliffe	2		2
Emptage	1		1
Fagan	5	1	6
Gunning	4	1	5
Haddington	6	1	7
Hart	27		27
McCourt	16		16
Meadows	11		11
Oakes	21		21
Paul	41	1	42
Phillips	37	1	38
Rigby	37		37
Smith	39	1	40
Spurdle	31	1	32
Trautmann	42	1	43
Turnbull	1		1
Westcott	40	1	41
Westwood	37	1	38
Williamson	6		6

Goalscorers

PLAYER	LEAGUE	CUP COMPETITION	TOTAL
		FA CUP	
Westcott	25		25
Smith	21		21
Hart	14		14
Clark	9		9
Haddington	4		4
Spurdle	4		4
Oakes	3		3
Paul	3		3
Cunliffe	2		2
Meadows	2		2
Turnbull	1		1
Westwood	1		1

Fact File

City managed to gain the point they needed from the last game of the season against Grimsby to secure a promotion place.

MANAGER: Les McDowall
CAPTAIN: Eric Westwood
TOP SCORER: Dennis Westcott
BIGGEST WIN: April 21, 1951 6-0 v Barnsley, Division 2
HIGHEST ATTENDANCE: October 28, 1950 45,693 v Hull City, drew 0-0, Division 1
MAJOR TRANSFERS IN: Roy Paul from Swansea City, Jimmy Meadows from Southport

Final Division 2 Table

		P	W	D	L	F	A	PTS
1	PRESTON NE	42	26	5	11	91	49	57
2	MANCHESTER CITY	42	19	14	9	89	61	52
3	CARDIFF C	42	17	16	9	53	45	50
4	BIRMINGHAM C	42	20	9	13	64	53	49
5	LEEDS U	42	20	8	14	63	55	48
6	BLACKBURN R	42	19	8	15	65	66	46
7	COVENTRY C	42	19	7	16	75	59	45
8	SHEFFIELD U	42	16	12	14	72	62	44
9	BRENTFORD	42	18	8	16	75	74	44
10	HULL C	42	16	11	15	74	70	43
11	DONCASTER R	42	15	13	14	64	68	43
12	SOUTHAMPTON	42	15	13	14	66	73	43
13	WEST HAM U	42	16	10	16	68	69	42
14	LEICESTER C	42	15	11	16	68	58	41
15	BARNSLEY	42	15	10	17	74	68	40
16	QPR	42	15	10	17	71	82	40
17	NOTTS CO	42	13	13	16	61	60	39
18	SWANSEA T	42	16	4	22	54	77	36
19	LUTON T	42	9	14	19	57	70	32
20	BURY	42	12	8	22	60	86	32
21	CHESTERFIELD	42	9	12	21	44	69	30
22	GRIMSBY T	42	8	12	22	61	95	28

Season 1951-52

Football League Division 1

DATE	OPPONENTS	SCORE	GOALSCORERS	ATTENDANCE
Aug 18	WOLVES	D 0-0		45,748
Aug 22	Huddersfield Town	L 1-5	Westcott	25,653
Aug 25	Sunderland	L 0-1		45,396
Aug 29	HUDDERSFIELD TOWN	W 3-0	Meadows, Hart, Westcott	30,863
Sep 1	ASTON VILLA	D 2-2	Paul, Westcott	30,018
Sep 5	Portsmouth	L 0-1		27,265
Sep 8	Derby County	W 3-1	Meadows, Hart, Williamson	22,073
Sep 15	MANCHESTER UNITED	L 1-2	Hart	52,571
Sep 22	ARSENAL	L 0-1		48,367
Sep 29	Blackpool	D 2-2	Hart, Westcott	33,858
Oct 6	Tottenham Hotspur	W 2-1	Clarke 2	57,550
Oct 13	PRESTON NORTH END	W 1-0	o.g.	57,566
Oct 20	Burnley	D 0-0		30,977
Oct 27	CHARLTON ATHLETIC	W 4-2	Meadows, Westcott, Broadis, Clarke	44,348
Nov 3	Fulham	W 2-1	Broadis, Revie	35,000
Nov 10	MIDDLESBROUGH	W 2-1	Meadows, Westcott	47,422
Nov 17	West Bromwich Albion	L 2-3	Hart, o.g.	28,000
Nov 24	NEWCASTLE UNITED	L 2-3	Meadows, Clarke	39,358
Dec 1	Bolton Wanderers	L 1-2	Meadows	45,008
Dec 8	STOKE CITY	L 0-1		20,397
Dec 15	Wolves	D 2-2	Westcott, Clarke	30,000
Dec 22	SUNDERLAND	W 3-1	Westcott 2, Clarke	28,535
Dec 25	Chelsea	W 3-0	Westcott, Broadis, Meadows	34,850
Dec 26	CHELSEA	W 3-1	Meadows, Revie, Westcott	49,700
Dec 29	Aston Villa	W 2-1	Meadows, Williamson	40,000
Jan 1	PORTSMOUTH	L 0-1		40,412
Jan 5	DERBY COUNTY	W 4-2	Hart 2, Broadis, Clarke	37,572
Jan 19	Manchester United	D 1-1	McCourt	54,254
Jan 26	Arsenal	D 2-2	Hart, Phoenix	54,527
Feb 9	BLACKPOOL	D 0-0		47,437
Feb 16	TOTTENHAM HOTSPUR	D 1-1	Revie	38,989
Mar 1	Preston North End	D 1-1	Hart	38,000
Mar 12	BURNLEY	L 0-1		20,132
Mar 15	Charlton Athletic	D 0-0		25,000
Mar 22	FULHAM	D 1-1	Hart	30,945
Mar 29	Middlesbrough	D 2-2	Hart, Revie	18,000
Apr 5	WEST BROMWICH ALBION	L 1-2	Revie	13,842
Apr 11	LIVERPOOL	L 1-2	Clarke	35,305
Apr 12	Newcastle United	L 0-1		40,000
Apr 14	Liverpool	W 2-1	Williamson, Clarke	34,404
Apr 19	BOLTON WANDERERS	L 0-3		28,297
Apr 26	Stoke City	L 1-3	Branagan	27,000

FA Cup

Jan 12	WOLVES	(Rd 3) D 2-2	Meadows, Revie	54,497
Jan 16	Wolves	(R) L 1-4	Clarke	43,865

League & Cup Appearances

PLAYER	LEAGUE	CUP COMPETITION FA CUP	TOTAL
Barnes	1		1
Branagan	32	2	34
Broadis	31	2	33
Clarke	41	2	43
Cunliffe	4		4
Davies	3		3
Gunning	3		3
Hannaway	35	2	37
Hart	26		26
McCourt	31		31
Meadows	37	2	39
Paul	35	2	37
Phillips	10		10
Phoenix	14		14
Revie	26	2	28
Rigby	38	2	40
Smith	3		3
Spurdle	9	2	11
Trautmann	41	2	43
Westcott	19	2	21
Westwood	7		7
Williams	1		1
Williamson	15		15

Goalscorers

PLAYER	LEAGUE	CUP COMPETITION FA CUP	TOTAL
Hart	11		11
Westcott	11		11
Clarke	9	1	10
Meadows	9	1	10
Revie	5	1	6
Broadis	4		4
Williamson	3		3
Branagan	1		1
McCourt	1		1
Paul	1		1
Phoenix	1		1
Opps' o.gs.	2		2

Fact File

Roy Clarke and Roy Paul were both regulars in the Wales international side this season.

MANAGER: Les McDowall

CAPTAIN: Roy Paul

TOP SCORER: Johnny Hart

BIGGEST WIN: August 29, 1951 3-0 v Huddersfield Town, Division 1; December 25, 1951 3-0 v Chelsea, Division 1

HIGHEST ATTENDANCE: October 13, 1951 57,566 v Preston North End, won 1-0, Division 1

MAJOR TRANSFERS IN: Ivor Broadis from Sunderland, Don Revie from Hull City

Final Division 1 Table

		P	W	D	L	F	A	Pts
1	MANCHESTER U	42	23	11	8	95	52	57
2	TOTTENHAM H	42	22	9	11	76	51	53
3	ARSENAL	42	21	11	10	80	61	53
4	PORTSMOUTH	42	20	8	14	68	58	48
5	BOLTON W	42	19	10	13	65	61	48
6	ASTON VILLA	42	19	9	14	79	70	47
7	PRESTON NE	42	17	12	13	74	54	46
8	NEWCASTLE U	42	18	9	15	98	73	45
9	BLACKPOOL	42	18	9	15	64	64	45
10	CHARLTON ATH	42	17	10	15	68	63	44
11	LIVERPOOL	42	12	19	11	57	61	43
12	SUNDERLAND	42	15	12	15	70	61	42
13	WBA	42	14	13	15	74	77	41
14	BURNLEY	42	15	10	17	56	63	40
15	MANCHESTER CITY	42	13	13	16	58	61	39
16	WOLVERHAMPTON W	42	12	14	16	73	73	38
17	DERBY CO	42	15	7	20	63	80	37
18	MIDDLESBROUGH	42	15	6	21	64	88	36
19	CHELSEA	42	14	8	20	52	72	36
20	STOKE C	42	12	7	23	49	88	31
21	HUDDERSFIELD T	42	10	8	24	49	82	28
22	FULHAM	42	8	11	23	58	77	27

Season 1952-53

Football League Division 1

DATE	OPPONENTS	SCORE	GOALSCORERS	ATTENDANCE
Aug 23	Stoke City	L 1-2	Smith	37,644
Aug 27	TOTTENHAM HOTSPUR	L 0-1		33,521
Aug 30	MANCHESTER UNITED	W 2-1	Broadis, Clarke	56,140
Sep 1	Tottenham Hotspur	D 3-3	Sowden 2, Meadows	40,870
Sep 6	LIVERPOOL	L 0-2		42,965
Sep 8	Burnley	L 1-2	Meadows	27,083
Sep 13	Middlesbrough	L 4-5	Revie 2, Broadis, Meadows	36,000
Sep 17	BURNLEY	D 0-0		24,884
Sep 20	WEST BROMWICH ALBION	L 0-1		33,043
Sep 27	Newcastle United	L 0-2		48,110
Oct 4	CARDIFF CITY	D 2-2	Revie, Branagan	35,000
Oct 11	Portsmouth	L 1-2	Williamson	33,644
Oct 18	BOLTON WANDERERS	L 1-2	Revie	42,270
Oct 25	Aston Villa	D 0-0		30,000
Nov 1	SUNDERLAND	L 2-5	Hart, Williamson	33,121
Nov 8	Wolves	L 3-7	Williamson 2, Davies	33,832
Nov 15	CHARLTON ATHLETIC	W 5-1	Meadows 3, Williamson, Clarke	23,362
Nov 22	Arsenal	L 1-3	Meadows	39,161
Nov 29	DERBY COUNTY	W 1-0	Hart	22,918
Dec 6	Blackpool	L 1-4	Williamson	19,496
Dec 13	CHELSEA	W 4-0	Meadows, Hart, Clark, o.g.	20,633
Dec 20	STOKE CITY	W 2-1	Williamson, Hart	13,562
Dec 26	Preston North End	L 2-6	Hart 2	38,000
Jan 3	Manchester United	D 1-1	Broadis	47,883
Jan 17	Liverpool	W 1-0	Hart	41,191
Jan 24	MIDDLESBROUGH	W 5-1	Spurdle 3, Williamson, Revie	26,715
Feb 7	West Bromwich Albion	L 1-2	Revie	25,000
Feb 14	NEWCASTLE UNITED	W 2-1	Meadows, Phoenix	25,000
Feb 21	Cardiff City	L 0-6		28,000
Feb 28	PORTSMOUTH	W 2-1	Meadows, Cunliffe	38,736
Mar 7	Bolton Wanderers	L 0-1		36,405
Mar 14	ASTON VILLA	W 4-1	Spurdle 3, Anders	32,566
Mar 21	Sunderland	D 3-3	Broadis 2, Williams	26,270
Mar 28	WOLVES	W 3-1	Spurdle, Whitfield, McCourt	27,127
Apr 3	SHEFFIELD WEDNESDAY	W 3-1	Broadis, Whitfield, Cunliffe	55,485
Apr 4	Charlton Athletic	W 2-1	Hart, McCourt	26,242
Apr 6	Sheffield Wednesday	D 1-1	Hart	43,520
Apr 11	ARSENAL	L 2-4	Spurdle 2	52,418
Apr 18	Derby County	L 0-5		15,618
Apr 22	PRESTON NORTH END	L 0-2		42,863
Apr 25	BLACKPOOL	W 5-0	Spurdle 2, McCourt, Cunliffe, Williamson	38,507
Apr 29	Chelsea	L 1-3	Williamson	48,594

FA Cup

Jan 10	SWINDON TOWN	(Rd 3) W 7-0	Hart 4, Williamson, Cunliffe, Broadis	28,953
Jan 31	LUTON TOWN	(Rd 4) D 1-1	Broadis	38,411
Feb 4	Luton Town	(R) L 1-5	Spurdle	21,991

League & Cup Appearances

PLAYER	LEAGUE	CUP COMPETITION FA CUP	TOTAL
Anders	12		12
Branagan	41	3	44
Broadis	34	3	37
Clarke	22		22
Cunliffe	20	3	23
Davies	5		5
Ewing	19	3	22
Gunning	6	1	7
Hannaway	18		18
Hart	20	1	21
Little	3	3	6
McCourt	13		13
Meadows	26	2	28
Paul	38	3	41
Phoenix	6		6
Revie	32	3	35
Rigby	18		18
Smith F	2		2
Sowden	9		9
Spurdle	27	2	29
Trautmann	42	3	45
Webster	1		1
Westwood	22		22
Whitfield	6		6
Williamson	19	3	22
Woosnam	1		1

Goalscorers

PLAYER	LEAGUE	CUP COMPETITION FA CUP	TOTAL
Hart	9	4	13
Spurdle	11	1	12
Williamson	11	1	12
Meadows	10		10
Broadis	6	2	8
Revie	6		6
Clarke	3		3
Cunliffe	3	1	4
McCourt	3		3
Sowden	2		2
Whitfield	2		2
Anders	1		1
Branagan	1		1
Davies	1		1
Phoenix	1		1
Smith F	1		1
Opps' o.g.	1		1

Fact File

The victory over neighbours United in August was City's only win in their first 16 games.

MANAGER: Les McDowall

CAPTAIN: Roy Paul

TOP SCORER: Billy Spurdle

BIGGEST WIN: January 10, 1953 7-0 v Swindon Town, FA Cup Round 3

HIGHEST ATTENDANCE: August 30, 1952 56,140 v Manchester United, won 2-1, Division 1

MAJOR TRANSFERS IN: Harry Anders from Preston North End

Final Division 1 Table

		P	W	D	L	F	A	Pts
1	ARSENAL	42	21	12	9	97	64	54
2	PRESTON NE	42	21	12	9	85	60	54
3	WOLVERHAMPTON W	42	19	13	10	86	63	51
4	WBA	42	21	8	13	66	60	50
5	CHARLTON ATH	42	19	11	12	77	63	49
6	BURNLEY	42	18	12	12	67	52	48
7	BLACKPOOL	42	19	9	14	71	70	47
8	MANCHESTER U	42	18	10	14	69	72	46
9	SUNDERLAND	42	15	13	14	68	82	43
10	TOTTENHAM H	42	15	11	16	78	69	41
11	ASTON VILLA	42	14	13	15	63	61	41
12	CARDIFF C	42	14	12	16	54	46	40
13	MIDDLESBROUGH	42	14	11	17	70	77	39
14	BOLTON W	42	15	9	18	61	69	39
15	PORTSMOUTH	42	14	10	18	74	83	38
16	NEWCASTLE U	42	14	9	19	59	70	37
17	LIVERPOOL	42	14	8	20	61	82	36
18	SHEFFIELD W	42	12	11	19	62	72	35
19	CHELSEA	42	12	11	19	56	66	35
20	MANCHESTER CITY	42	14	7	21	72	87	35
21	STOKE C	42	12	10	20	53	66	34
22	DERBY CO	42	11	10	21	59	74	32

The Essential History of Manchester City

Season 1953-54

Football League Division 1

DATE	OPPONENTS	SCORE	GOALSCORERS	ATTENDANCE
Aug 19	Sheffield Wednesday	L 0-2		48,000
Aug 22	WOLVES	L 0-4		20,039
Aug 24	Aston Villa	L 0-3		30,000
Aug 29	Sunderland	W 5-4	Hart 2, Whitfield, Clarke, Anders	49,434
Sep 2	ASTON VILLA	L 0-1		24,918
Sep 5	MANCHESTER UNITED	W 2-0	Revie, Hart	53,097
Sep 9	Huddersfield Town	D 1-1	Little	24,341
Sep 12	CARDIFF CITY	D 1-1	o.g.	31,915
Sep 16	HUDDERSFIELD TOWN	L 0-1		24,580
Sep 19	Arsenal	D 2-2	Spurdle, Hart	65,869
Sep 26	PORTSMOUTH	W 2-1	Revie, Hart	35,691
Oct 3	Blackpool	L 0-2		31,765
Oct 10	Bolton Wanderers	L 2-3	Revie 2	29,403
Oct 17	PRESTON NORTH END	L 1-4	Anders	43,295
Oct 24	Tottenham Hotspur	L 0-3		37,577
Oct 31	BURNLEY	W 3-2	Meadows 2, Cunliffe	32,353
Nov 7	Liverpool	D 2-2	Hart, Meadows	30,917
Nov 14	NEWCASTLE UNITED	D 0-0		34,150
Nov 21	Middlesbrough	W 1-0	o.g.	25,000
Nov 28	WEST BROMWICH ALBION	L 2-3	Hart, Revie	40,753
Dec 5	Charlton Athletic	L 1-2	Meadows	17,813
Dec 12	SHEFFIELD WEDNESDAY	W 3-2	Little, Revie, Davies	27,639
Dec 19	Wolves	L 1-3	Davies	27,606
Dec 25	Sheffield United	D 2-2	Revie, Hart	33,129
Dec 26	SHEFFIELD UNITED	W 2-1	Hart, o.g.	35,783
Jan 2	SUNDERLAND	W 2-1	McAdams, Revie	23,743
Jan 16	Manchester United	D 1-1	McAdams	46,379
Jan 23	Cardiff City	W 3-0	Revie, Clarke, Anders	22,000
Feb 6	ARSENAL	D 0-0		39,026
Feb 13	Portsmouth	L 1-4	McAdams	30,135
Feb 24	BLACKPOOL	L 1-4	Clarke	22,515
Feb 27	BOLTON WANDERERS	W 3-0	McAdams, Meadows, Revie	39,340
Mar 6	Preston North End	L 0-4		21,000
Mar 17	TOTTENHAM HOTSPUR	W 4-1	Hart, McAdams, Revie, Clarke	10,841
Mar 20	Burnley	L 1-3	Hart	23,054
Apr 3	Newcastle United	L 3-4	Hart, McAdams, Clarke	27,760
Apr 7	LIVERPOOL	L 0-2		12,593
Apr 10	MIDDLESBROUGH	W 5-2	Meadows 2, Clarke 2, Revie	28,445
Apr 16	Chelsea	W 1-0	Meadows	59,794
Apr 17	West Bromwich Albion	L 0-1		35,000
Apr 19	CHELSEA	D 1-1	Branagan	30,620
Apr 24	CHARLTON ATHLETIC	W 3-0	McAdams 2, Spurdle	19,549

FA Cup

Jan 9	Bradford City	(Rd 3)	W 5-2	McAdams 3, Revie, Clarke	22,194
Jan 30	TOTTENHAM HOTSPUR	(Rd 4)	L 0-1		50,576

League & Cup Appearances

PLAYER	LEAGUE	CUP COMPETITION FA CUP	TOTAL
Anders	19	1	20
Branagan	42	2	44
Broadis	9		9
Clarke	35	2	37
Cunliffe	10		10
Davidson	1		1
Davies	2		2
Ewing	42	2	44
Fagan	6	1	7
Hannaway	6		6
Hart	32	2	34
Hayes	11		11
Little	31		31
McAdams	17	2	19
McCourt	1		1
McTavish	20	2	22
Meadows	20	2	22
Paul	39	2	41
Revie	37	2	39
Sowden	2		2
Spurdle	24		24
Trautmann	42	2	44
Whitfield	7		7
Williamson	7		7

Goalscorers

PLAYER	LEAGUE	CUP COMPETITION FA CUP	TOTAL
Revie	12	1	13
Hart	12		12
McAdams	8	3	11
Meadows	8		8
Clarke	7	1	8
Anders	3		3
Davies	2		2
Little	2		2
Spurdle	2		2
Branagan	1		1
Cunliffe	1		1
Whitfield	1		1
Opps' o.gs.	3		3

Fact File

On 14 October 1953, City beat Hearts 6-3 in a friendly match in the first game under the Maine Road floodlights.

MANAGER: Les McDowall

CAPTAIN: Roy Paul

TOP SCORER: Don Revie

BIGGEST WIN: April 10, 1954 5-2 v Middlesbrough, Division 1; January 9, 1954 5-2 v Bradford City, FA Cup Round 3

HIGHEST ATTENDANCE: April 19, 1954 59,794 v Chelsea, drew 1-1, Division 1

MAJOR TRANSFERS IN: Billy McAdams from Distillery, Bill Leivers from Chesterfield

MAJOR TRANSFERS OUT: Ivor Broadis to Newcastle

Final Division 1 Table

		P	W	D	L	F	A	Pts
1	WOLVERHAMPTON W	42	25	7	10	96	56	57
2	WBA	42	22	9	11	86	63	53
3	HUDDERSFIELD T	42	20	11	11	78	61	51
4	MANCHESTER U	42	18	12	12	73	58	48
5	BOLTON W	42	18	12	12	75	60	48
6	BLACKPOOL	42	19	10	13	80	69	48
7	BURNLEY	42	21	4	17	78	67	46
8	CHELSEA	42	16	12	14	74	68	44
9	CHARLTON ATH	42	19	6	17	75	77	44
10	CARDIFF C	42	18	8	16	51	71	44
11	PRESTON NE	42	19	5	18	87	58	43
12	ARSENAL	42	15	13	14	75	73	43
13	ASTON VILLA	42	16	9	17	70	68	41
14	PORTSMOUTH	42	14	11	17	81	89	39
15	NEWCASTLE U	42	14	10	18	72	77	38
16	TOTTENHAM H	42	16	5	21	65	76	37
17	MANCHESTER CITY	42	14	9	19	62	77	37
18	SUNDERLAND	42	14	8	20	81	89	36
19	SHEFFIELD W	42	15	6	21	70	91	36
20	SHEFFIELD U	42	11	11	20	69	90	33
21	MIDDLESBROUGH	42	10	10	22	60	91	30
22	LIVERPOOL	42	9	10	23	68	97	28

Season 1954-55

Football League Division 1

DATE	OPPONENTS	SCORE	GOALSCORERS	ATTENDANCE
Aug 21	Preston North End	L 0-5		35,000
Aug 25	SHEFFIELD UNITED	W 5-2	Revie 2, Hart 2, Clarke	23,856
Aug 28	BURNLEY	D 0-0		38,201
Aug 30	Sheffield United	W 2-0	Revie, Hart	25,000
Sep 4	Leicester City	W 2-0	McAdams, Hart	32,825
Sep 8	ARSENAL	W 2-1	Hart, o.g.	38,146
Sep 11	CHELSEA	D 1-1	Paul	35,971
Sep 14	Arsenal	W 3-2	McAdams, Hart, Clarke	33,898
Sep 18	Cardiff City	L 0-3		30,000
Sep 25	MANCHESTER UNITED	W 3-2	Fagan, McAdams, Hart	54,105
Oct 2	EVERTON	W 1-0	Clarke	45,737
Oct 9	Wolves	D 2-2	Fagan 2	41,601
Oct 16	ASTON VILLA	L 2-4	Spurdle 2	36,384
Oct 23	Bolton Wanderers	D 2-2	McAdams, Revie	30,123
Oct 30	HUDDERSFIELD TOWN	L 2-4	Revie 2	34,246
Nov 6	Sheffield Wednesday	W 4-2	Williamson 2, Hart, Clarke	19,152
Nov 13	PORTSMOUTH	L 1-2	Fagan	24,564
Nov 20	Blackpool	W 3-1	McAdams 2, Williamson	21,734
Nov 27	CHARLTON ATHLETIC	L 1-5	Davies	25,799
Dec 4	Sunderland	L 2-3	Hart 2	33,733
Dec 11	TOTTENHAM HOTSPUR	D 0-0		27,052
Dec 18	PRESTON NORTH END	W 3-1	Hart 2, Hayes	26,615
Dec 25	NEWCASTLE UNITED	W 3-1	Hayes, Spurdle 2	26,664
Dec 27	Newcastle United	L 0-2		52,850
Jan 1	Burnley	L 0-2		25,931
Jan 15	LEICESTER CITY	D 2-2	Hayes, Clarke	13,648
Jan 22	Chelsea	W 2-0	Hayes, Clarke	34,160
Feb 5	CARDIFF CITY	W 4-1	Fagan, Hayes, Revie, Clarke	31,922
Feb 12	Manchester United	W 5-0	Fagan 2, Hayes 2, Hart	47,914
Feb 23	Everton	L 0-1		20,457
Mar 5	Tottenham Hotspur	D 2-2	Hart, Hayes	35,358
Mar 16	BOLTON WANDERERS	W 4-2	Hayes 3, Fagan	27,413
Mar 19	Huddersfield Town	D 0-0		31,065
Mar 30	SHEFFIELD WEDNESDAY	D 2-2	Hayes, Davies	14,825
Apr 2	Portsmouth	L 0-1		24,286
Apr 8	WEST BROMWICH ALBION	W 4-0	Johnstone, Spurdle, Hayes, Fagan	57,663
Apr 9	SUNDERLAND	W 1-0	Revie	60,611
Apr 11	West Bromwich Albion	L 1-2	Spurdle	30,000
Apr 16	Charlton Athletic	D 1-1	Johnstone	25,064
Apr 20	WOLVES	W 3-0	Fagan, Meadows, Williamson	50,705
Apr 23	BLACKPOOL	L 1-6	Fagan	44,339
Apr 30	Aston Villa	L 0-2		25,000

FA Cup

Jan 8	Derby County	(Rd 3) W 3-1	Barnes, Hayes, Revie	23,409
Jan 29	MANCHESTER UNITED	(Rd 4) W 2-0	Hayes, Revie	74,723
Feb 19	Luton Town	(Rd 5) W 2-0	Clarke 2	23,104
Mar 12	Birmingham City	(Rd 6) W 1-0	Hart	58,000
Mar 26	SUNDERLAND	(SF) W 1-0	Clarke	58,498
May 7	NEWCASTLE UNITED	(F) L 1-3	Johnstone	100,000

League & Cup Appearances

PLAYER	LEAGUE	CUP COMPETITION FA CUP	TOTAL
Anders	1		1
Barnes	40	6	46
Branagan	11	1	12
Clarke	33	5	38
Davies	3		3
Ewing	40	5	45
Fagan	36	6	42
Hannaway	1		1
Hart	31	4	35
Hayes	20	6	26
Johnstone	8	2	10
Leivers	2	1	3
Little	38	6	44
McAdams	19		19
McTavish	3		3
Meadows	36	5	41
Paul	41	6	47
Revie	32	6	38
Savage	2		2
Spurdle	16	1	17
Trautmann	40	6	46
Williamson	9		9

Goalscorers

PLAYER	LEAGUE	CUP COMPETITION FA CUP	TOTAL
Hart	14	1	15
Hayes	13	2	15
Fagan	11		11
Revie	8	2	10
Clarke	7	3	10
McAdams	6		6
Spurdle	6		6
Williamson	4		4
Davies	2		2
Johnstone	2	1	3
Meadows	1		1
Paul	1		1
Barnes		1	1
Opps' o.gs.	1		1

Fact File

'The Revie Plan' took City to Wembley, but 1-0 down after 20 minutes of the final, a Jimmy Meadows injury left them with only ten men for the rest of the match.

MANAGER: Les McDowall
CAPTAIN: Roy Paul
TOP SCORERS: Johnny Hart and Joe Hayes
BIGGEST WIN: Feburary 12, 1955 5-0 v Manchester United, Division 1
HIGHEST ATTENDANCE: May 7, 1955 100,000 v Newcastle United, lost 1-3, FA Cup final
MAJOR TRANSFERS IN: Bobby Johnstone from Hibernian

Final Division 1 Table

		P	W	D	L	F	A	PTS
1	CHELSEA	42	20	12	10	81	57	52
2	WOLVERHAMPTON W	42	19	10	13	89	70	48
3	PORTSMOUTH	42	18	12	12	74	62	48
4	SUNDERLAND	42	15	18	9	64	54	48
5	MANCHESTER U	42	20	7	15	84	74	47
6	ASTON VILLA	42	20	7	15	72	73	47
7	MANCHESTER CITY	42	18	10	14	76	69	46
8	NEWCASTLE U	42	17	9	16	89	77	43
9	ARSENAL	42	17	9	16	69	63	43
10	BURNLEY	42	17	9	16	51	48	43
11	EVERTON	42	16	10	16	62	68	42
12	HUDDERSFIELD T	42	14	13	15	63	68	41
13	SHEFFIELD U	42	17	7	18	70	86	41
14	PRESTON NE	42	16	8	18	83	64	40
15	CHARLTON ATH	42	15	10	17	76	75	40
16	TOTTENHAM H	42	16	8	18	72	73	40
17	WBA	42	16	8	18	76	96	40
18	BOLTON W	42	13	13	16	62	69	39
19	BLACKPOOL	42	14	10	18	60	64	38
20	CARDIFF C	42	13	11	18	62	76	37
21	LEICESTER C	42	12	11	19	74	86	35
22	SHEFFIELD W	42	8	10	24	63	100	26

Season 1955-56

Football League Division 1

DATE	OPPONENTS	SCORE	GOALSCORERS	ATTENDANCE
Aug 20	ASTON VILLA	D 2-2	Revie, Cunliffe	38,099
Aug 27	Wolves	L 2-7	Hayes, Revie	38,790
Aug 31	ARSENAL	D 2-2	Hayes 2	36,955
Sep 3	MANCHESTER UNITED	W 1-0	Hayes	59,192
Sep 6	Arsenal	D 0-0		30,864
Sep 10	CARDIFF CITY	W 3-1	Hayes 2, Johnstone	33,240
Sep 17	Huddersfield Town	D 3-3	Fagan, Johnstone, Clarke	20,443
Sep 24	BLACKPOOL	W 2-0	Revie, Johnstone	63,925
Oct 1	Chelsea	L 1-2	Meadows	44,538
Oct 8	Sheffield United	D 1-1	Dyson	24,000
Oct 15	PRESTON NORTH END	L 0-2		33,187
Oct 22	Birmingham City	L 3-4	Hayes, Dyson, Faulkner	28,500
Oct 29	WEST BROMWICH ALBION	W 2-0	Cunliffe, o.g.	25,081
Nov 5	Charlton Athletic	L 2-5	Hayes, Cunliffe	24,655
Nov 12	TOTTENHAM HOTSPUR	L 1-2	Hayes	24,094
Nov 19	Everton	D 1-1	Faulkner	34,612
Nov 26	NEWCASTLE UNITED	L 1-2	Clarke	32,860
Dec 3	Burnley	D 2-2	Hayes, Dyson	26,217
Dec 10	LUTON TOWN	W 3-2	Spurdle, Hayes, Clarke	14,499
Dec 17	Aston Villa	W 3-0	Spurdle, Dyson 2	20,000
Dec 24	WOLVES	D 2-2	Spurdle, Hayes	32,935
Dec 26	Bolton Wanderers	W 3-1	Spurdle, Dyson, o.g.	43,706
Dec 27	BOLTON WANDERERS	W 2-0	Paul, Clarke	38,405
Dec 31	Manchester United	L 1-2	Dyson	60,956
Jan 2	PORTSMOUTH	W 4-1	Johnstone 3, Hayes	43,133
Jan 14	Cardiff City	L 1-4	Johnstone	27,000
Jan 21	HUDDERSFIELD TOWN	W 1-0	Spurdle	21,076
Feb 4	Blackpool	W 1-0	Faulkner	17,014
Feb 11	CHELSEA	D 2-2	Hayes 2	26,642
Feb 25	Preston North End	W 3-0	Johnstone 2, Hayes	22,664
Mar 7	EVERTON	W 3-0	Spurdle, Johnstone, Clarke	15,227
Mar 10	West Bromwich Albion	W 4-0	Johnstone 2, Hayes, Dyson	32,000
Mar 21	CHARLTON ATHLETIC	L 0-2		13,998
Mar 24	Tottenham Hotspur	L 1-2	Hayes	31,622
Mar 30	Sunderland	W 3-0	Hayes, Revie, o.g.	40,394
Mar 31	BIRMINGHAM CITY	D 1-1	Hayes	44,777
Apr 2	SUNDERLAND	W 4-2	Hayes 2, Dyson 2	40,915
Apr 7	Newcastle United	L 1-3	Dyson	25,999
Apr 11	SHEFFIELD UNITED	W 3-1	Spurdle, Hayes, Faulkner	16,991
Apr 14	BURNLEY	L 1-3	Spurdle	29,087
Apr 21	Luton Town	L 2-3	Barnes, Clarke	18,189
Apr 28	Portsmouth	W 4-2	Dyson 2, Spurdle, Hart	24,684

FA Cup

Jan 7	BLACKPOOL	(Rd 3) D 1-1*	Dyson	32,577
Jan 11	BLACKPOOL	(Rd 3) W 2-1	Johnstone, Dyson	42,517
Jan 28	Southend United	(Rd 4) W 1-0	Hayes	29,500
Feb 18	LIVERPOOL	(Rd 5) D 0-0		70,640
Feb 22	Liverpool	(R) W 2-1	Hayes, Dyson	57,528
Mar 3	EVERTON	(Rd 6) W 2-1	Hayes, Johnstone	76,129
Mar 17	TOTTENHAM HOTSPUR	(SF) W 1-0	Johnstone	69,788
May 5	BIRMINGHAM CITY	(F) W 3-1	Johnstone, Hayes, Dyson	100,000

*Match abandoned.

League & Cup Appearances

PLAYER	LEAGUE	CUP COMPETITION FA CUP	TOTAL
Barnes	39	8	47
Branagan	15		15
Clarke	25	7	32
Cunliffe	6		6
Dyson	25	8	33
Ewing	39	8	47
Fagan	16		16
Faulkner	7		7
Hannaway	2		2
Hart	1		1
Hayes	42	8	50
Johnstone	31	8	39
Leivers	25	8	33
Little	42	8	50
Marsden	1		1
McTavish	5		5
Murray	1		1
Paul	36	8	44
Phoenix	6		6
Revie	21	2	23
Savage	2		2
Spurdle	35	7	42
Trautmann	40	8	48

Goalscorers

PLAYER	LEAGUE	CUP COMPETITION FA CUP	TOTAL
Hayes	23	4	27
Dyson	13	4	17
Johnstone	12	4	16
Spurdle	9		9
Clarke	6		6
Faulkner	4		4
Revie	4		4
Cunliffe	3		3
Barnes	1		1
Fagan	1		1
Hart	1		1
Marsden	1		1
Paul	1		1
Opps' o.gs.	3		3

Fact File

Footballer of the Year, Bert Trautmann played the last 15 minutes of City's Cup final victory with a broken neck.

MANAGER: Les McDowall

CAPTAIN: Roy Paul

TOP SCORER: Joe Hayes

BIGGEST WIN: March 10, 1956 4-0 v West Bromwich Albion, Division 1

HIGHEST ATTENDANCE: May 5, 1956 100,000 v Birmingham City, won 3-1, FA Cup final

MAJOR TRANSFERS IN: Cliff Sear from Oswestry Town

Final Division 1 Table

		P	W	D	L	F	A	Pts
1	MANCHESTER U	42	25	10	7	83	51	60
2	BLACKPOOL	42	20	9	13	86	62	49
3	WOLVERHAMPTON W	42	20	9	13	89	65	49
4	MANCHESTER CITY	42	18	10	14	82	69	46
5	ARSENAL	42	18	10	14	60	61	46
6	BIRMINGHAM C	42	18	9	15	75	57	45
7	BURNLEY	42	18	8	16	64	54	44
8	BOLTON W	42	18	7	17	71	58	43
9	SUNDERLAND	42	17	9	16	80	95	43
10	LUTON T	42	17	8	17	66	64	42
11	NEWCASTLE U	42	17	7	18	85	70	41
12	PORTSMOUTH	42	16	9	17	78	85	41
13	WBA	42	18	5	19	58	70	41
14	CHARLTON ATH	42	17	6	19	75	81	40
15	EVERTON	42	15	10	17	55	69	40
16	CHELSEA	42	14	11	17	64	77	39
17	CARDIFF C	42	15	9	18	55	69	39
18	TOTTENHAM H	42	15	7	20	61	71	37
19	PRESTON NE	42	14	8	20	73	72	36
20	ASTON VILLA	42	11	13	18	52	69	35
21	HUDDERSFIELD T	42	14	7	21	54	83	35
22	SHEFFIELD U	42	12	9	21	63	77	33

Season 1956-57

Football League Division 1

DATE	OPPONENTS	SCORE	GOALSCORERS	ATTENDANCE
Aug 18	Wolves	L 1-5	Revie	43,407
Aug 22	TOTTENHAM HOTSPUR	D 2-2	Clarke 2	32,718
Aug 25	ASTON VILLA	D 1-1	Clarke	24,326
Aug 29	Tottenham Hotspur	L 2-3	Johnstone, Paul	33,083
Sep 4	Luton Town	L 2-3	Hayes, McAdams	21,625
Sep 5	LEEDS UNITED	W 1-0	McAdams	34,185
Sep 8	SUNDERLAND	W 3-1	McAdams, Revie, Hayes	35,753
Sep 12	Leeds United	L 0-2		35,068
Sep 15	Charlton Athletic	L 0-1		18,533
Sep 22	Manchester United	L 0-2		53,515
Sep 29	BLACKPOOL	L 0-3		39,528
Oct 6	Arsenal	L 3-7	Clarke 2, Dyson	32,651
Oct 13	BURNLEY	L 0-1		35,981
Oct 20	Newcastle United	W 3-0	Fagan, Johnstone, Dyson	34,310
Oct 27	SHEFFIELD WEDNESDAY	W 4-2	Fagan, Hayes 2, Johnstone	29,259
Nov 3	Cardiff City	D 1-1	Dyson	28,000
Nov 10	BIRMINGHAM CITY	W 3-1	Johnstone 2, Hayes	21,005
Nov 17	West Bromwich Albion	D 1-1	Dyson	25,780
Nov 24	PORTSMOUTH	W 5-1	Fagan, Hayes 2, Johnstone, Clarke	24,364
Dec 1	Preston North End	L 1-3	o.g.	25,433
Dec 8	CHELSEA	W 5-4	Johnstone 3, Hayes 2	24,412
Dec 15	WOLVES	L 2-3	Johnstone 2	30,329
Dec 25	BOLTON WANDERERS	L 1-3	Fagan	19,731
Dec 26	Bolton Wanderers	L 0-1		20,865
Dec 29	LUTON TOWN	W 3-2	Dyson 2, Clarke	27,253
Jan 12	Sunderland	D 1-1	Fagan	34,119
Jan 19	CHARLTON ATHLETIC	W 5-1	Dyson 3, Johnstone, Fagan	22,108
Feb 2	MANCHESTER UNITED	L 2-4	Hayes, Clarke	63,872
Feb 4	Aston Villa	D 2-2	McClelland, Hayes	10,554
Feb 9	Blackpool	L 1-4	Johnstone	21,105
Feb 23	Sheffield Wednesday	D 2-2	Paul, Hayes	11,271
Mar 2	NEWCASTLE UNITED	L 1-2	Barnes	25,529
Mar 9	Chelsea	L 2-4	Fagan, Hayes	35,664
Mar 16	CARDIFF CITY	W 4-1	Johnstone 3, Dyson	26,395
Mar 20	ARSENAL	L 2-3	Barnes, Clarke	27,974
Mar 30	WEST BROMWICH ALBION	W 2-1	Paul, Fagan	26,361
Apr 6	Portsmouth	W 1-0	Dyson	24,949
Apr 13	PRESTON NORTH END	L 0-1		31,305
Apr 19	EVERTON	L 2-4	Fagan, Clarke	28,009
Apr 20	Burnley	W 3-0	Hayes, Dyson, Clarke	16,746
Apr 22	Everton	D 1-1	McAdams	28,887
Apr 27	Birmingham City	D 3-3	Kirkman 2, o.g.	23,700

FA Cup

Jan 5	Newcastle United	(Rd 3) D 1-1	Johnstone	57,890
Jan 9	NEWCASTLE UNITED	(R) L 4-5	Johnstone 2, Fagan, o.g.	46,988

FA Charity Shield

Oct 24	MANCHESTER UNITED	L 0-1		30,495

League & Cup Appearances

PLAYER	LEAGUE	CUP COMPETITION		TOTAL
		FA CUP	OTHER	
Barnes	31	2		33
Clarke	40	2	1	43
Dyson	32	2	1	35
Ewing	34	2	1	37
Fagan	31	2	1	34
Hannaway	2			2
Hart	4			4
Hayes	34		1	35
Johnstone	31	2	1	34
Kirkman	1			1
Leivers	42	2	1	45
Little	37	2	1	40
Marsden	9			9
McAdams	12	2		14
McClelland	4			4
McTavish	8			8
Paul	40	2	1	43
Phoenix	8			8
Revie	14		1	15
Savage	19		1	20
Sear	1			1
Spurdle	5			5
Thompson	2			2
Trautmann	21	2		23

Goalscorers

PLAYER	LEAGUE	CUP COMPETITION		TOTAL
		FA CUP	OTHER	
Johnstone	16	3		19
Hayes	14			14
Dyson	12			12
Clarke	11			11
Fagan	9	1		10
McAdams	4			4
Paul	3			3
Barnes	2			2
Kirkman	2			2
Revie	2			2
McClelland	1			1
Opps' o.gs.	2	1		3

Fact File

After seven months, Trautmann returns to the side in December despite having not fully recovered from his neck injury.

MANAGER: Les McDowall
CAPTAIN: Roy Paul
TOP SCORER: Bobby Johnstone
BIGGEST WIN: November 24, 1956 5-1 v Portsmouth, Division 1; January 19, 1957 5-1 v Charlton Athletic, Division 1
HIGHEST ATTENDANCE: February 2, 1957 63,872 v Manchester United, lost 2-4, Division 1
MAJOR TRANSFERS OUT: Don Revie to Sunderland

Final Division 1 Table

		P	W	D	L	F	A	Pts
1	MANCHESTER U	42	28	8	6	103	54	64
2	TOTTENHAM H	42	22	12	8	104	56	56
3	PRESTON NE	42	23	10	9	84	56	56
4	BLACKPOOL	42	22	9	11	93	65	53
5	ARSENAL	42	21	8	13	85	69	50
6	WOLVERHAMPTON W	42	20	8	14	94	70	48
7	BURNLEY	42	18	10	14	56	50	46
8	LEEDS U	42	15	14	13	72	63	44
9	BOLTON W	42	16	12	14	65	65	44
10	ASTON VILLA	42	14	15	13	65	55	43
11	WBA	42	14	14	14	59	61	42
12	BIRMINGHAM C	42	15	9	18	69	69	39
12	CHELSEA	42	13	13	16	73	73	39
14	SHEFFIELD W	42	16	6	20	82	88	38
15	EVERTON	42	14	10	18	61	79	38
16	LUTON T	42	14	9	19	58	76	37
17	NEWCASTLE U	42	14	8	20	67	87	36
18	MANCHESTER CITY	42	13	9	20	78	88	35
19	PORTSMOUTH	42	10	13	19	62	92	33
20	SUNDERLAND	42	12	8	22	67	88	32
21	CARDIFF C	42	10	9	23	53	88	29
22	CHARLTON ATH	42	9	4	29	62	120	22

Season 1957-58

Football League Division 1

DATE	OPPONENTS	SCORE	GOALSCORERS	ATTENDANCE
Aug 28	Chelsea	W 3-2	Barlow, Hayes, McAdams	43,722
Aug 31	Manchester United	L 1-4	Barnes	63,103
Sep 4	CHELSEA	W 5-2	Barlow 2, Fagan 2, McAdams	27,943
Sep 7	Nottingham Forest	L 1-2	Hayes	37,041
Sep 11	PRESTON NORTH END	W 2-0	Hayes, Fagan	24,439
Sep 14	PORTSMOUTH	W 2-1	Johnstone, Ewing	28,798
Sep 18	Preston North End	L 1-6	Fagan	22,034
Sep 21	West Bromwich Albion	L 2-9	Fagan, Clarke	25,900
Sep 28	TOTTENHAM HOTSPUR	W 5-1	Johnstone 2, Hayes 2, Barlow	22,497
Oct 5	Birmingham City	L 0-4		28,500
Oct 9	SHEFFIELD WEDNESDAY	W 2-0	Barlow, McAdams	24,016
Oct 12	LEICESTER CITY	W 4-3	Hayes 2, McAdams, Barlow	29,884
Oct 19	Blackpool	W 5-2	Hayes 2, Barnes, Barlow, McAdams	28,322
Oct 26	LUTON TOWN	D 2-2	Barlow, McAdams	30,633
Nov 2	Arsenal	L 1-2	McAdams	43,664
Nov 9	BOLTON WANDERERS	W 2-1	McAdams, Hayes	34,147
Nov 16	Leeds United	W 4-2	Hayes 2, McAdams, Barnes	23,885
Nov 23	WOLVES	L 3-4	Barnes 2, McAdams	45,121
Nov 30	Sunderland	L 1-2	McAdams	35,442
Dec 7	EVERTON	W 6-2	Barnes 3, McAdams 2, Hayes	20,912
Dec 14	Aston Villa	W 2-1	Hayes, o.g.	24,017
Dec 21	Sheffield Wednesday	W 5-4	Hayes 2, Kirkham 2, Johnstone	23,073
Dec 25	Burnley	L 1-2	Fagan	27,956
Dec 26	BURNLEY	W 4-1	Barlow, Kirkman, Hayes, Fagan	47,285
Dec 28	MANCHESTER UNITED	D 2-2	Hayes, o.g.	70,483
Jan 11	NOTTINGHAM FOREST	D 1-1	Johnstone	34,837
Jan 18	Portsmouth	L 1-2	Sambrook	26,254
Feb 1	WEST BROMWICH ALBION	W 4-1	McAdams 3, Barlow	38,702
Feb 8	Tottenham Hotspur	L 1-5	Hayes	37,539
Feb 22	Leicester City	L 4-8	Johnstone 2, McAdams, Barnes	31,017
Mar 1	BLACKPOOL	W 4-3	Barnes, Barlow, McAdams, o.g.	30,621
Mar 5	BIRMINGHAM CITY	D 1-1	Barlow	30,565
Mar 8	Luton Town	W 2-1	Sambrook, o.g.	16,004
Mar 15	ARSENAL	L 2-4	Barlow, Hayes	31,645
Mar 22	Wolves	D 3-3	Barlow 2, o.g.	34,932
Mar 29	LEEDS UNITED	W 1-0	McAdams	21,962
Apr 5	Bolton Wanderers	W 2-0	Barlow 2	27,733
Apr 7	NEWCASTLE UNITED	W 2-1	Warhurst, Hayes	33,995
Apr 12	SUNDERLAND	W 3-1	Hayes 2, Hart	31,166
Apr 14	Newcastle United	L 1-4	Warhurst	53,280
Apr 19	Everton	W 5-2	Hart 2, Hayes, Sambrook, Barnes	31,443
Apr 26	ASTON VILLA	L 1-2	Hayes	28,278

FA Cup

Jan 4	West Bromwich Albion	(Rd 3) L 1-5	Hayes	49,669

League & Cup Appearances

PLAYER	LEAGUE	CUP COMPETITION	TOTAL
		FA CUP	
Barlow	39	1	40
Barnes	39	1	40
Branagan	6	1	7
Cheetham	2		2
Clarke	6	1	7
Ewing	38	1	39
Fagan	29	1	30
Fidler	1		1
Fleet	1		1
Hart	5		5
Hayes	40	1	41
Johnstone	33	1	34
Kirkman	4		4
Leivers	36		36
Little	16		16
Marsden	4		4
McAdams	28		28
McCelland	3		3
McTavish	6		6
Phoenix	2		2
Sambrook	16		16
Savage	7		7
Sear	29	1	30
Taylor	1		1
Trautmann	34	1	35
Warhurst	37	1	38

Goalscorers

PLAYER	LEAGUE	CUP COMPETITION	TOTAL
		FA CUP	
Hayes	25	1	26
McAdams	19		19
Barlow	17		17
Barnes	11		11
Fagan	7		7
Johnstone	7		7
Hart	3		3
Kirkman	3		3
Sambrook	3		3
Warhurst	2		2
Clarke	1		1
Ewing	1		1
Opps' o.gs.	5		5

Fact File

City managed to score and concede over 100 goals in the season.

MANAGER: Les McDowall

CAPTAIN: Ken Barnes

TOP SCORER: Joe Hayes

BIGGEST WIN: December 7, 1957 6-2 v Everton, Division 1

HIGHEST ATTENDANCE: December 28, 1957 70,483 v Manchester United, drew 2-2, Division 1

MAJOR TRANSFERS IN: Roy Warhurst from Birmingham City

Final Division 1 Table

		P	W	D	L	F	A	Pts
1	WOLVERHAMPTON W	42	28	8	6	103	47	64
2	PRESTON NE	42	26	7	9	100	51	59
3	TOTTENHAM H	42	21	9	12	93	77	51
4	WBA	42	18	14	10	92	70	50
5	MANCHESTER CITY	42	22	5	15	104	100	49
6	BURNLEY	42	21	5	16	80	74	47
7	BLACKPOOL	42	19	6	17	80	67	44
8	LUTON T	42	19	6	17	69	63	44
9	MANCHESTER U	42	16	11	15	85	75	43
10	NOTTINGHAM F	42	16	10	16	69	63	42
11	CHELSEA	42	15	12	15	83	79	42
12	ARSENAL	42	16	7	19	73	85	39
13	BIRMINGHAM C	42	14	11	17	76	89	39
14	ASTON VILLA	42	16	7	19	73	86	39
15	BOLTON W	42	14	10	18	65	87	38
16	EVERTON	42	13	11	18	65	75	37
17	LEEDS U	42	14	9	19	51	63	37
18	LEICESTER C	42	14	5	23	91	112	33
19	NEWCASTLE U	42	12	8	22	73	81	32
20	PORTSMOUH	42	12	8	22	73	88	32
21	SUNDERLAND	42	10	12	20	54	97	32
22	SHEFFIELD W	42	12	7	23	69	92	31

Season 1958-59

Football League Division 1

DATE	OPPONENTS	SCORE		GOALSCORERS	ATTENDANCE
Aug 23	Burnley	W	4-3	Hayes 2, Johnstone 2	31,371
Aug 27	BOLTON WANDERERS	D	3-3	Barnes, Barlow, Sambrook	40,844
Aug 30	PRESTON NORTH END	D	1-1	McClelland	42,576
Sep 3	Bolton Wanderers	L	1-4	Hayes	39,727
Sep 6	Leicester City	L	1-3	McAdams	29,053
Sep 10	LUTON TOWN	D	1-1	Fagan	30,771
Sep 13	EVERTON	L	1-3	Barlow	35,437
Sep 17	Luton Town	L	1-5	Johnstone	18,160
Sep 20	Arsenal	L	1-4	Sambrook	47,878
Sep 27	MANCHESTER UNITED	D	1-1	Hayes	62,812
Oct 4	LEEDS UNITED	W	2-1	Barlow, Hayes	31,989
Oct 11	Wolves	L	0-2		33,769
Oct 18	PORTSMOUTH	W	3-2	Cheetham, Hayes, Fagan	31,330
Oct 25	Newcastle United	L	1-4	Hannah	54,330
Nov 1	TOTTENHAM HOTSPUR	W	5-1	Barlow 3, Hannah, Hayes	30,601
Nov 8	Nottingham Forest	L	0-4		31,004
Nov 15	CHELSEA	W	5-1	Leivers, Fagan, Barlow, Hayes, Sambrook	19,778
Nov 22	Blackpool	D	0-0		19,200
Nov 29	BLACKBURN ROVERS	L	0-1		16,405
Dec 6	Aston Villa	D	1-1	Kirkman	19,018
Dec 13	WEST HAM UNITED	W	3-1	Barlow 3	22,250
Dec 20	BURNLEY	L	1-4	Barnes	22,328
Dec 26	Birmingham City	L	1-6	Barlow	24,263
Dec 27	BIRMINGHAM CITY	W	4-1	Hayes 2, Barlow, Sambrook	29,276
Jan 3	Preston North End	L	0-2		21,208
Jan 31	Everton	L	1-3	Barlow	43,360
Feb 7	ARSENAL	D	0-0		31,819
Feb 14	Manchester United	L	1-4	Johnstone	59,604
Feb 21	Leeds United	W	4-0	Barlow 2, Barnes, Fidler	18,515
Feb 28	WOLVES	L	1-4	Hayes	42,776
Mar 7	Portsmouth	W	4-3	Fagan, McAdams, Hayes, Sambrook	19,919
Mar 14	NEWCASTLE UNITED	W	5-1	Hayes 2, Sambrook 2, Barnes	25,417
Mar 21	Tottenham Hotspur	L	1-3	McAdams	34,493
Mar 28	NOTTINGHAM FOREST	D	1-1	Barlow	28,146
Mar 30	WEST BROMWICH ALBION	L	0-2		25,551
Mar 31	West Bromwich Albion	L	0-3		32,076
Apr 4	Chelsea	L	0-2		32,554
Apr 11	BLACKPOOL	L	0-2		27,118
Apr 18	Blackburn Rovers	L	1-2	Hayes	24,616
Apr 20	West Ham United	L	1-5	Barlow	23,500
Apr 25	ASTON VILLA	D	0-0		39,661
Apr 29	LEICESTER CITY	W	3-1	McAdams, Hayes, Sambrook	46,936

FA Cup

Jan 10	Grimsby Town	(Rd 3) D	2-2	Barlow, Hayes	14,964
Jan 24	GRIMSBY TOWN	(R) L	1-2	Johnstone	35,840

League & Cup Appearances

PLAYER	LEAGUE	CUP COMPETITION FA CUP	TOTAL
Barlow	38	2	40
Barnes	40	2	42
Branagan	16	1	17
Cheetham	18		18
Ewing	30	2	32
Fagan	25		25
Fidler	4		4
Fleet	1		1
Hannah	23		23
Hayes	40	2	42
Horridge	3		3
Johnstone	18	2	20
Kirkman	2		2
Leivers	34	1	35
Lister	2		2
Little	1		1
McAdams	21	2	23
McClelland	1		1
McTavish	16		16
Pennington	1		1
Phoenix	16	2	18
Sambrook	33	2	35
Sear	31	2	33
Shawcross	4		4
Trautmann	41	2	43
Warhurst	3		3

Goalscorers

PLAYER	LEAGUE	CUP COMPETITION FA CUP	TOTAL
Barlow	17	1	18
Hayes	16	1	17
Sambrook	8		8
Barnes	4		4
Fagan	4		4
Johnstone	4	1	5
McAdams	4		4
Hannah	2		2
Cheetham	1		1
Fidler	1		1
Kirkman	1		1
Leivers	1		1
McClelland	1		1

Fact File

After winning their opening game of the season, City had to wait another ten games for their next victory.

MANAGER: Les McDowall

CAPTAIN: Ken Barnes

TOP SCORER: Colin Barlow

BIGGEST WIN: November 1, 1958 5-1 v Tottenham Hotspur, Division 1; November 15, 1958 5-1 v Chelsea, Division 1; March 14, 1958 5-1 v Newcastle United, Division 1

HIGHEST ATTENDANCE: September 27, 1958 62,812 v Manchester United, drew 1-1, Division 1

MAJOR TRANSFERS IN: George Hannah from Lincoln City

Final Division 1 Table

		P	W	D	L	F	A	Pts
1	WOLVERHAMPTON W	42	28	5	9	110	49	61
2	MANCHESTER U	42	24	7	11	103	66	55
3	ARSENAL	42	21	8	13	88	68	50
4	BOLTON W	42	20	10	12	79	66	50
5	WBA	42	18	13	11	88	68	49
6	WEST HAM U	42	21	6	15	85	70	48
7	BURNLEY	42	19	10	13	81	70	48
8	BLACKPOOL	42	18	11	13	66	49	47
9	BIRMINGHAM C	42	20	6	16	84	68	46
10	BLACKBURN R	42	17	10	15	76	70	44
11	NEWCASTLE U	42	17	7	18	80	80	41
12	PRESTON NE	42	17	7	18	70	77	41
13	NOTTINGHAM F	42	17	6	19	71	74	40
14	CHELSEA	42	18	4	20	77	98	40
15	LEEDS U	42	15	9	18	57	74	39
16	EVERTON	42	17	4	21	71	87	38
17	LUTON T	42	12	13	17	68	71	37
18	TOTTENHAM H	42	13	10	19	85	95	36
19	LEICESTER C	42	11	10	21	67	98	32
20	MANCHESTER CITY	42	11	9	22	64	95	31
21	ASTON VILLA	42	11	8	23	58	87	30
22	PORTSMOUTH	42	6	9	27	64	112	21

Season 1959-60

Football League Division 1

DATE	OPPONENTS	SCORE	GOALSCORERS	ATTENDANCE
Aug 22	NOTTINGHAM FOREST	W 2-1	Fagan, Johnstone	38,974
Aug 26	Fulham	L 2-5	Barlow, Colbridge	27,000
Aug 29	Sheffield Wednesday	L 0-1		33,479
Sep 2	FULHAM	W 3-1	McAdams 2, Colbridge	37,485
Sep 5	WOLVES	L 4-6	McAdams 3, Barlow	43,650
Sep 9	Luton Town	W 2-1	Hannah, Hayes	13,122
Sep 12	Arsenal	L 1-3	McAdams	38,392
Sep 16	LUTON TOWN	L 1-2	Colbridge	29,309
Sep 19	MANCHESTER UNITED	W 3-0	Hayes 2, Hannah	58,300
Oct 26	BLACKBURN ROVERS	W 2-1	McAdams, Hayes	41,687
Oct 3	Blackpool	W 3-1	Barlow, Hayes, Colbridge	33,226
Oct 10	Preston North End	W 5-1	McAdams 3, Barlow, Cheetham	31,546
Oct 17	LEICESTER CITY	W 3-2	McAdams 2, Hayes	33,896
Oct 24	Burnley	L 3-4	Hannah 2, Colbridge	28,653
Oct 31	TOTTENHAM HOTSPUR	L 1-2	Leivers	45,506
Nov 7	West Ham United	L 1-4	Hayes	25,243
Nov 14	CHELSEA	D 1-1	Dyson	24,364
Nov 21	West Bromwich Albion	L 0-2		24,219
Nov 28	NEWCASTLE UNITED	L 3-4	McAdams 3	29,416
Dec 5	Birmingham City	L 2-4	Hayes, Colbridge	18,661
Dec 12	LEEDS UNITED	D 3-3	Barlow 2, McAdams	19,715
Dec 19	Nottingham Forest	W 2-1	Barlow, o.g.	13,363
Dec 26	Everton	L 1-2	Barlow	30,580
Dec 28	EVERTON	W 4-0	Fagan, Barlow, McAdams, Hayes	43,531
Jan 2	SHEFFIELD WEDNESDAY	W 4-1	McAdams 2, Barlow, Hayes	44,167
Jan 16	Wolves	L 2-4	Barlow, Colbridge	27,864
Jan 23	ARSENAL	L 1-2	o.g.	28,441
Feb 6	Manchester United	D 0-0		59,450
Feb 13	Blackburn Rovers	L 1-2	Barlow	23,731
Feb 27	BIRMINGHAM CITY	W 3-0	Hayes 2, Barlow	23,479
Mar 5	Leicester City	L 0-5		24,009
Mar 9	BLACKPOOL	L 2-3	Barlow, Haydock	19,653
Mar 19	Leeds United	L 3-4	Barlow, Law, o.g.	32,545
Mar 30	WEST HAM UNITED	W 3-1	Barlow, Law, McAdams	29,572
Apr 2	Chelsea	L 0-3		36,044
Apr 9	WEST BROMWICH ALBION	L 0-1		24,342
Apr 15	BOLTON WANDERERS	W 1-0	Barlow	50,053
Apr 16	Tottenham Hotspur	W 1-0	McAdams	49,767
Apr 18	Bolton Wanderers	L 1-3	Barlow	35,591
Apr 23	PRESTON NORTH END	W 2-1	Barlow, Colbridge	29,812
Apr 30	Newcastle United	W 1-0	Hayes	27,812
May 2	BURNLEY	L 1-2	Colbridge	65,981

FA Cup

Jan 9	SOUTHAMPTON	(Rd 3) L 1-5	Barlow	42,065

League & Cup Appearances

PLAYER	LEAGUE	CUP COMPETITION FA CUP	TOTAL
Barlow	39	1	40
Barnes	37	1	38
Branagan	23		24
Cheetham	21		21
Colbridge	40	1	41
Dyson	6		6
Ewing	7		7
Fagan	10	1	11
Fleet	1		1
Hannah	26		26
Haydock	2		2
Hayes	41	1	42
Johnstone	3		3
Kerr	10		10
Law	7		7
Leigh	2		2
Leivers	28		28
McAdams	30	1	31
McTavish	35	1	36
Oakes	18	1	19
Phoenix	1		1
Sear	25	1	26
Shambrook	3		3
Shawcross	6		6
Trautmann	41	1	42

Goalscorers

PLAYER	LEAGUE	CUP COMPETITION FA CUP	TOTAL
McAdams	21		21
Barlow	19	1	20
Hayes	13		13
Colbridge	9		9
Hannah	4		4
Fagan	2		2
Law	2		2
Cheetham	1		1
Dyson	1		1
Haydock	1		1
Johnstone	1		1
Leivers	1		1
Opps' o.gs.	3		3

Fact File

British transfer record signing (£55,000) Denis Law scores on his debut at Elland Road in March.

MANAGER: Les McDowall
CAPTAIN: Ken Barnes
TOP SCORER: Billy McAdams
BIGGEST WIN: October 10, 1959 5-1 v Preston North End, Division 1
HIGHEST ATTENDANCE: May 2, 1960 65,981 v Burnley, lost 1-2, Division 1
MAJOR TRANSFERS IN: Denis Law from Huddersfield Town
MAJOR TRANSFERS OUT: Bobby Johnstone to Hearts

Final Division 1 Table

		P	W	D	L	F	A	PTS
1	BURNLEY	42	24	7	11	85	61	55
2	WOLVERHAMPTON W	42	24	6	12	106	67	54
3	TOTTENHAM H	42	21	11	10	86	50	53
4	WBA	42	19	11	12	83	57	49
5	SHEFFIELD W	42	19	11	12	80	59	49
6	BOLTON W	42	20	8	14	59	51	48
7	MANCHESTER U	42	19	7	16	102	80	45
8	NEWCASTLE U	42	18	8	16	82	78	44
9	PRESTON NE	42	16	12	14	79	76	44
10	FULHAM	42	17	10	15	73	80	44
11	BLACKPOOL	42	15	10	17	59	71	40
12	LEICESTER C	42	13	13	16	66	75	39
13	ARSENAL	42	15	9	18	68	80	39
14	WEST HAM U	42	16	6	20	75	91	38
15	EVERTON	42	13	11	18	73	78	37
16	MANCHESTER CITY	42	17	3	22	78	84	37
17	BLACKBURN R	42	16	5	21	60	70	37
18	CHELSEA	42	14	9	19	76	91	37
19	BIRMINGHAM C	42	13	10	19	63	80	36
20	NOTTINGHAM F	42	13	9	20	50	74	35
21	LEEDS U	42	12	10	20	65	92	34
22	LUTON T	42	9	12	21	50	73	30

Season 1960-61

Football League Division 1

DATE	OPPONENTS	SCORE	GOALSCORERS	ATTENDANCE
Aug 20	Nottingham Forest	D 2-2	Law, Hayes	30,133
Aug 24	BURNLEY	W 2-1	Barlow, Hayes	26,941
Aug 30	Burnley	W 3-1	Barlow, Law, Colbridge	28,547
Sep 3	ARSENAL	D 0-0		36,656
Sep 7	SHEFFIELD WEDNESDAY	D 1-1	Law	35,180
Sep 10	Newcastle United	W 3-1	Law, Hannah, Hayes	25,904
Sep 14	Sheffield Wednesday	L 1-3	Wagstaffe	28,796
Sep 17	CARDIFF CITY	W 4-2	Hayes 2, Barlow 2	30,932
Sep 24	West Bromwich Albion	L 3-6	Barlow, Hannah, Hayes	25,163
Oct 1	BIRMINGHAM CITY	W 2-1	Barlow, Law	27,665
Oct 10	Tottenham Hotspur	D 1-1	Colbridge	59,916
Oct 15	LEICESTER CITY	W 3-1	Barlow, Hayes, Sambrook	30,193
Oct 24	Everton	L 2-4	Barlow, Hayes	53,781
Oct 29	BLACKBURN ROVERS	W 4-0	Hayes 2, Law, Hannah	33,641
Nov 5	Bolton Wanderers	L 1-3	Law	34,005
Nov 12	WEST HAM UNITED	L 1-2	Barlow	33,721
Nov 19	Chelsea	L 3-6	Betts, Law, Baker	37,346
Dec 3	Aston Villa	L 1-5	Law	25,093
Dec 10	WOLVES	L 2-4	Baker, Law	30,078
Dec 17	NOTTINGHAM FOREST	L 1-2	Betts	18,252
Dec 24	FULHAM	W 3-2	Baker 2, Colbridge	18,469
Dec 26	Fulham	L 0-1		20,240
Dec 31	Manchester United	L 1-5	Barlow	61,123
Jan 14	Arsenal	L 4-5	Hayes 2, Betts, Barlow	36,440
Jan 21	NEWCASTLE UNITED	D 3-3	Barlow, Hayes, Law	19,746
Feb 4	Cardiff City	D 3-3	Hayes 2, Baker	15,478
Feb 11	WEST BROMWICH ALBION	W 3-0	Barlow 2, Betts	21,382
Feb 25	TOTTENHAM HOTSPUR	L 0-1		40,278
Mar 4	MANCHESTER UNITED	L 1-3	Wagstaffe	50,479
Mar 11	EVERTON	W 2-1	Shawcross, Baker	29,751
Mar 18	Blackburn Rovers	L 1-4	Hayes	19,733
Mar 22	Birmingham City	L 2-3	Law 2	18,092
Mar 25	BOLTON WANDERERS	D 0-0		21,816
Mar 31	PRESTON NORTH END	L 2-3	Law 2	31,164
Apr 1	Wolves	L 0-1		25,365
Apr 3	Preston North End	D 1-1	Baker	25,358
Apr 8	CHELSEA	W 2-1	Law, o.g.	27,720
Apr 15	West Ham United	D 1-1	Barlow	17,982
Apr 19	BLACKPOOL	D 1-1	Law	28,269
Apr 22	ASTON VILLA	W 4-1	Law 2, Barlow, Hayes	25,235
Apr 26	Leicester City	W 2-1	Baker 2	22,248
Apr 29	Blackpool	D 3-3	Barlow, Hayes, Wagstaffe	20,838

FA Cup

Jan 7	Cardiff City	(Rd 3) D 1-1	o.g.	30,000
Jan 11	CARDIFF CITY	(R) D 0-0		39,035
Jan 16	CARDIFF CITY	(2nd R) W 2-1	Law, Hayes	24,168
Jan 28	Luton Town	(Rd 4) W 6-2*	Law 6	23,727
Feb 1	Luton Town	(Rd 4) L 1-3	Law	15,783

*Match abandoned.

League Cup

Oct 18	STOCKPORT COUNTY	(Rd 2) W 3-0	Law 2, Hayes	21,065
Nov 21	Portsmouth	(Rd 3) L 0-2		10,368

League & Cup Appearances

PLAYER	LEAGUE	CUP COMPETITION		TOTAL
		FA CUP	LC	
Baker	22	2	1	25
Barlow	33	5	1	39
Barnes	31	5	2	38
Betts	42	5	2	49
Cheetham	7			7
Colbridge	19	1		21
Ewing	9			9
Fleet	2			2
Hannah	30	5	2	37
Hart	1			1
Haydock	1			1
Hayes	38	5	2	45
Law	37	5	2	44
Leivers	9	4		13
Oakes	22			22
Plenderleith	34	5	2	41
Sambrook	6	2	1	9
Sear	33	1	2	36
Shawcross	24	5	2	31
Trautmann	40	5	2	47
Wagstaffe	22			22

Goalscorers

PLAYER	LEAGUE	CUP COMPETITION		TOTAL
		FA CUP	LC	
Law	19	2	2	23
Hayes	18	1	1	20
Barlow	17			17
Baker	9			9
Hannah	3			3
Wagstaffe	3			3
Colbridge	3			3
Betts	4			4
Shawcross	1			1
Sambrook	1			1
Opps' o.gs.	1	1		2

Fact File

Denis Law scores six goals in an hour as City take a 6-2 lead in the FA Cup against Luton Town, only for the game to be abandoned two minutes later due to a waterlogged pitch.

MANAGER: Les McDowall

CAPTAIN: Ken Barnes

TOP SCORER: Denis Law

BIGGEST WIN: October 29, 1960 4-0 v Blackburn Rovers, Division 1; May 26, 1947 4-1 v Leeds United, Division 1

HIGHEST ATTENDANCE: December 31, 1960 61,123 v Manchester United, lost 1-5, Division 1

MAJOR TRANSFERS IN: Jackie Plenderleith from Hibernian

MAJOR TRANSFERS OUT: Denis Law to Torino

Final Division 1 Table

		P	W	D	L	F	A	Pts
1	TOTTENHAM H	42	31	4	7	115	55	66
2	SHEFFIELD W	42	23	12	7	78	47	58
3	WOLVERHAMPTON W	42	25	7	10	103	75	57
4	BURNLEY	42	22	7	13	102	77	51
5	EVERTON	42	22	6	14	87	69	50
6	LEICESTER C	42	18	9	15	87	70	45
7	MANCHESTER U	42	18	9	15	88	76	45
8	BLACKBURN R	42	15	13	14	77	76	43
9	ASTON VILLA	42	17	9	16	78	77	43
10	WBA	42	18	5	19	67	71	41
11	ARSENAL	42	15	11	16	77	85	41
12	CHELSEA	42	15	7	20	98	100	37
13	MANCHESTER CITY	42	13	11	18	79	90	37
14	NOTTINGHAM F	42	14	9	19	62	78	37
15	CARDIFF C	42	13	11	18	60	85	37
16	WEST HAM U	42	13	10	19	77	88	36
17	FULHAM	42	14	8	20	72	95	36
18	BOLTON W	42	12	11	19	58	73	35
19	BIRMINGHAM C	42	14	6	22	62	84	34
20	BLACKPOOL	42	12	9	21	68	73	33
21	NEWCASTLE U	42	11	10	21	86	109	32
22	PRESTON NE	42	10	10	22	43	71	30

Season 1961-62

Football League Division 1

DATE	OPPONENTS	SCORE	GOALSCORERS	ATTENDANCE
Aug 19	LEICESTER CITY	W 3-1	Kennedy, Barlow, Hayes	28,899
Aug 23	Fulham	W 4-3	Cheetham 2, Betts, Hayes	16,175
Aug 26	Ipswich Town	W 4-2	Dobing 2, Barlow, Hayes	21,473
Aug 30	FULHAM	W 2-1	Baker, Hayes	36,775
Sep 2	BURNLEY	L 1-3	Baker	38,171
Sep 6	Everton	W 2-0	Dobing, Baker	38,023
Sep 9	Arsenal	L 0-3		42,746
Sep 16	BOLTON WANDERERS	W 2-1	Baker, Hayes	27,275
Sep 20	EVERTON	L 1-3	Hayes	35,102
Sep 23	Manchester United	L 2-3	Kennedy, o.g.	55,933
Sep 30	West Bromwich Albion	D 2-2	Baker, o.g.	20,820
Oct 7	CARDIFF CITY	L 1-2	Sambrook	20,143
Oct 14	Tottenham Hotspur	L 0-2		40,344
Oct 21	NOTTINGHAM FOREST	W 3-0	Dobing, Barlow, Hayes	20,258
Oct 28	Wolves	L 1-4	Barlow	22,821
Nov 4	WEST HAM UNITED	L 3-5	Dobing 3	18,839
Nov 11	Sheffield United	L 1-3	Hannah	18,135
Nov 18	CHELSEA	D 2-2	Kennedy, Barlow	16,583
Nov 25	Aston Villa	L 1-2	Dobing	26,617
Dec 2	BLACKPOOL	L 2-4	Dobing, Barlow	15,971
Dec 9	Blackburn Rovers	L 1-4	Kennedy	13,892
Dec 16	Leicester City	L 0-2		15,196
Dec 23	IPSWICH TOWN	W 3-0	Young, Dobing, Hayes	18,376
Dec 26	Birmingham City	D 1-1	Dobing	21,902
Jan 13	Burnley	L 3-6	Young, Dobing, Hayes	22,728
Jan 20	ARSENAL	W 3-2	Young 2, o.g.	20,414
Feb 3	Bolton Wanderers	W 2-0	Hayes, Wagstaffe	18,454
Feb 10	MANCHESTER UNITED	L 0-2		49,959
Feb 21	WEST BROMWICH ALBION	W 3-1	Oakes, Dobing, Young	17,225
Feb 24	Cardiff City	D 0-0		19,600
Mar 3	TOTTENHAM HOTSPUR	W 6-2	Dobing 3, Young, Hayes, o.g.	31,706
Mar 10	Nottingham Forest	W 2-1	Young, Hayes	20,199
Mar 17	WOLVES	D 2-2	Dobing 2	28,407
Mar 24	West Ham United	W 4-0	Dobing 3, Hayes	25,808
Mar 31	SHEFFIELD UNITED	D 1-1	Hayes	19,157
Apr 7	Chelsea	D 1-1	Hayes	18,629
Apr 11	BIRMINGHAM CITY	L 1-4	o.g.	21,941
Apr 14	ASTON VILLA	W 1-0	Young	18,564
Apr 20	SHEFFIELD WEDNESDAY	W 3-1	Kennedy, Dobing, Hayes	32,131
Apr 21	Blackpool	L 1-3	Leivers	19,954
Apr 23	Sheffield Wednesday	L 0-1		22,084
Apr 28	BLACKBURN ROVERS	W 3-1	Young 2, Kennedy	22,253

FA Cup

Jan 6	Notts County	(Rd 3) W 1-0	Young	25,015
Jan 27	Everton	(Rd 4) L 0-2		56,980

League Cup

Sep 11	Ipswich Town	(Rd 1) L 2-4	Betts, o.g.	14,926

League & Cup Appearances

PLAYER	LEAGUE	CUP COMPETITION		TOTAL
		FA CUP	LC	
Aimson	2			2
Baker	15			15
Barlow	21		1	22
Benson	14			14
Betts	24	1	1	26
Cheetham	16	2	1	19
Colbridge	3			3
Dobing	41	2	1	44
Dowd	2			2
Ewing	21		1	22
Gomersall	2			2
Hannah	13	2	1	16
Hayes	39	2	1	42
Kennedy	42	2	1	45
Leivers	24	2		26
McDonald	5	1		6
Oakes	25			25
Pardoe	4			4
Plenderleith	2			2
Sambrook	4			4
Sear	35	2	1	38
Shawcross	2			2
Trautmann	40	2	1	43
Wagstaffe	42	2	1	45
Young	24	2		26

Goalscorers

PLAYER	LEAGUE	CUP COMPETITION		TOTAL
		FA CUP	LC	
Dobing	22			22
Hayes	16			16
Young	10	1		11
Barlow	6			6
Kennedy	6			6
Baker	5			5
Cheetham	2			2
Betts	1		1	2
Hannah	1			1
Leivers	1			1
Oakes	1			1
Sambrook	1			1
Wagstaffe	1			1
Opps' o.gs.	5		1	6

Fact File

15-year old Glyn Pardoe makes his debut against Birmingham City in April.

MANAGER: Les McDowall

CAPTAIN: Barrie Betts

TOP SCORER: Peter Dobing

BIGGEST WIN: March 3, 1962 6-2 v Tottenham Hotspur, Division 1

HIGHEST ATTENDANCE: January 27, 1962 56,980 v Everton, lost 0-2, FA Cup Round 4

MAJOR TRANSFERS IN: Peter Dobing from Blackburn Rovers, Bobby Kennedy from Kilmarnock

Final Division 1 Table

		P	W	D	L	F	A	Pts
1	IPSWICH T	42	24	8	10	93	67	56
2	BURNLEY	42	21	11	10	101	67	53
3	TOTTENHAM H	42	21	10	11	88	69	52
4	EVERTON	42	20	11	11	88	54	51
5	SHEFFIELD U	42	19	9	14	61	69	47
6	SHEFFIELD W	42	20	6	16	72	58	46
7	ASTON VILLA	42	18	8	16	65	56	44
8	WEST HAM U	42	17	10	15	76	82	44
9	WBA	42	15	13	14	83	67	43
10	ARSENAL	42	16	11	15	71	72	43
11	BOLTON W	42	16	10	16	62	66	42
12	MANCHESTER CITY	42	17	7	18	78	81	41
13	BLACKPOOL	42	15	11	16	70	75	41
14	LEICESTER C	42	17	6	19	72	71	40
15	MANCHESTER U	42	15	9	18	72	75	39
16	BLACKBURN R	42	14	11	17	50	58	39
17	BIRMINGHAM C	42	14	10	18	65	81	38
18	WOLVERHAMPTON W	42	13	10	19	73	86	36
19	NOTTINGHAM F	42	13	10	19	63	79	36
20	FULHAM	42	13	7	22	66	74	33
21	CARDIFF C	42	9	14	19	50	81	32
22	CHELSEA	42	9	10	23	63	94	28

Season 1962-63

Football League Division 1

DATE	OPPONENTS	SCORE	GOALSCORERS	ATTENDANCE
Aug 18	Wolves	L 1-8	o.g.	26,986
Aug 22	LIVERPOOL	D 2-2	Young 2	33,165
Aug 25	ASTON VILLA	L 0-2		29,524
Aug 29	Liverpool	L 1-4	Dobing	46,073
Sep 1	Tottenham Hotspur	L 2-4	Dobing, Harley	48,558
Sep 5	IPSWICH TOWN	W 2-1	Harley 2	24,825
Sep 8	WEST HAM UNITED	L 1-6	Barlow	24,069
Sep 11	Ipswich Town	D 0-0		18,849
Sep 15	Manchester United	W 3-2	Dobing, Harley, Hayes	49,193
Sep 22	Blackpool	D 2-2	Harley, Young	29,461
Sep 29	BLACKBURN ROVERS	L 0-1		23,249
Oct 6	LEYTON ORIENT	W 2-0	Harley, Hannah	19,706
Oct 13	Birmingham City	D 2-2	Young, Harley	21,114
Oct 20	SHEFFIELD WEDNESDAY	W 3-2	Harley 3	20,756
Oct 27	Burnley	D 0-0		30,595
Nov 3	EVERTON	D 1-1	Dobing	40,336
Nov 10	Bolton Wanderers	L 1-3	Oakes	21,700
Nov 17	LEICESTER CITY	D 1-1	Leivers	21,053
Nov 24	Fulham	W 4-2	Harley 2, Dobing, Hannah	17,871
Dec 1	ARSENAL	L 2-4	Harley 2	25,454
Dec 8	West Bromwich Albion	L 1-2	Dobing	12,402
Dec 15	WOLVES	D 3-3	Hayes, Dobing, Hannah	14,170
Feb 23	Leyton Orient	D 1-1	Harley	12,464
Mar 2	BIRMINGHAM CITY	W 2-1	Harley, Gray	28,798
Mar 9	Sheffield Wednesday	L 1-4	Harley	17,424
Mar 23	Everton	L 1-2	Wagstaffe	46,101
Mar 26	BURNLEY	L 2-5	Harley 2	21,985
Mar 29	FULHAM	L 2-3	Barlow, Gray	12,789
Apr 3	Sheffield United	L 1-3	Gray	16,710
Apr 6	Leicester City	L 0-2		27,092
Apr 12	NOTTINGHAM FOREST	W 1-0	Gray	25,793
Apr 13	BOLTON WANDERERS	W 2-1	Young, Dobing	18,551
Apr 15	Nottingham Forest	D 1-1	Harley	14,989
Apr 20	Arsenal	W 3-2	Gray 2, Hayes	20,569
Apr 24	SHEFFIELD UNITED	L 1-3	Hayes	19,277
Apr 27	WEST BROMWICH ALBION	L 1-5	Harley	14,995
May 1	Blackburn Rovers	L 1-4	Oakes	12,894
May 4	BLACKPOOL	L 0-3		19,062
May 8	Aston Villa	L 1-3	Dobing	17,707
May 11	TOTTENHAM HOTSPUR	W 1-0	Harley	27,784
May 15	MANCHESTER UNITED	D 1-1	Harley	52,424
May 18	West Ham United	L 1-6	Oakes	16,600

FA Cup

Mar 6	Walsall	(Rd 3) W 1-0	Harley	11,553
Mar 13	BURY	(Rd 4) W 1-0	Harley	41,575
Mar 16	NORWICH CITY	(Rd 5) L 1-2	Harley	31,217

League Cup

Sep 24	BLACKPOOL	(Rd 2 FL) D 0-0		12,064
Oct 8	Blackpool	(Rd 2 SL) D 3-3	Harley 2, Young	10,508
Oct 15	BLACKPOOL	(R) W 4-2	Harley 2, Oakes, Dobing	12,237
Oct 24	Newport County	(Rd 3) W 2-1	Harley, Hannah	9,898
Nov 14	LUTON TOWN	(Rd 4) W 1-0	Harley	8,682
Dec 11	Birmingham City	(Rd 5) L 0-6		18,010

League & Cup Appearances

PLAYER	LEAGUE	CUP COMPETITION		TOTAL
		FA CUP	LC	
Barlow	9			9
Batty	1			1
Benson	24	3	5	32
Betts	17	3	3	23
Chadwick	4		1	5
Cheetham	10			10
Dobing	41	3	6	50
Dowd	27	3	4	34
Fleet			1	1
Gray	18			18
Hannah	13	3	5	21
Harley	40	3	6	49
Hayes	21	1	4	26
Kennedy	41	3	5	49
Leivers	35	3	6	44
Oakes	34	2	4	40
Pardoe	5	1		6
Plenderleith	5			5
Sear	33	1	6	40
Shawcross	4			4
Trautmann	15		1	16
Wagstaffe	31	3	3	37
Wood	3			3
Young	31	1	6	38

Goalscorers

PLAYER	LEAGUE	CUP COMPETITION		TOTAL
		FA CUP	LC	
Harley	23	3	6	32
Dobing	9		1	10
Gray	6			6
Young	5		1	6
Hayes	4			4
Hannah	3		1	4
Oakes	3		1	4
Barlow	2			2
Leivers	1			1
Wagstaffe	1			1
Opps' o.gs.	1			1

Fact File

Controversial refereeing decisions cost City a point against relegation rivals United, before a heavy defeat at Upton Park doomed them to Division Two.

MANAGER: Les McDowall

CAPTAIN: Bill Leivers

TOP SCORER: Alex Harley

BIGGEST WIN: November 24, 1962 4-2 v Fulham, Division 1; October 15, 1962 4-2 v Blackpool, League Cup, Round 2 Second Leg replay

HIGHEST ATTENDANCE: May 15, 1963 52,424 v Manchester United, drew 1-1, Division 1

MAJOR TRANSFERS IN: Alex Harley from Third Lanark, Alan Ogley from Barnsley

Final Division 1 Table

		P	W	D	L	F	A	Pts
1	EVERTON	42	25	11	6	84	42	61
2	TOTTENHAM H	42	23	9	10	111	62	55
3	BURNLEY	42	22	10	10	78	57	54
4	LEICESTER C	42	20	12	10	79	53	52
5	WOLVERHAMPTON W	42	20	10	12	93	65	50
6	SHEFFIELD W	42	19	10	13	77	63	48
7	ARSENAL	42	18	10	14	86	77	46
8	LIVERPOOL	42	17	10	15	71	59	44
9	NOTTINGHAM F	42	17	10	15	67	69	44
10	SHEFFIELD U	42	16	12	14	58	60	44
11	BLACKBURN R	42	15	12	15	79	71	42
12	WEST HAM U	42	14	12	16	73	69	40
13	BLACKPOOL	42	13	14	15	58	64	40
14	WBA	42	16	7	19	71	79	39
15	ASTON VILLA	42	15	8	19	62	68	38
16	FULHAM	42	14	10	18	50	71	38
17	IPSWICH T	42	12	11	19	59	78	35
18	BOLTON W	42	15	5	22	55	75	35
19	MANCHESTER U	42	12	10	20	67	81	34
20	BIRMINGHAM C	42	10	13	19	63	90	33
21	MANCHESTER CITY	42	10	11	21	58	102	31
22	LEYTON ORIENT	42	6	9	27	37	81	21

Season 1963-64

Football League Division 2

DATE	OPPONENTS	SCORE	GOALSCORERS	ATTENDANCE
Aug 24	PORTSMOUTH	L 0-2		21,822
Aug 28	Cardiff City	D 2-2	Hannah, Kevan	25,352
Aug 31	Rotherham United	W 2-1	Kevan 2	11,418
Sep 4	CARDIFF CITY	W 4-0	Aimson 2, Young, Kevan	22,138
Sep 7	LEEDS UNITED	W 3-2	Young, Hannah, Kevan	29,186
Sep 10	Swindon Town	L 0-3		28,291
Sep 14	Sunderland	L 0-2		39,298
Sep 18	SWINDON TOWN	D 0-0		23,103
Sep 21	NORTHAMPTON TOWN	W 3-0	Oakes, Young, Wagstaffe	21,340
Sep 28	Bury	D 1-1	Hodgkinson	18,032
Oct 5	CHARLTON ATHLETIC	L 1-3	Gray	16,138
Oct 9	PLYMOUTH ARGYLE	D 1-1	Cunliffe	13,456
Oct 12	Grimsby Town	D 1-1	o.g.	9,754
Oct 19	PRESTON NORTH END	L 2-3	Aimson, Kevan	23,153
Oct 26	Derby County	W 3-1	Aimson, Oakes, Young	15,675
Nov 2	SWANSEA TOWN	W 1-0	Oakes	16,770
Nov 9	Southampton	L 2-4	Kevan, Murray	17,142
Nov 23	Newcastle United	L 1-3	Gray	21,200
Nov 30	HUDDERSFIELD TOWN	W 5-2	Murray 2, Kevan 2, Gray	16,192
Dec 7	Leyton Orient	W 2-0	Murray, Kevan	9,610
Dec 14	Portsmouth	D 2-2	Murray, Kevan	13,206
Dec 21	ROTHERHAM UNITED	W 6-1	Murray 3, Kevan 2, Young	11,060
Dec 26	SCUNTHORPE UNITED	W 8-1	Gray 3, Murray 3, Kevan 2	26,365
Dec 28	Scunthorpe United	W 4-2	Murray 2, Kevan, Wagstaffe	9,085
Jan 14	Leeds United	L 0-1		33,737
Jan 18	SUNDERLAND	L 0-3		31,136
Feb 1	Northampton Town	L 1-2	Kevan	12,330
Feb 8	BURY	D 1-1	Dowd	14,698
Feb 15	Charlton Athletic	L 3-4	Frost, Gray, Kevan	18,961
Feb 22	GRIMSBY TOWN	L 0-4		11,411
Feb 29	Middlesbrough	D 2-2	Gray, Kevan	12,763
Mar 7	DERBY COUNTY	W 3-2	Kevan 2, Murray	11,908
Mar 14	Plymouth Argyle	L 1-2	Kevan	11,761
Mar 17	MIDDLESBROUGH	W 1-0	Kevan	8,053
Mar 21	SOUTHAMPTON	D 1-1	Murray	13,481
Mar 27	NORWICH CITY	W 5-0	Kevan 3, Murray, Wagstaffe	29,212
Mar 28	Preston North End	L 0-2		24,796
Mar 30	Norwich City	W 2-1	Murray, Shawcross	17,482
Apr 4	NEWCASTLE UNITED	W 3-1	Kevan 2, Murray	15,450
Apr 11	Huddersfield Town	W 2-0	Pardoe, Murray	13,520
Apr 18	LEYTON ORIENT	W 2-0	Murray, Kevan	15,144
Apr 25	Swansea Town	D 3-3	Pardoe, Murray, Kevan	10,862

FA Cup

Jan 4	Swindon Town	(Rd 2) L 1-2	Oakes	18,065

League Cup

Sep 25	CARLISLE UNITED	(Rd 2) W 2-0	Aimson, Kevan	8,265
Oct 16	Hull City	(Rd 3) W 3-0	Aimson, Kevan, Young	13,880
Nov 27	LEEDS UNITED	(Rd 4) W 3-1	Kevan 2, Gray	10,984
Dec 17	Notts County	(Rd 5) W 1-0	Kevan	7,330
Jan 15	Stoke City	(SF FL) L 0-2		21,019
Feb 5	STOKE CITY	(SF SL) W 1-0	Kevan	16,894

Fact File

In the 1-1 draw with Bury in February, City's goal was scored by goalkeeper Harry Dowd, playing up front after breaking a finger. Bury's goal was scored by future Blue, Colin Bell.

MANAGER: George Poyser

CAPTAIN: Bobby Kennedy

TOP SCORER: Derek Kevan

BIGGEST WIN: December 26, 1963 8-1 v Scunthorpe United, Division 2

HIGHEST ATTENDANCE: September 14, 1963 39,298 v Sunderland, lost 0-2, Division 1

MAJOR TRANSFERS IN: Derek Kevan from Chelsea, Jimmy Murray from Wolves

MAJOR TRANSFERS OUT: Peter Dobing to Stoke City, Alex Harley to Birmingham City

League & Cup Appearances

PLAYER	LEAGUE	CUP COMPETITION		TOTAL
		FA CUP	LC	
Aimson	14		3	17
Batty	2			2
Benson	6			6
Betts	18		2	20
Chadwick	8		1	9
Cheetham	27		2	29
Cunliffe	3			3
Dowd	32	1	6	39
Frost	2			2
Gomersall	7			7
Gray	37	1	5	43
Hannah	9			9
Hayes	3		1	4
Hodgkinson	1		1	2
Kennedy	26	1	5	32
Kevan	40	1	5	46
Leivers	15	1	5	21
McAlinden	1			1
Murray	19	1	2	22
Oakes	41	1	6	48
Ogley	7			7
Panter	1		1	2
Pardoe	20		1	21
Sear	35	1	6	42
Shawcross	2			2
Trautmann	3			3
Wagstaffe	35	1	6	42
Wood	11	1	3	15
Young	37	1	5	43

Goalscorers

PLAYER	LEAGUE	CUP COMPETITION		TOTAL
		FA CUP	LC	
Kevan	30		6	36
Murray	21			21
Gray	8		1	9
Young	5		1	6
Aimson	4		2	6
Oakes	3	1		4
Wagstaffe	3			3
Hannah	2			2
Pardoe	2			2
Cunliffe	1			1
Dowd	1			1
Frost	1			1
Hodgkinson	1			1
Shawcross	1			1
Opps' o.gs.	1			1

Final Division 2 Table

		P	W	D	L	F	A	PTS
1	LEEDS	42	24	15	3	71	34	63
2	SUNDERLAND	42	25	11	6	81	37	61
3	PRESTON NE	42	23	10	9	79	54	56
4	CHARLTON ATH	42	19	10	13	76	70	48
5	SOUTHAMPTON	42	19	9	14	100	73	47
6	MANCHESTER CITY	42	18	10	14	84	66	46
7	ROTHERHAM U	42	19	7	16	90	78	45
8	NEWCASTLE U	42	20	5	17	74	69	45
9	PORTSMOUTH	42	16	11	15	79	70	43
10	MIDDLESBROUGH	42	15	11	16	67	52	41
11	NORTHAMPTON T	42	16	9	17	58	60	41
12	HUDDERSFIELD T	42	15	10	17	57	64	40
13	DERBY CO	42	14	11	17	56	67	39
14	SWINDON T	42	14	10	18	57	69	38
15	CARDIFF C	42	14	10	18	56	81	38
16	LEYTON ORIENT	42	13	10	19	54	72	36
17	NORWICH C	42	11	13	18	64	80	35
18	BURY	42	13	9	20	57	73	35
19	SWANSEA T	42	12	9	21	63	74	33
20	PLYMOUTH ARG	42	8	16	18	45	67	32
21	GRIMSBY T	42	9	14	19	47	75	32
22	SCUNTHORPE U	42	10	10	22	52	82	30

Season 1964-65

Football League Division 2

DATE	OPPONENTS	SCORE	GOALSCORERS	ATTENDANCE
Aug 22	Charlton Athletic	L 1-2	Kevan	19,299
Aug 26	LEYTON ORIENT	W 6-0	Murray 3, Oakes, Pardoe, Kevan	21,085
Aug 29	NORTHAMPTON TOWN	L 0-2		20,935
Aug 31	Leyton Orient	L 3-4	Gray, Pardoe, Kevan	11,512
Sep 5	PORTSMOUTH	W 2-0	Murray, Kevan	16,527
Sep 9	NORWICH CITY	L 0-2		16,191
Sep 12	Swindon Town	W 1-0	Kevan	17,353
Sep 16	Norwich City	L 1-4	Gray	22,309
Sep 19	DERBY COUNTY	W 2-0	Stobart, Kevan	16,214
Sep 26	Swansea Town	L 0-3		10,862
Oct 3	ROTHERHAM UNITED	W 2-1	Gray, Kevan	15,211
Oct 10	Southampton	L 0-1		18,412
Oct 14	NEWCASTLE UNITED	W 3-0	Kevan, Young, Oakes	10,215
Oct 17	HUDDERSFIELD TOWN	L 2-3	Kevan 2	15,704
Oct 24	Coventry City	D 2-2	Young, o.g.	28,693
Oct 31	CARDIFF CITY	W 2-0	Murray 2	13,146
Nov 7	Preston North End	W 5-2	Kevan 3, Young 2	19,374
Nov 14	IPSWICH TOWN	W 4-0	Murray 2, Kevan 2	16,835
Nov 21	Plymouth Argyle	L 2-3	Gray, Kevan	19,468
Nov 28	BOLTON WANDERERS	L 2-4	Ogden, Young	21,895
Dec 5	Middlesbrough	W 1-0	Kevan	13,873
Dec 19	Northampton Town	L 0-2		12,665
Dec 26	BURY	D 0-0		22,299
Dec 28	Bury	W 2-0	Murray, Kevan	11,279
Jan 2	Portsmouth	D 1-1	Young	12,500
Jan 16	SWINDON TOWN	L 1-2	Oakes	8,015
Jan 30	Derby County	L 0-2		14,765
Feb 6	SWANSEA TOWN	W 1-0	Murray	11,931
Feb 13	Rotherham United	D 0-0		10,917
Feb 20	SOUTHAMPTON	W 3-1	Young, Kennedy, Crossan	10,470
Feb 27	Huddersfield Town	L 0-1		14,405
Mar 6	MIDDLESBROUGH	D 1-1	Ogden	14,231
Mar 12	Cardiff City	D 2-2	Connor, Gray	9,094
Mar 20	PRESTON NORTH END	W 4-3	Murray 2, Connor, Crossan	12,884
Mar 27	Ipswich Town	L 1-4	Crossan	12,709
Apr 3	PLYMOUTH ARGYLE	W 2-1	Ogden, Oakes	10,929
Apr 10	Bolton Wanderers	L 0-4		15,885
Apr 16	CRYSTAL PALACE	L 0-2		15,885
Apr 17	COVENTRY CITY	D 1-1	Connor	10,804
Apr 19	Crystal Palace	D 1-1	Pardoe	12,175
Apr 24	Newcastle United	D 0-0		33,259
Apr 28	CHARLTON ATHLETIC	W 2-1	Murray, Young	8,409

FA Cup

Jan 9	SHREWSBURY TOWN	(Rd 3) D 1-1	Kevan	16,131
Jan 13	Shrewsbury Town	(R) L 1-3	Gray	15,924

League Cup

Sep 23	MANSFIELD TOWN	(Rd 2) L 3-5	Murray, Young, Kevan	8,789

League & Cup Appearances

PLAYER	LEAGUE	CUP COMPETITION		TOTAL
		FA CUP	LC	
Bacuzzi	41	2	1	44
Batty	10			10
Cheetham	11		1	12
Connor	24			24
Crossan	16			16
Dowd	21	2	1	24
Doyle	6			6
Gomersall	29			29
Gratrix	15			15
Gray	27	2	1	30
Hayes	2			2
Kennedy	38	2	1	41
Kevan	27	2	1	30
Murray	30	2	1	33
Oakes	41	2	1	44
Ogden	9			9
Ogley	21			21
Pardoe	14	2		16
Sear	7	2		9
Shawcross	5	1	1	7
Stobart	14			14
Wagstaffe	14		1	15
Wood	9	2		11
Young	31	1	1	33

Goalscorers

PLAYER	LEAGUE	CUP COMPETITION		TOTAL
		FA CUP	LC	
Kevan	18	1	1	20
Murray	13		1	14
Young	8		1	9
Gray	5	1		6
Oakes	4			4
Connor	3			3
Crossan	3			3
Gratrix	3			3
Ogden	3			3
Kennedy	1			1
Pardoe	1			1
Opps' o.gs.	5			5

Final Division 2 Table

		P	W	D	L	F	A	Pts
1	NEWCASTLE U	42	24	9	9	81	45	57
2	NORTHAMPTON T	42	20	16	6	66	50	56
3	BOLTON W	42	20	10	12	80	58	50
4	SOUTHAMPTON	42	17	14	11	83	63	48
5	IPSWICH T	42	15	17	10	74	67	47
6	NORWICH C	42	20	7	15	61	57	47
7	CRYSTAL PALACE	42	16	13	13	55	51	45
8	HUDDERSFIELD T	42	17	10	15	53	51	44
9	DERBY CO	42	16	11	15	84	79	43
10	COVENTRY C	42	17	9	16	72	70	43
11	MANCHESTER CITY	42	16	9	17	63	62	41
12	PRESTON NE	42	14	13	15	76	81	41
13	CARDIFF C	42	13	14	15	64	57	40
14	ROTHERHAM U	42	14	12	16	70	69	40
15	PLYMOUTH ARG	42	16	8	18	63	79	40
16	BURY	42	14	10	18	60	66	38
17	MIDDLESBROUGH	42	13	9	20	70	76	35
18	CHARLTON ATH	42	13	9	20	64	75	35
19	LEYTON ORIENT	42	12	11	19	50	72	35
20	PORTSMOUTH	42	12	10	20	56	77	34
21	SWINDON T	42	14	5	23	63	81	33
22	SWANSEA T	42	11	10	21	62	84	32

Fact File

The home tie against Swindon saw the lowest ever attendance (8,015) for a league game at Maine Road. Mike Summerbee scored for the visitors in their 2-1 win.

MANAGER: George Poyser

CAPTAIN: Bobby Kennedy

TOP SCORER: Derek Kevan

BIGGEST WIN: August 26, 1964 6-0 v Leyton Orient, Division 2

HIGHEST ATTENDANCE: April 24, 1965 33,259 v Newcastle United, drew 0-0, Division 2

MAJOR TRANSFERS IN: Johnny Crossan from Sunderland

Season 1965-66

Football League Division 2

DATE	OPPONENTS	SCORE	GOALSCORERS	ATTENDANCE
Aug 21	Middlesbrough	D 1-1	Murray	17,982
Aug 25	WOLVES	W 2-1	o.g. 2	25,572
Aug 28	BRISTOL CITY	D 2-2	Brand, o.g.	19,349
Aug 30	Wolves	W 4-2	Doyle, Crossan, Murray, o.g.	22,799
Sep 4	Coventry City	D 3-3	Young 2, Murray	29,403
Sep 11	CARLISLE UNITED	W 2-1	Pardoe 2	22,891
Sep 15	Norwich City	D 3-3	Pardoe 2, Crossan	16,381
Sep 18	Cardiff City	L 3-4	Murray, Pardoe, Gray	11,520
Sep 25	DERBY COUNTY	W 1-0	Murray	20,834
Oct 2	Southampton	W 1-0	Young	21,504
Oct 9	Huddersfield Town	D 0-0		31,876
Oct 16	CRYSTAL PALACE	W 3-1	Pardoe 2, Young	24,765
Oct 23	Preston North End	W 3-0	Young 2, Brand	25,117
Oct 27	NORWICH CITY	D 0-0		34,091
Oct 30	CHARLTON ATHLETIC	D 0-0		23,102
Nov 6	Plymouth Argyle	L 0-1		15,954
Nov 13	PORTSMOUTH	W 3-1	Murray 2, Pardoe	22,106
Nov 20	Bolton Wanderers	L 0-1		22,968
Nov 27	IPSWICH TOWN	W 2-1	Crossan 2	19,416
Dec 4	Birmingham City	L 1-3	Summerbee	10,442
Dec 11	LEYTON ORIENT	W 5-0	Young 3, Summerbee, Crossan	16,302
Dec 18	Crystal Palace	W 2-0	Doyle 2	12,847
Jan 1	HUDDERSFIELD TOWN	W 2-0	Doyle, Crossan	47,171
Jan 8	Portsmouth	D 2-2	Doyle, Summerbee	17,352
Jan 12	ROTHERHAM UNITED	W 3-1	Doyle 2, Crossan	25,526
Jan 15	PRESTON NORTH END	D 0-0		26,668
Jan 29	MIDDLESBROUGH	W 3-1	Summerbee 2, Young	25,278
Feb 5	Bristol City	D 1-1	Young	25,723
Feb 19	COVENTRY CITY	W 1-0	Crossan	40,190
Feb 26	Carlisle United	W 2-1	Summerbee, Pardoe	9,000
Mar 12	CARDIFF CITY	D 2-2	Connor, Young	29,642
Mar 19	Derby County	W 2-1	Bell, Young	22,533
Apr 2	PLYMOUTH ARGYLE	D 1-1	Crossan	24,087
Apr 8	BURY	W 1-0	Summerbee	43,104
Apr 12	Bury	L 1-2	Summerbee	21,437
Apr 16	BOLTON WANDERERS	W 4-1	Kennedy, Sear, Crossan, Connor	29,459
Apr 23	Ipswich Town	D 1-1	Crossan	15,995
Apr 30	BIRMINGHAM	W 3-1	Bell, Young, Crossan	28,409
May 4	Rotherham United	W 1-0	Bell	11,376
May 7	Leyton Orient	D 2-2	Bell, o.g.	6,109
May 13	Charlton Athletic	W 3-2	Oakes, Crossan, Connor	13,687
May 18	SOUTHAMPTON	D 0-0		34,653

FA Cup

Jan 22	Blackpool	(Rd 3) D 1-1	Pardoe	23,937
Jan 24	BLACKPOOL	(R) W 3-1	Summerbee, Doyle, Crossan	52,661
Feb 12	GRIMSBY TOWN	(Rd 4) W 2-0	Summerbee, o.g.	37,918
Mar 5	LEICESTER CITY	(Rd 5) D 2-2	Young 2	56,787
Mar 9	Leicester City	(R) W 1-0	Young	41,892
Mar 26	EVERTON	(Rd 6) D 0-0		63,034
Mar 29	Everton	(R) D 0-0		60,349
Apr 5	EVERTON	(2nd R) L 0-2		27,948

League Cup

Sep 22	LEICESTER CITY	(Rd 2) W 3-1	Murray, Pardoe, o.g.	13,246
Oct 13	COVENTRY CITY	(Rd 3) L 2-3	Crossan, Pardoe	18,213

Fact File

Colin Bell scores on his debut against Derby and heads the winner against Rotherham seven games later, to secure promotion.

MANAGER: Joe Mercer OBE

CAPTAIN: Johnny Crossan

TOP SCORER: Neil Young

BIGGEST WIN: December 11, 1965 5-0 v Leyton Orient, Division 2

HIGHEST ATTENDANCE: March 26, 1966 63,034 v Everton, drew 1-1, Division 2

MAJOR TRANSFERS IN: Ralph Brand from Rangers, Mike Summerbee from Swindon Town, Colin Bell from Bury, George Heslop from Everton

League & Cup Appearances (substitute)

PLAYER	LEAGUE	CUP COMPETITION		TOTAL
		FA CUP	LC	
Bacuzzi	15 (1)			15 (1)
Bell	11			11
Brand	17		1	18
Cheetham	12 (3)	2	1	15 (3)
Connor	29 (1)	8		37 (1)
Crossan	40	8	1	49
Dowd	38	8	1	47
Doyle	19 (1)	7		26 (1)
Gomersall	1			1
Gray	3 (3)		1	4 (3)
Heslop	34	8	1	43
Horne	15	5	1	21
Kennedy	35	8	2	45
Murray	11		1	12
Oakes	41	8	2	51
Ogley	4		1	5
Pardoe	40 (1)	8	1	50 (1)
Sear	19	3	2	24
Summerbee	42	8	2	52
Wood	1 (1)		1	2 (1)
Young	35	7	2	44

Goalscorers

PLAYER	LEAGUE	CUP COMPETITION		TOTAL
		FA CUP	LC	
Young	14	3		17
Crossan	13	1	1	15
Pardoe	9	1	2	12
Summerbee	8	2		10
Doyle	7	1		8
Murray	7		1	8
Bell	4			4
Connor	3			3
Brand	2			2
Gray	1			1
Kennedy	1			1
Oakes	1			1
Sear	1			1
Opps' o.gs.	5	1	1	7

Final Division 2 Table

		P	W	D	L	F	A	PTS
1	MANCHESTER CITY	42	22	15	5	76	44	59
2	SOUTHAMPTON	42	22	10	10	85	56	54
3	COVENTRY C	42	20	13	9	73	53	53
4	HUDDERSFIELD T	42	19	13	10	62	36	51
5	BRISTOL C	42	17	17	8	63	48	51
6	WOLVERHAMPTON W	42	20	10	12	87	61	50
7	ROTHERHAM U	42	16	14	12	75	74	46
8	DERBY CO	42	16	11	15	71	68	43
9	BOLTON W	42	16	9	17	62	59	41
10	BIRMINGHAM C	42	16	9	17	70	75	41
11	CRYSTAL PALACE	42	14	13	15	47	52	41
12	PORTSMOUTH	42	16	8	18	74	78	40
13	NORWICH C	42	12	15	15	52	52	39
14	CARLISLE U	42	17	5	20	60	63	39
15	IPSWICH T	42	15	9	18	58	66	39
16	CHARLTON ATH	42	12	14	16	61	70	38
17	PRESTON NE	42	11	15	16	62	70	37
18	PLYMOUTH ARG	42	12	13	17	54	63	37
19	BURY	42	14	7	21	62	76	35
20	CARDIFF C	42	12	10	20	71	91	34
21	MIDDLESBROUGH	42	10	13	19	58	86	33
22	LEYTON ORIENT	42	5	13	24	38	80	23

Season 1966-67

Football League Division 1

DATE	OPPONENTS	SCORE	GOALSCORERS	ATTENDANCE
Aug 20	Southampton	D 1-1	Summerbee	19,900
Aug 24	LIVERPOOL	W 2-1	Bell, Murray	50,320
Aug 27	SUNDERLAND	W 1-0	Oakes	34,948
Aug 30	Liverpool	L 2-3	Murray, Gray	51,645
Sep 3	Aston Villa	L 0-3		15,118
Sep 7	WEST HAM UNITED	L 1-4	Bell	31,079
Sep 10	ARSENAL	D 1-1	Pardoe	27,948
Sep 17	Manchester United	L 0-1		62,085
Sep 24	Blackpool	W 1-0	Crossan	25,761
Oct 1	CHELSEA	L 1-4	Young	31,989
Oct 8	TOTTENHAM HOTSPUR	L 1-2	Summerbee	32,551
Oct 15	Newcastle United	L 0-2		16,510
Oct 29	Burnley	W 3-2	Crossan 2, Bell	25,996
Nov 5	NEWCASTLE UNITED	D 1-1	Young	26,137
Nov 12	Stoke City	W 1-0	Summerbee	27,803
Nov 19	EVERTON	W 1-0	Bell	39,572
Nov 26	Fulham	L 1-4	Young	14,579
Dec 3	NOTTINGHAM FOREST	D 1-1	Kennedy	24,013
Dec 10	West Bromwich Albion	W 3-0	Pardoe, Jones, Crossan	16,908
Dec 17	SOUTHAMPTON	D 1-1	Bell	20,104
Dec 27	Sheffield Wednesday	L 0-1		34,005
Dec 31	Sunderland	L 0-1		28,826
Jan 2	SHEFFIELD WEDNESDAY	D 0-0		32,198
Jan 14	Arsenal	L 0-1		22,392
Jan 21	MANCHESTER UNITED	D 1-1	o.g.	62,983
Feb 4	BLACKPOOL	W 1-0	Bell	27,840
Feb 11	Chelsea	D 0-0		28,633
Feb 25	Tottenham Hotspur	D 1-1	Connor	33,822
Mar 4	BURNLEY	W 1-0	Bell	32,092
Mar 18	Leeds United	D 0-0		34,356
Mar 24	LEICESTER CITY	L 1-3	Crossan	35,396
Mar 25	WEST BROMWICH ALBION	D 2-2	Hince 2	22,780
Mar 28	Leicester City	L 1-2	Jones	17,361
Apr 1	Sheffield United	L 0-1		16,976
Apr 12	STOKE CITY	W 3-1	Bell 3	22,714
Apr 19	ASTON VILLA	D 1-1	Summerbee	21,817
Apr 22	FULHAM	W 3-0	Oakes, Bell, Crossan	22,752
Apr 29	Everton	D 1-1	Coleman	33,239
May 2	Nottingham Forest	L 0-2		32,000
May 6	SHEFFIELD UNITED	D 1-1	Crossan	21,267
May 8	LEEDS UNITED	W 2-1	Crossan, Young	24,316
May 13	West Ham United	D 1-1	Bell	17,186

FA Cup

Jan 28	LEICESTER CITY	(Rd 3) W 2-1	Doyle, Pardoe	38,529
Feb 18	Cardiff City	(Rd 4) D 1-1	o.g.	37,205
Feb 22	CARDIFF CITY	(R) W 3-1	Bell, Young, Crossan	41,616
Mar 11	IPSWICH TOWN	(Rd 5) D 1-1	Young	47,075
Mar 14	Ipswich Town	(R) W 3-0	Summerbee 2, o.g.	30,605
Apr 8	Leeds United	(Rd 6) L 0-1		48,887

League Cup

Sep 14	BOLTON WANDERERS	(Rd 2) W 3-1	Bell, Murray, Pardoe	9,006
Oct 5	West Bromwich Albion	(Rd 3) L 2-4	Summerbee, Young	19,193

League & Cup Appearances (substitute)

PLAYER	LEAGUE	CUP COMPETITION		TOTAL
		FA CUP	LC	
Bell	42	6	2	50
Book	41	6	2	49
Brand	3	1		4
Cheetham	1 (1)		1 (1)	2 (2)
Coleman	9			9
Connor	20 (4)	3		23 (4)
Crossan	38	6	1	45
Dowd	25	1	2	28
Doyle	14 (2)	5		19 (2)
Gray	2 (1)			2 (1)
Heslop	37	4	2	43
Hince	1			1
Horne	29 (1)	6	2	37 (1)
Jones	4 (1)			4 (1)
Kennedy	20 (1)	2	1	23 (1)
Murray	10		1 (1)	11 (1)
Oakes	39	6	2	47
Ogley	17	5		22
Pardoe	40	6	2	48
Summerbee	32	4	2	38
Young	38	5	2	45

Goalscorers

PLAYER	LEAGUE	CUP COMPETITION		TOTAL
		FA CUP	LC	
Bell	12	1	1	14
Crossan	8	1		9
Summerbee	4	2	1	7
Young	4	2	1	7
Pardoe	2	1	1	4
Murray	2		1	3
Oakes	2			2
Jones	2			2
Hince	2			2
Connor	1			1
Kennedy	1			1
Doyle		1		1
Coleman	1			1
Gray	1			1
Opps' o.gs.	1	2		3

Fact File

In their first home game back in the top flight the Blues beat reigning champions Liverpool in front of 50,320 spectators.

MANAGER: Joe Mercer OBE

CAPTAIN: Johnny Crossan

TOP SCORER: Colin Bell

BIGGEST WIN: December 10, 1966 3-0 v West Bromwich Albion, Division 1; April 22, 1967 3-0 v Fulham, Division 1; March 14, 1967 3-0 v Ipswich, FA Cup Round 5 Replay

HIGHEST ATTENDANCE: January 21, 1967 62,983 v Manchester United, drew 1-1, Division 1

MAJOR TRANSFERS IN: Tony Book from Plymouth Argyle

Final Division 1 Table

		P	W	D	L	F	A	Pts
1	MANCHESTER U	42	24	12	6	84	45	60
2	NOTTINGHAM F	42	23	10	9	64	41	56
3	TOTTENHAM H	42	24	8	10	71	48	56
4	LEEDS U	42	22	11	9	62	42	55
5	LIVERPOOL	42	19	13	10	64	47	51
6	EVERTON	42	19	10	13	65	46	48
7	ARSENAL	42	16	14	12	58	47	46
8	LEICESTER C	42	18	8	16	78	71	44
9	CHELSEA	42	15	14	13	67	62	44
10	SHEFFIELD U	42	16	10	16	52	59	42
11	SHEFFIELD W	42	14	13	15	56	47	41
12	STOKE C	42	17	7	18	63	58	41
13	WBA	42	16	7	19	77	73	39
14	BURNLEY	42	15	9	18	66	76	39
15	MANCHESTER CITY	42	12	15	15	43	52	39
16	WEST HAM U	42	14	8	20	80	84	36
17	SUNDERLAND	42	14	8	20	58	72	36
18	FULHAM	42	11	12	19	71	83	34
19	SOUTHAMPTON	42	14	6	22	74	92	34
20	NEWCASTLE U	42	12	9	21	39	81	33
21	ASTON VILLA	42	11	7	24	54	85	29
22	BLACKPOOL	42	6	9	27	41	76	21

Season 1967-68

Football League Division 1

DATE	OPPONENTS	SCORE	GOALSCORERS	ATTENDANCE
Aug 19	LIVERPOOL	D 0-0		49,343
Aug 23	Southampton	L 2-3	Bell, Coleman	23,675
Aug 26	Stoke City	L 0-3		22,426
Aug 30	SOUTHAMPTON	W 4-2	Bell 2, Young 2	22,002
Sep 2	NOTTINGHAM FOREST	W 2-0	Summerbee, Coleman	29,547
Sep 6	NEWCASTLE UNITED	W 2-0	Hince, Young	29,978
Sep 9	Coventry City	W 3-0	Hince, Bell, Summerbee	34,578
Sep 16	SHEFFIELD UNITED	W 5-2	Bowles 2, Summerbee, Young, Bell	31,922
Sep 23	Arsenal	L 0-1		41,567
Sep 30	MANCHESTER UNITED	L 1-2	Bell	62,942
Oct 7	Sunderland	L 0-1		27,885
Oct 14	WOLVES	W 2-0	Young, Doyle	36,476
Oct 21	Fulham	W 4-2	Summerbee 2, Lee, Young	22,108
Oct 28	LEEDS UNITED	W 1-0	Bell	39,713
Nov 4	Everton	D 1-1	Connor	47,144
Nov 11	LEICESTER CITY	W 6-0	Young 2, Lee 2, Doyle, Oakes	29,039
Nov 18	West Ham United	W 3-2	Lee 2, Summerbee	25,595
Nov 25	BURNLEY	W 4-2	Coleman 2, Summerbee, Young	37,098
Dec 2	Sheffield Wednesday	D 1-1	Oakes	38,207
Dec 9	TOTTENHAM HOTSPUR	W 4-1	Summerbee, Coleman, Young, Bell	35,792
Dec 16	Liverpool	D 1-1	Lee	53,268
Dec 23	STOKE CITY	W 4-2	Lee 2, Young, Coleman	40,121
Dec 26	West Bromwich Albion	L 2-3	Summerbee, Lee	44,897
Dec 30	WEST BROMWICH ALBION	L 0-2		45,754
Jan 6	Nottingham Forest	W 3-0	Summerbee, Young, Coleman	39,581
Jan 20	Sheffield United	W 3-0	Doyle, Bell, Lee	32,142
Feb 3	ARSENAL	D 1-1	Lee	42,392
Feb 24	SUNDERLAND	W 1-0	Lee	28,624
Mar 2	Burnley	W 1-0	Lee	23,486
Mar 9	COVENTRY CITY	W 3-1	Bell, Summerbee, Young	33,310
Mar 16	FULHAM	W 5-1	Young 2, Summerbee, Bell, Lee	30,773
Mar 23	Leeds United	L 0-2		51,818
Mar 27	Manchester United	W 3-1	Heslop, Lee, Bell	63,004
Apr 6	Leicester City	L 0-1		24,925
Apr 12	CHELSEA	W 1-0	Doyle	47,132
Apr 13	WEST HAM UNITED	W 3-0	Young 2, Doyle	38,754
Apr 16	Chelsea	L 0-1		37,171
Apr 20	Wolves	D 0-0		36,622
Apr 25	SHEFFIELD WEDNESDAY	W 1-0	o.g.	32,999
Apr 29	EVERTON	W 2-0	Book, Coleman	37,776
May 4	Tottenham Hotspur	W 3-1	Bell 2, Summerbee	51,242
May 11	Newcastle United	W 4-3	Young 2, Summerbee, Lee	46,300

FA Cup

Jan 27	READING	(Rd 3) D 0-0		40,343
Jan 31	Reading	(R) W 7-0	Summerbee 3, Young, Coleman, Heslop, Bell	25,659
Feb 17	LEICESTER CITY	(Rd 4) D 0-0		51,009
Feb 19	Leicester City	(R) L 3-4	Summerbee, Bell, Lee	39,112

League Cup

Sep 13	LEICESTER CITY	(Rd 2) W 4-0	Bowles 2, Book, Young	25,653
Oct 11	BLACKPOOL	(Rd 3) D 1-1	Summerbee	27,633
Oct 18	Blackpool	(R) W 2-0	Summerbee, o.g.	23,405
Nov 1	Fulham	(Rd 4) L 2-3	Oakes, Bell	11,732

MANAGER: Joe Mercer OBE

CAPTAIN: Tony Book

TOP SCORER: Neil Young

BIGGEST WIN: January 31, 1968 7-0 v Reading, FA Cup Round 3

HIGHEST ATTENDANCE: March 27, 1968 63,004 v Manchester United, won 3-1, Division 1

MAJOR TRANSFERS IN: Francis Lee from Bolton Wanderers

MAJOR TRANSFERS OUT: Johnny Crossan to Middlesbrough

League & Cup Appearances (substitute)

PLAYER	LEAGUE	CUP COMPETITION		TOTAL
		FA CUP	LC	
Bell	35	4	4	43
Book	42	4	4	50
Bowles	4		0 (1)	4 (1)
Cheetham	2 (1)			2 (1)
Clay	1 (1)			1 (1)
Coleman	38	4	4	46
Connor	10 (3)	0 (1)	0 (1)	10 (5)
Corrigan			2	2
Dowd	7		2	9
Doyle	37 (1)	4	3	44 (1)
Heslop	41	4	4	49
Hince	6		4	10
Horne	4 (1)		1	5 (1)
Jones	2			2
Kennedy	4 (2)			4 (2)
Lee	31	4		35
Mulhearn	33	4		37
Oakes	41	4	4	49
Ogley	2			2
Pardoe	41	4	4	49
Summerbee	41	4	4	49
Young	40	4	4	48

Goalscorers

PLAYER	LEAGUE	CUP COMPETITION		TOTAL
		FA CUP	LC	
Young	19	1	1	21
Summerbee	14	4	2	20
Lee	16	1		17
Bell	14	2	1	17
Coleman	8	1		9
Doyle	5			5
Oakes	2		1	3
Bowles	2		2	4
Book	1		1	2
Heslop	1	1		2
Hince	2			2
Connor	1			1
Opps' o.gs.	1		1	2

Fact File

In a season that saw Francis Lee and Stan Bowles make their debuts for the Blues, City steal the championship from under United's noses. An incredible victory in their last game at St James' Park brings the trophy to Maine Road.

Final Division 1 Table

		P	W	D	L	F	A	Pts
1	MANCHESTER CITY	42	26	6	10	86	43	58
2	MANCHESTER U	42	24	8	10	89	55	56
3	LIVERPOOL	42	22	11	9	71	40	55
4	LEEDS U	42	22	9	11	71	41	53
5	EVERTON	42	23	6	13	67	40	52
6	CHELSEA	42	18	12	12	62	68	48
7	TOTTENHAM H	42	19	9	14	70	59	47
8	WBA	42	17	12	13	75	62	46
9	ARSENAL	42	17	10	15	60	56	44
10	NEWCASTLE U	42	13	15	14	54	67	41
11	NOTTINGHAM F	42	14	11	17	52	64	39
12	WEST HAM U	42	14	10	18	73	69	38
13	LEICESTER C	42	13	12	17	64	69	38
14	BURNLEY	42	14	10	18	64	71	38
15	SUNDERLAND	42	13	11	18	51	61	37
16	SOUTHAMPTON	42	13	11	18	66	83	37
17	WOLVERHAMPTON W	42	14	8	20	66	75	36
18	STOKE C	42	14	7	21	50	73	35
19	SHEFFIELD W	42	11	12	19	51	63	34
20	COVENTRY C	42	9	15	18	51	71	33
21	SHEFFIELD U	42	11	10	21	49	70	32
22	FULHAM	42	10	7	25	56	98	27

Season 1968-69

Football League Division 1

DATE	OPPONENTS	SCORE	GOALSCORERS	ATTENDANCE
Aug 10	Liverpool	L 1-2	Young	51,236
Aug 14	WOLVES	W 3-2	Summerbee 2, Lee	35,835
Aug 17	MANCHESTER UNITED	D 0-0		63,052
Aug 21	Leicester City	L 0-3		30,076
Aug 24	Queens Park Rangers	D 1-1	Doyle	19,715
Aug 27	Arsenal	L 1-4	Bell	40,767
Aug 31	IPSWICH TOWN	D 1-1	Bell	31,303
Sep 7	Stoke City	L 0-1		22,015
Sep 14	SOUTHAMPTON	D 1-1	Coleman	29,031
Sep 21	Sunderland	W 4-0	Lee 2, Bell, Summerbee	31,687
Sep 28	LEEDS UNITED	W 3-1	Bell 2, Young	46,431
Oct 5	Everton	L 0-2		55,649
Oct 9	ARSENAL	D 1-1	Bell	33,830
Oct 12	TOTTENHAM HOTSPUR	W 4-0	Lee 2, Connor, Coleman	38,019
Oct 19	Coventry City	D 1-1	o.g.	30,670
Oct 26	NOTTINGHAM FOREST	D 3-3	Bell, Young, o.g.	32,937
Nov 2	Chelsea	L 0-2		40,700
Nov 9	SHEFFIELD WEDNESDAY	L 0-1		23,861
Nov 16	Newcastle United	L 0-1		36,400
Nov 23	WEST BROMWICH ALBION	W 5-1	Young 2, Bell 2, Doyle	24,867
Nov 30	West Ham United	L 1-2	Lee	33,082
Dec 7	BURNLEY	W 7-0	Bell 2, Young 2, Doyle, Lee, Coleman	31,009
Dec 14	Tottenham Hotspur	D 1-1	Lee	28,462
Dec 21	COVENTRY CITY	W 4-2	Young 2, Booth, o.g.	27,760
Dec 26	EVERTON	L 1-3	Bell	53,549
Jan 11	CHELSEA	W 4-1	Owen 2, Lee, Young	35,606
Jan 18	Sheffield Wednesday	D 1-1	Young	33,074
Mar 4	Burnley	L 1-2	Bell	18,348
Mar 8	Manchester United	W 1-0	Summerbee	63,388
Mar 11	Ipswich Town	L 1-2	Doyle	24,312
Mar 15	QUEENS PARK RANGERS	W 3-1	Lee, Young, Bowyer	28,869
Mar 24	Nottingham Forest	L 0-1		24,613
Mar 29	STOKE CITY	W 3-1	Bell, Owen, Doyle	27,337
Apr 4	LEICESTER CITY	W 2-0	Summerbee 2	42,022
Apr 5	Leeds United	L 0-1		43,176
Apr 8	Wolves	L 1-3	Lee	28,533
Apr 12	SUNDERLAND	W 1-0	Young	22,842
Apr 16	West Bromwich Albion	L 0-2		25,030
Apr 19	Southampton	L 0-3		26,254
Apr 30	WEST HAM UNITED	D 1-1	Pardoe	31,846
May 5	NEWCASTLE UNITED	W 1-0	Young	20,108
May 12	LIVERPOOL	W 1-0	Lee	28,309

FA Cup

Jan 4	LUTON TOWN	(Rd 3)	W 1-0	Lee	37,120
Jan 25	Newcastle United	(Rd 4)	D 0-0		55,680
Jan 29	NEWCASTLE UNITED	(R)	W 2-0	Owen, Young	60,844
Feb 24	Blackburn Rovers	(Rd 5)	W 4-1	Lee 2, Coleman 2	42,315
Mar 1	TOTTENHAM HOTSPUR	(Rd 6)	W 1-0	Lee	48,872
Mar 22	Everton	(SF)	W 1-0	Booth	63,025
Apr 26	LEICESTER CITY	(F)	W 1-0*	Young	100,000

* Played at Wembley.

League Cup

Sep 3	Huddersfield Town	(Rd 2)	D 0-0		23,426
Sep 11	HUDDERSFIELD TOWN	(R)	W 4-0	Summerbee 2, Bell, o.g.	26,948
Sep 25	Blackpool	(Rd 3)	L 0-1		23,795

FA Charity Shield

Aug 3	WEST BROMWICH ALBION	W 6-1	Owen 2, Lee 2, Young, o.g.	35,510

European Cup

Sep 18	FENERBACHE	(Rd 1 FL)	D 0-0		38,787
Oct 2	Fenerbache	(Rd 1 SL)	L 1-2	Coleman	45,000

MANAGER: Joe Mercer OBE

CAPTAIN: Tony Book

TOP SCORER: Francis Lee

BIGGEST WIN: December 7, 1968 7-0 v Burnley, Division 1

HIGHEST ATTENDANCE: March 26, 1969 100,000 v Leicester City, won 1-0, FA Cup final

MAJOR TRANSFERS IN: Bobby Owen from Bury, Arthur Mann from Hearts

---

League & Cup Appearances (substitute)

PLAYER	LEAGUE	CUP COMPETITION				TOTAL
		FA CUP	LC	OTHER	EUROPEAN	
Bell	39	5	3	1	2	50
Book	15	6				21
Booth	28	7	1			36
Bowles	1 (1)		0 (1)			1 (2)
Bowyer	3 (3)					3 (3)
Coleman	30 (1)	6	3		2	42 (1)
Connor	20 (1)	1		1	1	26 (1)
Corrigan	4					4
Dowd	27	7				34
Doyle	40	7	3	1	2	53
Glennon	0 (1)					0 (1)
Heslop	15 (1)		2	1	2	20 (1)
Kennedy	10		1		1	12
Lee	37	7	3	1	2	50
Mann	7 (1)	1				8 (1)
Mulhearn	11		3	1	2	17
Mundy	1 (1)					1 (1)
Oakes	39	7	3	1	2	52
Owen	16 (4)	3	1	1		21 (4)
Pardoe	39	7	2	1	2	51
Summerbee	39	6	3	1	2	51
Towers	1					1
Young	40	7	2	1	2	52

Goalscorers

PLAYER	LEAGUE	CUP COMPETITION				TOTAL
		FA CUP	LC	OTHER	EUROPEAN	
Lee	12	4		2		18
Young	14	2		1		17
Bell	14		1			15
Summerbee	6		2			8
Coleman	3	2			1	6
Owen	3	1		2		6
Doyle	5					5
Booth	1	1				2
Bowyer	1					1
Connor	1					1
Pardoe	1					1
Opps' o.gs.	3		1		1	5

Fact File

A goal by 19-year-old Tommy Booth in the last minute of the FA Cup semi-final booked City another place at Wembley. Joe Mercer then became the first to win the Cup as player and manager.

Final Division 1 Table

		P	W	D	L	F	A	Pts
1	LEEDS U	42	27	13	2	66	26	67
2	LIVERPOOL	42	25	11	6	63	24	61
3	EVERTON	42	21	15	6	77	36	57
4	ARSENAL	42	22	12	8	56	27	56
5	CHELSEA	42	20	10	12	73	53	50
6	TOTTENHAM H	42	14	17	11	61	51	45
7	SOUTHAMPTON	42	16	13	13	57	48	45
8	WEST HAM U	42	13	18	11	66	50	44
9	NEWCASTLE U	42	15	14	13	61	55	44
10	WBA	42	16	11	15	64	67	43
11	MANCHESTER U	42	15	12	15	57	53	42
12	IPSWICH T	42	15	11	16	59	60	41
13	MANCHESTER CITY	42	15	10	17	64	55	40
14	BURNLEY	42	15	9	18	55	82	39
15	SHEFFIELD W	42	10	16	16	41	54	36
16	WOLVERHAMPTON W	42	10	15	17	41	58	35
17	SUNDERLAND	42	11	12	19	43	67	34
18	NOTTINGHAM F	42	10	13	19	45	57	33
19	STOKE C	42	9	15	18	40	63	33
20	COVENTRY C	42	10	11	21	46	64	31
21	LEICESTER C	42	9	12	21	39	68	30
22	QPR	42	4	10	28	39	95	18

Season 1969-70

Football League Division 1

DATE	OPPONENTS	SCORE	GOALSCORERS	ATTENDANCE
Aug 9	SHEFFIELD WEDNESDAY	W 4-1	Young 2, Bell, Lee	32,583
Aug 12	Liverpool	L 2-3	Bowyer, o.g.	51,959
Aug 16	Newcastle United	L 0-1		46,850
Aug 20	LIVERPOOL	L 0-2		47,888
Aug 23	EVERTON	D 1-1	Bowyer	43,676
Aug 27	Sunderland	W 4-0	Bowyer 2, Oakes, Bell	21,515
Aug 30	Burnley	D 1-1	Bowyer	26,341
Sep 6	CHELSEA	D 0-0		35,995
Sep 13	Tottenham Hotspur	W 3-0	Oakes, Bell, Bowyer	41,644
Sep 20	COVENTRY CITY	W 3-1	Bell 2, Lee	34,320
Sep 27	Stoke City	L 0-2		29,739
Oct 4	WEST BROMWICH ALBION	W 2-1	Bell, Young	34,329
Oct 8	NEWCASTLE UNITED	W 2-1	Young, Lee	32,172
Oct 11	Nottingham Forest	D 2-2	Lee 2	30,037
Oct 18	Derby County	W 1-0	Lee	40,788
Oct 25	WOLVES	W 1-0	Doyle	34,425
Nov 1	Ipswich Town	D 1-1	Lee	24,124
Nov 8	SOUTHAMPTON	W 1-0	Bell	27,069
Nov 15	MANCHESTER UNITED	W 4-0	Bell 2, Young, o.g.	63,013
Nov 22	Arsenal	D 1-1	Bowyer	42,939
Nov 29	LEEDS UNITED	L 1-2	Lee	44,590
Dec 6	West Ham United	W 4-0	Bowyer 2, Lee, Doyle	27,440
Dec 13	TOTTENHAM HOTSPUR	D 1-1	Oakes	29,216
Dec 20	Chelsea	L 1-3	Summerbee	34,791
Dec 23	Everton	L 0-1		51,864
Jan 6	BURNLEY	D 1-1	Lee	22,074
Jan 10	Coventry City	L 0-3		29,386
Jan 17	STOKE CITY	L 0-1		31,565
Jan 31	West Bromwich Albion	L 0-3		30,722
Feb 7	NOTTINGHAM FOREST	D 1-1	Doyle	27,077
Feb 18	ARSENAL	D 1-1	Bowyer	25,504
Feb 21	Wolves	W 3-1	Summerbee 2, Bell	30,373
Feb 28	IPSWICH TOWN	W 1-0	Lee	29,376
Mar 11	CRYSTAL PALACE	L 0-1		25,381
Mar 21	WEST HAM UNITED	L 1-5	Lee	25,381
Mar 27	DERBY COUNTY	L 0-1		42,316
Mar 28	Manchester United	W 2-1	Lee, Doyle	60,286
Apr 4	SUNDERLAND	L 0-1		22,006
Apr 6	Crystal Palace	L 0-1		27,704
Apr 8	Southampton	D 0-0		24,384
Apr 18	Leeds United	W 3-1	Towers, Bell, Young	22,932
Apr 22	Sheffield Wednesday	W 2-1	Bowyer 2	45,258

FA Cup

Jan 3	Hull City	(Rd 3) W 1-0	Young	30,271
Jan 24	Manchester United	(Rd 4) L 0-3		63,417

League Cup

Sep 3	Southport	(Rd 2) W 3-0	Oakes, Bell, Lee	11,215
Sep 24	LIVERPOOL	(Rd 3) W 3-2	Doyle, Young, Bowyer	28,019
Oct 15	EVERTON	(Rd 4) W 2-0	Bell, Lee	45,643
Oct 29	QUEENS PARK RANGERS	(Rd 5) W 3-0	Bell 2, Summerbee	42,058
Dec 3	MANCHESTER UNITED	(SF 1) W 2-1	Bell, Lee (pen)	55,799
Dec 17	Manchester United	(SF 2) D 2-2	Bowyer, Summerbee	63,418
Mar 7	WEST BROMWICH ALBION	(F) W 2-1	Doyle, Pardoe	97,963

European Cup Winners Cup

Sep 17	Athletic Bilbao	(Rd 1 FL) D 3-3	Young, Booth, o.g.	45,000
Oct 1	ATHLETIC BILBAO	(Rd 1 SL) W 3-0	Oakes, Bell, Bowyer	49,664
Nov 12	SK Lierse	(Rd 2 FL) W 3-0	Lee 2, Bell	19,000
Nov 26	SK LIERSE	(RD 2 SL) W 5-0	Lee 2, Bell 2, Summerbee	26,486
Mar 4	Academica Coimbra	(Rd 3 FL) D 0-0		15,000
Mar 18	ACADEMICA COIMBRA	(Rd 3 SL) W 1-0	Towers	36,338
Apr 1	FC Schalke	(SF FL) L 0-1		38,000
Apr 15	FC SCHALKE	(SF SL) W 5-1	Doyle, Young 2, Lee, Bell	46,361
Apr 29	Gornik Zabrze	(F) W 2-1	Young, Lee (pen)	10,000

FA Charity Shield

Aug 2	Leeds United		L 1-2	Bell	35,510

MANAGER: Joe Mercer OBE   **CAPTAIN:** Tony Book

TOP SCORER: Francis Lee

BIGGEST WIN: November 26, 1969, 5-0 v SK Lierse, European Cup Winners Cup Round 2, Second Leg

HIGHEST ATTENDANCE: March 7, 1970 97,963 v West Bromwich Albion, won 2-1, League Cup final

MAJOR TRANSFERS OUT: Stan Bowles to Queens Park Rangers

League & Cup Appearances (substitute)

PLAYER	LEAGUE	CUP COMPETITION				TOTAL
		FA CUP	LC	ECWC	OTHER	
Bell	31	2	6	9	1	49
Book	38	2	7	9	1	57
Booth	41	2	6	9	1	59
Bowles	10 (1)		1			11 (1)
Bowyer	33 (1)	2	6 (1)	4 (1)		45 (3)
Carrodus	6			0 (1)		6 (1)
Coleman	5		0 (1)		1	6 (1)
Connor	8 (1)		2			10 (1)
Corrigan	34	1	7	8	1	51
Donachie	1 (2)					1 (2)
Dowd	2					2
Doyle	41	2	7	9	1	60
Glennon	3			0 (1)		3 (1)
Heslop	6 (1)		2	2 (3)		10 (4)
Jeffries	4 (3)			2		6 (3)
Lee	36	2	7	9	1	55
Mann	9		1	2		12
Mulhearn	6	1		1		8
Mundy	1					1
Oakes	40	2	7	9	1	59
Owen	2					2
Pardoe	38	2	6	9	1	56
Summerbee	32 (1)	2	7	7	1	49 (1)
Towers	6 (1)	0 (1)		2 (1)		8 (3)
Young	29	2	5	8	1	45

Goalscorers

PLAYER	LEAGUE	CUP COMPETITION				TOTAL
		FA CUP	LC	ECWC	OTHER	
Lee	13		3	6		22
Bell	11		5	5	1	22
Bowyer	12		2	1		15
Young	6	1	1	4		12
Doyle	4		2	1		7
Summerbee	3		2	1		6
Oakes	3		1	1		5
Towers	1			1		2
Booth				1		1
Pardoe			1			1
Opps' o.gs.	2			1		3

Fact File

City become the first English side to win a domestic and European trophy in the same season.

Final Division 1 Table

		P	W	D	L	F	A	Pts
1	EVERTON	42	29	8	5	72	34	66
2	LEEDS U	42	21	15	6	84	49	57
3	CHELSEA	42	21	13	8	70	50	55
4	DERBY CO	42	22	9	11	64	37	53
5	LIVERPOOL	42	20	11	11	65	42	51
6	COVENTRY C	42	19	11	12	58	48	49
7	NEWCASTLE U	42	17	13	12	57	35	47
8	MANCHESTER U	42	14	17	11	66	61	45
9	STOKE C	42	15	15	12	56	52	45
10	MANCHESTER CITY	42	16	11	15	55	48	43
11	TOTTENHAM H	42	17	9	16	54	55	43
12	ARSENAL	42	12	18	12	51	49	42
13	WOLVERHAMPTON W	42	12	16	14	55	57	40
14	BURNLEY	42	12	15	15	56	61	39
15	NOTTINGHAM F	42	10	18	14	50	71	38
16	WBA	42	14	9	19	58	66	37
17	WEST HAM U	42	12	12	18	51	60	36
18	IPSWICH T	42	10	11	21	40	63	31
19	SOUTHAMPTON	42	6	17	19	46	67	29
20	CRYSTAL PALACE	42	6	15	21	34	68	27
21	SUNDERLAND	42	6	14	22	30	68	26
22	SHEFFIELD W	42	8	9	25	40	71	25

Season 1970-71

Football League Division 1

DATE	OPPONENTS	SCORE	GOALSCORERS	ATTENDANCE
Aug 15	Southampton	D 1-1	Bell	24,599
Aug 19	Crystal Palace	W 1-0	Oakes	33,118
Aug 22	BURNLEY	D 0-0		36,599
Aug 26	BLACKPOOL	W 2-0	Bell, Lee	37,598
Aug 29	Everton	W 1-0	Bell	50,724
Sep 5	WEST BROMWICH ALBION	W 4-1	Bell 2, Summerbee, Lee	30,549
Sep 12	Nottingham Forest	W 1-0	Doyle	28,896
Sep 19	STOKE CITY	W 4-1	Book, Lee, Young, o.g.	35,473
Sep 26	Tottenham Hotspur	L 0-2		42,490
Oct 3	NEWCASTLE UNITED	D 1-1	Doyle	33,139
Oct 10	Chelsea	D 1-1	Bell	51,903
Oct 17	SOUTHAMPTON	D 1-1	Lee	31,998
Oct 24	Wolves	L 0-3		32,700
Oct 31	IPSWICH TOWN	W 2-0	Bell, Lee	27,317
Nov 7	Coventry City	L 1-2	Bell	25,287
Nov 14	DERBY COUNTY	D 1-1	Bell	31,817
Nov 21	WEST HAM UNITED	W 2-0	Lee 2	28,485
Nov 28	Leeds United	L 0-1		43,511
Dec 5	ARSENAL	L 0-2		33,027
Dec 12	Manchester United	W 4-1	Lee 3, Doyle	52,636
Dec 19	Burnley	W 4-0	Bell 2, Summerbee, Lee	19,917
Dec 26	HUDDERSFIELD TOWN	D 1-1	Bell	40,091
Jan 9	CRYSTAL PALACE	W 1-0	Book	27,442
Jan 12	Liverpool	D 0-0		45,985
Jan 16	Blackpool	D 3-3	Summerbee 2, Bell	29,356
Jan 30	LEEDS UNITED	L 0-2		43,517
Feb 6	Arsenal	L 0-1		36,122
Feb 20	West Ham United	D 0-0		30,168
Feb 26	Ipswich Town	L 0-2		20,685
Mar 6	WOLVES	D 0-0		24,663
Mar 13	Derby County	D 0-0		31,987
Mar 20	COVENTRY CITY	D 1-1	Lee	22,120
Mar 27	West Bromwich Albion	D 0-0		20,100
Apr 3	EVERTON	W 3-0	Doyle, Booth, Hill	26,885
Apr 9	NOTTINGHAM FOREST	L 1-3	Doyle	33,772
Apr 10	Huddersfield Town	L 0-1		21,992
Apr 12	Newcastle United	D 0-0		29,040
Apr 17	CHELSEA	D 1-1	Lee	26,120
Apr 24	Stoke City	L 0-2		14,836
Apr 26	LIVERPOOL	D 2-2	Carter, o.g.	17,975
May 1	TOTTENHAM HOTSPUR	L 0-1		19,674
May 5	MANCHESTER UNITED	L 3-4	Mellor, Lee, Hill	43,636

FA Cup

Jan 2	WIGAN ATHLETIC	(Rd 3) W 1-0	Bell	46,212
Jan 23	Chelsea	(Rd 4) W 3-0	Bell 2, Bowyer	50,176
Feb 17	ARSENAL	(Rd 5) L 1-2	Bell	45,105

League Cup

Sep 9	Carlisle United	(Rd 2) L 1-2	Lee	17,942

European Cup Winners Cup

Sep 9	LINFIELD	(Rd 1 FL) W 1-0	Bell	25,184
Sep 30	Linfield	(Rd 1 SL) W 1-2*	Lee	24,000
Oct 21	Honved	(Rd 2 FL) W 1-0	Lee	14,000
Nov 4	HONVED	(Rd 2 SL) W 2-0	Bell, Lee	28,770
Mar 10	Gornik Zabrze	(Rd 3 FL) L 0-2		100,000
Mar 24	GORNIK ZABRZE	(Rd 3 SL) W 2-0	Mellor, Doyle	31,950
Mar 31	Gornik Zabrze	(R) W 3-1†	Booth, Lee, Young	12,100
Apr 14	Chelsea	(SF FL) L 0-1		45,955
Apr 28	CHELSEA	(SF SL) L 0-1		43,663

*Won on away goals. †Played at Copenhagen.

MANAGER: Joe Mercer OBE

CAPTAIN: Tony Book

TOP SCORER: Colin Bell

BIGGEST WIN: December 19, 1970 4-0 v Burnley, Division 1

HIGHEST ATTENDANCE: March 24, 1971 100,000 v Gornik Zabrze, lost 2-0, European Cup Winners Cup Round 3, First Leg

MAJOR TRANSFERS IN: Freddie Hill from Halifax Town

MAJOR TRANSFERS OUT: Ian Bowyer to Orient

League & Cup Appearances (substitute)

PLAYER	LEAGUE	FA CUP	LC	ECWC	OTHER	TOTAL
Bell	34	3	1	7	2	47
Book	33 (1)	3	1	6	2	45 (1)
Booth	26	3	1	6	1	37
Bowyer	6 (3)	2	(1)	1 (2)		9 (6)
Brennan	0 (2)					0 (2)
Carrodus	5 (1)	(1)				5 (2)
Carter	4 (1)			(1)		4 (2)
Connor	11 (1)		4			15 (1)
Corrigan	33	3	1	6	2	45
Donachie	11		3 (1)			14 (1)
Doyle	37	3	1	7	2	50
Healey	9		3			12
Heslop	19 (1)	2		3	1	25 (1)
Hill	20 (3)			4	1	25 (3)
Jeffries	18 (2)	2		6		26 (2)
Johnson	4 (1)			2		6 (1)
Lee	38	2	1	9	2	52
Mann	16 (2)	3		1 (1)		20 (3)
Mellor	5 (1)			1		6 (1)
Oakes	30	3	1	4	2	40
Pardoe	19		1	4	2	26
Summerbee	26	2	1	6	1 (1)	36 (1)
Towers	33 (1)		1	9	2	45 (1)
White	1					1
Young	24	2 (1)	1	7	2	36 (1)

Goalscorers

PLAYER	LEAGUE	FA CUP	LC	ECWC	OTHER	TOTAL
Lee	14		1	4	1	20
Bell	13	4		2		19
Doyle	5			1		6
Summerbee	4					4
Book	2					2
Booth	1			1		2
Hill	2					2
Mellor	1			1		2
Young	1			1		2
Bowyer		1				1
Carter	1					1
Oakes	1					1
Heslop				1		1
Opps' o.gs.	2					2

Fact File

After a victory over Crystal Palace in January, City would win only one more league game all season as boardroom battles raged in the background.

Final Division 1 Table

		P	W	D	L	F	A	Pts
1	ARSENAL	42	29	7	6	71	29	65
2	LEEDS U	42	27	10	5	72	30	64
3	TOTTENHAM H	42	19	14	9	54	33	52
4	WOLVERHAMPTON W	42	22	8	12	64	54	52
5	LIVERPOOL	42	17	17	8	42	24	51
6	CHELSEA	42	18	15	9	52	42	51
7	SOUTHAMPTON	42	17	12	13	56	44	46
8	MANCHESTER U	42	16	11	15	65	66	43
9	DERBY CO	42	16	10	16	56	54	42
10	COVENTRY C	42	16	10	16	37	38	42
11	MANCHESTER CITY	42	12	17	13	47	42	41
12	NEWCASTLE U	42	14	13	15	44	46	41
13	STOKE C	42	12	13	17	44	48	37
14	EVERTON	42	12	13	17	54	60	37
15	HUDDERSFIELD T	42	11	14	17	40	49	36
16	NOTTINGHAM F	42	14	8	20	42	61	36
17	WBA	42	10	15	17	58	75	35
18	CRYSTAL PALACE	42	12	11	19	39	57	35
19	IPSWICH T	42	12	10	20	42	48	34
20	WEST HAM U	42	10	14	18	47	60	34
21	BURNLEY	42	7	13	22	29	63	27
22	BLACKPOOL	42	4	15	23	34	66	23

Season 1971-72

Football League Division 1

DATE	OPPONENTS	SCORE	GOALSCORERS	ATTENDANCE
Aug 14	LEEDS UNITED	L 0-1		38,566
Aug 18	CRYSTAL PALACE	W 4-0	Lee 2, Davies, Booth	27,103
Aug 21	Chelsea	D 2-2	Lee 2	38,425
Aug 24	Wolves	L 1-2	Lee	26,663
Aug 28	TOTTENHAM HOTSPUR	W 4-0	Bell, Summerbee, Davies, Lee	36,483
Sep 1	LIVERPOOL	W 1-0	Mellor	45,144
Sep 4	Leicester City	D 0-0		25,238
Sep 11	NEWCASTLE UNITED	W 2-1	Bell, Lee	32,710
Sep 18	Nottingham Forest	D 2-2	Davies, Lee	21,468
Sep 25	SOUTHAMPTON	W 3-0	Bell, Davies, Lee	27,897
Oct 2	West Bromwich Albion	W 2-0	Lee, Connor	25,834
Oct 9	EVERTON	W 1-0	Lee	33,538
Oct 16	Leeds United	L 0-3		36,004
Oct 23	SHEFFIELD UNITED	W 2-1	Doyle, Lee	41,688
Oct 30	Huddersfield Town	D 1-1	Carter	20,153
Nov 6	MANCHESTER UNITED	D 3-3	Summerbee, Bell, Lee	63,326
Nov 13	Arsenal	W 2-1	Mellor, Bell	47,443
Nov 20	West Ham United	W 2-0	Davies, Lee	33,694
Nov 27	COVENTRY CITY	W 4-0	Bell 2, Lee 2	31,003
Dec 4	Derby County	L 1-3	Lee	35,354
Dec 11	IPSWICH TOWN	W 4-0	Bell, Davies, Lee, Mellor	26,900
Dec 18	LEICESTER CITY	D 1-1	Lee	29,524
Dec 27	Stoke City	W 3-1	Book, Lee, Towers	43,007
Jan 1	NOTTINGHAM FOREST	D 2-2	Davies, Lee	38,777
Jan 8	Tottenham Hotspur	D 1-1	Davies	36,470
Jan 22	Crystal Palace	W 2-1	Lee, o.g.	31,480
Jan 29	WOLVES	W 5-2	Lee 3, Booth, Towers	37,639
Feb 12	Sheffield United	D 3-3	Lee 2, Bell	38,184
Feb 19	HUDDERSFIELD TOWN	W 1-0	Booth	36,421
Feb 26	Liverpool	L 0-3		50,074
Mar 1	WEST BROMWICH ALBION	W 2-1	Bell 2	25,677
Mar 4	ARSENAL	W 2-0	Lee 2	44,213
Mar 11	Everton	W 2-1	Hill, o.g.	44,646
Mar 18	CHELSEA	W 1-0	Booth	53,322
Mar 25	Newcastle United	D 0-0		37,460
Apr 1	STOKE CITY	L 1-2	Lee	49,392
Apr 3	Southampton	L 0-2		27,374
Apr 8	WEST HAM UNITED	W 3-1	Marsh 2, Bell	38,491
Apr 12	Manchester United	W 3-1	Lee 2, Marsh	56,362
Apr 15	Coventry City	D 1-1	Towers	34,225
Apr 18	Ipswich Town	L 1-2	Summerbee	24,365
Apr 22	DERBY COUNTY	W 2-0	Lee, Marsh	55,026

FA Cup

Jan 15	MIDDLESBROUGH	(Rd 3) D 1-1	Lee	42,620
Jan 18	Middlesbrough	(R) L 0-1		37,917

League Cup

Sep 8	WOLVES	(Rd 2) W 4-3	Bell 2, Lee, Davies	29,156
Oct 5	Bolton Wanderers	(Rd 3) L 0-3		42,039

League & Cup Appearances (substitute)

PLAYER	LEAGUE	CUP COMPETITION		TOTAL
		FA CUP	LC	
Bell	33	2	1	36
Book	40	2	2	44
Booth	40	2	2	44
Carter	0 (1)			0 (1)
Connor	8			8
Corrigan	35	2	2	39
Davies	40	2	2	44
Donachie	35 (2)	2	2	39 (2)
Doyle	41	2	2	45
Healey	7			7
Henson	0 (1)			0 (1)
Heslop	7		1	8
Hill	4 (2)		1	5 (2)
Jeffries	9 (3)		1 (1)	10 (4)
Johnson	0 (1)			0 (1)
Lee	42	2	2	46
Marsh	7 (1)			7 (1)
Mellor	21 (1)	1		22 (1)
Oakes	31 (1)	2		33 (1)
Summerbee	40	2	2	44
Towers	19 (2)	2	1	22 (2)
Young	3 (2)			3 (2)

Goalscorers

PLAYER	LEAGUE	CUP COMPETITION		TOTAL
		FA CUP	LC	
Lee	33	1	1	35
Bell	12		2	14
Davies	8		1	9
Booth	4			4
Marsh	4			4
Mellor	3			3
Summerbee	3			3
Towers	3			3
Book	1			1
Carter	1			1
Connor	1			1
Doyle	1			1
Hill	1			1
Opps' o.gs.	2			2

Fact File

Francis Lee's 35 goals included a record-breaking 13 League penalties.

MANAGER: Joe Mercer OBE/Malcolm Allison

CAPTAIN: Tony Book

TOP SCORER: Francis Lee

BIGGEST WIN: August 18, 1971 4-0 v Crystal Palace, Division 1; August 28, 1971 4-0 v Tottenham Hotspur, Division 1; November 27, 1971 4-0 v Coventry City, Division 1; December 11, 1972 4-0 v Ipswich Town, Division 1

HIGHEST ATTENDANCE: November 6, 1971 63,326 v Manchester United, drew 3-3, Division 1

MAJOR TRANSFERS IN: Wyn Davies from Newcastle United, Rodney Marsh from Queens Park Rangers

Final Division 1 Table

		P	W	D	L	F	A	PTS
1	DERBY CO	42	24	10	8	69	33	58
2	LEEDS U	42	24	9	9	73	31	57
3	LIVERPOOL	42	24	9	9	64	30	57
4	MANCHESTER CITY	42	23	11	8	77	45	57
5	ARSENAL	42	22	8	12	58	40	52
6	TOTTENHAM H	42	19	13	10	63	42	51
7	CHELSEA	42	18	12	12	58	49	48
8	MANCHESTER U	42	19	10	13	69	61	48
9	WOLVERHAMPTON W	42	18	11	13	65	57	47
10	SHEFFIELD U	42	17	12	13	61	60	46
11	NEWCASTLE U	42	15	11	16	49	52	41
12	LEICESTER C	42	13	13	16	41	46	39
13	IPSWICH T	42	11	16	15	39	53	38
14	WEST HAM U	42	12	12	18	47	51	36
15	EVERTON	42	9	18	15	37	48	36
16	WBA	42	12	11	19	42	54	35
17	STOKE C	42	10	15	17	39	56	35
18	COVENTRY C	42	9	15	18	44	67	33
19	SOUTHAMPTON	42	12	7	23	52	80	31
20	CRYSTAL PALACE	42	8	13	21	39	65	29
21	NOTTINGHAM F	42	8	9	25	47	81	25
22	HUDDERSFIELD T	42	6	13	23	27	59	25

Season 1972-73

Football League Division 1

DATE	OPPONENTS	SCORE	GOALSCORERS	ATTENDANCE
Aug 12	Liverpool	L 0-2		55,383
Aug 16	EVERTON	L 0-1		38,676
Aug 19	NORWICH CITY	W 3-0	Lee 2, Bell	31,171
Aug 23	Derby County	L 0-1		31,173
Aug 26	Chelsea	L 1-2	Mellor	30,845
Aug 29	Crystal Palace	L 0-1		24,731
Sep 2	LEICESTER CITY	W 1-0	Marsh	27,233
Sep 9	Birmingham City	L 1-4	Towers	32,983
Sep 16	TOTTENHAM HOTSPUR	W 2-1	Marsh 2	31,755
Sep 23	Stoke City	L 1-5	Lee	26,448
Sep 30	WEST BROMWICH ALBION	W 2-1	Booth, Lee	27,332
Oct 7	WOLVES	D 1-1	Marsh	31,301
Oct 14	Coventry City	L 2-3	Summerbee, Marsh	24,560
Oct 21	WEST HAM UNITED	W 4-3	Marsh 2, Summerbee, Towers	30,890
Oct 28	Arsenal	D 0-0		45,536
Nov 4	DERBY COUNTY	W 4-0	Bell, Marsh, Carrodus, o.g.	35,829
Nov 11	Everton	W 3-2	Lee 2, o.g.	32,924
Nov 18	MANCHESTER UNITED	W 3-0	Bell 2, o.g.	52,050
Nov 25	Leeds United	L 0-3		39,879
Dec 2	IPSWICH TOWN	D 1-1	Lee	27,839
Dec 9	Sheffield United	D 1-1	Bell	19,208
Dec 16	SOUTHAMPTON	W 2-1	Marsh 2	24,825
Dec 23	Newcastle United	L 1-2	Mellor	24,249
Dec 26	STOKE CITY	D 1-1	Mellor	36,334
Dec 30	Norwich City	D 1-1	Towers	24,203
Jan 20	Leicester City	D 1-1	Bell	18,761
Jan 27	BIRMINGHAM CITY	W 1-0	Donachie	31,882
Feb 10	Tottenham Hotspur	W 3-2	Lee 2, Marsh	30,944
Feb 17	LIVERPOOL	D 1-1	Booth	41,709
Mar 3	Wolves	L 1-5	Marsh	25,047
Mar 6	Southampton	D 1-1	Lee	16,188
Mar 10	COVENTRY CITY	L 1-2	Booth	30,448
Mar 17	West Ham United	L 1-2	Doyle	30,156
Mar 24	ARSENAL	L 1-2	Booth	32,031
Mar 27	CHELSEA	L 0-1		23,974
Mar 31	LEEDS UNITED	W 1-0	Towers	35,772
Apr 7	Ipswich Town	D 1-1	Oakes	19,109
Apr 14	SHEFFIELD UNITED	W 3-1	Bell, Marsh, Lee	26,811
Apr 18	NEWCASTLE UNITED	W 2-0	Booth, Marsh	25,156
Apr 21	Manchester United	D 0-0		61,500
Apr 25	West Bromwich Albion	W 2-1	Lee, Towers	21,193
Apr 28	CRYSTAL PALACE	L 2-3	Lee 2	34,784

FA Cup

Jan 13	STOKE CITY	(Rd 3) W 3-2	Summerbee, Bell, Marsh	38,648
Feb 3	Liverpool	(Rd 4) D 0-0		56,296
Feb 7	LIVERPOOL	(R) W 2-0	Bell, Booth	49,572
Feb 24	SUNDERLAND	(Rd 5) D 2-2	Towers, o.g.	54,478
Feb 27	Sunderland	(R) L 1-3	Lee	51,782

League Cup

Sep 6	ROCHDALE	(Rd 2) W 4-0	Marsh 2, Bell, Lee	17,222
Oct 3	Bury	(Rd 3) L 0-2		16,614

UEFA Cup

Sep 13	VALENCIA	(Rd 1 FL) D 2-2	Mellor, Marsh	21,698
Sep 27	Valencia	(Rd 1 SL) L 1-2	Marsh	35,000

FA Charity Shield

Aug 5	Aston Villa	W 1-0	Lee	34,859

MANAGER: Malcolm Allison/Johnny Hart

CAPTAIN: Tony Book

TOP SCORER: Rodney Marsh

BIGGEST WIN: November 4, 1972 4-0 v Derby County, Division 1; September 6, 1972 4-0 v Rochdale, League Cup Round 2

HIGHEST ATTENDANCE: April 21, 1972 61,500 v Manchester United, drew 0-0, Division 1

MAJOR TRANSFERS OUT: Wyn Davies to Manchester United, Ian Mellor to Norwich

League & Cup Appearances (substitute)

PLAYER	LEAGUE	CUP COMPETITION				TOTAL
		FA CUP	LC	UEFA	OTHER	
Barrett	14 (1)		1	1		16 (1)
Bell	39	5	2	2	1	49
Book	29 (1)	5	1	2	1	38 (1)
Booth	34	5	2	2	1	44
Brennan	1 (1)					1 (1)
Carrodus	6 (4)					6 (4)
Corrigan	30	5	1	1	1	38
Davies	5		1	1		7
Donachie	40	5	1	2	1	49
Doyle	38 (2)	5	2	1	1	47 (2)
Healey	12		1	1	(1)	14 (1)
Hill	4 (2)					4 (2)
Jeffries	33 (1)	5	1	1		40 (1)
Lee	35	5	2	2	1	45
Marsh	37	5	2	2	1	47
Mellor	10 (2)	2 (1)	1		(1)	13 (4)
Oakes	13 (1)		2			15 (1)
Pardoe	6					6
Summerbee	38	4	1	2	1	46
Towers	35	4	2	2	1	44
Whelan	3					3

Goalscorers

PLAYER	LEAGUE	CUP COMPETITION				TOTAL
		FA CUP	LC	UEFA	OTHER	
Marsh	14	1	2	2		19
Lee	14	1	1		1	17
Bell	7	2	1			10
Booth	5	1				6
Towers	5	1				6
Mellor	3			1		4
Summerbee	2	1				3
Carrodus	1					1
Donachie	1					1
Doyle	1					1
Oakes	1					1
Opps' o.gs.	3	1				4

Fact File

Wyn Davies played for Manchester United in their 3-0 defeat by City in November, just three days after signing from the Blues.

Final Division 1 Table

		P	W	D	L	F	A	Pts
1	LIVERPOOL	42	25	10	7	72	42	60
2	ARSENAL	42	23	11	8	57	43	57
3	LEEDS U	42	21	11	10	71	45	53
4	IPSWICH T	42	17	14	11	55	45	48
5	WOLVERHAMPTON W	42	18	11	13	66	54	47
6	WEST HAM U	42	17	12	13	67	53	46
7	DERBY CO	42	19	8	15	56	54	46
8	TOTTENHAM H	42	16	13	13	58	48	45
9	NEWCASTLE U	42	16	13	13	60	51	45
10	BIRMINGHAM C	42	15	12	15	53	54	42
11	MANCHESTER CITY	42	15	11	16	57	60	41
12	CHELSEA	42	13	14	15	49	51	40
13	SOUTHAMPTON	42	11	18	13	47	52	40
14	SHEFFIELD U	42	15	10	17	51	59	40
15	STOKE C	42	14	10	18	61	56	38
16	LEICESTER C	42	10	17	15	40	46	37
17	EVERTON	42	13	11	18	41	49	37
18	MANCHESTER U	42	12	13	17	44	60	37
19	COVENTRY C	42	13	9	20	40	55	35
20	NORWICH C	42	11	10	21	36	63	32
21	CRYSTAL PALACE	42	9	12	21	41	58	30
22	WBA	42	9	10	23	38	62	28

Season 1973-74

Football League Division 1

DATE	OPPONENTS	SCORE	GOALSCORERS	ATTENDANCE
Aug 25	BIRMINGHAM CITY	W 3-1	Law 2, Bell	34,178
Aug 29	Derby County	L 0-1		31,295
Sep 1	Stoke City	D 1-1	Law	22,434
Sep 5	COVENTRY CITY	W 1-0	Marsh	30,931
Sep 8	NORWICH CITY	W 2-1	Bell, Lee	31,209
Sep 11	Coventry City	L 1-2	Marsh	27,394
Sep 15	Leicester City	D 1-1	Bell	28,466
Sep 22	CHELSEA	W 3-2	Lee 2, Towers	32,118
Sep 29	Burnley	L 0-3		24,492
Oct 6	SOUTHAMPTON	D 1-1	Marsh	27,727
Oct 13	Newcastle United	L 0-1		35,225
Oct 20	Sheffield United	W 2-1	Law, o.g.	25,234
Oct 27	LEEDS UNITED	L 0-1		45,346
Nov 3	Wolves	D 0-0		21,499
Nov 10	ARSENAL	L 1-2	Lee	31,041
Nov 17	QUEENS PARK RANGERS	W 1-0	Lee	30,486
Nov 24	Ipswich Town	L 1-2	Leman	19,143
Dec 8	West Ham United	L 1-2	Lee	20,790
Dec 15	Tottenham Hotspur	W 2-0	Bell, Booth	17,066
Dec 22	BURNLEY	W 2-0	Doyle, Bell	28,114
Dec 26	Everton	L 0-2		36,007
Dec 29	Norwich City	D 1-1	Law	24,303
Jan 1	STOKE CITY	D 0-0		35,009
Jan 12	LEICESTER CITY	W 2-0	Marsh, Law	27,488
Jan 19	Birmingham City	D 1-1	Law	31,401
Feb 2	TOTTENHAM HOTSPUR	D 0-0		24,652
Feb 6	DERBY COUNTY	W 1-0	Bell	22,845
Feb 9	Chelsea	L 0-1		20,206
Feb 23	Southampton	W 2-0	Law, Marsh	19,234
Mar 9	Leeds United	L 0-1		36,578
Mar 13	MANCHESTER UNITED	D 0-0		51,331
Mar 16	SHEFFIELD UNITED	L 0-1		26,220
Mar 23	Arsenal	L 0-2		25,319
Mar 27	NEWCASTLE UNITED	W 2-1	Lee 2	21,590
Mar 30	WOLVES	D 1-1	Lee	25,236
Apr 2	EVERTON	D 1-1	Tueart	22,918
Apr 6	IPSWICH TOWN	L 1-3	Summerbee	22,269
Apr 9	Queens Park Rangers	L 0-3		20,461
Apr 12	LIVERPOOL	D 1-1	Lee	43,248
Apr 16	Liverpool	L 0-4		50,781
Apr 20	WEST HAM UNITED	W 2-1	Booth, Bell	29,700
Apr 27	Manchester United	W 1-0	Law	56,966

FA Cup

Jan 5	Oxford United	(Rd 3) W 5-2	Law 2, Summerbee 2 Marsh	13,435
Jan 27	Notts County	(Rd 4) L 1-4	Carrodus	14,472

League Cup

Oct 2	Walsall	(Rd 2) D 0-0		12,943
Oct 22	WALSALL	(R) D 0-0		19,428
Oct 30	WALSALL	(2nd R) W 4-0*	Lee 3, Bell	13,646
Nov 6	Carlisle United	(Rd 3) W 1-0	Lee	14,472
Nov 21	York City	(Rd 4) D 0-0		15,360
Dec 5	YORK CITY	(R) W 4-1	Marsh 3, Lee	17,972
Dec 19	Coventry City	(Rd 5) D 2-2	Booth, Leman	12,661
Jan 16	COVENTRY CITY	(R) W 4-2	Lee 2, Summerbee, Law	25,409
Jan 23	Plymouth Argyle	(SF FL) D 1-1	Booth	30,390
Jan 30	PLYMOUTH ARGYLE	(SF SL) W 2-0	Bell, Lee	40,117
Mar 3	WOLVES	(F) L 1-2†	Bell	100,000

*Played at Old Trafford. †Played at Wembley.

FA Charity Shield

Aug 18	BURNLEY	L 0-1	34,859

MANAGER: Johnny Hart/Ron Saunders

CAPTAIN: Rodney Marsh

TOP SCORER: Francis Lee

BIGGEST WIN: January 5, 1974 5-2 v Oxford United, FA Cup Round 3

HIGHEST ATTENDANCE: April 27, 1974 56,966 v Manchester United, won 1-0, Division 1

MAJOR TRANSFERS IN: Denis Law from Manchester United, Dennis Tueart from Sunderland, Keith McRae from Motherwell

League & Cup Appearances (substitute)

PLAYER	LEAGUE	FA CUP	LC	OTHER	TOTAL
Barrett	16 (1)	2	4		22 (1)
Bell	41	2	11	1	55
Book	4		1 (1)	1	6 (1)
Booth	40	2	11	1	54
Carrodus	16 (3)	1	3		20 (3)
Corrigan	15	1		1	17
Daniels	2 (1)				2 (1)
Donachie	42	2	11	1	56
Doyle	39	2	11	1	53
Healey	2		1		3
Henson	0 (1)			1	1 (1)
Horswill	7 (1)				7 (1)
Law	22 (2)	1	4		27 (2)
Lee	29 (1)	2	11		42 (1)
Leman	9 (4)	(1)	2 (2)		11 (7)
Lester	1				1
MacRae	25	1	10		36
Marsh	23 (1)	2	8	1	34 (1)
Oakes	28		5	1	34
Pardoe	31 (1)		7		38 (1)
Summerbee	39	2	11	1	53
Towers	23 (1)	2	10		35 (1)
Tueart	8			1	9
Whelan	0 (3)				0 (3)

Goalscorers

PLAYER	LEAGUE	FA CUP	LC	OTHER	TOTAL
Lee	10		8		18
Law	9	2	1		12
Bell	7		3		10
Marsh	5	1	3		9
Booth	2		2		4
Summerbee	1	2	1		4
Leman	1		1		2
Carrodus		1			1
Doyle	1				1
Towers	1				1
Tueart	1				1
Opps' o.gs.	1				1

Fact File

Denis Law is back in blue, scoring two on his return in the season's opening game and finished the campaign with the infamous back-heel that 'relegated' United to Division Two.

Final Division 1 Table

		P	W	D	L	F	A	Pts
1	LEEDS U	42	24	14	4	66	31	62
2	LIVERPOOL	42	22	13	7	52	31	57
3	DERBY CO	42	17	14	11	52	42	48
4	IPSWICH T	42	18	11	13	67	58	47
5	STOKE C	42	15	16	11	54	42	46
6	BURNLEY	42	16	14	12	56	53	46
7	EVERTON	42	16	12	14	50	48	44
8	QPR	42	13	17	12	56	52	43
9	LEICESTER C	42	13	16	13	51	41	42
10	ARSENAL	42	14	14	14	49	51	42
11	TOTTENHAM H	42	14	14	14	45	50	42
12	WOLVERHAMPTON W	42	13	15	14	49	49	41
13	SHEFFIELD U	42	14	12	16	44	49	40
14	MANCHESTER CITY	42	14	12	16	39	46	40
15	NEWCASTLE U	42	13	12	17	49	48	38
16	COVENTRY C	42	14	10	18	43	54	38
17	CHELSEA	42	12	13	17	56	60	37
18	WEST HAM U	42	11	15	16	55	60	37
19	BIRMINGHAM C	42	12	13	17	52	64	37
20	SOUTHAMPTON	42	11	14	17	47	68	36
21	MANCHESTER U	42	10	12	20	38	48	32
22	NORWICH C	42	7	15	20	37	62	29

Season 1974-75

Football League Division 1

DATE	OPPONENTS	SCORE	GOALSCORERS	ATTENDANCE
Aug 17	WEST HAM UNITED	W 4-0	Marsh 2, Tueart, Doyle	30,240
Aug 21	TOTTENHAM HOTSPUR	W 1-0	Hartford	31,549
Aug 24	Arsenal	L 0-4		27,143
Aug 28	Tottenham Hotspur	W 2-1	Bell, Booth	20,079
Aug 31	LEEDS UNITED	W 2-1	Summerbee, Bell	37,919
Sep 7	Coventry City	D 2-2	Oakes, Marsh	15,440
Sep 14	LIVERPOOL	W 2-0	Marsh, Tueart	45,194
Sep 21	Middlesbrough	L 0-3		30,256
Sep 24	Carlisle United	D 0-0		17,900
Sep 28	QUEENS PARK RANGERS	W 1-0	Marsh	30,674
Oct 5	CHELSEA	D 1-1	Bell	32,412
Oct 12	Burnley	L 1-2	Tueart	23,406
Oct 16	ARSENAL	W 2-1	Tueart 2	26,658
Oct 19	LUTON TOWN	W 1-0	Summerbee	30,649
Oct 26	Ipswich Town	D 1-1	Bell	25,171
Nov 2	Everton	L 0-2		43,905
Nov 9	STOKE CITY	W 1-0	Marsh	30,966
Nov 16	Birmingham City	L 0-4		35,143
Nov 23	LEICESTER CITY	W 4-1	Daniels 2, Bell, Tueart	31,628
Nov 30	Newcastle United	L 1-2	Marsh	37,600
Dec 7	SHEFFIELD UNITED	W 3-2	Hammond, Marsh, Bell	29,675
Dec 14	West Ham United	D 0-0		33,908
Dec 21	WOLVES	D 0-0		29,326
Dec 26	Liverpool	L 1-4	Bell	46,062
Dec 28	DERBY COUNTY	L 1-2	Bell	40,180
Jan 11	Sheffield United	D 1-1	Booth	25,190
Jan 18	NEWCASTLE UNITED	W 5-1	Tueart 3, Bell, Hammond	32,021
Feb 1	Stoke City	L 0-4		32,007
Feb 8	EVERTON	W 2-1	Bell, Tueart	44,718
Feb 22	BIRMINGHAM CITY	W 3-1	Bell, Royle, Tueart	33,240
Mar 1	Leeds United	D 2-2	Oakes, Donachie	47,489
Mar 8	Leicester City	L 0-1		23,059
Mar 15	Queens Park Rangers	L 0-2		22,102
Mar 19	CARLISLE UNITED	L 1-2	Barnes	24,049
Mar 22	COVENTRY CITY	W 1-0	Tueart	25,903
Mar 28	MIDDLESBROUGH	W 2-1	Bell, Marsh	37,772
Mar 29	Wolves	L 0-1		21,716
Apr 1	Derby County	L 1-2	Bell	32,966
Apr 12	Chelsea	W 1-0	Hartford	26,249
Apr 19	BURNLEY	W 2-0	Bell, Tueart	30,723
Apr 23	IPSWICH TOWN	D 1-1	Bell	29,391
Apr 26	Luton Town	D 1-1	Tueart	20,768

FA Cup

Jan 4	Newcastle United	(Rd 3) L 0-2*		37,625

*Match played at Maine Road because of an FA ruling into crowd trouble at St James' Park.

League Cup

Sep 10	SCUNTHORPE UNITED	(Rd 2) D 6-0	Bell 3, Barrett, Marsh, Doyle	14,790
Oct 9	Manchester United	(Rd 3) W 0-1		55,225

League & Cup Appearances (substitute)

PLAYER	LEAGUE	CUP COMPETITION		TOTAL
		FA CUP	LC	
Barnes	3	1		4
Barrett	17 (1)		1	18 (1)
Bell	42	1	2	45
Booth	18			18
Clarke	13		2	15
Corrigan	15	1		16
Daniels	7 (3)			7 (1)
Donachie	40	1	1	42
Doyle	42	1	2	45
Hammond	26	1	1	28
Hartford	29 (1)	1	1	31 (1)
Henson	12 (2)	0 (1)	1	13 (3)
Horswill	4 (2)	1		5 (2)
Keegan	3 (2)			3 (2)
Leman	0 (1)			0 (1)
MacRae	27		2	29
Marsh	37	1	2	40
Oakes	40	1	2	43
Pardoe	6		1	7
Royle	16			16
Summerbee	26 (1)		2	28 (1)
Tueart	39	1	2	42

Goalscorers

PLAYER	LEAGUE	CUP COMPETITION		TOTAL
		FA CUP	LC	
Bell	15		3	18
Tueart	14			14
Marsh	9		1	10
Booth	2			2
Daniels	2			2
Doyle	1		1	2
Hammond	2			2
Hartford	2			2
Oakes	2			2
Summerbee	2			2
Barnes	1			1
Barrett	1		1	1
Donachie	1			1
Royle	1			1

Fact File

Peter Barnes made his full debut against Burnley in October.

MANAGER: Tony Book

CAPTAIN: Rodney Marsh

TOP SCORER: Colin Bell

BIGGEST WIN: September 10, 1974 6-0 v Scunthorpe United, FA Cup Round 2

HIGHEST ATTENDANCE: October 9, 1974 55,225 v Manchester United, lost 0-1, FA Cup Round 3

MAJOR TRANSFERS IN: Asa Hartford from West Bromwich Albion, Joe Royle from Everton

MAJOR TRANSFERS OUT: Denis Law (retired), Francis Lee to Derby County

Final Division 1 Table

		P	W	D	L	F	A	Pts
1	DERBY CO	42	21	11	10	67	49	53
2	LIVERPOOL	42	20	11	11	60	39	51
3	IPSWICH T	42	23	5	14	66	44	51
4	EVERTON	42	16	18	8	56	42	50
5	STOKE C	42	17	15	10	64	48	49
6	SHEFFIELD U	42	18	13	11	58	51	49
7	MIDDLESBROUGH	42	18	12	12	54	40	48
8	MANCHESTER CITY	42	18	10	14	54	54	46
9	LEEDS U	42	16	13	13	57	49	45
10	BURNLEY	42	17	11	14	68	67	45
11	QPR	42	16	10	16	54	54	42
12	WOLVERHAMPTON W	42	14	11	17	57	54	39
13	WEST HAM U	42	13	13	16	58	59	39
14	COVENTRY C	42	12	15	15	51	62	39
15	NEWCASTLE U	42	15	9	18	59	72	39
16	ARSENAL	42	13	11	18	47	49	37
17	BIRMINGHAM C	42	14	9	19	53	61	37
18	LEICESTER C	42	12	12	18	46	60	36
19	TOTTENHAM H	42	13	8	21	52	63	34
20	LUTON T	42	11	11	20	47	65	33
21	CHELSEA	42	9	15	18	42	72	33
22	CARLISLE U	42	12	5	25	43	59	29

Season 1975-76

Football League Division 1

DATE	OPPONENTS	SCORE	GOALSCORERS	ATTENDANCE
Aug 16	NORWICH CITY	W 3-0	Tueart 2, Bell	29,103
Aug 20	LEICESTER CITY	D 1-1	o.g.	28,557
Aug 23	Coventry City	L 0-2		21,097
Aug 27	Aston Villa	L 0-1		35,212
Aug 30	NEWCASTLE UNITED	W 4-0	Royle 2, Tueart 2	31,875
Sep 6	West Ham United	L 0-1		29,752
Sep 13	MIDDLESBROUGH	W 4-0	Marsh 2, Royle, Tueart	30,353
Sep 20	Derby County	L 0-1		23,250
Sep 24	STOKE CITY	W 1-0	Marsh	28,915
Sep 27	MANCHESTER UNITED	D 2-2	Royle, o.g.	46,931
Oct 4	Arsenal	W 3-2	Hartford, Royle, Marsh	24,928
Oct 11	BURNLEY	D 0-0		35,003
Oct 18	Tottenham Hotspur	D 2-2	Bell, Watson	30,502
Oct 25	IPSWICH TOWN	D 1-1	Bell	30,644
Nov 1	Sheffield United	D 2-2	Barnes, Booth	24,670
Nov 8	BIRMINGHAM CITY	W 2-0	Bell 2	28,329
Nov 15	Everton	D 1-1	Booth	32,077
Nov 22	TOTTENHAM HOTSPUR	W 2-1	Oakes, Tueart	31,456
Nov 29	Wolves	W 4-0	Hartford 2, Barnes, Tueart	20,867
Dec 6	QUEENS PARK RANGERS	D 0-0		36,066
Dec 13	COVENTRY CITY	W 4-2	Oakes, Barnes, Booth, Tueart	27,256
Dec 20	Norwich City	D 2-2	Royle, Tueart	19,692
Dec 26	LEEDS UNITED	L 0-1		48,077
Dec 27	Liverpool	L 0-1		53,386
Jan 10	Middlesbrough	L 0-1		22,358
Jan 17	WEST HAM UNITED	W 3-0	Royle 2, Oakes	32,147
Jan 31	Leicester City	L 0-1		21,723
Feb 7	ASTON VILLA	W 2-1	Hartford, Booth	32,331
Feb 14	Birmingham City	L 1-2	Hartford	22,445
Feb 21	EVERTON	W 3-0	Hartford, Royle, Tueart	33,148
Mar 6	SHEFFIELD UNITED	W 4-0	Hartford 2, Royle, Tueart	33,510
Mar 13	Burnley	D 0-0		24,278
Mar 20	WOLVES	W 3-2	Keegan, Doyle, Tueart	32,761
Mar 27	Queens Park Rangers	L 0-1		29,883
Apr 2	Stoke City	D 0-0		18,798
Apr 7	Ipswich Town	L 1-2	Keegan	21,290
Apr 10	DERBY COUNTY	W 4-3	Tueart 2, Royle, Power	42,061
Apr 14	Newcastle United	L 1-2	Royle	21,095
Apr 17	Leeds United	L 1-2	Bell	33,154
Apr 19	LIVERPOOL	L 0-3		50,439
Apr 24	ARSENAL	W 3-1	Hartford, Booth 2	31,003
May 4	Manchester United	L 0-2		59,528

FA Cup

Jan 3	HARTLEPOOL UNITED	(Rd 3) W 6-0	Tueart 2, Booth 2, Hartford, Oakes	26,863
Jan 28	Stoke City	(Rd 4) L 0-1		38,072

League Cup

Sep 10	Norwich City	(Rd 2) D 1-1	Watson	18,332
Sep 17	NORWICH CITY	(R) D 2-2	Royle, Tueart	29,667
Sep 24	Norwich City	(Rd 2) W 6-1	Tueart 3, Doyle, Royle, o.g.	6,238
Oct 8	NOTTINGHAM FOREST	(Rd 3) W 2-1	Bell, Royle	26,536
Nov 12	MANCHESTER UNITED	(Rd 4) W 4-0	Tueart 2, Royle, Hartford	50,182
Dec 3	MANSFIELD TOWN	(Rd 5) W 4-2	Hartford, Royle, Tueart, Oakes	30,022
Jan 13	Middlesbrough	(SF FL) L 0-1		35,000
Jan 21	MIDDLESBROUGH	(SF SL) W 4-0	Keegan, Oakes, Barnes, Royle	44,426
Feb 28	Newcastle United	(F) W 2-1	Barnes, Tueart	100,000

MANAGER: Tony Book

CAPTAIN: Mike Doyle

TOP SCORER: Dennis Tueart

BIGGEST WIN: January 3, 1975 6-0 v Hartlepool United, FA Cup Round 3

HIGHEST ATTENDANCE: February 20, 1975 100,000 v Newcastle United, won 2-1, League Cup final

MAJOR TRANSFERS IN: Dave Watson from Sunderland

League & Cup Appearances (substitute)

PLAYER	LEAGUE	CUP COMPETITION		TOTAL
		FA CUP	LC	
Barnes	27 (1)	1	6 (1)	34 (2)
Barrett	3	1	2	6
Bell	20		5	25
Booth	25 (1)	2	3 (1)	30 (2)
Clements	26 (1)	1	7	34 (1)
Corrigan	41	2	9	52
Docherty	1			1
Donachie	40	2	9	51
Doyle	41	2	9	52
Hammond	7 (1)			7 (1)
Hartford	39	2	9	50
Keegan	17 (1)	0 (1)	2	19 (2)
Leman	1 (2)			1 (2)
MacRae	1			1
Marsh	12		4	16
Oakes	38 (1)	2	9	49 (1)
Owen	4			4
Power	14 (5)	2	2 (1)	18 (6)
Royle	37	2	9	48
Telford	0 (1)			0 (1)
Tueart	37 (1)	2	7	46 (1)
Watson	31	1	7	39

Goalscorers

PLAYER	LEAGUE	CUP COMPETITION		TOTAL
		FA CUP	LC	
Tueart	14	2	8	24
Royle	12		6	18
Hartford	9	1	2	12
Booth	6	2		8
Bell	6		1	7
Oakes	3	1	2	6
Barnes	3		2	5
Marsh	4			4
Keegan	2		1	3
Doyle	1		1	2
Watson	1		1	2
Power	1			1
Opps' o.gs.	2		1	3

Fact File

Colin Bell injured his knee in the 4-0 thrashing of United in the League Cup. The injury would keep him out of the team for two years.

Peter Barnes is named this season's Young Footballer of the Year.

Final Division 1 Table

		P	W	D	L	F	A	PTS
1	LIVERPOOL	42	23	14	5	66	31	60
2	QPR	42	24	11	7	67	33	59
3	MANCHESTER U	42	23	10	10	68	42	56
4	DERBY CO	42	21	11	10	75	58	53
5	LEEDS U	42	21	9	12	65	46	51
6	IPSWICH T	42	16	14	12	54	48	46
7	LEICESTER C	42	13	19	10	48	51	45
8	MANCHESTER CITY	42	16	12	15	64	46	43
9	TOTTENHAM H	42	14	15	13	63	63	43
10	NORWICH C	42	16	10	16	58	58	42
11	EVERTON	42	15	12	15	60	66	42
12	STOKE C	42	15	11	16	48	50	41
13	MIDDLESBROUGH	42	15	10	17	46	45	40
14	COVENTRY C	42	13	14	15	47	57	40
15	NEWCASTLE U	42	15	9	18	71	62	39
16	ASTON VILLA	42	11	17	14	51	59	39
17	ARSENAL	42	13	10	19	47	53	36
18	WEST HAM U	42	13	10	19	48	71	36
19	BIRMINGHAM C	42	13	7	22	57	75	33
20	WOLVERHAMPTON W	42	10	10	22	51	68	30
21	BURNLEY	42	9	10	23	43	66	28
22	SHEFFIELD U	42	6	10	26	33	82	22

Season 1976-77

Football League Division 1

DATE	OPPONENTS		SCORE	GOALSCORERS	ATTENDANCE
Aug 12	Leicester City	D	2-2	Royle, Tueart	22,612
Aug 25	ASTON VILLA	W	2-0	Tueart, Watson	41,007
Aug 28	STOKE CITY	D	0-0		39,878
Sep 4	Arsenal	D	0-0		35,132
Sep 11	BRISTOL CITY	W	2-1	Barnes, Tueart	35,891
Sep 18	Sunderland	W	2-0	Royle, Tueart	37,397
Sep 25	MANCHESTER UNITED	L	1-3	Tueart	48,861
Oct 2	WEST HAM UNITED	W	4-2	Tueart 2, Owen, Hartford	37,795
Oct 5	Everton	D	2-2	Hartford, Power	31,370
Oct 16	QUEENS PARK RANGERS	D	0-0		40,751
Oct 23	Ipswich Town	L	0-1		25,041
Oct 30	Norwich City	W	2-0	Kidd, Royle	22,861
Nov 6	NEWCASTLE UNITED	D	0-0		40,049
Nov 20	WEST BROMWICH ALBION	W	1-0	Tueart	36,656
Nov 27	Birmingham City	D	0-0		29,722
Dec 4	DERBY COUNTY	W	3-2	Kidd 2, Tueart	34,179
Dec 7	Middlesbrough	D	0-0		18,000
Dec 11	Tottenham Hotspur	D	2-2	Kidd, Power	24,608
Dec 18	COVENTRY CITY	W	2-0	Kidd, Tueart	32,227
Dec 27	Leeds United	W	2-0	Kidd 2	48,708
Dec 29	LIVERPOOL	D	1-1	Royle	50,020
Jan 22	LEICESTER CITY	W	5-0	Kidd 4, Doyle	37,609
Feb 3	Stoke City	W	2-0	Royle, Tueart	27,139
Feb 12	ARSENAL	W	1-0	Royle	45,368
Feb 16	Newcastle United	D	2-2	Kidd, Tueart	27,920
Feb 19	Bristol City	L	0-1		27,601
Mar 1	NORWICH CITY	W	2-0	Tueart 2	36,021
Mar 5	Manchester United	L	1-3	Royle	58,595
Mar 9	SUNDERLAND	W	1-0	Tueart	44,439
Mar 12	West Ham United	L	0-1		24,974
Mar 22	Queens Park Rangers	D	0-0		17,619
Apr 2	IPSWICH TOWN	W	2-1	Kidd, Watson	42,780
Apr 8	LEEDS UNITED	W	2-1	Kidd 2	47,727
Apr 9	Liverpool	L	1-2	Kidd	55,283
Apr 11	MIDDLESBROUGH	W	1-0	Hartford	37,735
Apr 16	West Bromwich Albion	W	2-0	Kidd, Tueart	24,889
Apr 19	BIRMINGHAM CITY	W	2-1	Kidd 2	36,203
Apr 30	Derby County	L	0-4		29,127
May 4	Aston Villa	D	1-1	Tueart	36,190
May 7	TOTTENHAM HOTSPUR	W	5-0	Booth, Barnes, Kidd, Tueart, Hartford	37,919
May 10	EVERTON	D	1-1	Kidd	38,004
May 14	Coventry City	W	1-0	Conway	21,429

FA Cup

Jan 8	WEST BROMWICH ALBION (Rd 3)	D	1-1	Kidd	38,195
Jan 11	West Bromwich Albion (R)	W	1-0	Royle	27,494
Jan 29	Newcastle United (Rd 4)	W	3-1	Owen, Royle, o.g.	45,300
Feb 26	Leeds United (Rd 5)	L	0-1		47,731

League Cup

Sep 1	Aston Villa (Rd 2)	L	0-3		34,585

UEFA Cup

Sep 15	JUVENTUS (Rd 2)	W	1-0	Kidd	36,955
Sep 29	Juventus	L	0-2		55,000

Fact File

The defeat at Derby at the end of April effectively lost City the championship as they completed the season just a point behind champions Liverpool.

MANAGER: Tony Book

CAPTAIN: Mike Doyle

TOP SCORER: Brian Kidd

BIGGEST WIN: January 22, 1977 5-0 v Leicester City, Division 1; January 22, 1977 5-0 v Tottenham Hotspur, Division 1

HIGHEST ATTENDANCE: March 5, 1977 58,595 v Manchester United, lost 1-3, Division 1

MAJOR TRANSFERS IN: Brian Kidd from Arsenal

MAJOR TRANSFERS OUT: Alan Oakes to Chester City

League & Cup Appearances (substitute)

PLAYER	LEAGUE	CUP COMPETITION			TOTAL
		FA CUP	LC	UEFA	
Barnes	16 (5)		1	1	18 (5)
Booth	14 (1)		0 (1)	1	15 (2)
Clements	35	4			39
Conway	11 (2)	1	1	1	14 (2)
Corrigan	42	4	1	2	49
Docherty	7		1	2	10
Donachie	42	4	1	2	49
Doyle	33	4	1	2	40
Hartford	40	4	1	2	47
Henry	0 (2)				0 (2)
Keegan	8			1	9
Kidd	39	4		2	45
Lester	0 (1)			0 (1)	0 (2)
Owen	30 (1)	3			33 (1)
Power	27 (2)	4	1	0 (1)	32 (3)
Royle	39	4	1	2	46
Tueart	38	4	1	2	45
Watson	41	4	1	2	48

Goalscorers

PLAYER	LEAGUE	CUP COMPETITION			TOTAL
		FA CUP	LC	UEFA	
Kidd	21	1		1	23
Tueart	18				18
Royle	7	2			9
Hartford	4				4
Barnes	2				2
Owen	1	1			2
Power	2				2
Watson	2				2
Booth	1				1
Conway	1				1
Doyle	1				1
Opps' o.gs.		1			1

Final Division 1 Table

		P	W	D	L	F	A	Pts
1	LIVERPOOL	42	23	11	8	62	33	57
2	MANCHESTER CITY	42	21	14	7	60	34	56
3	IPSWICH T	42	22	8	12	66	39	56
4	ASTON VILLA	42	22	7	13	76	50	51
5	NEWCASTLE U	42	18	13	11	64	49	49
6	MANCHESTER U	42	18	11	13	71	62	47
7	WBA	42	16	13	13	62	56	45
8	ARSENAL	42	16	11	15	64	59	43
9	EVERTON	42	14	14	14	62	64	42
10	LEEDS U	42	15	12	15	48	51	42
11	LEICESTER C	42	12	18	12	47	60	42
12	MIDDLESBROUGH	42	14	13	15	40	45	41
13	BIRMINGHAM C	42	13	12	17	63	61	38
14	QPR	42	13	12	17	47	52	38
15	DERBY CO	42	9	19	14	50	55	37
16	NORWICH C	42	14	9	19	47	64	37
17	WEST HAM U	42	11	14	17	46	65	36
18	BRISTOL C	42	11	13	18	38	48	35
19	COVENTRY C	42	10	15	17	48	59	35
20	SUNDERLAND	42	11	12	19	46	54	34
21	STOKE C	42	10	14	18	28	51	34
22	TOTTENHAM H	42	12	9	21	48	72	33

Season 1977-78

Football League Division 1

DATE	OPPONENTS	SCORE	GOALSCORERS	ATTENDANCE
Aug 20	LEICESTER CITY	D 0-0		45,963
Aug 24	Aston Villa	W 4-1	Tueart 3, Booth	40,121
Aug 27	West Ham United	W 1-0	Royle	25,278
Sep 3	NORWICH CITY	W 4-0	Channon 2, Hartford, Power	41,269
Sep 10	MANCHESTER UNITED	W 3-1	Kidd 2, Channon	50,856
Sep 17	Queens Park Rangers	D 1-1	Royle	24,668
Sep 24	BRISTOL CITY	W 2-0	Barnes, Owen	41,897
Oct 1	Everton	D 1-1	Hartford	43,286
Oct 4	Coventry City	L 2-4	Barnes, Tueart	19,586
Oct 8	ARSENAL	W 2-1	Barnes, Tueart	43,177
Oct 15	Nottingham Forest	L 1-2	Kidd	35,572
Oct 22	WOLVES	L 0-2		42,730
Oct 29	LIVERPOOL	W 3-1	Channon, Royle, Kidd	49,207
Nov 5	Ipswich Town	L 0-1		23,636
Nov 12	LEEDS UNITED	L 2-3	Barnes, Channon	42,651
Nov 19	West Bromwich Albion	D 0-0		27,159
Nov 26	CHELSEA	W 6-2	Tueart 3, Barnes, Channon, o.g.	34,345
Dec 3	Derby County	L 1-2	Power	26,888
Dec 10	BIRMINGHAM CITY	W 3-0	Owen, Channon, Tueart	36,671
Dec 17	Leeds United	L 0-2		37,380
Dec 26	NEWCASTLE UNITED	W 4-0	Tueart 3, Kidd	45,811
Dec 27	Middlesbrough	W 2-0	Hartford, Owen	26,879
Dec 31	ASTON VILLA	W 2-0	Kidd, Barnes	46,074
Jan 2	Leicester City	W 1-0	Owen	24,041
Jan 14	WEST HAM UNITED	W 3-2	Barnes, Booth, Kidd	43,627
Jan 21	Norwich City	W 3-1	Kidd 2, Owen	20,397
Feb 11	QUEENS PARK RANGERS	W 2-1	Channon, Bell	39,860
Feb 17	Bristol City	D 2-2	Kidd, Booth	25,834
Feb 25	EVERTON	W 1-0	Kidd	46,817
Mar 4	Arsenal	L 0-3		34,003
Mar 15	Manchester United	D 2-2	Barnes, Kidd	54,426
Mar 18	Wolves	D 1-1	Bell	20,583
Mar 25	MIDDLESBROUGH	D 2-2	Channon 2	37,944
Mar 29	Newcastle United	D 2-1	Palmer 2	20,246
Apr 1	IPSWICH TOWN	W 2-1	Channon, Palmer	34,975
Apr 11	NOTTINGHAM FOREST	D 0-0		43,428
Apr 15	WEST BROMWICH ALBION	L 1-3	Kidd	36,521
Apr 22	Birmingham City	W 4-1	Kidd 2, Owen, Power	25,294
Apr 25	COVENTRY CITY	W 3-1	Owen, Kidd, Hartford	32,412
Apr 29	DERBY COUNTY	D 1-1	Channon	39,175
May 2	Liverpool	L 0-4		44,528
May 5	Chelsea	D 0-0		18,782

FA Cup

Jan 7	Leeds United	(Rd 3) W 2-1	Barnes, Tueart	38,516
Jan 31	Nottingham Forest	(Rd 4) W 1-2	Kidd	38,509

League Cup

Aug 31	Chesterfield	(Rd 2) W 1-0	Kidd	14,282
Oct 25	Luton Town	(Rd 3) D 1-1	Barnes	16,443
Nov 1	LUTON TOWN	(R) D 0-0		28,254
Nov 9	Luton Town	(2 R) W 3-2*	Channon, Kidd, Tueart	13,043
Nov 29	Ipswich Town	(Rd 4) W 2-1	Kidd, Tueart	22,645
Jan 18	ARSENAL	(Rd 5) D 0-0		42,435
Jan 24	Arsenal	(R) L 0-1		57,548

*Played at Old Trafford.

UEFA Cup

Sep 14	WIDZEW LODZ	(Rd 1) D 2-2	Barnes, Channon	33,695
Sep 28	Widzew Lodz		D 0-0	40,000

MANAGER: Tony Book
CAPTAIN: Dave Watson
TOP SCORER: Brian Kidd
BIGGEST WIN: November 26, 1977 6-2 v Chelsea, Division 1
HIGHEST ATTENDANCE: January 24, 1977 57,548 v Arsenal, lost 0-1, League Cup final
MAJOR TRANSFERS IN: Mike Channon from Southampton
MAJOR TRANSFERS OUT: Dennis Tueart to New York Cosmos, Joe Royle to Everton

League & Cup Appearances (substitute)

PLAYER	LEAGUE	CUP COMPETITION			TOTAL
		FA CUP	LC	UEFA	
Barnes	33 (1)	2	6 (1)	2	43 (2)
Bell	16 (1)	2	2		20 (1)
Booth	39	2	6	2	49
Channon	33 (1)	(1)	5 (1)	1	39 (3)
Clements	40 (2)	2	7	1 (1)	50 (3)
Corrigan	42	2	7	2	53
Donachie	39	2	7	1	49
Doyle	13 (1)		3	1	17 (1)
Hartford	37	2	5	2	46
Henry	1				1
Keegan	0 (2)		1	1	0 (2)
Kidd	39	2	7	2	50
Owen	33	2	4	2	41
Palmer	4 (1)				4 (1)
Power	29		4	1	34
Royle	6 (1)		2	1 (1)	9 (2)
Tueart	17	2	5	1	25
Watson	41	2	6	2	51

Goalscorers

PLAYER	LEAGUE	CUP COMPETITION			TOTAL
		FA CUP	LC	UEFA	
Kidd	16	1	3		20
Tueart	12	1	2		15
Channon	12		1	1	14
Barnes	8	1	1	1	11
Owen	7				7
Hartford	4				4
Booth	3				3
Palmer	3				3
Power	3				3
Royle	3				3
Bell	2				2
Opps' o.gs.	1				1

Fact File

Colin Bell returned to the side on Boxing Day to inspire the team to eight victories in the next nine games.

Final Division 1 Table

		P	W	D	L	F	A	Pts
1	NOTTINGHAM F	42	25	14	3	69	24	64
2	LIVERPOOL	42	24	9	9	65	34	57
3	EVERTON	42	22	11	9	76	45	55
4	MANCHESTER CITY	42	20	12	10	74	51	52
5	ARSENAL	42	21	10	11	60	37	52
6	WBA	42	18	14	10	62	53	50
7	COVENTRY C	42	18	12	12	75	62	48
8	ASTON VILLA	42	18	10	14	57	42	46
9	LEEDS U	42	18	10	14	63	53	46
10	MANCHESTER U	42	16	10	16	67	63	42
11	BIRMINGHAM C	42	16	9	17	55	60	41
12	DERBY CO	42	14	13	15	54	59	41
13	NORWICH C	42	11	18	13	52	66	40
14	MIDDLESBROUGH	42	12	15	15	42	54	39
15	WOLVERHAMPTON W	42	12	12	18	51	64	36
16	CHELSEA	42	11	14	17	46	69	36
17	BRISTOL C	42	11	13	18	49	53	35
18	IPSWICH T	42	11	13	18	47	61	35
19	QPR	42	9	15	18	47	64	33
20	WEST HAM U	42	12	8	22	52	69	32
21	NEWCASTLE U	42	6	10	26	42	78	22
22	LEICESTER C	42	5	12	25	26	70	22

Season 1978-79

Football League Division 1

DATE	OPPONENTS	SCORE	GOALSCORERS	ATTENDANCE
Aug 19	Derby County	D 1-1	Kidd	26,480
Aug 22	Arsenal	D 1-1	Kidd	39,506
Aug 26	LIVERPOOL	L 1-4	Kidd	46,710
Sep 2	Norwich City	D 1-1	Channon	18,607
Sep 9	LEEDS UNITED	W 3-0	Palmer 2, Watson	40,125
Sep 16	Chelsea	W 4-1	R Futcher 3, Channon	29,980
Sep 23	TOTTENHAM HOTSPUR	W 2-0	R Futcher, Owen	43,471
Sep 30	Manchester United	L 0-1		55,317
Oct 7	Birmingham City	W 2-1	R Futcher, Kidd	18,378
Oct 14	COVENTRY CITY	W 2-0	Owen 2	36,723
Oct 21	Bolton Wanderers	D 2-2	Palmer, Owen	32,249
Oct 28	WEST BROMWICH ALBION	D 2-2	Channon, Hartford	40,521
Nov 4	Aston Villa	D 1-1	Owen	32,724
Nov 11	DERBY COUNTY	L 1-2	Owen	37,376
Nov 18	Liverpool	L 0-1		47,765
Nov 25	IPSWICH TOWN	L 1-2	Hartford	38,527
Dec 9	SOUTHAMPTON	L 1-2	Power	33,450
Dec 16	Queens Park Rangers	L 1-2	Channon	12,902
Dec 23	NOTTINGHAM FOREST	D 0-0		37,012
Dec 26	Everton	L 0-1		46,996
Dec 30	Bristol City	D 1-1	R Futcher	25,253
Jan 13	Leeds United	D 1-1	Kidd	36,303
Jan 20	CHELSEA	L 2-3	Power, R Futcher	31,876
Feb 3	Tottenham Hotspur	W 3-0	Channon, Kidd, Barnes	32,037
Feb 10	MANCHESTER UNITED	L 0-3		46,151
Feb 24	Coventry City	W 3-0	Channon 2, Kidd	20,116
Feb 27	NORWICH CITY	D 2-2	Owen 2	29,852
Mar 3	BOLTON WANDERERS	W 2-1	Owen, Channon	41,127
Mar 24	Arsenal	D 1-1	Channon	35,041
Mar 27	Wolves	D 1-1	Channon	19,998
Mar 31	Ipswich Town	L 1-2	Silkman	20,773
Apr 4	West Bromwich Albion	L 0-4		22,314
Apr 7	WOLVES	W 3-1	Channon, Silkman, Palmer	32,298
Apr 14	EVERTON	D 0-0		39,711
Apr 17	Middlesbrough	L 0-2		19,676
Apr 21	QUEENS PARK RANGERS	W 3-1	Owen 2, Silkman	30,694
Apr 24	MIDDLESBROUGH	W 1-0	Deyna	28,264
Apr 28	Southampton	L 0-1		19,764
May 1	BIRMINGHAM CITY	W 3-1	Deyna 2, Power	27,366
May 5	BRISTOL CITY	W 2-0	Deyna, Hartford	29,739
May 9	Nottingham Forest	L 1-3	o.g.	21,104
May 15	ASTON VILLA	L 2-3	Deyna 2	30,028

FA Cup

Jan 15	ROTHERHAM UNITED	(Rd 3) D 0-0		26,029
Jan 17	Rotherham United	(R) W 4-2	Kidd 2, Barnes, Owen	13,758
Jan 27	Shrewsbury Town	(Rd 4) L 0-2		14,215

League Cup

Aug 29	GRIMSBY TOWN	(Rd 3) W 2-0	Palmer, o.g.	21,481
Oct 4	Blackpool	(Rd 4) D 1-1	Channon	18,886
Oct 1	BLACKPOOL	(R) W 3-0	Owen 2, Booth	26,213
Nov 8	Norwich City	(Rd 5) W 3-1	Channon 2, Barnes	19,413
Dec 12	Southampton	(Rd 6) L 1-2	o.g.	21,523

UEFA Cup

Sep 13	FC Twente Enschede	(Rd 1) D 1-1	Watson	12,000
Sep 27	FC TWENTE ENSCHEDE	W 3-2	Kidd, Bell, o.g.	29,330
Oct 18	STANDARD LIEGE	(Rd 2) W 4-0	Kidd 2, Palmer, Hartford	27,489
Nov 1	Standard Liege	L 0-2		25,000
Nov 23	AC Milan	(Rd 3) D 2-2	Kidd, Power	40,000
Dec 6	AC MILAN	W 3-0	Booth, Hartford, Kidd	38,026
Mar 7	BORUSSIA MONCHENGLADBACH	(Rd 4) D 1-1	Channon	39,005
Mar 20	Borussia Monchengladbach	L 1-3	Deyna	30,000

MANAGER: Tony Book   **CAPTAIN:** Dave Watson

TOP SCORER: Mike Channon

BIGGEST WIN: October 18, 1977 4-0 v Standard Liege, UEFA Cup Round 2

HIGHEST ATTENDANCE: September 30, 1977 55,317 v Manchester United, lost 0-1, Division 1

MAJOR TRANSFERS IN: Paul Futcher from Luton, Kaziu Deyna from Legia Warsaw

MAJOR TRANSFERS OUT: Mike Doyle to Stoke City, Brian Kidd to Everton

League & Cup Appearances (substitute)

PLAYER	LEAGUE	CUP COMPETITION			TOTAL
		FA CUP	LC	UEFA	
Barnes	29	3	3 (1)	6	41 (1)
Bell	10	1 (1)	1	3 (1)	15 (2)
Bennett	0 (1)				0 (1)
Booth	20		5	6	31
Channon	36	3	4	6	49
Clements	15		4	5	24
Corrigan	42	2	5	8	57
Deyna	11 (2)	2	1	(1)	14 (3)
Donachie	38	3	4	6	51
Futcher P	24	3	1	2	30
Futcher R	10 (7)	1	2 (1)		13 (8)
Hartford	39	3	5	8	55
Henry	13 (2)			1	14 (2)
Keegan	4		1	1 (2)	6 (2)
Kidd	19 (1)	3	4	6	32 (1)
MacRae	1				1
Owen	34 (1)	2	5	3	44 (1)
Palmer	10 (4)		2 (1)	4 (4)	16 (5)
Power	32	3	3	6	44
Ranson	8	1			9
Reid	7 (1)			2	9 (1)
Silkman	12				12
Viljoen	16		1	(1) 7	24 (1)
Watson	33	2	4	8	47

Goalscorers

PLAYER	LEAGUE	CUP COMPETITION			TOTAL
		FA CUP	LC	UEFA	
Channon	11		3	1	15
Kidd	7	2		5	14
Owen	11	1	2		14
Deyna	6			1	7
Futcher R	7				7
Hartford	3		2		5
Palmer	4		1	1	6
Power	3		1		4
Silkman	3				3
Barnes	1	1		1	3
Watson	1			1	2
Bell				1	1
Booth			1	1	2
Opps' o.gs.	1		2	1	4

Fact File

Three of City's goals in the 4-0 victory over Standard Liege at Maine Road came in the last five minutes.

Final Division 1 Table

		P	W	D	L	F	A	Pts
1	LIVERPOOL	42	30	8	4	85	16	68
2	NOTTINGHAM F	42	21	18	3	61	26	60
3	WBA	42	24	11	7	72	35	59
4	EVERTON	42	17	17	8	52	40	51
5	LEEDS U	42	18	14	10	70	52	50
6	IPSWICH T	42	20	9	13	63	49	49
7	ARSENAL	42	17	14	11	61	48	48
8	ASTON VILLA	42	15	16	11	59	49	46
9	MANCHESTER U	42	15	15	12	60	63	45
10	COVENTRY C	42	14	16	12	58	68	44
11	TOTTENHAM H	42	13	15	14	48	61	41
12	MIDDLESBROUGH	42	15	10	17	57	50	40
13	BRISTOL C	42	15	10	17	47	51	40
14	SOUTHAMPTON	42	12	16	14	47	53	40
15	MANCHESTER CITY	42	13	13	16	58	56	39
16	NORWICH C	42	7	23	12	51	57	37
17	BOLTON W	42	12	11	19	54	75	35
18	WOLVERHAMPTON W	42	13	8	21	44	68	34
19	DERBY CO	42	10	11	21	44	71	31
20	QPR	42	6	13	23	45	73	25
21	BIRMINGHAM C	42	6	10	26	37	64	22
22	CHELSEA	42	5	10	27	44	92	20

Season 1979-80

Football League Division 1

DATE	OPPONENTS	SCORE	GOALSCORERS	ATTENDANCE
Aug 18	CRYSTAL PALACE	D 0-0		40,681
Aug 21	Middlesbrough	L 0-3		24,002
Aug 25	BRIGHTON & HOVE ALBION	W 3-2	Power, Robinson, Channon	34,557
Sep 1	Tottenham Hotspur	L 1-2	MacKenzie	30,901
Sep 8	SOUTHAMPTON	L 0-1		34,920
Sep 15	West Bromwich Albion	L 0-4		22,236
Sep 22	COVENTRY CITY	W 3-0	Robinson 2, MacKenzie	30,869
Sep 29	Leeds United	W 2-1	Power, Deyna	29,592
Oct 6	Arsenal	D 0-0		34,668
Oct 10	MIDDLESBROUGH	W 1-0	Deyna	29,384
Oct 13	NOTTINGHAM FOREST	W 1-0	Deyna	41,683
Oct 20	Norwich City	D 2-2	Bennett 2	18,000
Oct 27	LIVERPOOL	L 0-4		48,128
Nov 3	Crystal Palace	L 0-2		29,443
Nov 10	MANCHESTER UNITED	W 2-0	Henry, Robinson	50,067
Nov 17	Bolton Wanderers	W 1-0	Daley	25,515
Nov 24	Bristol City	L 0-1		18,296
Dec 1	WOLVES	L 2-3	Palmer, Deyna	33,894
Dec 8	Ipswich Town	L 0-4		18,221
Dec 15	DERBY COUNTY	W 3-0	Henry, Robinson, o.g.	27,667
Dec 22	Everton	W 2-1	Henry, Daley	26,308
Dec 26	STOKE CITY	D 1-1	Power	36,286
Dec 29	Brighton & Hove Albion	L 1-4	Lee	28,093
Jan 12	TOTTENHAM HOTSPUR	D 1-1	Robinson	34,337
Jan 19	Southampton	L 1-4	Power	21,422
Feb 2	WEST BROMWICH ALBION	L 1-3	Lee	32,904
Feb 9	Coventry City	D 0-0		17,114
Feb 16	LEEDS UNITED	D 1-1	Power	34,392
Feb 23	Nottingham Forest	L 0-4		27,255
Feb 27	Aston Villa	D 2-2	Robinson, Power	29,139
Mar 1	NORWICH CITY	D 0-0		32,248
Mar 11	Liverpool	L 0-2		40,443
Mar 15	ARSENAL	L 0-3		33,792
Mar 22	Manchester United	L 0-1		56,384
Mar 29	BOLTON WANDERERS	D 2-2	Tueart 2	33,500
Apr 2	EVERTON	D 1-1	Deyna	33,473
Apr 5	Stoke City	D 0-0		20,451
Apr 7	ASTON VILLA	D 1-1	Power	32,943
Apr 12	Wolves	W 2-1	Tueart, Reeves	23,850
Apr 19	BRISTOL CITY	W 3-1	Deyna, Tueart, Robinson	32,745
Apr 26	Derby County	L 1-3	Tueart	22,572
May 3	IPSWICH TOWN	W 2-1	Henry, Reeves	31,648

FA Cup

Jan 5	Halifax Town	(Rd 3) L 0-1		12,599

League Cup

Aug 28	Sheffield Wednesday	(Rd 2 FL) D 1-1	Viljoen	24,095
Sep 4	SHEFFIELD WEDNESDAY	(Rd 2 SL) W 2-1	Henry 2	24,074
Sep 26	SUNDERLAND	(RD 3) D 1-1	Robinson	26,181
Oct 3	Sunderland	(R) L 0-1		33,559

League & Cup Appearances (substitute)

PLAYER	LEAGUE	CUP COMPETITION		TOTAL
		FA CUP	LC	
Bennett	23 (2)	1	1	25 (2)
Booth	24		2	26
Caton	42	1	4	47
Channon	2		1	3
Corrigan	42	1	4	47
Daley	33	1	2	36
Deyna	21 (1)		1	22 (1)
Donachie	19		3	22
Futcher P	12 (1)		2	14 (1)
Henry	29 (3)	1	1	31 (3)
Lee	6 (1)			6 (1)
MacKenzie	17 (2)		4	21 (2)
Palmer	5 (2)		(1)	5 (3)
Power	41	1	4	46
Ranson	40	1	4	45
Reeves	9			9
Reid	22 (1)	1		23 (1)
Robinson	29 (1)	1	4	34 (1)
Shinton	5	1		6
Silkman	7		2	9
Stepanovic	13 (1)		4	17 (1)
Sugrue	1			1
Tueart	11			11
Viljoen	9 (2)	1	1	11 (2)

Goalscorers

PLAYER	LEAGUE	CUP COMPETITION		TOTAL
		FA CUP	LC	
Robinson	8		1	9
Power	7			7
Deyna	6			6
Henry	4		2	6
Tueart	5			5
Bennett	2			2
Daley	2			2
Lee	2			2
MacKenzie	2			2
Reeves	2			2
Channon	1			1
Palmer	1			1
Viljoen			1	1
Opps' o.gs.	1			1

Fact File

City went 18 games without a win between December and April.

MANAGER: Malcolm Allison

CAPTAIN: Dragoslav Stepanovic

TOP SCORER: Michael Robinson

BIGGEST WIN: December 15, 1979 3-0 v Derby County, Division 1

HIGHEST ATTENDANCE: March 22, 1980 56,384 v Manchester United, lost 0-1, Division 1

MAJOR TRANSFERS IN: Steve MacKenzie from Crystal Palace, Michael Robinson from Preston, Bobby Shinton from Wrexham, Dragaslav Stepanovic from Rekovac, Steve Daley from Wolves, Dennis Tueart from New York Cosmos, Kevin Reeves from Norwich City

MAJOR TRANSFERS OUT: Gary Owen to West Bromwich Albion, Peter Barnes to West Bromwich Albion, Dave Watson to Werder Bremen, Asa Hartford to Nottingham Forest, Mike Channon to Southampton

Final Division 1 Table

		P	W	D	L	F	A	PTS
1	LIVERPOOL	42	25	10	7	81	30	60
2	MANCHESTER U	42	24	10	8	65	35	58
3	IPSWICH T	42	22	9	11	68	39	53
4	ARSENAL	42	18	16	8	52	36	52
5	NOTTINGHAM F	42	20	8	14	63	43	48
6	WOLVERHAMPTON W	42	19	9	14	58	47	47
7	ASTON VILLA	42	16	14	12	51	50	46
8	SOUTHAMPTON	42	18	9	15	65	53	45
9	MIDDLESBROUGH	42	16	12	14	50	44	44
10	WBA	42	11	19	12	54	50	41
11	LEEDS U	42	13	14	15	46	50	40
12	NORWICH C	42	13	14	15	58	66	40
13	CRYSTAL PALACE	42	12	16	14	41	50	40
14	TOTTENHAM H	42	15	10	17	52	62	40
15	COVENTRY C	42	16	7	19	56	66	39
16	BRIGHTON & HA	42	11	15	16	47	57	37
17	MANCHESTER CITY	42	12	13	17	43	66	37
18	STOKE C	42	13	10	19	44	58	36
19	EVERTON	42	9	17	16	43	51	35
20	BRISTOL C	42	9	13	20	37	66	31
21	DERBY CO	42	11	8	23	47	67	30
22	BOLTON W	42	5	15	22	38	73	25

Season 1980-81

Football League Division 1

DATE	OPPONENTS	SCORE	GOALSCORERS	ATTENDANCE
Aug 16	Southampton	L 0-2		23,320
Aug 20	SUNDERLAND	L 0-4		33,271
Aug 23	ASTON VILLA	D 2-2	Ranson, Tueart	30,017
Aug 30	Middlesbrough	D 2-2	MacKenzie, Reeves	15,761
Sep 6	ARSENAL	D 1-1	Tueart	32,223
Sep 13	Nottingham Forest	L 2-3	Henry, Bennett	23,184
Sep 20	STOKE CITY	L 1-2	Tueart	29,507
Sep 27	Manchester United	D 2-2	Palmer, Reeves	55,926
Oct 4	LIVERPOOL	L 0-3		41,022
Oct 8	Leeds United	L 0-1		19,134
Oct 11	West Bromwich Albion	L 1-3	Daley	19,515
Oct 18	BIRMINGHAM CITY	L 0-1		30,041
Oct 22	TOTTENHAM HOTSPUR	W 3-1	Daley, MacKenzie, Reeves	28,788
Oct 25	Brighton & Hove Albion	W 2-1	Tueart 2	18,368
Nov 1	NORWICH CITY	W 1-0	Power	33,056
Nov 8	Leicester City	D 1-1	Tueart	19,104
Nov 12	Sunderland	L 0-2		23,387
Nov 15	SOUTHAMPTON	W 3-0	Bennett, Gow, Reeves	32,661
Nov 22	COVENTRY CITY	W 3-0	Bennett, Power, Reeves	30,047
Nov 29	Crystal Palace	W 3-2	Gow 2, Reeves	16,578
Dec 6	IPSWICH TOWN	D 1-1	Gow	32,215
Dec 13	Tottenham Hotspur	L 1-2	Boyer	23,883
Dec 20	LEEDS UNITED	W 1-0	Reeves	31,866
Dec 26	Everton	W 2-0	Gow, Power	36,194
Dec 27	WOLVES	W 4-0	Hutchison 2, McDonald, Reeves	37,817
Jan 10	Coventry City	D 1-1	MacKenzie	18,248
Jan 17	MIDDLESBROUGH	W 3-2	Hutchison, Reeves, McDonald	30,774
Jan 31	Aston Villa	L 0-1		33,682
Feb 7	NOTTINGHAM FOREST	D 1-1	Power	39,524
Feb 21	MANCHESTER UNITED	W 1-0	MacKenzie	50,114
Feb 24	Arsenal	L 0-2		24,790
Mar 14	WEST BROMWICH ALBION	W 2-1	McDonald, Tueart	36,581
Mar 18	Stoke City	L 1-2	McDonald	15,842
Mar 21	Birmingham City	L 0-2		16,160
Mar 28	BRIGHTON & HOVE ALBION	D 1-1	McDonald	30,122
Mar 31	LEICESTER CITY	D 3-3	Reeves 2, Henry	26,144
Apr 4	Norwich City	L 0-2		17,957
Apr 18	Wolves	W 3-1	Bennett 2, Tueart	17,371
Apr 20	EVERTON	W 3-1	Bennett, MacKenzie, Reeves	34,434
Apr 25	Ipswich Town	L 0-1		22,684
May 2	CRYSTAL PALACE	D 1-1	Bennett	31,017
May 19	Liverpool	L 0-1		24,462

FA Cup

Jan 3	CRYSTAL PALACE	(Rd 3) W 4-0	Reeves 2, Power, Boyer	39,347
Jan 24	NORWICH CITY	(Rd 4) W 6-0	Reeves, Gow, MacKenzie, Bennett, Power, McDonald	38,919
Feb 14	Peterborough	(Rd 5) W 1-0	Booth	27,780
Mar 7	Everton	(Rd 6) D 2-2	Power, Gow	52,791
Mar 11	EVERTON	(R) W 3-1	McDonald 2, Power	52,532
Apr 11	Ipswich Town	(SF) W 1-0	Power	46,537
May 9	Tottenham Hotspur	(F) D 1-1*	Hutchison	100,000
May 14	Tottenham Hotspur	(R) L 2-3*	Reeves (pen), MacKenzie	92,500
				*Played at Wembley.

League Cup

Aug 27	Stoke City	(Rd 2 FL) D 1-1	Henry	13,176
Sep 9	STOKE CITY	(Rd 2 SL) W 3-0	Bennett 2, Henry	21,356
Sep 23	Luton Town	(Rd 3) W 2-1	Henry, Bennett	10,030
Oct 29	NOTTS COUNTY	(Rd 4) W 5-1	Tueart 4, Bennett	26,363
Dec 3	WEST BROMWICH ALBION	(Rd 5) W 2-1	Henry, Bennett	35,611
Jan 14	LIVERPOOL	(SF FL) L 0-1		48,045
Feb 10	Liverpool	(SF SL) D 1-1	Reeves	46,711

MANAGER: Malcolm Allison/John Bond

CAPTAIN: Paul Power

TOP SCORER: Kevin Reeves

BIGGEST WIN: January 24, 1981 6-0 v Norwich City, FA Cup Round 4

HIGHEST ATTENDANCE: May 9, 1981 100,000 v Tottenham Hotspur, drew 1-1, FA Cup final

MAJOR TRANSFERS IN: Bobby McDonald and Tommy Hutchison from Coventry City, Gerry Gow from Bristol City

League & Cup Appearances (substitute)

PLAYER	LEAGUE	CUP COMPETITION		TOTAL
		FA CUP	LC	
Bennett	20 (6)	4 (1)	6	30 (7)
Booth	30	2	5	37
Boyer	6 (1)	2	2	10 (1)
Buckley	4 (2)		2	6 (2)
Caton	29 (1)	7	6	42 (1)
Corrigan	37	8	6	51
Daley	14 (1)		3	17 (1)
Deyna	2 (1)			2 (1)
Gow	20	8		28
Henry	25 (2)	2 (1)	6 (1)	33 (4)
Hutchison	24	8		32
Kinsey	1			1
MacKenzie	39	8	6	53
MacRae	3		1	4
May	0 (1)			0 (1)
McDonald	28	8		36
Palmer	3 (2)		1 (1)	4 (3)
Power	42	8	7	57
Ranson	32 (1)	6	7	45 (1)
Reeves	38 (1)	8	7	53 (1)
Reid	37	7	7	51
Stepanovic	1			1
Sugrue	4 (1)		(1)	4 (2)
Tueart	21 (1)	2 (1)	5	28 (2)
Williams	2			2

Goalscorers

PLAYER	LEAGUE	CUP COMPETITION		TOTAL
		FA CUP	LC	
Reeves	12	4	1	17
Bennett	7	1	5	13
Tueart	8		4	12
Power	4	5		9
MacKenzie	6	2		8
Gow	5	2		7
McDonald	4	3		7
Henry	2		4	6
Hutchison	3	1		4
Boyer	1	1		2
Daley	2			2
Booth		1		1
Palmer	1			1
Ranson	1			1

Fact File

Paul Power's extra-time free-kick curled around the Ipswich wall to take City to the hundredth ever FA Cup final.

Final Division 1 Table

		P	W	D	L	F	A	Pts
1	ASTON VILLA	42	26	8	8	72	40	60
2	IPSWICH T	42	23	10	9	77	43	56
3	ARSENAL	42	19	15	8	61	45	53
4	WBA	42	20	12	10	60	42	52
5	LIVERPOOL	42	17	17	8	62	46	51
6	SOUTHAMPTON	42	20	10	12	76	56	50
7	NOTTINGHAM F	42	19	12	11	62	44	50
8	MANCHESTER U	42	15	18	9	51	36	48
9	LEEDS U	42	17	10	15	39	47	44
10	TOTTENHAM H	42	14	15	13	70	68	43
11	STOKE C	42	12	18	12	51	60	42
12	MANCHESTER CITY	42	14	11	17	56	59	39
13	BIRMINGHAM C	42	13	12	17	50	61	38
14	MIDDLESBROUGH	42	16	5	21	53	61	37
15	EVERTON	42	13	10	19	55	58	36
16	COVENTRY C	42	13	10	19	48	68	36
17	SUNDERLAND	42	14	7	21	52	53	35
18	WOLVERHAMPTON W	42	13	9	20	43	55	35
19	BRIGHTON & HA	42	14	7	21	54	67	35
20	NORWICH C	42	13	7	22	49	73	33
21	LEICESTER C	42	13	6	23	40	67	32
22	CRYSTAL PALACE	42	6	7	29	47	83	19

Season 1981-82

Football League Division 1

DATE	OPPONENTS	SCORE	GOALSCORERS	ATTENDANCE
Aug 29	WEST BROMWICH ALBION	W 2-1	Tueart, Hutchison	36,187
Sep 1	Notts County	D 1-1	McDonald	14,546
Sep 5	Stoke City	W 3-1	Francis 2, Boyer	25,256
Sep 12	SOUTHAMPTON	D 1-1	Reeves	42,003
Sep 19	Birmingham City	L 0-3		20,109
Sep 23	LEEDS UNITED	W 4-0	Tueart 2, Reeves 2	35,077
Sep 26	TOTTENHAM HOTSPUR	L 0-1		39,085
Oct 3	Brighton & Hove Albion	L 1-4	Reeves	18,300
Oct 10	MANCHESTER UNITED	D 0-0		52,037
Oct 17	Arsenal	L 0-1		25,470
Oct 24	NOTTINGHAM FOREST	D 0-0		34,881
Oct 31	Everton	W 1-0	Tueart	31,305
Nov 7	MIDDLESBROUGH	W 3-2	Tueart, Reeves, Francis	32,025
Nov 21	SWANSEA CITY	W 4-0	Reeves 2, Tueart 2	34,774
Nov 28	Ipswich Town	L 0-2		20,476
Dec 5	ASTON VILLA	W 1-0	Tueart	32,487
Dec 12	Coventry City	W 1-0	Tueart	12,398
Dec 19	SUNDERLAND	L 2-3	Francis 2	29,462
Dec 26	Liverpool	W 3-1	Reeves, Bond, Hartford	37,929
Dec 28	WOLVES	W 2-1	Francis, Hartford	40,298
Jan 9	STOKE CITY	D 1-1	Francis	31,941
Jan 30	BIRMINGHAM CITY	W 4-2	Reeves 2, Francis 2	28,438
Feb 2	West Ham United	D 1-1	Bond	26,552
Feb 6	Southampton	L 1-2	McDonald	22,645
Feb 13	BRIGHTON & HOVE ALBION	W 4-0	McDonald, Reeves, Francis, o.g.	30,038
Feb 20	Tottenham Hotspur	L 0-2		46,181
Feb 27	Manchester United	D 1-1	Reeves	57,872
Mar 6	ARSENAL	D 0-0		30,288
Mar 10	Leeds United	W 1-0	Reeves	20,797
Mar 13	Nottingham Forest	D 1-1	Caton	20,927
Mar 20	EVERTON	D 1-1	Bond	33,002
Mar 27	Middlesbrough	D 0-0		11,709
Apr 3	WEST HAM UNITED	L 0-1		30,875
Apr 10	LIVERPOOL	L 0-5		40,112
Apr 12	Wolves	L 1-4	McDonald	14,891
Apr 17	Swansea City	L 0-2		19,212
Apr 21	West Ham United	W 1-0	Francis	11,703
Apr 24	IPSWICH TOWN	D 1-1	Hartford	30,329
May 1	Aston Villa	D 0-0		22,150
May 5	NOTTS COUNTY	W 1-0	Power	24,443
May 8	COVENTRY CITY	L 1-3	Francis	27,580
May 15	Sunderland	L 0-1		26,167

FA Cup

Jan 2	CARDIFF CITY	(Rd 3)	W 3-1	Francis 2, McDonald	31,547
Jan 23	COVENTRY CITY	(Rd 4)	L 1-3	Bond	31,276

League Cup

Oct 7	STOKE CITY	(Rd 2 FL)	W 2-0	Hartford, o.g.	23,146
Oct 28	Stoke City*	(Rd 2 SL)	L 0-2		17,373
Nov 11	NORTHAMPTON TOWN	(Rd 3)	W 3-1	Tueart 2, McDonald	21,139
Dec 2	Barnsley	(Rd 4)	L 0-1		33,792

*City won 9-8 on penalties.

League & Cup Appearances (substitute)

PLAYER	LEAGUE	CUP COMPETITION		TOTAL
		FA CUP	LC	
Bond	32 (1)	2	4	38 (1)
Booth	1			1
Boyer	10 (2)		1	11 (2)
Caton	39	2	4	45
Corrigan	39	2	4	45
Elliott	1			1
Francis	26	2	1	29
Gow	6	2		8
Hareide	9 (7)		0 (1)	9 (8)
Hartford	30	2	4	36
Henry	0 (2)			0 (2)
Hutchison	20 (2)	2	3 (1)	25 (3)
Jackson	6 (2)			6 (2)
Kinsey	13 (3)	0 (1)		13 (4)
May	3 (3)			3 (3)
McDonald	36	2	2	40
O'Neill	12 (1)		3	15 (1)
Power	25	1	1	27
Ranson	36	1	4	41
Reeves	42	2	4	48
Reid	36	2	4	42
Ryan	19			19
Tueart	15		4	19
Williams	3			3
Wilson	3 (1)		1	4 (1)

Goalscorers

PLAYER	LEAGUE	CUP COMPETITION		TOTAL
		FA CUP	LC	
Francis	12	2		14
Reeves	13			13
Tueart	9		2	11
McDonald	4	1	1	6
Bond	3	1		4
Hartford	3		1	4
Boyer	1			1
Caton	1			1
Hutchison	1			1
Power	1			1
Opps' o.gs.	1		1	2

Fact File

Trevor Francis scored two goals on his City debut against Stoke City.

MANAGER: John Bond

CAPTAIN: Paul Power

TOP SCORER: Trevor Francis

BIGGEST WIN: September 23, 1981 4-0 v Leeds United, Division 1; November 21, 1981 4-0 v Swansea City, Division 1; February 13, 1981 4-0 v Brighton and Hove Albion, Division 1

HIGHEST ATTENDANCE: February 27, 1982 57,872 v Manchester United, drew 1-1, Division 1

MAJOR TRANSFERS IN: Martin O'Neill from Norwich City, Trevor Francis from Nottingham Forest

Final Division 1 Table

		P	W	D	L	F	A	PTS
1	LIVERPOOL	42	26	9	7	80	32	87
2	IPSWICH T	42	26	5	11	75	53	83
3	MANCHESTER U	42	22	12	8	59	29	78
4	TOTTENHAM H	42	20	11	11	67	48	71
5	ARSENAL	42	20	11	11	48	37	71
6	SWANSEA C	42	21	6	15	58	51	69
7	SOUTHAMPTON	42	19	9	14	72	67	66
8	EVERTON	42	17	13	12	56	50	64
9	WEST HAM U	42	14	16	12	66	57	58
10	MANCHESTER CITY	42	15	13	14	49	50	58
11	ASTON VILLA	42	15	12	15	55	53	57
12	NOTTINGHAM F	42	15	12	15	42	48	57
13	BRIGHTON & HA	42	13	13	16	43	52	52
14	COVENTRY C	42	13	11	18	56	62	50
15	NOTTS CO	42	13	8	21	61	69	47
16	BIRMINGHAM C	42	10	14	18	53	61	44
17	WBA	42	11	11	20	46	57	44
18	STOKE C	42	12	8	22	44	63	44
19	SUNDERLAND	42	11	11	20	38	58	44
20	LEEDS U	42	10	12	20	39	61	42
21	WOLVERHAMPTON W	42	10	10	22	32	63	40
22	MIDDLESBROUGH	42	8	15	19	34	52	39

Season 1982-83

Football League Division 1

DATE	OPPONENTS	SCORE	GOALSCORERS	ATTENDANCE
Aug 28	Norwich City	W 2-1	Power, Cross	22,638
Sep 1	STOKE CITY	W 1-0	Cross	27,847
Sep 4	WATFORD	W 1-0	Tueart	29,617
Sep 7	Notts County	L 0-1		9,736
Sep 11	Tottenham Hotspur	W 2-1	Baker 2	32,483
Sep 18	ASTON VILLA	L 0-1		28,650
Sep 25	West Ham United	L 1-4	Boyer	23,883
Oct 2	COVENTRY CITY	W 3-2	Baker, Caton, Cross	25,105
Oct 9	Everton	L 1-2	Cross	25,158
Oct 16	SUNDERLAND	D 2-2	Cross, Reeves	25,053
Oct 23	Manchester United	D 2-2	Tueart, Cross	57,334
Oct 30	SWANSEA CITY	W 2-1	Tueart, Hartford	25,021
Nov 6	SOUTHAMPTON	W 2-0	McDonald, Reeves	25,115
Nov 13	Ipswich Town	L 0-1		19,523
Nov 20	BIRMINGHAM CITY	D 0-0		23,174
Nov 27	Nottingham Forest	L 0-3		18,845
Dec 4	ARSENAL	W 2-1	Caton 2	23,057
Dec 11	Luton Town	L 1-3	Cross	11,013
Dec 18	BRIGHTON & HOVE ALBION	D 1-1	Bond	20,615
Dec 27	Liverpool	L 2-5	Caton, Cross	44,664
Dec 28	WEST BROMWICH ALBION	W 2-1	Kinsey, o.g.	25,172
Jan 1	Birmingham City	D 2-2	Bond, Bodak	16,362
Jan 3	Watford	L 0-2		20,049
Jan 15	NORWICH CITY	W 4-2	Cross 2, Bond, Hartford	22,000
Jan 22	Aston Villa	D 1-1	Hartford	20,415
Feb 5	TOTTENHAM HOTSPUR	D 2-2	Tueart, Cross	26,357
Feb 12	Coventry City	L 0-4		9,527
Feb 19	NOTTS COUNTY	L 0-1		21,199
Feb 26	Sunderland	L 2-3	Reeves, Caton	15,124
Mar 2	EVERTON	D 0-0		22,253
Mar 5	MANCHESTER UNITED	L 1-2	Reeves	45,400
Mar 12	Swansea City	L 1-4	McDonald	9,884
Mar 19	Southampton	L 1-4	Reeves	17,201
Mar 26	IPSWICH TOWN	L 0-1		21,845
Apr 2	West Bromwich Albion	W 2-0	Reeves, Cross	13,654
Apr 4	LIVERPOOL	L 0-4		35,647
Apr 9	Stoke City	L 0-1		15,372
Apr 16	WEST HAM UNITED	W 2-0	McDonald, Tueart	23,015
Apr 23	Arsenal	L 0-3		16,810
Apr 30	NOTTINGHAM FOREST	L 1-2	Baker	23,563
May 7	Brighton & Hove Albion	W 1-0	Reeves	17,794
May 14	LUTON TOWN	L 0-1		42,843

FA Cup

Jan 8	Sunderland	(Rd 3) D 0-0		21,518
Jan 12	SUNDERLAND	(R) W 2-1	Cross, Hartford	22,356
Jan 29	Brighton & Hove Albion	(Rd 4) L 0-4		16,804

League Cup

Oct 5	Wigan Athletic	(Rd 2 FL) D 1-1	Tueart	12,194
Oct 27	WIGAN ATHLETIC	(Rd 2 SL) W 2-0	Power 2	16,083
Nov 10	SOUTHAMPTON	(Rd 3) D 1-1	Tueart	17,463
Nov 24	Southampton	(R) L 0-4		19,298

League & Cup Appearances (substitute)

PLAYER	LEAGUE	FA CUP	LC	TOTAL
Baker	27		4	31
Bodak	12 (2)	2 (1)		14 (3)
Bond	40	3	4	47
Boyer	1		1	2
Caton	38	2	4	44
Corrigan	25	3	3	31
Cross	31	3	4	38
Davies	2			2
Golac	2			2
Hareide	8			8
Hartford	38	3	4	45
Hildersley	1			1
Jones	3			3
Kinsey	12 (1)	3		15 (1)
Lomax	1			1
May	4 (4)			4 (4)
McDonald	32	0 (1)	3	35 (1)
Park	0 (2)			0 (1)
Power	33	3	4	40
Ranson	40	3	4	47
Reeves	40	3	4	47
Reid	24 (1)	3	1	28 (1)
Simpson	1 (2)			1 (2)
Tueart	30 (6)	2 (1)	3	35 (7)
Williams	17		1	18

Goalscorers

PLAYER	LEAGUE	FA CUP	LC	TOTAL
Cross	12	1		13
Tueart	5		2	7
Reeves	7			7
Caton	5			5
Power	1		2	3
Baker	4			4
Hartford	3	1		4
Bond	3			3
McDonald	3			3
Bodak	1			1
Boyer	1			1
Kinsey	1			1
Opps' o.gs.	1			1

Fact File

A shoulder injury to Joe Corrigan forced Bobby McDonald to take over in goal in the third minute of the home match against Watford. He kept a clean sheet as City won 1-0.

Luton's victory in the last game of the season meant they survived and City were relegated.

MANAGER: John Bond/John Benson

CAPTAIN: Paul Power

TOP SCORER: David Cross

BIGGEST WIN: January 15, 1983 4-2 v Norwich City, Division 1

HIGHEST ATTENDANCE: October 23, 1982 57,872 v Manchester United, drew 2-2, Division 1

MAJOR TRANSFERS OUT: Trevor Francis to Sampdoria

Final Division 1 Table

		P	W	D	L	F	A	Pts
1	LIVERPOOL	42	24	10	8	87	37	82
2	WATFORD	42	22	5	15	74	57	71
3	MANCHESTER U	42	19	13	8	56	38	70
4	TOTTENHAM H	42	20	9	13	65	50	69
5	NOTTINGHAM F	42	20	9	13	62	50	69
6	ASTON VILLA	42	21	5	16	62	50	68
7	EVERTON	42	18	10	14	66	48	64
8	WEST HAM U	42	20	4	18	68	62	64
9	IPSWICH T	42	15	13	14	64	50	58
10	ARSENAL	42	16	10	16	58	56	58
11	WBA	42	15	12	15	51	49	57
12	SOUTHAMPTON	42	15	12	15	54	58	57
13	STOKE C	42	16	9	17	53	64	57
14	NORWICH C	42	14	12	16	52	58	54
15	NOTTS CO	42	15	7	20	55	71	52
16	SUNDERLAND	42	12	14	16	48	61	50
17	BIRMINGHAM C	42	12	15	16	40	55	50
18	LUTON T	42	12	13	17	65	84	49
19	COVENTRY C	42	13	9	20	48	59	48
20	MANCHESTER CITY	42	13	8	21	47	70	47
21	SWANSEA C	42	10	11	21	51	69	41
22	BRIGHTON & HA	42	9	13	20	38	68	40

The Essential History of Manchester City

Football League Division 2

DATE	OPPONENTS	SCORE	GOALSCORERS	ATTENDANCE
Aug 27	Crystal Palace	W 2-0	May, Parlane	13,382
Aug 29	Cardiff City	L 1-2	Tolmie	8,899
Sep 3	BARNSLEY	W 3-2	Tolmie 2, Parlane	25,105
Sep 7	FULHAM	D 0-0		23,356
Sep 10	Portsmouth	W 2-1	Parlane, Tolmie	18,852
Sep 17	BLACKBURN ROVERS	W 6-0	Parlane 3, Baker, Tolmie, May	25,433
Sep 24	Leeds United	W 2-1	Parlane, Baker	21,918
Oct 1	GRIMSBY TOWN	W 2-1	Caton, Tolmie	25,000
Oct 8	SWANSEA CITY	W 2-1	Parlane, Davidson	23,571
Oct 15	Charlton Athletic	L 0-1		7,639
Oct 22	MIDDLESBROUGH	W 2-1	Parlane, Tolmie	24,466
Oct 29	Newcastle United	L 0-5		33,588
Nov 5	Shrewsbury Town	W 3-1	May, Caton, Kinsey	9,471
Nov 12	BRIGHTON & HOVE ALBION	W 4-0	Baker 2, Parlane, Tolmie	24,562
Nov 19	Carlisle United	L 0-2		8,745
Nov 26	DERBY COUNTY	D 1-1	Parlane	22,689
Dec 3	Chelsea	W 1-0	Tolmie	29,142
Dec 10	SHEFFIELD WEDNESDAY	L 1-2	Bond	41,862
Dec 17	Cambridge United	D 0-0		5,204
Dec 26	OLDHAM ATHLETIC	W 2-0	Parlane, Kinsey	35,898
Dec 27	Huddersfield Town	W 3-1	Lomax, Baker, Kinsey	23,497
Dec 31	Barnsley	D 1-1	Parlane	17,148
Jan 2	LEEDS UNITED	D 1-1	Tolmie	34,441
Jan 14	CRYSTAL PALACE	W 3-1	Power, Baker, Kinsey	20,144
Jan 21	Blackburn Rovers	L 1-2	Tolmie	18,199
Feb 4	Grimsby Town	D 1-1	Parlane	11,986
Feb 11	PORTSMOUTH	W 2-1	Tolmie, Reid	23,138
Feb 18	NEWCASTLE UNITED	L 1-2	Kinsey	41,767
Feb 25	Middlesbrough	D 0-0		9,343
Mar 3	SHREWSBURY TOWN	W 1-0	Reid	20,083
Mar 10	Brighton & Hove Albion	D 1-1	Hartford	14,132
Mar 17	Fulham	L 1-5	McNab	9,684
Mar 24	CARDIFF CITY	W 2-1	Baker, Johnson	20,140
Mar 31	CHARLTON ATHLETIC	L 0-1		19,147
Apr 7	Swansea City	W 2-0	Parlane, Kinsey	7,254
Apr 14	CARLISLE UNITED	W 3-1	May, Smith, Parlane	20,760
Apr 20	Oldham Athletic	D 2-2	Bond, McCarthy	19,952
Apr 23	HUDDERSFIELD TOWN	L 2-3	Bond 2	23,247
Apr 28	Derby County	L 0-1		14,470
May 4	CHELSEA	L 0-2		21,713
May 7	Sheffield Wednesday	D 0-0		36,763
May 12	CAMBRIDGE UNITED	W 5-0	Power, May, Baker, Tolmie, Kinsey	20,787

FA Cup

Jan 7	Blackpool	(Rd 3)	L 1-2	o.g.	15,377

League Cup

Oct 5	Torquay United	(Rd 2 FL)	D 0-0		6,439
Oct 25	TORQUAY UNITED	(Rd 2 SL)	W 6-0	Parlane 3, Tolmie 2, Hoyland	14,021
Nov 9	Aston Villa	(Rd 3)	L 0-3		23,922

League & Cup Appearances (substitute)

PLAYER	LEAGUE	CUP COMPETITION		TOTAL
		FA CUP	LC	
Baker	36	1	3	40
Bond	33 (1)	1		34 (1)
Caton	16		3	19
Dalziel	4 (1)	(1)		4 (2)
Davidson	2 (4)		1	3 (4)
Davies	5		1	6
Hartford	7			7
Hoyland	1		0 (1)	1 (1)
Johnson	4 (2)			4 (2)
Kinsey	16 (7)		1	17 (7)
Lomax	16 (1)	1		17 (1)
May	42	1	3	46
McCarthy	24	1		25
McNab	33	1	2	36
Parlane	40 (1)	1	3	44 (1)
Power	37	1	3	41
Ranson	25 (1)		3	28 (1)
Reid	18 (1)		2	20 (1)
Smith	9			9
Sullivan	1			1
Tolmie	38 (3)	1	3	42 (3)
Walsh	3 (1)	1	1 (1)	5 (2)
Williams	42	1	3	46
Wilson	11			11

Goalscorers

PLAYER	LEAGUE	CUP COMPETITION		TOTAL
		FA CUP	LC	
Parlane	16		3	19
Tolmie	13		2	15
Baker	8			8
Kinsey	7			7
May	5			5
Bond	4			4
Caton	2			2
Power	2			2
Reid	2			2
Davidson	1			1
Hartford	1			1
Hoyland			1	1
Johnson	1			1
Lomax	1			1
McCarthy	1			1
McNab	1			1
Smith	1			1
Opps' o.gs.		1		1

Fact File

City were well in the running for promotion before three defeats in April took the wind out of their sails.

MANAGER: Billy McNeill MBE

CAPTAIN: Paul Power

TOP SCORER: Derek Parlane

BIGGEST WIN: September 17, 1983 6-0 v Blackburn Rovers, Division 2; October 25, 1983 6-0 v Torquay United, League Cup, Round 2 Second Leg

HIGHEST ATTENDANCE: December 10, 1983 41,862 v Sheffield Wednesday, lost 1-2, Division 2

MAJOR TRANSFERS IN: Jim Tolmie from FC Lokeren, Neil McNab from Brighton, Mick McCarthy from Barnsley, Derek Parlane from Leeds.

MAJOR TRANSFERS OUT: Tommy Caton to Arsenal

Final Division 2 Table

		P	W	D	L	F	A	Pts
1	CHELSEA	42	25	13	4	90	40	89
2	SHEFFIELD W	42	26	10	6	72	34	88
3	NEWCASTLE U	42	24	8	10	85	53	80
4	MANCHESTER CITY	42	20	10	12	66	48	70
5	GRIMSBY T	42	19	13	10	60	47	70
6	BLACKBURN R	42	17	16	9	57	46	67
7	CARLISLE U	42	16	16	10	48	41	64
8	SHREWSBURY T	42	17	10	15	49	53	61
9	BRIGHTON & HA	42	17	9	16	69	60	60
10	LEEDS U	42	16	12	14	55	56	60
11	FULHAM	42	15	12	15	60	53	57
12	HUDDERSFIELD T	42	14	15	13	56	49	57
13	CHARLTON ATH	42	16	9	17	53	64	57
14	BARNSLEY	42	15	7	20	57	53	52
15	CARDIFF C	42	15	6	21	53	66	51
16	PORTSMOUTH	42	14	7	21	73	64	49
17	MIDDLESBROUGH	42	12	13	17	41	47	49
18	CRYSTAL PALACE	42	12	11	19	42	52	47
19	OLDHAM ATH	42	13	8	21	47	73	47
20	DERBY CO	42	11	9	22	36	72	42
21	SWANSEA C	42	7	8	27	36	85	29
22	CAMBRIDGE U	42	4	12	26	28	77	24

Season 1984-85

Football League Division 2

DATE	OPPONENTS	SCORE	GOALSCORERS	ATTENDANCE
Aug 24	Wimbledon	D 2-2	Smith, Parlane	8,365
Aug 27	GRIMSBY TOWN	W 3-0	Bond, Smith, Parlane	21,137
Sep 1	FULHAM	L 2-3	Parlane 2	21,071
Sep 4	Wolves	L 0-2		13,255
Sep 8	Carlisle United	D 0-0		6,641
Sep 15	HUDDERSFIELD TOWN	W 1-0	Baker	20,201
Sep 22	Cardiff City	W 3-0	Smith, Cunningham, Wilson	6,089
Sep 29	CRYSTAL PALACE	W 2-1	Smith, Kinsey	20,252
Oct 6	OXFORD UNITED	W 1-0	Kinsey	24,755
Oct 13	Shrewsbury Town	L 0-1		8,563
Oct 20	Middlesbrough	L 1-2	Kinsey	7,737
Oct 27	BLACKBURN ROVERS	W 2-1	o.g., May	23,798
Nov 3	Brighton & Hove Albion	D 0-0		14,034
Nov 10	BIRMINGHAM CITY	W 1-0	Phillips	25,369
Nov 17	Sheffield United	D 0-0		16,605
Nov 24	PORTSMOUTH	D 2-2	Kinsey, Smith	23,700
Dec 1	Oldham Athletic	W 2-0	Smith, Melrose	14,129
Dec 8	NOTTS COUNTY	W 2-0	Phillips, Melrose	20,109
Dec 15	Charlton Athletic	W 3-1	Phillips, Smith, Melrose	6,247
Dec 22	Fulham	L 2-3	Baker, Melrose	6,847
Dec 26	BARNSLEY	D 1-1	Melrose	27,131
Dec 29	WOLVES	W 4-0	Phillips, Smith, Baker, Wilson	22,022
Jan 1	Leeds United	D 1-1	Melrose	22,626
Jan 12	Huddersfield Town	W 2-0	Smith, Wilson	15,640
Jan 19	WIMBLEDON	W 3-0	Phillips, Smith, Baker	23,303
Feb 2	Crystal Palace	W 2-1	Phillips, Wilson	7,668
Feb 9	CARLISLE UNITED	L 1-3	Phillips	21,347
Feb 23	BRIGHTON & HOVE ALBION	W 2-0	Phillips, Smith	20,227
Mar 2	Blackburn Rovers	W 1-0	Kinsey	22,099
Mar 9	MIDDLESBROUGH	W 1-0	Phillips	22,399
Mar 16	SHREWSBURY TOWN	W 4-0	Smith, May, Power, Kinsey	20,828
Mar 19	Birmingham City	D 0-0		18,004
Mar 23	Oxford United	L 0-3		13,096
Mar 30	CARDIFF CITY	D 2-2	Simpson, Kinsey	20,047
Apr 6	Barnsley	D 0-0		12,930
Apr 8	LEEDS UNITED	L 1-2	Tolmie	33,535
Apr 13	Grimsby Town	L 1-4	Simpson	8,362
Apr 20	SHEFFIELD UNITED	W 2-0	Clements, Tolmie	21,132
Apr 27	Portsmouth	W 2-1	Phillips, Simpson	22,232
May 4	OLDHAM ATHLETIC	D 0-0		28,933
May 6	Notts County	L 2-3	Simpson 2	17,812
May 11	CHARLTON ATHLETIC	W 5-1	Phillips 2, May, Simpson, Melrose	47,285

FA Cup

Jan 5	Coventry City	(Rd 3) L 1-2	Power	15,642

League Cup

Sep 25	BLACKPOOL	(Rd 2 FL) W 4-2	Cunningham 2, McCarthy Wilson	13,344
Oct 9	Blackpool	(Rd 2 SL) W 3-1	Tolmie 2, Smith	10,966
Oct 31	WEST HAM UNITED	(Rd 3) D 0-0		20,510
Nov 6	West Ham United	(R) W 2-1	Cunningham, Kinsey	17,461
Nov 12	Chelsea	(Rd 4) L 1-4	Smith	17,461

Fact File

Needing a win at home to Charlton in the last game of the season, City went up in style winning 5-1.

MANAGER: Billy McNeill MBE

CAPTAIN: Paul Power

TOP SCORER: Gordon Smith

BIGGEST WIN: May 11, 1985 5-1 v Charlton Athletic, Division 2

HIGHEST ATTENDANCE: May 11, 1985 47,285 v Charlton Athletic, won 5-1, Division 2

MAJOR TRANSFERS IN: Jim Melrose from Celtic

League & Cup Appearances (substitute)

PLAYER	LEAGUE	FA CUP	LC	TOTAL
Baker	29	1	3	33
Beckford	1 (3)		0 (1)	1 (4)
Bond	3			3
Clements	11 (1)			11 (1)
Cunningham	16 (2)	(1)	5	21 (3)
Hoyland	1			1
Kinsey	33 (2)	1	5	39 (2)
Lomax	6 (1)	1	1	8 (1)
May	39	1	4	44
McCarthy	39	1	4	44
McNab	15 (3)		2	17 (3)
McNaught	7			7
Melrose	23 (1)	1		24 (1)
Parlane	7			7
Phillips	42	1	5	48
Power	42	1	5	48
Reid	31 (1)		5	36 (1)
Simpson	9 (1)			9 (1)
Sinclair	1		1	2
Smith	31 (1)	1	5	37 (1)
Tolmie	7 (10)		(2)	7 (12)
Williams	42	1	5	48
Wilson	27	1	5	33

Goalscorers

PLAYER	LEAGUE	FA CUP	LC	TOTAL
Smith	12		2	14
Phillips	12			12
Kinsey	7		1	8
Melrose	7			7
Simpson	6			6
Wilson	4		1	5
Baker	4			4
Cunningham	1		3	4
Parlane	4			4
Tolmie	2		2	4
May	3			3
Power	1	1		2
Bond	1			1
Clements	1			1
McCarthy			1	1
Opps' o.gs.	1			1

Final Division 2 Table

		P	W	D	L	F	A	Pts
1	Oxford U	42	25	9	8	84	36	84
2	Birmingham C	42	25	7	10	59	33	82
3	Manchester City	42	21	11	10	66	40	74
4	Portsmouth	42	20	14	8	69	50	74
5	Blackburn R	42	21	10	11	66	41	73
6	Brighton & HA	42	20	12	10	54	34	72
7	Leeds U	42	19	12	11	66	43	69
8	Shrewsbury T	42	18	11	13	66	53	65
9	Fulham	42	19	8	15	68	64	65
10	Grimsby T	42	18	8	16	72	64	62
11	Barnsley	42	14	16	12	42	42	58
12	Wimbledon	42	16	10	16	71	75	58
13	Huddersfield T	42	15	10	17	52	64	55
14	Oldham Ath	42	15	8	19	49	67	53
15	Crystal Palace	42	12	12	18	46	65	48
16	Carlisle U	42	13	8	21	50	67	47
17	Charlton Ath	42	11	12	19	51	63	45
18	Sheffield U	42	10	14	18	54	66	44
19	Middlesbrough	42	10	10	22	41	57	40
20	Notts Co	42	10	7	25	45	73	37
21	Cardiff C	42	9	8	25	47	79	35
22	Wolverhampton W	42	8	9	25	37	79	33

Season 1985-86

Football League Division 1

DATE	OPPONENTS	SCORE	GOALSCORERS	ATTENDANCE
Aug 17	Coventry City	D 1-1	McIlroy	14,550
Aug 21	LEICESTER CITY	D 1-1	Lillis	25,528
Aug 24	SHEFFIELD WEDNESDAY	L 1-3	Simpson	26,934
Aug 26	West Bromwich Albion	W 3-2	Simpson, Wilson, Lillis	12,122
Aug 31	TOTTENHAM HOTSPUR	W 2-1	Simpson, o.g.	27,789
Sep 3	Birmingham City	L 0-1		11,706
Sep 7	Southampton	L 0-3		14,308
Sep 14	MANCHESTER UNITED	L 0-3		48,773
Sep 21	WEST HAM UNITED	D 2-2	Lillis, Melrose	22,001
Sep 28	Oxford United	L 0-1		9,796
Oct 5	CHELSEA	L 0-1		20,104
Oct 12	Watford	L 2-3	Lillis, McNab	15,418
Oct 19	Queens Park Rangers	D 0-0		13,471
Oct 26	EVERTON	D 1-1	Simpson	28,807
Nov 2	Arsenal	L 0-1		22,264
Nov 9	IPSWICH TOWN	D 1-1	Lillis	20,853
Nov 16	Nottingham Forest	W 2-0	Wilson, Simpson	15,140
Nov 23	NEWCASTLE UNITED	W 1-0	Lillis	25,179
Nov 30	Luton Town	L 1-2	Lillis	10,096
Dec 7	Leicester City	D 1-1	Davies	10,289
Dec 14	COVENTRY CITY	W 5-1	Davies 2, Simpson 2, Lillis	20,075
Dec 21	Sheffield Wednesday	L 2-3	McNab, Lillis	23,177
Dec 26	LIVERPOOL	W 1-0	Wilson	35,384
Dec 28	BIRMINGHAM CITY	D 1-1	McNab	24,955
Jan 1	Aston Villa	W 1-0	Lillis	14,215
Jan 11	SOUTHAMPTON	W 1-0	Phillips	21,674
Jan 18	Tottenham Hotspur	W 2-0	Lillis, Davies	17,009
Feb 1	WEST BROMWICH ALBION	W 2-1	Davies, Power	20,540
Feb 8	QUEENS PARK RANGERS	W 2-0	Davies, Simpson	20,414
Feb 11	Everton	L 0-4		30,006
Mar 1	OXFORD UNITED	L 0-3		20,099
Mar 8	Chelsea	L 0-1		17,573
Mar 15	WATFORD	L 0-1		18,899
Mar 22	Manchester United	D 2-2	Wilson, o.g.	52,174
Mar 29	ASTON VILLA	D 2-2	Wilson, McNab	20,935
Mar 31	Liverpool	L 0-2		43,316
Apr 5	ARSENAL	L 0-1		19,590
Apr 12	Ipswich Town	D 0-0		13,986
Apr 19	NOTTINGHAM FOREST	L 1-2	Davies	19,715
Apr 26	Newcastle United	L 1-3	Davies	22,689
Apr 28	West Ham United	L 0-1		27,153
May 3	LUTON TOWN	D 1-1	Davies	20,361

FA Cup

Jan 4	Walsall	(Rd 3) W 3-1	Simpson 2, Davies	10,779
Jan 25	WATFORD	(Rd 4) D 1-1	Davies	31,623
Feb 3	Watford	(R) D 0-0		19,347
Feb 6	WATFORD	(2nd R) L 1-3	Kinsey	27,260

Milk Cup

Sep 25	Bury	(Rd 2 FL) W 2-1*	Wilson, Melrose	11,377
Oct 8	BURY	(Rd 2 SL) W 2-1	Lillis, Melrose	9,766
Oct 30	ARSENAL	(Rd 3) L 1-2	Davies	18,279

*Played at Old Trafford.

Full Members' Cup

Oct 14	LEEDS UNITED	(Gp 3) W 6-1	Davies 3, Baker, Lillis Power	4,029
Oct 22	Sheffield United	(Gp 3) W 2-1	Phillips, Baker	3,420
Nov 4	SUNDERLAND	(SF) D 0-0†		6,642
Nov 26	Hull City	(Northern Final FL) L 1-2	Phillips	5,213
Dec 11	HULL CITY	(Northern Final SL) W 2-0	Phillips, Melrose	10,180
Mar 23	Chelsea	(F) L 4-5	Lillis 2, Kinsey, o.g.	68,000

†Won 5-4 on penalties.

MANAGER: Billy McNeill MBE

CAPTAIN: Paul Power

TOP SCORERS: Gordon Davies and Mark Lillis

BIGGEST WIN: October 14, 1985 6-1 v Leeds United, Full Members Cup, Group 3

HIGHEST ATTENDANCE: March 23, 1986 68,000 v Chelsea, lost 4-5, Full Members' Cup final

MAJOR TRANSFERS IN: Sammy McIlroy from Manchester United, Mark Lillis from Huddersfield Town

League & Cup Appearances (substitute)

PLAYER	LEAGUE	CUP COMPETITION			TOTAL
		FA CUP	MILK	FMC	
Baker	9 (1)		2	2 (1)	13 (2)
Barrett	1				1
Beckford	2 (1)				2 (1)
Clements	30	4	3	4	41
Davies	26	4	1	5	36
Johnson	4			3	7
Kinsey	12 (1)	0 (2)		1	13 (3)
Lillis	39	4	3	5	51
May	36 (1)	4	2	6	48 (1)
McCarthy	38	4	3	3	48
McIlroy	12		1	2	15
McNab	37	4	2	4	47
Melrose	4 (6)		2 (1)	2 (2)	8 (9)
Moulden	1 (1)	0 (1)		0 (1)	1 (3)
Nixon	28	4	3	6	41
Phillips	39	4	3	5	51
Power	36	4	3	6	49
Redmond			1		10
Reid	30	4	1	6	41
Siddall	6				6
Simpson	30 (7)	4		3 (3)	40 (10)
Smith	0 (1)			0 (1)	0 (2)
Tolmie	1 (2)			(1)	1 (3)
Williams	8				8
Wilson	24 (1)		3	2	29 (1)

Goalscorers

PLAYER	LEAGUE	CUP COMPETITION			TOTAL
		FA CUP	MILK	FMC	
Davies	9	2	1	3	15
Lillis	11		1	3	15
Simpson	8	2			10
Wilson	5		1		6
McNab	4				4
Melrose	1		2	1	3
Baker				2	2
Kinsey		1		1	2
McIlroy	1				1
Phillips	1		3		1
Power	1		1		1
Opps' o.gs.	2				2

Fact File

City beat United in this season's FA Youth Cup Final with a team that included Hinchcliffe, White, Lake and Brightwell.

Final Division 1 Table

		P	W	D	L	F	A	PTS
1	LIVERPOOL	42	26	10	6	89	37	88
2	EVERTON	42	26	8	8	87	41	86
3	WEST HAM U	42	26	6	10	74	40	84
4	MANCHESTER U	42	22	10	10	70	36	76
5	SHEFFIELD W	42	21	10	11	63	54	73
6	CHELSEA	42	20	11	11	57	56	71
7	ARSENAL	42	20	9	13	49	47	69
8	NOTTINGHAM F	42	19	11	12	69	53	68
9	LUTON T	42	18	12	12	61	44	66
10	TOTTENHAM H	42	19	8	15	74	52	65
11	NEWCASTLE U	42	17	12	13	67	72	63
12	WATFORD	42	16	11	15	69	62	59
13	QPR	42	15	7	20	53	64	52
14	SOUTHAMPTON	42	12	10	20	51	62	46
15	MANCHESTER CITY	42	11	12	19	43	57	45
16	ASTON VILLA	42	10	14	18	51	67	44
17	COVENTRY C	42	11	10	21	48	71	43
18	OXFORD U	42	10	12	20	62	80	42
19	LEICESTER C	42	10	12	20	54	76	42
20	IPSWICH T	42	11	8	23	32	55	41
21	BIRMINGHAM C	42	8	5	29	30	73	29
22	WBA	42	4	12	26	35	89	24

Season 1986-87

Football League Division 1

DATE	OPPONENTS	SCORE	GOALSCORERS	ATTENDANCE
Aug 23	WIMBLEDON	W 3-1	Baker 2, Christie	20,756
Aug 25	Liverpool	D 0-0		39,989
Aug 30	Tottenham Hotspur	L 0-1		23,764
Sep 3	NORWICH CITY	D 2-2	Christie 2	19,122
Sep 6	COVENTRY CITY	L 0-1		18,320
Sep 13	Oxford United	D 0-0		8,245
Sep 20	QUEENS PARK RANGERS	D 0-0		17,774
Sep 27	Luton Town	L 0-1		9,371
Oct 4	LEICESTER CITY	L 1-2	Hopkins	18,033
Oct 11	Newcastle United	L 1-3	Simpson	21,780
Oct 18	Chelsea	L 1-2	Varadi	12,990
Oct 26	MANCHESTER UNITED	D 1-1	McCarthy	32,440
Nov 1	Southampton	D 1-1	Baker	14,352
Nov 8	ASTON VILLA	W 3-1	Moulden 2, Varadi	22,875
Nov 15	CHARLTON ATHLETIC	W 2-1	Moulden, Simpson	20,578
Nov 22	Arsenal	L 0-3		29,009
Nov 29	EVERTON	L 1-3	Moulden	27,097
Dec 6	Nottingham Forest	L 0-2		19,129
Dec 13	WEST HAM UNITED	W 3-1	Varadi 2, White	19,067
Dec 21	Coventry City	D 2-2	Redmond 2	12,430
Dec 26	SHEFFIELD WEDNESDAY	W 1-0	Simpson	30,193
Dec 28	Charlton Athletic	L 0-5		7,697
Jan 1	Watford	D 1-1	Varadi	15,514
Jan 3	OXFORD UNITED	W 1-0	McNab	20,724
Jan 17	LIVERPOOL	L 0-1		35,336
Jan 24	Wimbledon	D 0-0		5,667
Feb 14	Norwich City	D 1-1	Brightwell	16,094
Feb 21	LUTON TOWN	D 1-1	Lake	17,507
Feb 28	Queens Park Rangers	L 0-1		12,739
Mar 7	Manchester United	L 0-2		48,619
Mar 14	CHELSEA	L 1-2	McNab	19,819
Mar 21	NEWCASTLE UNITED	D 0-0		23,060
Mar 28	Leicester City	L 0-4		10,743
Apr 4	Aston Villa	D 0-0		18,241
Apr 11	SOUTHAMPTON	L 2-4	Stewart, Moulden	18,193
Apr 15	TOTTENHAM HOTSPUR	D 1-1	McNab	21,460
Apr 18	WATFORD	L 1-2	McNab	18,541
Apr 20	Sheffield Wednesday	L 1-2	Varadi	19,769
Apr 25	ARSENAL	W 3-0	Varadi 2, Stewart	18,072
May 2	Everton	D 0-0		37,541
May 4	NOTTINGHAM FOREST	W 1-0	Varadi	21,405
May 9	West Ham United	L 0-2		18,413

FA Cup

Jan 10	Manchester United	(Rd 3) L 0-1		54,297

Littlewoods Cup

Sep 23	Southend United	(Rd 2 FL) D 0-0		6,182
Oct 8	SOUTHEND UNITED	(Rd 2 SL) W 2-1	McNab, Simpson	9,373
Oct 28	Arsenal	(Rd 3) L 1-3	Simpson	21,604

Full Members' Cup

Nov 4	WIMBLEDON	(Rd 2) W 3-1	Moulden 2, Clements	4,914
Nov 26	WATFORD	(Rd 3) W 1-0	Moulden	6,393
Jan 31	IPSWICH TOWN	(Rd 4) L 2-3	Varadi 2	11,027

League & Cup Appearances (substitute)

PLAYER	LEAGUE	CUP COMPETITION			TOTAL
		FA CUP	LITTLEWOODS	FMC	
Baker	13 (2)	0 (1)	1 (1)	1	15 (4)
Barnes	8			1	9
Barrett	1 (1)		1		2 (1)
Beckford	4				4
Brightwell	12 (4)	0 (1)	2		14 (5)
Christie	9		1		10
Clements	39	1	2	2	44
Davies	5		1		6
Gidman	22	1	1	2	26
Grealish	11	1		3	15
Hopkins	7		2		9
Lake	3			1	4
Langley	9				9
May	17 (5)		1	1 (1)	19 (6)
McCarthy	39	1	3	3	46
McIlroy	1				1
McNab	42	1	2	2	47
Moulden	16 (4)		1 (1)	2	19 (5)
Nixon	5				5
Redmond	28 (2)	1	3	2	34 (2)
Reid	6 (1)				6 (1)
Simpson	27 (5)	1	3	3	34 (5)
Stewart	11				11
Suckling	37	1	3	3	44
Varadi	29 (1)	1	1	2	33 (1)
White	19 (5)	1	2 (1)	2	24 (6)
Wilson	42	1	3	3	49

Goalscorers

PLAYER	LEAGUE	CUP COMPETITION			TOTAL
		FA CUP	LITTLEWOODS	FMC	
Varadi	9			2	11
Moulden	5			3	8
McNab	4		1		5
Simpson	3		2		5
Christie	3				3
Baker	3				3
Redmond	2				2
Stewart	2				2
Brightwell	1				1
Clements				1	1
Hopkins	1				1
Lake	1				1
McCarthy	1				1
White	1				1

Fact File

Billy McNeill left after the Queens Park Rangers match in September, but ironically City's next win came in November when he brought his new team Aston Villa to Maine Road.

MANAGER: Jimmy Frizzell

CAPTAIN: Mick McCarthy

TOP SCORER: Imre Varadi

BIGGEST WIN: April 25, 1987 3-0 v Arsenal, Division 1

HIGHEST ATTENDANCE: January 10, 1987 54,297 v Manchester United, lost 0-1, FA Cup Round 3

MAJOR TRANSFERS IN: Paul Stewart from Blackpool

MAJOR TRANSFERS OUT: Paul Power to Everton

Final Division 1 Table

		P	W	D	L	F	A	Pts
1	EVERTON	42	26	8	8	76	31	86
2	LIVERPOOL	42	23	8	11	72	42	77
3	TOTTENHAM H	42	21	8	13	68	43	71
4	ARSENAL	42	20	10	12	58	35	70
5	NORWICH C	42	17	17	8	53	51	68
6	WIMBLEDON	42	19	9	14	57	50	66
7	LUTON T	42	18	12	12	47	45	66
8	NOTTINGHAM F	42	18	11	13	64	51	65
9	WATFORD	42	18	9	15	67	54	63
10	COVENTRY C	42	17	12	13	50	45	63
11	MANCHESTER U	42	14	14	14	52	45	56
12	SOUTHAMPTON	42	14	10	18	69	68	52
13	SHEFFIELD W	42	13	13	16	58	59	52
14	CHELSEA	42	13	13	16	53	64	52
15	WEST HAM U	42	14	10	18	52	67	52
16	QPR	42	13	11	18	48	64	50
17	NEWCASTLE U	42	12	11	19	47	65	47
18	OXFORD U	42	11	13	18	44	69	46
19	CHARLTON ATH	42	11	11	20	45	55	44
20	LEICESTER C	42	11	9	22	54	76	42
21	MANCHESTER CITY	42	8	15	19	36	57	39
22	ASTON VILLA	42	8	12	22	45	79	36

Season 1987-88

Barclays League Division 2

DATE	OPPONENTS	SCORE	GOALSCORERS	ATTENDANCE
Aug 15	PLYMOUTH ARGYLE	W 2-1	Stewart, Varadi	20,046
Aug 22	Oldham Athletic	D 1-1	Varadi	15,964
Aug 31	Aston Villa	D 1-1	Scott	16,282
Sep 5	BLACKBURN ROVERS	L 1-2	Scott	20,372
Sep 12	Shrewsbury Town	D 0-0		6,280
Sep 16	MILLWALL	W 4-0	Gidman, White, Stewart, Scott	15,430
Sep 19	STOKE CITY	W 3-0	Varadi 3	19,322
Sep 26	Leeds United	L 0-2		25,358
Sep 29	Hull City	L 1-3	Stewart	9,650
Oct 3	LEICESTER CITY	W 4-2	Stewart 2, Varadi 2	16,441
Oct 10	SHEFFIELD UNITED	L 2-3	White, Brightwell	18,377
Oct 17	Ipswich Town	L 0-3		12,711
Oct 21	Bradford City	W 4-2	Stewart 2, Lake, White	14,818
Oct 24	BARNSLEY	D 1-1	Varadi	17,063
Oct 31	Swindon Town	W 4-3	White 2, Varadi, Simpson	11,536
Nov 4	MIDDLESBROUGH	D 1-1	Hinchcliffe	18,434
Nov 7	HUDDERSFIELD TOWN	W 10-1	White 3, Adcock 3, Stewart 3, McNab	19,583
Nov 14	Reading	W 2-0	Stewart 2	10,052
Nov 21	BIRMINGHAM CITY	W 3-0	White 2, Stewart	22,690
Nov 28	West Bromwich Albion	D 1-1	Adcock	15,452
Dec 1	Bournemouth	W 2-0	White, Stewart	9,499
Dec 5	CRYSTAL PALACE	L 1-3	Lake	23,161
Dec 12	Millwall	W 1-0	Adcock	10,477
Dec 19	OLDHAM ATHLETIC	L 1-2	Stewart	22,518
Dec 26	LEEDS UNITED	L 1-2	White	30,153
Dec 28	Stoke City	W 3-1	Stewart 2, Brightwell	18,020
Jan 2	SHREWSBURY TOWN	L 1-3	Lake	21,455
Jan 16	Plymouth Argyle	L 2-3	Stewart, McNab	13,291
Jan 23	ASTON VILLA	L 0-2		24,668
Feb 6	Blackburn Rovers	L 1-2	Varadi	13,508
Feb 13	BOURNEMOUTH	W 2-0	Stewart, Varadi	16,161
Feb 27	Leicester City	L 0-1		13,852
Mar 2	HULL CITY	W 2-0	Varadi 2	16,040
Mar 5	IPSWICH TOWN	W 2-0	Morley, Varadi	17,402
Mar 8	Sheffield United	W 2-1	White, Morley	13,906
Mar 19	SWINDON TOWN	D 1-1	Stewart	17,022
Mar 26	Barnsley	L 1-3	Varadi	9,061
Apr 2	Huddersfield Town	L 0-1		7,835
Apr 4	READING	W 2-0	Stewart 2	15,172
Apr 9	Middlesbrough	L 1-2	Thompstone	19,443
Apr 23	BRADFORD CITY	D 2-2	Brightwell, Morley	20,335
Apr 30	Birmingham City	W 3-0	Brightwell 2, Varadi	8,014
May 2	WEST BROMWICH ALBION	W 4-2	Stewart 2, Morley, Varadi	16,490
May 7	Crystal Palace	L 0-2		17,555

FA Cup

Jan 9	Huddersfield Town	(Rd 3) D 2-2	Brightwell, Gidman	18,102
Jan 12	HUDDERSFIELD TOWN	(R) D 0-0		24,565
Jan 25	Huddersfield Town	(2nd R) W 3-0	Hinchcliffe, White, Varadi	21,510
Jan 30	Blackpool	(Rd 4) D 1-1	Lake	10,835
Feb 3	BLACKPOOL	(R) W 2-1	Stewart, Simpson	26,503
Feb 20	PLYMOUTH ARGYLE	(Rd 5) W 3-1	Scott, Simpson, Moulden	29,206
Mar 13	LIVERPOOL	(Rd 6) L 0-4		44,047

Littlewoods Cup

Sep 22	WOLVES	(Rd 2 FL) L 1-2	Adcock	8,551
Oct 6	Wolves	(Rd 2 SL) W 2-0	Gidman, Hinchcliffe	13,843
Oct 27	NOTTINGHAM FOREST	(Rd 3) W 3-0	Varadi 2, Stewart	15,168
Nov 17	WATFORD	(Rd 4) W 3-1	White 2, Stewart	20,357
Jan 20	Everton	(Rd 5) L 0-2		40,014

Full Members' Cup

Nov 10	PLYMOUTH ARGYLE	(Rd 1) W 6-0	Hinchcliffe, Adcock 3, Stewart, Lake	5,051
Dec 16	CHELSEA	(Rd 2) L 0-2		6,402

MANAGER: Mel Machin

CAPTAIN: Steve Redmond

TOP SCORER: Paul Stewart

BIGGEST WIN: November 7, 1988 10-1 v Huddersfield Town, Division 2

HIGHEST ATTENDANCE: March 13, 1988 44,047 v Liverpool, lost 0-4, FA Cup Round 6

League & Cup Appearances (substitute)

PLAYER	LEAGUE	CUP COMPETITION			TOTAL
		FA CUP	LITTLEWOODS	FMC	
Adcock	12 (3)	2	2 (1)	2	18 (4)
Barnes			0 (1)		0 (1)
Beckford	5				5
Brightwell	32 (1)	3 (2)	4	0 (1)	39 (4)
Clements	24 (1)	5	3	1	33 (1)
Gidman	30 (1)	7	4	2	44 (1)
Hinchcliffe	42	7	4	2	55
Lake	30 (3)	4	4	2	40 (3)
Lennon	1				1
McNab	36 (1)	7	5	2	50 (1)
Mimms	3				3
Morley	13 (2)				13 (2)
Moulden	2 (4)	1 (2)			3 (6)
Nixon	25	6	5	2	38
Redmond	44	7	5	2	58
Scott	19 (4)	3	2 (1)	0 (2)	24 (7)
Seagraves	13 (4)	1	1	1	16 (4)
Simpson	31 (7)	5 (2)	4	2	42 (9)
Stewart	40	6	4	2	52
Stowell	14	1			15
Suckling	2				2
Thompstone	(1)				0 (1)
Varadi	26 (6)	5 (1)	3 (2)	0 (1)	34 (10)
White	40 (4)	7	4	2	53 (4)

Goalscorers

PLAYER	LEAGUE	CUP COMPETITION			TOTAL
		FA CUP	LITTLEWOODS	FMC	
Stewart	24	1	2	1	28
Varadi	16	1	2		19
White	13	1	2		16
Adcock	5		1	3	9
Brightwell	5	1			6
Lake	3	1		1	5
Hinchcliffe	1	1	1	1	4
Morley	4				4
Scott	3	1			4
Gidman	1	1	1		3
Simpson	1	2			3
McNab	2				2
Moulden		1			1
Thompstone	1				1

Fact File

Highlight of the season was the 10-1 victory over Huddersfield Town. Stewart, Adcock and White all claimed hat-tricks in the match.

Final Division 2 Table

		P	W	D	L	F	A	Pts
1	MILLWALL	44	25	7	12	72	52	82
2	ASTON VILLA	44	22	12	10	68	41	78
3	MIDDLESBROUGH	44	22	12	10	63	36	78
4	BRADFORD C	44	22	11	11	74	54	77
5	BLACKBURN R	44	21	14	9	68	52	77
6	CRYSTAL PALACE	44	22	9	13	86	59	75
7	LEEDS U	44	19	12	13	61	51	69
8	IPSWICH T	44	19	9	16	61	52	66
9	MANCHESTER CITY	44	19	8	17	80	60	65
10	OLDHAM ATH	44	18	11	15	72	64	65
11	STOKE C	44	17	11	16	50	57	62
12	SWINDON T	44	16	11	17	73	60	59
13	LEICESTER C	44	16	11	17	62	61	59
14	BARNSLEY	44	15	12	17	61	62	57
15	HULL C	44	14	15	15	54	60	57
16	PLYMOUTH ARG	44	16	8	20	65	67	56
17	BOURNEMOUTH	44	13	10	21	56	68	49
18	SHREWSBURY T	44	11	16	17	42	54	49
19	BIRMINGHAM C	44	11	15	18	41	66	48
20	WBA	44	12	11	21	50	69	47
21	SHEFFIELD U	44	13	7	24	45	74	46
22	READING	44	10	12	22	44	70	42
23	HUDDERSFIELD T	44	6	10	28	41	100	28

Season 1988-89

Barclays League Division 2

DATE	OPPONENTS	SCORE	GOALSCORERS	ATTENDANCE
Aug 27	Hull City	L 0-1		11,653
Aug 29	OLDHAM ATHLETIC	L 1-4	Lake	22,594
Sep 4	WALSALL	D 2-2	Morley, McNab	17,104
Sep 10	Leeds United	D 1-1	McNab	23,122
Sep 17	BRIGHTON & HOVE ALBION	W 2-1	Brightwell, Moulden	16,033
Sep 20	Chelsea	W 3-1	Brightwell 2, Moulden	8,858
Sep 24	Barnsley	W 2-1	White, Morley	9,300
Oct 1	BLACKBURN ROVERS	W 1-0	Biggins	22,111
Oct 5	PORTSMOUTH	W 4-1	Biggins, White, Moulden, Lake	17,202
Oct 8	Ipswich Town	L 0-1		15,521
Oct 15	Plymouth Argyle	W 1-0	Gayle	10,158
Oct 22	BIRMINGHAM CITY	D 0-0		20,205
Oct 26	West Bromwich Albion	L 0-1		14,258
Oct 29	SUNDERLAND	D 1-1	Hinchcliffe	22,398
Nov 5	Leicester City	D 0-0		14,080
Nov 12	WATFORD	W 3-1	Biggins 2, Moulden	21,142
Nov 19	Bournemouth	W 1-0	Moulden	9,500
Nov 26	OXFORD UNITED	W 2-1	Morley, Redmond	20,145
Dec 3	Crystal Palace	D 0-0		12,444
Dec 10	BRADFORD CITY	W 4-0	Moulden 2, Brightwell 2	20,129
Dec 17	SHREWSBURY TOWN	D 2-2	Hinchcliffe 2	19,613
Dec 26	Stoke City	L 1-3	Gleghorn	24,056
Dec 31	Swindon Town	W 2-1	Beckford, Gayle	10,776
Jan 2	LEEDS UNITED	D 0-0		33,034
Jan 14	Oldham Athletic	W 1-0	Megson	19,200
Jan 21	HULL CITY	W 4-1	Biggins 2, White, Moulden	20,485
Feb 4	Portsmouth	W 1-0	Gleghorn	13,307
Feb 11	IPSWICH TOWN	W 4-0	Biggins 2, Morley, Gayle	22,145
Feb 18	Birmingham City	W 2-0	Gleghorn, McNab	11,707
Feb 25	PLYMOUTH ARGYLE	W 2-0	Biggins, McNab	22,451
Mar 1	WEST BROMWICH ALBION	D 1-1	Moulden	25,109
Mar 4	Watford	L 0-1		15,747
Mar 11	LEICESTER CITY	W 4-2	Morley 3, o.g.	22,266
Mar 14	Sunderland	W 4-2	White 2, Morley, Gleghorn	16,101
Mar 18	CHELSEA	L 2-3	Taggart, Moulden	40,070
Mar 25	Walsall	D 3-3	Moulden 2, Oldfield	7,562
Mar 27	STOKE CITY	W 2-1	Oldfield, Hinchcliffe	28,303
Apr 1	Brighton & Hove Albion	L 1-2	Morley	12,072
Apr 4	Shrewsbury Town	W 1-0	Morley	8,271
Apr 8	SWINDON TOWN	W 2-1	Hinchcliffe, Oldfield	22,663
Apr 15	Blackburn Rovers	L 0-4		16,727
Apr 22	BARNSLEY	L 1-2	Lake	21,274
Apr 29	Oxford United	W 4-2	Gleghorn, White, Brightwell, o.g.	7,762
May 1	CRYSTAL PALACE	D 1-1	Gleghorn	33,456
May 6	BOURNEMOUTH	D 3-3	Moulden 2, Morley	30,564
May 13	Bradford City	D 1-1	Morley	12,479

FA Cup

Jan 7	LEICESTER CITY	(Rd 3) W 1-0	McNab	23,838
Jan 28	Brentford	(Rd 4) L 1-3	Gleghorn	12,000

Littlewoods Cup

Sep 18	PLYMOUTH ARGYLE	(Rd 2 FL) W 1-0	White	9,454
Oct 12	Plymouth Argyle	(Rd 2 SL) W 6-3	Gleghorn 2, Biggins, Moulden, McNab, Lake	8,794
Nov 2	SHEFFIELD UNITED	(Rd 3) W 4-2	Moulden 3, Morley	16,609
Nov 29	Luton Town	(Rd 4) L 1-3	White	10,178

Full Members' Cup

Dec 13	Blackburn Rovers	(Rd 2) L 2-3	Gleghorn, o.g.	5,763

League & Cup Appearances (substitute)

PLAYER	LEAGUE	CUP COMPETITION			TOTAL
		FA CUP	LITTLEWOODS	FMC	
Beckford	2 (6)		1 (3)		3 (9)
Biggins	29 (3)	2	4		35 (3)
Bradshaw	1 (4)	0 (1)		0 (1)	1 (6)
Brightwell	24 (2)	2	2	1	29 (2)
Cooper	8				8
Dibble	38	2	4	1	45
Gayle	41	2	4		47
Gleghorn	25 (7)	0 (1)	2 (1)	1	28 (9)
Hinchcliffe	37 (2)	2	3	1	43 (2)
Hughes	1				1
Lake	37 (1)	2	2	1	42 (1)
McNab	42	2	4	1	49
Megson	22	1		1	24
Morley	39 (1)	1	4	1	45 (1)
Moulden	29 (7)	1	4	1	35 (7)
Oldfield	8 (3)				8 (3)
Redmond	46	2	4	1	53
Scott	1	0 (1)	1		2 (1)
Seagraves	21 (2)	2	2	1	26 (2)
Simpson	1		0 (1)		1 (1)
Taggart	9 (2)				9 (2)
Varadi	1 (2)				1 (2)
White	44 (1)	2	3	1	50 (1)
Williams	0 (1)				0 (1)

Goalscorers

PLAYER	LEAGUE	CUP COMPETITION			TOTAL
		FA CUP	LITTLEWOODS	FMC	
Moulden	13		4		17
Morley	12		1		13
Biggins	9		1		10
Gleghorn	6	1	2	1	10
White	6		2		8
McNab	5	1	1		7
Brightwell	6				6
Hinchcliffe	5				5
Lake	3		1		4
Gayle	3				3
Oldfield	3				3
Beckford	1				1
Megson	1				1
Redmond	1				1
Taggart	1				1
Opps' o.gs.	2		1		3

Fact File

Trevor Morley's goal with four minutes to go in the final match of the season at Bradford, earned City a direct promotion.

Final Division 2 Table

		P	W	D	L	F	A	Pts
1	CHELSEA	46	29	12	5	96	50	99
2	MANCHESTER CITY	46	23	13	10	77	53	82
3	CRYSTAL PALACE	46	23	12	11	71	49	81
4	WATFORD	46	22	12	12	74	48	78
5	BLACKBURN R	46	22	11	13	74	59	77
6	SWINDON T	46	20	16	10	68	53	76
7	BARNSLEY	46	20	14	12	66	58	74
8	IPSWICH T	46	22	7	17	71	61	73
9	WBA	46	18	18	10	65	41	72
10	LEEDS U	46	17	16	13	59	50	67
11	SUNDERLAND	46	16	15	15	60	60	63
12	BOURNEMOUTH	46	18	8	20	53	62	62
13	STOKE C	46	15	14	17	57	72	59
14	BRADFORD C	46	13	17	16	52	59	56
15	LEICESTER C	46	13	16	17	56	63	55
16	OLDHAM ATH	46	11	21	14	75	72	54
17	OXFORD U	46	14	12	20	62	70	54
18	PLYMOUTH ARG	46	14	12	20	55	66	54
19	BRIGHTON & HA	46	14	9	23	57	66	51
20	PORTSMOUTH	46	13	12	21	53	62	51
21	HULL C	46	11	14	21	52	68	47
22	SHREWSBURY T	46	8	18	20	40	67	42
23	BIRMINGHAM C	46	8	11	27	31	76	35
24	WALSALL	46	5	16	25	41	80	31

MANAGER: Mel Machin

CAPTAIN: Steve Redmond

TOP SCORER: Andy Moulden

BIGGEST WIN: September 18, 1988 6-3 v Plymouth Argyle, League Cup, Round 2 Second Leg

HIGHEST ATTENDANCE: March 18, 1989 40,070 v Chelsea, lost 2-3, Division 1

MAJOR TRANSFERS IN: Brian Gayle from Wimbledon, Wayne Biggins from Norwich City

MAJOR TRANSFERS OUT: Paul Stewart to Tottenham Hotspur

Season 1989-90

Barclays League Division 1

DATE	OPPONENTS	SCORE	GOALSCORERS	ATTENDANCE
Aug 19	Liverpool	L 1-3	Hinchliffe	37,628
Aug 23	SOUTHAMPTON	L 1-2	Gleghorn	25,416
Aug 26	TOTTENHAM HOTSPUR	D 1-1	White	32,004
Aug 30	Coventry City	L 1-2	White	16,111
Sep 9	QUEENS PARK RANGERS	W 1-0	Allen	23,420
Sep 16	Wimbledon	L 0-1		6,815
Sep 23	MANCHESTER UNITED	W 5-1	Oldfield 2, Hinchliffe, Bishop, Morley	43,246
Sep 30	LUTON TOWN	W 3-1	Bishop, Oldfield, Brightwell	23,863
Oct 14	Arsenal	L 0-4		40,414
Oct 22	ASTON VILLA	L 0-2		23,354
Oct 28	Chelsea	D 1-1	Allen	21,917
Nov 4	CRYSTAL PALACE	W 3-0	White, Morley, Allen	23,768
Nov 11	Derby County	L 0-6		19,239
Nov 18	NOTTINGHAM FOREST	L 0-3		26,238
Nov 25	Charlton Athletic	D 1-1	Allen	8,852
Dec 2	LIVERPOOL	L 1-4	Allen	31,641
Dec 9	Southampton	L 1-2	Allen	15,832
Dec 17	Everton	D 0-0		21,737
Dec 26	NORWICH CITY	W 1-0	Allen	29,534
Dec 30	MILLWALL	W 2-0	White 2	28,084
Jan 1	Sheffield Wednesday	L 0-2		28,756
Jan 13	Tottenham Hotspur	D 1-1	Hendry	26,384
Jan 20	COVENTRY CITY	W 1-0	White	24,345
Feb 3	Manchester United	D 1-1	Brightwell	40,274
Feb 10	WIMBLEDON	D 1-1	Hendry	24,126
Feb 24	CHARLTON ATHLETIC	L 1-2	White	24,030
Mar 3	Nottingham Forest	L 0-1		22,644
Mar 10	ARSENAL	D 1-1	White	29,087
Mar 17	Luton Town	D 1-1	Allen	9,765
Mar 21	CHELSEA	D 1-1	Quinn	24,670
Apr 1	Aston Villa	D 2-1	Reid, Ward	24,797
Apr 7	Millwall	D 1-1	Ward	10,265
Apr 11	Queens Park Rangers	W 3-1	Allen, Hendry, Ward	8,437
Apr 14	SHEFFIELD WEDNESDAY	W 2-1	Quinn, Heath	33,022
Apr 16	Norwich City	W 1-0	Heath	18,914
Apr 21	EVERTON	W 1-0	Quinn	32,144
Apr 28	DERBY COUNTY	L 0-1		29,542
May 5	Crystal Palace	D 2-2	Quinn, Allen	20,056

FA Cup

Jan 6	MILLWALL	(Rd 3) D 0-0		25,038
Jan 9	Millwall	(R) D 1-1	Hendry	17,616
Jan 15	Millwall	(2nd R) L 1-3	Lake	17,771

Littlewoods Cup

Sep 19	Brentford	(Rd 2 FL) L 1-2	Oldfield	6,065
Oct 4	BRENTFORD	(Rd 2 SL) W 4-1	Morley 2, White, Oldfield	17,874
Oct 25	NORWICH CITY	(Rd 3) W 3-1	Allen, White, Bishop	20,126
Nov 22	COVENTRY CITY	(Rd 4) L 0-1		23,355

Full Members' Cup

Nov 29	Nottingham Forest	(Rd 2) L 2-3	White, Oldfield	9,279

League & Cup Appearances (substitute)

PLAYER	LEAGUE	CUP COMPETITION			TOTAL
		FA CUP	LITTLEWOODS	FMC	
Allen	23 (7)	3	2		28 (7)
Beckford	1 (4)				1 (4)
Bishop	18 (1)		4	1	23 (1)
Brightwell	14 (14)		1 (1)	0 (1)	15 (16)
Clarke	4 (5)				4 (5)
Cooper	7		2		9
Dibble	31	3	2	1	37
Fashanu	0 (2)				0 (2)
Fleming	13 (1)		4	1	18 (1)
Gayle	14		4	1	19
Gleghorn	2				2
Harper	21	3			24
Heath	7 (5)				7 (5)
Hendry	25	3	1		29
Hinchliffe	28 (3)	3	4	1	36 (3)
Lake	31	3	4	1	37
McNab	11 (1)		3	1	15 (1)
Megson	19	3			22
Morley	17		3	1	21
Oldfield	10 (5)		2 (1)	0 (1)	12 (7)
Quinn	9				9
Redmond	38	3	4	1	46
Reid	18	3			21
Seagraves	2				2
Taggart	1		1		2
Ward A	0 (1)	0 (2)			0 (3)
Ward M	19	3			22
White	35 (2)	3	4	1	43 (2)

Goalscorers

PLAYER	LEAGUE	CUP COMPETITION			TOTAL
		FA CUP	LITTLEWOODS	FMC	
Allen	10		1		11
White	8		2	1	11
Oldfield	3		2	1	6
Hendry	3	1			4
Morley	2		2		4
Quinn	4				4
Bishop	2		1		3
Ward M	3				3
Brightwell	2				2
Heath	2				2
Hinchliffe	2				2
Gleghorn	1				1
Lake		1			1
Reid	1				1

Fact File

City's 5-1 victory over United in September was their best ever derby result at Maine Road.

MANAGER: Mel Machin/Howard Kendall
CAPTAIN: Steve Redmond
TOP SCORERS: Clive Allen and David White
BIGGEST WIN: September 23, 1989 5-1 v Manchester United, Division 1;
HIGHEST ATTENDANCE: September 23, 1989 43,246 v Manchester United, won 5-1, Division 1
MAJOR TRANSFERS IN: Ian Bishop from Bournemouth, Clive Allen from Bordeaux, Niall Quinn from Arsenal
MAJOR TRANSFERS OUT: Andy Moulden to Bournemouth

Final Division 1 Table

		P	W	D	L	F	A	PTS
1	LIVERPOOL	38	23	10	5	78	37	79
2	ASTON VILLA	38	21	7	10	57	38	70
3	TOTTENHAM H	38	19	6	13	59	47	63
4	ARSENAL	38	18	8	12	54	38	62
5	CHELSEA	38	16	12	10	58	50	60
6	EVERTON	38	17	8	13	57	46	59
7	SOUTHAMPTON	38	15	10	13	71	63	55
8	WIMBLEDON	38	13	16	9	47	40	55
9	NOTTINGHAM F	38	15	9	14	55	47	54
10	NORWICH C	38	13	14	11	44	40	53
11	QPR	38	13	11	14	45	44	50
12	COVENTRY C	38	14	7	17	39	59	49
13	MANCHESTER U	38	13	9	16	46	47	48
14	MANCHESTER CITY	38	12	12	14	43	52	48
15	CRYSTAL PALACE	38	13	9	16	42	66	48
16	DERBY CO	38	13	7	28	43	40	46
17	LUTON T	38	10	13	15	43	57	43
18	SHEFFIELD W	38	11	10	17	35	51	43
19	CHARLTON ATH	38	7	9	22	31	57	30
20	MILLWALL	38	5	11	22	39	65	26

Season 1990-91

Barclays League Division 1

DATE	OPPONENTS	SCORE	GOALSCORERS	ATTENDANCE
Aug 25	Tottenham Hotspur	L 1-3	Quinn	33,501
Sep 1	EVERTON	W 1-0	Heath	31,456
Sep 5	ASTON VILLA	W 2-1	Ward (pen), Pointon	30,199
Sep 8	Sheffield United	D 1-1	White	21,895
Sep 15	NORWICH CITY	W 2-1	Quinn, Brennan	26,247
Sep 22	Chelsea	D 1-1	Ward (pen)	20,924
Sep 29	Wimbledon	D 1-1	Allen	6,158
Oct 6	COVENTRY CITY	W 2-0	Harper, Quinn	26,198
Oct 20	Derby County	D 1-1	Ward (pen)	17,884
Oct 27	MANCHESTER UNITED	D 3-3	White 2, Hendry	36,427
Nov 3	Sunderland	D 1-1	White	23,137
Nov 10	LEEDS UNITED	L 2-3	Ward (pen), White	27,782
Nov 17	Luton Town	D 2-2	White, Redmond	9,564
Nov 24	Liverpool	D 2-2	Ward (pen), Quinn	37,849
Dec 1	QUEENS PARK RANGERS	W 2-1	Quinn 2	25,080
Dec 15	TOTTENHAM HOTSPUR	W 2-1	Redmond, Ward (pen)	31,263
Dec 22	CRYSTAL PALACE	L 0-2		25,321
Dec 26	Southampton	L 1-2	Quinn	16,029
Dec 29	Nottingham Forest	W 3-1	Quinn 2, Clarke	24,937
Jan 1	ARSENAL	L 0-1		30,579
Jan 13	Everton	L 0-2		22,774
Jan 19	SHEFFIELD UNITED	W 2-0	Ward 2	25,741
Feb 2	Norwich City	W 2-1	Quinn, White	15,194
Feb 9	CHELSEA	W 2-1	Megson, White	25,116
Mar 2	Queens Park Rangers	L 0-1		12,376
Mar 5	LUTON TOWN	W 3-0	Quinn 2, Allen (pen)	20,404
Mar 9	LIVERPOOL	L 0-3		33,150
Mar 16	WIMBLEDON	D 1-1	Ward (pen)	21,089
Mar 23	Coventry City	L 1-3	Allen	13,198
Mar 30	SOUTHAMPTON	D 3-3	Allen, Brennan, White	23,163
Apr 1	Crystal Palace	W 3-1	Quinn 3	18,001
Apr 6	NOTTINGHAM FOREST	W 3-1	Ward (pen), Quinn, Redmond	25,169
Apr 10	Leeds United	W 2-1	Hill, Quinn	28,757
Apr 17	Arsenal	D 2-2	Ward (pen), White	38,412
Apr 20	DERBY COUNTY	W 2-1	Quinn, White	24,037
Apr 23	Aston Villa	W 5-1	White 4, Brennan	24,848
May 4	Manchester United	L 0-1		45,286
May 11	SUNDERLAND	W 3-2	Quinn 2, White	39,194

FA Cup

Jan 6	Burnley	(Rd 3) W 1-0	Hendry	20,331
Jan 26	Port Vale	(Rd 4) W 2-1	Quinn, Allen	19,132
Feb 16	Notts County	(Rd 5) L 0-1		18,979

Rumbelows Cup

Sep 26	Torquay	(Rd 2 FL) W 4-0	Harper, Hendry, Allen, Beckford	5,429
Oct 10	TORQUAY	(Rd 2 SL) D 0-0		12,204
Oct 30	ARSENAL	(Rd 3) L 1-2	Allen	26,825

Full Members' Cup

Dec 19	MIDDLESBROUGH	(Rd 2) W 2-1	White, Quinn	6,406
Jan 22	Sheffield United	(Rd 3) W 2-0	Ward 2	5,106
Feb 20	Leeds United	(Rd 4) L 0-2		11,898

Fact File

The Blues' fifth place finish was their best since 1977-78.

MANAGER: Howard Kendall/Peter Reid

CAPTAIN: Steve Redmond

TOP SCORER: Niall Quinn

BIGGEST WIN: April 23, 1990 5-1 v Aston Villa, Division 1

HIGHEST ATTENDANCE: May 4, 1990 45,286 v Manchester United, lost 0-1, Division 1

MAJOR TRANSFERS IN: Tony Coton from Watford, Neil Pointon from Everton

MAJOR TRANSFERS OUT: Andy Hinchcliffe to Everton

League & Cup Appearances (substitute)

PLAYER	LEAGUE	CUP COMPETITION				TOTAL
		FA CUP	RUMBELOWS	FMC		
Allen	8 (12)	1 (2)	2 (1)	2		13 (15)
Beckford	0 (2)		0 (1)			0 (3)
Brennan	12 (4)	1	2	1		16 (4)
Brightwell I	30 (3)	3	2 (1)	2 (1)		37 (5)
Clarke	3 (4)	1		1		5 (4)
Coton	33	3	3	3		42
Dibble	3					3
Harper	25 (4)	3	3	3		34 (4)
Heath	31 (4)	1 (1)	2 (1)	0 (1)		34 (7)
Hendry	32	2	3	3		40
Hill	7 (4)			1		8 (4)
Hughes	0 (4)					0 (4)
Lake	3					3
Margetson	2		0 (1)			2 (1)
Megson	19	3	2	2		26
Pointon	35	3	3	3		44
Quinn	38	2	3	3		46
Redmond	35 (2)	3	3	2		43 (2)
Reid	28 (2)	1	1			30 (2)
Ward M	36	3	3	3		45
White	38	3	1	3		45

Goalscorers

PLAYER	LEAGUE	CUP COMPETITION				TOTAL
		FA CUP	RUMBELOWS	FMC		
Quinn	20	1		1		22
White	16			1		17
Ward M	11			2		13
Allen	4	1	2			7
Brennan	3					3
Hendry	1	1	1			3
Redmond	3					3
Harper	1		1			2
Beckford			1			1
Clarke	1					1
Heath	1					1
Hill	1					1
Megson	1					1
Pointon	1					1

Final Division 1 Table

		P	W	D	L	F	A	Pts
1	ARSENAL	38	24	13	1	74	18	83
2	LIVERPOOL	38	23	7	8	77	40	76
3	CRYSTAL PALACE	38	20	9	9	50	41	69
4	LEEDS U	38	19	7	12	65	47	64
5	MANCHESTER CITY	38	17	11	10	64	53	62
6	MANCHESTER U	38	16	12	10	58	45	59
7	WIMBLEDON	38	14	14	10	53	46	56
8	NOTTINGHAM F	38	14	12	12	65	50	54
9	EVERTON	38	13	12	13	50	46	51
10	TOTTENHAM H	38	11	16	11	51	50	49
11	CHELSEA	38	13	10	15	58	69	49
12	QPR	38	12	10	16	44	53	46
13	SHEFFIELD U	38	13	7	18	36	55	46
14	SOUTHAMPTON	38	12	9	17	58	69	45
15	NORWICH C	38	13	6	19	41	64	45
16	COVENTRY C	38	11	11	16	42	49	44
17	ASTON VILLA	38	9	14	15	46	58	41
18	LUTON T	38	10	7	21	42	61	37
19	SUNDERLAND	38	8	10	20	38	60	34
20	DERBY CO	38	5	9	24	37	75	24

Arsenal had two points deducted, Manchester U had one point deducted for disciplinary reasons

Season 1991-92

Barclays League Division 1

DATE	OPPONENTS	SCORE	GOALSCORERS	ATTENDANCE
Aug 17	Coventry City	W 1-0	Quinn	18,013
Aug 21	LIVERPOOL	W 2-1	White 2	37,322
Aug 24	CRYSTAL PALACE	W 3-2	Brennan 2 (2 pen), White	28,023
Aug 28	Norwich City	D 0-0		15,376
Aug 31	Arsenal	L 1-2	Brightwell	35,009
Sep 4	NOTTINGHAM FOREST	W 2-1	Quinn, Hill	29,146
Sep 7	Leeds United	L 0-3		29,986
Sep 14	SHEFFIELD WEDNESDAY	L 0-1		29,453
Sep 17	EVERTON	L 0-1		27,509
Sep 21	West Ham United	W 2-1	Redmond (pen), Hendry	25,588
Sep 28	OLDHAM ATHLETIC	L 1-2	White	31,271
Oct 6	Notts County	W 3-1	Sheron, Allen	11,878
Oct 19	Tottenham Hotspur	W 1-0	Quinn	30,502
Oct 26	SHEFFIELD UNITED	W 3-2	Sheron, Quinn, Hughes	25,495
Nov 2	Southampton	W 3-0	Quinn, Sheron, o.g.	13,933
Nov 16	MANCHESTER UNITED	D 0-0		38,180
Nov 23	Luton Town	D 2-2	Curle, Quinn	10,031
Nov 30	WIMBLEDON	D 0-0		22,429
Dec 7	Aston Villa	L 1-3	White	26,265
Dec 14	QUEENS PARK RANGERS	D 2-2	White, Curle	21,437
Dec 20	Liverpool	D 2-2	White 2	36,743
Dec 26	NORWICH CITY	W 2-1	Quinn, White	28,164
Dec 28	ARSENAL	W 1-0	White	32,325
Jan 1	Chelsea	D 1-1	Sheron	18,196
Jan 11	Crystal Palace	D 1-1	Curle (pen)	14,766
Jan 18	COVENTRY CITY	W 1-0	White	23,005
Feb 1	TOTTENHAM HOTSPUR	W 1-0	White	30,123
Feb 8	Sheffield United	L 2-4	Curle (pen), Hill	26,562
Feb 15	LUTON TOWN	W 4-0	White 2, Hill, Heath	22,137
Feb 22	Wimbledon	L 1-2	Sheron	5,082
Feb 29	ASTON VILLA	W 2-0	Quinn, White	28,268
Mar 7	Queens Park Rangers	L 0-4		10,779
Mar 15	SOUTHAMPTON	L 0-1		24,265
Mar 21	Nottingham Forest	L 0-2		24,115
Mar 28	CHELSEA	D 0-0		23,633
Apr 4	LEEDS UNITED	W 4-0	Hill, Sheron, Quinn, Brennan	30,239
Apr 7	Manchester United	D 1-1	Curle (pen)	46,781
Apr 11	Sheffield Wednesday	L 0-2		32,138
Apr 18	WEST HAM UNITED	W 2-0	Pointon, W Clarke	25,601
Apr 20	Everton	W 2-1	Quinn 2	21,101
Apr 25	NOTTS COUNTY	W 2-0	Simpson, Quinn	23,426
May 2	Oldham Athletic	W 5-2	Mike, White 3, Sheron	18,588

FA Cup

Jan 4	Middlesbrough	(Rd 3) L 1-2	Reid	21,174

Rumbelows Cup

Sep 25	CHESTER CITY	(Rd 2 FL) W 3-1	White 2, Quinn	10,987
Oct 8	Chester City	(Rd 2 SL) W 3-0	Allen, Sheron, Brennan	4,146
Oct 29	QUEENS PARK RANGERS	(Rd 3) D 0-0		15,512
Nov 20	Queens Park Rangers	(R) W 3-1	Heath 2, Quinn	11,033
Dec 4	Middlesbrough	(Rd 4) L 1-2	White	17,286

Full Members' Cup

Oct 23	Sheffield Wednesday	(Rd 2) L 2-3	Hendry 2	7,951

Fact File

City topped the table after three matches, but eventually had to be satisfied with fifth place and a tremendous victory over champions-to-be Leeds.

MANAGER: Peter Reid

CAPTAIN: Keith Curle

TOP SCORER: David White

BIGGEST WIN: February 15, 1992 4-0 v Luton Town, Division 1

HIGHEST ATTENDANCE: April 7, 1992 46,781 v Manchester United, drew 1-1, Division 1

MAJOR TRANSFERS IN: Keith Curle from Wimbledon, Steve McMahon from Liverpool

League & Cup Appearances (substitute)

PLAYER	LEAGUE	CUP COMPETITION			TOTAL
		FA CUP	RUMBELOWS	FMC	
Allen C	0 (3)		1 (1)		1 (4)
Brennan	13		2	1	16
Brightwell D	3 (1)				3 (1)
Brightwell I	36 (4)	1	5	1	43 (4)
Clarke W	0 (5)				0 (5)
Coton	37	1	5		43
Curle	40	1	4	1	46
Dibble	2				2
Heath	20 (8)	1	5	1	27 (8)
Hendry	0 (6)		0 (1)	1	1 (7)
Hill	36		5		41
Hoekman	0 (1)		0 (2)		0 (3)
Hughes	24	1	5	1	31
Margetson	3			1	4
Mauge				0 (1)	0 (1)
McMahon	18	1			19
Megson	18 (4)	0 (1)	3		21 (5)
Mike	2				2
Pointon	39	1	5	1	46
Quigley	0 (5)			1	1 (5)
Quinn	35	1	4		40
Redmond	31	1	5	1	38
Reid	29 (2)	1	1		31 (2)
Sheron	20 (9)	0 (1)	2 (1)	1	23 (11)
Simpson	9 (2)				9 (2)
Vonk	8 (1)				8 (1)
White	39	1	3		43

Goalscorers

PLAYER	LEAGUE	CUP COMPETITION			TOTAL
		FA CUP	RUMBELOWS	FMC	
White	18		3		21
Quinn	12		2		14
Sheron	7		1		8
Curle	5				5
Brennan	3		1		4
Hill	4				4
Allen C	2		1		3
Heath	1		2		3
Hendry	1			2	3
Brightwell I	1				1
Clarke W	1				1
Hughes	1				1
Mike	1				1
Pointon	1				1
Redmond	1				1
Reid		1			1
Simpson	1				1
Opps' o.gs.	1				1

Final Division 1 Table

		P	W	D	L	F	A	Pts
1	LEEDS U	42	22	16	4	74	37	82
2	MANCHESTER U	42	21	15	6	63	33	78
3	SHEFFIELD W	42	21	12	9	62	49	75
4	ARSENAL	42	19	15	8	81	46	72
5	MANCHESTER CITY	42	20	10	12	61	48	70
6	LIVERPOOL	42	16	16	10	47	40	64
7	ASTON VILLA	42	17	9	16	48	44	60
8	NOTTINGHAM F	42	16	11	15	60	58	59
9	SHEFFIELD U	42	16	9	17	65	63	57
10	CRYSTAL PALACE	42	14	15	13	53	61	57
11	QPR	42	12	18	12	48	47	54
12	EVERTON	42	13	14	15	52	51	53
13	WIMBLEDON	42	13	14	15	53	53	53
14	CHELSEA	42	13	14	15	50	60	53
15	TOTTENHAM H	42	15	7	20	58	63	52
16	SOUTHAMPTON	42	14	10	18	39	55	52
17	OLDHAM ATH	42	14	9	19	63	67	51
18	NORWICH C	42	11	12	19	47	63	45
19	COVENTRY C	42	11	11	20	35	44	44
20	LUTON T	42	10	12	20	38	71	42
21	NOTTS CO	42	10	10	22	40	62	40
22	WEST HAM U	42	9	11	22	37	59	38

Season 1992-93

Premier League

DATE	OPPONENTS	SCORE	GOALSCORERS	ATTENDANCE
Aug 17	QUEENS PARK RANGERS	D 1-1	White	24,471
Aug 19	Middlesbrough	L 0-2		15,369
Aug 22	Blackburn Rovers	L 0-1		19,433
Aug 26	NORWICH CITY	W 3-1	White 2, McMahon	23,183
Aug 29	OLDHAM ATHLETIC	D 3-3	Quinn, Vonk, White	27,288
Sep 1	Wimbledon	W 1-0	White	4,714
Sep 5	Sheffield Wednesday	W 3-0	White 2, Vonk	27,169
Sep 12	MIDDLESBROUGH	L 0-1		25,244
Sep 20	CHELSEA	L 0-1		22,420
Sep 28	Arsenal	L 0-1		21,504
Oct 3	NOTTINGHAM FOREST	D 2-2	Holden, Simpson	22,571
Oct 17	Crystal Palace	D 0-0		14,005
Oct 24	SOUTHAMPTON	W 1-0	Sheron	20,089
Oct 31	Everton	W 3-1	Sheron 2, White	20,242
Nov 7	LEEDS UNITED	W 4-0	Sheron, White, Hill, Brightwell	27,255
Nov 21	Coventry City	W 3-2	Sheron, Quinn, Curle (pen)	14,590
Nov 28	TOTTENHAM HOTSPUR	L 0-1		25,496
Dec 6	Manchester United	L 1-2	Quinn	35,408
Dec 12	Ipswich Town	L 1-3	Flitcroft	16,833
Dec 19	ASTON VILLA	D 1-1	Flitcroft	23,525
Dec 26	SHEFFIELD UNITED	W 2-0	White 2	27,455
Dec 28	Liverpool	D 1-1	Quinn	43,037
Jan 9	Chelsea	W 4-2	White, Sheron 2, o.g.	15,939
Jan 16	ARSENAL	L 0-1		25,041
Jan 26	Oldham Athletic	W 1-0	Quinn	14,903
Jan 30	BLACKBURN ROVERS	W 3-2	Sheron, Curle (pen), White	29,122
Feb 6	Queens Park Rangers	D 1-1	Sheron	13,003
Feb 20	Norwich City	L 1-2	Sheron	16,386
Feb 23	SHEFFIELD WEDNESDAY	L 1-2	Quinn	23,619
Feb 27	Nottingham Forest	W 2-0	White, Flitcroft	25,956
Mar 10	COVENTRY CITY	W 1-0	Flitcroft	20,092
Mar 13	Leeds United	L 0-1		30,840
Mar 20	MANCHESTER UNITED	D 1-1	Quinn	37,136
Mar 24	Tottenham Hotspur	L 1-3	Sheron	27,247
Apr 3	IPSWICH TOWN	W 3-1	Quinn, Holden, Vonk	20,680
Apr 9	Sheffield United	D 1-1	o.g.	18,231
Apr 12	LIVERPOOL	D 1-1	Flitcroft	28,098
Apr 18	Aston Villa	L 1-3	Quinn	33,108
Apr 21	WIMBLEDON	D 1-1	Holden	19,524
May 1	Southampton	W 1-0	White	11,830
May 5	CRYSTAL PALACE	D 0-0		21,167
May 8	EVERTON	L 2-5	White, Curle (pen)	25,180

FA Cup

Jan 2	READING	(Rd 3) D 1-1	Sheron		20,523
Jan 13	Reading	(R) W 4-0	Sheron, Holden, Flitcroft, Quinn		12,065
Jan 23	Queens Park Rangers	(Rd 4) W 2-1	White, Vonk		18,652
Feb 13	BARNSLEY	(Rd 5) W 2-0	White 2		32,807
Mar 7	TOTTENHAM HOTSPUR	(Rd 6) L 2-4	Sheron, Phelan		34,050

Coca-Cola Cup

Sep 23	BRISTOL ROVERS	(Rd 2 FL) D 0-0			9,967
Oct 7	Bristol Rovers	(Rd 2 SL) W 2-1	o.g., Holden		7,822
Oct 28	TOTTENHAM HOTSPUR	(Rd 3) L 0-1			18,399

League & Cup Appearances (substitute)

PLAYER	LEAGUE	CUP COMPETITION		TOTAL
		FA CUP	COCA-COLA	
Brightwell D	4 (4)	0 (1)		4 (5)
Brightwell I	21	1	3	25
Coton	40	5	3	48
Curle	39	4	3	46
Dibble	1 (1)			1 (1)
Flitcroft	28 (4)	5	1 (1)	34 (5)
Hill	23 (1)	2 (1)	3	28 (2)
Holden	40 (1)	5	3	48 (1)
Ingebritsen	2 (5)			2 (5)
Kerr	0 (1)			0 (1)
Lake	2			2
Margetson	1			1
McMahon	24 (3)	2	2	28 (3)
Mike	1 (2)			1 (2)
Phelan	37	5	3	45
Quigley	1 (4)			1 (4)
Quinn	39	5	3	47
Ranson	17	1		18
Reid	14 (6)	2	1 (1)	17 (7)
Sheron	33 (5)	5	2	40 (5)
Simpson	27 (2)	4	3	34 (2)
Vonk	26	3 (1)		29 (1)
White	42	5	3	50

Goalscorers

PLAYER	LEAGUE	CUP COMPETITION		TOTAL
		FA CUP	COCA-COLA	
White	16	3		19
Sheron	11	3		14
Quinn	9	1		10
Flitcroft	5	1		6
Holden	3	1	1	5
Vonk	3	1		4
Curle	3			3
Phelan	1	1		2
Brightwell I	1			1
Hill	1			1
McMahon	1			1
Simpson	1			1
Opps' o.gs.	1		1	2

Fact File

Paul Lake returned from injury at the beginning of the season, but was carried off in the second game after just eight minutes with a knee injury.

Final Premier League Table

		P	W	D	L	F	A	Pts
1	MANCHESTER U	42	24	12	6	67	31	84
2	ASTON VILLA	42	21	11	10	57	40	74
3	NORWICH C	42	21	9	12	61	65	72
4	BLACKBURN R	42	20	11	11	68	46	71
5	QPR	42	17	12	13	63	55	63
6	LIVERPOOL	42	16	11	15	62	55	59
7	SHEFFIELD W	42	15	14	13	55	51	59
8	TOTTENHAM H	42	16	11	15	60	66	59
9	MANCHESTER CITY	42	15	12	15	56	51	57
10	ARSENAL	42	15	11	16	40	38	56
11	CHELSEA	42	14	14	14	51	54	56
12	WIMBLEDON	42	14	12	16	56	55	54
13	EVERTON	42	15	8	19	53	55	53
14	SHEFFIELD U	42	14	10	18	54	53	52
15	COVENTRY C	42	13	13	16	52	57	52
16	IPSWICH T	42	12	16	14	50	55	52
17	LEEDS U	42	12	15	15	57	62	51
18	SOUTHAMPTON	42	13	11	18	54	61	50
19	OLDHAM ATH	42	13	10	19	63	74	49
20	CRYSTAL PALACE	42	11	16	15	48	61	49
21	MIDDLESBROUGH	42	11	11	20	54	75	44
22	NOTTINGHAM F	42	10	10	22	41	62	40

MANAGER: Peter Reid

CAPTAIN: Keith Curle

TOP SCORER: David White

BIGGEST WIN: November 7, 1992 4-0 v Leeds United, Premier League; January 13, 1993 4-0 v Reading, FA Cup Round 3 replay

HIGHEST ATTENDANCE: December 28, 1992 43,037 v Liverpool, drew 1-1, Premier League

MAJOR TRANSFERS IN: Rick Holden from Oldham, Terry Phelan from Wimbledon

MAJOR TRANSFERS OUT: Steve Redmond and Neil Pointon to Oldham

Season 1993-94

Premier League

DATE	OPPONENTS	SCORE	GOALSCORERS	ATTENDANCE
Aug 14	LEEDS UNITED	D 1-1	Flitcroft	32,366
Aug 17	Everton	L 0-1		26,025
Aug 21	Tottenham Hotspur	L 0-2		24,535
Aug 24	BLACKBURN ROVERS	L 0-2		25,185
Aug 27	COVENTRY CITY	D 1-1	Sheron	21,537
Sep 1	Swindon Town	W 3-1	Vonk, Quinn, Mike	16,067
Sep 11	QUEENS PARK RANGERS	W 3-0	Quinn, Sheron, Flitcroft	24,445
Sep 20	Wimbledon	L 0-1		8,533
Sep 25	Sheffield United	W 1-0	Sheron	20,067
Oct 4	OLDHAM ATHLETIC	D 1-1	Sheron	21,401
Oct 16	Arsenal	D 0-0		29,567
Oct 23	LIVERPOOL	D 1-1	White	30,403
Nov 1	West Ham United	L 1-3	Curle (pen)	16,605
Nov 7	MANCHESTER UNITED	L 2-3	Quinn 2	35,155
Nov 20	Norwich City	D 1-1	Quinn	16,626
Nov 22	Chelsea	D 0-0		10,128
Nov 27	SHEFFIELD WEDNESDAY	L 1-3	Sheron	23,416
Dec 4	Leeds United	L 2-3	Sheron, Griffiths	33,820
Dec 8	EVERTON	W 1-0	Griffiths	20,513
Dec 11	TOTTENHAM HOTSPUR	L 0-2		21,566
Dec 18	Blackburn Rovers	L 0-2		19,479
Dec 28	SOUTHAMPTON	D 1-1	Phelan	24,712
Jan 1	Newcastle United	L 0-2		35,585
Jan 15	ARSENAL	D 0-0		25,642
Jan 22	Liverpool	L 1-2	Griffiths	41,872
Feb 5	IPSWICH TOWN	W 2-1	Griffiths, Flitcroft	28,188
Feb 12	WEST HAM UNITED	D 0-0		29,118
Feb 19	Coventry City	L 0-4		11,739
Feb 22	Aston Villa	D 0-0		19,254
Feb 25	SWINDON TOWN	W 2-1	o.g., Rocastle	26,360
Mar 5	Queens Park Rangers	D 1-1	Rocastle	13,474
Mar 12	WIMBLEDON	L 0-1		23,981
Mar 19	SHEFFIELD UNITED	D 0-0		25,448
Mar 26	Oldham Athletic	D 0-0		16,462
Mar 29	Ipswich Town	D 2-2	Walsh, Rosler	12,871
Apr 2	ASTON VILLA	W 3-0	Beagrie, Walsh, Rosler	26,075
Apr 4	Southampton	W 1-0	Karl	16,377
Apr 9	NEWCASTLE UNITED	W 2-1	Walsh, D Brightwell	33,774
Apr 16	NORWICH CITY	D 1-1	Rosler	28,020
Apr 23	Manchester United	L 0-2		44,333
Apr 30	CHELSEA	D 2-2	Rosler, Walsh	33,594
May 7	Sheffield Wednesday	D 1-1	Rosler	33,589

FA Cup

Jan 8	LEICESTER CITY	(Rd 3) W 4-1	Ingebritsen, Kernaghan	22,613
Jan 29	Cardiff City	(Rd 4) L 0-1		20,486

Coca-Cola Cup

Sep 9	READING	(Rd 2 FL) D 1-1	White	9,280
Oct 6	Reading	(Rd 2 SL) W 2-1	Lomas, Quinn	10,052
Oct 26	CHELSEA	(Rd 3) W 1-0	White	16,713
Dec 1	Nottingham Forest	(Rd 4) D 0-0		22,195
Dec 15	NOTTINGHAM FOREST	(R) L 1-2	Vonk	14,117

League & Cup Appearances (substitute)

PLAYER	LEAGUE	CUP COMPETITION		TOTAL
		FA CUP	COCA-COLA	
Beagrie	9			9
Brightwell D	19 (3)	1	1	21 (3)
Brightwell I	6 (1)			6 (1)
Coton	31	2	4	37
Curle	29	1	5	35
Dibble	11	0 (1)	1	12 (1)
Edghill	22 (1)	1	4	27 (1)
Flitcroft	19 (2)	1	4	24 (2)
Foster	1	1		2
Griffiths	11 (5)	2		13 (5)
Groenendijk	9 (1)	2	1	12 (1)
Hill	15 (2)			15 (2)
Holden	9			9
Ingebritsen	2 (6)	2		4 (6)
Karl	4 (2)			4 (2)
Kernaghan	23 (1)	2	5	30 (1)
Kerr	2			2
Lomas	17 (6)	1 (1)	4	22 (7)
McMahon	35		5	40
Mike	1 (8)		1 (1)	2 (9)
Phelan	30	2	4	36
Quigley	2			2
Quinn	14 (1)		3	17 (1)
Reid	1 (3)			1 (3)
Rocastle	21	2		23
Rosler	12			12
Sheron	29 (4)	0 (2)	5	34 (6)
Shutt	5 (1)			5 (1)
Simpson	12 (3)		2 (1)	14 (4)
Vonk	34 (1)	2	2 (1)	38 (2)
Walsh	11			11
White	16		4	20

Goalscorers

PLAYER	LEAGUE	CUP COMPETITION		TOTAL
		FA CUP	COCA-COLA	
Quinn	5		1	6
Sheron	6			6
Rosler	5			5
Griffiths	4			4
Walsh	4			4
Flitcroft	3			3
Ingebritsen		3		3
White	1		2	3
Rocastle	2			2
Vonk	1		1	2
Beagrie	1			1
Brightwell D	1			1
Curle	1			1
Karl	1			1
Kernaghan		1		1
Lomas			1	1
Mike	1			1
Phelan	1			1
Opps' o.gs.	1			1

Fact File

This season was the last for the famous Kippax Street Stand which was demolished in the summer of 1994.

MANAGER: Brian Horton

CAPTAIN: Keith Curle

TOP SCORER: Niall Quinn

BIGGEST WIN: January 8, 1994 4-1 v Leicester City, FA Cup Round 3 Replay

HIGHEST ATTENDANCE: April 23, 1994 44,333 v Manchester United, lost 0-2, Premier League

MAJOR TRANSFERS IN: David Rocastle from Leeds, Paul Walsh from Portsmouth, Peter Beagrie from Everton, Uwe Rosler from FC Nurnburg, Alan Kernaghan from Middlesbrough

MAJOR TRANSFERS OUT: David White to Leeds

Final Premier League Table

		P	W	D	L	F	A	Pts
1	MANCHESTER U	42	27	11	4	80	38	92
2	BLACKBURN R	42	25	9	8	63	36	84
3	NEWCASTLE U	42	23	8	11	82	41	77
4	ARSENAL	42	18	17	7	53	28	71
5	LEEDS U	42	18	16	8	65	39	70
6	WIMBLEDON	42	18	11	13	56	53	65
7	SHEFFIELD W	42	16	16	10	76	54	64
8	LIVERPOOL	42	17	9	16	59	55	60
9	QPR	42	16	12	14	62	61	60
10	ASTON VILLA	42	15	12	15	46	50	57
11	COVENTRY C	42	14	14	14	43	45	56
12	NORWICH C	42	12	17	13	65	61	53
13	WEST HAM U	42	13	13	16	47	58	52
14	CHELSEA	42	13	12	17	49	53	51
15	TOTTENHAM H	42	11	12	19	54	59	45
16	MANCHESTER CITY	42	9	18	15	38	49	45
17	EVERTON	42	12	8	22	42	63	44
18	SOUTHAMPTON	42	12	7	23	49	66	43
19	IPSWICH T	42	9	16	17	35	58	43
20	SHEFFIELD U	42	8	18	16	42	60	42
21	OLDHAM ATH	42	9	13	20	42	68	40
22	SWINDON T	42	5	15	22	47	100	30

Season 1994-95

Premier League

DATE	OPPONENTS	SCORE	GOALSCORERS	ATTENDANCE
Aug 20	Arsenal	L 0-3		38,368
Aug 24	WEST HAM UNITED	W 3-0	Walsh, Beagrie, Rosler	19,150
Aug 27	EVERTON	W 4-0	Rosler 2, Walsh 2	19,867
Aug 31	Chelsea	L 0-3		21,740
Sep 10	CRYSTAL PALACE	D 1-1	Walsh	19,971
Sep 17	Sheffield Wednesday	D 1-1	Walsh	26,585
Sep 24	NORWICH CITY	W 2-0	Quinn, Rosler	21,031
Oct 1	Leeds United	L 0-2		30,938
Oct 8	NOTTINGHAM FOREST	D 3-3	Quinn 2, Lomas	23,150
Oct 15	Queens Park Rangers	W 2-1	Flitcroft, Walsh	13,631
Oct 22	TOTTENHAM HOTSPUR	W 5-2	Walsh 2, Quinn, Lomas, Flitcroft	25,473
Oct 29	Coventry City	L 0-1		15,802
Nov 5	SOUTHAMPTON	D 3-3	Walsh 2, Beagrie	21,589
Nov 10	Manchester United	L 0-5		43,738
Nov 20	Leicester City	W 1-0	Quinn	19,006
Nov 26	WIMBLEDON	W 2-0	Flitcroft, Rosler	21,131
Dec 3	Ipswich Town	W 2-1	Flitcroft, Rosler	13,754
Dec 12	Arsenal	L 1-2	Simpson	20,500
Dec 17	West Ham United	L 0-3		17,286
Dec 26	BLACKBURN ROVERS	L 1-3	Quinn	23,387
Dec 28	Liverpool	L 0-2		38,122
Dec 31	ASTON VILLA	D 2-2	Rosler 2	22,513
Jan 2	Newcastle United	D 0-0		34,437
Jan 14	COVENTRY CITY	D 0-0		20,232
Jan 25	LEICESTER CITY	L 0-1		21,007
Feb 4	Southampton	D 2-2	Kernaghan, Flitcroft	14,902
Feb 11	MANCHESTER UNITED	L 0-3		26,368
Feb 22	IPSWICH TOWN	W 2-0	Quinn, Rosler	21,430
Feb 25	LEEDS UNITED	D 0-0		22,892
Mar 4	Norwich City	D 1-1	Simpson	16,266
Mar 8	CHELSEA	L 1-2	Gaudino	21,880
Mar 15	Everton	D 1-1	Gaudino	28,485
Mar 18	SHEFFIELD WEDNESDAY	W 3-2	Rosler 2, Walsh	23,355
Mar 21	Wimbledon	L 0-2		5,268
Apr 1	Crystal Palace	L 1-2	Rosler	13,451
Apr 11	Tottenham Hotspur	L 1-2	Rosler	27,410
Apr 14	LIVERPOOL	W 2-1	Summerbee, Gaudino	7,055
Apr 17	Blackburn Rovers	W 3-2	Curle (pen), Rosler, Walsh	27,851
Apr 29	NEWCASTLE UNITED	D 0-0		27,389
May 3	Aston Villa	D 1-1	Rosler	30,133
May 6	Nottingham Forest	L 0-1		28,882
May 14	QUEENS PARK RANGERS	L 2-3	Quinn, Curle (pen)	27,850

FA Cup

DATE	OPPONENTS		SCORE	GOALSCORERS	ATTENDANCE
Jan 8	Notts County	(Rd 3)	D 2-2	Beagrie, D Brightwell	12,376
Jan 18	NOTTS COUNTY	(R)	W 5-2	Rosler 4, Gaudino	14,261
Jan 28	ASTON VILLA	(Rd 4)	W 1-0	Walsh	21,177
Feb 19	Newcastle United	(Rd 5)	L 1-3	Rosler	33,219

Coca-Cola Cup

DATE	OPPONENTS		SCORE	GOALSCORERS	ATTENDANCE
Sep 20	Barnet	(Rd 2 FL)	L 0-1		3,120
Oct 5	BARNET	(Rd 2 SL)	W 4-1	Quinn 2, Walsh, Summerbee	11,545
Oct 25	Queens Park Rangers	(Rd 3)	W 4-3	Summerbee, Curle (pen), Beagrie, Lomas	11,701
Nov 30	NEWCASTLE UNITED	(Rd 4)	D 1-1	Rosler	25,162
Dec 21	Newcastle United	(R)	W 2-0	Rosler, Walsh	30,156
Jan 11	Crystal Palace	(Rd 5)	L 0-4		16,668

MANAGER: Brian Horton

CAPTAIN: Keith Curle

TOP SCORER: Uwe Rosler

BIGGEST WIN: August 27, 1994 4-0 v Everton, Premier League

HIGHEST ATTENDANCE: November 10, 1994 43,738 v Manchester United, lost 0-5, Premier League

MAJOR TRANSFERS IN: Nicky Summerbee from Swindon

MAJOR TRANSFERS OUT Mike Sheron to Norwich, David Rocastle to Chelsea

League & Cup Appearances (substitute)

PLAYER	LEAGUE	CUP COMPETITION		TOTAL
		FA CUP	COCA-COLA	
Beagrie	33 (4)	4	6	43 (4)
Brightwell D	9	3 (1)	1 (1)	13 (2)
Brightwell I	29 (1)	4		33 (1)
Burridge	3 (1)			3 (1)
Coton	22 (1)	1	1	24 (1)
Curle	31	3	3	37
Dibble	14 (1)	3	5	22 (1)
Edghill	14		3	17
Flitcroft	37	4	5	46
Foster	9 (2)	1 (1)	0 (1)	10 (4)
Gaudino	17 (3)	3	1 (1)	21 (4)
Griffiths	(2)		0 (1)	0 (3)
Hill	10 (3)			10 (3)
Kernaghan	18 (4)	3	5	26 (4)
Kerr	2			2
Lomas	18 (2)	1	6	25 (2)
McMahon	6 (1)		1	7 (1)
Mike	1 (1)	0 (1)		1 (2)
Phelan	26 (1)	1	3	30 (1)
Quinn	24 (11)	1 (3)	4 (2)	29 (16)
Rosler	29 (2)	4	3 (1)	36 (3)
Simpson	10 (6)	0 (1)		10 (7)
Summerbee	39 (2)	4	6	49 (2)
Thomas	0 (2)			0 (2)
Tracey	3			3
Vonk	19 (2)	1	0 (1)	20 (3)
Walsh	39	3	6	48

Goalscorers

PLAYER	LEAGUE	CUP COMPETITION		TOTAL
		FA CUP	COCA-COLA	
Rosler	15	5	2	22
Walsh	12	1	2	15
Quinn	8		2	10
Flitcroft	5			5
Beagrie	2	1	1	4
Gaudino	3	1		4
Curle	2		1	3
Lomas	2		1	3
Summerbee	1		2	3
Simpson	2			2
Brightwell D		1		1
Kernaghan	1			1

Fact File

The 4-3 away win against Queens Park Rangers was achieved despite City having Richard Edghill and Andy Dibble sent off.

Final Premier League Table

		P	W	D	L	F	A	Pts
1	BLACKBURN R	42	27	8	7	80	39	89
2	MANCHESTER U	42	26	10	6	77	28	88
3	NOTTINGHAM F	42	22	11	9	72	43	77
4	LIVERPOOL	42	21	11	10	65	37	74
5	LEEDS U	42	20	13	9	59	38	73
6	NEWCASTLE U	42	20	12	10	67	47	72
7	TOTTENHAM H	42	16	14	12	66	58	62
8	QPR	42	17	9	16	61	59	60
9	WIMBLEDON	42	15	11	16	48	65	56
10	SOUTHAMPTON	42	12	18	12	61	63	54
11	CHELSEA	42	13	15	14	50	55	54
12	ARSENAL	42	13	12	17	52	49	51
13	SHEFFIELD W	42	13	12	17	49	57	51
14	WEST HAM U	42	13	11	18	44	48	50
15	EVERTON	42	11	17	14	44	51	50
16	COVENTRY C	42	12	14	16	44	62	50
17	MANCHESTER CITY	42	12	13	17	53	64	49
18	ASTON VILLA	42	11	15	16	51	56	48
19	CRYSTAL PALACE	42	11	12	19	34	49	45
20	NORWICH C	42	10	13	19	37	54	43
21	LEICESTER C	42	6	11	25	45	80	29
22	IPSWICH T	42	7	6	29	36	93	27

Season 1995-96

Premier League

DATE	OPPONENTS	SCORE	GOALSCORERS	ATTENDANCE
Aug 19	TOTTENHAM HOTSPUR	D 1-1	Rosler	30,827
Aug 23	Coventry City	L 1-2	Rosler	16,568
Aug 26	Queens Park Rangers	L 0-1		14,212
Aug 30	EVERTON	L 0-2		28,432
Sep 10	ARSENAL	L 0-1		23,984
Sep 16	Newcastle United	L 1-3	Creaney	36,501
Sep 23	MIDDLESBROUGH	L 0-1		25,865
Sep 30	Nottingham Forest	L 0-3		25,620
Oct 14	Manchester United	L 0-1		35,707
Oct 21	LEEDS UNITED	D 0-0		26,390
Oct 28	Liverpool	L 0-6		39,267
Nov 4	BOLTON WANDERERS	W 1-0	Summerbee	28,397
Nov 18	Sheffield Wednesday	D 1-1	Lomas	24,422
Nov 22	WIMBLEDON	W 1-0	Quinn	23,617
Nov 25	ASTON VILLA	W 1-0	Kinkladze	28,017
Dec 2	Leeds United	W 1-0	Creaney	33,249
Dec 9	Middlesbrough	L 1-4	Kinkladze	29,469
Dec 18	NOTTINGHAM FOREST	D 1-1	Rosler	24,287
Dec 23	CHELSEA	L 0-1		28,668
Dec 26	Blackburn Rovers	L 0-2		28,915
Jan 1	WEST HAM UNITED	W 2-1	Quinn 2	26,024
Jan 13	Tottenham Hotspur	L 0-1		31,438
Jan 20	COVENTRY CITY	D 1-1	Rosler	25,710
Jan 31	Southampton	D 1-1	Rosler	15,172
Feb 3	QUEENS PARK RANGERS	W 2-0	Clough, Symons	27,509
Feb 10	Everton	L 0-2		37,354
Feb 24	NEWCASTLE UNITED	D 3-3	Quinn 2, Rosler	31,115
Mar 2	BLACKBURN ROVERS	D 1-1	Lomas	20,078
Mar 5	Arsenal	L 1-3	Creaney	34,519
Mar 12	Chelsea	D 1-1	Clough	17,078
Mar 16	SOUTHAMPTON	W 2-1	Kinkladze 2	29,550
Mar 23	West Ham United	L 2-4	Quinn 2	24,017
Mar 30	Bolton Wanderers	D 1-1	Quinn	21,050
Apr 6	MANCHESTER UNITED	L 2-3	Kavelashvili, Rosler	29,688
Apr 8	Wimbledon	L 0-3		11,844
Apr 13	SHEFFIELD WEDNESDAY	W 1-0	Rosler	30,898
Apr 27	Aston Villa	W 1-0	Lomas	39,336
May 5	LIVERPOOL	D 2-2	Rosler (pen), Symons	31,436

FA Cup

Jan 6	Leicester City	(Rd 3) D 0-0		20,640
Jan 17	LEICESTER CITY	(R) W 5-0	Rosler, Kinkladze, Quinn, Lomas, Creaney	19,980
Feb 7	Coventry City	(Rd 4) D 2-2	Flitcroft, o.g.	18,709
Feb 14	COVENTRY CITY	(R) W 2-1	Clough, Quinn	22,419
Feb 18	Manchester United	(Rd 5) L 1-2	Rosler	42,692

Coca-Cola Cup

Sep 9	Wycombe Wanderers	(Rd 2 FL) D 0-0		7,443
Oct 4	WYCOMBE WANDERERS	(Rd 2 SL) W 4-0	Rosler 2, Quinn, Curle (pen)	11,474
Oct 25	Liverpool	(Rd 3) L 0-4		29,394

League & Cup Appearances (substitute)

PLAYER	LEAGUE	CUP COMPETITION		TOTAL
		FA CUP	COCA-COLA	
Beagrie	4 (1)	2	2	8 (1)
Brightwell I	26 (3)	1	1	28 (3)
Brown	16 (5)		0 (2)	16 (7)
Clough	15			15
Creaney	6 (9)	0 (3)		6 (12)
Curle	32	3	3	38
Edghill	13	3	3	19
Ekelund	2 (2)	0 (1)		2 (3)
Flitcroft	25	1	1	27
Foster	4	1	1	6
Frontzeck	11 (1)			11 (1)
Hiley	2 (4)			2 (4)
Immel	38	3	3	44
Ingram	5			5
Kavelashvili	3 (1)			3 (1)
Kernaghan	4 (2)			4 (2)
Kerr	0 (1)			0 (1)
Kinkladze	37	3	3	43
Lomas	32 (1)	3	3	38 (1)
Margetson			0 (1)	0 (1)
Mazzarelli	0 (2)			0 (2)
Phelan	9	1	1	11
Phillips	2 (9)			2 (9)
Quinn	24 (8)	3	3	30 (8)
Rosler	34 (2)	3	3	40 (2)
Summerbee	33 (4)	1 (2)	1 (2)	35 (8)
Symons	38	3	3	44
Walsh	3			3

Goalscorers

PLAYER	LEAGUE	CUP COMPETITION		TOTAL
		FA CUP	COCA-COLA	
Rosler	9	2	2	13
Quinn	8	2	1	11
Kinkladze	4	1		5
Creaney	3	1		4
Lomas	3	1		4
Clough	2	1		3
Symons	2			2
Curle			1	1
Flitcroft	1			1
Kavelashvili	1			1
Summerbee	1			1
Opps' o.gs.		1		1

Fact File

After coming back from a 2-0 scoreline against Liverpool, City believed they had secured the point they needed for Premier League survival. However, they were mistaken: Coventry and Southampton had both drawn and City were to be relegated on goal difference.

MANAGER: Alan Ball

CAPTAIN: Keith Curle

TOP SCORER: Uwe Rosler

BIGGEST WIN: January 17, 1996 5-0 v Leicester City, FA Cup Round 3 replay

HIGHEST ATTENDANCE: February 18, 1996 42,692 v Manchester United, lost 1-2, FA Cup Round 5

MAJOR TRANSFERS IN: Georgiou Kinkladze from Dinamo Tblisi, Kit Symons from Portsmouth, Nigel Clough from Liverpool

Final Premier League Table

		P	W	D	L	F	A	PTS
1	MANCHESTER U	38	25	7	6	73	35	82
2	NEWCASTLE U	38	24	6	8	66	37	78
3	LIVERPOOL	38	20	11	7	70	34	71
4	ASTON VILLA	38	18	9	11	52	35	63
5	ARSENAL	38	17	12	9	49	32	63
6	EVERTON	38	17	10	11	64	44	61
7	BLACKBURN R	38	18	7	13	61	47	61
8	TOTTENHAM H	38	16	13	9	50	38	61
9	NOTTINGHAM F	38	15	13	10	50	54	58
10	WEST HAM U	38	14	9	15	43	52	51
11	CHELSEA	38	12	14	12	46	44	50
12	MIDDLESBROUGH	38	11	10	17	35	50	43
13	LEEDS U	38	12	7	19	40	57	43
14	WIMBLEDON	38	10	11	17	55	70	41
15	SHEFFIELD W	38	10	10	18	48	61	40
16	COVENTRY C	38	8	14	16	42	60	38
17	SOUTHAMPTON	38	9	11	18	34	52	38
18	MANCHESTER CITY	38	9	11	18	33	58	38
19	QPR	38	9	6	23	38	57	33
20	BOLTON W	38	8	5	25	39	71	29

Season 1996-97

Nationwide League Division 1

DATE	OPPONENTS	SCORE	GOALSCORERS	ATTENDANCE
Aug 16	IPSWICH TOWN	W 1-0	Lomas	29,129
Aug 20	Bolton Wanderers	L 0-1		18,257
Aug 24	Stoke City	L 1-2	Rosler	21,116
Sep 3	CHARLTON ATHLETIC	W 2-1	Rosler (pen), Creaney	25,963
Sep 7	BARNSLEY	L 1-2	Clough	26,464
Sep 10	Port Vale	W 2-0	Rosler, Dickov	10,770
Sep 14	Crystal Palace	L 1-3	Kavelashvili	17,638
Sep 21	BIRMINGHAM CITY	W 1-0	Kinkladze (pen)	26,757
Sep 28	Sheffield United	L 0-2		20,867
Oct 12	Queens Park Rangers	D 2-2	Brightwell, Kinkladze (pen)	16,265
Oct 15	Reading	L 0-2		11,724
Oct 19	NORWICH CITY	W 2-1	Clough, Dickov	28,269
Oct 27	WOLVES	L 0-1		27,296
Oct 29	Southend United	W 3-2	Rosler, Kinkladze 2 (1 pen)	8,707
Nov 2	Swindon Town	L 0-2		14,374
Nov 13	OXFORD UNITED	L 2-3	Dickov, Brightwell	23,079
Nov 16	Portsmouth	L 1-2	Rodger	12,841
Nov 19	HUDDERSFIELD TOWN	D 0-0		23,314
Nov 23	TRANMERE ROVERS	L 1-2	Summerbee	26,531
Nov 27	WEST BROMWICH ALBION	W 3-2	Rosler, Kinkladze 2 (2 pen)	24,200
Dec 1	Wolves	L 0-3		23,911
Dec 7	BRADFORD CITY	W 3-2	Kinkladze (pen), Dickov, Whitley	25,015
Dec 21	Oldham Athletic	L 1-2	Kinkladze	12,992
Dec 26	PORT VALE	L 0-1		30,344
Dec 28	Barnsley	L 0-2		17,159
Jan 11	CRYSTAL PALACE	D 1-1	o.g.	27,395
Jan 18	Huddersfield Town	D 1-1	Lomas	18,358
Jan 29	SHEFFIELD UNITED	D 0-0		26,551
Feb 2	Oxford United	W 4-1	o.g., Kinkladze 2, Rosler	8,824
Feb 8	SOUTHEND UNITED	W 3-0	Rosler 2, Kinkladze	26,261
Feb 22	SWINDON TOWN	W 3-0	Horlock, Summerbee, Rosler	27,262
Mar 1	Bradford City	W 3-1	Rosler 2 (1 pen), Horlock	17,609
Mar 5	PORTSMOUTH	D 1-1	Horlock	26,051
Mar 8	OLDHAM ATHLETIC	W 1-0	Rosler	30,729
Mar 11	Birmingham City	L 0-2		20,084
Mar 15	Grimsby Town	D 1-1	Kavelashvili	8,732
Mar 18	Tranmere Rovers	D 1-1	o.g.	12,019
Mar 22	STOKE CITY	W 2-0	Atkinson, Lomas	28,497
Apr 5	Charlton Athletic	D 1-1	Brennan	19,000
Apr 9	BOLTON WANDERERS	L 1-2	Kinkladze	28,026
Apr 12	West Bromwich Albion	W 3-1	Rosler 2, Horlock	20,087
Apr 16	GRIMSBY TOWN	W 3-1	Atkinson, Summerbee 2	23,334
Apr 19	QUEENS PARK RANGERS	L 0-3		27,580
Apr 22	Ipswich Town	L 0-1		15,824
Apr 25	Norwich City	D 0-0		14,080
May 3	READING	W 3-2	Dickov, Rosler, Heaney	27,260

FA Cup

Jan 25	Brentford	(Rd 3) W 1-0	Summerbee	12,019
Feb 5	WATFORD	(Rd 4) W 3-1	Heaney, Summerbee, Rosler	24,031
Feb 15	MIDDLESBROUGH	(Rd 5) L 0-1		30,462

Coca-Cola Cup

Sep 17	Lincoln City	(Rd 2 FL) L 1-4	Rosler	7,599
Sep 24	LINCOLN CITY	(Rd 2 SL) L 0-1		14,242

Fact File

An astonishing season that saw City employ five different managers, including caretaker manager Asa Hartford and Phil Neal.

MANAGER: Alan Ball/Steve Coppell/Frank Clark
CAPTAIN: Kit Symons
TOP SCORER: Uwe Rosler
BIGGEST WIN: February 2, 1997 4-1 v Oxford United, Division 1
HIGHEST ATTENDANCE: March 8, 1997 30,729 v Oldham Athletic, won 1-0, Division 1
MAJOR TRANSFERS IN: Paul Dickov from Arsenal
MAJOR TRANSFERS OUT: Niall Quinn to Sunderland

League & Cup Appearances (substitute)

PLAYER	LEAGUE	CUP COMPETITION		TOTAL
		FA CUP	COCA-COLA	
Atkinson	7 (1)			7 (1)
Beagrie	0 (1)	0 (1)		0 (2)
Beesley	6			6
Brannan	11			11
Brightwell I	36 (1)	2		38 (1)
Brown	7 (4)	1	1 (1)	9 (5)
Clough	18 (5)		2	20 (7)
Creaney	1 (4)	0 (1)		1 (5)
Crooks	8 (7)	2	0 (1)	10 (8)
Dibble	12 (1)		2	14 (1)
Dickov	25 (4)	0 (1)	2	27 (5)
Foster	3			3
Frontzeck	8 (3)	1		9 (3)
Greenacre	0 (4)			0 (4)
Heaney	10 (5)	2		12 (5)
Hiley	2 (1)			2 (1)
Horlock	18			18
Immel	4			4
Ingram	13 (5)	3	1	17 (5)
Kavelashvili	6 (18)		0 (1)	6 (19)
Kernaghan	9 (1)	2		11 (1)
Kinkladze	39	3	1	43
Lomas	35	3	2	40
Margetson	17	3		20
McGoldrick	33	3	1	37
Phillips	1 (3)		0 (1)	1 (4)
Rodger	8			8
Rosler	43 (1)	3	2	48 (1)
Summerbee	43 (1)	3	2	48 (1)
Symons	44	3	2	49
Wassall	14 (1)		2	16 (1)
Whitley	12 (11)		1	13 (11)
Wright	13			13

Goalscorers

PLAYER	LEAGUE	CUP COMPETITION		TOTAL
		FA CUP	COCA-COLA	
Rosler	15	1	1	17
Kinkladze	12			12
Summerbee	4	2		6
Dickov	5			5
Horlock	4			4
Lomas	3			3
Atkinson	2			2
Brightwell I	2			2
Clough	2			2
Heaney	1	1		2
Kavelashvili	2			2
Brannan	1			1
Creaney	1			1
Rodger	1			1
Whitley	1			1
Opps' o.gs.	3			3

Final Division 1 Table

		P	W	D	L	F	A	Pts
1	BOLTON W	46	28	14	4	100	53	98
2	BARNSLEY	46	22	14	10	76	55	80
3	WOLVERHAMPTON W	46	22	10	14	68	51	76
4	IPSWICH T	46	20	14	12	68	50	74
5	SHEFFIELD U	46	20	13	13	75	52	73
6	CRYSTAL PALACE	46	19	14	13	78	48	71
7	PORTSMOUTH	46	20	8	18	59	53	68
8	PORT VALE	46	17	16	13	58	55	67
9	QPR	46	18	12	16	64	60	66
10	BIRMINGHAM C	46	17	15	14	52	48	66
11	TRANMERE R	46	17	14	15	63	56	65
12	STOKE C	46	18	10	18	51	57	64
13	NORWICH C	46	17	12	17	63	68	63
14	MANCHESTER CITY	46	17	10	19	59	60	61
15	CHARLTON ATH	46	16	11	19	52	66	59
16	WBA	46	14	15	17	68	72	57
17	OXFORD U	46	16	9	21	64	68	57
18	READING	46	15	12	19	58	67	57
19	SWINDON T	46	15	9	22	52	71	54
20	HUDDERSFIELD T	46	13	15	18	48	61	54
21	BRADFORD C	46	12	12	22	47	72	48
22	GRIMSBY T	46	11	13	22	60	81	46
23	OLDHAM ATH	46	10	13	23	51	66	43
24	SOUTHEND U	46	8	15	23	42	86	39

Season 1997-98

Nationwide League Division 1

DATE	OPPONENTS	SCORE	GOALSCORERS	ATTENDANCE
Aug 9	PORTSMOUTH	D 2-2	Rosler, Wiekens	30,474
Aug 15	Sunderland	L 1-3	Kinkladze (pen)	38,894
Aug 22	TRANMERE ROVERS	D 1-1	Horlock	26,336
Aug 30	Charlton Athletic	L 1-2	Wiekens	14,009
Sep 3	Nottingham Forest	W 3-1	Brannan 2, Dickov	23,681
Sep 12	Bury	D 1-1	Morley	11,216
Sep 20	NORWICH CITY	L 1-2	Bradbury	27,258
Sep 27	SWINDON TOWN	W 6-0	Kinkladze, o.g., Horlock, Dickov 2, Bradbury	26,646
Oct 4	Ipswich Town	L 0-1		14,322
Oct 18	READING	D 0-0		26,488
Oct 22	STOKE CITY	L 0-1		25,333
Oct 26	Queens Park Rangers	L 0-2		14,451
Oct 29	CREWE ALEXANDRA	W 1-0	Greenacre	27,384
Nov 1	Oxford United	D 0-0		8,592
Nov 4	PORT VALE	L 2-3	Wiekens, Dickov	24,554
Nov 7	HUDDERSFIELD TOWN	L 0-1		24,425
Nov 15	Sheffield United	D 1-1	Horlock	23,780
Nov 22	BRADFORD CITY	W 1-0	Vaughan	29,746
Nov 29	Stockport County	L 1-3	Brannan	11,351
Dec 2	West Bromwich Albion	W 1-0	Dickov	17,904
Dec 6	WOLVES	L 0-1		28,999
Dec 13	Birmingham City	L 1-2	Shelia	21,014
Dec 20	MIDDLESBROUGH	W 2-2	Rosler (pen), Dickov	28,097
Dec 26	Crewe Alexandra	L 0-1		5,759
Dec 28	NOTTINGHAM FOREST	L 2-3	Shelia, Dickov	31,839
Jan 10	Portsmouth	W 3-0	Russell, Kinkladze, Rosler	13,612
Jan 17	SUNDERLAND	L 0-1		31,715
Jan 28	CHARLTON ATHLETIC	D 2-2	Dickov (pen), Symons	24,058
Jan 31	Tranmere Rovers	D 0-0		12,830
Feb 7	Norwich City	D 0-0		15,274
Feb 14	BURY	L 0-1		28,885
Feb 18	IPSWICH TOWN	L 1-2	Symons	27,156
Feb 21	Swindon Town	W 3-1	Rosler 2, Bradbury	12,280
Feb 24	Reading	L 0-3		11,513
Feb 28	WEST BROMWICH ALBION	W 1-0	Rosler	28,460
Mar 3	Huddersfield Town	W 3-1	Wiekens, Briscoe, Tskhadadze	15,694
Mar 7	OXFORD UNITED	L 0-2		28,720
Mar 14	Port Vale	L 1-2	Wiekens	13,122
Mar 21	SHEFFIELD UNITED	D 0-0		28,496
Mar 28	Bradford City	L 1-2	Jeff Whitley	17,099
Apr 4	STOCKPORT COUNTY	W 4-1	Goater, Jobson, Bradbury 2	31,855
Apr 11	Wolves	D 2-2	Pollock, Horlock	24,458
Apr 13	BIRMINGHAM CITY	L 0-1		29,569
Apr 17	Middlesbrough	L 0-1		30,182
Apr 25	QUEENS PARK RANGERS	D 2-2	Kinkladze, Bradbury	32,040
May 3	Stoke City	W 5-2	Goater 2, Dickov, Bradbury, Horlock	26,664

FA Cup

Jan 3	BRADFORD CITY	(Rd 3) W 2-0	Rosler, Brown	23,686
Jan 25	WEST HAM UNITED	(Rd 4) L 1-2	Kinkladze	26,495

Coca-Cola Cup

Aug 11	Blackpool	(Rd 1 FL) L 0-1		8,084
Aug 26	BLACKPOOL*	(Rd 1 SL) L 1-1	Horlock	12,563

*Blackpool won 4-2 on penalties.

Fact File

City conceded two goals in a seven minute period in injury time to lose 2-1 at Birmingham in December.

MANAGER: Frank Clark/Joe Royle

CAPTAIN: Kit Symons

TOP SCORER: Paul Dickov

BIGGEST WIN: September 27, 1997 6-0 v Swindon Town, Division 1

HIGHEST ATTENDANCE: August 15, 1997 38,894 v Sunderland, lost 1-3, Division 1

MAJOR TRANSFERS OUT: Lee Bradbury from Portsmouth, Shaun Goater from Bristol City, Richard Jobson from Leeds United

League & Cup Appearances (substitute)

PLAYER	LEAGUE	CUP COMPETITION		TOTAL
		FA CUP	COCA-COLA	
Beardsley	5 (1)			5 (1)
Beesley	4 (3)			4 (3)
Bishop	4 (2)			4 (2)
Bradbury	23 (4)		2	25 (4)
Brannan	27 (5)	1	1	29 (5)
Brightwell	19 (2)	2	2	23 (2)
Briscoe	5			5
Brown	18 (8)	2		20 (8)
Conlon	1 (6)			1 (6)
Creaney	1			1
Crooks	3 (2)			3 (2)
Dickov	21 (9)	2	0 (1)	23 (10)
Edghill	36	1		37
Goater	7			7
Greenacre	2 (1)	0 (1)		2 (2)
Heaney	3			3
Horlock	25		2	27
Jobson	6			6
Kelly	1			1
Kernaghan	1		1	2
Kinkladze	29 (1)	2	2	33 (1)
Margetson	28		2	30
McGoldrick	6 (1)		0 (1)	6 (2)
Morley	1 (2)			1 (2)
Pollock	8			8
Rosler	23 (6)	2	2	27 (6)
Russell	17 (7)	2		19 (7)
Scully	1 (8)			1 (8)
Shelia	12	2		14
Summerbee	4 (5)		2	6 (5)
Symons	42	1	1	44
Tskhadadze	10			10
Van Blerk	10 (9)	0 (1)	0 (1)	10 (11)
Vaughan	19		2	21
Whiteley Jim	17 (2)	1 (1)		18 (3)
Whitley Jeff	14 (3)	1		15 (3)
Wiekens	35 (2)	1	2	38 (2)
Wright	18	2		20

Goalscorers

PLAYER	LEAGUE	CUP COMPETITION		TOTAL
		FA CUP	COCA-COLA	
Dickov	9			9
Bradbury	7			7
Rosler	6	1		7
Horlock	5		1	6
Kinkladze	4	1		5
Wiekens	5			5
Brannan	3			3
Goater	3			3
Shelia	2			2
Symons	2			2

The following scored 1: Briscoe, Brown, Greenacre, Jobson, Morley, Pollock, Russell, Tskhadadze, Vaughan, Whitley (Jeff)

Final Division 1 Table

		P	W	D	L	F	A	PTS
1	NOTTINGHAM F	46	28	10	8	82	42	94
2	MIDDLESBROUGH	46	27	10	9	77	41	91
3	SUNDERLAND	46	26	12	8	86	50	90
4	CHARLTON ATH	46	26	10	10	80	49	88
5	IPSWICH T	46	23	14	9	77	43	83
6	SHEFFIELD U	46	19	17	10	69	54	74
7	BIRMINGHAM C	46	19	17	10	60	35	74
8	STOCKPORT CO	46	19	8	19	71	69	65
9	WOLVERHAMPTON W	46	18	11	17	57	53	65
10	WBA	46	16	12	17	50	56	61
11	CREWE ALEX	46	18	5	23	58	65	59
12	OXFORD U	46	16	10	20	60	64	58
13	BRADFORD C	46	14	15	17	46	59	57
14	TRANMERE R	46	14	14	18	54	57	56
15	NORWICH C	46	14	13	19	52	69	55
16	HUDDERSFIELD T	46	14	11	21	50	72	53
17	BURY	46	11	19	16	42	58	52
18	SWINDON T	46	14	10	22	42	73	52
19	PORT VALE	46	13	10	23	56	66	49
20	PORTSMOUTH	46	13	10	23	51	63	49
21	QPR	46	10	19	17	51	63	49
22	MANCHESTER CITY	46	12	12	22	56	57	48
23	STOKE C	46	11	13	22	44	74	46
24	READING	46	11	9	26	39	78	42

Season 1998-99

Nationwide League Division 2

DATE	OPPONENTS	SCORE	GOALSCORERS	ATTENDANCE
Aug 8	BLACKPOOL	W 3-0	Tskhadadze, Goater, Bradbury	32,134
Aug 14	Fulham	L 0-3		14,284
Aug 22	WREXHAM	D 0-0		27,677
Aug 29	Notts County	D 1-1	Goater	10,316
Sep 2	WALSALL	W 3-1	Goater 2, Dickov	24,291
Sep 8	Bournemouth	W 2-1	Dickov, Allsopp	26,696
Sep 12	Macclesfield Town	W 1-0	Goater	6,381
Sep 19	CHESTERFIELD	D 1-1	Bradbury	27,500
Sep 26	Northampton Town	D 2-2	Goater, Dickov	7,557
Sep 29	Millwall	D 1-1	Bradbury	12,726
Oct 3	BURNLEY	D 2-2	Goater, Allsopp	30,722
Oct 12	PRESTON NORTH END	L 0-1		28,779
Oct 17	Wigan Athletic	W 1-0	Goater	6,700
Oct 20	Lincoln City	L 1-2	o.g.	7,338
Oct 24	READING	L 0-1		24,365
Oct 31	COLCHESTER UNITED	W 2-1	Horlock, Morrison	24,820
Nov 7	Oldham Athletic	W 3-0	Horlock 2, Morrison	12,976
Nov 10	Wycombe Wanderers	L 0-1		8,129
Nov 21	GILLINGHAM	D 0-0		26,529
Nov 28	Luton Town	D 1-1	Morrison	9,070
Dec 12	BRISTOL ROVERS	D 0-0		24,976
Dec 19	York City	L 1-2	Russell	7,527
Dec 26	Wrexham	W 1-0	Wiekens	9,048
Dec 28	STOKE CITY	W 2-1	Dickov, Taylor	30,478
Jan 9	Blackpool	D 0-0		9,752
Jan 16	FULHAM	W 3-0	Horlock, Goater, Taylor	30,251
Jan 23	Walsall	D 1-1	Pollock	9,517
Jan 29	Stoke City	W 1-0	Wiekens	13,679
Feb 6	MILLWALL	W 3-0	Horlock, Dickov, Cooke	29,862
Feb 13	Bournemouth	D 0-0		10,964
Feb 20	MACCLESFIELD TOWN	W 2-0	Goater, Taylor	31,086
Feb 27	Chesterfield	D 1-1	Crooks	8,245
Mar 6	NORTHAMPTON TOWN	D 0-0		27,999
Mar 9	Burnley	W 6-0	Goater 3, Horlock, Allsopp, Morrison	17,251
Mar 16	NOTTS COUNTY	W 2-1	Brown, Cooke	26,502
Mar 20	Colchester United	D 1-1	Goater	6,554
Mar 27	Reading	W 3-1	Goater, Cooke 2	20,055
Apr 3	WIGAN ATHLETIC	W 1-0	Cooke	31,058
Apr 5	Preston North End	D 1-1	Brown	20,857
Apr 10	LINCOLN CITY	W 4-0	Dickov 3, Horlock	26,298
Apr 14	LUTON TOWN	W 2-0	Vaughan, Dickov	26,130
Apr 17	Gillingham	W 2-0	Cooke, Horlock	10,400
Apr 24	WYCOMBE WANDERERS	L 1-2	Goater	29,337
May 1	Bristol Rovers	D 2-2	Goater, Cooke	8,033
May 8	YORK CITY	W 4-0	Horlock, Dickov, Allsopp, Jeff Whitley	32,471

FA Cup

Nov 13	HALIFAX TOWN	(Rd 1) W 3-0	Russell 2, Goater	11,106
Dec 4	Darlington	(Rd 2) D 1-1	Dickov	7,250
Dec 15	DARLINGTON	(R) W 1-0	Brown	8,595
Jan 2	Wimbledon	(Rd 3) L 0-1		11,226

Worthington Cup

Aug 11	Notts County	(Rd 1 FL) W 2-0	Tskhadadze, Allsopp	5,795
Aug 19	NOTTS COUNTY	(Rd 1 SL) W 7-1	Goater 2, Dickov 2, Mason, Jim Whitley, Bradbury	10,063
Sep 16	Derby County	(Rd 2 FL) D 1-1	Tiatto	22,986
Sep 23	DERBY COUNTY	(Rd 2 SL) L 0-1		19,622

Auto Windscreen Shield

Dec 8	MANSFIELD TOWN	(Rd 1) 1-2	Allsopp	3,007

Second Division Play-Offs

May 15	Wigan Athletic	(SF FL) D 1-1	Dickov	6,762
May 19	WIGAN ATHLETIC	(SF SL) W 1-0	Goater	31,350
May 30	Gillingham*	(F) W 2-2	Horlock, Dickov	76,935

*Played at Wembley. Result after extra time. Won 3-1 on penalties.

Fact File

Of the 23 other clubs in the division, 19 had their highest crowd of the season when City visited.

League & Cup Appearances (substitute)

PLAYER	LEAGUE	CUP COMPETITION			TOTAL
		FA CUP	WORTHINGTON	OTHER	
Allsopp	3 (23)		0 (3)	1 (1)	4 (27)
Bailey				0 (1)	0 (1)
Bishop	21 (1)	1 (1)		0 (1)	22 (3)
Bradbury	11 (2)		4		15 (2)
Branch	4				4
Brown	29 (5)	2 (1)	0 (1)	4	35 (7)
Conlon			0 (1)		0 (1)
Cooke	24 (4)	3		3	30 (4)
Crooks	35 (2)			3	38 (2)
Dickov	25 (13)	2 (2)	3 (1)	3 (1)	33 (16)
Edghill	41	2	4	3	50
Fenton	15		3	1	19
Goater	44 (2)	4	3	3	54 (2)
Greenacre	1				1
Heaney				1	1
Horlock	39 (1)	3	3	3	48 (1)
Mason	18	2	3		23
Morrison	22 (1)	4		1	27 (1)
Pollock	24 (3)	3 (1)	4 (1)	1 (1)	32 (5)
Rimmer				1	1
Robins	0 (2)				0 (2)
Russell	5 (2)	3 (1)			8 (3)
Shelia	3				3
Taylor	20 (9)	3		1 (3)	24 (12)
Tiatto	8 (9)	0 (1)	1	1	10 (10)
Tskhadadze	2		1		3
Vaughan	37 (4)	3	4	3 (1)	47 (5)
Weaver	45	4	3	3	55
Whitley Jeff	4 (7)		0 (1)	4	8 (8)
Whitley Jim	10 (7)	1	3 (1)		14 (9)
Wiekens	43	4	4	3	54
Wright	1		1	1	3

Goalscorers

PLAYER	LEAGUE	CUP COMPETITION			TOTAL
		FA CUP	WORTHINGTON	OTHER	
Goater	18	1	2	1	22
Dickov	12	1	2	2	17
Horlock	10			1	11
Cooke	7				7
Allsopp	4		1	1	6
Bradbury	3		1		4
Morrison	4				4
Taylor	4				4
Russell	1	2			3
Brown	2	1			3
Tskhadadze	1		1		2
Wiekens	2				2
Crooks	1				1
Mason			1		1
Pollock	1				1
Vaughan	1				1
Whitley Jeff	1				1
Whitley Jim			1		1
Tiatto			1		1
Opps' o.gs.	1				1

Final Division 2 Table

		P	W	D	L	F	A	Pts
1	FULHAM	46	31	8	7	79	32	101
2	WALSALL	46	26	9	11	63	47	87
3	MANCHESTER CITY	46	22	16	8	69	33	82
4	GILLINGHAM	46	22	14	10	75	44	80
5	PRESTON N E	46	22	13	11	78	50	79
6	WIGAN ATHLETIC	46	22	10	14	75	48	76
7	BOURNEMOUTH	46	21	13	12	63	41	76
8	STOKE CITY	46	21	6	19	59	63	69
9	CHESTERFIELD	46	17	13	16	46	44	64
10	MILLWALL	46	17	11	18	52	59	62
11	READING	46	16	13	17	54	63	61
12	LUTON TOWN	46	16	10	20	51	60	58
13	BRISTOL ROVERS	46	13	17	16	65	56	56
14	BLACKPOOL	46	14	14	18	44	54	56
15	BURNLEY	46	13	16	17	54	73	55
16	NOTTS COUNTY	46	14	12	20	52	61	54
17	WREXHAM	46	13	14	19	43	62	53
18	COLCHESTER U	46	12	16	18	52	70	52
19	WYCOMBE WAND	46	13	12	21	52	58	51
20	OLDHAM ATHLETIC	46	14	9	23	48	66	51
21	YORK CITY	46	13	11	22	56	80	50
22	NORTHAMPTON T	46	10	18	18	43	57	48
23	LINCOLN CITY	46	13	7	26	42	74	46
24	MACCLESFIELD T	46	11	10	25	43	63	43

Season 1999-2000

Football League Division 1

DATE	OPPONENTS	SCORE	GOALSCORERS	ATTENDANCE
Aug 8	WOLVES	L 0-1		31,755
Aug 14	Fulham	D 0-0		16,754
Aug 21	SHEFFIELD UNITED	W 6-0	Horlock 2 (2 pen), Goater Dickov, G Taylor, Kennedy	30,110
Aug 28	Bolton Wanderers	W 1-0	Kennedy	21,671
Aug 30	NOTTINGHAM FOREST	W 1-0	Goater	31,857
Sep 11	CRYSTAL PALACE	W 2-1	G Taylor, Jobson	31,541
Sep 18	Walsall	W 1-0	Goater	7,260
Sep 26	Ipswich Town	L 1-2	Goater	19,406
Sep 28	Norwich City	L 0-1		15,130
Oct 2	PORT VALE	W 2-1	Bishop 2	31,608
Oct 16	Tranmere Rovers	D 1-1	Horlock (pen)	13,208
Oct 19	Birmingham City	W 1-0	Jobson	22,126
Oct 23	BLACKBURN ROVERS	W 2-0	Edghill, Jeff Whitley	33,027
Oct 27	IPSWICH TOWN	W 1-0	Horlock	32,799
Oct 30	Port Vale	W 2-1	Granville, o.g.	10,250
Nov 3	PORTSMOUTH	W 4-2	G Taylor 2, Pollock, Jeff Whitley	31,660
Nov 6	Queens Park Rangers	D 1-1	Horlock	19,002
Nov 20	Charlton Athletic	W 1-0	Goater	20,043
Nov 24	BARNSLEY	W 3-1	Horlock, Goater, G Taylor	32,692
Nov 27	HUDDERSFIELD TOWN	L 0-1		32,936
Dec 3	Wolves	L 1-4	Goater	21,635
Dec 7	STOCKPORT COUNTY	L 1-2	Wiekens	32,686
Dec 18	SWINDON TOWN	W 3-0	Goater, Pollock, R Taylor	31,751
Dec 26	West Bromwich Albion	W 2-0	Goater, Granville	19,589
Dec 28	GRIMSBY TOWN	W 2-1	Horlock 2	32,607
Jan 3	Crewe Alexandra	D 1-1	Crooks	10,066
Jan 16	FULHAM	W 4-0	Goater 3, Horlock (pen)	30,057
Jan 22	Sheffield United	L 0-1		23,862
Feb 5	Nottingham Forest	W 3-1	Goater 2, R Taylor	25,846
Feb 12	NORWICH CITY	W 3-1	Kennedy 2, Goater	32,681
Feb 18	Huddersfield Town	D 1-1	Goater	18,173
Feb 26	WALSALL	D 1-1	Goater	32,438
Mar 4	Crystal Palace	D 1-1	R Taylor	21,052
Mar 8	QUEENS PARK RANGERS	L 1-3	Jeff Whitley	31,353
Mar 11	Barnsley	L 1-2	Goater	22,650
Mar 19	CHARLTON ATHLETIC	D 1-1	Goater	32,139
Mar 21	Stockport County	D 2-2	Pollock, Jobson	11,212
Mar 25	WEST BROMWICH ALBION	W 2-1	Goater, Kennedy	32,062
Apr 1	Swindon Town	W 2-0	Goater, Kennedy	12,397
Apr 5	BOLTON WANDERERS	W 2-0	Horlock, Dickov	32,927
Apr 8	CREWE ALEXANDRA	W 4-0	Dickov 2, Prior, Kennedy	32,433
Apr 15	Grimsby Town	D 1-1	Prior	8,166
Apr 22	TRANMERE ROVERS	W 2-0	Goater, Jeff Whitley	32,842
Apr 24	Portsmouth	D 2-2	Prior, R Taylor	19,015
Apr 28	BIRMINGHAM CITY	W 1-0	Goater	32,062
May 7	Blackburn Rovers	W 4-1	Goater, Kennedy, Dickov, o.g.	29,913

FA Cup

Dec 12	Chester City	(Rd 3) W 4-1	Goater 2, Bishop, o.g.	5,469
Jan 9	LEEDS UNITED	(Rd 4) L 2-5	Goater, Bishop	29,240

Worthington Cup

Aug 11	BURNLEY	(Rd1 FL) W 5-0	Kennedy 2, Horlock, Goater, G Taylor	11,074
Aug 24	Burnley	(Rd1 SL) W 1-0	Cooke	3,647
Sep 15	SOUTHAMPTON	(Rd2 FL) D 0-0		17,476
Sep 21	Southampton	(Rd2 FL) L 3-4	Goater 2, Dickov	10,960

Fact File

City needed to avoid defeat in the last game of the season to ensure promotion. Trailing 1-0 at half-time, they stormed home to win 4-1.

MANAGER: Joe Royle

CAPTAIN: Andy Morrison

TOP SCORER: Shaun Goater

BIGGEST WIN: August 21, 1999 6-0 v Sheffield United, Division 1;

HIGHEST ATTENDANCE: October 23, 1999 33,027 v Blackburn Rovers, won 2-0, Division 1

MAJOR TRANSFERS IN: Mark Kennedy from Wimbledon, Danny Granville from Leeds United, Robert Taylor from Gillingham

League & Cup Appearances (substitute)

PLAYER	LEAGUE	CUP COMPETITION		TOTAL
		FA CUP	WORTHINGTON	
Allsopp	0 (4)	0 (4)		0 (8)
Bishop	25 (12)	2 (2)	2	29 (14)
Cooke	6 (7)	3 (1)		9 (8)
Crooks	9 (11)	3 (1)		12 (12)
Dickov	23 (12)	2	1	26 (12)
Edghill	40 (1)	3	2	45 (1)
Fenton		0 (1)		1 (1)
Goater	40	3	2	45
Grunt	4 (3)		1	5 (3)
Granville	28 (8)		2	30 (8)
Horlock	36 (2)	3	2	41 (2)
Jobson	43 (1)	3	2	48 (1)
Kennedy	41	4	2	47
Morrison	12	2		14
Peacock	4 (4)		1 (1)	5 (5)
Pollock	17 (7)	1	1	19 (7)
Prior	9			9
Taylor G	8 (10)	2 (1)		10 (11)
Taylor R	14 (2)			14 (2)
Tiatto	26 (9)	3		29 (9)
Vaughan	0 (1)	0 (1)		0 (2)
Weaver	45	4	2	51
Whitley Jeff	0 (1)		2	2 (1)
Whitley Jim	41 (1)	3	0 (2)	44 (3)
Wiekens	32 (1)	2	2	36 (1)
Wright	1			1

Goalscorers

PLAYER	LEAGUE	CUP COMPETITION		TOTAL
		FA CUP	WORTHINGTON	
Goater	23	3	3	29
Horlock	10		1	11
Kennedy	8		2	10
Dickov	5		1	6
Taylor G	5		1	6
Taylor R	5			5
Whitley Jeff	4			4
Bishop	2	2		4
Jobson	3			3
Pollock	3			3
Peacock				2
Prior	3			1
Crooks	1			1
Edghill	1			1
Granville	1			1
Wiekens	1			1
Cooke			1	1

Final Division 1 Table

		P	W	D	L	F	A	Pts
1	CHARLTON A	46	27	10	9	79	45	91
2	MANCHESTER CITY	46	26	11	9	78	40	89
3	IPSWICH T	46	25	12	9	71	42	87
4	BARNSLEY	46	24	10	12	88	67	82
5	BIRMINGHAM C	46	22	11	13	65	44	77
6	BOLTON W	46	21	13	12	69	50	76
7	WOLVERHAMPTON W	46	21	11	14	64	48	74
8	HUDDERSFIELD T	46	21	11	14	62	49	74
9	FULHAM	46	17	16	13	49	41	67
10	QPR	46	16	18	12	62	53	66
11	BLACKBURN R	46	15	17	14	55	51	62
12	NORWICH C	46	14	15	17	45	50	57
13	TRANMERE R	46	15	12	19	57	68	57
14	NOTTINGHAM F	46	14	14	18	53	55	56
15	CRYSTAL PALACE	46	13	15	18	57	67	54
16	SHEFFIELD U	46	13	15	18	59	71	54
17	STOCKPORT CO	46	13	15	18	55	67	54
18	PORTSMOUTH	46	13	12	21	55	66	51
19	CREWE ALEX	46	14	9	23	46	67	51
20	GRIMSBY T	46	13	12	21	41	67	51
21	WBA	46	10	19	17	43	60	49
22	WALSALL	46	11	13	22	52	77	46
23	PORT VALE	46	7	15	24	48	69	36
24	SWINDON T	46	8	12	26	38	77	36

Season 2000-01

FA Carling Premiership

DATE	OPPONENTS	SCORE	GOALSCORERS	ATTENDANCE
Aug 19	Charlton Athletic	L 0-4		20,043
Aug 23	SUNDERLAND	W 4-2	Wanchope 3, Haaland	34,410
Aug 26	COVENTRY CITY	L 1-2	Horlock	34,140
Sep 5	Leeds United	W 2-1	Wiekens, Howey	40,055
Sep 9	Liverpool	L 2-3	Horlock, Weah	44,692
Sep 17	MIDDLESBROUGH	D 1-1	Wanchope	32,053
Sep 23	Tottenham Hotspur	D 0-0		36,069
Sep 30	NEWCASTLE UNITED	L 0-1		34,497
Oct 14	BRADFORD CITY	W 2-0	Haaland, Dickov	34,229
Oct 23	Southampton	W 2-0	Tiatto, Dickov	15,056
Oct 28	Arsenal	L 0-5		38,049
Nov 4	LEICESTER CITY	L 0-1		34,279
Nov 11	West Ham United	L 1-4	Prior	26,022
Nov 18	MANCHESTER UNITED	L 0-1		34,429
Nov 25	IPSWICH TOWN	L 2-3	Wanchope, Howey	33,741
Dec 3	Chelsea	L 1-2	Dickov	34,971
Dec 9	EVERTON	W 5-0	Wanchope, Howey, Dickov, Goater, o.g.	34,516
Dec 16	Aston Villa	D 2-2	Haaland, Wanchope	29,281
Dec 23	Sunderland	L 0-1		47,475
Dec 26	DERBY COUNTY	D 0-0		34,321
Dec 30	CHARLTON ATHLETIC	L 1-4	Huckerby	33,280
Jan 1	Coventry City	D 1-1	Wanchope	21,999
Jan 13	LEEDS UNITED	L 0-4		34,288
Jan 20	Derby County	D 1-1	Howey	31,174
Jan 31	LIVERPOOL	D 1-1	Tiatto	34,629
Feb 3	Middlesbrough	D 1-1	o.g.	31,794
Feb 10	TOTTENHAM HOTSPUR	L 0-1		34,399
Feb 24	Newcastle United	W 1-0	Goater	51,981
Mar 3	SOUTHAMPTON	L 0-1		33,990
Mar 17	Bradford City	D 2-2	Wiekens, Goater	19,117
Mar 31	ASTON VILLA	L 1-3	Goater	34,243
Apr 8	Everton	L 1-3	Whitley	36,561
Apr 11	ARSENAL	L 0-4		33,444
Apr 14	Leicester City	W 2-1	Wanchope, Goater	20,224
Apr 21	Manchester United	D 1-1	Howey	67,535
Apr 28	WEST HAM UNITED	W 1-0	Goater	33,737
May 7	Ipswich Town	L 1-2	Goater	25,004
May 19	CHELSEA	L 1-2	Howey	34,479

FA Cup

Jan 6	BIRMINGHAM CITY	(Rd 3) W 3-2	Goater, Morrison, Huckerby	19,380
Jan 27	COVENTRY CITY	(Rd 4) W 1-0	Goater	24,637
Feb 17	Liverpool	(Rd 5) L 2-4	Goater, Kanchelskis	36,231

Worthington Cup

Sep 20	GILLINGHAM	(Rd 2 FL) D 1-1	Weah	17,408
Sep 26	Gillingham	(Rd 2 SL) W 4-2*	Weah 2, Kennedy, Dickov	6,520
Nov 1	Aston Villa	(Rd 3) W 1-0	Horlock	24,138
Nov 29	WIMBLEDON	(Rd 4) W 2-1	Wanchope, Goater	19,513
Dec 12	IPSWICH TOWN**	(Rd 5) D 1-1	Dickov	23,260
Dec 19	IPSWICH TOWN	(R) L 1-2*	Goater	31,252

*After extra time. ** Match abandoned.

League & Cup Appearances (substitute)

PLAYER	LEAGUE	CUP COMPETITION		TOTAL
		FA CUP	WORTHINGTON	
Allsopp	0 (1)			0 (1)
Bishop	3 (6)	0 (1)	2 (3)	5 (10)
Charvet	16 (4)	0 (1)		16 (5)
Crooks	0 (2)		2	2 (2)
Dickov	15 (6)	0 (1)	2 (1)	17 (8)
Dunfield	0 (1)			0 (1)
Dunne	24 (1)	3		27 (1)
Edghill	6	1		7
Goater	20 (6)	2 (1)	3	25 (7)
Grant	5 (5)	1 (1)		6 (6)
Granville	16 (3)	3	0 (3)	19 (6)
Haaland	35	3	5	43
Horlock	14		4	18
Howey	38	1	2	41
Huckerby	8 (5)	3		11 (5)
Jobson			1 (2)	1 (2)
Kanchelskis	7 (3)	1		8 (3)
Kennedy	15 (8)	1 (3)		16 (11)
Morrison	3	3	1	7
Nash	6			6
Ostenstad	1 (3)			1 (3)
Prior	18 (2)	2 (1)	4	24 (3)
Ritchie	11 (1)	1	3	15 (1)
Tiatto	31 (2)	2	4	37 (2)
Wanchope	25 (2)	1	3	29 (2)
Weah	5 (2)		2	7 (2)
Weaver	31	3	5	39
Whitley	28 (3)	1	5	34 (3)
Wiekens	29 (5)	2 (1)	3 (1)	34 (7)
Wright	1			1
Wright-Phillips	9 (6)		3 (1)	12 (7)

Not including abandoned match.

Goalscorers

PLAYER	LEAGUE	CUP COMPETITION		TOTAL
		FA CUP	WORTHINGTON	
Goater	7	3	2	12
Wanchope	9		1	10
Howey	6			6
Dickov	4		1	5
Weah	1		3	4
Haaland	3			3
Horlock	2		1	3
Tiatto	2			2
Huckerby	1	1		2
Wiekens	2			2
Kanchelskis		1		1
Kennedy			1	1
Morrison	1			1
Prior	1			1
Whitley	1			1
Opps' o.gs.	2			2

Fact File

The Blues lost 2-1 at Ipswich in the penultimate game and suffered relegation. Despite this, an average home attendance of more than 34,000 was the highest of any relegated club since the Premiership began in 1992.

MANAGER: Joe Royle   **CAPTAIN:** Alfie Haaland

TOP SCORER: Shaun Goater

BIGGEST WIN: December 9, 2000 5-0 v Everton, Premier League

HIGHEST ATTENDANCE: April 2, 2001 67,535 v Manchester United, drew 1-1, Premier League

MAJOR TRANSFERS IN: Paulo Wanchope from West Ham United, Alfie Haaland and Darren Huckerby from Leeds United, Richard Dunne from Everton, Carlo Nash from Stockport County

MAJOR TRANSFERS OUT: Ian Bishop to Miami Fusion, Tommy Wright to Bolton Wanderers, Richard Jobson to Tranmere Rovers

Final Premier League Table

		P	W	D	L	F	A	Pts
1	MANCHESTER UNITED	38	24	8	6	79	31	80
2	ARSENAL	38	20	10	8	63	38	70
3	LIVERPOOL	38	20	9	9	71	39	69
4	LEEDS UNITED	38	20	8	10	64	43	68
5	IPSWICH TOWN	38	20	6	12	57	42	66
6	CHELSEA	38	17	10	11	68	45	61
7	SUNDERLAND	38	15	12	11	46	41	57
8	ASTON VILLA	38	13	15	10	46	43	54
9	CHARLTON ATHLETIC	38	14	10	14	50	57	52
10	SOUTHAMPTON	38	14	10	14	40	48	52
11	NEWCASTLE UNITED	38	14	9	15	44	50	51
12	TOTTENHAM HOTSPUR	38	13	10	15	47	54	49
13	LEICESTER CITY	38	14	6	18	39	51	48
14	MIDDLESBROUGH	38	9	15	14	44	44	42
15	WEST HAM UNITED	38	10	12	16	45	50	42
16	EVERTON	38	11	9	18	45	59	42
17	DERBY COUNTY	38	10	12	16	37	59	42
18	MANCHESTER CITY	38	8	10	20	41	65	34
19	COVENTRY CITY	38	8	10	20	36	63	34
20	BRADFORD CITY	38	5	11	22	30	70	26

Season 2001-02

Football League Division 1

DATE	OPPONENTS	SCORE	GOALSCORERS	ATTENDANCE
Aug 11	WATFORD	W 3-0	Goater, Berkovic, Pearce	33,939
Aug 18	Norwich City	L 0-2		18,745
Aug 25	CREWE ALEXANDRA	W 5-2	Goater 2, Wanchope 2, Pearce	32,844
Aug 27	Burnley	W 4-2	Goater 3, Wanchope	19,603
Sep 8	West Bromwich Albion	L 0-4		23,524
Sep 15	BIRMINGHAM CITY	W 3-0	Goater 2, Dunne	31,714
Sep 19	Coventry City	L 3-4	Horlock, Benarbia, o.g.	18,804
Sep 22	Sheffield Wednesday	W 6-2	Goater 2, Wanchope 2, Benarbia, Granville	25,731
Sep 25	WALSALL	W 3-0	Goater, Wanchope, Benarbia	31,525
Sep 29	WIMBLEDON	L 0-4		32,989
Oct 13	STOCKPORT COUNTY	D 2-2	Goater, Benarbia	34,214
Oct 16	SHEFFIELD UNITED	D 0-0		32,454
Oct 21	Preston North End	L 1-2	Huckerby	21,014
Oct 23	GRIMSBY TOWN	W 4-0	Huckerby 2, Howey, Goater	30,797
Oct 28	Nottingham Forest	D 1-1	Goater	28,226
Oct 31	Barnsley	W 3-0	Pearce, Goater, Huckerby	15,159
Nov 3	GILLINGHAM	W 4-1	Goater 3, Huckerby	33,067
Nov 17	Portsmouth	L 1-2	Huckerby	19,103
Nov 24	ROTHERHAM UNITED	W 2-1	Negouai, Benarbia	34,223
Dec 1	Grimsby Town	W 2-0	Goater, Huckerby	7,960
Dec 4	Millwall	W 3-2	Goater, Huckerby, Wright-Phillips	13,026
Dec 8	Crystal Palace	L 1-2	Goater	22,080
Dec 11	WOLVERHAMPTON W.	W 1-0	Horlock	33,639
Dec 16	BRADFORD CITY	W 3-1	Horlock, Wright-Phillips, Mettomo	30,749
Dec 26	WEST BROMWICH ALBION	D 0-0		34,407
Dec 29	BURNLEY	W 5-1	Wanchope 3, Berkovic, Huckerby	34,250
Jan 1	Sheffield United	W 3-1	Berkovic, Goater, Wright-Phillips	26,291
Jan 13	NORWICH CITY	W 3-1	Berkovic 2, Wanchope	31,794
Jan 20	Watford	W 2-1	Wanchope, o.g.	17,074
Jan 30	MILLWALL	W 2-0	Goater 2	30,238
Feb 3	Wimbledon	L 1-2	Benarbia	10,664
Feb 10	PRESTON NORTH END	W 3-2	Howey, Wanchope, Wright-Phillips	34,220
Feb 23	Walsall	D 0-0		7,618
Feb 27	SHEFFIELD WEDNESDAY	W 4-0	Berkovic, Goater, Huckerby, Horlock	33,682
Mar 3	COVENTRY CITY	W 4-2	Wright-Phillips 2, Tiatto, Huckerby	33,335
Mar 5	Birmingham City	W 2-1	Horlock, Jensen	24,160
Mar 8	Bradford City	W 2-0	Huckerby, Macken	18,168
Mar 12	Crewe Alexandra	W 3-1	Goater, Huckerby, Benarbia	10,092
Mar 16	CRYSTAL PALACE	W 1-0	Horlock	33,637
Mar 19	Stockport County	L 1-2	Macken	9,537
Mar 23	Rotherham United	D 1-1	Benarbia	11,426
Mar 30	NOTTINGHAM FOREST	W 3-0	Huckerby 3	34,345
Apr 1	Wolverhampton W.	W 2-0	Wright-Phillips 2	28,015
Apr 6	BARNSLEY	W 5-1	Huckerby 3, Macken 2	33,628
Apr 13	Gillingham	W 3-1	Horlock, Goater, Huckerby	9,494
Apr 21	PORTSMOUTH	W 3-1	Howey, Goater, Macken	34,657

FA Cup

Jan 5	SWINDON TOWN	(Rd 3) W 2-0	Wanchope, Horlock	21,581
Jan 27	Ipswich Town	(Rd 4) W 4-1	Goater 2, Berkovic, Huckerby	21,199
Feb 17	Newcastle United	(Rd 5) L 0-1		51,020

Worthington Cup

Sep 11	Notts. County	(Rd 2) W 4-2	Goater, Dickov, Huckerby, Shuker	5,972
Oct 10	BIRMINGHAM CITY	(Rd 3) W 6-0	Huckerby 4, Goater, o.g.	13,912
Nov 28	Blackburn Rovers	(Rd 4) L 0-2		17,907

Fact File

City equal their most League goals ever in one season and win the First Division Championship for the first time since 1968.

League & Cup Appearances (substitute)

PLAYER	LEAGUE	CUP COMPETITION		TOTAL
		FA CUP	WORTHINGTON	
Benarbia	38	2	2	42
Berkovic	20 (5)	3	2 (1)	25 (6)
Charvet	3			3
Colosimo	0 (6)		1	1 (6)
Dickov	0 (7)		0 (1)	0 (8)
Dunne	41 (2)	3	3	47 (2)
Edghill	9 (2)	1 (1)		10 (3)
Etuhu	11 (1)		1	12 (1)
Goater	42	1 (1)	2	45 (1)
Grant	2 (1)		1	3 (1)
Granville	12 (4)		1 (1)	13 (5)
Haaland	0 (3)			0 (3)
Horlock	33 (9)	3	2	38 (9)
Howey	34	2	2	38
Huckerby	30 (10)	3	2 (1)	35 (11)
Jensen	16 (2)	2		18 (2)
Killen	0 (3)			0 (3)
Macken	4 (4)			4 (4)
Mears	0 (1)			0 (1)
Mettomo	17 (6)		1 (1)	18 (7)
Mike	1 (1)			1 (1)
Nash	22 (1)	1	1	24 (1)
Negouai	2 (3)	0 (1)	1	3 (4)
Pearce	38	1 (1)	3	42 (1)
Ritchie	0 (8)	2	0 (1)	2 (9)
Shuker	0 (2)		0 (1)	0 (3)
Sun	2 (5)			2 (5)
Tiatto	36 (1)	1	2	39 (1)
Toure	0 (1)		0 (1)	0 (2)
Wanchope	14 (1)	2	1	17 (1)
Weaver	24 (1)	2	2	28 (1)
Whitley	0 (2)			0 (2)
Wiekens	24 (5)	1	2	27 (5)
Wright-Phillips	31 (4)	3	1 (1)	35 (5)

Goalscorers

PLAYER	LEAGUE	CUP COMPETITION		TOTAL
		FA CUP	WORTHINGTON	
Goater	28	2	2	32
Huckerby	20	1	5	26
Wanchope	12	1		13
Benarbia	8			8
Horlock	7	1		8
Wright-Phillips	8			8
Berkovic	6	1		7
Macken	5			5
Howey	3			3
Pearce	3			3

The following scored 1: Dunne, Granville, Jensen, Mettomo, Negouai, Tiatto, Dickov, Shuker.

Final Division 1 Table

		P	W	D	L	F	A	Pts
1	MANCHESTER CITY	46	31	6	9	108	52	99
2	WBA	46	27	8	11	61	29	89
3	WOLVERHAMPTON W	46	25	11	10	76	43	86
4	MILLWALL	46	22	11	13	69	48	77
5	BIRMINGHAM C	46	21	13	12	70	49	76
6	NORWICH C	46	22	9	15	60	51	75
7	BURNLEY	46	21	12	13	70	62	75
8	PRESTON NE	46	20	12	14	71	59	72
9	WIMBLEDON	46	18	13	15	63	57	67
10	CRYSTAL PALACE	46	20	6	20	70	62	66
11	COVENTRY C	46	20	6	20	59	53	66
12	GILLINGHAM	46	18	10	18	64	67	64
13	SHEFFIELD U	46	15	15	16	53	54	60
14	WATFORD	46	16	11	19	62	56	59
15	BRADFORD C	46	15	10	21	69	76	55
16	NOTTINGHAM F	46	12	18	16	50	51	54
17	PORTSMOUTH	46	13	14	19	60	72	53
18	WALSALL	46	13	12	21	51	71	51
19	GRIMSBY T	46	12	14	20	50	72	50
20	SHEFFIELD WED	46	12	14	20	49	71	50
21	ROTHERHAM U	46	10	19	17	52	66	49
22	CREWE ALEX	46	12	13	21	47	76	49
23	BARNSLEY	46	11	15	20	59	86	48
24	STOCKPORT CO	46	6	8	32	42	102	26

Manchester City in celebration. Clockwise from top left: Tony Book, George Heslop, Roy Paul, Nicky Weaver and Francis Lee.

Complete Players' Career Records

(records up to and including season 2001-02)

Other = Wartime, Charity Shield, Play Offs, Test Matches, Full Members' Cup, Associate Members' Cup, Anglo-Scottish Cup, Tennent-Caledonian Cup, Anglo-Italian Cup, Texaco Cup and the Football Alliance

Player	Birthplace	From	Year Joined	Year Left	To	League App	Sub	Goals
ABAZAJ, E	Albania	Benfica	1995		On Loan	-		
ABBOTT, J	Patricroft	Eccles Borough	1913	1915	Released	3		2
ADCOCK, A	Bethnal Green	Colchester United	1987	1988	Northampton Town	12	3	5
AIMSON, P	Prestbury	Stafford Boys	1958	1964	York City	16		4
ALBINSON, G	Prestwich	Manchester United	1921	1923	Crewe Alexandra	3		
ALISON, J	Peebles	Falkirk	1949	1952	Aldershot	19		
ALLAN, J	Glasgow	Scottish Interim League	1927	1928	Scottish Interim League	8		1
ALLEN, A	Manchester	Glossop North End	1915	1924	Southport	52		
ALLEN, C	Stepney	Bordeaux	1989	1991	Chelsea	31	22	16
ALLMARK, J	Liverpool	Colwyn Bay	1937	1938	New Brighton	1		
ALLSOPP, D	Melbourne, Australia	Port Melbourne Sharks	1998	2000	Notts. County	3	26	4
ANDERS, H	St Helens	Preston North End	1953	1956	Port Vale	32		4
ANGUS, H	St Helens	West Manchester	1892	1893	Released	2		
ANGUS, J		Third Lanark	1892	1892	Stockport County	7		3
APPLETON, F	Hyde	Marple FC	1924	1929	Released	2		
ARMITT, G		Blackburn Rovers	1893	1893	Released	1		
ASHWORTH, S	Fenton, Stoke	Stoke City	1903	1904	Everton	18		
ATKINSON, D	Shrewsbury	Fenerbache, Turkey	1997		On Loan	7	1	2
AUSTIN, S	Arnold	Norwich City	1924	1931	Chesterfield	160		43
BACON, A	Birdholme	Derby County	1928	1929	Reading	5		1
BACUZZI, D	Islington	Arsenal	1964	1966	Reading	56	1	
BAILEY, A	Macclesfield	Trainee	1997	1999	Stockport County	-		
BAKER, G	New York	St Mirren	1960	1961	Hibernian	37		14
BAKER, G	Southampton	Southampton	1982	1987	Southampton	114	3	19
BAKER, J		Local League	1893	1895	Released	3		1
BALDWIN, W		Sale Holmfield	1904	1908	Reading	2		
BANKS, W	Hurlford	Kilmarnock	1905	1908	Atherton Canbee	25		1
BANNISTER, C	Burton-on-Trent	Newtown	1896	1897	Lincoln City	18		2
BANNISTER, E		Buxton	1907	1910	Preston North End	1		
BANNISTER, J	Leyland	Chorley	1902	1906	Manchester United	45	21	2
BARBER, L	Wombwell	Halifax Town	1927	1932	Retired	92		
BARKAS, S	Wardley	Bradford City	1934	1947	Workington	175		1
BARLOW, C	Collyhurst	Tarporley Boys	1956	1963	Oldham Athletic	179		78
BARNES, H	Wadsley Bridge	Derby County	1914	1924	Preston North End	217		120
BARNES, K	Birmingham	Stafford Rangers	1950	1961	Wrexham	258		19
BARNES, P	Rugeley	Manchester Boys	1972	1979	West Bromwich Albion ⎱	116	7	15
		Manchester United	1987	1988	Hull City ⎰			
BARNETT, L	Bramley, Rotherham	Blackpool	1930	1936	Retired	84		
BARR, A	Ballymena	Glentoran	1936	1940	Released	4		2
BARRASS, M	Seaham Harbour	Sheffield Wednesday	1926	1933	Ashton National	162		14
BARRETT, C	Cheadle Heath	Cheadle Heath Nomads	1970	1976	Nottingham Forest	50	3	
BARRETT, E	Rochdale	Y.T.S.	1984	1987	Oldham Athletic	2	1	
BARRETT, F	Dundee	Newton Heath	1901	1902	Dundee	5		
BATTY, M	Manchester	Apprentice	1960	1966	Rhyl	13		
BEAGRIE, P	North Ormesby	Everton	1994	1997	Bradford City	46	6	3
BEARDSLEY, P	Newcastle	Bolton Wanderers	1998		On Loan	5	1	
BECKFORD, D	Burnage	Manchester Boys	1984	1987	Port Vale	7	4	
BECKFORD, J	Burnage	Manchester Boys	1986	1992	Birmingham City	8	12	1
BEEBY, A	Ashbourne	Liverpool	1911	1912	Released	11		
BEECH, C	Congleton	Trainee	1992	1997	Cardiff City	-		
BEESLEY, P	Liverpool	Leeds United	1997	1998	Port Vale	10	3	
BELL, C	Hesleden	Bury	1966	1979	Retired	393	1	117
BELL, P	Ferryhill	Raith Rovers	1926	1928	Falkirk	42		7
BENARBIA, A	Oran, Algeria	Paris St.Germain	2001			38		8
BENNETT, A		Local Leagues	1893	1896	Released	12		6
BENNETT, D	Manchester	Manchester Boys	1976	1981	Cardiff City	43	9	9
BENNETT, E	Bristol	Wrexham	1926	1929	Norwich City	19		
BENSON, J	Arbroath	Stockport Boys	1958	Torquay	United (1964)	44		
BENTLEY, H	Knutsford	Macclesfield Town	1910	1912	Released	1		
BENZIE, R	Greenock	Doncaster Rovers	1925	1928	Welsh League	13		
BERKOVIC, E	Hiafa, Israel	Glasgow Celtic	2001			20	5	6
BETTS, B	Barnsley	Stockport County	1960	1964	Scunthorpe United	101		5
BEVAN, F	Hackney	Millwall Athletic	1901	1903	Reading	8		1
BIGGINS, W	Sheffield	Norwich City	1988	1989	Stoke City	29	3	9

Complete Players' Career Records: Abazaj – Biggins

In the appearance columns "-" indicates that although eligible to appear in the tournament the player did not appear. A "0" indicates the player was an unsued substitute. The information in this section has been provided by www.citystat.net

FAC Apps	Sub	Goals	FLC Apps	Sub	Goals	European Apps	Sub	Goals	Others Apps	Sub	Goals	Totals Apps	Sub	Goals
0												0		
-												3		2
2			2	1	1				2		4	18	4	9
-			3		2							19		6
-												3		
1												20		
1												9		1
4									4			60		
4	2	1	5	2	4				2			42	26	21
-									-			1		
0			0	7	1				1	1	1	4	34	6
1									4			33		4
-									1		1	3		1
1												8		3
1												3		
												1		
4												22		
												7	1	2
12		4										172		47
-												5		1
2			1									59	1	
-			-						0	1		0	1	
1			1									39		14
2	1		13	1					3	1	2	132	6	21
-												3		1
-												2		
1												26		1
-												18		2
-												1		
-		1									47		21	
7												99		
20									76		3	271		4
8		2	2									189		80
18		5							73		73	308		198
23			2						-			283		19
7		2	16	5	4	9	1		2			150	12	22
8									1			93		
-												4		2
10		1										172		15
3	1		8			1	1		3			65	4	1
-			1						0			3	1	
4												9		
-			-									13		
4	1	1	8			1						58	7	5
												5	1	
-			0	1					-			7	5	
0			1	4	1				-			9	16	2
-												11		
0			-									0		
			-									10	3	
33	1	9	40		18	23	1	8	9		1	498	3	153
-												42		7
2			2									42		8
-												12		6
5	1	1	7		5	-						55	10	15
1												20		
3			5									52		
-												1		
-												13		
3		1	2	1								25	6	7
8			8								1	117		6
1												9		1
2			4			1			-			35	3	10

Player	Birthplace	From	Year Joined	Year Left	To	League App	Sub	Goals
BISHOP, I	Liverpool	Bournemouth	1989	1989	West Ham United	} 71	25	4
		West Ham United	1998	2001	Miami Fusion USA			
BLACK, A	Stirling	Heart of Midlothian	1946	1950	Stockport County	139		47
BLACKSHAW, B	Ashton-under-Lyne	Audenshaw United	1937	1946	Oldham Athletic	3		
BLAIR, J	Dumfries	Woolwich Arsenal	1906	1910	Bradford City	76		
BLAIR, T	Glasgow	Kilmarnock	1920	1922	Canada	38		
BLEW, H	Wrexham	Wrexham	1906		On Loan	1		
BODAK, P	Birmingham	Manchester United	1982	1983	Seiko, Hong Kong	12	2	1
BOND, K	West Ham	Seattle Sounders	1981	1984	Southampton	108	2	11
BOOK, T	Bath	Plymouth Argyle	1966	1974	Retired	242	2	4
BOOTH, F	Hyde	Stockport County	1902	1906	Bury	94		18
BOOTH, T	Langley	Middleton Boys	1965	1981	Preston North End	380	2	25
BOOTLE, W	Ashton-under-Lyne	Junior	1943	1951	Wigan Athletic	5		
BOTTOMLEY, W	Mossley	Oldham Athletic	1908	1919	Retired	98		2
BOWLES, S	Moston	Manchester Boys	1965	1970	Crewe Alexandra	15	2	2
BOWMAN, W	Canada	Accrington Stanley	1892	1900	Retired	47		3
BOWYER, I	Little Sutton	Mid-Cheshire Boys	1966	1971	Orient	42	8	13
BOYER, P	Nottingham	Southampton	1980	1983	Retired	17	3	3
BRADBURY, L	Oswestry	Portsmouth	1997	1998	Crystal Palace	34	6	10
BRADFORD, L	Eccles	Hurst FC	1925	1926	Ashton National	5		1
BRADSHAW, C	Sheffield	Sheffield Wednesday	1988	1989	Sheffield United	1	4	
BRANAGAN, K	Salford	North Salford YC	1948	1960	Oldham Athletic	196		3
BRANCH, M	Liverpool	Everton	1998		On Loan	4		
BRAND, R	Edinburgh	Glasgow Rangers	1965	1967	Sunderland	20		2
BRANNAN, G	Prescot	Tranmere Rovers	1997	1998	Motherwell	38	5	4
BRAY, J	Oswaldtwistle	Manchester Central	1929	1947	Watford	260		10
BRENNAN, J	Manchester	Bradford City	1914	1922	Rochdale	56		4
BRENNAN, M	Rossendale	Middlesbrough	1990	1992	Oldham Athletic	25	4	6
BRENNAN, M	Salford	Lancashire Schools	1968	1973	Rochdale	1	3	
BRIGHTWELL, D	Lutterworth	Y.T.S.	1988	1995	Bradford City	35	8	1
BRIGHTWELL, I	Lutterworth	Midas Junior Club	1985	1998	Coventry City	285	36	18
BRISCOE, L	Pontefract	Sheffield Wednesday	1998		On Loan	5		1
BROAD, T	Stalybridge	Bristol City	1915	1921	Stoke City	42		
BROADHURST, C	Moston	Ashton National	1927	1930	Blackpool	33		25
BROADIS, I	Isle of Dogs	Sunderland	1951	1953	Newcastle United	74		10
BROOK, E	Mexborough	Barnsley	1928	1940	Retired	452		158
BROOKS, G	Radcliffe	Longfield	1911	1918	Killed in Action	3		1
BROOMFIELD, H	Audlem, nr Nantwich	Manchester United	1908	1910	Manchester United	4		
BROWELL, T	Walbottle	Everton	1913	1926	Blackpool	222		122
BROWN, H		Crewe Alexandra	1910	1911	Tredagar	2		
BROWN, J		Orrell	1908	1910	Stoke	6		
BROWN, M	Hartlepool	Trainee	1994	1999	Sheffield United	78	22	2
BUCHAN, J	Perth	Woolwich Arsenal	1905	1911	Motherwell	155		8
BUCKLEY, F	Urmston	Aston Villa	1907	1909	Birmingham	11		
BUCKLEY, G	Manchester	Salford Boys	1977	1981	Preston North End	4	2	
BURGESS, C	Talke, Staffordshire	Stoke	1908	1911	Released	32		
BURGESS, H	Openshaw	Glossop North End	1903	1906	Manchester United	85		2
BURRIDGE, J	Workington	Dumbarton	1994	1994	Falkirk	} 3	1	
		Falkirk	1994	1995	Notts County			
BUSBY, M	Orbiston	Denny Hibs	1928	1936	Liverpool	202		11
CAINE, J		Local League	1892	1894	Liverpool	1		
CALDERWOOD, J	Busby, Lanark	Manchester Calico Ptrs	1922	1927	Grimsby Town	35		
CALLAGHAN, T		Glossop North End	1907	1909	Partick Thistle	2		
CALVEY, M		Blackburn Rovers	1894	1894	Baltimore, USA	7		5
CAMPBELL, B	Ayr	Ayr United	1890	1892	Darwen	~		
CANN, S	Babbicombe	Torquay United	1930	1935	Charlton Athletic	42		
CAPEL, T	Droylsden	Droylsden	1941	1947	Chesterfield	9		2
CARDWELL, L	Whitegate, nr Blackpool	Blackpool	1938	1947	Netherfield	42		
CARRODUS, F	Altrincham	Altrincham	1969	1974	Aston Villa	33	9	1
CARROLL, F	Beesbrook	Belfast Celtic	1920	1925	Newry Town	18		
CARSON, A	Glasgow	Newton Heath	1893	1894	Liverpool	9		3
CARTER, S	Great Yarmouth	Norfolk Schools	1968	1972	Notts County	4	2	2
CARTWRIGHT, J	Warrington	Northwich Victoria	1914	1921	Crystal Palace	38		3
CASSIDY, J	Dalziel	Newton Heath	1900	1901	Middlesbrough	31		14
CASSIDY, J	Lurgan	Newry Town	1935	1937	Tranmere Rovers	3		
CATON, T	Kirby	Liverpool Boys	1979	1983	Arsenal	164	1	8
CHADWICK, G	Oldham	Manchester Boys	1959	1983	Walsallx	12		
CHANNON, M	Orcheston	Southampton	1977	1979	Southampton	71	1	24
CHAPLOW, H		Chorley	1909	1911	Middlesbrough	7		
CHAPLIN, J	Dundee	Dundee	1910	1913	Leeds City	15		

FAC Apps	Sub	Goals	FLC Apps	Sub	Goals	European Apps	Sub	Goals	Others Apps	Sub	Goals	Totals Apps	Sub	Goals
3	2	2	8	5	1				1	1		83	33	7
7		5										146		52
									8		2	11		2
5		1										81		1
3												41		
												1		
2	1		-									14	3	1
6		1	8									122	2	12
28			19	1	1	17			6			312	3	5
9		1										103		19
27		5	44	2	3	25		3	11			487	4	36
1									32		6	38		6
5									32			135		2
-			1	2	2	-			-			16	4	4
2									-			49		3
4		1	6	2	2	5	3	1				57	13	17
2		1	4									23	3	4
0			6		1							40	6	11
-												5		1
0	1		-						0	1		1	6	
12									-			208		3
												4		
1			1									22		2
1			2									41	5	4
20									180		11	460		21
									94		4	154		4
1			4		1				2			32	4	7
-			-			-			2			3	3	
5	2	1	2	1					-			42	11	2
19	4	1	29	2					4	3		337	45	19
												5		1
2									46		2	88		4
3		1										36		26
5		2										79		12
41		19							7		2	501		179
-												3		1
												4		
25		17							33		18	280		157
-												2		
												6		
10	1	2	2	4					4			94	27	4
9		2										164		10
-												11		
-			2									6	2	
-												32		
9												94		2
0			0									3	1	
24		3							1			227		14
												1		
2												37		
												2		
-												7		5
1			2									1		2
4												46		
4			2						1			14		4
6									45			93		
1	1	1	3			0		1	-			37	11	2
2												20		
-												9		3
-			-			0		1	1			5	3	2
9		2							60		9	107		14
1												32		14
-												3		
12			21									197	1	8
-			2									14		
3	1		10	1	4	7		2				91	3	30
-												7		
2												17		

Player	Birthplace	From	Year Joined	Year Left	To	League App	Sub	Goals
CHAPMAN, T	Newtown	Newtown	1895	1896	Grimsby Town	26		3
CHAPPELL, T	Buxton	West Manchester	1896	1900	Retired	8		
CHARVET, L	Beziers, France	Newcastle United	2000			19	4	
CHEETHAM, R	Eccles	Manchester Boys	1955	1968	Detroit Cougars	127	5	4
CHRISTIE, J	Sale	Manchester United	1904	1907	Bradford Park Avenue	10		
CHRISTIE, T	Cresswell	Derby County	1986	1986	Walsall	9		3
CLARE, T	Congleton	Stoke	1897	1899	Burslem Port Vale	1		
CLARK, G	Gainsborough	Southend United	1936	1947	Hyde United	55		
CLARKE, J	Pontefract	Apprentice	1971	1975	Sunderland	13		
CLARKE, R	Newport	Cardiff City	1947	1958	Stockport County	349		73
CLARKE, W	Willenhall	Leicester City	1990	1992	Walsall	7	14	2
CLAY, J	Stockport	Stockport Boys	1962	1968	Macclesfield Town	1	1	
CLAYTON, R	Retford	Retford	1935	1938	Bristol City	3		2
CLEMENTS, K	Middleton	Middleton Youth Club	1971	1979	Oldham Athletic	} 220	5	1
		Oldham Athletic	1985	1988	Bury			
CLIFFORD, H		Stoke	1895	1896	Released	4		1
CLOUGH, N	Sunderland	Liverpool	1996	1998	Burton Albion	33	5	4
CODLING, R	Durham	Croydon Common	1910	1911	Released	5		
COLBRIDGE, C	Hull	Crewe Alexandra	1959	1962	Wrexham	62		12
COLEMAN, T	Liverpool	Doncaster Rivers	1965	1967	Sheffield Wednesday	82	1	12
COLOSIMO, S	Australia	South Melbourne Lakers	2001	2002	Racing Genk, Belgium	0	6	
COMRIE, M	Denny	Brentford	1932	1934	Burnley	17		1
CONLIN, J	Consett	Bradford City	1904	1911	Birmingham	161		28
CONLON, B	Drogheda	Queens Park Rangers	1997	1998	Southend United	1	6	
CONNOR, D	Wythenshaw	Manchester Boys	1962	1972	Preston North End	} 130	11	10
		Preston North End	1974	1975	Macclesfield Town			
CONSTANTINE, J	Ashton-under-Lyne	Rochdale	1944	1947	Bury	18		12
CONWAY, J	Dublin	Fulham	1976	1978	Portland Timbers	11	2	1
COOKE, T	Marston Green	Manchester United	1999			27	8	7
COOKSON, S	Manchester	Macclesfield Town	1918	1928	Bradford	285		
COOPER, P	Brierley Hill	Leicester City	1989	1990	Stockport County	15		
CORBETT, F	Birmingham	Torquay United	1930	1936	Lincoln City	15		
CORBETT, V	Birmingham	Hereford United	1933	1935	Southend United	5		
CORRIGAN, J	Rusholme	Sale Grammar School	1966	1983	Seattle Sounders	476		
COTON, T	Tamworth	Watford	1990	1996	Manchester United	162	1	
COUPE, D	Worksop		1908	1910	Released	1		
COUPLAND, C	Grimsby	Mansfield Town	1925	1927	Grimsby Town	24		2
COWAN, S	Chesterfield	Doncaster Rivers	1924	1935	Bradford City	369		19
COWAN, W	Edinburgh	Newcastle United	1926	1927	St Mirren	22		11
COWIE, A	Lockee, Fifeshire	Gravesend United	1898	1899	Queens Park Rangers	11		3
COX, W	Southampton	Millwall Athletic	1900	1901	Bury	1		
CRAWSHAW, R	Manchester	Stockport County	1919	1922	Halifax Town	25		6
CREANEY, G	Coatbridge	Portsmouth	1995	1998	St Mirren	8	13	4
CROOKS, L	Wakefield	Trainee	1995	2001	Barnsley	52	23	2
CROSS, D	Heywood	West Ham United	1982	1983	Vancouver Whitecaps	31		12
CROSSAN, J	Londonderry	Sunderland	1965	1967	Middlesbrough	94		24
CUMMING, J	Alexandria	Clydebank Juniors	1913	1920	West Ham United	35		3
CUNLIFFE, R	Manchester	Apprentice	1960	1965	York City	3		1
CUNLIFFE, R	Bryn	Garswood St Andrew	1945	1956	Chesterfield	44		9
CUNNINGHAM, T	Kingston, Jamaica	Sheffield Wednesday	1984	1985	Newcastle United	16	2	1
CURLE, K	Bristol	Wimbledon	1991	1996	Wolverhampton W	171		11
DALE, B	Manchester	Manchester United	1931	1938	Ipswich Town	237		
DALEY, S	Barnsley	Wolverhampton Wanderers	1979	1981	Seattle Sounders	47	1	4
DALZIEL, G	Motherwell	Glasgow Rangers	1983	1984	Partick Thistle	4	1	
DANIELS, A	Mossley	Mossley	1920	1926	Watford	31		
DANIELS, B	Salford	Ashton United	1971	1975	Chester	9	4	2
DARTNELL, H		Wellingborough	1900	1901	Barnsley	4		
DAVIDSON, A	Beith, Ayrshire	Glossop North End	1900	1901	Reading	7		1
DAVIDSON, D	Govan Hill	Glentyne Thistle	1951	1958	Workington Town	1		
DAVIDSON, D	Elgin	Sea Bees, Hong Kong	1983	1984	Highland Leagues	2	4	1
DAVIDSON, R	West Calder	Glasgow Celtic	1902	1904	Airdrieonians	32		
DAVIES, F	Birkenhead	Glossop North End	1906	1910	Released	6		
DAVIES, G	Manchester	Ashton United	1951	1957	Chester	13		5
DAVIES, G	Merthyr Tydfil	Chelsea	1985	1986	Fulham	31		9
DAVIES, I	Bristol	Newcastle United	1982	1984	Carlisle United	7		
DAVIES, J	Chirk	Chirk	1891	1894	Sheffield United	} 35		13
		Sheffield United	1895	1896	Millwall Athletic			
		Reading	1900	1901	Stockport County			
DAVIES, R	Stafford	Stafford Rangers	1911	1912	Pontypridd	6		
DAVIES, W	Caernarvon	Newcastle United	1971	1972	Manchester United	45		8

Complete Players' Career Records: Chapman – Davies, W

FAC			FLC			European			Others			Totals		
Apps	Sub	Goals	Apps	Sub	Goals	Apps	Sub	Goals	Apps	Sub	Goals	Apps	Sub	Goals
~									2			28		3
-												8		
	1											19	5	
4			6	1								137	6	4
-												10		
			1									10		3
												1		
9									180			244		
-			2									15		
20		6							1			370		79
1			-						1			9	14	2
-			-									1	1	
1									-			4		2
17			26			6	1		7		1	276	6	2
~												4		1
3		1	2									38	5	5
-												5		
2			1									65		12
10		3	7	1		2		1	1			102	2	16
			1									1	6	
-												17		1
14		2										175		30
-			0	1								1	7	
12	1		5	1		5			2	1		154	14	10
4		4							34		25	56		41
1			1			1						14	2	1
0			3	1	1				3			33	9	8
21		1										306		1
-			2						-			17		
-												15		
1												6		
37			52			27			12		1	604	1	
12			16						3			193	1	
-												1		
3												27		2
37		5							1			407		24
1												23		11
-												11		3
-												1		
1												26		6
0	4	1	-						-			8	17	5
5			5	2					3			65	25	2
3		1	4									38		13
14		2	2			1						110		27
6									-			41		3
-												3		1
4		1							1			49		10
0	1		5	3								21	3	4
14			18	2					1			204		13
32									2			271		
1			5									53	1	4
0	1		-									4	2	
1												32		
-			-						0	1		9	5	2
-												4		
-												7		1
-												1		
-			1									3	4	1
-												32		
-												6		
-												13		5
4		2	2	1					5		3	42		15
-			1									8		
3									24	8		62		21
-												6		
2			3	1		-			2			52		9

Player	Birthplace	From	Year Joined	Year Left	To	League App	Sub	Goals
DELLOW, R	Crosby	Mansfield Town	1935	1936	Tranmere Rovers	10		4
DENNISON, J	Manchester	Sale Holmfield	1903	1906	Released	1		2
DENNISON, R	Arnold	Brighton & Hove Albion	1925	1926	Clapton Orient	8		4
DEYNA, K	Starsgrad	Legia Warsaw	1978	1981	San Diego Sockers	34	4	12
DIBBLE, A	Cwmbran	Luton Town	1988	1997	Glasgow Rangers	113	3	
DICKOV, P	Livingstone	Arsenal	1996	2002	Leicester City	105	51	33
DITCHFIELD, J	Blackburn	Rossendale	1895	1896	Released	12		1
DOBING, P	Manchester	Blackburn Rovers	1961	1963	Stoke City	82		31
DOCHERTY, M	Preston	Burnley	1976	1976	Sunderland	8		
DOHERTY, P	Magherafelt	Blackpool	1936	1945	Derby County	119		74
DONACHIE, W	Castlemilk, Glasgow	Glasgow Celtic	1968	1980	Portland Timbers	347	4	2
DONALDSON, A	Barrhead	Sunderland	1923	1924	Chorley	7		
DONNELLY, R	Craigneuk	Partick Thistle	1935	1937	Morton	37		1
DORAN, J	Belfast	Brighton & Hove Albion	1922	1924	Crewe Alexandra	3		1
DORSETT, G	Brownhills	West Bromwich Albion	1901	1912	Retired	193		62
DORSETT, J	Brownhills	West Bromwich Albion	1910	1920	Southend United	132		17
DOUGAL, G	Edinburgh	Hibernian	1898	1901	Glossop North End	75		13
DOUGLAS, W	Dundee	Dundee Our Boys	1890	1894	Newton Heath	36		
DOWD, H	Salford	Blackley ICI	1958	1970	Oldham Athletic	181		1
DOYLE, M	Manchester	Stockport Boys	1962	1978	Stoke City	441	7	31
DRUMMOND, J	Glasgow	Glasgow Celtic	1902	1903	Partick Thistle	28		5
DUNFIELD, T	Vancouver, Canada	Trainee	2000			0	1	
DUNKLEY, M	Kettering	Northampton Town	1938	1947	Kettering Town	54		6
DUNNE, L	Dublin	Drumcondra	1933	1935	Hull City	3		
DUNNE, R	Dublin	Everton	2000			65	3	1
DYER, F	Bishopbriggs, Strathclyde	Royal Arsenal	1893	1898	Retired	36		3
DYSON, J	Oldham	Nelson	1951	1961	Stirling Albion	63		26
EADIE, B	Greenock	Greenock Morton	1906	1914	Derby County	185		6
EASTWOOD, E	Heywood	Heywood St James	1935	1947	Port Vale	16		
EDELSTON, J	Appleby Bridge	Hull City	1920	1920	Fulham	6		
EDEN, J	Manchester	Local League	1910	1912	Released	1		
EDGE, A	Stoke	Northwich Victoria	1894	1894	Released	1		
EDGHILL, R	Oldham	Trainee	1992	2002	Released	178	3	1
EDMONDSON, J	Accrington	Accrington Stanley	1902	1906	Bolton Wanderers	38		
EGAN, W	Chirk	Fairfield	1893	1894	Burnley	7		
EKELUND, R	Denmark	Barcelona	1995		On Loan	2	2	
ELLIOTT, A	Ashton-under-Lyne	Derby Boys	1980	1982	Sligo Rovers	1		
ELWOOD, J	Belfast	Glentoran	1924	1927	Chesterfield	31		
EMPTAGE, A	Grimsby	Scunthorpe United	1937	1951	Stockport County	136		1
ESPIE, J	Hamilton	Burnley	1896	1896	Released	1		
ETHERINGTON, R	Manchester	Leyland	1921	1924	Rotherham County	12		
ETUHU, D	Kano, Nigeria	Trainee	1998	2002	Preston North End	11	1	
EWING, D	Perth	Luncarty Juniors	1949	1962	Crewe Alexandra	279		1
EYRES, S	Droylsden	Failsworth	1907	1908	Colne	1		1
FAGAN, F	Dublin	Hull City	1953	1960	Derby County	153		34
FAGAN, J	Liverpool	Earlstown Bohemians	1938	1951	Nelson	148		2
FAIRCLOUGH, A	St.Helens	Eccles Borough	1913	1920	Southend United	5		1
FAIRCLOUGH, P	St Helens	Eccles Borough	1913	1920	Released	5		
FARRELL, T	Earlstown	Woolwich Arsenal	1905	1908	Airdrieonians	3		
FASHANU, J	Hackney	Edmonton, Canada	1989	1989	West Ham United	0	2	
FAULKNER, R	Manchester	Junior	1953	1957	Walsall	7		4
FAYERS, F	King's Lynn	Stockport County	1920	1923	Halifax Town	73		5
FELTON, B	Heyworth	Sheffield Wednesday	1929	1932	Tottenham Hotspur	73		
FENTON, N	Preston	Trainee	1996	2000	Notts. County	15		
FERGUSON, A		Preston North End	1894	1894	Baltimore, USA	2		
FIDLER, D	Stockport	Manchester United	1956	1960	Port Vale	5		1
FINNERHAN, P	Northwich	Northwich Victoria	1894	1897	Liverpool	85		27
FINNEY, S	Hexham	Preston North End	1993	1995	Swindon Town	0		
FINNIGAN, D	Wrexham	Connah's Quay & Shotton	1926	1927	Accrington Stanley	8		
FISHER, J	Glasgow	Brighton & Hove Albion	1906	1907	Bradford Park Avenue	5		2
FLEET, S	Salford	Bolton Wanderers	1953	1963	Wrexham	5		
FLEMING, G	Apprentice	Nottingham Forest	1989	1990	Barnsley	13	1	
FLETCHER, E	Turnstall. Staffordshire	Crewe Alexandra	1911	1926	Watford	301		2
FLETCHER, L	Helsby	Amateur	1932	1935	Watford	5		1
FLITCROFT, G	Bolton	Bolton Boys	1989	1996	Blackburn Rovers	109	6	13
FORD, J	Newcastle-upon-Tyne	Spen Black & White	1921	1922	Seaton Delaval	4		
FORRESTER, T		Local League	1892	1894	Released	10		2
FOSTER, C	Rotherham	Morecombe	1927	1928	Oldham Athletic	3		
FOSTER, H		Local League	1896	1898	Darwen	7		1
FOSTER, J	Blackley	Trainee	1990	1998	Carlisle United	17	2	

FAC Apps	Sub	Goals	FLC Apps	Sub	Goals	European Apps	Sub	Goals	Others Apps	Sub	Goals	Totals Apps	Sub	Goals
-												10		4
												1		2
2												10		4
2			2			0	1	1				38	5	13
8	1		14						2			137	4	
5	4	1	9	4	5				3		2	122	59	41
~												15		1
5			7	1								94		32
			1			2			2			13		
11		5							91		61	221		140
21			40			13	1		10			431	5	2
												7		
-												37		1
-												3		1
18		3										211		65
6									7		3	145		20
2												77		13
5									22			63		
22			16			-			-			219		1
44		2	43	4		23		2	14		1	565	7	40
-												28		5
												0	1	
7		1							61		15	122		22
-												3		
6			3									74	3	1
1												37		3
9		3	-						1			73		29
20												205		6
-									163			179		
												6		
-												1		
-												1		
8	1		17						3			206	4	1
2												40		
												7		
1	1											3	3	
-			-									1		
1												32		
8									34		5	178		6
												1		
-												12		
				1								12	1	
22			1						1			303		
-												1		1
11		1							1			165		35
10									12			170		2
-									6		8	11		9
-									102		13	107		13
-												3		
-			-									0	2	
									-			7		4
4												77		5
10												83		
-			3	1					1			19	1	
												2		
-												5		1
-									4			89		27
-			-									0		
-												8		
-												5		2
-			1									6		
-			4						1			18	1	
26									133		3	460		5
-												5		1
14		2	11	1					-			134	7	15
-												4		
-												10		2
-												3		
1												8		1
2	1		2	1								21	4	

Player	Birthplace	From	Year Joined	Year Left	To	League App	Sub	Goals
FRANCIS, T	Plymouth	Nottingham Forest	1981	1982	Sampdoria	26		12
FREEMAN, R	Droitwich	Bromsgrove Rovers	1935	1939	Exeter City	4		1
FRONTZECK, M	Odenkirchen	Borussia Mönchengladbach	1996	1997	Freiburg	19	4	
FROST, R	Hazel Grove	Stockport Boys	1962	1965	Kettering	2		1
FROST, S	Poplar	Millwall	1901	1907	Millwall	103		4
FURR, G	Watford	Watford	1909	1910	Watford	3		
FUTCHER, P	Chester	Luton Town	1978	1980	Oldham Athletic	36	1	
FUTCHER, R	Chester	Luton Town	1978	1979	Minnesota Kicks	10	7	7
GARNER, W	Manchester	Heaton Park	1912	1919	Southport	5		
GARTLAND, P	Seaham	Seaham Harbour	1914	1917	Retired	1		
GAUDINO, M	Brule	Eintracht Frankfurt	1994		On Loan	17	3	3
GAUGHAN, W	Cardiff	Cardiff City	1914	1919	Newport County	10		
GAYLE, B	Kingston	Wimbledon	1988	1990	Ipswich Town	55		3
GIBBONS, S	Darlaston	Cradley Heath	1927	1930	Fulham	10		
GIBSON, T	Glasgow	Bridgetown Waverley	1926	1927	South Shields	2		2
GIDMAN, J	Liverpool	Manchester United	1986	1988	Stoke City	52	1	1
GILL, R	Manchester	Local League	1941	1951	Chester	8		
GILLESPIE, B	Strathclyde	Lincoln City	1897	1905	South Africa	218		126
GILLIES, A	Fife	Bolton Wanderers	1896	1896	Heart of Midlothian	3		
GLEGHORN, N	Seaham	Ipswich Town	1988	1989	Birmingham City	27	7	7
GLENNON, C	Manchester	Manchester Boys	1965	1971	Northwich Victoria	3	1	
GOATER, S	Hamilton, Bermuda	Bristol City	1998			150	8	78
GODFREY, J		Coventry City	1919	1920	Merthyr Town	9		1
GODWIN, V		Blackburn Rovers	1948	1949	Stoke City	8		3
GOLAC, I		Bournemouth	1983	1983	Bjelasica, Yugoslavia	2		
GOMERSALL, V	Manchester	Junior	1958	1966	Swansea Town	39		
GOODCHILD, J	Southampton	Southampton Common	1911	1927	Guildford City	204		
GOODWIN, E	Chester-le-Street	Leeds City	1919	1921	Rochdale	20		3
GORRINGE, F	Salford	Manchester Docks	1926	1928	Lincoln City	1		2
GOULD, W	Burton-on-Trent	Bradford City	1909	1912	Tranmere Rovers	8		2
GOW, G	Glasgow	Bristol City	1980	1982	Rotherham United	26		5
GRANT, A	Liverpool	Everton	1999	2001	Burnley	11	10	
GRANVILLE, D	Islington	Leeds United	1999	2001	Crystal Palace	56	14	3
GRATRIX, R	Salford	Blackpool	1964	1965	Toronto, Canada	15		
GRAY, A	Tredegar	Oldham Athletic	1927	1929	Manchester Central	68		
GRAY, G	Bolton	Local League	1919	1922	Released	3		
GRAY, M	Renfrew	Third Lanark	1963	1967	Port Elizabeth	87	4	21
GREALISH, T	Paddington	West Bromwich Albion	1986	1987	Rotherham United	11		
GREENACRE, C	Wakefield	Trainee	1995	1999	Mansfield Town	3	5	1
GREENWOOD, J	Manchester	Junior	1946	1949	Exeter City	1		
GREGG, W	Woodhouse, Sheffield	Accrington Stanley	1937	1938	Chester	9		
GREGORY, C	Doncaster	Doncaster Rivers	1930	1934	Reading	21		2
GREGORY, J	Manchester	Bury	1905	1906	Bolton Wanderers	3		
GRIEVE, R	Greenock	Greenock Morton	1906	1909	Accrington Stanley	44		18
GRIFFITHS, C	Welshpool	Shrewsbury Town	1993	1995	Portsmouth	11	7	4
GROENENDIJK, A	Leiden, Netherlands	Ajax Amsterdam	1993	1994	Sparta Rotterdam	9		
GUNN, J		Bolton Wanderers	1896	1897	Clyde	21		4
GUNNING, J	Helensburgh	Hibernian	1950	1954	Barrow	13		
HAALAND, A.I.	Stavanger, Norway	Leeds United	2000			35	3	3
HADDINGTON, R	Scarborough	Oldham Athletic	1950	1951	Stockport County	6		4
HALL, J	Bolden	Barnsley	1913	1920	Bristol Rovers	1		
HALL, W		Bolton Wanderers	1906	1907	Crystal Palace	11		
HALLIDAY, D	Dumfries	Arsenal	1930	1933	Clapton Orient	76		47
HALLOWS, H		Southport Central	1900	1901	Southport Central	1		
HAMBLETT, G		St Francis Gorton	1905	1908	St Helens Rangers	1		
HAMILL, M	Belfast	Belfast Celtic	1920	1924	Fall River, Boston	118		1
HAMMOND, G	Sudbury	Ipswich Town	1974	1976	Charlton Athletic	33	1	2
HANNAH, G	Liverpool	Lincoln City	1958	1964	Notts County	114		15
HANNAWAY, J	Bootle	Seaforth Fellowship	1950	1957	Gillingham	64		
HANNEY, T	Reading	Reading	1913	1919	Coventry City	68		1
HANVEY, K	Manchester	Apprentice	1971	1972	Swansea City	-		
HAREIDE, Å	Isle of Hareid, Norway	Molde FK	1981	1982	Norwich City	17	7	
HARGREAVES, J		Northwich Victoria	1893	1895	Blackburn Rovers	8		
HARLEY, A	Glasgow	Third Lanark	1962	1963	Birmingham City	40		23
HARPER, A	Plumstead	Sheffield Wednesday	1989	1991	Everton	46	4	1
HARPER, J		Newtown	1895	1898	Chatham	33		
HARPER, W	Wishaw	Sunderland	1923	1924	Crystal Palace	4		
HARRISON, J	Rhyl	Rhyl	1929	1930	Sheffield United	2		1
HART, J	Golborne	Loughton YC	1944	1963	Retired	169		67

FAC Apps	Sub	Goals	FLC Apps	Sub	Goals	European Apps	Sub	Goals	Others Apps	Sub	Goals	Totals Apps	Sub	Goals
2		2	1									29		14
-												4		1
1			1									21	4	
-			-									2		1
9												112		4
-												3		
3			3	1		2						44	2	
1			2			-						13	7	7
-												5		
-									-			1		
3		1	1	1								21	4	4
-									-			10		
2			8						1			66		3
1												11		
-												2		2
8		1	6		1				4			70	1	3
1												9		
13		6										231		132
									2			5		
0	1	1	2	1	2				1		1	30	9	11
-			-			0	1		-			3	2	
9	2	9	11		9				3		1	173	10	97
-												9		1
-												8		3
												2		
-			-									39		
13									130			347		
1		2										21		5
-												1		2
-												8		2
10		1	-									36		6
2	1		1									14	11	
5			1	4								62	18	3
-												15		
2									5			75		
-												3		
3		1	7		1							97	4	23
1									3			15		
0	1		-									3	6	1
-												1		
-									-			9		
-												21		2
-												3		
2		1										46		19
2			0	1								13	8	4
2			1									12		
4		1										25		5
2												15		
3	1		5									43	4	3
1												7		4
-												1		
-												11		
6		4										82		51
-												1		
												1		
10		1										128		2
1			1						1			36	1	2
9			8		1							131		16
2												66		
10									3			81		1
-									1			1		
-			0	1								17	8	
-												8		
3		3	6		6							49		32
6			3		1				3			58	4	2
1									1			35		
-												4		
-												2		1
9		6	-						4		1	182		74

Player	Birthplace	From	Year Joined	Year Left	To	League App	Sub	Goals
HARTFORD, A	Clydebank	West Bromwich Albion	1974	1979	Nottingham Forest ⎱	259	1	29
		Everton	1981	1984	Fort Lauderdale Sun ⎰			
HARVEY, H		Burslem Port Vale	1900	1901	Burton United	7		1
HAYDOCK, J		Bolton Wanderers	1890	1891	Blackburn Rovers			
HAYDOCK, W	Salford	Buxton Town	1959	1961	Crewe Alexandra	3		1
HAYES, J	Kearsley	Junior	1953	1965	Barnsley	331		142
HEALE, J	Bristol	Bristol City	1934	1945	Retired	86		39
HEALEY, R	Manchester	Manchester Boys	1966	1974	Cardiff City	30		
HEANEY, N	Middlesbrough	Southampton	1996	1999	Darlington	13	5	1
HEATH, A	Stoke-on-Trent	Aston Villa	1990	1992	Stoke City	58	17	4
HEDLEY, F	Monkseaton	Nelson	1930	1931	Chester	2		2
HEINEMANN, G	Stafford	Stafford Rangers	1928	1931	Coventry City	21		
HENDERSON, J		Abercorn	1901	1902	Released	5		1
HENDERSON, J	Cowdenbeath	St Barnard's	1914	1920	Southend United	5		
HENDREN, E	Turnham Green	Brentford	1908	1909	Coventry City	2		
HENDRY, C	Keith	Blackburn Rovers	1989	1991	Blackburn Rovers	57	6	5
HENRY, A	Houghton-le-Spring	Durham Boys	1974	1981	Bolton Wanderers	68	11	6
HENRY, W	Glasgow	Leicester Fosse	1911	1920	St Barnard's	143		1
HENSON, P	Manchester	Brookdale YC	1969	1975	Sheffield Wednesday	12	4	
HERD, A	Bowhill, nr Selkirk	Hamilton Academicals	1933	1948	Stockport County	257		107
HESHAM, F	Manchester	Junior	1896	1901	Crewe Alexandra	3		
HESLOP, G	Wallsend	Everton	1965	1971	Cape Town, S Africa	159	3	1
HICKS, G	Salford	Droylsden	1923	1928	Birmingham	123		40
HIGGS, F	Willington	Barnsley	1932	1933	Aldershot	1		
HILDERSLEY, R	Kirkcaldy	Kirkcaldy Schools	1981	1984	Chester City	1		
HILEY, S	Plymouth	Birmingham City	1996	1998	Southampton	4	5	
HILL, A	Maltby	Bury	1990	1995	Port Vale	91	7	6
HILL, F	Sheffield	Halifax Town	1969	1973	Peterborough United	28	7	3
HILL, P		Everton	1906	1909	Airdrie	38		
HILL, R		Sheffield United	1895	1897	Released	21		9
HILLMAN, J	Tavistock	Burnley	1902	1906	Millwall	116		
HINCE, P	Manchester	Local League	1966	1968	Charlton Athletic	7		4
HINCHCLIFFE, A	Manchester	Manchester Boys	1985	1990	Everton	107	5	8
HINDMARSH, J	Whitburn	Stockport County	1912	1919	Newport County	28		1
HITCHCOCK, E		Aston Villa	1909	1909	Released	1		
HOAD, S	Blackpool	Blackpool	1911	1920	Rochdale	64		1
HODGETTS, J		Local League	1886	1891	Released			
HODGKINSON, D	Banwell	Margate	1961	1964	Stockport County	1		1
HODGSON, R	Birkenhead	Tranmere Rovers	1944	1947	Southport	1		
HODGSON, S	Macclesfield	Trainee	1998	2001	Released	-		
HOEKMAN, D	Nijmegen, Holland	Den Haag	1991	1991	Blackburn Rovers	0	1	
HOGAN, B	Salford	Junior	1942	1949	Carlisle United	3		
HOLDEN, R	Skipton	Oldham Athletic	1992	1993	Oldham Athletic	49	1	3
HOLFORD, T	Hanley	Stoke	1908	1914	Stoke	172		34
HOLMES, W	Darley Jillside, Matlock	Chesterfield Municipal	1896	1905	Clapton Orient	156		4
HOPE, J	East Wemyss	Ardear Recreation	1939	1947	Queen of the South	7		
HOPKINS, R	Halt Green, Birmingham	Birmingham City	1983	1986	West Bromwich Albion	7		1
HOPKINS, W		Derby County	1891	1894	Released	23		
HORLOCK, K	Bexley	Swindon Town	1997			162	12	37
HORNE, A	Birmingham	Southend United	1928	1929	Preston North End	11		2
HORNE, S	Clanfield	Aston Villa	1965	1969	Fulham	48	2	
HORRIDGE, P	Manchester	Newton Heath Parish	1951	1959	Crewe Alexandra	3		
HORSWILL, M	Annfield Plain	Sunderland	1974	1975	Plymouth Argyle	11	3	
HOSIE, J	Glasgow	Blackburn Rovers	1901	1902	Stockport County	39		3
HOWARD, F	Walkden	Walkden Wednesday	1912	1920	Pontypridd	79		40
HOWE, F	Bredbury	Liverpool	1938	1938	Grimsby Town	6		5
HOWEY, S	Sunderland	Newcastle United	2000			72		9
HOYLAND, J	Sheffield	Sheffield Schools	1982	1986	Bury	2		
HUCKERBY, D	Nottingham	Leeds United	2000			38	15	21
HUGHES, E	Wrexham	Wrexham	1912	1920	Aberdare Athletic	77		2
HUGHES, J		Local League	1894	1895	Released	2		
HUGHES, M	Larne	Carrick Rangers	1988	1992	Strasbourg	25	1	1
HUMPHREYS, R	Oswestry	Oswestry Town	1910	1912	Released	3		
HUNTER, R		Local League	1898	1902	Stockport County	7		
HURST, D	Cockermouth	Workington	1901	1902	Manchester United	15		
HUTCHINSON, G		Local League	1894	1896	Released	7		
HUTCHISON, T	Cardenden	Coventry City	1980	1982	Bulova, Hong Kong	44	2	4
HYNDS, T	Hurlford	Glasgow Celtic	1901	1906	Woolwich Arsenal	158		9
IMMEL, E	Marburg, Germany	VFB Stuttgart	1995	1998	Retired	42		

FAC Apps	Sub	Goals	FLC Apps	Sub	Goals	European Apps	Sub	Goals	Others Apps	Sub	Goals	Totals Apps	Sub	Goals
17		2	29		3	12	2		5		1	322	1	37
-												7		1
1												1		
-			-									3		1
24		9	8		1				1			364		152
5		2							43		33	134		74
-			2			4	1		2		3	38	1	
2		1	-						1			16	5	2
2	1		7	1	2				1	2		68	21	6
-												2		2
3												24		
-												5		1
-									33			38		
-												2		
5		2	4	1	1				4		2	70	7	10
3	1		7	1	6	1			1			80	13	12
15									25			183		1
0	1		1			-			1	1		14	6	
30		17							91		61	378		185
-												3		
18		1	12			7	3		2		1	198	6	3
12		8										135		48
-												1		
-			-									1		
-			-									4	5	
2	1		11						1			105	8	6
-			-			4			2			34	7	3
2												40		
-									1			22		9
8												124		
-					4							11		4
12	1		11		1				4		1	134	5	11
7	1											35		2
-												1		
5		1							3		1	72		3
1		2										1		2
-			1									2		1
-									5			6		
-			0									0		
-			0	2					0			0	3	
-									5		1	8		1
5		1	3		1							57	1	5
12		4										184		38
10												166		4
-									1			8		
-			2									9		1
1												24		
11	1		14		3				3		1	190	12	42
-												11		2
11			4	1		-			-			63	3	
-												3		
1			-									12	3	
4												43		3
12		3							7		4	98		47
-												6		5
3			4									79		9
-			0	1	1				-			2	1	1
6		2	2	1	5							46	16	28
12		1							65		2	154		5
-												2		
1			5						1			32	1	1
-												3		
-												7		
-												15		
-												7		
10		1	3	1								57	3	5
14												172		9
5			3									50		

Player	Birthplace	From	Year Joined	Year Left	To	League App	Sub	Goals
INGEBRIGSTEN, K	Trondheim, Norway	Rosenborg	1993	1994	Lillestrom	4	10	
INGHAM, T W	Manchester	Local League	1921	1923	Released	2		1
INGRAM, Rae	Manchester	Trainee	1991	1998	Macclesfield Town	18	5	
JACKSON, G	Swinton	Manchester Boys	1981	1985	Exeter City	6	2	
JACKSON, H	Blackburn	Burnley	1956	1947	Preston North End	8		2
JAMES, F		Halesowen	1909	1910	Exeter City	2		
JARVIS, H	Manchester	Local League	1919	1921	Released	2		
JEFFRIES, D	Manchester	Manchester Boys	1966	1973	Crystal Palace	64	9	
JENSEN, N	Denmark	FC Kobenhaun	2002			16	2	1
JOBLING, L	Sunderland	Norwich City	1912	1913	Hartlepools United	2		
JOBSON, R	Holderness	Leeds United	1998	2001	Tranmere Rovers	49	1	4
JOHNSON, D	Liverpool	Everton	1984	1984	Tulsa Roughnecks, USA	4	2	1
JOHNSON, J	Cardiff	Welsh Schools	1970	1973	Crystal Palace	4	2	
JOHNSON, N	Rotherham	Rotherham United	1985	1987	Rotherham United	4		
JOHNSON, T	Dalton-in-Furniss	Dalton	1919	1930	Everton	328		158
JOHNSTONE, R	Selkirk	Hibernian	1955	1959	Hibernian	124		42
JONES, A	Llandudno	Small Heath	1893	1894	Released	2		1
JONES, C H	Jersey	Tottenham Hotspur	1982	1982	Crystal Palace	3		
JONES, C M	Altrincham	Cheshire Boys	1962	1968	Swindon Town	6	1	2
JONES, D	Oswestry	Bolton Wanderers	1898	1902	Died	114		1
JONES, R S	Liverpool	Everton	1894	1895	South Shore	18		
JONES, R T	Lambeth	Millwall Athletic	1901	1902	Millwall Athletic	9		2
JONES, W J	Liverpool	Local League	1948	1951	Chester	3		
JONES, W L	Chirk	Rushton Druids	1903	1919	Southend United	281		69
KANCHELSKIS, A	Kirovgrad, Ukraine	Glasgow Rangers	2001		On Loan	7	3	
KARL, S	Germany	Borussia Dortmund	1994		On Trial	4	2	1
KAVELASHVILI, M	Tbilisi, Georgia	Spartak Vladikavkaz	1996	1999	FC Zurich	9	19	3
KEARY, A	Liverpool	Liverpool Dominion	1911	1912	Port Vale	8		1
KEEGAN, G	Little Horton	Apprentice	1971	1979	Oldham Athletic	32	5	2
KELLY, P	Kilco	Belfast Celtic	1920	1923	West Ham United	25		1
KELLY, R	Ballinasloe	Athlone Town	1994	1999	Released	1		
KELLY, W	Newcastle	Newcastle United	1911	1913	Blyth Spartans	10		
KELSO, T	Renton	Third Lanark	1906	1913	Dundee	138		3
KENNEDY, R	Motherwell	Kilmarnock	1961	1969	Grimsby Town	216	3	9
KENNEDY, M	Dublin	Wimbledon	1999	2001	Wolverhampton W	56	8	8
KERNAGHAN, A	Otley	Middlesbrough	1993	1997	St Johnstone	55	8	1
KERR, A	Lugar Bothwell	Partick Thistle	1959	1959	Kilmarnock	10		
KERR, D	Dumfries	Y.T.S.	1990	1996	Mansfield Town	4	2	
KEVAN, D	Ripon	Chelsea	1963	1965	Crystal Palace	67		48
KIDD, B	Collyhurst	Arsenal	1976	1979	Everton	97	1	44
KILLEN, C	Wellington, New Zealand	Trialist	1999			0	3	
KINKLADZE, G	Tbilisi, Georgia	Dynamo Tbilisi	1995	1998	Ajax Amsterdam	105	1	20
KINSEY, S	Gorton	Manchester Boys	1979	1986	Minnesota Kicks, USA	87	14	15
KIRKMAN, A	Bolton	Bacup Borough	1955	1959	Rotherham United	7		6
KNOWLES, F	Hyde	Hartlepools United	1919	1920	Stalybridge Celtic	2		
LAKE, P	Denton	Blue Star YC	1985	1996	Retired	106	4	7
LAMBIE, W	Larkhall	Queens Park	1890	1893	Queens Park	3		1
LAMPH, T	Gateshead	Leeds City	1919	1920	Derby County	11		
LANGFORD, L	Alfreton	Nottingham Forest	1930	1934	Manchester United	112		
LANGLEY, K	St Helens	Everton	1987	1988	Birmingham City	9		
LAW, D	Aberdeen	Huddersfield Town	1960	1961	Torino, Italy	} 66	2	30
		Manchester United	1973	1974	Retired			
LAWRENCE, V	Arbroath	Forfar Athletic	1911	1913	Oldham Athletic	20		
LEE, F	Westhoughton	Bolton Wanderers	1967	1974	Derby County	248	1	112
LEE, S	Manchester	Stockport County	1978	1980	Portland Timbers, USA	6	1	2
LEIGH, P	Wythenshaw	Stamford LC	1957	1961	Crewe Alexandra	2		
LEIVERS, W	Bolsover	Chesterfield	1953	1964	Doncaster Rovers	250		4
LEMAN, D	Newcastle	Newcastle Boys	1970	1976	Sheffield Wednesday	10	7	1
LENNON, N	Lugan	Belfast Boys	1987	1990	Crewe Alexandra	1		
LEONARD, P		St Mirren	1897	1898	New Brompton	} 16		5
		Thames Ironworks	1899	1900	Released			
LESLIE, A	Methil, Greenock	St Mirren	1923	1925	Tranmere Rovers	1		
LESTER, M	Manchester	Oldham Athletic	1973	1977	Washington Diplomats	1	1	
LEWIS, W	Chester	Chester	1896	1897	Chester	12		4
LEYLAND, J	Northwich	Witton Albion	1920	1923	Manchester North End	3		
LIEVESLEY, R	Netherthorpe	Staveley	1919	1920	Southend United	2		
LILLIS, M	Didsbury	Huddersfield Town	1985	(1986)	Derby County	39		11
LINACRE, W	Chesterfield	Chesterfield	1947	1949	Middlesbrough	75		6
LISTER, B	Manchester	Manchester Boys	1954	1960	Oldham Atheltic	2		

FAC Apps	Sub	Goals	FLC Apps	Sub	Goals	European Apps	Sub	Goals	Others Apps	Sub	Goals	Totals Apps	Sub	Goals
2		3	0									6	10	3
-												2		1
4			1									23	5	
-			-									6	2	
1		1										9		3
-												2		
												2		
7			2	1		9			2	1		84	11	
2												18	2	1
-												2		
2			4	2					-			55	3	4
												4	2	1
-			-			2			1			7	2	
-									3			7		
26		8							5		4	359		170
14		9							1			139		51
~												2		1
			-									3		
-			-									6	1	2
4												118		1
-												18		
4												13		2
-												3		
21		5							37		6	339		80
1		1										8	3	1
												4	2	1
0	1		-									9	20	3
-												8		1
0	1		4	1	1	3	2		2			41	9	3
4		2	-						-			29		3
-			-									1		
-									-			10		
13												151		3
18			16			1			-			251	3	9
2			5	3	3							63	11	11
7		1	8									70	8	2
-												10		
-			0									4	2	
3		1	6		7							76		56
9		4	11		3	10		6	2		2	129	1	59
												0	3	
9		2	6									120	1	22
4	3	1	6			1			1		1	98	17	18
-												7		6
-									1			3		
9		2	10			1			5		1	130	4	11
-												3		1
-												11		
13												125		
-			-						-			9		
5		4	6		3				3		1	80	2	38
2												22		
24		7	26		14	22		10	8	1	5	328	2	148
0												6	1	2
-			-									2		
20			11						1			282		4
0	1		2	2	1	-			1	2	1	13	12	3
-			-						-			1		
1												17		5
-												1		
-			-			0	1		0	1		1	3	
1												13		4
-												3		
-												2		
4			3		1				5		3	51		15
4		1										79		7
												2		

Player	Birthplace	From	Year Joined	Year Left	To	League App	Sub	Goals
LITTLE, R	Manchester	Greenwich Victoria	1949	1958	Brighton & Hove Albion	168		2
LITTLE, T	Derby	Derby County	1892	1894	Baltimore, USA			
		Baltimore, USA	1894	1895	Ashton North End	16		5
LIVINGSTONE, G	Dumbarton	Liverpool	1903	1907	Glasgow Rangers	81		19
LLOYD, N	Salford	Manchester Central	1932	1935	New Brighton	3		
LOMAS, S	Hannover, Germany	Y.T.S.	1990	1997	West Ham United	102	9	8
LOMAX, G	Droylsden	Manchester Boys	1981	1985	Carlisle United	23	2	1
LYALL, Jack	Dundee	Sheffield Wednesday	1909	1911	Dundee	40		
LYON, W	Clanchuscudden	Bristol Rovers	1903	1904	Preston North End	6		
MACKEN, J	Manchester	Preston North End	2002			4	4	5
MACKENZIE, S	Romford	Crystal Palace	1979	1981	West Bromwich Albion	56	2	8
MALEY, W	Newry, Co Down	Glasgow Celtic	1896		On Loan	1		
MANN, A	Burntisland	Heart of Midlothian	1968	1972	Notts County	32	3	
MANN, G	East Stirlingshire	Blackburn Rovers	1894	1897	Bristol City	59		7
MANSFIELD, E		Northern Nomads	1909	1909	Released	1		
MARGETSON, M	West Neath	Y.T.S.	1988	1998	Southend United	51		
MARSDEN, K	Darley Dale	Chesterfield	1955	1959	Accrington Stanley	14		1
MARSH, R	Hatfield	Queens Park Rangers	1972	1976	Tampa Bay Rowdies	116	2	36
MARSHALL, R	Hucknall	Sunderland	1928	1939	Stockport County	325		70
MASON, G	Edinburgh	Trainee	1996	2000	Dunfermline	18	1	
MAUGE, R	Islington	Bury	1991		On Loan	-		
MAY, A	Bury	Bury Schools	1980	1987	Huddersfield Town	141	9	8
MAZZARELLI, G		FC Zurich	1996	1996	Grasshoppers Zurich	0	2	
McADAMS, W	Belfast	Distillery Belfast	1953	1960	Bolton Wanderers	127		62
McALINDEN, R	Salford	Salford Boys	1962	1965	Toronto	1		
McBRIDE, J	Renton	Liverpool	1894	1897	Ashton North End	70		1
McCABE, A		Rotherham Town	1896	1896	Rochdale	1		
McCARTHY, M	Barnsley	Barnsley	1983	1987	Glasgow Celtic	140		2
McCLELLAND, J	Bradford	Manchester YMCA	1953	1958	Lincoln City	8		2
McCLOY, P	Uddington	Ayr United	1925	1932	Irish Leagues	147		
McCONNELL, A	Moss End, Glasgow	Moss End Swifts	1896	1897	Woolwich Arsenal	2		
McCORMACK, M	Glasgow	Glasgow Rangers	1947	1947	Blackpool	1		
McCOURT, F	Portadown	Bristol Rovers	1950	1954	Colchester United	61		4
McCOURT, J	Glasgow	Sheffield United	1924	1925	Dykehead	4		
McCULLOUGH, K	Larne	Belfast Celtic	1935	1938	Northampton Town	17		1
McDONALD, R	Kilpatrick	Vale of Leven	1956	1963	Bournemouth	5		
McDONALD, R	Kincorth, Aberdeen	Coventry City	1980	1983	Oxford United	96		11
McDOWALL, L	Gunga Pur, India	Sunderland	1938	1949	Wrexham	117		8
McDOWELL, A		Local League	1893	1895	Released	4		
McGOLDRICK, E	Islington	Arsenal	1996	1998	Retired	39	1	
McGUIRE, P	Manchester	Hurst FC	1912	1916	Killed in Action	15		
McILROY, S	Belfast	Stoke City	1985	1987	Orgyte, Sweden	13		1
McKINNEY, R	Ballymena	Ballymena	1999	2001	Swindon Town	0		0
McLEOD, E	Glasgow	East Fife	1938	1940	Hibernian	4		2
McLEOD, J	Glasgow	Larne	1935	1937	Millwall	12		9
McLUCKIE, J	Stonehouse	Hamilton Academicals	1933	1934	Aston Villa	32		1
McMAHON, J		Preston North End	1902	1906	Bury	100		1
McMAHON, S	Liverpool	Liverpool	1991	1994	Swindon Town	83	4	1
McMORRAN, E	Larne	Belfast Celtic	1947	1949	Leeds United	33		14
McMULLEN, J	Denny	Partick Thistle	1926	1933	Oldham Athletic	220		10
McNAB, N	Greenock	Brighton & Hove Albion	1983	1990	Tranmere Rovers	216	5	16
McNAUGHT, K	Kirkcaldy	West Bromwich Albion	1984		On Loan	7		
McOUSTRA, W	Glasgow	Glasgow Celtic	1902	1907	Blackpool	65		6
MacRAE, K	Glasgow	Motherwell	1973	1981	Portland Timbers, USA	56		
McREDDIE, W		Stoke	1894	1895	Bolton Wanderers	31		12
McTAVISH, J	Glasgow	Dalry Thistle	1952	1960	St Mirren	93		
McVICKERS, J		Accrington Stanley	1892	1894	Macclesfield	26		
McWHINNIE, W	Scotland	Ayr United	1890	1892	Walsall Town Swifts	~		
MEADOWS, J	Bolton	Southport	1951	1957	Retired	130		30
MEARS, T	Failsworth	Trainee	1999	2002	Preston North End	0	1	
MEECHAN, P	Broxburn	Southampton	1900	1901	Barrow	6		
MEGSON, G	Manchester	Sheffield Wednesday	1989	1992	Norwich City	78	4	2
MELLOR, I	Sale	Wythenshaw Schools	1967	1973	Norwich City	36	4	7
MELROSE, J	Glasgow	Glasgow Celtic	1984	1986	Charlton Athletic	27	7	8
MEREDITH, W	Black Park, Chirk	Chirk	1894	1906	Manchester United			
		Manchester United	1921	1924	Retired	366		145
METTOMO, L	Douala, Cameroon	St.Etienne	2001			17	6	1
MIDDLETON, H		Derby Junction	1892	1894	Loughborough Town	36		4
MIKE, A	Manchester	Y.T.S.	1990	1995	Stockport County	5	11	2

FAC			FLC			European			Others			Totals		
Apps	Sub	Goals	Apps	Sub	Goals	Apps	Sub	Goals	Apps	Sub	Goals	Apps	Sub	Goals
18									1			187		2
~												16		5
7		1										88		20
-												3		-
10	1	1	15		2							127	10	11
2			1						-			26	2	1
4												44		
-												6		
									4			4	4	5
8		2	10									74	2	10
												1		
4					1	3	1		-			40	4	
1									4			64		7
												1		
3			2	2					1			57	2	
-									-			14		1
8		2	16		6	2		2	8		1	150	2	47
30		10							1			356		80
2			3		1				-			23	1	1
									0	1		0		1
6			10						7	1		164	10	8
									0			0	2	
7		3										134		65
-									-			1		
1									4	1		75		2
												1		
7			10		1				6			163		3
-									-			8		2
10												157		
-												2		
												1		
-												61		4
-												4		
1												18		1
1			-									6		
10	1	4	5		1							111	1	16
9									115		8	241		16
-												4		
3			1	1								43	2	
-												15		
-			1						2			16		1
-			0		0							0		0
-												4		2
2		2										14		11
5									1			38		1
9												109		1
3			8									94	4	1
3												36		14
22		2										242		12
15		1	20		2				10			261	5	19
												7		
-												65		6
2			13			-			1			72		
-												31		12
3			-						-			96		
3									2			31		
2		2							11	2		13		4
11		1							-			141		31
												0	1	
-												6		
7	1		5						2			92		2
2	1		1	1		2	1	2	1	1	1	42	8	10
1			2	1	2				2	2	1	32	10	11
24		5							111		8	501		158
			1	1								18	7	1
3									2			41		4
0	1		1	1					-			6	13	2

The Essential History of Manchester City

Player	Birthplace	From	Year Joined	Year Left	To	League App	Sub	Goals
MIKE, L	Manchester	Trainee	1998	2001	Aberdeen	1	1	
MILARVIE, B	Gorton	Newton Heath	1891	1896	Released	50		9
MILLAR, J	Edinburgh	Hamilton Academicals	1902	1903	South Africa	8		2
MILLER, J		Bolton Wanderers	1896	1896	Bolton Wanderers	2		
MILLS, L	Mexborough	Bradford City	2000		On Loan	1	2	
MILNE, J		Bolton Wanderers	1890	1894	Released	18		3
MILSOM, J	Bedminster	Bolton Wanderers	1938	1940	Retired	33		22
MIMMS, R	York	Everton	1987		On Loan	3		
MITCHELL, J	Manchester	Preston North End	1922	1926	Leicester Fosse	99		
MOFFAT, J	Paisley	St Mirren	1903	1906	Kilmarnock	20		4
MOFFAT, R	Dumfries	St Mirren	1895	1907	Kilmarnock	156		7
MOONEY, F	Liverpool	Bootle	1892	1895	Bury	9		4
MORGAN, H	Lanarkshire	Newton Heath	1901	1902	Accrington Stanley	12		1
MORLEY, D	St Helens	Trainee	1996	1998	Southend United	1	2	1
MORLEY, T	Nottingham	Northampton Town	1988	1989	West Ham United	69	3	18
MORRIS, H	Chirk	Chirk	1891	1893	Sheffield United }	44		21
		Sheffield United	1895	1896	Grimsby Town }			
MORRIS, H	Hardgate	Clyde	1922	1924	Nottingham Forest	57		
MORRISON, A	Inverness	Huddersfield Town	1998	2002	Released	36	1	4
MOULDEN, P	Farnworth	Bolton Boys	1984	1989	Bournemouth	48	16	18
MULHEARN, K	Liverpool	Stockport County	1967	1971	Shrewsbury Town	50		
MULLIGAN, J	Belfast	Belfast Celtic	1920	1923	Southport	3		
MUNDY, J	Wythenshaw	Ashland Rovers	1966	1971	Bangor City	2	1	
MUNN, S	Glasgow	Grimsby Town	1897	1901	Released	20		
MUNRO, J	Garmouth	Waterford	1947	1950	Oldham Athletic	25		4
MURPHY, W	St Helens	Alexandra Victoria	1918	1926	Southampton	209		30
MURRAY, H	Drybridge	Dalry Thistle	1954	1960	Altrincham	1		
MURRAY, J	Dover	Wolverhampton Wanderers	1963	1967	Walsall	70		43
MURRAY, W	Burnley	Arbroath	1950	1950	Macclesfield Town	20		1
NASH, C	Bolton	Stockport County	2001			28	1	
NASH, J	Uxbridge	Nelson	1894	1895	Released	17		1
NAYLOR, J	High Crompton	Newcastle United	1932	1934	Macclesfield Town	1		
NEGOUAI, C	Fort-de-France, Morocco	Charleroi	2001			2	3	1
NEILSON, R	Blackhall	Dawdon Colliery	1935	1947	Droylsden	16		1
NELSON, J	Manchester	Local League	1911	1912	Released	8		
NEWTON, W	Romiley	Droylsden	1916	1920	Southend United	2		
NICHOLLS, J	Bilston	Bilston United	1932	1934	Brentford	16		
NIXON, E	Manchester	Curzon Ashton	1983	1988	Tranmere Rovers	58		
NORGROVE, F	Hyde	Glossop North End	1904	1912	Released	94		1
OAKES, A	Winsford	Mid-Cheshire Boys	1958	1976	Chester	561	3	26
OAKES, J	Hamilton	Blackburn Rovers	1948	1951	Queen of the South	77		9
OAKES, T	Manchester	Manchester United	1947	1948	Goslings FC	1		
O'BRIEN, J		Local League	1893	1893	Walsall Town Swifts	2		
OGDEN, T	Culcheth	Junior	1963	1965	Doncaster Rovers	9		3
OGLEY, A	Barnsley	Barnsley	1963	1967	Stockport County	51		
OLDFIELD, D	Perth, Australia	Luton Town	1989	1990	Leicester City	18	8	6
O'NEILL, M	Kilrea	Norwich City	1981	1982	Norwich City	12	1	
ORR, W		Glossop North End	1899	1903	Fulham	36		
OSTENSTAD, E	Haguesund, Norway	Blackburn Rovers	2001		On Loan	1	3	
OWEN, G	Whiston	Warrington & Dist. Sch.	1974	1979	West Bromwich Albion	101	2	19
OWEN, R	Farnworth	Bury	1968	1970	Carlisle United	18	4	3
OWEN, W	Llanfairfechan	Northwich Victoria	1934	1936	Tranmere Rovers	9		3
OXFORD, K	Oldham	Ardwick Lads Club	1946	1950	Chesterfield	1		
PALMER, R	Manchester	Manchester Boys	1975	1980	Oldham Athletic	22	9	9
PANTER, D	Blackpool	Chorlton Lads Club	1960	1964	Torquay United	1		
PARDOE, G	Winsford	Mid-Cheshire Boys	1961	1976	Retired	303	2	17
PARK, T	Liverpool	Stockport County	1983		On Loan	0	2	
PARLANE, D	Helensburgh	Leeds United	1983	1985	Swansea City	47	1	20
PATTERSON, W	Edinburgh	Hibernian	1896	1897	Stockport County	1		
PAUL, R	Gelli Pentre	Swansea Town	1950	1957	Worcester City	270		9
PAYNE, J	Southall	Brentford	1931	1934	Brighton & Hove Albion	4		1
PEACOCK, L	Paisley	Mansfield Town	1999	2000	Bristol City	4	4	
PEARCE, S	Hammersmith	West Ham United	2001	2002	Retired	38		3
PEARSON, F	Manchester	Preston North End	1903	1905	Chelsea	7		2
PEARSON, H	Stockport	Bredbury	1921	1923	Released	1		
PENNINGTON, J	Golborne	Junior	1955	1961	Crewe Alexandra	1		
PERCIVAL, J	Low Patrington	Durham City	1932	1947	Bournemouth	161		8
PERCIVAL, P	Reddish	Ashton National	1931	1935	Sheffield Wednesday	2		
PHELAN, T	Salford	Wimbledon	1992	1995	Chelsea	102	1	2

FAC Apps	Sub	Goals	FLC Apps	Sub	Goals	European Apps	Sub	Goals	Others Apps	Sub	Goals	Totals Apps	Sub	Goals
												1	1	
4		1							19		4	73		14
												8		2
									2			4		
												1	2	
1									18		5	37		8
2		2							1			36		24
												3		
10												109		
2												22		4
7												163		7
												9		4
3		1										15		2
			0									1	2	1
1			7		3				2			79	3	21
3									26		10	73		31
4												61		
7			3						1			47	1	5
2	3	1	5	1	4				3		3	58	20	26
5			3					3	1			62		
												3		
-								-	-			2	1	
												20		
												25		4
11		1							23		2	243		33
									-			1		
3			5	1	3							78	1	46
									4			24		1
1					1							30	1	
~												17		1
-												1		
0	1				1							3	4	1
4									25			45		1
-												8		
-									14		1	16		1
-												16		
10			8						8			84		
4												98		1
41		2	46	1	5	17		1	11			676	4	34
2												79		9
-												1		
-												2		
-												9		3
5			1									57		
			2	1	2				0	1	1	20	10	9
-			3									15	1	
5												41		
												1	3	
7	2		9		2	5			-			122	2	23
3	1		1					-	1		2	23	4	6
1												10		3
-												1		
-			3	3	1	4		1				29	12	11
					1							2		
30		1	26		4	15			4			378	2	22
												0	2	
1			3		3							51	1	23
-												1		
23									1			294		9
-												4		1
1	1											5	5	
1	1		3									42	1	3
1												8		2
-												1		
-			-									1		
12									38		3	211		11
-												2		
8		1	11									121	1	3

Player	Birthplace	From	Year Joined	Year Left	To	League App	Sub	Goals
PHILLIPS, D	Wegburg, Germany	Plymouth Argyle	1984	1986	Coventry City	81		13
PHILLIPS, E	North Shield	Ashington	1947	1951	Hull City	80		
PHILLIPS, J	Weston Rhyn	Chirk	1925	1927	Retired	1		
PHILLIPS, M	Exeter	Exeter City	1995	1998	Portsmouth	3	12	
PHOENIX, R	Stretford	Humphrey Park	1950	1960	Rochdale	53		2
PICKFORD, E		Local League	1893	1894	Released	8		3
PLATT, J		Local League	1896	1897	Released	1		
PLENDERLEITH, J	Belshill	Hibernian	1960	1963	Queen of the South	41		
POINTON, N	Church Warsop	Everton	1985	1992	Oldham Athletic	74		2
POLLOCK, J	Stockton-on-Tees	Bolton Wanderers	1998	2000	Crystal Palace	49	9	5
PORTEOUS, T	Rotherham	Rotherham Town	1896	1896	Rotherham Town	5		
POTTER, S	Belper	Apprentice	1973	1974	Swansea City	-		
POWELL, R	Knighton	Knighton Town	1948	1952	Chesterfield	12		
POWER, P	Openshaw	Leeds Polytechnic	1973	1986	Everton	358	7	26
PRINGLE, C	Nitshill	St Mirren	1922	1928	Manchester Central	197		1
PRIOR, S	Rochford	Derby County	2000	2001	Cardiff City	27	2	4
PRITCHARD, J	Meriden	Crystal Palace	1938	1947	Southend United	22		5
QUIGLEY, M	Manchester	Y.T.S.	1987	1995	Hull City	3	9	
QUINN, N	Dublin	Arsenal	1990	1996	Sunderland	183	20	66
RACE, H	Evenswood	Liverpool	1930	1933	Nottingham Forest	10		3
RAMSEY, J	Wishaw	Wishaw	1909	1910	Released	1		
RANKIN, B	Glasgow	West Bromwich Albion	1907	1907	Luton Town	2		
RANSON, R	St Helens	Apprentice	1976	1984	Birmingham City	198	2	1
		Newcastle United	1993	1993	Reading			
RAY, D	Newcastle-under-Lyme	Burslem Port Vale	1896	1900	Macclesfield Town	83		3
		Macclesfield Town	1902	1903	Stockport County			
READ, T	Manchester	Streford	1895	1902	Manchester United	115		2
REDMOND, S	Liverpool	Liverpool Boys	1984	1992	Oldham Athletic	231	4	7
REEVES, K	Burley	Norwich City	1980	1983	Burnley	129	1	34
REGAN, E		Local League	1893	1894	Burslem Port Vale	21		
REGAN, R	Falkirk	Partick Thistle	1936	1937	Dundee	4		
REID, J	Hebburn-on-Tyne	South Shields	1919	1920	Stockport County	3		1
REID, N	Davyhulme	Whitehall Juniors	1977	1982	Seattle Sounders, USA	211	6	2
		Seattle Sounders, USA	1982	1987	Blackburn Rovers			
REID, P	Huyton	Queens Park Rangers	1989	1993	Southampton	90	13	1
REVIE, D	Middlesbrough	Hull City	1951	1956	Sunderland	162		37
RIDDING, W	Heswall	Tranmere Rovers	1930	1931	Manchester United	9		4
RIDLEY, M	Mickley	South Shield	1927	1933	Reading	174		
RIGBY, J	Lowton	Bryn Boys Brigade	1946	1954	Peterborough United	100		
RIMMER, S	Liverpool	Trainee	1995	1999	Port Vale	-		
RITCHIE, P	Kirkcaldy	Glasgow Rangers	2000			11	9	
ROBERTS, C	Halesowen	Brentford	1930	1932	Exeter City	8		2
ROBERTS, F	Sandbach	Bolton Wanderers	1922	1929	Manchester Central	216		116
ROBERTSON, D		Local League	1893	1894	Released	7		3
ROBERTSON, G	Failsworth	Ashton National	1927	1933	Southend United	14		
ROBERTSON, J		Stoke	1896	1896	Released	3		2
ROBINS, M	Ashton-under-Lyme	Panionios	1999	1999	Walsall	0	2	
ROBINSON, J	Oswaldtwistle	Accrington Stanley	1937	1946	Bury	2		
ROBINSON, M	Leicester	Preston North End	1979	1980	Brighton & Hove Albion	29	1	8
ROBINSON, P	Manchester	Juniors	1940	1947	Chesterfield	1		
ROBINSON, R		Local League	1893	1894	Wolverhampton Wanderers	4		2
ROBINSON, W	Prescott	Bolton Wanderers	1902	1905	Hull City	1		
ROBSON, D	Ayr	Ayr United	1890	1894	Wolverhampton W.	86		1
		Wolverhampton Wanderers	1894	1896	Millwall			
ROCASTLE, D	Lewisham	Leeds United	1993	1994	Chelsea	21		2
RODGER, C	Ayr	Ayr United	1935	1938	Northampton Town	19		7
RODGER, S	Shoreham	Crystal Palace	1996		On Loan	8		1
ROGERS, J	Normanton	Oswestry Town	1935	1938	Chesterfield	11		1
RÖSLER, U	Altenburg, Germany	Nürnburg	1994	1998	Kaiserlautern	141	11	50
ROSS, D	Over Darwen	Norwich City	1907	1912	Dundee	59		19
ROSS, J	Edinburgh	Burnley	1897	1902	Died	67		21
ROWAN, A		Burton Swifts	1894	1896	Released	45		23
ROWLANDS, A	Anglesey	Trainee	1995	1998	Released	-		
ROWLEY, H	Bilston	Manchester United	1931	1933	Oldham Athletic	18		4
ROYLE, J	Liverpool	Everton	1974	1977	Bristol City	98	1	23
ROYLE, S	Stockport	Heaton Chapel	1918	1922	Released	1		
RUDD, J	Hull	Teremure Athletic	1938	1947	York City	2		
RUSHTON, W		Bolton Wanderers	1890	1892	Released	~		
RUSSELL, C	South Shields	Sunderland	1997	2000	St. Johnstone	22	9	2

FAC Apps	Sub	Goals	FLC Apps	Sub	Goals	European Apps	Sub	Goals	Others Apps	Sub	Goals	Totals Apps	Sub	Goals
5			8						5		3	99		16
2												82		
-												1		
-			0	1								3	13	
2									-			55		
~												8		3
-												1		
4			2									47		
4			8									90		2
4	1		5						4			59	11	5
-			-						1	1		5		
									0			0		
1		5										13		
28		6	37	1	2	7	1	1	6		1	436	9	36
19												216		1
2	1		4									33	3	4
3									48		9	73		14
-			-						1			4	9	
13	3	4	20	2	7				3		1	219	25	78
1												11		3
												1		
												2		
13			22			-						233	2	1
6														
4												89		3
17			24									119		2
13		4	15		1				11			283	4	7
1												157	1	39
-												22		
-												4		
-												3		1
17			20			2			6			256	6	2
7	1		3	1					-			100	14	2
15		4							1			178		41
-												9		4
11												185		
2												102		
-			-						1			1		
3			3	1								17	10	
-												8		2
21		14										237		130
-												7		3
1												15		
-												3		2
-									-			0	2	
									56			58		
1			4		1							34	1	9
1									32		2	34		2
-												4		2
-												1		
5									23			114		1
2												23		2
1												20		7
												8		1
3												14		1
14		9	10	1	5							165	12	64
4												63		19
3	1											70		22
-			-									48		25
0									3		2	0		
-												18		4
6		2	12		6	3		1	5		1	124	2	32
-												1		
-									14		3	16		3
1	2								-			1		2
5	2		-						-			27	9	4

Player	Birthplace	From	Year Joined	Year Left	To	League App	Sub	Goals
RUSSELL, D		Nottingham Forest	1892	1893	Heart of Midlothian	17		3
RYAN, J	Lewisham	Sheffield United	1982	1983	Stockport County	19		
SADDINGTON, A		Local League	1893	1894	Released	6		
SALT, G		Local League	1911	1913	Released	1		
SAMBROOK, R	Wolverhampton	Coventry City	1958	1962	Doncaster Rovers	62		13
SAVAGE, J	Bromley	Halifax Town	1953	1958	Walsall	30		
SCOTSON, J	Manchester	Local League	1898	1903	Stockport County	6		
SCOTT, I	Radcliffe	Bury Boys	1984	1989	Stoke City	20	4	3
SCOTT, S	Macclesfield	Northwich Victoria	1913	1921	Norwich City	15		
SCULLY, A	Dublin	Crystal Palace	1997	1998	Queens Park Rangers	1	8	
SEAGRAVES, M	Bootle	Liverpool	1987	1990	Bolton Wanderers	36	6	
SEAR, C	Rhostyllen	Oswestry Town	1955	1968	Chester	248		1
SHADWELL, J	Bury	Turton	1933	1936	Exeter City	2		
SHARP, S	Manchester	Bolton Wanderers	1918	1929	Crewe Alexandra	176		
SHARPLES, J	Blackburn	Rossendale	1894	1897	Millwall Athletic	39		20
SHAWCROSS, D	Stretford	Manchester Boys	1956	1965	Stockport County	47		2
SHELIA, M	Georgia	Alania Vladikavkaz	1997	2000	Released	15		2
SHERON, M	Liverpool	Y.T.S.	1988	1994	Norwich City	82	18	24
SHINTON, R	West Bromwich	Wrexham	1979	1980	Newcastle United	5		
SHUKER, C	Liverpool	Trainee	2000			0	2	
SHUTT, C	Sheffield	Birmingham City	1993		On Loan	5	1	
SIDDALL, B	Ellesmere Port	Stoke City	1986		On Loan	6		
SILKMAN, B	Stepney	Plymouth Argyle	1979	1980	Brentford	19		3
SIMON, A	Manchester	Amateur	1890	1890	Released	~		
SIMPSON, A	Salford	Local League	1921	1923	Released	1		
SIMPSON, F	Trowbridge	Swindon Town	1992	1995	Portsmouth	58	13	4
SIMPSON, P	Carlisle	Cumbria Boys	1982	1988	Oxford United	99	22	18
SINCLAIR, G	Paisley	Glasgow Celtic	1984		On Loan	1		
SLATER, P		Blackburn Rovers	1900	1904	Bury	20		
SMELT, T	Rotherham	Morecambe	1927	1928	Oldham Athletic	2		1
SMITH, F	Draycott	Sheffield United	1952	1952	Grimsby Town	2		1
SMITH, G	Fleetwood	Salford Adelphi Lads Club	1938	1951	Chesterfield	166		75
SMITH, G D	Kilwinnig	Brighton & Hove Albion	1984	1986	Oldham Athletic	40	2	13
SMITH, H	Manchester	Blackburn Rovers	1894	1895	Stalybridge Rovers	18		
SMITH, J	Burton-upon-Trent	Burton United	1909	1914	South Shields	18		6
SMITH, R	Walkden	Walkden	1920	1924	Pontypridd	6		
SMITH, W E	Leicester	Leicester Fosse	1906	1920	Port Vale	232		
SMITH, W	Buxton	Buxton	1897	1902	Released	144		5
SMITH, W	Stockport	Stockport County	1897	1900	Stockport County	54		22
SOWDEN, W	Manchester	Greenwood Victoria	1949	1954	Chesterfield	11		2
SPITTLE, A		Local League	1893	1894	Released	1		1
SPOTTISWOODE, J	Carlisle	Carlisle United	1913	1914	Bury	6		
SPROSTON, B	Elworth, nr Sandbach	Tottenham Hotspur	1938	1950	Ashton United	125		5
SPURDLE, W	St Peter's Port, Guernsey	Oldham Athletic	1950	1956	Port Vale	160		32
STEELE, A	Newmilns, Ayrshire	Ayr United	1906	1908	Tottenham Hotspur	30		1
STEELE, F		Local League	1892	1894	Released	17		1
STENSON, J		Local League	1893	1894	Released	2		
STEPANOVIC, D	Rekovac, Serbia	Vfr Wormatia Worms	1979	1981	Vfr Wormatia Worms	14	1	
STEWART, G	Wishaw	Hibernian	1906	1911	Partick Thistle	93		11
STEWART, P	Wythenshawe	Blackpool	1987	1988	Tottenham Hotspur	51		26
STOBART, B	Doncaster	Wolverhampton Wanderers	1964	1964	Aston Villa	14		1
STONES, H	Manchester	Local League	1892	1894	Newton Heath	12		
STOWELL, M	Preston	Everton	1987		On Loan	14		
SUCKLING, P	Leyton	Coventry City	1986	1988	Crystal Palace	39		
SUGDEN, F	Gorton	Droylsden	1917	1920	Tranmere Rovers	6		
SUGRUE, P	Coventry	Nuneaton Borough	1980	1981	Cardiff City	5	1	
SULLIVAN, D	Glasgow	Glasgow Celtic	1983		On Loan	-		
SUMMERBEE, M	Preston	Swindon Town	1965	1975	Burnley	355	2	47
SUMMERBEE, N	Altrincham	Swindon Town	1994	1997	Sunderland	119	12	6
SUN, J	China	Dalian Shide	2002			2	5	
SWANN, J	Broughton	Northern Nomads	1909	1912	Released	1		
SWIFT, F	Blackpool	Fleetwood	1932	1949	Retired	341		
SYME, R G	South Queensferry	Dunfermline	1930	1934	Burnley	11		2
SYMONS, K	Basingstoke	Portsmouth	1995	1998	Fulham	124		4
TAGGART, G	Belfast	Belfast Boys	1987	1990	Barnsley	10	2	1
TAIT, D	Renton	Renton	1896	1897	Darwen	4		2
TAIT, T	Hetton-le-Hole	Southport	1928	1930	Bolton Wanderers	61		43
TAYLOR, G	Weston-super-Mare	Sheffield United	1998	2001	Burnley	28	15	9
TAYLOR, H	Fegg Hayes, Burslem	Huddersfield Town	1912	1921	Released	91		27

FAC			FLC			European			Others			Totals		
Apps	Sub	Goals	Apps	Sub	Goals	Apps	Sub	Goals	Apps	Sub	Goals	Apps	Sub	Goals
2												19		3
-			-									19		
												6		
-												1		
4			1									67		13
-									1			31		
2	1											8		1
3	1	1	3	1					0	2		26	8	4
1									10			26		
0			-						0			1	8	
3			3						2			44	6	
14			17									279		1
												2		
6		1										182		1
1									-			40		20
5			3									55		2
2			-						-			17		2
5	3	3	9	1	1				1			97	22	28
1			-									6		
			0	1	1							0	3	1
												5	1	
												6		
-			2									21		3
1												1		
-												1		
4	1		5	1								67	15	4
10	2	4	10	1	2				8	3		127	28	24
			1									1		
3												23		
-												2		1
												2		1
13		5							90		45	269		125
1			5		2				0	1		46	3	15
~												18		
2		1										20		7
-												6		
24									8			264		
10		3										154		8
3												57		22
-												11		2
												1		1
												6		
6									74		5	205		10
12		1										172		33
2												32		1
1												18		1
~												2		
-					4							18	1	
9	2											102		13
6	1		4		2				2		1	63		30
			-									14		1
-												12		
1												15		
1			3						3			46		12
-									39			45		
-			0	1								5	2	
			1									1		
34	11		36		8	16		1	8	1	1	449	3	68
12	2		11	2	2							142	14	10
												2	5	
												1		
35									136			512		
-												11		2
9			6									139		4
-			-						1			11	2	1
-												4		2
3	3											64		46
3			2	1	1				1	3		34	19	10
10	1								32	14		133		42

Player	Birthplace	From	Year Joined	Year Left	To	League App	Sub	Goals
TAYLOR, K	Manchester	Manchester Transport	1954	1960	Burton Albion	1		
TAYLOR, R	Norwich	Gillingham	1999	2000	Wolverhampton Wanderers	14	2	5
TELFORD, W	Carlisle	Burnley	1975		On Trial	0	1	
THOMAS, S	Bury	Trainee	1991	1998	Released	0	2	
THOMPSON, F	Egerton	Atherton	1921	1927	Swindon Town	33		
THOMPSON, G	Swallow Nest, Maltby	Preston North End	1956	1957	Carlisle United	2		
THOMPSON, J	Chadderton	Oldham Athletic	1920	1921	Stalybridge Celtic	2		
THOMPSTONE, I	Bury	Y.T.S.	1987	1990	Oldham Athletic	0	1	1
THORNLEY, I	Hayfield, Glossop	Glossop North End	1904	1912	South Shields	192		92
THRELFALL, F	Preston	Local League	1898	1905	Fulham	67		8
THURLOW, A	Depwade	Huddersfield Town	1946	1950	Retired	21		
TIATTO, D	Melbourne, Australia	Baden, Switzerland	1998			101	21	3
TILSON, F	Barnsley	Barnsley	1928	1938	Northampton Town	245		110
TOLMIE, J	Glasgow	SC Lokeren, Belgium	1983	1986	Sweden	46	15	15
TOMPKINSON, H		Longsight St John's	1894	1894	Released	6		1
TONGE, J		Local League	1896	1900	Released	4		
TOSELAND, E	Kettering	Coventry City	1929	1939	Sheffield Wednesday	368		61
TOURE, A	St. Denis, France	Nantes	2001	2002	Paris St.Germain	0	1	
TOWERS, A	New Moston	Manchester Boys	1967	1974	Sunderland	117	5	10
TOWNLEY, W	Blackburn	Darwen	1896	1897	Released	3		
TRACEY, S	Woolwich	Sheffield United	1994		On Loan	3		
TRAUTMANN, B	Bremen, Germany	St Helens	1949	1964	Retired	508		
TSKHADADZE, K	Rustavi, Georgia	Alaniya Vladikavkaz	1998	2000	Retired	12		2
TUEART, D	Newcastle	Sunderland	1974	1978	New York Cosmos	216	8	86
		New York Cosmos, USA	1980	1983	Stoke City			
TURNBULL, A	Hurlford	Hurlford Thistle	1902	1906	Manchester United	110		53
TURNBULL, R	Newbiggin	Sunderland	1949	1951	Swansea Town	30		5
TURNER, H		Stoke	1893	1893	Released	1		
TYLER, H	Sheffield	Sheffield Wednesday	1916	1921	Stalybridge Celtic	44		
UTLEY, G	Elscar	Sheffield United	1922	1923	Bristol City	1		
VAN BLERK, J	Sydney, Australia	Millwall	1997	1998	West Bromwich Albion	10	9	
VARADI, I	Paddington	West Bromwich Albion	1986	1988	Sheffield Wednesday	56	9	26
VAUGHAN, A	Manchester	Ipswich Town	1997	2000	Nottingham Forest	54	4	2
VILJOEN, C	Johannesburg, S. Africa	Ipswich Town	1978	1980	Chelsea	25	2	
VONK, M	Alkmaar, Netherlands	SVV / Dordrecht '90	1992	1995	Sheffield United	87	4	4
WAGSTAFFE, D	Manchester	Manchester Boys	1958	1964	Wolverhampton W	144		8
WALKER, J	Alexandria, Dumbarton	Everton	1894	1895	Leicester Fosse	19		1
WALL, L J	Shrewsbury	Glossop North End	1910	1913	Dundee	41		2
WALLACE, A		Blackpool	1894	1894	Baltimore, USA	6		1
WALLACE, W	Blaydon-on-Tyne	Newburn	1911	1914	Bolton Wanderers	43		9
WALMSLEY, C	Burnley	Burnley	1931	1932	Reading	2		
WALSH, M	Blackley	Fort Lauderdale, USA	1983	1984	Blackpool	3	1	
WALSH, P	Plumstead	Portsmouth	1994	1995	Portsmouth	54		16
WALSH, W	Dublin	Manchester United	1936	1951	Chelmsford City	109		1
WANCHOPE, P	San Jose, Costa Rica	West Ham United	2000			39	3	21
WARD, A	Middleton	Cheadle Town	1987	1991	Leicester City	0	1	
WARD, M	Huyton	West Ham United	1989	1991	Everton	55		14
WARDLE, W	Houghton-le-Spring	Southport	1937	1939	Grimsby Town	6		
WARHURST, R	Handsworth, Sheffield	Birmingham City	1957	1959	Crewe Alexandra	40		2
WARNER, J	Woolwich	Custom House	1921	1926	Watford	76		15
WASSALL, D	Edgbaston	Derby County	1996		On Loan	14	1	
WATSON, D	Stapleford	Sunderland	1975	1979	Werder Bremen	146		4
WATSON, L		Southport Central	1901	1902	Blackburn Rovers	1		
WEAH, G	Monrovia, Liberia	A.C.Milan	2000	2000	Marseille, France	5	2	1
WEAVER, N	Sheffield	Mansfield Town	1997			150	1	
WEBB, C	Higham Ferrers	Dundee	1908	1909	Airdrieonians	22		3
WEBB, G	Wanstead	West Ham United	1912	1912	Retired	2		
WEBSTER, E	Manchester	Local League	1952	1953	Released	1		
WEIR, D	Aldershot	Bolton Wanderers	1890	1893	Bolton Wanderers	14		8
WESTCOTT, D	Wallasey	Blackburn Rovers	1950	1952	Chesterfield	72		37
WESTWOOD, E	Manchester	Manchester United	1937	1953	Altrincham	248		3
WHARTON, J	Bolton	Preston North End	1947	1948	Blackburn Rovers	23		2
WHELAN, A	Salford	Manchester United	1973	1974	Rochdale	3	3	
WHITE, D	Urmston	Salford Boys	1984	1993	Leeds United	273	12	78
WHITE, H	Timperley	Cheshire Boys	1970	1973	Bangor City	1		
WHITEHEAD, J	Church	Blackburn Rovers	1897	1899	Retired	24		7
WHITFIELD, K	Bishop Aukland	Wolverhampton Wanderers	1953	1954	Brighton & Hove Albion	13		3
WHITLEY, Jeff	Zambia	Trainee	1996			96	27	8
WHITLEY, Jim	Zambia	Trainee	1994	2001	Wrexham	27	11	

FAC Apps	Sub	Goals	FLC Apps	Sub	Goals	European Apps	Sub	Goals	Others Apps	Sub	Goals	Totals Apps	Sub	Goals
-												1		
												14	2	5
									1			1	1	
-			-									0	2	
3												36		
-									-			2		
-												2		
-			-						-			0	1	1
9		1										201		93
7												74		8
-												21		
3	1		10		1				1			115	22	4
28		22							2			275		132
1			3	2	4				0	1		50	18	19
~												6		1
1												5		
41		14							2			411		75
			0	1								0	2	
8	1	1	14			13	2	1	5			157	8	12
-												3		
			0									3		
33			4						-			545		
-			1		1				-			13		3
13	2	3	27		18	3			6		2	265	10	109
9		7										119		60
1												31		5
												1		
3									94		7	141		7
-												1		
0	1		0	1								10	11	
6	1	1	4	2	2				2	1	2	68	13	31
3			6	1					3	1		66	6	2
1			2	1	1	7						35	3	1
6	1	1	3	2	1							96	7	6
6			11									161		8
~												19		1
-												41		2
~												6		1
3												46		12
-												2		
1			1	1								5	2	
3		1	6		2							63		19
9									229		8	347		9
3		1	4		1							46	3	23
0	2		-						-			0	3	
6			3						3		2	67		16
1												7		
1												41		2
2												78		15
			2									16	1	
9			18		1	12	1		3			188		6
-												1		
			2		3							7	2	4
11			14						3			178	1	
												22		3
												2		
												1		
-														
2		3							18		2	34		13
3												75		37
12		2							29		1	289		6
3												26		2
-			-						-			3	3	
22		4	24	2	11				9		2	328	14	95
-			-			-			-			1		
2												26		7
-												13		3
2	2		9	1					4			111	30	8
2	1		3	1	1				0	1		32	14	1

Player	Birthplace	From	Year Joined	Year Left	To	League App	Sub	Goals
WHITTAKER, J		Barnsley	1904	1906	Clapton Orient	6		1
		Clapton Orient	1907	1908	Clapton Orient			
WHITTLE, D		Halliwell	1890	1894	Bolton Wanderers	30		3
WIEKENS, G	Nordster, Holland	BV Veendam	1997			162	14	10
WIFFILL, D	Bristol	Bath City	1980	1982	Bulova, Hong Kong	0		
WILKINSON, J	Darlington	Darlington St Augustine's	1906	1912	Released	31		2
WILLEY, W		Local League	1893	1894	Released	1		
WILLIAMS, A	Moss Side	Manchester Boys	1978	1986	Port Vale	114		
WILLIAMS, C	Welling	Royal Arsenal	1894	1902	Tottenham Hotspur	221		1
WILLIAMS, D	Mold	Mold Alexandra	1951	1954	Mold Alexandra	1		
WILLIAMS, E	Manchester	Brindle Heath	1945	1951	Halifax Town	38		
WILLIAMS, F	Manchester	Blackpool South Shore	1896	1902	Manchester United	125		38
WILLIAMS, W	Littleborough	Stockport County	1988	1988	Stockport County	0	1	
WILLIAMSON, J	Manchester	Manchester Transport	1949	1956	Blackburn Rovers	59		14
WILSON, C	Greenheys	Moss Side Amateurs	1979	1987	Chelsea	107	2	9
		Chelsea	1987		On Loan			
WILSON, J		Lincoln City	1897	1898	Released	1		
WILSON, W	Middlesbrough	Hurst FC	1921	1927	Stockport County	48		
WOOD, A	Macclesfield	Apprentice	1961	1966	Shrewsbury Town	24	1	
WOOD, J		Derby County	1907	1909	Plymouth Argyle	28		6
WOODCOCK, W	Ashton-under-Lyme	Manchester United	1920	1922	Stockport County	15		2
WOODROFFE, L	Portsmouth	Military	1945	1947	Watford	9		1
WOOSNAM, M	Newtown	Chelsea	1919	1925	Northwich Victoria	86		4
WOOSNAM, P	Caersws, Montgomeryshire	Bangor University	1951	1954	Sutton United	1		
WRIGHT, N	Ushaw Moor	Accrington Stanley	1933	1935	Watford	3		1
WRIGHT, T	Belfast	Nottingham Forest	1997	2001	Bolton Wanderers	34		
WRIGHT-PHILLIPS, S	London	Nottingham Forest	1998			42	12	8
WRIGHTSON, F	Shildon, Co Durham	Darlington	1930	1932	Fulham	22		4
WYNN, G	Oswestry	Wrexham	1909	1919	Coventry City	119		54
YATES, J	Sheffield	Burnley	1892	1893	Sheffield United	20		9
YOUNG, A	Slamannan, Stirling	Tottenham Hotspur	1911	1912	South Liverpool	13		2
YOUNG, J	Glasgow	Port Glasgow Authority	1905	1907	Glasgow League	1		
YOUNG, N	Fallowfield	Manchester Boys	1959	1972	Preston North End	332	2	86
YUILL, J	Manchester	Northern Nomads	1906	1907	Stockport County			
		Stockport County	1907	1909	Wrexham			
		Wrexham	1909	1909	Pendlebury	3		1

Top 10 Appearances

Player	Seasons Played	League	FA Cup	FLC	Europe	Other	TOTAL
Alan Oakes	1959-76	561/3	41	46/1	17	11	676/4
Joe Corrigan	1967-83	476	37	52	27	12/1	604/1
Mike Doyle	1964-78	441/7	44	43	23	14	565/7
Bert Trautmann	1949-64	508	33	4	/		545
Colin Bell	1965-79	393/1	33/1	40	23/1	9	498/3
Eric Brook	1927-39	452	41	/	/		493
Tommy Booth	1968-82	380/2	27	44/2	25	11	487/4
Mike Summerbee	1965-75	355/2	34	36	16	8/1	449/3
Paul Power	1975-86	358/7	28	37/1	7/1	6	436/9
Willie Donachie	1969-80	347/4	21	40	13/1	10	431/5

Top 10 Goalscorers

Player	Seasons Played	League	FA Cup	FLC	Europe	Other	TOTAL
Eric Brook	1927-39	158	19	/	/		177
Tommy Johnson	1919-30	158	8	/	/		166
Colin Bell	1966-79	117	9	18	8	1	153
Joe Hayes	1953-65	142	9	1	/		152
Billy Meredith	1894-05 & 1921-24	145	5	/	/		150
Francis Lee	1967-74	112	7	14	10	5	148
Tommy Browell	1913-26	122	17	/	/		139
Fred Tilson	1928-38	110	22	/	/		132
Billy Gillespie	1896-05	126	6	/	/		132
Frank Roberts	1922-29	116	14	/	/		130

Complete Players' Career Records: Whittaker – Yuill

FAC Apps	Sub	Goals	FLC Apps	Sub	Goals	European Apps	Sub	Goals	Others Apps	Sub	Goals	Totals Apps	Sub	Goals
-												6		1
	1											31		3
10	1		13	1					3			188	16	10
-			-									0		
-												31		2
~												1		
2			9						-			125		
7									4			232		1
-												1		
3									10			51		
5												130		38
									-			0	1	
3		1										62		15
2			10		2				5			124	2	11
-												1		
5												53		
3			4									31	1	
5	3											33		9
-									2	1		17		3
-									6	2		15		3
7												93		4
-												1		
-												3		1
2			1						1			38		
3			4	3								49	15	8
-												22		4
9	5								30	9		158		68
1												21		9
2												15		2
-												1		
32	1	10	28		6	17		5	4		1	413	3	108
-												3		1

Manchester City Managers

Lawrence Furniss 1889 to 1893
Joshua Parlby 1893 to 1895
Sam Ormerod 1895 to 1902
Tom Maley 1902 to 1906
Harry Newbould 1906 to 1912
Ernest Mangnall 1912 to 1924
David Ashworth 1924 to 1925
Peter Hodge 1926 to 1932
Wilf Wild 1932 to 1946
Sam Cowan 1946 to 1947
Jock Thomson 1947 to 1950

Les McDowall 1950 to 1963
George Poyser 1963 to 1965
Joe Mercer OBE 1965 to 1972
Malcolm Allison 1972 to 1973
Johnny Hart 1973
Ron Saunders 1973 to 1974
Tony Book 1974 to 1979
Malcolm Allison 1979 to 1980
John Bond 1980 to 1983
John Benson 1983
Billy McNeill MBE 1983 to 1986

Jimmy Frizzell 1986 to 1987
Mel Machin 1987 to 1989
Howard Kendall 1989 to 1990
Peter Reid 1990 to 1993
Brian Horton 1993 to 1995
Alan Ball 1995 to 1996
Steve Coppell 1996
Frank Clark 1997 to 1998
Joe Royle 1998 to 2001
Kevin Keegan 2001 to present

Manchester Derby Matches (league and cup)

CITY V	PLAYED	WON	DREW	LOST	FOR	AGAINST
UNITED	136	36	46	54	182	199

Chronology

- **1879** The church of St.Mark's (West Gorton) forms a working mens' club.
- **1880** The men's club football team plays its first game on some rough land in the Thomas Street/Clowes Street area.
- **1881** The club moves to a new venue for home games: Kirkmanshulme Cricket Club.
- **1882** The cricketers object to the state of their pitch and the footballers move again, this time to Queen's Road/Clemington Park.
- **1883** Reports indicate that that the side played more than fifteen games but could only field eleven players three times.
- **1884** Gorton AFC comes into being, playing their home games at Pink Bank Lane.
- **1885** Another new ground, this time behind The Bull's Head Hotel on Reddish Lane.
- **1886** Gorton lost 11-1 to Newton Heath in the Manchester Cup.
- **1887** The club changes its name to Ardwick FC and moves to a permanent ground just off Hyde Road.
- **1888** A 1,000 capacity grandstand is built at the new ground.
- **1889** Ardwick lost 3-2 to Newton Heath in a floodlit charity match at Belle Vue. The game was watched by some 12,000 and raised £140 for the Hyde Road Colliery disaster fund.
- **1890** In an attempt to strengthen the side, Ardwick signed twelve players, none of whom are from Manchester.
- **1891** Entered the FA Cup for the first time, beating Liverpool Stanley 12-0, still a club record score in the FA Cup.
- **1892** Ardwick become a founder member of the Football League Division Two.
- **1893** Joshua Parlby takes over as secretary/manager from Lawrence Furniss.
- **1894** Ardwick FC becomes Manchester City FC and Billy Meredith signs.
- **1895** City beat Lincoln City 11-3 in Division Two, still a club record victory in the league.
- **1896** City finished second in Division Two, missing out on promotion after losing heavily in the Test Matches at the end of the season.
- **1897** Preston North End beat City 6-0 in the First Round of the FA Cup, still the club's record FA Cup defeat.
- **1898** Meredith and Whitehead both score hat-tricks as Burton United are crushed 9-0 in the last game of the season. City finished 3rd.
- **1899** City win the Second Division Championship for the first time in their history.
- **1900** Average attendance is more than 15,000 as City finish their first season in the top division in 7th place.

- **1901** City beat Newton Heath 4-2 in the final of the Manchester Senior Cup.
- **1902** City finished 18th (and bottom) of the First Division and are relegated.
- **1903** Centre forward Billy Gillespie is top scorer with 30 goals as City win the Second Division
- **1904** Thanks to a Billy Meredith goal, City beat Bolton Wanderers 1-0 in the FA Cup Final at Crystal Palace to clinch the trophy for the first time. They also finished runners-up in Division One, missing out on the double by three points to Sheffield Wednesday.
- **1905** Billy Meredith is suspended for alleged match-fixing in a game against Aston Villa.
- **1906** The FA finally reports its findings into the bribery scandal and seventeen players and four officials are banned and fined. New manager Harry Newbould takes over a dying club. City beat United 3-0 in the first Manchester derby.
- **1907** Hyde Road has an average attendance of 21,670, the first time the 20,000 figure has been reached.
- **1908** Amazingly, Newbould's completely rebuilt side finishes third in Division One.
- **1909** City finish 19th and are relegated on goal average alongside Leicester Fosse. Their nearest rivals Bradford City beat Manchester United 1-0 in the last game of the season to survive.
- **1910** City won the Second Division Championship for the third time.
- **1911** City won the Manchester Senior Cup, beating neighbours United 3-1 in the final.
- **1912** Ernest Mangnall took over from Harry Newbould and became City's sixth manager.
- **1913** The Blues lose 2-0 in the FA Cup Second Round to Sunderland, after crowd trouble at Hyde Road had forced the first game to be abandoned.
- **1914** New signing Tommy 'Boy' Browell is top scorer with thirteen league goals in the season.
- **1915** City finished 5th in the First Division. It was to be the last league season for five years.
- **1919** City won the wartime Lancashire Section Subsidiary Tournament.
- **1920** A fire at Hyde Road completely destroys the all wooden Main Stand.
- **1921** A crowd of more than 50,000 watched City beat Championship rivals Burnley 3-0 at Hyde Road. Burnley would eventually clinch the title, with City finishing in second place. Now aged 47, Billy Meredith rejoined City.
- **1922** Max Woosnam breaks a leg in the last game of the season against Newcastle. The injury effectively finished his career.
- **1923** City moved to the brand-new 90,000 capacity

Maine Road stadium. Sheffield United were the first visitors with City winning 2-1.

- **1924** At 49 years and 245 days old, Billy Meredith played against Newcastle United in the FA Cup semi-final.
- **1925** Tommy Browell scored five times as Burnley were beaten 8-3 at Maine Road in a league game.
- **1926** The Blues beat United 6-1 at Old Trafford in the league in January. The season finished badly as City lost 1-0 to Bolton Wanderers in the FA Cup final and were also relegated.
- **1927** With Tommy Johnson scoring 25 times, City finished third in Division Two.
- **1928** City become Second Division Champions for the fourth time, scoring exactly 100 goals.
- **1929** Tommy Johnson's club record breaking season 1928-29. He scored 38 goals in 39 league games.
- **1930** Swindon Town were beaten 10-1 in the FA Cup 4th Round at Maine Road with Bobby Marshall scoring five times.
- **1931** Bill Dale signed for the Blues from neighbours United. He would become the regular left-back for the next seven years.
- **1932** The Blues lost 1-0 to Arsenal in the semi-final of the FA Cup. Frank Swift signed from Fleetwood.
- **1933** A Dixie Dean inspired Everton beat City 3-0 in the FA Cup final at Wembley. Wilf Wild became the new manager, taking over from Peter Hodge.
- **1934** Two goals from Freddie Tilson are enough to beat Portsmouth and clinch the FA Cup for the second time in the club's history. A record crowd of 84,569 saw City's quarter-final game with Stoke at Maine Road.
- **1935** City beat Wolves 5-0 in the last game of the season to finish 4th in Division One.
- **1936** Possibly City's greatest ever player, Peter Doherty, signed from Blackpool for £10,000.
- **1937** With Doherty scoring 30 times, City are crowned First Division Champions for the first time.
- **1938** Despite the success of the previous year, and scoring more goals than any other side in the division, City finished 21st and were relegated.
- **1939** The outbreak of World War II forced League Football to be suspended after just three games of the 1939-40 season.
- **1946** The first season back after the war saw former captain Sam Cowan take over the manager's reigns from Wilf Wild.
- **1947** The Blues won the Second Division Championship for the fifth time. Sam Cowan's short time in charge ended when Jock Thomson took over in November.
- **1948** An average crowd of 42,725 saw the Blues' home games in the 1947-48 season, a then record.
- **1949** Former German prisoner-of-war Bert Trautmann took over goalkeeping duties from Frank Swift. After some initial resistance, Trautmann would go on to become a legend at Maine Road.
- **1950** City were once again relegated to the Second Division. It cost Jock Thomson his job. He was replaced by former player Les McDowall.
- **1951** The Blues finished second to Preston North End and earned promotion.
- **1952** More than 56,000 saw City beat United 2-1 at Maine Road thanks to goals from Ivor Broadis and Roy Clarke.
- **1953** Floodlights were installed at Maine Road and used for the first time in a friendly against Hearts.
- **1954** The 1954-55 season started with the introduction of a new style of play, 'The Revie Plan'. City lost 5-0 at Preston on the opening day.
- **1955** City reached Wembley only to lose 3-1 to Newcastle United in the FA Cup final.
- **1956** The Blues returned to Wembley and a 3-1 triumph over Birmingham City. Remarkably goalkeeper Bert Trautmann played the last quarter of an hour with a broken neck.
- **1957** Another new style of play, 'The Marsden Plan', was quickly abandoned, as City were humbled 9-2 at West Bromwich.
- **1958** The Blues scored 104 goals in the league as well as conceding 100.
- **1959** City avoided relegation by just a single point.
- **1960** Manager Les McDowall broke the British transfer record when he bought Denis Law from Huddersfield Town for £55,000.
- **1961** Law scored six times in an abandoned FA Cup-tie at Luton. City lost the replay 3-1, Law scored again.
- **1962** Glyn Pardoe made his debut in City's first team. At just 15 years and 314 days old, he became the youngest player ever to appear in the senior side.
- **1963** City lost 6-1 in the last game of the season at West Ham and were relegated. George Poyser became the new manager.
- **1964** Bert Trautmann's Testimonial game was played in front of a crowd of 48,000 at Maine Road.
- **1965** Joe Mercer and Malcolm Allison began a managerial partnership that heralded the greatest period in the club's history. Mike Summerbee was signed from Swindon Town.
- **1966** Colin Bell signed from Bury as City won promotion from the Second Division for the sixth time.
- **1967** Francis Lee signed from Bolton Wanderers for a then club record transfer fee of £60,000.
- **1968** The Blues won 4-3 at Newcastle to clinch the First Division Championship for only the second time, but fell at the first hurdle in the European Cup.
- **1969** Neil Young's goal at Wembley was enough to win the FA Cup against Leicester.
- **1970** City became the first English side to win both a domestic and European trophy following successes in the League Cup and European Cup Winners' Cup.
- **1971** A disappointing year: the club finished 11th in Division One and failed to win a trophy! They did reach the semi-final of the European Cup-Winners' Cup only to lose to Chelsea.

- **1972** Malcolm Allison signed the flamboyant Rodney Marsh for a new club record fee of £200,000. City finished fourth in the First Division, only one point behind eventual Champions Derby County.
- **1973** Ron Saunders became the new manager following the earlier departures of both Joe Mercer and Malcolm Allison.
- **1974** Colin Bell's goal in the League Cup final proved City's only consolation as Wolves win 2-1. Former captain Tony Book took over from Ron Saunders. The recently returned Denis Law scored his famous goal for City at Old Trafford.
- **1975** Mike Summerbee left the club for Burnley with Dave Watson arriving from Sunderland.
- **1976** A spectacular goal from Dennis Tueart won the League Cup for City against Newcastle United. Colin Bell suffered a serious knee injury in a game against Manchester United.
- **1977** The Blues missed out on the First Division title by just one point to Liverpool.
- **1978** City reserves won the Central League for the first time. The Blues' were watched by an average 41,687, still a club record. AC Milan were beaten 3-0 in a UEFA Cup-tie.
- **1979** Malcolm Allison returned to the club as 'Coaching Overlord'. Unfortunately it was not a success. Steve Daley became City's first £1 million player.
- **1980** Tony Book and Malcolm Allison both lost their jobs as John Bond took over. City lost in the FA Cup to Fourth Division Halifax.
- **1981** Tommy Hutchison scored for both sides as City drew 1-1 with Tottenham in the 100th FA Cup final. Unfortunately the Blues lost the replay 3-2.
- **1982** The first season of three points for a win. City finished 10th in Division One.
- **1983** City lost 1-0 at home to Luton Town in the last game of the season and were relegated. Billy McNeill became City's 13th manager since the war.
- **1984** The Blues finished 4th in Division Two with Derek Parlane top scorer.
- **1985** A thrilling 5-1 victory against Charlton Athletic clinched promotion back to the top division.
- **1986** City's youngsters won the FA Youth Cup for the first time, beating Manchester United in the two-legged final. The first team lost 5-4 to Chelsea in the final of the Full Members' Cup. Billy McNeill left for Aston Villa with Jimmy Frizzell taking over.
- **1987** City are relegated to the Second Division. Mel Machin became the new manager.
- **1988** Paul Stewart is sold to Tottenham for a then club record transfer fee received of £1,700,000.
- **1989** Promoted to the First Division as runners-up to Chelsea. City beat neighbours United 5-1 in the most memorable derby game of recent times. Despite Machin's successes, he was replaced by Howard Kendall in December.
- **1990** Kendall's short-lived reign ended when he returned to his 'first love', Everton. Peter Reid became the club's first player/manager. Joe Mercer passed away on his 76th birthday.
- **1991** David White scored four times in a 5-1 win at Aston Villa. The old Platt Lane Stand was demolished. City finished the 1990-91 season in 5th place. Keith Curle signed for a new club record fee of £2.5 million.
- **1992** Terry Phelan signed from Wimbledon to equal the record transfer fee. City played their first game (a 1-1 draw with QPR) in the newly formed FA Premier League.
- **1993** Peter Reid was sacked to be replaced by Brian Horton. The new Umbro Stand was opened on the same day as City lost 4-2 to Tottenham in the FA Cup quarter-final. Peter Swales resigned as club chairman.
- **1994** After lengthy negotiations, former player Francis Lee was appointed as the new chairman. The famous Kippax Stand was demolished after 71 years service. Uwe Rosler signed from FC Nurnburg.
- **1995** Gio Kinkladze signed from Dynamo Tblisi. Alan Ball became the new manager following the dismissal of Brian Horton. The new Kippax Street stand was unveiled.
- **1996** City drew 2-2 with Liverpool on the last day of the season and were relegated from the Premier League. Alan Ball's resignation made him the first of five men in charge in a period of less than six months.
- **1997** Lee Bradbury signed from Portsmouth for a club record fee of £3 million by new manager Frank Clark. Eastlands Stadium plans are unveiled – City's proposed move planned for 2003.
- **1998** In February, with City second from bottom in Division One, Joe Royle replaced Frank Clark. Unfortunately he cannot prevent City from relegation to the Second (actually Third) Division, the lowest point in the club's history. Chairman Francis Lee resigned to be replaced by David Bernstein.
- **1999** The Blues won an amazing Second Division play-off game against Gillingham at Wembley to earn promotion.
- **2000** On May 7 City won 4-1 at Blackburn to end their remarkable back-to-back promotion seasons and re-enter the Premiership after four years.
- **2001** Tragically though City were unable to maintain their tremendous run of the last two years and were subsequently relegated. Joe Royle lost his job at the end of the season.
- **2002** New manager Kevin Keegan revitalised the Blues into one of the most attacking and entertaining sides in the country. After equalling the record number of goals scored (108), City were crowned First Division Champions, their first trophy since 1976. Peter Schmeichel and new record signing Nicolas Anelka arrived in the summer as the Blues looked to establish themselves in the Premiership with the new stadium just 12 months away.